C0-GAR-731

Multiple Wives,
Multiple Pleasures

Multiple Wives, Multiple Pleasures

Representing the Harem, 1800–1875

Joan DelPlato

Madison • Teaneck
Fairleigh Dickinson University Press
London: Associated University Presses

© 2002 by Rosemont Publishing & Printing Corp.

All rights reserved. Authorization to photocopy items for internal or personal use, or the internal or personal use of specific clients, is granted by the copyright owner, provided that a base fee of $10.00, plus eight cents per page, per copy is paid directly to the Copyright Clearance Center, 222 Rosewood Drive, Danvers, Massachusetts 01923. [0-8386-3880-5/02 $10.00+ 8¢ pp, pc.]

Associated University Presses
440 Forsgate Drive
Cranbury, NJ 08512

Associated University Presses
16 Barter Street
London WC1A 2AH, England

Associated University Presses
P.O. Box 338, Port Credit
Mississauga, Ontario
Canada L5G 4L8

The paper used in this publication meets the requirements of the American National Standard for Permanence of Paper for Printed Library Materials Z39.48-1984.

Library of Congress Cataloging-in-Publication Data

DelPlato, Joan, 1953–
Multiple wives, multiple pleasures : representing the harem, 1800–1875 / Joan DelPlato.
p. cm.
Includes bibliographical references and index.
ISBN 0-8386-3880-5 (alk. paper)
1. Harem in art. 2. Arts, British—19th century—Themes, motives. 3. Arts, French—19th century—Themes, motives. I. Title.

NX650.H37 D45 2002
757'.4'094209034—dc21 2001040689

Publication of this book has been aided by a grant from the Millard Meiss Publication Fund of the College Art Association.

MM

PRINTED IN THE UNITED STATES OF AMERICA

For my parents, Lewis and Helen Del Plato

Contents

Preface 9
Acknowledgments 15

1. Introduction 19
   - The Appeal of the Harem for a Varied Nineteenth-Century Public in Britain and France 19
   - Harem Representation and the Politics of Aesthetic Positivism in England and France 24
   - Revealing the Hidden: Harem Images and the New *Scientia Sexualis* in the Nineteenth Century 25
   - Identity and Difference: "Western" Reconstructions of Sex, Class, and Race in "Eastern" Garb 27

2. The Colonial Contexts for the Harem Representation 30
   - Introduction: The Role of the Muslim Harem in the Rhetoric of International Politics 30
   - France, England, and the Harem 31
   - Napoleon Bonaparte and Vivant Denon on the Harem 32
   - Harem Representations Specifying Ethnicity/Nationality/"Race" 36
   - Conclusion 56

3. Depictions of Slavery and the Making of the Harem 58
   - Introduction 58
   - Protest and Defense; Titillation and Ambivalence: Harem Slavery and the Slave Market Represented by a Range of Observers 59
   - Representing the "Happy Slave" In or Bound for the Harem 67
   - Slave Market Pictures and Unveiling Scenes 73
   - The Greek War of Independence and Harem Women as War Prisoners 90
   - Freedom, Enslavement, and Domesticity: The Open Window and the Closed Harem 103
   - The Paradox of British and French Sentiment on Harem Slavery and the Slave Market: Freeing the Harem Victim from Life in a "Luxurious Prison" 108

4. Setting the Stage: Harem Props as Fetishized Accoutrements 110
   - Introduction: Eros and Science: Fetishizing the Harem 110
   - To Smoke and to Drink: The Pipe and Coffee 111
   - Harem Animals: Gazelles, Birds, and Cats 121
   - Lute Music 134
   - Symbolic Flowers 138
   - Jewelry and Slippers 143
   - The Harem Space 154

5. The Harem Fetishized: Harem Women as Immoral 162
   - Introduction 162
   - Morality and Art: Examining the Argument that the Faces of Harem Women Can Not Be Beautiful 163
   - Negative Stereotypes of Harem Women 165
   - Rococo-Revival Harem Imagery and the Critique of Tyranny as an Enlightenment Inheritance 195
   - Summary 201

6. The Harem Fetishized: Muslim Women as Moral: Angels in Heaven and the House 202
   - Introduction 202

Pure Creatures in Heavenly and Earthly Gardens 203
Things Are Not What They Seem: "Good" Harem Women and Readings of *Memento mori* 225
The Interdependence of Positive and Negative Stereotyping 228

7. Conclusions 230
The End of the Phenomenon of the Harem Representation 230
Britain: The Critical Reaction to Lewis's Late Harem Painting 230
France: Pre-Impressionist "Modern" Harem Painting 231
Conclusion 238

Notes 241
Bibliography 261
Index 269

Preface

To undertake a study of "the harem" as it was represented in nineteenth-century England and France presents some thorny problems. Where shall the researcher go in order to locate an accurate description of the harem against which to compare western pictorial and written interpretations of it? Commentators of the time often claimed that their information about the harem was accurate, and pictures of the harem were often presumed to be true. But closer analysis reveals these claims as deeply flawed. I am compelled to disrupt these cultural texts' presumption of authenticity. In critiquing these claims, I want to consider what purposes such assertions might have served. And I want to identify the widespread nineteenth-century *preoccupation* with accuracy, a positivist principle that characterized much official and popular culture. Still there is no document which will tell the absolute truth about the harem; there are only "representations" of it.

Whether Eugène Delacroix really did get to see a harem firsthand in Morocco to be able to paint his 1834 *Women of Algiers*,[1] or whether western women writers write about harem women more accurately than men are unanswerable questions, in my view. And they are incidental to my major project. A hunt for the truth about the harem is not only impossible, but a scholar's obsession over it could preclude investigation into broader questions of epistemology and British and French self-reflexivity.

Investigations of the harem in the nineteenth and twentieth centuries often begin with an etymology of the English word "harem." (The word is the same in French.) The assumption here is that the word will allow a discussion of origins, logically the beginning of the harem "story." Though the assumption is subject to debate, I will begin this way too. The term harem itself derives from the Arabic *harim* or *haram* (which come into English as "hareem" or "harem") having connotations of the sacred and the forbidden.[2] By extension harem referred to the assembly of women living in the polygynous Muslim home. From a term describing territory that is "off-limits," it came to mean the female quarters of a Turkish house (*haremlik*).[3] The English and French term odalisque (rarely odalique) derives from the Turkish *oda*, meaning "chamber"; thus an odalisque originally meant a chamber girl or attendant. In western usage, the term has come to refer specifically to the harem concubine. By the eighteenth century the term odalisque referred to the eroticized artistic genre in which a nominally eastern woman lies on her side on display for the spectator. Written accounts on the harem often presume that information about the origin of a term like "harem" provide a kernel of truth about it. The alternative I propose is to chart contextually varied uses of harem terminology: to locate how the words are used at particular historical moments, in reference to what visual images, and having what kinds of associations.

Consulting the *Qur'an* has been another way to understand the harem representation in the West. Leila Ahmed has done valuable work in questioning the scholarly analysis of Arab women when it is based largely on Qur'anic exhortations. She has shown that the seclusion of women which underpins the harem dates from the time of Muhammad, who created it as a distance between his wives and the community he founded, "the distance appropriate for the wives of the now powerful leader of a new, unambiguously patriarchal society," though it is unknown how Muhammad's secluding his wives became a more widespread practice within the community.[4] There are three Qur'anic scriptures that are used as justification for the seclusion of women and veiling (24:31–32; 33:54 and 60). As for the sanctioning of polygyny, it is attributed to this verse from the *Qur'an*:

> And if you fear that you cannot act equitably towards orphans, then marry such women as seem good to you, two and three and four; but if you fear that you will not do justice (between them), then (marry) only one or what your right hands possess; this is more proper that you may not deviate from the right course. (4:3)

But the harem's existence cannot be understood by its Qur'anic sanction alone. As Judith E. Tucker cautions, it would be an oversimplification to read Islamic texts as monolithic and dictatorial in shaping the harem as a rigid, unchanging institution over time and place.[5] Ahmed provides two more arguments in favor of a more nuanced understanding of the harem: one, this same verse has been used to argue that men should not be polygamous, given the conditional verb form that introduces it; in Arabic it has a "negative connoting permanent impossibility," and two, that the *Qur'an* is open to radically different readings on the status of women.[6] Another way to avoid presenting a monolithic Islam on the harem would be to analyze several case studies of the social and political life of elite women of nineteenth-century palaces as well as less wealthy harems considering memoirs of the women themselves.[7]

According to some nineteenth-century western writers, the Islamic rationale for the harem was to protect the women housed within it from undesirable contact with unrelated men. However, some twentieth-century scholars have argued that the social functions of harem seclusion and veiling were less purely chivalrous and had more direct gynophobic aspects: rather than protecting women from men, it was sometimes thought to protect men from the animality women supposedly emanate.[8] This difference in conception of the harem—one as protection of vulnerable women versus the other as restraint on the erotic magnetism of "the feminine"—at first seems to presume different understandings of female sexual prowess. But the belief that women are both pathetically weak and frighteningly powerful is a recurrent paradox under patriarchy, whether eastern or western. For some Victorians, the view of the harem as sanctuary for the women within constituted an eastern version of the cult of domesticity in England or bourgeois France. Of course, the harem supported multiple wives, and in this way differed from a Victorian home in the extent of those dependent on its supporter. Whether located in the West or the East, that the lady (or ladies) of the house did not work outside the home for wages could be considered a privilege for the woman and a sign of financial success for the husband/pasha who could afford to support her, their children, and several servants.

The harem can be analyzed from a number of viewpoints—religious, social, cultural, geographical, political. My project to differentiate the harem from the harem representation can be facilitated by also considering the harem as a spatial entity. The space of the harem as unitary and commonsensical—as a transparent container holding women, children, servants, and occasionally the master—can be subjected to what Henri Lefebvre has called "a critique of Cartesian space."[9] I propose some distinctions based on Lefebvre's categorizations, each of which is a site for the play of ideology.

First, there were the lived spaces of the harem and its representation. This includes the space that was inhabited by actual women in the specific geographical locales within the Arab world, women whose lives are alluded to in western paintings and poetry. The events and routines that took place in the physical harem space, where people made sense of their lives, was the reality that so many writers and artists claimed to know. But the harem encompassed social practices that inevitably exceeded the westerner's naming of them as "eastern" or "Muslim" or "polygynous." And the lived space of the harem *representation*, which is really my topic here, probes the ways British and French individuals, families, classes, and societies made sense of the harem as that other lived space—however vaguely understood—and how they may have integrated knowledge about it into the sense they made of their own lives on a day-to-day basis.

Secondly, there was "the harem space" as constructed by cultural purveyors, who had greater power to affect others' notions of the harem. It became a packageable entity, a cultural commodity. For example, editors of French and British newspapers who agreed to publish travel accounts about the harem put forth notions of the harem space that evolved from their own agenda to capture the attention of a reading public and sell "news." Scholarly attention to this second kind of harem space might also consider how it was used by politicians and government elites as a discourse to maintain social control. On occasion, the harem was evoked by foreign policymakers in London's Parliament linked to decisions about colonial intervention. It was also at issue when particular government officials decided to purchase one of the hundreds of harem or odalisque pictures exhibited at the Salon in Paris from 1800 until 1875.

Third, there were the spaces in which the harem functioned as a means of cultural resistance. This might have occurred in a private studio when Edouard Manet, leader of the new French school of painting, first showed to his circle of friends his disruptive *La Sultane* around 1870 as a manifesto of rebellion against the harem subject grown stale at the hands of Academic painters and popular printmakers. Or this kind of harem space might have coalesced at the table located just under a cheap print of a harem pinned on the wall in a radical working-class eatery in the suburbs of Paris around 1848. How a harem picture could function there would be quite different from its high art contexts carved out by Manet's work.

However categorized, the "harem spaces" were varied and ubiquitous in nineteenth-century England and France. Rather than simply containing such activities, each harem space was actually constructed by those social actions and needs. At each level myth, fantasy, projection, identity formation, and capitalist relationships are actively constituted within harem spaces. And the three types of space are an inextricable triad.[10] Each kind of harem space had a particular relationship with the other types, and each was a site for social and political struggle. Each instance of the harem space functioned as a microcosm of the East—another larger space that was also (1) lived in, (2) manipulated, and (3) resisted in complex ways.

In this study I want to reestablish the fluidity of the relationships among these three broad categories for considering the harem space. And I want to identify how both economics and language help create the several kinds of harem spaces. As for the latter, Ashcroft, Griffiths, and Tiffin assert, "in some sense place *is* language, something in constant flux, a discourse in process."[11] Timothy Mitchell goes so far as to claim that the East might be not a place at all, as the term is used by the West, but a "series of representations."[12]

Given my struggles in writing about the harem today, I am struck by the confidence with which so many nineteenth-century writers and artists apparently believed it was possible to describe the harem in terms that were truthful, objective, or based on highly reliable sources. Such writers who claimed evenhandedness were reacting against the exaggeration and rumor, the outrageous melodrama with which the subject of the harem had been treated at times. In part, this positivist revision of the harem in this period contrasts with an excess—one which the British considered "French" or the French considered "aristocratic." What interests me in this study of both countries' representations of the harem is not settling the question of whether the British or the French were more emotionally excessive, accurate, erotic, scientific in their picturing the harem. Instead I am interested in the functions of various truth-claims, whether about the French, the British, the Arab, the easterner, or the harem. None of these can be objectively represented. Rather we are given access to these concepts through visual and verbal representation, mediations of experience shaped by the creative agent and the work's audience.

Like pictures, written literature on the harem exploded in popularity in the nineteenth century. This is due in part to a dramatic increase in travel literature. A greater number of British books on Egypt were published in the first half of the nineteenth century than ever before.[13] In this study I draw upon written records of the harem such as travel accounts published in monographs and the periodical press, but I also consult sources as diverse as the critical reaction to art about the harem and the rhetoric of the abolitionist movement. Without ignoring how different harem texts (popular and elite, even "good" and "bad" painting) interpellated different audiences, I try to consider texts democratically, as documents equally worthy of scholarly attention. A brief comment on a harem picture written by an anonymous journalist in the *Illustrated London News* is potentially as significant for conveying cultural meaning as a poem by Byron. A cheap French lithograph is as revealing as a fine art painting exhibited at the Salon.

There was considerable overlap in the nineteenth century between high and low visual art forms—paintings and prints—in France and England. In this study the majority of harem prints analyzed are French lithographs housed at the Cabinet des Estampes at the Bibliothèque Nationale and done after 1815. The larger cache of prints to which these fifty or so harem pictures belong—and which survive due to the law passed during the French Revolution that one copy of any printed text be stored in the national library—marks the beginnings of commercial lithography in France.[14] Beatrice Farwell writes that French popular prints were produced for an international market that ranged in the thousands. Correspondingly, the functions for these printed harem images, whether they survive singly or in bound volumes, were quite varied. Some were reproductions of Salon paintings, occasionally published in art periodicals. Some were wall decorations in homes or the local eatery. Some served as private pornography. They drew the attention of passersby when displayed in a lithographer's shop window. Their public was varied in nationality and class. French prints were also purchased by British consumers. Their buyers were drawn from the working class as well as the more comfortable classes. Even Empress Eugénie, who traveled to Egypt, commissioned a harem printmaker to paint a gouache of a privileged Turkish harem woman.[15]

As a survey of harem representation produced in nineteenth-century England and France, this study reflects the limitations and hopefully the value of the survey approach. This is by no means a complete historical analysis of any one of the images selected. I have made choices to discuss some images in great detail and to consider them at more than one point in this study, while others are briefly mentioned, choices which often reflect the availability of research material. Nonetheless, my survey approach can hopefully become a tool with which to identify widespread harem motifs and themes, which themselves can be connected to social and political issues.

I also compare British and French imagery. No one will deny that there were distinctive French and British schools of art in the first three-quarters of the nineteenth century, the period of this study. But to consider the schools separately, as is more typically done in nineteenth-century art history, is to overlook how they might have had overlapping concerns, and producing a harem picture was one of them. Opposing the French and British schools also overlooks the historical entity like the binational group which included several painters of the harem whose work will be discussed here: Richard Parkes Bonington, Delacroix, the Devéria Brothers, Alexandre Colin, Henry William Pickersgill, Jules Robert Auguste, and John Frederick Lewis, artists active in the years 1827–55, when, as Marcia Pointon demonstrates, there was a strong market in both countries for watercolors of Oriental subjects,[16] including harem pictures.

In this study I describe the dynamic nature of the harem phenomenon over time, how its representation changed until about 1875. While each representation of the harem emerged from a specific historical moment, harem pictures conform to some pictorial formulas, inviting comparisons to each other. Noteworthy for their sameness, there are innumerable variations of the reclining odalisque, often nude or semi-nude, surrounded by eastern bric-a-brac. This consistency became the formula by which harem pictures could be distinguished from other erotic images. This web of interwoven referents can be seen as what comprises the tradition of "the harem" as understood in nineteenth-century England and France.[17] That harem pictures are so repetitive is not to say that they are artistically unimaginative or of poor quality; some are semantically quite subtle and many technically proficient. Still the repetition of certain motifs in the harem suggests an obsession with the harem woman. In this study I make the question of this stereotyping of harem women one of my central concerns. Stereotyping is, after all, based in repetition and obsession, practices that can be interpreted in Lacanian terms. Here the work of Homi K. Bhabha will be useful.[18] The desire to represent the harem woman at all marks a point on a continuum of psychosexual colonialism; other points of intensity are marked by the desire to possess, name, and dissect her, to borrow Malek Alloula's terms.[19]

When a harem's locale is specified in painting titles or travel literature, it is most frequently named as either Turkey, Egypt, or North Africa. For the most part, however, representations of the harem and attitudes toward it differed imperceptibly whether it was located in Algeria, Egypt, Turkey, or Persia, countries which were not often thought to have distinct identities as nations.[20] In art and letters "turquerie" was a catchall term used to describe faddish orientalism having a tie to cultures as far west as Morocco and as far east as India; Farwell calls "turquerie" "indisputably the most pervasive element in French exoticism."[21] A distinction was drawn between most harems and the sultan's harem in Constantinople, which was understood as simply more extravagant. This misconception of Islam as a monolithic whole helps to keep intact stereotypes about it.

Any commentary on or representation of "the harem" produced in England or France is inescapably western. The topic and the term are western inventions. Just as Foucault describes the invention of "the criminal" or "the insane" set against the development of the institution created to accommodate each, so too is "the harem inmate" a type that is constructed and situated in a particular institution called the harem. (Interestingly, the English word "inmate" is used to describe the inhabitant of the jail, the asylum, or the harem.) The British-born feminist Harriet Martineau at mid-century draws a startling parallel of these institutions. After having visited a harem, she wrote about it with "a heaviness of heart greater than I have ever brought away from Deaf and Dumb Schools, Lunatic Asylums or even Prisons. As such are my impressions of hareems."[22] Early nineteenth-century discourses on the pathos of confinement accompany the rise of the romantic cult of individual freedom. Many other commentators on the harem woman would see her as a type whose nature was thought to be determined by her physical context,[23] as we shall see.

In Muslim societies where it existed the harem was considered an integral part of the home. It could not be understood apart from its historical specificity: how the institution may have differed from one society to another and over time. However, western observers—writers and artists and their audiences—have decontextualized and fetishized the harem, using misconceptions of it for their own ends. I hope to articulate what presumed knowledge about the harem is formed in that process in England and France. I will explore how this knowledge is linked to the formation of both power and pleasure.[24]

Thus my critical approach to a study of the harem subject attempts to avoid truth claims about its real nature, which cannot be named. It also entails an acknowledgment of my own feminist, class- and race-conscious perspective using some analytical tools of a politicized deconstruction, a perspective that is inevitably that of a western intellectual. This study suggests the needs the harem served for sexual organization and social control in British and French societies. And though I am not an Islamicist, I occasionally point out what Edward Said has called the "contrapuntal" views of the harem expressed by divergent western writers as well as eastern traditions or spokesmen.[25] Yet I attempt to critique both sets of rationales on the harem. Furthermore, I accept Gayatri Chakravorty Spivak's deconstructivist claim that there is no chance for the (female) subaltern—the harem woman herself—to speak, given the ways patriarchy and imperialism have constructed the positions of Self (Subject) and Other (Object), manipulating her agency.[26] The voice of "the harem woman" herself is, alas, missing from this study as well.

At times the art historical methodology employed here may resemble traditional iconographical analysis, because in attempting to decode pictures and symbols within them I draw upon many other pictures and written accounts having similar subjects. Pictures of harem women are in effect an oriental variation on the Venus tradition which permeates western art, as Marilyn Brown has noted.[27] Comparing scenes depicting these women allows me to articulate types and degrees of eroticism, making judgments which are inevitably relative. Comparing texts also lets me identify conventions and their disruptions. Variations within those conventions then become important road markers that warrant inquiry into the historical moment in which they were produced to assess possible determinants. Thus I attempt to contextualize the motifs in harem paintings, establishing the structures and conventions of a tradition of harem texts not yet fully recognized by current scholarship. But while I employ a frequently used tool of art history, it is put in the service of a critique of cultural texts.

Though politics is my concern, I can rarely document with certainty the state of political consciousness for any of the artists or writers whose work is under consideration here. But their texts are clearly part of an interlocking mental, cultural, and political web whose extent I hope to demonstrate. I want to treat these interrelated representations of the harem as capable of conveying cultural messages. Meaning does not reside within the single representation of the harem. Indeed, its meanings fluctuate in relationship to various texts. As Terry Eagleton writes: "Reading a text is more like tracing this process of constant flickering than it is like counting the beads on a necklace."[28] Comparisons with related texts thus open up harem pictures and written accounts to a wide range of interpretations. My study focuses on the processes of devising possible meanings, and thus it differs from traditional art history that has been content to put forth a single, "correct" reading of an art object while claiming an epistemological and political objectivity. A goal of this study is, on the one hand, to broadly sketch in the outlines of pictorial genres and, on the other, to establish in-depth histories of selected pictures. To do so I draw from some theories that originated outside art history proper and make a leap into an analysis of the pictorial.

In this study power relations of various kinds are foregrounded. Gender politics is at issue in critics' commentary when masculine and feminine roles are read as part of the narrative fiction of the harem picture or in the presumed interactions of depicted female and the fictive (male) spectator. Class politics are inevitably played out in all representations of the harem, in some cases more explicitly than others, since the institution itself depended on a social hierarchy, as did the nineteenth-century society in which its viewers lived. A third locus for power relations which the images suggest is in the constellation of issues evoked by the concepts "eastern" and "western" cultures. This study is postcolonial in its refusal to accept the terms of dominance inherent in the naming (or picturing) of the eastern Other by a western artist. Moreover, when eastern race or ethnicities are specified in harem paintings' titles and in the critics' reactions to them, these categories must be addressed by the researcher.

Much theoretical work has been written in recent years critiquing the terms "East" and "West" and their ethnocentric bases indebted to Edward Said's now-classic *Orientalism* (1978), which has spawned a tremendously rich literature that has permeated nearly every field in the humanities and social sciences.[29] My study is indebted to that literature and uses it as a springboard. Indeed, this book can be seen as a response to the call issued by Said in his later *Culture and Imperialism* (1993) for critical studies which insist on relating art production to the complex needs of imperialism. Even though 1878, 1882, and 1884 have been the more conventional dates for the official beginning of imperialism in Egypt, the French invaded Algeria in 1830. New interpretation recognizes that all of the nineteenth century can be called an "age of empire" for England and France. After all, imperialism is not only about the actual acquisition of land; it also refers to the development of a colonizing ideology, which implicates the production of culture.[30] It is daunting, and some would say an oxymoron, to connect the spheres of art and politics, as powerful forces in the art world traditionally defy such a linkage. Art is simultaneously pleasurable and one of the most elevated concerns (as conceived for example by critic John Ruskin), while the politics of imperialism are fundamentally ugly in their forceful brutality.[31] Like pleasure, imperialism is one of the motivating contexts for the production of French and British harem texts. By analyzing the dialectical contexts of great enjoyment and what might be called social control, one can in fact develop a fuller understanding of how these pictures functioned to both delight their original viewer and obfuscate political events taking place at home and overseas. These pictures function in a similar way today: they might move us aesthetically, but they continue to obscure how they served as tools of cross-cultural compulsion, contributing to the ongoing conception of art's history as a parade of beautiful masterpieces and art history as a disinterested chronicle of aesthetics.

The development of my argument is also indebted to the first volume of Michel Foucault's *History of Sexuality*. His thesis about the nature of Victorian sexuality continues to run against the grain of popular thinking about the nineteenth century. He counters the very concept of "sexuality" that had historically preexisted the Victorians only to be hidden from view by "repressed" society, claiming instead that sexuality is continually constituted anew in representation. In addition, his thesis about the new nineteenth-century thinking on sex—giving expression to a subject previously thought hidden—is particularly germane to representations of harem women: their clandestine glamor, hidden before artists and writers discovered it, is given pictorial form and thereby exposed to a public view, becoming a commodity spectacle. Foucault's observations are less about vision and more about a bringing of sexuality to consciousness. Jacques Derrida writes that presence is established by way of "'ocular metaphors.'"[32] In other words, picturing the harem establishes it as real in the world. This may sound obvious, but once it is acknowledged that pictures are mediated truths, the radical nature of the statement becomes clearer. Derrida's writing also reinforces the power of visual art to fix a reality in the here-and-now. Critical theories on the gaze are especially relevant to analyzing harem images, which presume a potent and mastering view of a forbidden sight.[33]

The exposure of the hidden female to the eyes of the West is a fundamental premise of the harem picture. Harem women are dually invaded by imperialism and its concurrent mania for picturing them. Imperialism abroad and a cultural fad at home converge to produce what Douthwaite has called a "rhetoric of exoticism" characterized by the discourses of both colonialism and "sexual anxieties, self-loathing and apprehension of religious, class or national differences."[34]

That the exotic is positioned as female is the particular problematic that this study addresses. In these pictures the female body becomes the highly charged site over which serious ideological wars are waged. That the female body is multivalent is inevitable, given the many meanings "female" and "body" connoted in the nineteenth century. A study of these images can richly demonstrate "how gender conflict can be used to nuance or uncover the friction of cross-cultural encounters."[35]

Throughout the nineteenth century, painted and written texts of the harem functioned ethnographically to preserve a dying, exotic institution.[36] Yet what is captured in this collection of British and French representations is not the truth of the institution but many historically specific views of it imbued with fears about difference in culture, race, religion, class and gender—made more manageable through the pleasure of representation.

Acknowledgments

Many people contributed to the making of this book and its considerable expansion and reconceptualization from the manuscript that was my dissertation in art history at UCLA under the guidance of David Kunzle and Albert Boime. Looking back over these years, I am struck by the generosity of those who helped me in completing this project. Susan Casteras enthusiastically supported the book project from its early to late stages with a kindness and exemplary mentorship to which I aspire. Beatrice Farwell Duncan, who lent crucial materials for the dissertation, generously lent them again for publication. Alan Wallach, Abigail Solomon-Godeau, and Irvin Schick gave sound advice and encouragement at crucial junctures. I am extremely appreciative to all these distinguished scholars.

I am deeply grateful to several librarians, registrars, and photo keepers. This includes Katie Archey Kerwood, Dana Cummings, and Joan Goodkind of the Simon's Rock Alumni Library and Susan Roeper of the Sterling and Francine Clark Art Institute library. I am especially grateful to Barbara Thompson at the Witt Photo Archives at the Courtauld in London and Elisabeth Molle of the Réunion des Musées Nationaux whose investigative skills and rapid responses allowed a large number of crucial images to be included in the book.

In obtaining permissions to reproduce artworks in this study several people helped me, often through email, including art historians, curators, and other scholars, private collectors, people in museums, auction houses, and galleries in the U.K., France, Germany, The Netherlands, Japan, Russia, Switzerland, and the U.S.: Luann Wilkins Abrahams, Leila Ahmed, Giselda Adler, Siobhan Anderson, Martha Asher, Robyn Asleson, Kenneth P. Bendiner, Marla Berns, Claire Q. Bellanti, Roberto Bersano, Liz Boyle, Irene Bierman, Lesley A. Black, Yvonne Brandt, Jules Breeze, Cindy M. Buckner, Muriel S. Butkin, Elizabeth Byrns, Beverly Carter, Catherine Casley, Mark Cattanach, Zeynep Çelik, JoAnne Charlton, Catherine Collyer, Jennifer Cozens, Ute Creutz, Henrietta Dalmahoy, Nadège Danet, Walter B. Denny, Stephen Duffy, Martin Durrant, Sonia Edard, Paul Evans, J. David Farmer, Vera Faulkner, Mayalen Gauthier, Christina Geiger, Christopher Gibbs, Kimberly Gilhooly, Susan Glenn, Melissa L. Gold, Barbara C. Goldstein, Elizabeth Gombosi, Catherine Gordon, Randi Jean Greenberg, Adam Grummitt, Felicity Harvey, Julian Hartnoll, Audrey W. Hall, Iain J. Harrison, Penny Haworth, Perry Hewitt, Diane Hudson, Nicole Hungerford, Chloe Johnson, Michelle Kemp, Melinda Kennedy, Christopher Knapton, Vivien Knight, Barbara Lewis, Stephanie B. Lindskog, Erika Lindt, Ed Lonergan, Briony Llewellyn, Brian MacDermott, Rupert Maas, James MacGregor, Guido Martini, Danielle Maternati-Baldouy, Vladimir Matveyev, Anastasia Mikliaeva, Miyuki Nakasendo, Scott Miller, Elizabeth Molle, Charles Newton, Charles Nugent, Octavio Olvera, Victoria Osborne, Richard Ormond, Henrietta Pattinson, Harley Preston, Nancy Boyle Press, Steffi Reh, Jennifer Reis, Donald A. Rosenthal, Leah Ross, Rebecca Rubin, Sandra M. Rushing, Julian Schuckburgh, Tracey Schuster, David Scrase, Howard Shaw, Janet Skidmore, Skylar Smith, Amber Lee Stafford, Angela Summerfield, Cherie Summers, Vern G. Swanson, Keiko Tatsumichi, Gordon Theil, Barbara Thompson, Gary Tinterow, J. M. Twelves, Kathrin Umbach, Susanna van Langenberg, Laura Valentine, Babs Vaughan, Françoise Vicente, Peter Walsh, Jeremy Warren, Michael Watson, Genevieve Webb, Ed Whitley, Pauline Wickham, Don Williamson, Wim de Wit, Lynne Withey, Christy Wood, Suzanne Wynne, and George Zombakis. I also want to thank those who helped and wish to remain anonymous.

The College Art Association's Millard Meiss Publication Fund grant for manuscript preparation and the Simon's Rock College Faculty Development Fund made this book possible by off-setting the intimidating publication costs. Judy Samoff and her staff at Bard College's office of grants helped me research funding sources. Thomas R. Wilson was exceptionally generous and competent. At Associated University Presses Julien Yoseloff, Harry Keyishian, and Christine Retz provided ongoing support.

My students at Simon's Rock College understood and shared my enthusiasm for the subject of the harem picture, for which I am grateful. My talented research assistants, Angela Labrador and John McGuire, readily adapted software to my needs and assured me that even nineteenth-century scholars could master the latest technology at the turn of the millennium. Adam Miller, Michael Mark, Roseanne Frieri, and Tony and Steve Carlotta helped with photos. Rochelle Duffy, David Reed, Colleen Ramsey, and especially Maria T. Crespo and Russell Miller provided logistical assistance.

My Simon's Rock colleague friends contributed much. Riding back from Bard College on a cold New England autumn night, Barbara Resnik invented the first half of the book's title in a flash of inspiration. Wendy Shifrin, Nancy Yanoshak, Patricia Sharpe, and Fran Mascia-Lees read the manuscript thoughtfully. I regret that my revisions could never do justice to the insightful, often brilliant suggestions they offered for the manuscript's improvement. Gabriel Asfar's expertise in French and Arabic language usage and Islamic culture allowed me to correct a number of errors. Other language faculty helped with translating permission forms. Any mistakes or misunderstandings that are left even after my colleagues pointed them out to me I shall have to consider part of the risk of writing a book that is too wide-ranging and "out-of-field" for a more reasonable scholar to have undertaken. Pat has provided enormous support in her roles as both dean and friend; I want to thank her for both kinds of help. Abdelmajid Hannoum, David Naylor, Bob Shanks, Amy Tucker, and Rich Michi gave encouragement in the final stages.

John Copoulos helped keep the project alive by asking about the book during its dormancy and reminding me about the risk of endless diversion that "reading theory" can present. He has been unfailingly supportive over the years and from thousands of miles.

Nance, who has been a most enduring and endearing friend, has listened sympathetically to all phases of the book's evolution and what seemed to be its inextricable connection to the complexities of my life. Not even Socrates himself could use the well-formed question to teach me so much about what I say. Karen, Don, and Nora have been cherished friends through the whole process and long before.

My siblings and their families, and my friends, especially Fran, have understood that I sometimes needed to be absent from festive gatherings to work on the book.

I am grateful to Jilla for recognizing that a mother who is made happy by writing is a mother who should be writing. Her simple acceptance of this fact has facilitated my own.

And finally I want to thank my parents for always having encouraged my independence and thereby my independent thinking. Now that I have completed this book I see how writing it has allowed me to channel my more youthful rebelliousness using the old-fashioned work ethic by which they have always lived. In appreciation for their gifts of wisdom, good humor, and love, I dedicate this book to them.

Multiple Wives,
Multiple Pleasures

1
Introduction

This is a history of how the harem was understood in nineteenth-century England and France as evidenced in pictures and verbal accounts. Observers were intrigued by the existence of the eastern harem, widely known as the portion of the wealthy Muslim home housing its female members. It could include up to four legal wives, as many concubines as affordable, the master's mother, his unmarried sisters and all his young children. The harem was understood to be secluded, attended by slaves and sometimes guarded (traditionally by a black eunuch). Europeans constructed a multifaceted mythology about this alternative kind of marriage and social organization, a mythology that survives in pictures and written form. One myth featured a collection of opium-smoking, lightly clad women shut up in a luxurious space, hungrily awaiting the arrival of the husband-master whom they shared. Another myth was that harem women were victims, sometimes Christian, forced into confinement and submitting to the will of a perverse master. In British and French art the women typically were beautiful, servile, and put on display for the western voyeur.

Cultural representations of the harem functioned as a necessary counterpart to the Europeans' construction of their own social, political, and psychosexual identity. In articulating their perceptions about the radical differences between eastern and western styles of sex and marriage, observers revealed a range of attitudes on several topics, most notably for this study the roles of women and men, servants and masters, and blacks and whites in both the East and the West.

The Appeal of the Harem for a Varied Nineteenth-Century Public in Britain and France

Western observers were profoundly ambivalent about the "primitive" harem and the multiple pleasures offered by the idea of multiple wives. This study explores this ambivalence by considering the negative and positive stereotyping of harem women. It considers the historical significance of the harem in the discourse of international politics including the debate over the existence of slavery, on which the harem was based. One goal of this book is to lay out the multiplicity of attitudes that the harem has provoked. The ambivalence (or multivalence) of colonialist attitudes is especially significant to document, as it suggests vulnerable sites within formal authority and the potential for the colonizer's effective resistance to it.[1] Whether attacking or defending it, French and British public comments on polygyny and slavery, as we shall explore, marked a new and growing "institutional incitement to speak about [sex]" which Foucault has argued proliferated in nineteenth-century Europe.[2]

Many observers severely criticized the harem. Early ethnographers and political analysts claimed the harem belonged to a society which was left at an earlier stage of evolution, one morally inferior to the stage represented by European bourgeois society. The tyrant's fundamentally evil harem would flourish within a despotic society. Such thinking is based in a definition of the ideal social arrangement—family and marriage that were enlightened (based on love and free choice) appropriate to the democratic governments of nineteenth-century England and France.

Sometimes the harem was criticized in the context of addressing population problems. This constituted an historically new area of surveillance in which institutions felt compelled to investigate the sex lives of their own citizens (and foreign peoples) ostensibly to evaluate the stability of the nation.[3] "Backward" polygynous society failed to thrive despite the plethora of available women, because more wives put greater demands on a master's virility; excessive couplings were thought to weaken a male. The perceived inability of the East to replenish its population was considered a key factor in the political demise of the Ottoman Empire, the "sick man of Europe," and some blamed the harem system. In 1792 the feminist Mary Wollstonecraft, writing *Vindication of the Rights of Woman,* endorses the view that polygynous men were weakened from too much sex in parts of the world where the climate is warmer. She decries the empire's political despotism "which desolates Turkey, and renders the men, as well as the soil, unfruitful."[4] In his 1721 *Persian Letters* Montesquieu makes the same point when he addresses the question of thinning of the world's population, especially in Constantinople. Usbek, the harem master who travels to France and whose correspondence to and from Persia forms the book's structure, claims that polygyny and the related phenomena of eunuchs and virgin slaves in the harem contribute to the eastern lack of vitality and that weak and sickly children result from too frequent demands on the harem master.[5] Montesquieu lampoons this kind of "knowledge" and "news" about the East when Usbek's cotraveler, Rica, criticizes early journalistic surveillance complaining about the French "newsmongers [who] know how many wives our august sultan has and how many children he fathers each year" (*PL* 230–31).

In the nineteenth century the issues raised by Wollstonecraft in England and Montesquieu in France are resuscitated in public debate over the "Eastern Question." Discourse over the harem becomes intertwined with disagreements over British policies with Russia and the crumbling Ottoman Empire. Focus turns to Georgia and Circassia in the Caucasus Mountains, traditionally the two locales for obtaining the most highly prized white female concubine-slaves for the harem. Turkey had formally ceded the two areas to Russia (in 1801 and 1829 respectively), but the Circassians resisted Russian domination until 1864, when they were subdued. Moreover, the British mistakenly believed Russia had designs on the Ottoman Empire. For these reasons Circassians were perceived in England as freedom-loving and fiercely independent. Understood this way, Circassians could be viewed positively or negatively depending on one's political position on the Eastern Question: advocacy for Turkey (such as that of Lord Palmerston, foreign secretary from 1830–41 and 1846–51, and prime minister from 1855–58 and 1859–65) meant support for the patriotic Circassians and the harems their women inhabited, while advocacy for Russia (the official British policy for a time) meant excoriating the savage, untamable Circassians and a corresponding anti-harem stance.

Criticism of the seclusion of harem women could constitute an indirect criticism of Muslim men, from whom the West felt obliged to protect native women. As Gayatri Chakravorty Spivak writes, "imperialism's image as the establisher of the good society is marked by the espousal of the woman as *object* of protection from her own kind."[6] The private domestic sphere traditionally associated with women was now viewed as a necessary adjunct to the public world of men and nation-building. The harem became part of the "white man's burden" providing one more justification for meddling in eastern affairs: colonists would bring the superior system of Christian marriage to the uncivilized natives. The attention given to issues of the Oriental domestic sphere and the insistence that they were vitally linked to the political sphere was characteristic of imperialist thinking about the formerly private world of the sex life of foreign peoples. Making the private world of the Other within the Other a public issue was also a projection of a newly developing consciousness about the relationship of the female and male spheres in England. This new attention helped solidify those spheres—public/male and private/female—by sanctioning the view that English women should remain at home and perform domestic tasks.

For Christian orthodoxy harem polygyny was inherently immoral, an atavistic remnant from the earliest Judeo-Christian tradition. The harem was thought to spawn idleness and debauchery. Moreover, polygyny was interpreted as sexual license, itself sinful and thus a sign of the falsity of Islam.[7] Of course, writers acknowledged that the nuclear family too was structured around gender relationships, but the harem was considered more imbued with unrestrained sex. The objection to polygyny is voiced in the eighteenth century, just as the concept of the married couple is sentimentalized,[8] and it is fully developed in the nineteenth century, when the couple is enshrined in bourgeois culture.

In Muslim society the institution of the harem denied the view of women to all men except a few close relatives, so pictures of it in England and France titillated the cognizant viewer by their inherent sense of moral transgression. Furthermore, the Islamic sanction against figural representation in religious art (upheld with varying degrees of rigor over time and geography) added an additional layer of transgression to the secular depiction of harem women, for viewers who conflated the prohibition. Even for the viewer unaware of these Muslim restrictions, a representation of Woman provides a kind of visual mastery over her. In the case of pictures of the forbidden harem woman, the viewer's privilege is amplified.

For educated feminists at least from Mary Wollstonecraft and continuing through the 1870s' *Englishwoman's Review* (and beyond) the harem severely oppressed women. They abhorred the confinement of eastern women to the domestic sphere and the value placed on them only for their beauty and procreative ability. As a single harem master could take up to four wives and as many concubines as he could afford, the harem presumed the superiority of men: it took several women to equal one man's worth within the system. Based on simple arithmetic, polygyny suggested female inferiority.[9] Wollstonecraft wrote: "if polygamy be necessary, woman must be inferior to man, and made for him" (*VRW* 164). In this regard the harem was a metaphor for women's inferior status in British or French industrialized society, where one male factory owner might oversee many female garment workers or the family patriarch might own a wife and many pretty daughters who paid him homage and respect. This reading of the harem as the institutionalization of female subservience contrasts with that of the late eighteenth-century aristocratic feminist, Lady Mary Wortley Montagu, who exhorted her reader to respect the harem, claiming that it offered eastern women certain kinds of freedom.[10]

Like feminists, nineteenth-century abolitionists condemned the harem because they thought it could shield from the law slaveholders who abused innocent women and girls. Reports of the London-based abolitionist Anti-Slavery Society were chivalrous as they described female slaves purchased for the harem. The Society and at times even Parliament issued the call to rescue maidens in distress. This reached frantic proportions in the Philhellenic literature which decried the Turks' abduction of Greek virgins for use in the harem; on this theme a substantive group of pictures were produced a few of which will be examined in this study. There are other examples of Victorian art in which the rescue of the female is bound up with middle-class definitions of masculinity.[11] One of the impulses for the western chivalrous tradition, to which the abolitionist movement is partially indebted, is a displacement of subliminal sexual desire.

Condemnation of the harem, and the slave trade which supplied it with many of its inhabitants, may be considered an allusion to class conflict at home. Social critics had sharpened the debate by an incendiary use of the term "slavery" to describe poorly paid servants. Most noteworthy, John Ruskin, a critic of Victorian art and society, compared the exploitation endured by both servants and slaves. Moreover, the British lower classes had for centuries practiced wife-selling as a form of divorce. Condemning the harem and the slave trade in which women were bought and sold might be related to a speaker's disdain for the low-class British practice of wife-selling.

While most French and British observers deplored the harem system, others defended it as a legitimate means of social and sexual organization which could ensure the dignity of both men and women and allow for the responsible raising of children and the constructing of a nation. The harem's socially acceptable system of concubinage was also considered a more desirable alternative to the flagrant illegitimacy of births in England and France.[12] Travelers who had spent long periods of time in the East sometimes adopted this early, culturally relativist position on the harem. They argued that though it differed in structure from European bourgeois society, its design fulfilled the same functions as family: emotional stability and social regulation.

For apologists who idealized the harem it proffered a simple model of natural social harmony viewed from the perspective of an increasingly complex and mechanized industrial society. The harem system offered a paradigm of orderliness in which the sexes peaceably coexisted in separate spheres for writers disturbed by a relaxation of domestic morals and the disintegration of the family marked by unstable gender roles in England and France. Each sex seemed to know its place and acted accordingly, the man dominant and even cruel, if necessary, the woman always receptive and resigned. According to this "natural" reading, the harem guaranteed that male masters did not compete with other men for the same woman (even though women within the harem were popularly thought to vie for their master's attention). This was tantamount to a form of "free love"—but only for the man. The harem represented a return to a truer form of society, in which layers of an overly industrialized system were stripped away.

Natives in warm climates of the East were thought to be more focused on their bodies. They supposedly matured earlier and married sooner in part because of the increased heat, hence the alleged origins of polygyny and the harem.[13] Correspondingly, tourists from the cool West traveling to the warm East develop a sexual/body awareness. Henri Lefebvre has recently linked the consumer's physical gratification with travel.[14] Writing about advanced industrial society, he articulates the tourist's heightened attention to the body that occurs within the geographical spaces of vacation resorts. His observation is also relevant to the nineteenth century, when bourgeois vacation travel burgeoned: in leisure spots a "'culture of the body'" developed which imitated the natural.[15] This new consciousness of the body can refer to the vacationers' own body and its relationship to indigenous bodies. That the harem woman was generally not seen on trips to the East failed to dislodge her as the desire of the vacationer's fantasy. To the contrary, it may have increased the enthusiasm (and anxiety) for her to materialize in representations made back home. Images of her functioned as fetishized souvenirs—always promising more than could actually be had by the West, always granting less.

For the less serious armchair traveler the harem was a bemusing oddity that provided exotic but safe entertainment. One could flaunt his or her familiarity with the Muslim system as a sign of worldly sophistication. The harem could be a cross-cultural aberration, like pygmies or cannibals, that indicated world diversity but ultimately assured the reader of the superiority of European bourgeois culture.

The tendency for the harem to be treated by some writers as a light, partly fictive entertainment prone to hyperbole gave rise to innumerable testimonies from other writers and travelers as to the truth of their observations, made with their own eyes or else drawn from a highly reliable source. These claims to veracity emerge from a society that revered documentation. However else representations of the harem may have functioned, they always presumed to offer a view into an institution that was traditionally off-limits to foreigners and unrelated males past puberty. It was shrouded in the secrecy mandated by a mysterious and "strange" Islam.

For a disgruntled middle-class husband the harem could be seen as an escape from the responsibilities of the nuclear family. It provided a tangible locale for his fantasy of sex with multiple partners, women who were all compliant and undemanding. In this regard, the harem could function as the expression of wish-fulfillment. Because profligate sexual activity was considered one of the privileges of the aristocracy, the bourgeois male might use the fantasy of the harem as a vehicle for class envy. Conversely, the harem could become a projection of the fear of the *femme fatale*, who, in the company of her harem inmates, might overpower and devour the lone male. This is also implicit in the comment that the harem greatly contributed to the "impotence" of the Ottoman Empire.

These modes of thinking about the cross-cultural phenomenon of the harem, to be developed in this study, are problematic. The premise that the harem is much like Christian bourgeois marriage is a relativist statement. According to Douthwaite, relativism suggests that all peoples are fundamentally the same and that there are no significant differences among cultures. The harem is considered as valid as Christian bourgeois marriage. By contrast, an essentialist perspective is that western marriage and the eastern harem are fundamentally different, that each is monolithic and unchanging. This essentialist view names the harem as more natural and Christian marriage as overly complex. Both relativism and essentialism represent modes of thinking that project the West onto the "East." And values of the West remain the standard of evaluation. Each viewpoint prevents more nuanced considerations of historical change, power, and conflict in both societies; each fails to recognize the great variety of practices that are grouped under the rubric "the harem" or "Christian marriage." Both essentialism and relativism fail to acknowledge understandings of the institution for Muslim subjects. In different ways, both viewpoints support the status quo.[16] They still function to reassert Christian bourgeois values of home, family, and religion today. In Stanley Diamond's words, "'Relativism is the bad faith of the conqueror, who has become secure enough to become a tourist.'"[17]

Recent scholarship has established the fact that modernist representation is known to value vision over other senses and that the point of view established is male, for the most part.[18] The harem picture presents a particular case study for privileging male vision. The French or British female was the other reader of the harem and its representation in the nineteenth century. The opinions of several women are considered in this study. One way of addressing the issue of "the female view" is to show it as diverse: women in nineteenth-century England and France undoubtedly responded to the harem in a great number of ways depending on their class, religion, education, travel experience, their attitudes toward slavery, and the vicissitudes of international politics at the moment in which each spoke. There are several nineteenth-century articles and books claiming to be written by women authors, occasionally called "an anonymous lady," on the subject of harem life. There is nothing discernibly feminine about the viewpoint of some of them.[19] There is a curious dichotomy over which gender was to represent the harem and in what genre. In nineteenth-century written discourse, the harem subject was often considered a woman's topic. Its femininity is implied by the plethora of gossipy detail describing eastern family relationships as well as the exotic objects found in the harem: jewelry, costumes, cosmetics, furnishings, service ware. However, brilliant women writers took on the harem subject for ends which were hardly gossipy.[20] Yet the harem picture, fashioned by masculine artists for the most part, was pitched erotically toward the presumed male spectator. And when jewelry, costumes, cosmetics and other objects were depicted visually, in paint or lithography, they were perceived as more erotic, functioning as fetishes for the harem woman herself, as I hope to demonstrate.

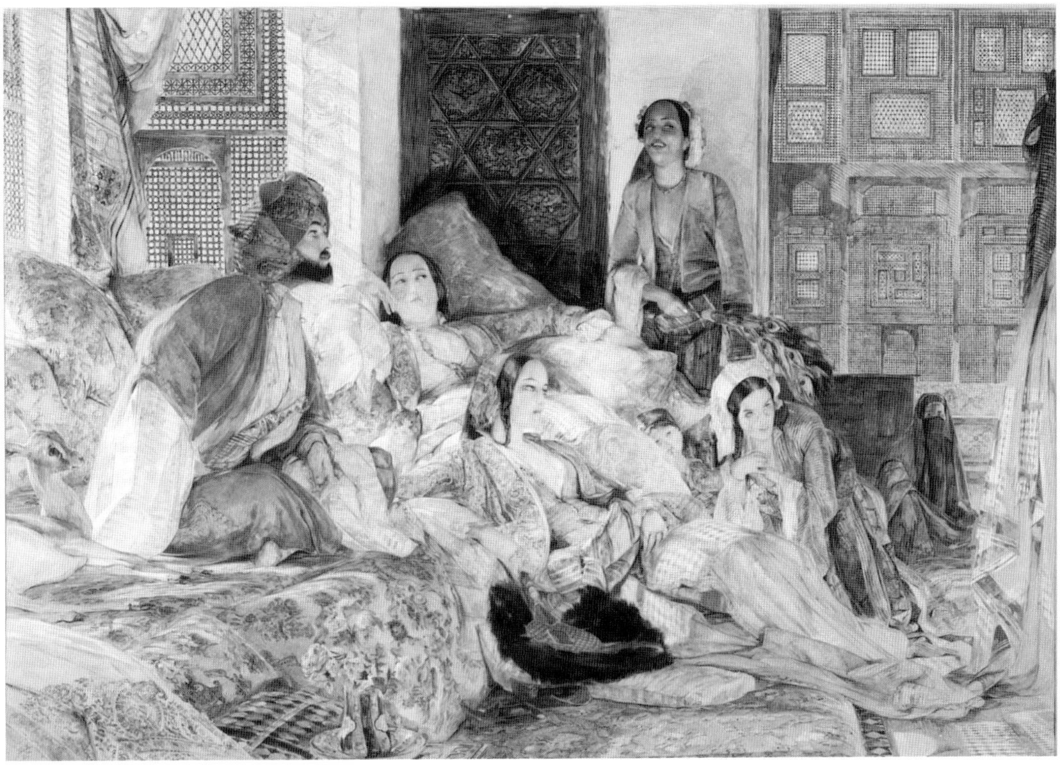

Fig. 1.1. John Frederick Lewis. *Hhareem.* Watercolor. Courtesy of the Trustees of the Victoria and Albert. V&A Picture Library.

As for female viewers of harem pictures, some historical evidence survives, but it is inconclusive about the gender dynamics between the female viewer and the female viewed. Carol Ockman has pieced together an early nineteenth-century group of odalisques ordered by women, including Ingres's *Grande Odalisque*, commissioned by Caroline Bonaparte Murat, one of Napoleon's sisters and queen of Naples. The work was a pendant to the now-lost *Sleeper of Naples.*[21] Women like Caroline Murat paid for these works, but it is an open (and complex) question how these women might have viewed such works and positioned their own gender in response to them. A very different situation is reported in London at mid-century, when women literally walked away from a harem picture. In response to the showing at the Old Water-Colour Society of John Lewis's 1850 *Hhareem* (Plate 1) in which a new, half-dressed slave is introduced into a harem scene of several wives and a pasha, we read in the *Illustrated London News* that "This is a marvellous picture; such as men love to linger around, but such as women, we observed, pass rapidly by."[22] (The Victoria and Albert houses a related image, which closely resembles a portion of this composition [Fig. 1.1]). If the reviewer's observations are reliable, the dichotomy is confirmed between respectable, (ladylike) written descriptions of the harem and disreputable male pictorial renderings of the harem—in that historical moment.

At a deeper level, the question about how women reacted to pictures and writing about the harem can be answered in another way without essentializing women or forcing them to conform to the psychoanalytical male model for the role of desire in identity formation. In using imagery to formulate identity, women can "masquerade" as men, replicating the visual dynamics of male mastery and identification described by Freud, Lacan, and a host of recent feminist scholars. The Self can be formulated as consisting of both male and female elements. Identification is a fluid process, especially for women, as some feminists have argued. In other words, a female viewer may use harem pictures to "try on" masculine and feminine identities and take them off again. Douthwaite's recent observation about gendered views of the liberation/destruction of the harem in Montesquieu's *Persian Letters* implies an eighteenth-century view of the harem that was stratified along gender lines: the harem women call the harem a prison which forces them to be idle, while Usbek refers to it as a "'sweet retreat, where you find innocence and self-security, where no danger makes you afraid.' "[23]

How female viewers might have responded to harem pictures over the course of the nineteenth century in England and France is not yet fully answerable. If gender definitions indeed are fluid, bourgeois women viewers of the harem saw it both similarly and differently from men. Women sometimes see "as women," while women are also capable of seeing as men do. In this way women have the capacity for exercising "double vision" even more so than men, some scholars have argued. If readings of women today offer some of the range of possibilities for the ways in which nineteenth-century women read the harem, it was met with feelings of fascination, disgust, desire, repression, identification, humor, and titillation.

My study is based on the assumption that the harem trope provided the means for the British and French to construct their political and psychosexual self-images. That the Other is constructed on the basis of the Self has been a premise of much cross-cultural analysis. Paintings, prints, essays, short stories, travel accounts, and novels about the harem—all cultural representations—provided the arena for the playing out of deeply held and often unnamed beliefs, revealing a great deal about thinking on class, race, and gender distinctions in the nineteenth century. Even today for thinkers wrestling with the tensions inherent in the domestication of women in industrialized countries at the start of the new millennium, the configuration of an exotic woman of privileged leisure confined to the home could not but be self-referential, inviting contrasts and comparisons between the exotic harem woman, the bourgeois lady at home, and the American feminist scholar. To the extent that literate western societies were ambivalent toward their own forms of marriage, they would be ambivalent toward what they construct as its opposite—harem polygyny.

Thus the harem texts to be examined in this study can be correlated to one or several of the attitudes outlined here by analyzing their narrative emphases and intertextual references, using written reactions to these pictures and to the harem more generally. Nineteenth-century representations of the harem were intertwined with several other political issues of the day, including the abolition of slavery (harem and nonharem alike); the Woman Question and one of its correlatives, the newly developed cult of domesticity; the Eastern Question and international political position-taking. A focus on these representations can yield a remarkably rich fabric in the history of polemics.

Harem Representation and the Politics of Aesthetic Positivism in England and France

Representations of the harem whether in visual or written form are grounded in what I would like to call aesthetic positivism.[24] These images are presented as having a referent in reality, one lived by actual women in Turkey, Egypt, the Maghreb, and elsewhere. The spoken public discourse surrounding visual and printed representations of the harem—such as comments in Parliament or at a meeting of the Anti-Slavery Society—helped establish the reality of the harem experience for nineteenth-century readers and viewers, but such speech also constituted representation. What makes these pictures positivist is the presumption that they refer to and unproblematically replicate that lived reality. And a particular configuration of realist stylistic techniques reinforce the truth of such pictures and written texts. For the moment I want to by-pass the period-style Realism as it is conventionally used in art history along with the categories Rococo, Romantic, Rococo-revival (categories I myself will use for the sake of convenience in this study, however). Going beyond the stylistic differences of national schools, I maintain that both British and French harem pictures are based in aesthetic positivism, admittedly an unusual art historical approach which attempts to consider what harem pictures produced in the two countries have in common.

Several British and French images evoke the comparison of the realist harem picture with the realist photograph, regularly constructed as the epitome of mimesis since its invention. A constant belief evoked by the nineteenth-century photograph is that it captures/holds still evidence of a lived experience, that someone or something was there at one time. This is also implied by harem pictures. Thus the "implicit positivism"[25] of the orientalist photograph can be extended to cover a much broader range of orientalist pictures, including images of the harem.[26]

This paradox of the highly mediated nature of harem paintings' aesthetic positivism is articulated by the *Art Journal* in 1869 when it judges John Lewis's *Intercepted Correspondence* as "one of the highly realistic yet supremely artificial compositions of Mr. Lewis."[27] Similarly, when the French art critic Edmond About calls Lewis's *Hhareem* "strange"[28] in 1855 (Plate 1), the term refers to the excess of realism on which Lewis's picture is premised. The painting obsessively records a reality that must be precisely spelled out, since it is only imagined. No one will doubt that the harem pictures of Lewis or the writings of Edward Lane are realistic, in their highly detailed, illuminating, and straightforward presentation of information. Critics pointed this out and lauded them for it. It is riskier to argue that the French harem picture in the nineteenth century is also grounded in positivism. What allows the use of the term for Ingres's *Grande Odalisque* (1814)? Or Delacroix's *Women of Algiers* (1834)? Or one of the many popular lithographs of the harem dating from the July Monarchy which will be studied here? Even the images of Gérôme, perhaps a fairer comparison to Lewis in both time and technique, are readable as more "French" (read: more eroticized) and thus inherently different from the British images. French harem pictures could more readily be given the descriptor "erotic" while British harem pictures are relatively more "scientific" (ethnographic).

There are many ways to approach this perceived dichotomy between British and French harem pictures. Nineteenth-century harem representations produced in both countries, images premised on close description and a link to first-hand observation, utilize the guise of science to present the erotic. In each case science and the erotic are emphasized to varying degrees. John Lewis's meticulous harem pictures were eroticized in their fetishization of the female body through luxurious fabrics, jewels, and even (arguably) the colored latticed windows. And Gérôme's racy slave market pictures were scientific in their interest in precision and ethnography. In fact, in writing as well as in visual texts, highly detailed or repetitious representations of the harem requiring intense effort to produce can help alleviate anxiety—the writer's, the artist's, the reader's, the viewer's—elicited by the subjects of sexuality and subordination. Long descriptive passages or great numbers of similar themes can work "to domesticate the alien,"[29] a phrase which has special resonance when the subject is the harem, which is both domestic and alien to western observers. The "scientizing" of the harem itself can be considered a technique to distance the writer from its potentially erotic titillation[30]—or provide an excuse for it.

Aesthetic positivism can be characterized not only by its realistic look but also by its function. I want to link the positivist style to the politics of gender, class, and protoimperialism. In response to Edward Said's call for a search for the formal vocabulary of cultural imperialism,[31] I want to study the syntax of the harem representation. This study establishes the building blocks of the harem representation, their common vocabulary of themes and objects. These in turn contributed to the aesthetic positivism fundamental to establishing their truth.[32] In this regard they can be read as ideological. Bhabha describes the colonialist text as having "transparency," which produces "an effect of authority."[33] Harem images which were produced in the first three-quarters of the nineteenth century had an authority in the art worlds—visual and literary, official and popular—and in the realm of international/colonialist politics, as I describe at length in the next chapter. The artistic and political realms are inseparable. Thus, the harem representation, grounded upon positivist premises, is a significant site for cultural and political readings.

Bhabha further writes that in order to be accepted as authoritative, seemingly transparent texts must adhere to "rules of recognition."[34] If texts do not conform, the colonial program becomes ambivalent, subject to critique and dismantling. The "rules of recognition," conventions for portraying and thinking about the "transparent" harem picture in the nineteenth century, will be described in subsequent chapters. Those "rules," which operate from the beginning of the nineteenth century, start to crumble c. 1875 as the authority of the harem picture breaks down on the cusp of the new wave of colonization, as outlined in my concluding chapter.

Revealing the Hidden: Harem Images and the New *Scientia Sexualis* in the Nineteenth Century

Nineteenth-century harem representations—of whatever "style"—participate in a particular kind of scientific systemizing of sex: *scientia sexualis.* Theorized by Michel Foucault in his 1976 *History of Sexuality*, volume 1, the term characterizes nineteenth-century bourgeois thinking on sex. Foucault posits a division between Victorian societies in which a *scientia sexualis* reigned, and Chinese, Japanese, Indian, and "Arabo-Moslem societies" characterized by an *ars erotica.* His contribution to our understanding of Victorian notions of sexuality in this volume is his rejection of the characterization of the era as repressed. He suggests instead that the culture was excessive in its productive discourses about sex. One such discourse was that on the Muslim harem.

Foucault writes that sex in the nineteenth century was understood not simply as pleasure of the experience but as pleasure enhanced by the telling and revealing of it. Such a telling is possible by means of the self-confession, which produces a presumed truth about sex. I believe harem pictures constitute a pleasurable pictorial confession about the polygynous sexual arrangement thought to reveal the fundamental truth of eastern society. The pleasure of telling or revealing the truth about the harem comes from speaking about what was thought to be unspoken. Foucault's insight about the pleasure in revelation is played out in the nineteenth century by a particular kind of contestation over the truth about harem women. It is precisely the struggle over what constituted the truth about harem women that makes these texts so productive. Was she moral or immoral? oversexed or virginal? confined or free? a good mother or bad? happy with her life or not? beautiful or not? There was compelling urgency and great pleasure for participants in culture to gain the upper hand, to have the last word, to produce the definitive "picture," of the harem woman. Bhabha provides a useful point of analysis about how this process was affected by the seemingly transparent text: the truth emerges only after a false view can be established.[35] The outmoded view of the harem was constantly being denounced and superseded by observers who claimed the authentic, allegedly firsthand experience of the harem.

This struggle to reveal the truth about the harem was curiously presumptuous, because western artists and writers recreated the confession of an experience that they cannot have had directly. Typical of nineteenth-century discourses on "deviant" sexualities, the harem is understood in reference to the speaker's "normal" sexuality. In binary fashion, eastern sexual and social experience constructs western sexual and social experience. This formation of eastern identity through representation was ultimately self-referential.

These nineteenth-century texts contribute to a specialized knowledge about harem women produced by "luring [pleasure and truth] out in the open."[36] Foucault is writing about an individual confession which produces the necessary fiction of the self; the Victorian self confesses publicly and indirectly as it tells the truth about the Other. Whether individual or cultural, religious, or psychological, the confessional model is useful. In order to be effective the confession of the sexual experience needs to be "thorough, meticulous, [. . .] constant [. . .] and scientific."[37] It is this cluster of four terms that I would like to define as the collective "style" of harem pictures analyzed here.

"Meticulous" and "constant," the harem accoutrements found in these pictures—pipes, coffee, musical instruments, animals, flowers, jewelry (examined as symbolic motifs in chapter 4)—are much more than indicators of an eastern setting. Highly detailed and occurring from picture to picture (or text to text), they are positivist ciphers, assurances of the authenticity of the scene before the viewer. The specialized knowledge about the harem woman these pictures produce for their original audiences (what I name as pseudo-knowledge) is information about her character, both incorrigibly immoral—adulterous, negligent, perverse, indolent, whorish, jealous (see chapter 5)—and exceedingly moral—virginal, silent, cordial, obedient, patient, maternal (see chapter 6). The scientific aspect of harem pictures is that they subject the vague, the rumored, the out-of-sight to visual scrutiny. The sacred/secreted is pinned down, pictured and exposed to observation. In this regard the impulse behind harem representation, visual and verbal alike, anticipates the sciences of anthropology and ethnography which seek to view, record, and preserve the fundamentally different, the primitive. Because the primitive is conceived of as a stage of human civilization, the recording attempts to hold still what is thought to be fundamentally ephemeral. As harem representations epitomize the Female ("the sex") they cannot but elicit pleasure, the double pleasures of looking and knowing.

When Foucault uses the word "lure" to describe the bringing out into the light of day the pleasure and truth of Victorian notions of sex, it has particular resonance for the pleasures of viewing harem pictures in which the fictional woman represented becomes complicit in the very transgression of the picture. Harem pictures examined here mark different points on the continuum between the secretive/private and the scientific/public; the British tend to look more scientific and the French more private. But all of them are fetishized, that is, all negate any living, breathing harem woman located in her indigenous culture. All these representations present merely a fragment of her experience and instrumentalize her invented persona to serve as a foil for western identity formation. These are some of the "strategies of power"[38] that are inherent in the "will to knowledge" about harem women which underlies the whole phenomenon.

Timothy Mitchell takes this one step further. He believes that the opening up of the harem to the observation of the West was part of the colonial program to reform the perceived chaos and corruption of the Egyptian home, which was thought to impede national progress. If the new state, in imitation of the French and British model, was to be organized and disciplined, "it was necessary to break down existing patterns of association and segregation, mystified and romanticised under such labels as 'the harem.'"[39] Immoral (polygynous) mothers would be rectified, and there would be hope for Egypt's future generations. Penetration of such private space, as represented in art and literature, parallels the actual destruction of the harem.

Identity and Difference: "Western" Reconstructions of Sex, Class, and Race in "Eastern" Garb

A history of nineteenth-century harem pictures, viewed against the texts to which they are dependent for their meanings, raises a host of issues which I will develop in subsequent chapters. These include: high politics, that is, international relations over abolition and the Eastern Question; the politics of multiple interpretations revealing the speaker's own interests and attitudes, contributing to his or her own ongoing process of identity formation; domestic class and gender politics about the position of servants and women. I want to maintain my reader's consciousness of my own politics: gender-, class-, and race-sensitive and indebted to critical postmodern theories about the value of multivalent and intertextual analyses of culture. Some of the issues raised by new theories of representation are crucial to any study of representations of colonized women.[40] The very subject of this study mandates a politicizing of these theories that might otherwise be applied neutrally or conservatively. Some of those questions require more development.

Harem representation is linked to class analysis in England and France. For some commentators in the eighteenth and nineteenth centuries criticism of the harem was a "veiled" critique of the eighteenth-century leisured aristocracy from whose amorality the middle class attempted to distance itself as part of its self-definition. At the same time, some considered the harem a parallel phenomenon for well-to-do middle-class women's leisure touted publicly as a status symbol for themselves and their husbands who could afford to keep them from working for wages. In fact the bourgeois woman's leisured status only appeared as such and was possible through a great deal of her own work and organization of others' labor within the home.[41] The harem discourse about busyness/idleness certainly draws from this tension between public expectations for women's leisurely life and the reality of managerial organization that underpinned them.

Harem representation is implicated in ideological debates over colonialist intervention in the Arab world. To address this, one needs to consider how the image of the harem woman might reinforce stereotypes of the Other, contributing to a dehumanization of the eastern people, which allows for their economic and cultural exploitation. Pictures made in and for the official art world have enormous influence on the making of stereotypes about the foreigner, whether male or female, all the more powerful for their unarticulated connection to the world of high politics. On the one hand, some of the harem pictures analyzed here seem to legitimize customs of the native, for example, those that draw from Islamic theological traditions. On the other hand, even when harem pictures can be read to validate Muslim marriage, they always presume British/French superiority and of course visual dominance in violating a sacrosanct institution.

What are the functions of harem pictures in French and British society charged with debate over slavery in all its forms—foreign and domestic, white and black, male and female? Positive and negative typing of women is part of cultural ambivalence toward both women and the Other and especially their overlap: the female Other. Harem pictures are not only about women. They are also about class relationships. And they are about racial relations. They present the opportunity to express notions about how women, servants, and people of various "races" or nationalities are expected to look and behave, expectations that can help us dismantle the construction of white European bourgeois male identity.

To what extent did British and French observers believe that harem wives and mothers were like their western counterparts? Responses to the question are explicit in a few cultural texts on the harem. In the pair of French lithographs done in 1854 after Desandré, *Une anglaise romanesque* and *Une persane boudeuse* (Fig. 1.2), the two women depicted have similar facial and body types. Still there is a sharp contrast in the women's essential natures suggested by their clothing, pose, and activities. The romantic Englishwoman seeks escape in novels, tea, and reverie, while the sulky Persian finds pleasure in the pipe and love, symbolized by the bouquet on the floor. Her provocative body pose and the signs of her interests indicate a freer, more sexualized existence than the straightlaced Englishwoman's. There is more than one binary at play here: though English and Persian women may be Other to a French audience, they are set in explicit opposition to each other by the mere fact that this is a pair of prints whose individual characters take on meaning in relationship to each other.

These prints have a literary parallel in Gérard de Nerval's *Voyage to the Orient.* He is extremely ambivalent about the way in which Otherness and identity might be reconciled. He writes that a foreign woman is "captivating and irresistible," and because he cannot understand her language, she has "none of those vulgar shortcomings to which we have become only too accustomed among the women of our own country."[42] In effect, familiarity breeds contempt,

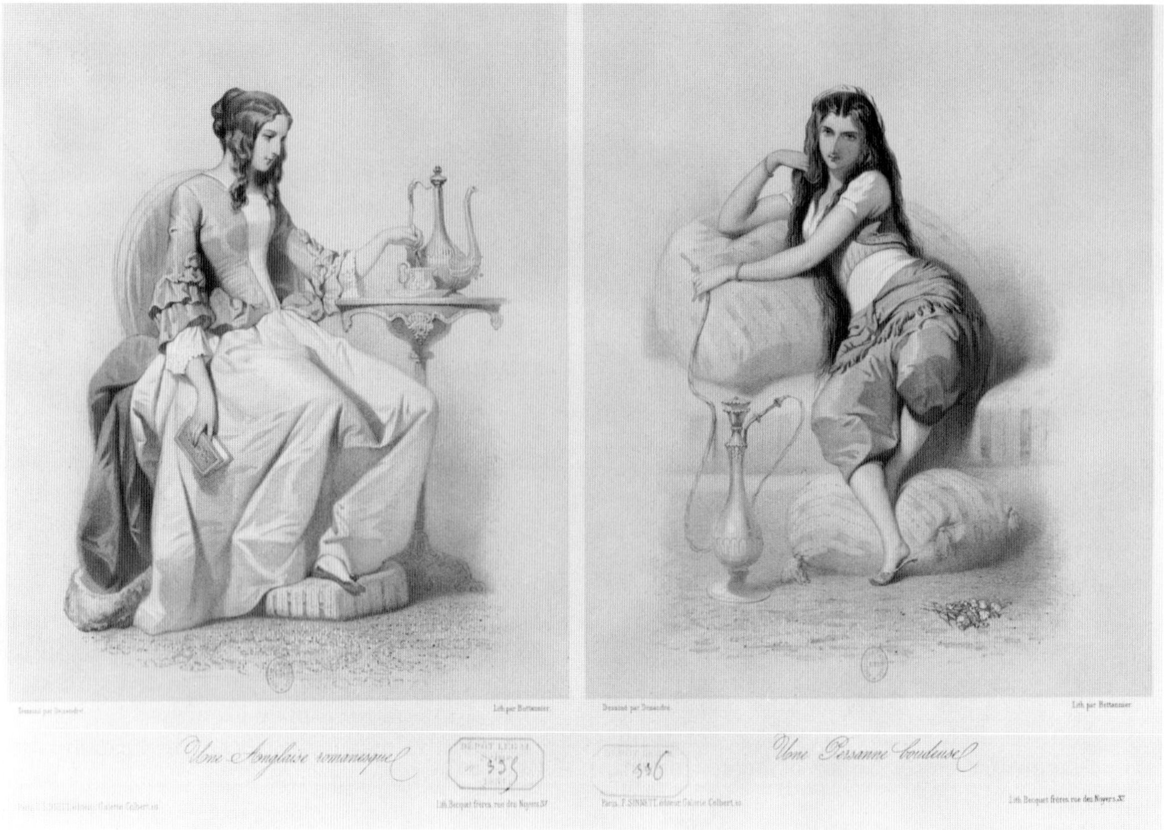

Fig. 1.2. Bettannier after Desandré. ***Une anglaise romanesque*** **and** ***Une persane boudeuse.*** **1854. Lithographs. Cliché Bibliothèque nationale de France, Paris. Farwell,** ***FPLI,*** **v. 11, 1B3 B82233.**

while the strange is enchanting. (Or, when you don't speak the same language, your woman can't nag.) Nerval reinforces the traditional binary in his conception of women. And when it is suggested that he marry his slave Zetnaybia and return to Paris with her—a test of reconciling the polarities—his writing reveals great anxiety. The formerly "captivating" woman out of context would suddenly be viewed as "hideous" as "a cannibal," to use his words. Nerval, until now the lover of things oriental, is concerned with how Zetnaybia could ever measure up to European gender expectations: "How can such a woman become my equal?" (*VO* 77).

In a similar way, Alphonse de Lamartine notes a contrast between a Maltese woman and an English woman whom he claims to see sitting on a nearby terrace: the Maltese strums her guitar and "plays an old national air, wild as the climate" while the Englishwoman "turns over the pages of the immortal poets of her country."[43] While the western women reads a book as a means of coming to terms with her heritage, the more spontaneous and uncivilized eastern woman uses music. Her nationality or "race" expresses her essence, in Lamartine's view. In the prints of the English and Persian women and in Lamartine's writings, difference and identity are conceived as (1) visible, thus knowable and (2) inevitable and unchanging.

Like Nerval, Alexandre Dumas sets up a neat dichotomy between eastern and western women and more generally between our culture and theirs. The tenor of his observations is also that we are civilized while they are not. But his writing vacillates in determining whether civilization is better because it offers personal liberties or whether it restrains too much making us "almost always troubled and careworn," which an Arab "never" is.[44] The Muslim "sensual paradise," polygyny, and physical violence are understood as corporeal sloppiness as compared to French marital restraint reinforced by protective laws. Arab women emerge as the disadvantaged who in contradistinction to women of western Europe are "prisoners in their homes" (*AA* 186). Morever they must submit to male authority, even though any show of disrespect toward them might be met with women's "vengeance" (*AA* 118).

Dumas's is a typical dichotomy. Curiously for this study of visual art, the rigid bifurcation between eastern and western is threatened when he sees on a wall of a room in Philippesville four lithographs of French paintings (whose identification is not revealed to the reader). This is an important moment, though Dumas writes about it in a brief, offhand way. It is a moment when the terms East and West could potentially be blurred, a moment when the rigid poles might instead be shown to be points on a continuum of experience. No such revelation occurs for Dumas. At the sight of those unnamed reproductions, unconscious reminders of his own identity in a foreign context, he merely expresses "disappointment" for how they disrupt the purity of his own vicarious experience of otherness (*AA* 160).[45] A blip of dissonance, they are taken in and forgotten.

As the writing of Dumas, Lamartine, and Nerval suggests, constructing eastern and western women stereotypically can also defuse the Woman Question as it was understood back home. Compared to eastern women, western women don't have it so bad. Tapper captures the paradox: "their own domestic subordination seems insignificant by contrast, while at the same time their achievements in the public arena seem more significant than perhaps they are."[46]

Visual and verbal texts which dwell on the ways in which eastern women are like western women generally fail to admit the possibility that western bourgeois women (and men) might be like eastern harem women. If harem women are wicked or oversexed, it is presumed that western (bourgeois) women can be neither. The relationship to the speaker is one of difference. This process of constantly splitting the Self from that which is perceived as different becomes a way to repress fears about one's self. This seems to support Bhabha's stunningly perceptive observation about how discrimination or stereotyping strategies work:

> Produced through the strategy of disavowal, the *reference* of discrimination is always to a process of splitting as the condition of subjection: a discrimination between the mother culture and its bastards, the self and its doubles, where the trace of what is disavowed is not repressed but repeated as something *different*—a mutation, a hybrid.[47]

It is ironic then that in representations of the harem the process of making the Orient the Other happens in the nineteenth century, the very time when colonial powers began "collecting" countries. In effect, the harem is a popular subject for colonialist agents to decry in part because they themselves are establishing a "harem" of colonies.[48] Perhaps crudely put, as European powers become the owners of collections of colonies, which they construct as the Other, their own process of identity-formation requires that they split off the characteristics of both despicable master and weak/vulnerable outsider and project them onto, respectively, the male and female Other. The next chapter explores in greater depth the colonial contexts of the nineteenth-century harem picture.

2
The Colonial Contexts for the Harem Representation

Introduction: The Role of the Muslim Harem in the Rhetoric of International Politics

In this chapter I want to address the question of how the public world of nineteenth-century high politics considered the private world of the harem within the discourse on the Eastern Question. Instead of writing a history of this phenomenon called the harem, a self-contained arena of sexual life ghettoized from high politics, I want to link private and public, to show that notions of the harem affected governmental decisions about international politics which in turn contributed to French and British thinking about the harem. To use the terms of historian Joan Wallach Scott, I am in search of "the reciprocal nature of gender and society and [. . .] the particular and contextually specific ways in which politics constructs gender and gender constructs politics."[1] The history of East-West international relations in the nineteenth century needs a rewriting which considers the issue of the harem.

In this chapter I attempt to expand the parameters of high politics. And I want to acknowledge how the conception of the center of political life depends on its construction of the margins, or as Lefebvre names it, "'an elsewhere.'"[2] Western European identity is formulated as it constructs the harem space and its inhabitants as peripheral. The perception of the harem as outré marriage custom must be dislodged through my remapping.

When we inquire into French or British attitudes toward the Middle Eastern Muslim harem and toward each other we encounter epistemological questions. For example, what does it mean for Britain to maintain a stereotypical attitude toward the East or France for that matter? In learned British circles observers described national differences, often antagonistic toward France as well as the East and its institutions: legal, religious, social. My own goal is not to argue that British or French observers in fact describe any essential character of those countries. I want to document the *perception* of writers and artists that countries could hold attitudes toward each other and what those viewpoints entailed.

The classical western tradition has often expressed sexual desire in the language of war, correlating women's bodies to the battleground.[3] The impulse to possess the land can be linked to the impulse to possess the women who live there. Representations of the harem become the repository for the expression of both territorial and sexual urges. An association between land and women, the public and private spheres, is fundamental to the formation of a modern western identity: the Self, whether at the psychological, sociological, or national level, cannot be defined without constant reference to an Other.

As modern western monogamous society, supposedly based on free choice of one's life partner, becomes more deeply institutionalized, it is understood as the polar opposite to the Muslim harem, thought to be based on coercion and tyranny. The objection to polygyny thus becomes especially acute when monogamy is increasingly perceived as the only real moral choice. And the outrage over harem slavery becomes heightened when the concept of freedom is used to define one's self, one's class, and one's nation.

Though this is a study of British and French misunderstanding of the harem, it must be acknowledged that the East was also in a state of flux on the issues of the harem and slavery in the nineteenth century. Research has been done about changes in women's lives in Egypt, a forerunner among eastern countries in two areas of modernization, feminism and Islamic reform.[4] Innovation in these areas, especially acute under the leadership of Mohamed Ali (ruled 1805–1848), contributed to the gradual demise of the harem in the nineteenth century.

Judith Tucker believes that the existence of slavery in Egypt was exaggerated by the West in the nineteenth century, as it accounted for 0.5 percent of the population and was dwindling.[5] In the eighteenth century, the great mameluke houses had recruited slaves: males served in militias having loyalty to the private house, and females served in plush harems, symbols of mameluke wealth and prestige.

But as capitalism began to take root, the economy grew more dependent upon wage labor. Smaller private armies gave way to Muhammad Ali's state-controlled army. Private households held less power as the state became consolidated. And the harem began to lose its politically symbolic value throughout the century, though it (and slavery more generally) continued to provide "comfort and pleasure."[6] Even before the British forced campaigns to free slaves, manumission—for which there was a long and much-lauded tradition within Islamic texts—was commonplace among slaveholders contributing to a large-scale "erosion" of the harem in the 1860s and 1870s.[7] Never widespread, the harem survived only in the wealthiest "museum-like" homes such as that of the Khedive Ismail (ruled 1863–79).[8] By the turn of the century the harem concubine was considered "an anachronism."[9]

The liberation of women from the harem was one goal in indigenous reformist movements, influenced in part by debates originating within Islam and in part by ideas imported from the West and reworked into nationalist traditions. Later in the century in Egypt polygyny, concubinage, and the enslavement of women were denounced as anti-Muslim by Sheik Mohamed Abduh (1849–1905), who called for a reinterpretation of the *Qur'an*, which he also felt approved of female education.[10] In Turkey the call to limit the sultan to one wife dates to a 1912 manifesto issued by the Young Turks Movement.[11] The proposed reforms were part of a cultural and religious asceticism which advocated curbs on the privileges of the elites and a democratization of resources.

In eighteenth-century French representation, the harem's dissolution accompanies the breakdown of political absolutism. Montesquieu correlates the liberation of the harem with the destruction of tyrannical political authority, as the Persian harem master Usbek and especially his friend Rica become more understanding of a western mode of governance during their sojourn in Paris. In the libretto from Mozart's 1782 opera *Abduction from the Seraglio* the pasha Selim makes a decision to forfeit his captured slave Constanza, in effect dissolving his harem, because of an enlightened decision to allow her to reunite with her beloved Belmonte. The pasha is praised as a wise and noble ruler for his forgiveness of Belmonte and his man Pedrillo, who come to rescue her and her maid Blonde. The closing lyrics to the opera's grand finale reiterate this: "Ever proudly we shall hail him and his noble virtue's fame."[12] Eighteenth-century writing that views political and sexual tyranny as interconnected in the harem is analyzed in more detail in chapter 5.

In nineteenth-century French and British representation as well the tyranny of the harem unfolds within the context of political or juridical tyranny. In Delacroix's painted *Sardanapalus* (see Fig. 4.53), the sadistic king watches nonchalantly the destruction of his harem, proof of the arbitrariness of his judgment and testament to his political authority, despite the invading foreigners at his door. But Byron's Assyrian king Sardanapalus provokes more complex questions of whether an enlightened leader can also own a harem. His 1821 play by the same name, which struggles with the definition of good governance, appeared during the Restoration in France, when the political legitimacy of kingship was being scrutinized in light of the revolution's legacy. Sardanapalus is nonviolent; he wears flowers in his hair—and delights in the pleasures of the harem. In act 1 his brother-in-law Salemenes twice criticizes him as "effeminate," a reference to his style of clothing and presumably his brand of leadership, in which he is overly attentive to the needs of his people. When his rule is threatened by outsiders, Sardanapalus undergoes a transformation from slothful (soft-hearted?) ruler to warrior, as he finally accepts the role of forceful ruler expected by his august lineage. But he does so too late to be effective. By the end of the play he admits to his favorite slave Myrrha that he would have been a better ruler except for his having maintained a harem: "Had I never loved / But thee, I should have been an unopposed / Monarch of honouring nations."[13] The struggle for Sardanapalus is between his heart, his feminine side, and his head, indebted to tradition. Harem-holding has been an emotional indulgence that has distracted him from his primary public duty.

Harem texts raise questions about the nature of government and individual liberty. And harem representations are shaped by the vicissitudes of international politics as well.

France, England, and the Harem

Harem representation can be understood by considering the political contestation between England and France. British and French religion, language, and aesthetic traditions differed, yet the nations had similar goals. In the East each sought material profit, and in art production each wanted a proud national school. Old animosities and new alliances appeared throughout the century over relations with the East. Cultural antagonism surfaces as a leitmotif in the dignified British response to naughty French harem pictures. While British harem pictures underscore the foreignness of the Muslim institution, their different look reasserts a distance from France, alluding to and rekindling old rivalries manifest in both culture and politics. The divergent look of British and French harem images was in part an artistic manifestation of their long-standing competition played out over a new issue, the Eastern Question.

In their cultural practices Britain and France blended their artistic concepts of the harem. The art centers of Paris and London had some close ties, including a privileged clientele of travelers, traders, and diplomats who circulated information about the customs of distant countries, and a leisured consumer audience receptive to such observations. French artists exhibited their works at the Royal Academy, and English artists showed at the annual Salon, beginning enthusiastically in the second quarter of the nineteenth century. Books with engraved illustrations of the harem and other aspects of Middle Eastern life had appeared often in English and French at least since the seventeenth century. By the nineteenth century, harem prints readily circulated between the two countries, often produced by a printer having offices in both London and Paris. As for watercolors, Oriental subjects became "a major factor" in the success of those markets from the 1830s.[14]

Cultural antagonism between France and Britain could carry a moral edge. As feminist Mary Wollstonecraft characterized it in the late eighteenth century, "the French character" is associated with "sensuality," while modesty "has been more grossly insulted in France than even in England" (*VRW* 86). Yet this stereotype was not without ambivalence. Some British artists and writers were also attracted to France's so-called freer ways, and the admiration could be reciprocal.

British-French rivalry was a real factor in the development of colonization in the Middle East. While Britain was building its overseas trade, the period 1800–1815 was marked by ongoing economic and political conflict with France. British observers saw French trade as stifled by government regulations and class traditions, while business leaders saw their own finances as relatively unencumbered. By his own admission in 1797, Napoleon would begin his Egyptian Campaign in order to secure markets for France and undermine British power.[15]

Napoleon's political expedition to Egypt begun in 1798 included a crew of 165 savants. In his yearlong sojourn Napoleon set up several councils, including the Grand Divan in Cairo, which were bilingual but headed by French commissioners. In Cairo the core of the French intelligentsia set up the *Institut d'Egypte* and a French-Arabic printing press. The French expedition ended in 1801 when they were expelled, but their presence left a permanent mark on elite cultural life. The French also published detailed information on Egyptian society in the encyclopedic *Description de l'Egypte* issued by the imperial press from 1809–28. Napoleon's double defeat by 1815 marked a culmination in early nineteenth-century Franco-British political and economic antagonism. France had dominated the Mediterranean in the eighteenth century, but the nineteenth century brought Great Britain naval and industrial superiority. Commercially, Britain predominated in the Middle East, while France provided a palpable cultural force. Though the British were unequivocally the leaders in naval strength by the nineteenth century, they still feared French encroachments on Turkish integrity, especially in the second quarter of the century. The construction of the Suez Canal intensified their rivalry. Granted rights to the canal by Mohammed Ali's son Said (r. 1854–63) in 1856, French construction efforts met with the continued opposition of Lord Palmerston, operating through the Porte. French-British alliances were brief and motivated by immediate crises.[16]

Napoleon Bonaparte and Vivant Denon on the Harem

My quivering lips pour forth the words
That cluster in his name of glory—
The star gigantic with its rays of swords
Whose gleams irradiate all modern story.

—Victor Hugo, "My Napoleon," *Les Orientales* (1828)

Napoleon Bonaparte's name is fundamental to a study of the early-nineteenth-century French presence in Egypt, and it is manifest not only in politics but also in culture (as demonstrated in Hugo's panegyric within his volume of eastern poetry).[17] An illustrated book translated into English in 1803, Vivant Denon's *Travels in Upper and Lower Egypt*,[18] dedicated to the "hero" Napoleon Bonaparte and published under his patronage, contains three images of the harem. Both images and texts were produced by Baron Dominique Vivant Denon (1747–1825), artist, man of letters, and member of the Institute of Cairo selected to accompany Napoleon on his campaign and record, under military escort, the noteworthy Egyptian monuments, especially the ancient archeological ruins.[19] It is useful to read the three harem pictures along with Denon's written commentaries on the harem taken from his *Travels* and Napoleon's recorded comments about

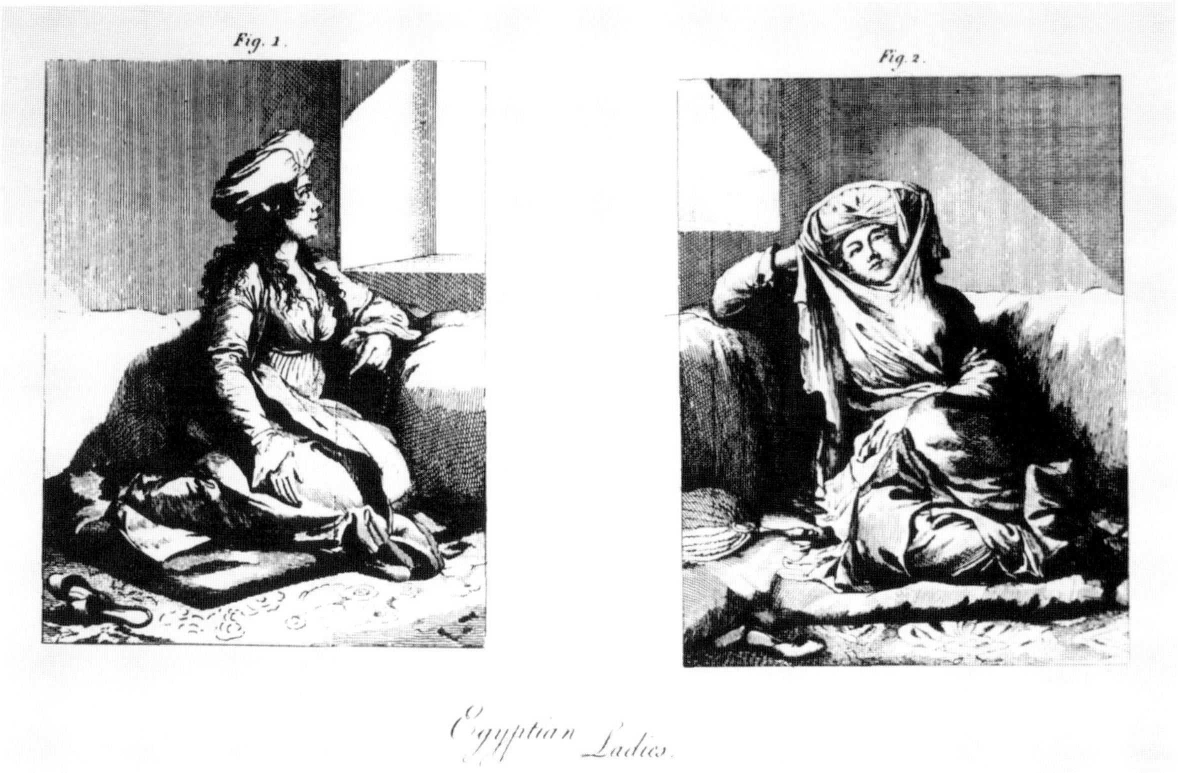

Fig. 2.1. After Dominique Vivant Denon. *Egyptian Ladies.* Engraving. *Travels in Upper and Lower Egypt,* 1803.

the harem and eastern slavery, several of which survive in his memoirs, dictated while in exile on St. Helena from the year of his surrender to the British at Waterloo until his death in 1821.

Two of the three harem pictures from Denon's *Egypt* are a pair of engravings titled *Egyptian Ladies* (Fig. 2.1). The women are located in a harem according to the fuller title, given in the description to the plates: "Egyptian Ladies in the Haram." Each woman dressed in eastern garb sits alone near an open window. In each composition her shoes appear in the lower left as signs of each scene's intimacy. The woman in Denon's figure 1 shown in profile looks out the window and fingers her worry beads. The woman in his figure 2 leaning on her right elbow makes eye contact with the spectator, a lute at her side. The setting and poses of his figures, already formulaic by the early nineteenth century, belie both the authenticity and the spontaneity that are claimed for his image-making in the preface, where he writes that these engravings are done after "drawings which I made most frequently on my knee, or standing, or even on horseback" (*E* 1:vii).

Early on in Denon's account he writes with astounding arrogance about the French ability to penetrate and change the harem. His comments contextualize the pair of plates as scenes "invaded" by the eyes of the French: "I also deferred the pleasure of drawing the Egyptian women, until we should, by our own influence over the manners of the eastern nations, remove the veil by which they are covered" (*E* 1:219). The "influence" in question is a favor done for a rich native, who in return invited Denon to breakfast with them at his home. Denon describes the woman shown in his figure 2, whose beauty was "accompanied by a soft tinge of melancholy. She was extremely fair, and her hands uncommonly delicate and handsome" (*E* 1:222). His choice of terms presumes that her beauty is what led to her confinement in the harem, and her sadness resulted from it. She also had a "negligent and pensive air," which he believed she affected, convinced that by doing so "she should become superior to all the magnificence by which she was surrounded and covered" (*E* 1:223). Is her pose, leaning back with head on elbow, eyes slightly drawn meant to be read as Denon's observation of her emotional aloofness? The lack of connection is common between early-nineteenth-century book illustration and its accompanying text. A clear correlation between image and verbal text is difficult to draw.

Denon claims that the other woman shown in the pair of *Egyptian Ladies* (his figure 1) was the seemingly submissive wife of a jealous man, his neighbor whose marital spats he overheard. The author claims he became her (platonic) confidant, and listened to her troubles. Denon later learned that when the plague broke out in Egypt, it took her, her husband—and, surprisingly, her lover. Her willingness to bare her soul to Denon anticipates his revelation about her marital infidelity to her Frankish husband. Compositionally, her gaze, which focuses out the window, may be a visual clue about her infidelity. Left unanswered is the question of why a "Frank" would have a harem at all.

Napoleon's own comments on the harem, though they are issued a decade later, are relevant to a reading of this pair of plates. The placement of these women alone is the main visual indicator of their confinement of which he clearly approves. As he says, "Each father of a family in the Orient has an absolute power over his wife, his children, and his slaves which public authority cannot modify."[20] Though his comments are ostensibly about Egypt, they function as a point of reference for French ideals. The Egyptian home thus mirrors the French legal ideal described in his *Code Napoléon*—patriarchal, orderly, and ultimately private, a microcosm of his political ideology.

Napoleon contrasts eastern polygyny with western monogamy. While "the Orientals shut up their women, ours share in all our rights."[21] That French women shared in "all our rights" has a peculiar phrasing. Its implication, that French women had a share in all the rights of French men, was of course far from the truth. Or again when Napoleon compares the rights of eastern and western women, his tone turns sarcastic, as he interprets "women's rights" as the right to go to the baths or to church (too) often:

> these women have their rights as ours have theirs. One cannot prevent them from going to the public bath, any more than one can prevent our women from going to church; the one (group) abuses it as the other.[22]

Napoleon admires the fact that Easterners are successful in guarding their women, while the French are forced to rely on women's virtue. His comment reveals a profound distrust of women while it asserts the classic double standard based on gender. In this passage from the *Mémorial* dated 3 June 1816 easterners have a better idea for how women should be treated: as property and not as equal partners:

> We Western peoples do not understand anything about women. We have treated them too well and made them almost our equals. The Eastern peoples have much more sense and feeling of what is the right approach. They have declared them the property of man, and indeed nature has made them to be our slaves. It is only because of our own silly ideas that they claim to be our sovereigns.[23]

Similarly, Napoleon's major apology for polygyny may be this statement of 23 September 1816:

> Everything is arranged among the Orientals so that they can guard their wives well and be sure of them. Our whole life in the West, on the contrary, is such that we cannot guard them, and we are obliged to rely on them. We have to depend on the women's sense of honour and to have blind confidence in them.[24]

The social historian John Cairncross suggested that Napoleon's sympathy with the Muslim system be explained in part by the proximity of his native Corsica to the Arab world. Cairncross also points out the autobiographical component in Napoleon's comment, as he had close tabs kept on his wife Josephine, who was unfaithful, and continued this same surveillance with his Empress Marie Louise.

In these passages, Napoleon vacillates as to whether Catholic monogamous marriage is superior to Muslim polygynous marriage. When directly posing the problem of whether monogamy or polygyny is the better system, Napoleon claims that it is "'a very big question,'" and relying upon personal happiness as the indicator of a successful marital system, he calls it a draw.[25]

Under the guise of cross-cultural respect, Napoleon celebrates the harem. It presumes that women are property and slaves, not equals, and this he calls the natural state of male-female relations. In a memorable analogy, he claims women are the fruit trees which produce fruit (progeny), while men are the gardeners who own both the trees and the fruit (women and children), and unlike men to whom women and children belong, women can own nothing but "beauty, graces, seduction, obligations, dependence; submission."[26]

In his most baldly misogynist and orientalist comment, Napoleon claims that Circassian mamelukes[27] (one of what he calls the three races of Egypt) have few children in part because of the disgusting nature of their women, who are fat and can hardly walk, though they affect sweetness. They spend their entire days lying on couches. It is these lazy, negligent, and recumbent women whom Napoleon blames for the widespread homosexuality in Egypt, comparing its practice in ancient Greece and Rome. He explains the profligacy of Egyptian homosexuality ("this monstrous inclination") and what he sees as its virtual nonexistence in France by the differences between

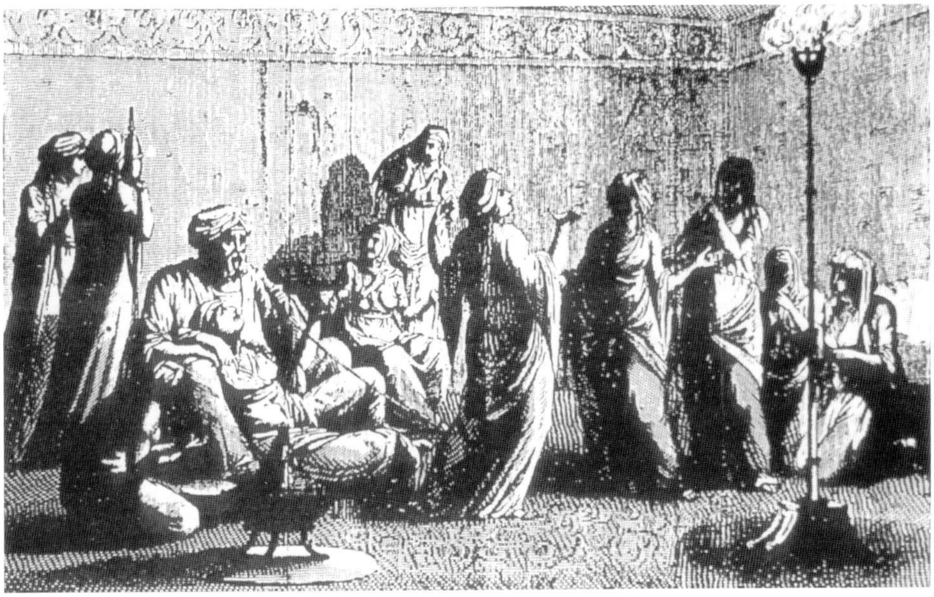

Fig. 2.2. After Dominique Vivant Denon. *Entertainment in the Harem*. Engraving. *Travels in Upper and Lower Egypt*, 1803.

Egyptian and French women; Oriental women fail to take care of themselves, losing their body shape, vivacity, and charm.[28]

Besides the basic fact of her seclusion, indicators in the pair of harem pictures of a possible "Napoleonic" view of the harem are her identity as Body—full, substantial, weighted. With little indication of any other activity, these women are presumed to be lazy, focused only on the memory of lovemaking or their anticipation of it. Their partly seated, semi-reclining position can be read as another indicator of their submission. Whether Denon intended the women portrayed to be read as beautiful or disgusting is an open question.

Unlike this pair of plates on the harem where the multiple wives of the harem are only suggested by the pictorial representation of two, each in seclusion, Denon's third plate on the subject, *Entertainment in the Harem* (Fig. 2.2), shows a number of women of varied social status. Those who stand and two seated to the far right appear to be the musicians and dancers. One male, presumably the master, is depicted with a long chibouk in one hand and a current favorite in the other. In front of them another woman bows in subservience. Like the pair of plates showing single women, this image illustrates an event that actually occurred, Denon claims. His text asserts that dancing girls called *almées*, outsiders brought in to celebrate a special occasion, performed in front of two hundred soldiers, a feat that required some military persuasion of the sheiks, wary of "the polluted [. . .] inspection of infidels" (*E* 1:230). Denon brags that the presence of a general and the soldiers and some old offenses for which the sheiks owed an atonement account for why the foreigners were finally allowed to enter. The *almées'* famous dance, referred to frequently in the history of nineteenth-century harem pictures,[29] degenerates from (in Denon's words) "voluptuous" and "lascivious" to a translation "in the grossest and most indecent way, [of] the giddy transports of passion" (*E* 1:232).

Despite his claim that it is authentic, the setting of Denon's engraving is fanciful. The image itself is focused as much on the amorous pasha and his female lover as on the *almées*. In the print there is no suggestion of an audience of two hundred soldiers. The male-female interaction, in which the large impassive master smoking is support for the smaller female lounging between his knees, her own legs splayed as she gazes deeply into his eyes, is formulaic in harem imagery. A binary relationship of the powerful and the powerless is echoed in the subservience of the menial slave who attends to the couple's needs. In the fiction of the scene, the male pasha's dominance is made explicit by the women's subservient positions. He is in fact an analog for the powerful French soldiers whom Denon claimed watched the scene, for Denon whose efforts allow the scene to become visible, and for the western viewer c. 1803 who is the picture's consumer. The frieze-like movement of the female figures repeated in the wall decoration and the detailed interest in the lamp and tandour recall the archeological/scientific trend in French paintings and prints set in antiquity and produced in the late eighteenth and early nineteenth centuries. This image would in fact be used for scientific ends: it served as the basis for a color engraving by John Chapman after Denon (Plate 2) that illustrated the *Encyclopaedia Londinensis* (London 1810), the earliest English encyclopedia I have found to carry an entry under the term "harem." Here the scene is depicted more clearly, and it contains fewer figures. The odalisque's breasts, now exposed, and Chapman's red coloration of the liquid in the vessel she raises emphasize orgiastic transgression. The fantasy is exaggerated even more so than in Denon's earlier print, despite its use within the authoritative source of the encyclopedia.

Just as Napoleon's later comments on the harem reveal ambivalence toward Muslim women, whether beautiful or disgusting, so too does Denon initially delight in the appearance of the *almées* ("we all joined in a general exclamation when they disclosed their features" [*E* 1:233]) and then, finding himself drawn to the beauty of one of them named Josephine (coincidentally [?] the name of Napoleon's wife), he laments: "I could have wished, I must confess, that Josephine had not resembled the others in her [suggestive] style of dancing (*E* 1:234)." Denon implies that women to be ogled can be provocative, but a woman to be favored should be modest.

Even without information about the *almées*—consider an early-nineteenth-century viewer of this print who passes over the verbal commentary—the image could easily be read as a scene of moral transgression. That it contains one amorous pasha and many attractive women intent upon entertainment might have conjured up associations of unbridled sexual activity in the harem or even an eastern whorehouse. Indeed, Napoleon's reading of Egyptian polygyny resembles one bourgeois justification for prostitution in his claim that it is acceptable because it is natural: while Nature has made the female sexually unavailable at times (presumably due to pregnancy, lactation, menstruation, and related illnesses) the male suffers no such "inconveniences; (and) must therefore have several women, etc."[30] The "Orientals," whom Napoleon believes have more "*d'esprit*" and (curiously) justice than the French, have recognized the truth that women are "the veritable property of man; and in fact nature has made them our slaves."[31] This is the scene of an orgy, where one's natural impulses get expressed. It goes without saying, however, that this sexual freedom for the male is not a female prerogative. Napoleon claims unequivocally that a woman's infidelity is "beyond redemption" ("irreparable").[32] Thus polygyny, like prostitution, assures an adequate pool of available women for the ever-ready male. Polygyny and prostitution are conflated in this image.

The picture's composition is initially unclear about which women serve which functions within the harem. This lack of pictorial clarity may have a political parallel in what Napoleon saw as a less hierarchal Egyptian society. He admired Egyptian society for its social mobility, where even slaves, male and female alike, could experience social ascendance. He contrasts this with the more "rigid" and "debasing" system in the French colonies.[33]

In sharp contrast to Denon's view is a British condemnation of French orientalism, found in the Advertisement by Arthur Aikin in his English translation of Denon's 1803 *Egypt*. He politely introduces Denon to the reader, comments on the division of the book into chapters—and proceeds to excoriate the French colonial presence in Egypt:

> We see a dreadful licence of lust, rapine and slaughter, the French troops were allowed to indulge in, and how whole villages were exterminated upon the bare suspicion of mediating resistance to the ravishers of their women, the desolators of their fields, the incendiaries of their houses. (*E* 1:vi)

Aikin denounces French militarism in the East. Yet, he justifies his own role in translating the book on the grounds that Denon is principally an artist who produces an interesting and unique account. The fact remains that after Aikin vents his moral outrage, he admires Denon and aids in the dissemination of his book throughout the English-speaking world in the name of artistic and scientific progress. The advancement of art and science would become a pervasive nineteenth-century rationale for producing and reproducing representations of the harem.

Harem Representations Specifying Ethnicity/Nationality/"Race"

Representations of harem pictures specifying the ethnicity, race, or nationality of the woman depicted presume an air of authenticity. In pinpointing a fact about the female subject's presumed origins the artist or writer situates her in a world that is segmented into ethnic, racial, and/or geographical entities. On the one hand, this might seem a positive, historicizing impulse, the desire to disrupt the romantic fantasy of the generic harem woman and ground her in a time and place—granting her some means of identity. On the other hand, this practice of specifying an ethnic or racial origin for the harem woman in fact did not lead to a better understanding of her. Instead, artists and writers fell into stereotypical conventions for addressing the nature of difference of a particular race.[34] And it became one more curious fact about the harem woman. Race could be indicated by her skin or hair color, culinary taste, or style of clothing, all of which were perceived as essential and unchanging. As an expression of tourist thinking, the implications of one's origins were meant to bemuse.

The presentation of race presumed western ethnic and nationalistic superiority.[35] At the same time, specifying the nationality of harem slaves could be considered evidence of the enemy countries the Ottomans had conquered.[36] Such titles in nineteenth-century representations could indicate the Turkish infidel's illicit war booty, souvenirs of the reach and power of the Turkish presence. The multiple ethnicities of the women in the harem assembled by the Veiled Prophet of Khorassan suggest his power in Thomas Moore's 1817 *Lalla Rookh.* Moore specifies a great diversity of origins, including the British Isles.

> Well hath the Prophet-Chief his bidding done;
> And every beauteous race beneath the sun,
> From those who kneel at Brahma's burning founts,
> To the fresh nymphs bounding o'er Yemen's mounts;
> From Persia's eyes of full and fawn-like ray,
> To the small, half-shut glances of Kathay;
> And Georgia's bloom, and Azab's darker smiles,
> And the gold ringlets of the Western Isles;
> All, all are there; - each Land its flower hath given,
> To form that fair young Nursery for Heaven![37]

Passages like Moore's or titles of paintings which contain referents to race or ethnicity can function to assert colonialist ends. Homi K. Bhabha argues that one colonial tactic is to construct the colonized "as a population of degenerative types on the basis of racial origin."[38]

As for the concept of "race," Henry Louis Gates, Jr. calls for its rethinking. Rather than a self-evident category having essential truths, he calls race "the ultimate trope of difference" arbitrarily applied and "dangerous," based on pseudosciences of the eighteenth and nineteenth centuries.[39] Bhabha further points out that skin color has been "a visible fetish of difference."[40] This is extremely apt for describing the French protagonist's project in Gérard de Nerval's story "Zetnaybia," published as the first of his three-part *Voyage to the Orient* of 1851. Having decided to purchase a slave to settle his domestic living arrangements while in Egypt, he seeks out a slave having the right skin tone.

> It didn't take me long to inspect them, for though their savage appearance was interesting it hardly encouraged cohabitation. Most of them were disfigured by a mass of tattoos, grotesque incisions, blue stars and suns cut into the greyish black of their skin. [. . .] "I find their colour too dark, let's look at some lighter tints." (*VO* 35–36)

Though he initially searches for an Abyssinian slave, the man in this fictionalized autobiography finally chooses to buy a slave who is Javanese and of "the yellow race." Amidst a collection of dark-skinned women, Zetnaybia is perceived as an Other whom he desires among the others: "Nor can I explain my sudden, overwhelming inclination for the strange and unexpected which quickly led me to decide in her favor" (*VO* 46). At the end of the story, Nerval grows disillusioned with Zetnaybia, whom he places in a school. The search for the Other is endlessly deferred.[41]

Skin is only one cipher for racial difference. Face and body parts and even costume are read as indicators of racial identity. Lamartine, who professes love and admiration for the "Mohammedan" peoples, carries this to an extreme by claiming to be able to identify race or ethnicity based on the subtlest traits of physiognomy, observations that today seem extremely arbitrary. His evidence of racial differences among eastern women is taken from his stolen glimpses of them on their terraces in the moonlight. He concludes

> They have the Italian eye, but softer, more timid, more filled with tenderness and love. They possess likewise the Grecian figure, but more rounded, and with movements more supple and graceful. Their foreheads are high, smooth, white and polished like those of the handsomest English or Swiss women; but the straight and broad outline of the nose gives more of majesty and antique nobleness to their physiognomy. [. . .] it [the eastern female face] is so sweet to an European accustomed to the jaded features and contracted countenances of European women. (*PHL* 76–77)

Similarly, he waxes poetic at the extraordinary and unusual clothing of the women he claims to observe. As for one beauty, he claims "Her oriental costume added much to the charms of this young maiden's person" (*PHL* 173). He goes on to describe in lovingly obsessive detail the plaits of her light-colored hair and its decoration. Lamartine's lengthy descriptions are not merely aesthetic appreciation for eastern beauty in face, body, and clothing. Nor can they be dismissed as gossipy, feminized interests in the *minutiae* of the mundane. They are notably scientific in their closely observed, positivist claims of comparative racial truths at the same time that they are eroticized

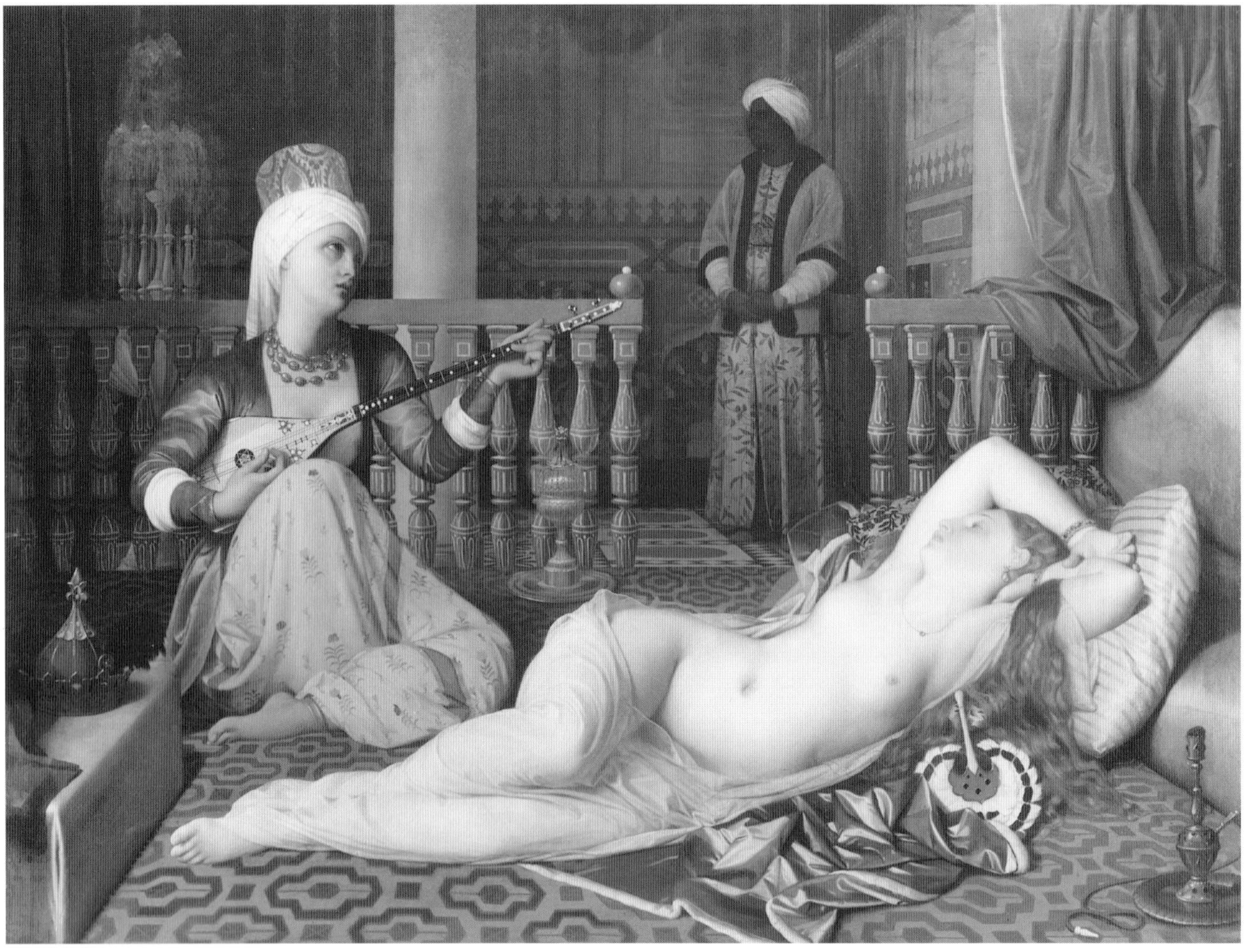

Fig. 2.3. Jean Auguste Dominique Ingres. *Odalisque with Slave.* 1842. Oil on canvas. Courtesy of the Fogg Art Museum, Harvard University Art Museums, Bequest of Grenville L. Winthrop. Photographic Services. © President and Fellows of Harvard College, Harvard University.

and niggling. In this way, clothing functions as a cipher of difference.[42] Fraught as they were with arbitrary judgments, descriptions of origin produce a pseudoknowledge about the harem women and peoples they purport to know.

The themes I want to explore in examining harem pictures in this section are the binary attitudes of scientism (the desire to objectively respond to the harem) and exoticizing (the desire to perpetuate the harem as titillating curiosity) and how these attitudes might be suggested visually. In fact, such seemingly opposed impulses might coexist within the same image.

Pictures of the harem typically indicate its hierarchy on the basis of ethnic or racial difference. The highest ranking harem inhabitants are nearly always the lightest-skinned, the lowest ranking are nearly always the darkest-skinned. But this is not a case of western artists accurately reporting a Muslim tendency to racism. Indicators are that social hierarchies in Egypt were more fluid and less strictly bound to racial determinants than in Europe in the nineteenth century.[43] Writers and artists represented what they expected to be the case, projecting western attitudes onto the East.

A French painting that suggests the formulaic quality of western expectations about race and status in the harem is J. A. D. Ingres's *Odalisque avec esclave* of 1842 (Fig. 2.3). Here the most highly privileged slave has the lightest skin. She is the pasha's feast and is given to us (the viewer) for our visual delectation. She is the whitest and in her passive display the most exaggeratedly feminine. The darkest-skinned figure is the menial and the male protector, standing and actively watchful, the desexualized substitute for the pasha's presence who denies public access to the female body that the pasha (and viewer) are able to have. In between those two extremes and occupying the middle ground between them (spatially and figuratively) is the brown-skinned female. Similarly, her activity level is a median between those of the white woman and black man: seated rather than supine or standing, she serves the white woman, entertains her with lute music but does not directly answer to the pasha nor appeal to the viewer to the same degree.

The juxtaposition of all three figures reinforces western notions of a strict harem hierarchy derived from the "actual symbiotic intermingling of [. . .] racial and sexual themes."[44] All three skin types, rendered unambiguously by Ingres's use of a precisely chiseled line, reflect the ultimate fantasy of subservience each maintains to the unseen, powerful pasha—and to the powerful western viewer. The ruler here is not the women's only master, however; so is the nineteenth-century spectator who assumes a scopic mastery in viewing these pictures.

Circassian and Georgian Women

By far the most frequently mentioned ethnicities or "races" of harem women were Circassian and Georgian associated with the Caucasus Mountains. Ranked above all other female harem inmates on the basis of their "white" ("Caucasian") skin color, they became known to western commentators as the premium, most desired slaves who, because of their rarefied light skin or eyes, were most likely to be promoted within the harem to the rank of wife. Even when writers name no other race of harem slaves, they are likely to specify a Circassian or Georgian inmate. French and British representations of these groups contributed to a pseudoknowledge about their essential characteristics.

Western writers and artists often considered Circassian and Georgian women Christian. In point of fact, much of the two land areas had converted to Islam in the seventeenth century. Thus by the nineteenth century, Circassians and Georgians practiced a provincial amalgam of the two religions. Perhaps the western understanding of their faith as Christian constituted a reading of their light skin color. Or the latter led to the former.

Circassia was often considered along with Georgia, territory located in the west Caucasian mountains, but each had distinct histories. Georgia had been under Russian domination from the eighteenth century and did not maintain the strong sense of independence that Circassia did. In 1801 Georgia became part of the Russian Empire. Turkey ceded additional lands to Russia by 1829. While Georgia fought on the side of Russia in the Crimean War, the Circassians for the most part refused to ally themselves with their conquerors. Russia thus blockaded Circassia in an effort to quell resistance. In the aftermath of the war, however, Russia realized it had more to gain by lifting its blockade and allowing emigration to depopulate the rebellious areas. Emigrants then fled to Constantinople, Cairo, and other parts of the Ottoman Empire. So while the supply of female Georgian slaves dwindled, Circassian women were more plentiful for use in the harem in the second half of the nineteenth century.

The alleged characteristics of Circassian and Georgian women are articulated by the author Emma Reeve in 1839. She differentiates between the blond Circassians who are "indolent and graceful, their voices low and sweet" and what she calls the slightly darker-skinned Georgians who are "more animated" and have more "intelligence and vivacity than their delicate rivals."[45] Similar descriptions of the Circassian harem women appear in Florence Nightingale's travel journal, her only piece of writing not on the subject of nursing. She calls them "the most graceful, and the most sensual-looking creatures I ever saw (like dancers)."[46] This (backhanded) compliment appears in the context of her overall judgement about the hellish nature of the harem, which she allegedly visited on her five-month sojourn to Egypt in 1849.

A related condemnation of the harem—and the opinion that the Circassians and Georgians are its only saving virtue—appears in the writing of the feminist-activist Harriet Martineau. Mothers from these two groups produce "the finest children," and if they were to be excluded from the harem the upper class in Egypt would be doomed (*EL* 264).

A much less conciliatory comment about Circassians was Napoleon's c. 1815. He describes the acquiring of Circassian boys sold "by their mothers"[47] to merchants, who in turn sell them at Cairo and Constantinople. The same attitude appears much later in the century in England by Mrs. John Blunt. They are distrusted, uneducated and thus "unchecked" by "evil passions"; they are "thievish, haughty [. . .], cowardly, cruel and false." Echoing Napoleon's condemnation, she claims Circassians are child-sellers, and even cannibals.[48] She claims that the name Circassian can be ranked below even that of the gypsy.[49] Blunt's acceptance of a hierarchy based on racial origin is explicit.

Politically, the issue of Circassian independence heats up in the early 1830s. They were a reputedly proud and independent group of men and women who resisted Russian domination from 1829, when Turkey ceded Circassia to Russia, until 1864. In those intervening years the Circassians became known in England as a democratic but "wild" tribe capable of great "fierceness" for the cause of country.[50]

The major defender of the Turkish harem in Victorian politics arrived at such a stance as a diplomat in his support of the Circassian cause. David Urquhart (1805–1877), a zealous Turcophile and Russophobe attached to the Turkish embassy in 1835 and later a member of Parliament (1847–52), came to prominence with the 1838 publication of his *Spirit of the East*.[51] His defense of the harem was a means of expressing both his protectionism toward Turkey and the Ottoman Empire and his antagonism toward Russian encroachments on it.[52]

Urquhart reported he had been anti-Turkish before the mid-1830s. (He and his brother Charles Gordon had been active Philhellenes.) Urquhart recounts the stages by which he changed his impressions of the harem, a process that undoubtedly contributed to his change from an anti-Turkish to a pro-Turkish stance.[53] Invited to visit the Imam's harem, he was initially incredulous. When he had arrived and was seated by the fire, he saw the foolishness of the mystique surrounding it: "The veil at once was rent, and the mystery had vanished" (*SE* 2:370). Instead of an erotic fantasy come true, Urquhart finds a family scene, one in which the women cover their faces in his presence.

Urquhart devotes a sixth of the second volume of *Spirit of the East* to the harem. He apologizes for his prolixity but argues that a thorough discussion is necessary to connect the private and the public and the harem debate to international political questions (quoted in *ME* 1:69 n. 2). As he reprimands the French in general for their insensitivity to Middle Eastern customs,[54] he disputes Napoleon's views on the harem, quoting two of them at length: one sanctioning polygyny, the other on the value of the absolute, private power of the husband over his wife. He challenges Napoleon's interpretation of the harem as a microcosm for French colonialism generally. Overall Urquhart implies the superiority of British to French principles in matters of social customs, morality, and international policy (*SE* 2:242).

Urquhart attempts to debunk several other myths associated with the harem. He discounts the notion that British and Turkish social customs are diametrically opposed. He calls for an acknowledgment of the importance of Muslim women as an integral part of the polity. He writes that westerners understand little about harem life, as it requires a thorough knowledge of the social system of which it is part. For obscuring a true understanding of Muslim customs, he blames party politics. He claims westerners are wrong to think of the harem as inferior to their own social organization and that so-called slavery is a better alternative to the class antagonism ravaging England. Moreover, the harem system of concubinage, in which resulting children have legal protection, is vastly preferable to the fact of illegitimate offspring in Great Britain.

He counters the stereotypical notion that harem women are ignorant: he claims that girls receive as much education as boys and that they are active, industrious and happy. Harem women do have rights, he insists, and they express them. The notion that they live in fear and trembling of their husbands is false. Urquhart does admit that polygyny is a trying experience for harem inmates. He also acknowledges that barrenness is a real cause for the scorn of women. In culminating his analysis, Urquhart claims that the harem is not the locale for "sloth" and "indolence;" instead, he calls it "home" (with all its Victorian associations): "security, protection, filial duties, paternal authority, love, delicacy of manners and of intercourse" (*SE* 2:410). Urquhart also corrects the western misconception about the Turk who spends too much time enjoying his harem. Europeans believe they seclude themselves

> to slothful and ignoble indolence behind the walls and lattices of the Harem [. . .] Wholly unconscious of those claims, duties, attractions and occupations, we can account for the Turk's attachment to his Harem only by supposing that sensual gratifications are concealed behind the mystery that envelopes it; and we therefore distrust any observations, and disregard any fact that tends to an opposite conclusion. (*SE* 2:410)

In Urquhart's view, the Turk who likes to spend time in his harem is not a moral degenerate but its opposite—an attentive husband and father.

He says that his beliefs, if reflected in British international policy, would also help safeguard potential Turkish markets. Urquhart explicitly links his views on the private harem to the public world of national politics. In asking "'Is not the nation an aggregate of families?'"[55] he implies a commonality of British and Turkish values and lends legitimacy to the harem institution. There he claimed that Turkey had the potential to become "'the largest mart in the world for English manufactures'"[56] and that trade could be facilitated by cutting back on government interference.

At a time when Turkey was considered "the sick man of Europe" he was optimistic about the possibility of the Ottoman renewal; he thought the Ottoman Empire could be given new life. Yet he claimed it would be only with British help that the empire could achieve true and lasting reform. Supportive as he was of Turkish reform, he also opposed in 1833 a Turkish constitution, advocating instead the theory of enlightened despotism. An ardent advocate of

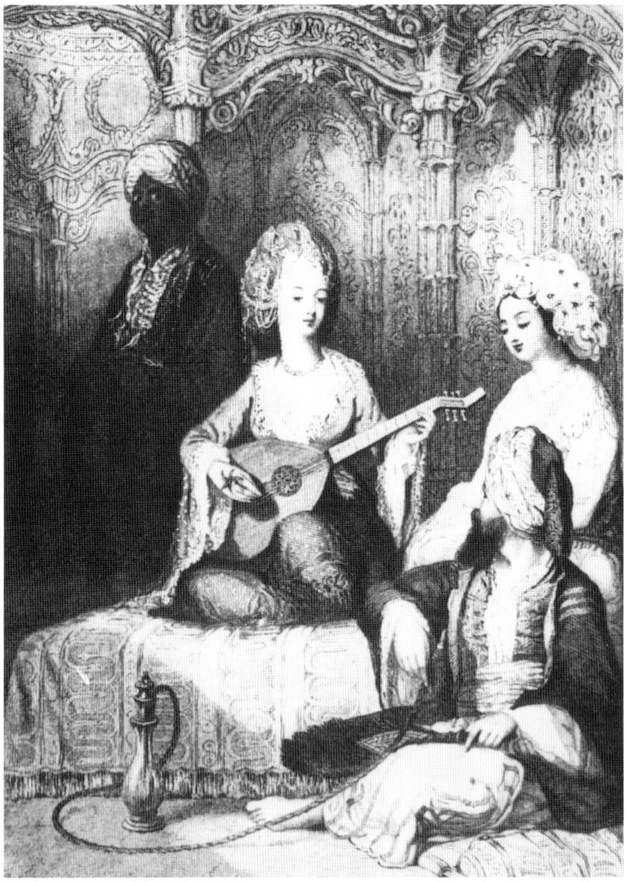

Fig. 2.4. After Thomas Allom. *Circassian Slaves*. Engraving. Robert Walsh, *Constantinople and the Scenery of the Seven Churches of Asia*. 1838. Photo Adam Miller.

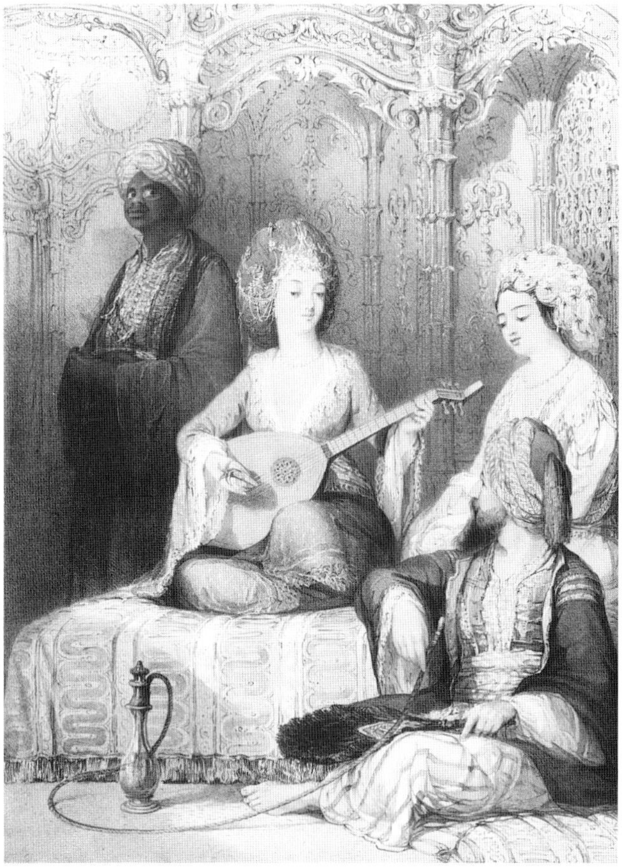

Fig. 2.5. C. Hullmandel after Thomas Allom. *Circassian Slaves, Constantinople*. Emma Reeve, *Character and Costume in Turkey and Italy*. 1839. Lithograph. Yale Center for British Art, Paul Mellon Fund.

free enterprise, Urquhart claimed to respect Muslim society while expressing his respect paternalistically. He was a spokesman for early Victorian informal colonization and, curiously, respect for the harem and support of the Circassians were part of that policy.

Some images of harem women done by British artists and named as Circassian make an illuminating comparison in addressing the issue of ethnic or racial stereotyping. Thomas Allom's *Circassian Slaves*, appeared in both engraved and lithographic forms of book illumination in 1838 and 1839, respectively (Figs. 2.4 and 2.5). In their rendering, these prints after Allom are extremely precise. Descriptions of fabrics, architecture, the shadow over the left corner of the sofa, and objects such as the lute and the hookah are painstaking. In their content as well, the prints after Allom show a harem as orderly. The four figures represent strata of power, the master seated on the floor in a chivalrous manner, his attention riveted to his lady, the lower ranking-female off to the right demure (in her lowered eyes) and cooperative, the black eunuch looming protectively in the background. The Circassian is the emotional center of the scene. She is its raison d'être and through her musical talent, charm, and feminine delicacy, she assures the smooth and orderly running of its parts, much as the ideal western mistress of the house might do with her servants and husband. The Circassian woman here is likened to the ideal Victorian lady, in that spirit of relativist thinking that characterized Urquhart's comments.

Another picture is titled *Circassian* (Fig. 2.6), an undated sketch attributed to John Lewis[57] and having no known exhibition record. In contrast to the prints after Allom, Lewis executes an extremely loose rendering of this Circassian. The daring *décolletage*, the dramatic drapery, the hurried background, the exotic larger-featured face make his painterly image a Romantic interpretation of a Circassian resembling Delacroix's political heroines more than Allom's demure Circassian. Might this rendering of a harem inmate suggest the admirably wild, freedom-loving Circassian championed by Urquhart in the

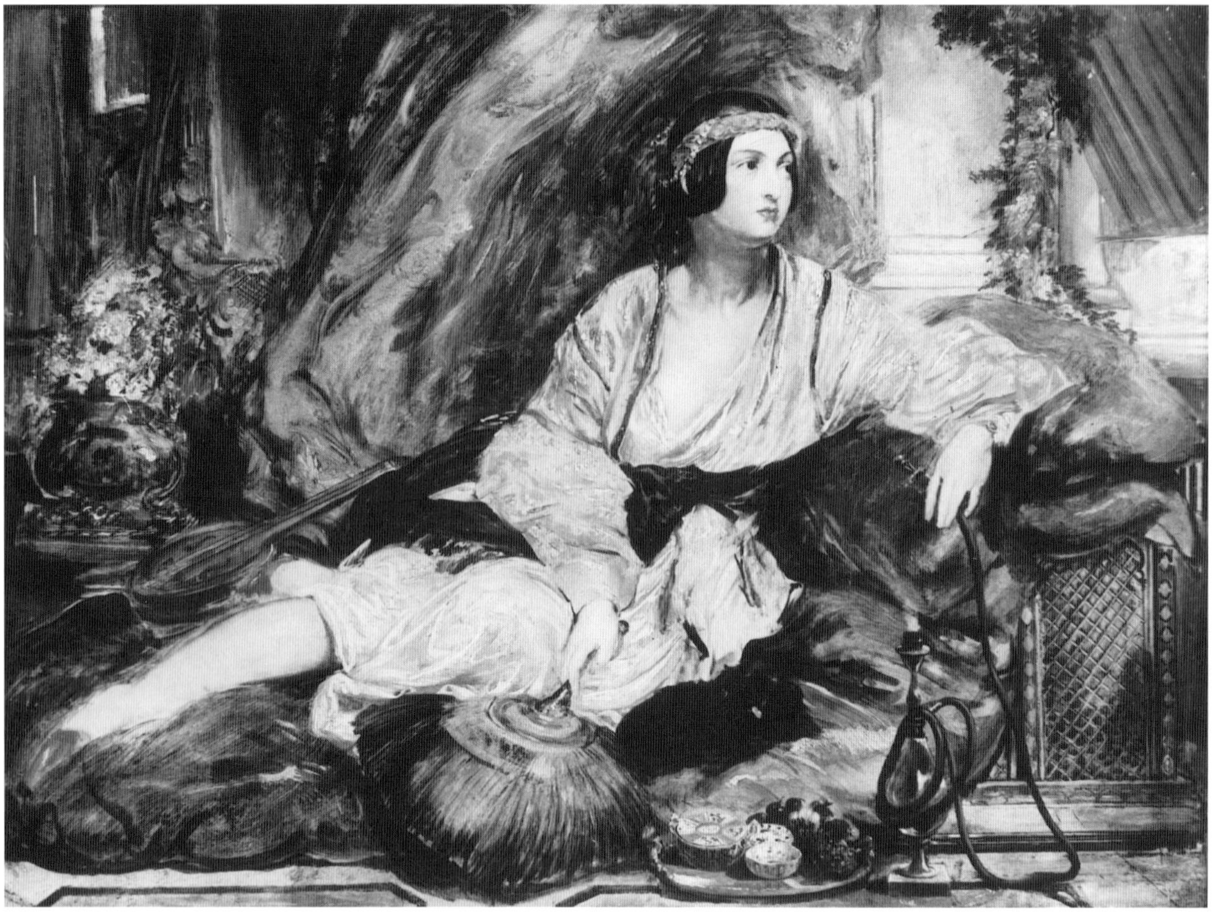

Fig. 2.6. Attributed to John Frederick Lewis. *Circassian.* N.d. Sketch. Private Collection. By permission of Sotheby's. Photo Courtesy Witt Library, Courtauld Institute, London.

long period from 1829–64 when that group resisted Russian dominance?

A picture of a Georgian woman is the 1843 print *La marchande d'oiseaux des tropiques: georgienne* (Fig. 2.7) done after W. Bleigh Barker by Régnier. This may be an illustration to *1001 Nights* in which Dalila works in the public sphere of Bagdad selling birds for her father, a carrier-pigeon official.[58] Ironically, she is a mere bird-seller, but her light eyes, elaborate dress, multi-strand pearl necklace, the barred windows, and her affinity with such exotic creatures suggest a social privilege associated with the harem life of a premium Georgian.

Circassian and Georgian ethnicity/"race" connoted favoritism and privilege in French and British texts. As such and on the basis of their alleged race and religion (white and Christian) these types of slaves functioned as the closest parallel to the western Self and thus could be constructed as the repository for a western projection, a proxy westerner who maintains a distance from the harem life in which she is forced to participate.

Armenian Women

In the Victorian period it was unusual for an artist to name an Armenian in the title of a harem picture.[59] More commonly she would have been called a Georgian or Circassian. An official source claimed there were "somewhat under 2,000 Armenians" in Egypt in 1840.[60] Most Armenians were Christians (*L* 1:410)—some orthodox, others Roman Catholic—and an Armenian woman in a Muslim harem may have arrived there as a captured prisoner of war. Stereotypically, Armenian women "do not take kindly to slavery and are difficult to manage."[61] When they are named Armenian, artists may be alluding to the taking of reluctant women into the harem—unlike Circassian women who, some writers claim, went gladly.[62]

In 1855 Armenia, under joint control by both Turkey and Russia since the early nineteenth century, was experiencing a cultural renascence and a growing national identity. All of the area bordering the Black Sea was undergoing profound change in the wake of the Crimean War. Armenians also formed

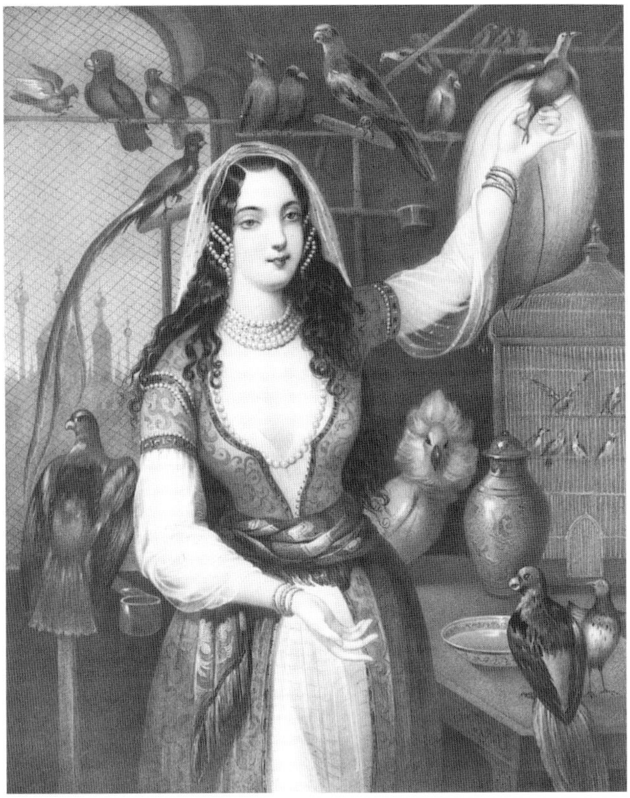

Fig. 2.7. Régnier after W. Bleigh Barker. *La Marchande d'oiseaux des tropiques georgienne.* 1843. Lithograph. Cliché Bibliothèque nationale de France, Paris. Farwell, *FPLI*, v. 9, 5E7 B81846.

one of the largest minorities in the adjacent country of Georgia, controlled by Russia since the early nineteenth century. During the war Russia blockaded Armenia to prohibit emigrations of refugees from both Circassia and Georgia. As a result of its defeat, Russia was forced to lift the blockade and failed to prevent great numbers of Caucasian immigrants from flooding Constantinople and Cairo in the next decade. An Armenian woman painted in this context could be read as a refugee from that war-ravaged area, specifically a Christian prisoner of war captured by force and sold for service.

An example of nineteenth-century French exotic ethnography appears in Louis Dupré's 1825 lithograph (reissued in 1838), *Un prince arménien et sa femme (Duz-Oglou)* (Fig. 2.8). Fully clothed, both the prince and his wife make eye contact with the spectator, who is less a voyeur of the blatantly erotic (even though this may be a bedchamber) than the privately exotic. His exotic marker is his elaborate headdress worn indoors, while hers are her dark, blunt facial features, her free-flowing hair and especially the connected eyebrows. While the man's exotic character is culturally determined (and removable), woman's exotic indicator is found on her body itself. The title pays deference to his public rank, but the picture focuses more on her body, as was customary in western portraits of married couples, in which she is made a reflection of his power. Moreover, the image conflates the traditional indicators of harem iconography—sofa, chibouk, reclining figure, and couple dressed in elaborate ethnic regalia—and peoples it with figures that were typically Christian.[63] Thus this work mimics western conventions but exoticizes them.

Such pictorial ciphers of the female body as exotic parallel the pseudoknowledge about Armenian women to be found in both French and British writing. In the 1830s Lamartine decides that Armenian women's beauty surpasses that of many of the women he had previously described in their transparent, rose-leaf complexions, their silvery voices, and the softness of their eyes. He claims, additionally, that Armenian women maintain their beauty longer than many other "races" of women because of the more moderate climate, the family-based homelife and the lack of distraction by "the artificial passions of society" (*PHL* 344).

In an 1858 article in the British periodical press Armenian women are characterized by their admirable aesthetic sensibility manifest in their clothing and body decoration; the author approves of "the delicacy and harmony of the colours of their stuffs, the richness and good taste of the embroidery with which their bodices are covered, and the style of wearing their hair."[64] In contrast, Mrs. John Blunt, a resident of Turkey for twenty years, has mostly unflattering comments about Armenian women. Though they are known for their beauty and the "languid expression of their eyes," they are reputedly "very backward in every respect." Tasteless in dress and toilette, they don't wash their hair, and so "it abounds in live stock of a most migratory character." What's more they have a "fancy for toad-eating" (*PT* 1:131–33). In describing their life among animals, large and small, they themselves become animal-like.

Ethnic/racial identity is linked to exotic costume in Charles Landelle's 1866 painting, *An Armenian Woman* (Fig. 2.9), in the Wallace Collection. A diadem of tiny gold medallions and ornate earrings alert us to her foreignness. The kerchief and flowing hair indicate her origins in a primitive culture. The swell of her left hip serves to feminize the body otherwise hidden by layers of dress. In its indebtedness to Lane's illustration *A Lady Adorned with the Ckoor's and Suf'a, etc.* (Fig. 2.10) in *Modern Egyptians* (*ME* 1:54), Landelle has consulted a reputably accurate and even

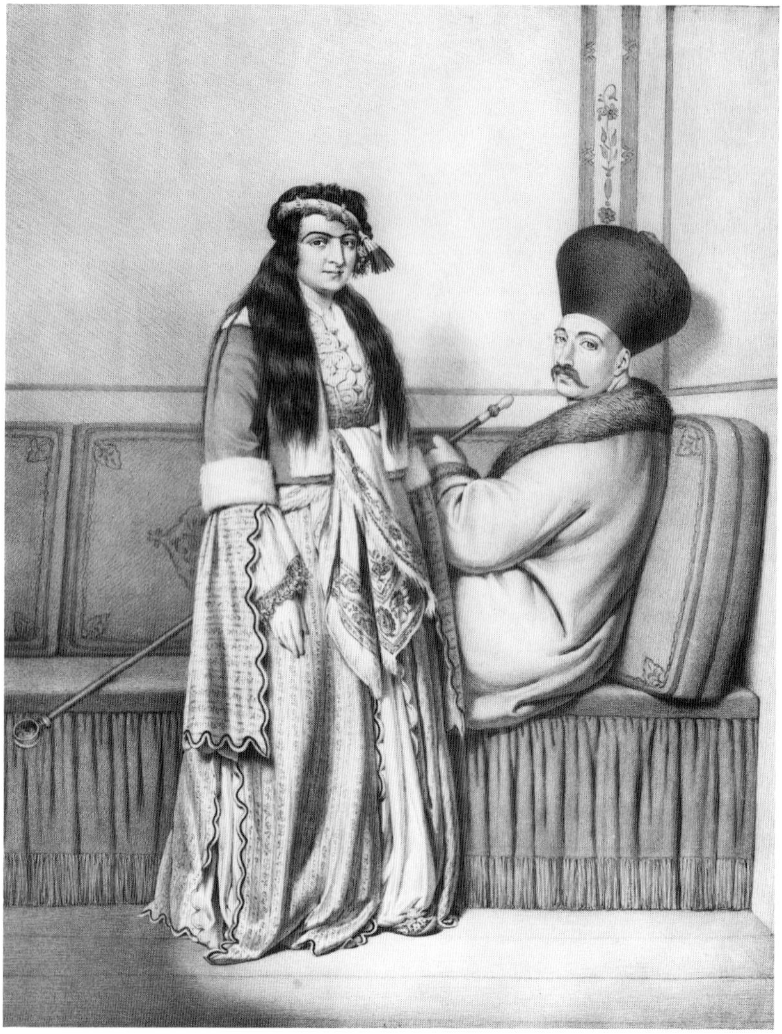

Fig. 2.8. Louis Dupré. *Un prince arménien et sa femme (Duz-Oglou)*. 1825, reissued 1838. Lithograph. Cliché Bibliothèque nationale de France, Paris. Farwell, *FPLI*, v. 9, 6B5 B85272.

scientific source, though his specifying an Armenian identity seems arbitrary.

In 1855 John Lewis exhibited *An Armenian Lady, Cairo*, in which a single woman dressed in voluminous garb represents a whole harem.[65] For the critic John Ruskin it was not a completely successful work. While praising the "precision and purity" of this oil painting ("here everything is exquisitely, ineffably right") he declares, oddly, that the harem is an "uninteresting" subject.[66] Given the lively discussion of harems and harem pictures in the press, we cannot take him literally; in 1855 the issue was just coming into its own in the wake of the Crimean War.[67] Ruskin is caught between morality and aesthetics. His contradictory comments are symptomatic of a modern paradigm within art historical analysis that separates a painting's form from its content; here its rendering is excellent but its subject inappropriate. His critical comments about the harem subject could be expected from such a public figure whose written words were closely evaluated by an artistic community to whom he preached the moral obligation of art, as I explore in another chapter.

Spanish Women

"Be a Christian, noble King!
For it were a grievous thing:
For to seek and find too well
In the arms of infidel.
Spain with cry of shame would ring,
If from honour faithful fell."

—Victor Hugo, "[Juana] The Obdurate Beauty," *Les Orientales* (*WB* 68).

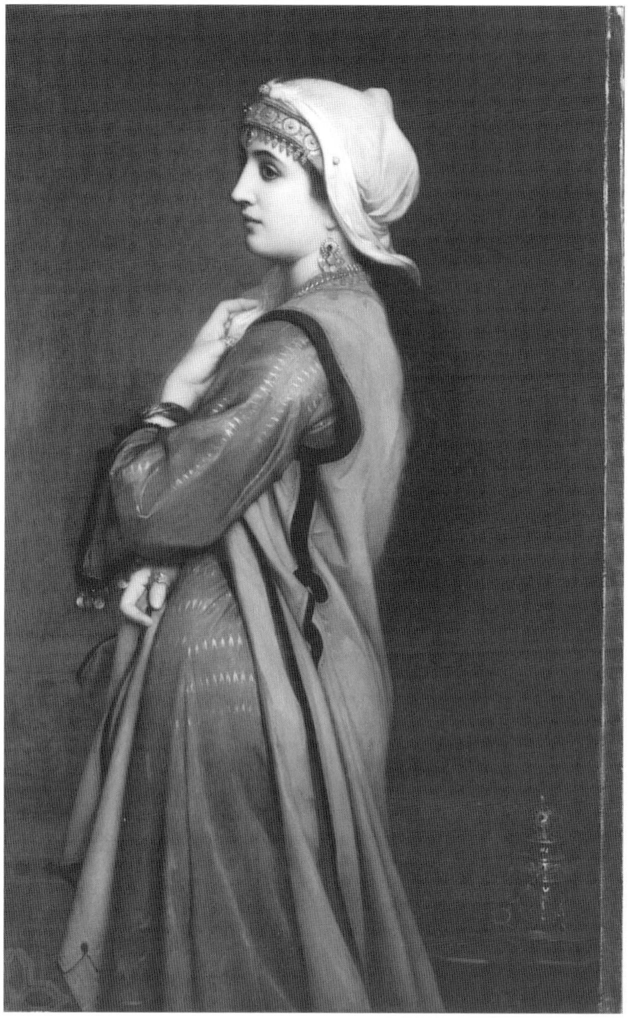

Fig. 2.9. Charles Landelle. *An Armenian Woman.* 1866. Reproduced by permission of the Trustees of the Wallace Collection, London.

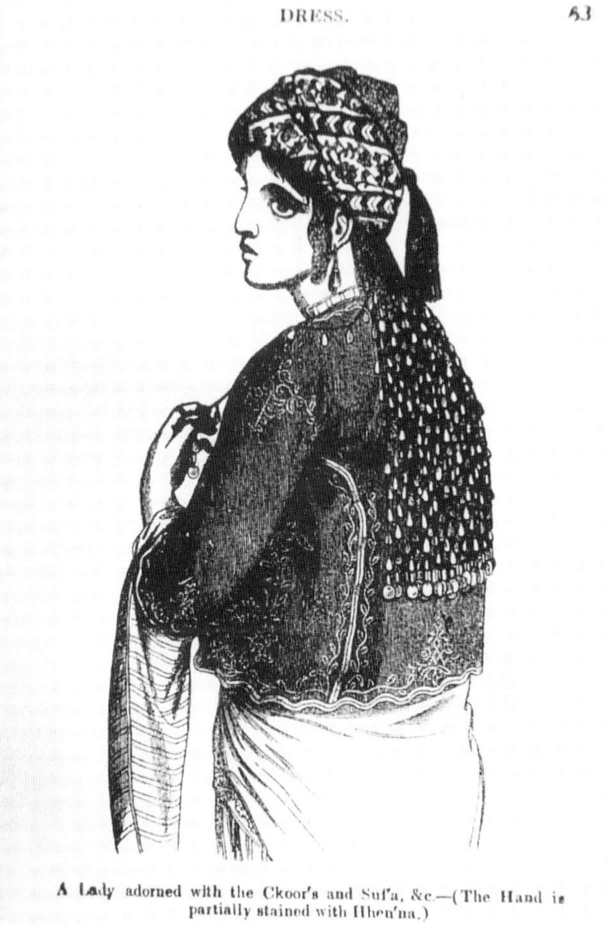

Fig. 2.10. Edward William Lane. *Lady Adorned with the Ckoor's and Suf'a, etc.* Engraving. *Manners and Customs of the Modern Egyptians,* 1836. Photo Adam Miller.

In Hugo's poem a politically powerful sultan patiently asks Juana, his beautiful Spanish virgin-slave, how he can win her love. She responds that this can happen only by his converting to Christianity. The poem provides the opportunity for Hugo to draw upon the stereotype of the emotional and proud Spanish, notions traceable to writers in the eighteenth century. Montesquieu believes Spanish men, like Hugo's Juana, are highly devout. He writes that they are also prone to jealousy and passion: "No one on earth is more willing to die of love-sickness under their mistresses' windows . . ." (*PL* 156), a courtly image that has great resonance for harem imagery, as analyzed in the next chapter. The Spanish woman in the harem can offer a study in contrast between Christianity and Islam, us and them. Though the Spanish were predominantly Catholic like the French, the lack of any substantive political or industrial revolution in Spain meant that the culture could be perceived as fundamentally other to its French neighbor. Thus a Spanish woman in the harem could be considered an inferior type of European whose place is more understandable in a harem than, say, a French woman's.[68]

Spanish women in a harem appear in the eighteenth-century writing of Lady Mary Wortley Montagu. To one of her correspondents she describes the story of a Spanish woman traveling with her family at the time when Naples was under Turkish domination. When the family was attacked in a ship raid, the Turkish admiral "took" (using Lady Mary's euphemism) the Spanish woman. Struck by her beauty and suffering (which he had caused!), he freed her brother and their attendants, who returned to Spain and sent £4,000 ransom to the sister's Turkish captor, who then freed her. The woman considered her options. If she chose to return to Spain her Catholic family would most likely place her in a nunnery "as the kindest thing they could do for her in her present Circumstances." Instead she chose to offer herself in marriage to the Turk, her ransom money becoming a dowry. Lady Mary recounts the honorable (monogamous) ending: "He marry'd her and never married again, and (as she says her selfe) she never had any reason to repent the choice she made" (*L* 1:408–9).

Spain in the nineteenth century was the site for Napoleonic meddling in 1808 (resisted by guerrillas who were supported by England). And it was also an increasingly popular vacation locale for European tourists in search of an exotic, preindustrial "primitive" that was still relatively close. Alexandre Dumas recounts that his son fell in love with a Spanish woman, whom he first spied "on one of those magic balconies." He serenaded her; they smiled to each other, and she "slipped her tiny hand through the lattice to receive his burning kisses." He claims they even met once. But her family intervened, and they were forced to part "each mourning a broken dream" (*AA* 55). Dumas's tale is a classically romanticized scenario of the guarded women who, for the sake of love, violates the unreasonable physical restrictions placed on her by a tyrannical society. Typically, it is with a western man that she plots. And usually the affair is doomed because of insurmountable cultural and religious differences. Dumas's fictionalized account is made Spanish, but it could just as easily have a Turkish or Egyptian setting.

After his trip to Spain from 1832 to 1840, John Lewis had earned the nickname "Spanish Lewis," since much of his resulting imagery centered on Spanish themes. This was long before his Middle Eastern scenes became popular beginning in the 1850s. In 1876, the last year of his life, John Lewis painted two harem pictures having Spanish references, both rather indirect. The pose of the main figure in his 1876 *Harem* (Fig. 2.11) owes a debt to Francisco Goya's *Clothed Maja* c. 1797–98 (Fig. 2.12), an image Lewis had copied many years earlier in his Spanish period.[69] A unique element in the scene is the Spaniel dog, a rare breed in the Middle East whose origins indicate further affinities to Spain; Lewis, who loved to sketch animals, drew Spaniels as early as 1826.[70] Here a white woman admires herself in a mirror held by a black servant; the *vanitas* theme so typical in harem representation is explicit in this picture. The mirror, used by a white-skinned woman and supported by a dark-skinned woman, serves as a prop to allow for the reading of racial subservience.

In the title of his second harem picture suggesting Spain, *Siesta* (Fig. 2.13), signed and dated 1876, there might be a question as to whether Lewis has painted a harem picture at all or just a Spanish woman napping. However, several elements here are common to his many harem compositions that predate this image: low couches and side table, latticed windows, patterns of light, a view out each window, fruit, fan, and flowers. Two of the three large red poppies, symbol of oblivion,[71] face the slumbering woman. The costume too is similar to that worn by women in his other pictures whose harem setting is clearly indicated in the title.

That Lewis chose to show a woman asleep is in keeping with a French tradition of harem imagery which is more explicitly eroticized than Lewis's picture. Her sleep is not for the night, as the filtered sunlight proves, but for a siesta, a convenient time for the painter to allow a harem woman's inherent indolence to slip into somnolence. Her half-conscious state and the whiteness of her partially exposed breast heighten her vulnerability.

Much earlier Richard Parkes Bonington had used the same Spanish title in his watercolor of a (harem?) woman napping, *La Siesta* (Fig. 2.14), dated 1828.[72] In Delacroix's painting *Reclining Odalisque* (Fig. 2.15) of 1827–28 the woman may have been asleep but is now becoming energized. The picture is a classic formulation of the aroused and languorous female body in French erotic art—recumbent, back arched, mouth open, sex draped loosely and positioned to receive the gaze of the spectator. But here she is given an eastern flavor by way of a few strategic objects: turban, pipe, ankle and wrist bracelets, and her light-colored hair (suggesting a Circassian identity). Her passivity gives way to revitalization precisely because of the presence of the desirous viewer.

A harem woman, asleep and ill, and thus doubly vulnerable is described in the 1824 account told by "an eastern physician," Meerza Ahmed Tubeeb. Just as in Lewis's painting, the woman is alone, and the author has fetishized the surrounding accoutrements—colored brocades, henna-stained nails, and a fan. In both Lewis's painting and the description that preceded it by over half a century the observer is a voyeur. In the early article a first-person narrative and a self-consciousness heighten the immediacy of its visual eroticism: "all this, and ten thousand other beauties, rivetted me to the spot. I gazed and gazed, and scarcely dared to draw my breath—and strained my sight till my eyes grew dim."[73] Lewis's voyeurism is less explicit than the physician's; the painter/spectator remains at a greater distance from the woman. Yet in both cases she is the passive spectacle; the reader/viewer plays the role of the powerful (male) presence creating the total environment through his privileged gaze.

Western women too recorded their process of watching harem women asleep. In 1837 Julia Pardoe's

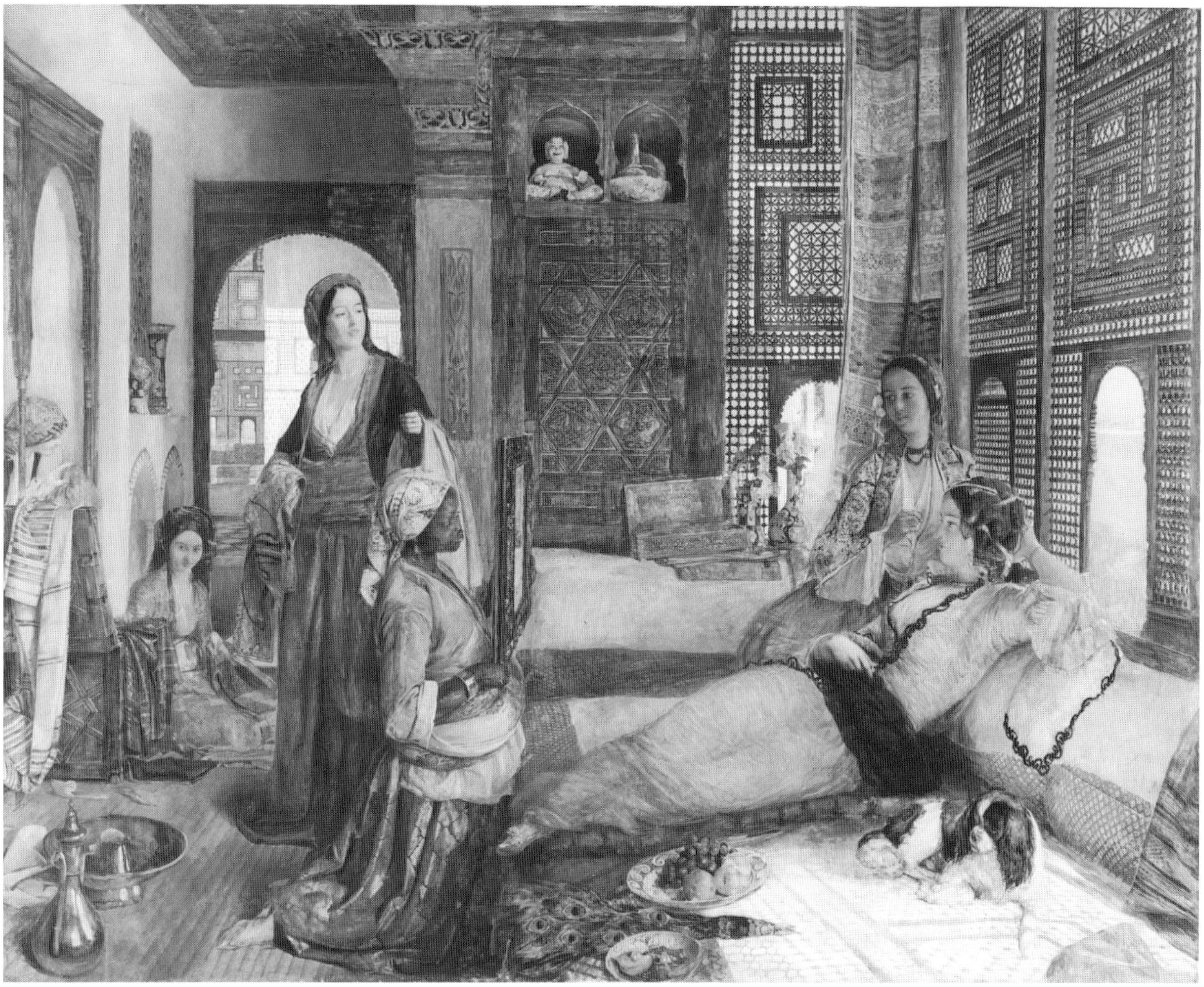

Fig. 2.11. John Frederick Lewis. *Harem*. 1876. Birmingham Museums & Art Gallery.

playful description of sleepy harem girls had less of the physician's intense scrutiny. But she too fetishizes the "bevy of fair girls" in focusing on fragmented body parts: "What eyes, and lips, and teeth, were grouped together." And like Tubeeb she makes the transition from the women's idleness to sleep: "with their delicate fingers clasped together, and almost making their idleness look graceful. Here and there one lay fast asleep, with her cheek pillowed upon her hand, and a smile upon her lips" (*CS* 1:312–13). Again indolence leads to somnolence for Pardoe in describing the slave girl, who is not Spanish but Circassian; she has the "softest sleepiest expression—the lowest voice—and the most indolently graceful movements [. . .]. As she pillows her pure, pale cheek upon her small dimpled hands, you feel no inclination to arouse her into exertion" (*CS* 2:212). The sleeping harem woman embodies the viewer's dreamlike fantasy of life in the harem. She displays one set of feminine ideals: malleability, dependence, helplessness, and passivity, all accentuated by her slumber.[74]

But what of the association between sleepy harem women and their Spanish identity? There is a short leap from recumbent harem women to lazy peoples. The "lazy native" is a stereotype that has been used to justify imperialism/cross-cultural dominance, discussed more fully below. These images suggest a construction of the Other as more inclined to the siesta and its corollary, sexual activity, than the "upright," industrious and productive western Self. As such these harem images picture people whose lives are both inviting and inferior, seductive and fearsome. For visitors to a poor country who are in search of the picturesque, the harem woman can be all of these things: inviting, inferior, fearsome, somnolent—and a pretty, exotic picture. Tourists to Spain are hardly Napoleonic invaders. But the stereotypes tourists

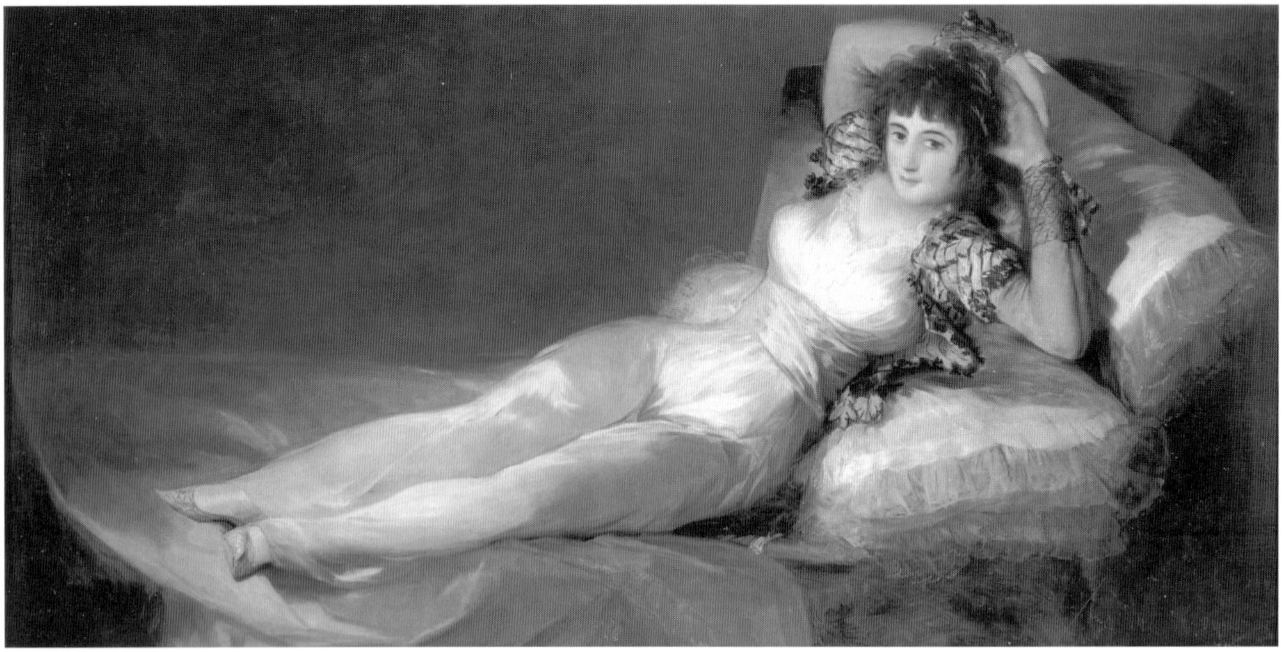

Fig. 2.12. Francisco Goya. *Clothed Maja*. Ca. 1797–98. Museo Nacional del Prado-Madrid.

harbored formed the bases for attitudes that sanctioned Napoleon's political imperialism.

Abyssinian Women

In contemporary sources listing the hierarchy of harem slaves in their accounts of Muslim slavery in Egypt and Turkey, Abyssinia (present-day Ethiopia) on the east African coast was thought to be the site of particularly beautiful "brown-skinned" women often used in harems. The word "Abyssinian" came to refer to a skin color as much as a geographical locale.[75] A woman of this "race" was considered the second most desirable type of harem slave, surpassed only by the white Circassian and Georgian slaves in wealthy harems where owners could afford to maintain distinctions of rank based on skin color. The influential Egyptologist Edward William Lane says the "handsome" Abyssinian woman ranks in price and esteem below the white slave-girl and above the black menial. The pseudoknowledge he produces about Abyssinian women is that they are "of delicate constitution" based on his impression that while in the foreign land of Egypt they are particularly susceptible to consumption (*ME* 1:234).

Lane was probably read by Sir Richard Burton, another major British Orientalist (in the sense of both scholarship on the East and misconceptions of the East). Like Lane, Burton decides that female Abyssinian slaves are a "tender race" and "they suffer when first transported to Egypt from many complaints, especially consumption, dysentery and varicose veins."[76] Burton claims he was able to study Abyssinians at some length, and the result of all his observation was a set of conclusions which reveal his love of thoroughbred horses (and gastronomy) more than any truth about this "race" of women. Burton's paralleling of the women slaves with animals was perhaps intended as tongue-in-cheek, but the effect is insulting:

> They were average specimens of the steatopygous Abyssinian breed, broad-shouldered, thin-flanked, fine-limbed, and with haunches of a prodigious size. None of them had handsome features, but the short curly hair that stands on end being concealed under a kerchief, there was something pretty in the brow, eyes and upper part of the nose, coarse and sensual in the pendent [*sic*] lips, large jowl and projecting mouth, whilst the whole had a combination of piquancy with sweetness. (*PNP* 1:87)

At another point in Burton's account, he uses skin as a cipher of racial difference in his claim that Abyssinian girls are prized "because their skins are always cool in the hottest weather" (*PNP* 2:272). This is an indirect reference to skin color in which difference is perceived in innate, biological terms.

Nerval produced another kind of knowledge about the Abyssinian slave, the type he initially wanted to purchase. He changed his mind about her

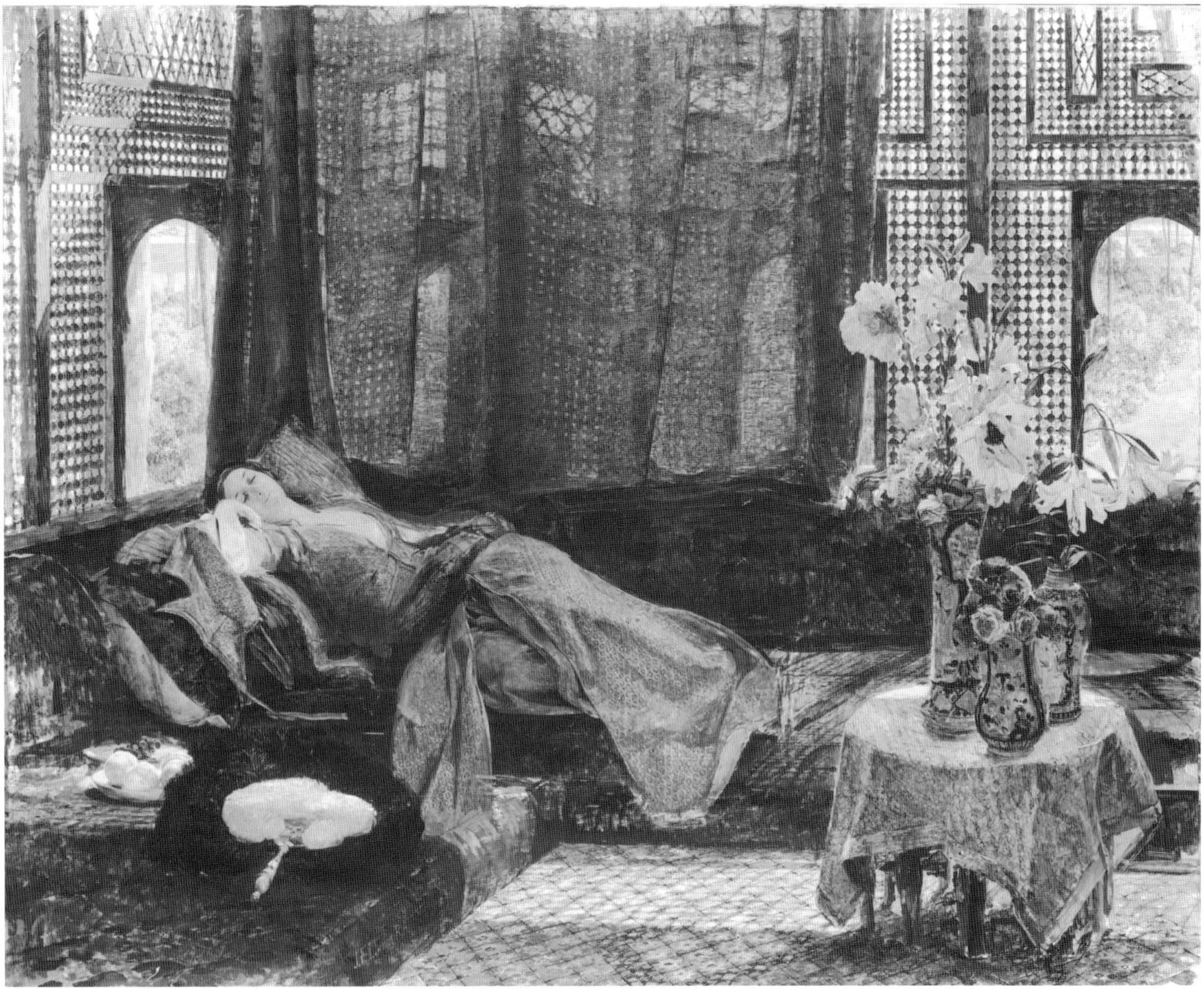

Fig. 2.13. John Frederick Lewis. *Siesta*. 1876. Tate Gallery, London 1999.

desirability after deciding "they all looked alike, which is what generally occurs among these primitive races" (*VO* 46).

Another public discourse on the Abyssinian woman in (or bound for) the harem described her as beautiful but oppressed. Mention of her appears in the *Anti-Slavery Reporter* at least twice in November 1843 alone. On 15 November it is reported that Abyssinians were included in the mass liberation of 7,000 Christian slaves and hundreds of pagan slaves.[77] Again on 29 November a physician-traveler reports on the rape and mistreatment of Abyssinian girls he witnessed as part of a slave caravan. He claims two-thirds of the females were under age fourteen (*ASR* [29 November 1843], 221–22). Lane too reports on the "brutal violence" suffered by Abyssinian girls and boys (*ME* 1:236).

An image of an Abyssinian woman in the harem appears in the 1848 illustrated luxury book *Oriental Album*. In *Habesh or Abyssinian Slave, Cairo* (Fig. 2.16), done after A. C. T. E. Prisse d'Avennes, the woman's skin color is again an indicator of inferior social status, as her job, like that of a European domestic, is to attend to her mistress's baby. The mother holds her own child—but only temporarily. In the course of a day she attends to more varied occupations, a result of her social privilege, while the monotony of childcare that the darker-skinned Habesh provides is her central function in the harem, a monotony broken briefly in the scene shown here.

Given the perception of a white-dominated hierarchy of harem slaves, the Abyssinian identity given the main slave being unveiled in John Lewis's watercolor titled *Hhareem* at its first showing at the 1850 OWCS is retitled *Hareem of a Mameluke Bey, Cairo: The Introduction of an Abyssinian Slave* (See Plate 1) at its second public showing in 1855 at the Royal Scottish Academy in Edinburgh. Its longer title constructs a

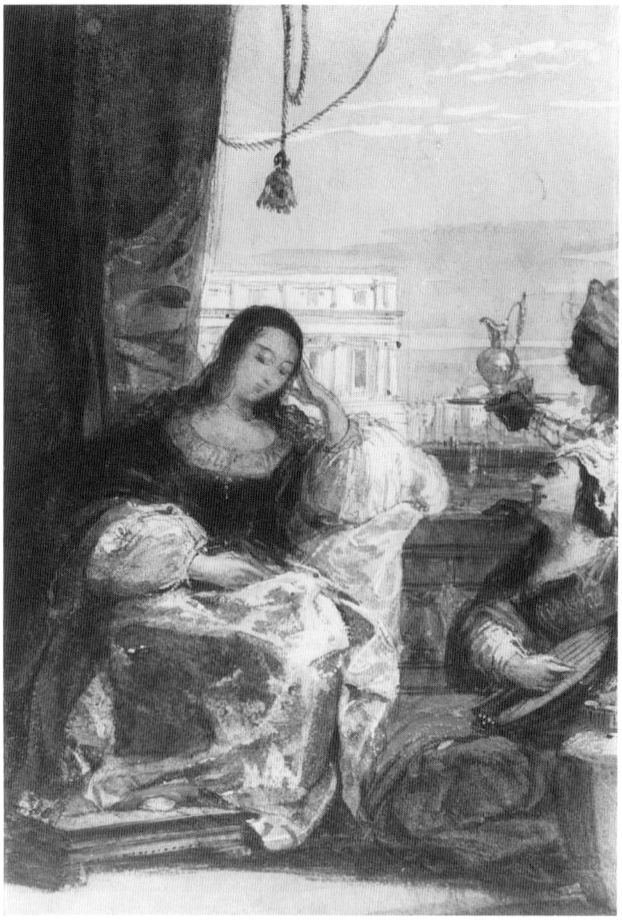

Fig. 2.14. Bonington. *La Siesta*. 1828. Watercolor. Reproduced by permission of the Trustees of the Wallace Collection, London.

new narrative for it. She is the newly acquired slave, one who ranks below the white women to our left, presumably the official wives, but below the black menials in the background. Indeed her skin tone is a shade between the two groups of women; at its first showing one critic described her as being "of dark complexion."[78] Both pasha and white women scrutinize her, making her the object of their joint gazes; she is an object because of her skin color and state of partial undress. Though she ranks below them, she is a potential usurper of their favored status.

By specifying Abyssinia in its longer title in 1853[79] the work takes on a more timely slant at its showing in Scotland, birthplace of Lord Byron and David Urquhart (and his Philhellenic brother Charles Gordon), a country which had a history of supporting social causes at least since the Greek War of Independence. In 1853 a local leader, Ras Kassa, (1820–68) was emerging as ad hoc ruler of Abyssinia.[80]

Lewis's watercolor had a contemporary relevance in 1853, though its meaning remained ambiguous. Did it advocate the abolition of the harem slavery system which wrenched this young woman from her home and to this foreign locale where she was subjected to evaluation and possible censure? Or was she fortunate to have been purchased to live out her life in this "luxurious prison"? The picture could be read either way.

Maghrebian Women (Algerian, Tunisian, Moroccan)

When French nineteenth-century artists specified a regional identity for the women depicted in their images of the harem, the most frequently named subject by far is the woman belonging to an Algerian, Tunisian, or Moroccan "race." To generalize, I am using the Arabic-based term "Maghrebian" women, which refers not to people eastern at all but to the western portion of the Ottoman Empire. My deliberate usage of the term elicits the inadequacy of the European-based concept of eastern land and eastern women.

The French had set their sights on Algeria and surrounding lands even before the July Monarchy, but by 1830 France had occupied that country. In fact, the diplomatic and commercial events leading up to the French occupation were intertwined with the events marking *les trois glorieuses*, the three glorious days that ushered in the July Monarchy and King Louis-Philippe's eighteen-year reign. A history of the French harem picture in this period must be constructed against the backdrop of a deepening French colonial foothold in the Maghreb. In this period a study of two specific images bracket a growing self-consciousness about the colonial process and the role of harem women's representations in chronicling that process: Delacroix's *Femmes d'Alger* and Vernet's *Capture of the Smala of 'Abd Al-Qadir*.

Eugène Delacroix's *Femmes d'Alger dans leur appartement* (Fig. 2.17) was on display for nearly three months in the Salon of 1834. Critical reactions to it were more directly connected to the art politics of the July Monarchy than to international and sexual politics, which I believe can be read nonetheless. The painting put in the context of its critical reaction marks an important case study in the reception of a Romantic harem picture and the subtle ways in which aesthetic discourse can be linked to colonialist attitudes toward Algeria and women.

The painting uses several traditional indicators of the harem setting. Three white harem women sit on the floor in a shadowy interior. Two on the right appear to share the mouthpiece to a narghile; a third looks out from the picture plane. They are

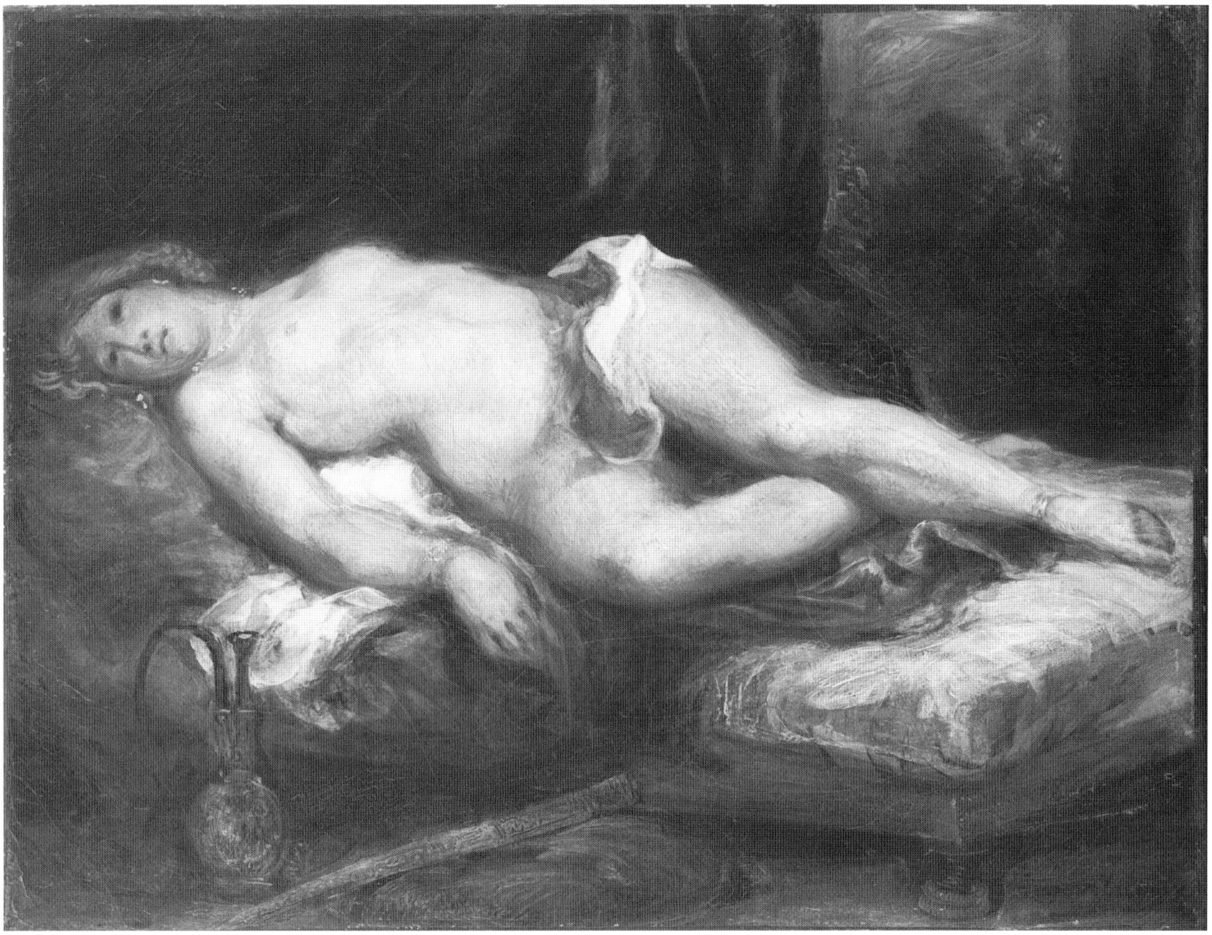

Fig. 2.15. Eugène Delacroix. *Reclining Odalisque.* 1827–28. Reproduction by permission of the Syndics of the Fitzwilliam Museum, Cambridge.

attended by a standing darker-skinned female slave with her back toward the spectator, a sign of her subservience, as she pushes aside a luxurious curtain and reveals them to the viewer. In the background are a window, mirror, and wall decoration including a pseudo-Qur'anic inscription and partially opened cupboards revealing exotic objects.

Both leftist and mainstream critics comment on Delacroix's handling of color, the hallmark of his "Liberal Romanticism." Of the critics on the left[81] who comment on Delacroix's painting, most evaluate it favorably, four of whom are briefly surveyed here.

Gustave Planche makes a token formal criticism of *Femmes d'Alger*, that the women's arms are out of proportion, but overall he praises the job Delacroix has done, calling it his best work to date. He says Delacroix's manner is "large and fecund," suggesting that the women are the same. On the topic of the women he writes that they are not sentimentalized nor frivolous and that the artist has a serious attitude toward his subject. Indeed, the women are clothed and fail to "flirt" with the spectator, unlike many in harem prints dating from the July Monarchy. From these comments it seems that Planche legitimizes Delacroix's choice of subject as high Art in contradistinction to sentimental frivolity, characteristics of rococo and rococo-revivalist harem imagery. Planche, unlike David d'Angers (quoted in a later chapter), constructs a new category for harem pictures, one distinct from debased aristocratic indulgence. Indeed, he says explicitly that *Femmes d'Alger* is about the art of painting.[82]

Barthélemy Hauréau had made two points that Planche would reuse two weeks later. Hauréau explicitly states it is Delacroix's "beauties," that is, the women themselves and not his overall manner which is "large and powerful."[83] And again for Hauréau *Femmes d'Alger* is about the art of painting. Both points suggest that Hauréau works to legitimize the harem as a subject for fine art. He judges that Delacroix is talented but undisciplined and that there are only hints of his virtues and all of his vices in this work.

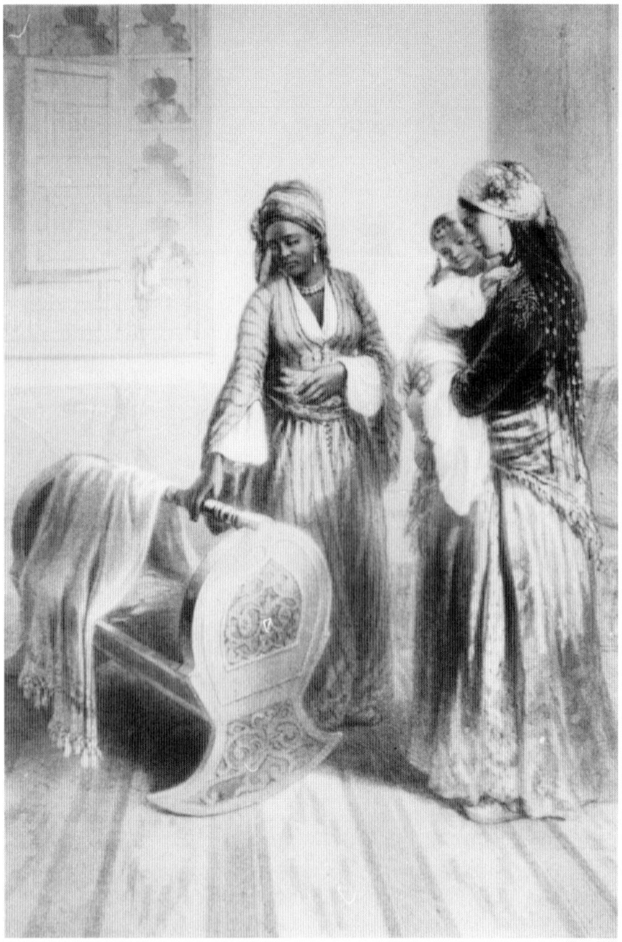

Fig. 2.16. Mouilleron after Prisse d'Avennes. *Habesh or Abyssinian Slave, Cairo.* Lithograph. *Oriental Album*, plate 5. 1848. Photo Adam Miller.

And, importantly, he complains that the work is not contemporary.

The response of Théophile Thoré-Bürger forms an interesting counterpart to the comments of his contemporaries. His reaction is itself a poetic evocation of the painting's mood, typical of Romantic aesthetics.[84] Equivalents in the mood of each text are suggested. Thoré's repetition of terms ("c'est un[e]" and "sans doute") functions to induce a litany-like altered consciousness appropriate to the exotic locale of the interior. Against the background of calm interiority produced by the women's smoking, Thoré overlays onomatopoeia, pleasant noises, metallic tinkling, in the line characterized by "t" and hard "c" sounds like the sounds of metal jewelry in motion as he names the objects: "des tentures éclatantes, des cassolettes et des *narguileck*." The painting's tactility is recounted in Thoré's line: "and over all there reigns a harmony and a vapor which caresses the long dark eyelashes of the women, which undulates over their supple clothes," in which "vapor," "caress," "eyelashes," "undulate," and "supple" all suggest touch. And his description of the physiological effects of the painting on the poet/(re)viewer might be considered a transposition of the visual into the physical-emotional. Thus rather than a description or evaluative comment on the narrative of Delacroix's painting or the politics of harem women, Thoré's writing functions as a literary parallel to the evocations of the painting. And a subtle politics emerges.

Both Thoré and Planche use the word *nonchalance*, a red flag in the critical discourse on the harem woman. Littré's 1876 dictionary definition gives the term erotic overtones.[85] For Thoré "adorable nonchalance" describes the overall mood of the picture, while for Planche the women's attitudes are "full of softness and nonchalance." These terms connote both pleasure and moral transgression premised on female passivity. In the narrative of the painting the women's inactivity is induced by the opium smoking. This narrative and Delacroix's formal choices give rise to critical readings of profound feminine receptivity; the woman who waits for a male agent is a recurrent theme in harem imagery. It is closely related to the "lazy native" stereotype, whether male or female, that is also fundamental to colonialist thinking. When the native is female, she is doubly passive.[86]

Thoré's comments on nonchalance and his evocation of the mood of Delacroix's *Femmes d'Alger* are particularly noteworthy given his conviction expressed this very same year about how art should follow a political and social direction. A Saint-Simonian, Thoré writes in *L'Artiste* that artists' goal should be "to depict current events, to penetrate to the core of the age, to give the fine arts their social character."[87] Why Delacroix's painting was exempt has to do with its feminine subject, ostensibly excluded from public political events.

In contrast to these leftist writers, one of the few strongly critical comments is issued by Etienne Jean Delécluze, hostile to Delacroix's work since 1826. His is the only centrist comment I have discovered to speak to the painting's subject matter. He criticizes the women's exotic looks, and his brief comment is snide: "if these are the type of *houris* of Muhammed, we will not be made Turks so soon."[88] French observers too were aware of the conflation of harem women and *houris.* Delécluze may have intended his "humor" to reveal his anti-Romantic position, but it also reveals his Orientalist attitude.

Delacroix's *Femmes d'Alger* was purchased for the state for 3,000 francs by Louis Adolphe Thiers, minister of the interior in 1832 and 1834–36, and minister of commerce and public works from 1833–34.

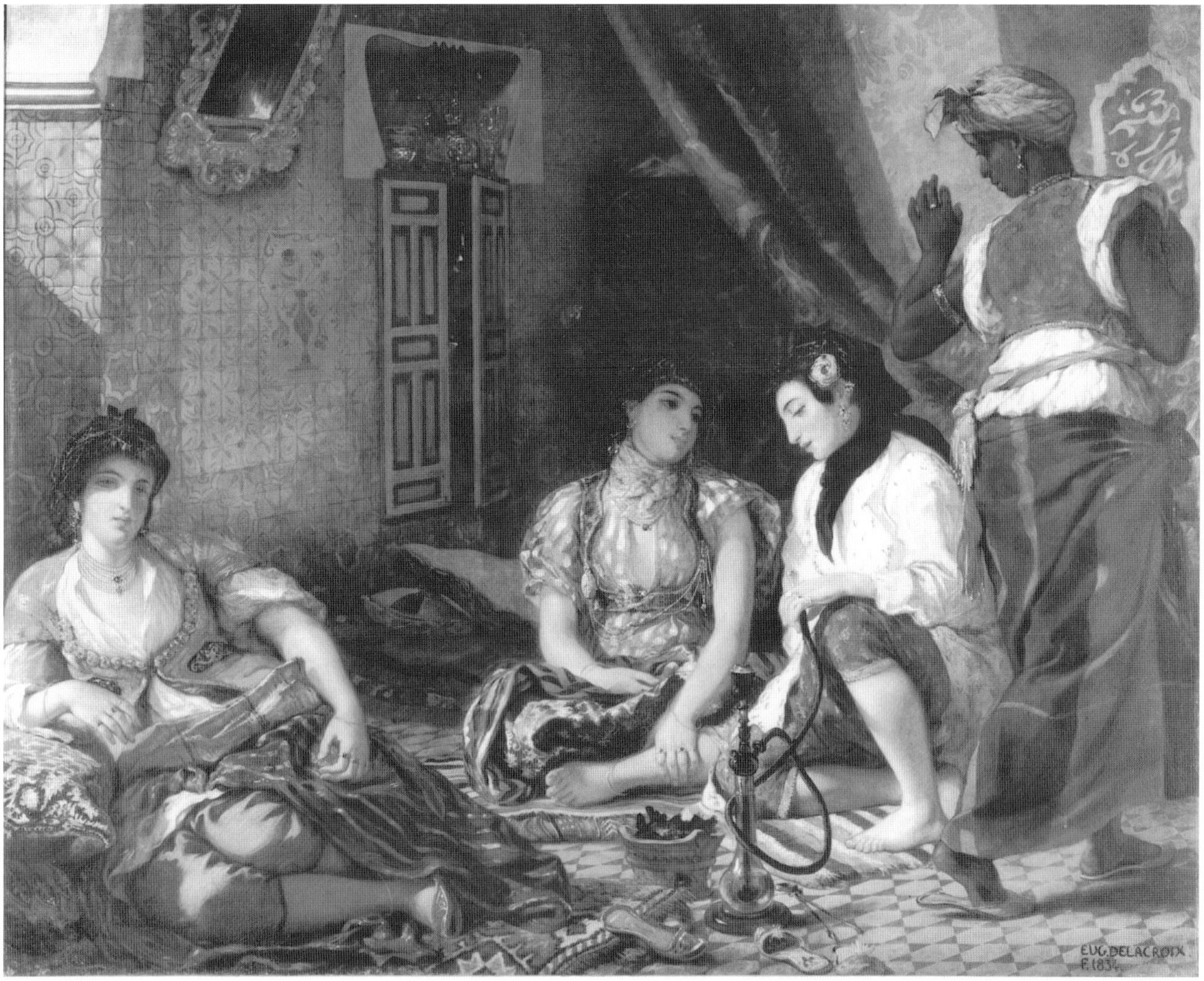

Fig. 2.17. Eugène Delacroix. *Femmes d'Alger dans leur appartement/Women of Algiers in their Apartment.* 1834 Salon. Musée du Louvre, Paris. © Photo RMN.

There are several possible explanations for why Thiers bought the picture. He may have felt it necessary to justify the commission the government had recently given to Delacroix to adorn the throne room of the Palais Bourbon,[89] a project in which Delacroix envisioned one of six subjects as the "Conquest of Algiers."[90] A supporter of both Louis-Philippe and Eugène Delacroix, Thiers may also have been eager to maintain the unraveling alliance between the king and the Liberals who ushered him into power in the 1830 July Revolution. In the 1831 Salon Delacroix's *Liberty Leading the People* had been purchased in a reassertion of support, though Louis-Philippe's subsequent domestic policies from 1831–34 were repressive. The two paintings by Delacroix are quite different—one public and contemporary, the other private and (ostensibly) removed from Parisian life—but the revolution to which *Liberty* refers was bound up with the history of the conquest of Algiers in 1830. Thiers may have read *Femmes d'Alger* as an assertion of the monarchy's successful, if ambiguous, military campaign in Algeria at a time when the government was besieged for its repressive domestic policies.

The work can be considered an assertion of the exotic-passive female as symbol for the Romantic imagination and its concomitant left Liberalism.[91] In the second half of the century as well representations of women's bodies would continue to be the battleground over which the aesthetic battles of French modernity would be waged.[92]

Historically harem women had been defined by their difference from a bustling Parisian bourgeois life. In Thoré's words on Delacroix's *Femmes d'Alger*: "There is an immense contrast with the French character which has never dreamt of economizing movement and activity." Delacroix's painting, despite what we might call its contemporary title, was apparently considered apolitical in that its referent is passive, calm, "nonchalant" women and not, say, North African resistance fighters (who would become increasingly more vociferous against the French invaders into the 1830s). Perhaps Delacroix's reference to the Eternal Female rather than the changing Historical Male is Hauréau's point when he claims that the subject is not contemporary. As long as the harem hovered in the grey area of Parisian consciousness between fact and fantasy, the mystique of the exotic harem woman could be maintained.

Themes suggested to us today by Delacroix's *Femmes d'Alger* are not openly articulated in the critical response: slavery, race, the harem hierarchy, concubinage/polygyny (euphemized by Delécluze as houris), or colonialism in Algiers. This critical reluctance to name colonialism may be understandable, given Algeria's ambiguous political status as unofficial colony at the time of these writings; not until July 1834 was it declared French. Moreover, the subject of the harem picture was traditionally apolitical, even though Algiers is part of Delacroix's title. The critics' apparent reluctance to link the erotic-exotic aesthetic to the economic and political was a project outside the scope of French art criticism in 1834. Mention of slavery or race even in the leftist press would have politicized the work and removed it from the category "Art." The development of the mechanism of art criticism in the early July Monarchy was premised on its removal from politics in part to justify its own elevated status.

There are several interesting postscripts to *Femmes d'Alger* besides Delacroix's own later version completed in 1849 (Fig. 2.18), a work that is more removed and dematerialized than its prototype. Alexandre Dumas's description of Moorish and Arab women's clothing can be considered in some ways a verbal transposition of the painting. Alongside "facts" such as the women's temperament and their tendency to age quickly, he writes a detailed account of their clothing and jewelry presumably in an effort to uncover harem women's perceived essence:

> Their usual dress is a fine, transparent chemise and short, wide trousers of red, blue or green silk reaching to the knees. Below, their legs are bare, and on their feet are embroidered velvet slippers, though when women are sitting at ease their slippers are generally strewn around them on the floor. Moorish women usually wear headdresses, collars and bracelets of gold pieces, sometimes as many as 2 or 3 hundred gold coins called *maboules*, and these they never lay aside, not even in their tenderest, most passionate moments. (*AA* 115)

Dumas does not explicitly acknowledge Delacroix here, but he does so at several other places in the book. Delacroix's *Femmes d'Alger*, which might be considered today a highly romanticized painting, seems a likely source for Dumas's claims.

Another postscript to *Femmes d'Alger*[93] appears in the writing of the well-known poet and critic Charles Baudelaire, who purchased from Delacroix a print of the painting.[94] After the artist's death Baudelaire makes some interesting comments about Delacroix's retrograde sexual politics. The portrait of Delacroix to emerge from Baudelaire's account is a youthful enthusiast of women who later grows to distrust them for their ability to be "disobedient and disturbing once one throws open the door of one's heart to her, and gluttonously devouring of time and strength."[95] The poet likens the artist to a Muslim man who sees Woman as soulless:

> Had he been a Mohammedan, he would not perhaps have gone so far as to drive her out of his mosques, but he would have been amazed to see her entering them, not being quite able to understand what sort of converse she could have with Allah.[96]

Delacroix's understanding of woman as *femme fatale* was what Baudelaire terms part of his obsession with "the oriental idea" on women. Unlike the discourse of Delacroix's contemporaneous art criticism, the poet's retrospective comments suggest the deeper psychological meanings the artistic subject of the Oriental woman may have had for the painter. While woman was "an object of art, delightful and well suited to excite the mind," Baudelaire claims Delacroix the misogynist excluded women from his later life.

In no other painting is the colonialist desecration of the harem more vividly represented than in Horace Vernet's enormous (sixty-six-feet-long) contemporary military painting *Capture of the Smala of 'Abd Al-Qadir* shown at the 1845 Salon and accompanied by the longest *livret* description that year. In physical size, verbal description, and political position, the spectacular picture is about French military excess. The panoramic canvas celebrates the seizure led by Duke of Aumale, son of King Louis-Philippe, of the traveling capital consisting of about 30,000 civilians and belonging to the leader of the Algerian resistance from 1832 until his surrender in 1847. The event was the surprise attack of 16 May 1843. Using 600 horsemen, the French defeated 5,000 Algerian guards. Three hundred Algerians were killed by the French, who also took 3,000 people, including members of 'Abd Al-Qadir's family, along with his treasury and other booty.[97] In the eight years of the

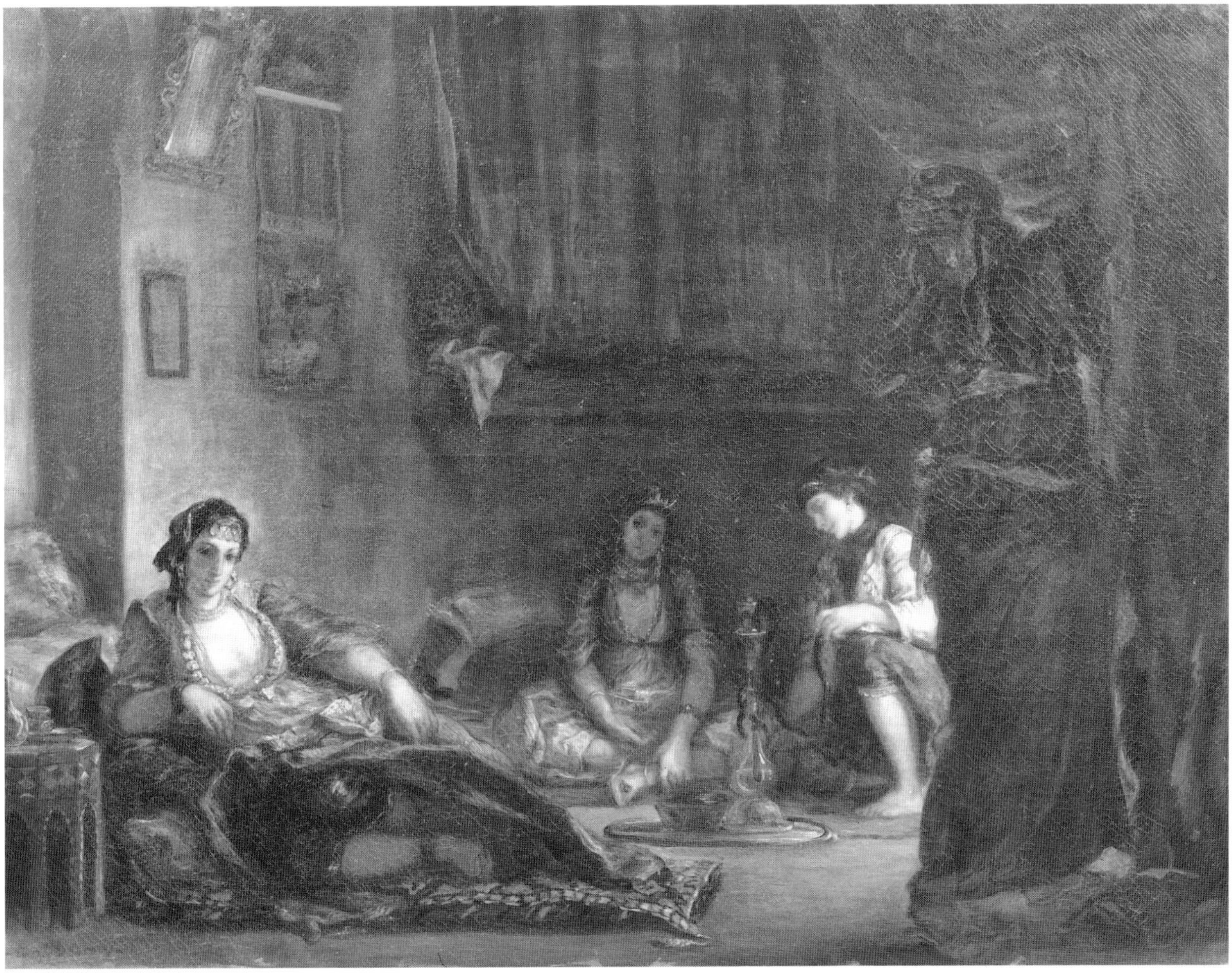

Fig. 2.18. Eugène Delacroix. *Femmes d'Alger dans l'Intérieur/Women of Algiers in their Apartment.* 1849. Musée Fabre, Montpellier. © Photo RMN.

French-Algerian war (1839–47) the Algerian population would be decimated by about ten per cent.[98] Painted in the stage of the French colonization of Algeria that called for total conquest, it reflects the harsh clarity of the French prerogative to destroy the indigenous state. Commissioned by the king from Vernet, his official state painter, the work served as propaganda justifying its regular outlay of revenue in Algeria. The picture bespeaks French military glory from its locale of the newly renovated War Gallery of Versailles. The destruction of the harem was a significant part of the painting's narrative and its ideological function.

The vignette of the harem's disruption (Plate 3) is indicated by the jostling of two women who desperately struggle to keep themselves atop a litter even as they tumble to the ground. Both are still veiled, in effect: Vernet gives us only the back view of one woman, while the face of the other is covered by her upper arm. A third woman is visible. She may be read as the first wife, given her physical elevation in the painting and the fact that she seems to occupy her own litter. She is not yet as affected by the commotion except that she affixes her diaphanous veil to look out at the scene below, revealing an "Egyptian" profile, fine jewels and long, unfettered locks of hair. In this scene the luxurious stuffs, the ungainly feminine poses, the foil of white women and black men, and the injured animals recall Delacroix's *Sardanapalus* (see Fig. 4.53) shown eighteen years earlier, while the black man desperately trying to right the structure seems to have a formal connection to figures in the Italian Mannerist painting *Descent from the Cross* by Pontormo. As a pro-French image *Capture of the Smala* shows harem women in need of liberation from their uncivilized life lead in the company of animals and subservient humans. The prominently displayed bare foot of one of the three women remind us of her "natural," uncivilized state, as does the ungirdled breast and their lightly clad torsos.

The Salon *livret* was similarly patriotic. The scene served "to give their native soldiers a new and brilliant example of our national valor."[99] *L'Illustration* also complimented Vernet for avoiding the "banal horror" of the capture and admired the "quick sentiment and happy inspiration" of the scene, in effect, its testament to the efficiency of the French military machinery, which wipes out both the personal and professional grounding of the resistance leader in this watershed event.[100] Despite cries of protest from fez-capped boy and camel (cries that add to the picturesque quality), the picture boldly asserts that the harem must go as part of the inexorable Frenchification of Algeria.

Several other images of Maghrebian women produced by French painters will be analyzed in this study.[101] That so many of them can be integrated into preexisting categories of harem women suggests the extent to which stereotypes operate to produce crudely generalized knowledge of a fundamental essence of eastern woman, an essence that was perceived to be representable through material objects. In all of these pictures, clothing, jewelry, and exotic objects function as indicators of racial difference.

The practice of enshrining such objects by their representation within pictorial art continues in Alexandre Dumas's *Adventures in Algeria*. One of Dumas's explicit intertextual references in his writing is Delacroix's portraits of a Jewish woman in Morocco. In his travel account Dumas is shown innumerable examples of tourist art by a dealer, David Azercot, who functions as a kind of magic genie granting all his wishes for luxurious things. Dumas inventories them: "copper vessels, mother-of-pearl caskets, tobacco jars and strange, Eastern design, Turkish *chibouques*, hookahs, anything that came into my head," and each time he asks David returns with the object Dumas wanted "till I was almost panic-stricken to see my wishes taking shape before me" (*AA* 28). Suddenly Dumas remembers Delacroix's painting of a Moroccan Jewess that he had seen in his studio. And the culmination of Dumas's desires is wanting to see a living female artifact, "a similar model" to the "Jewess wearing the loveliest traditional robes" (*AA* 28–29) painted by Delacroix. Coincidentally, the house Delacroix had visited in the early 1830s was Azercot's, and the woman he painted, Rachel, was his sister-in-law. Azercot warns that she is fifteen years older and offers a younger substitute, his cousin Molly, who "'will be waiting for you, dressed as Rachel was'" (*AA* 28). The women's bodies are interchangeable; it is the Maghrebian native dress that intrigues Dumas, because it functions as the indicator of her exotic essence.

At the end of his travel book, Alphonse de Lamartine outlines a justification for continuing French domination in Algeria. Though he expresses great respect for the "Mohammedan" religion and admiration for the beauty of its women, the "coast of Africa" is not inhabited by the laudable races of Turks or Arabs but rather by Barbary regencies which are independent of the Turks. He claims they are neither respectable nor indigenous. Rather they are

> colonies of freebooters, superfluous to the soil, and which take no root in it; which have neither right, nor title, nor family among the nations; which, like a vessel without a flag, are the legitimate prey of the cannon; upon which whoever will may fire. Turkey is not there. (*PHL* 483)

Apparently, the fact that the French too had no root in Maghrebian soil was not germane.

Conclusion

The image of a harem inmate having a specific nationality functions in still another way. According to Grosrichard, her foreignness acts as an *exemplum* of the ruler's subject peoples and confirms their submission to him; the harem woman is not simply one but "the Other chosen from many."[102] In other words, specifying ethnicity suggests the great extent of Ottoman rule—but also its fragmentation. Within such a system of political decay, the ethnicized woman is made somewhat more precise in her identity, but only in an arbitrary and perfunctory way. She is thus readable as a female body, a private vehicle for the expression of international political concerns.

As for French international politics, Alphonse de Lamartine's explicit ideological program for European expansion into the East claims knowledge of the will of God himself. The author sees Europe and the East as existing in binary opposition to each other. The crisis of overproduction in Europe is paralleled by an underproduction, indeed a "stagnation" and "a state of exhaustion and torpidity" in the East (*PHL* 482). He sees western expansion as a mutually beneficial arrangement: Europe stands to gain new markets for its goods and a restoration of its social order threatened by "those perpetually increasing masses of the populace, armed, undisciplined, and struggling between poverty on the one hand, and pillage on the other" (*PHL* 482). Such social tension is to be released in the East so as to safeguard private property at home: it is here that the East becomes feminized as the receptacle ("outlet") to European "excess of life" and "excess of force" (*PHL* 482). At the same time, the East also stands to gain. While it renews Europe's "vigor" (*PHL* 491), colonization will also make the East fecund again. "Anarchy and disorganized barbarism, territories devoid of inhabitants, and a people destitute of rulers" (*PHL* 482) will cease. The Turks are an honorable race, and while Lamartine does not advocate their extinction, they will be extinct nonetheless without Europe's help. "As a race of men, they must be saved," and western capitalism has the "duty" to do so (*PHL* 491). In the process Europe will learn from the East, given to Europe by God to civilize, construct, educate, discover, explore, and codify their legal and religious traditions. Lamartine's love and respect for eastern women and religion occur within an ideological framework of incipient economic domination, an early statement of "white man's burden."

Lamartine feels the issue of colonization is of the greatest political import. The stakes are high. He writes hyperbolically: "unless the anticipative wisdom of the European governments devise a preservation against them, the ruin of the known social world is inevitable within a given time" (*PHL* 482). He writes in the 1830s in response to the informal colonization of Algeria. He is also responding to the threat of Mohammed Ali's Egyptian army to overturn the sultan. As a result, the Russian czar orders troops to help defend Turkey. Fearing a Russian takeover in the East, France and England intervene. In this context, Lamartine criticizes Mohammed Ali as selfishly exploitive of his country's resources. He claims that after his leadership wanes, a power vacuum will arise, one which must be filled: "After him, she [Arabia] knows she must fall under some yoke, and cares not of whom (*PHL* 483).

Lamartine's conviction about the necessity of European colonization and his patronizing attitudes toward eastern women are particularly noteworthy, given his prominence in both French letters and politics in the first half of the century. The poet whose *Poetic Meditations* established his reputation in 1820 would become minister of foreign affairs of the Provisional Government at Louis-Philippe's abdication in 1848. His writing on Muslim women bridges the discourses of poetics and politics.

3

Depictions of Slavery and the Making of the Harem

Introduction

> No European goes to the East with a clear idea of a slave market. He has seen fanciful French lithographs, and attractive scenes in Eastern ballets, where the pretty girls appeared ready, on the shortest notice, and in the most bewitching costumes, to dance the Gitana, Romaika, Tarantella, Redowa, or any other characteristic *pas* that might be required of them. Or, if not schooled into these impressions, he takes the indignant view of the subject, and thinks of nothing but chains and lashes, and finds, at last, that one is just as false as the other.[1]

The slave market was one of the means by which slaves were secured to build a harem or diversify its functions. Some writers, like Albert Smith quoted above, were conscious of the polemical nature of representations of the slave market. Imbued with Enlightenment ideas of personal freedom as the foundation of human society, observers in England and France had difficulty reconciling harem slavery and the slave market with their own social structures. An analysis of these issues becomes a fascinating study in the conflicts inherent in the construction of cultural identity and difference in the nineteenth century.

Apologists for harem slavery frequently compared it to plantation slavery and found living in a wealthy pasha's home to be vastly superior to the moral degradation and harsh physical conditions endured by American field slaves. Yet even those who could accept harem slavery as legitimate were pained at the idea of selling of human beings at a slave market. To other observers the slave's life of material ease once she reached the harem compensated for the indignities she had suffered along the way. This last pattern of thinking, in which suffering is a necessary stage leading to material improvement, can be considered a projection of the ideologies of self-help and the work ethic. In their perceptions of the process that took harem women from the slave market to the harem's "paradise," such writers may be recounting a familiar story, the bourgeois ideal of social ascendance from working-class to middle-class status.

That the harem offered a life of material luxury was an argument used to counter complaints about how it imprisoned women. By reputation, prospective slaves sometimes went gladly into the harem via the slave market as a way to secure their futures, ensuring financial stability for themselves and perhaps their families as well. Sophie Lane Poole, sister of the renowned Edward William Lane whose book forms a feminine counterpart to his own, called the harem a "luxurious prison."[2] Similarly, in the western European cult of domesticity women were protected from the outside world in a comfortable home but were confined to it. Discussions of the slave in the harem and the means by which she was brought there could serve as an allegory for the western bourgeois female condition. The claim that these women too were slaves was part of feminist discourse since Mary Wollstonecraft's 1792 *Vindication of the Rights of Women.* She claims that it is not only exotic peoples who keep women enslaved. Maintaining a binary opposition between rational creatures and slaves, she insists that women be considered beings capable of rational thought (*VRW* 120–21). When women are treated like slaves, they begin to resemble indolent harem women, who cannot be virtuous because they are not free:

> Liberty is the mother of virtue, and if women be, by their very constitution, slaves, and not allowed to breathe the sharp invigorating air of freedom they must ever languish like exotics, and be reckoned beautiful flaws in nature. (121–22)

Her early conceptualization of woman as a kind of slave gets resuscitated in mid-nineteenth-century abolitionist rhetoric. There the liberation of women is seen as an extension of the impulse to free the slaves. This is articulated explicitly at the American 1848 Seneca Falls Convention, a gathering of mostly white middle-class feminists with a notable appearance by the former slave Frederick Douglass, one of the male signers of the *Declaration of the Rights of Women.*

Some Victorian observers of conscience failed to accept the concept of either voluntary or mild servitude and focused their protest instead on the woman who joined the harem in a brutal and forceful manner: when she was taken as a prisoner of war and sold against her will into a life of slavery. Though westerners had expressed concern over harem inmates as political prisoners for centuries, the Greek War of Independence from the Turks in the 1820s provided a new occasion for the eruption and development of these patterns of thinking, recording, and picturing. Christian Philhellenes saw little possibility of an earthly paradise for the Greek woman captured for harem service. She was expected to break completely with her old life, learn a new language, and accept an alien culture. Her daily life was profoundly changed. She would live secluded from the outside world and almost exclusively in the company of women. Above all, she would apostatize.

Islam issued myriad judgments on slavery. Just as there is no monolith Islam that unequivocally sanctions and determines the character of the harem, there is none to approve of slave-holding universally. Classic Muslim jurists saw slavery as the exceptional condition and advocated freedom for the majority of subjects. The practice of slave-holding varied widely over geography and chronology, ethnicity and psychology. "Edicts" about a slave's status are really "a set of scattered opinions," while the slave in Muslim jurisprudence has rights acknowledging his/her ambiguous status—sometimes property, sometimes person.[3] The slave's personhood is presumed by some rules governing the treatment of concubines (slave women with whom a master would cohabit for procreation and pleasure): that the master refrain from cohabiting with slaves other than his own; that a concubine could not be shared; that a concubine could not be prostituted.[4] On the other hand, the slave was property according to some practices. The most extreme assertion of this and of the master's right of ownership—killing his slave—had few repercussions; in nineteenth-century Egypt "the logic of the law suggests" he would not be punished.[5] Though the law specifies the slave must be treated humanely, this is a judgment open to wide interpretation.

In point of fact, not all harem women were slaves. Some harem wives, especially the senior wife, had most likely never been slaves but were married into families of rank and wealth comparable to their own through the process of arranged marriage more familiar in the West. And slave status was not immutable. If a concubine produced a child whom the master acknowledged to be his, that child was free and enjoyed all the rights of belonging to his family; also the concubine-mother could not be resold.[6] Such a child could inherit property and rank just as children born in wedlock. If a concubine slave married the master, she lost her slave status. These instances of social mobility appeared in British accounts as a way to defend the harem against the myth of a monolithic and rigidly oppressive Islam.

Protest and Defense; Titillation and Ambivalence: Harem Slavery and the Slave Market Represented by a Range of Observers

The Anti-Slavery Society and Diplomats

The provocative nature of the slave market—and by implication artistic representations of it—is evident in texts issued by the London-based Anti-Slavery Society in the early Victorian period with an emphasis on the 1840s. Close examination of these texts shows that rather than unequivocal protest against slavery, however, authors express degrees of ambivalence toward the issues which harem slavery elicits: race, gender, and freedom.

Humanitarian concern for the enslaved harem woman appeared in travel accounts as early as the sixteenth and seventeenth centuries.[7] Popularized in the eighteenth century by Enlightenment thinkers in both England and France, sympathy grew from the conviction that harem women were unfree and that individual freedom should be universally applied. These ideas contributed to the ideological basis of the abolitionist movement which took up the cause of women of the harem—black and white alike—in the emancipation of all slaves worldwide. The crusade to abolish the harem is most clearly articulated by the abolitionist movement, specifically the London-based Anti-Slavery Society. As late as 1878 the society continued lobbying for the liberation of white slaves from the harem, long after the British government gave up the cause.

In 1840 the Anti-Slavery Society worked in concert with the British government, an early and rare alliance between the two bodies that claimed to share similar goals but could hardly agree on the means. One of the functions of British pressure on the Ottoman Turks to reform the laws and practice of white harem slavery was to convince the British public, especially sympathizers with the dispossessed, that lawmakers were true humanitarians sensitive to principles of liberty and justice.[8] Evidence of

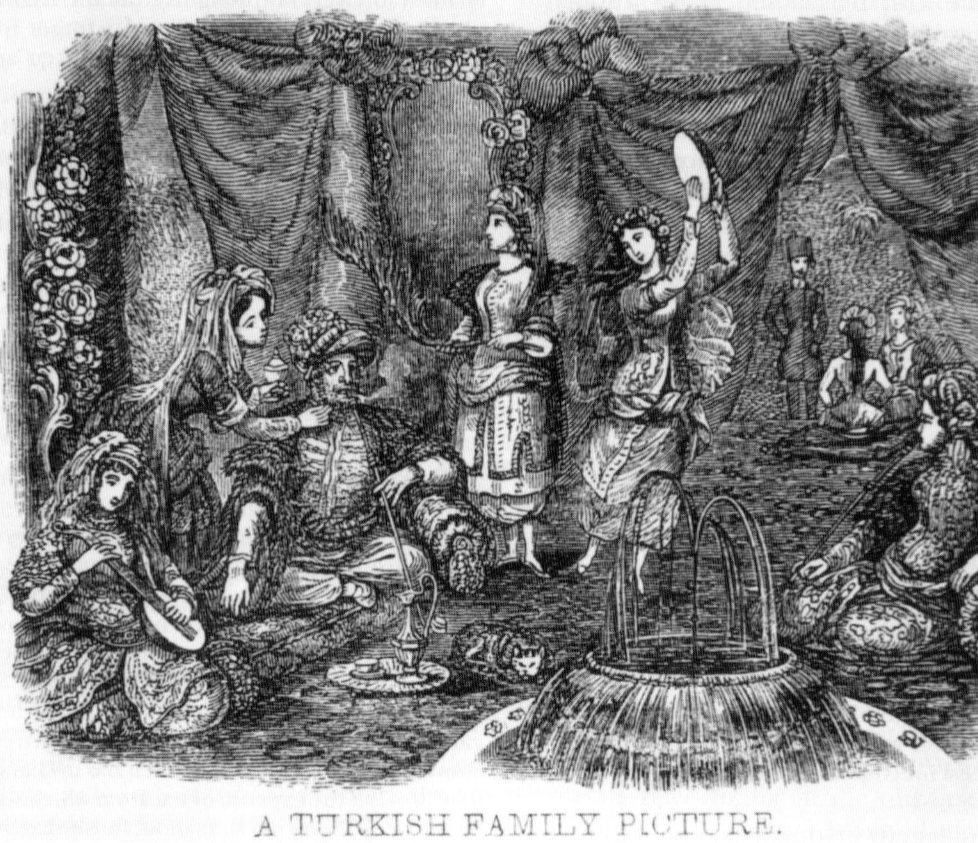

Fig. 3.1. Anonymous. *A Turkish Family Picture.* 1837. Engraving. Frontispiece to Edmund Spencer, *Travels in Circassia.* Photo Adam Miller.

country, that had sacrificed millions to eradicate this stain of barbarism from every land over which her flag waved."[28]

Spencer does not indicate explicitly whether his condemnation of the slave market extended to the harem, but the illustration on the title page of his book suggests a very different attitude. Despite Spencer's condemnation of the slave market in his text, the illustration, *A Turkish Family Picture* (Fig. 3.1), conveys none of his sense of moral outrage or "disgust." Here is a sumptuous interior which contains several of the harem signs (to be discussed more fully in subsequent chapters): pipes, musical instruments, coffee service, mirror, fine fabrics, flowers, fountain, and feline. The pasha is attended by two women, while an *almée* dances and a fourth woman plays the *ood.* A fifth woman sitting to the right smokes a chibouk like her master. The illustration is called a family scene, but there are no small children present. Instead the women conduct themselves as Victorian daughters toward their father. There is a hierarchy based on gender, but its erotic component differs significantly from that found in many French prints of the harem. The pasha seems a benevolent old patriarch whom all women try to please, not at all the cruel "barbarian Osmanli" or "licentious libertine" from whom slave women need to be saved.

In the background is another man. He is a rarity in the harem pictorial tradition, which more typically shows women secluded. He wears a fez and frockcoat, trousers and boots, indicating a second wave of Ottoman reform of the traditional dress of turban and flowing robes dating from 1828 and required for the Turkish army.[29] A travel writer from 1850 applauds the ideological import of such reform, comparing the fez to the Phrygian cap: "The fezz, like the bonnet rouge of the French republicans, is the great symbol of equality."[30] The point of the print seems to be that in modern Turkey the harem too is undergoing reform and moving closer to the western family. One is reminded of the viewpoint of David Urquhart, one of whose books appeared the year after Spencer's in which the harem is celebrated as the locale of domestic harmony. He defines the harem woman's independence, integrity, and significance within the Turkish polity and the

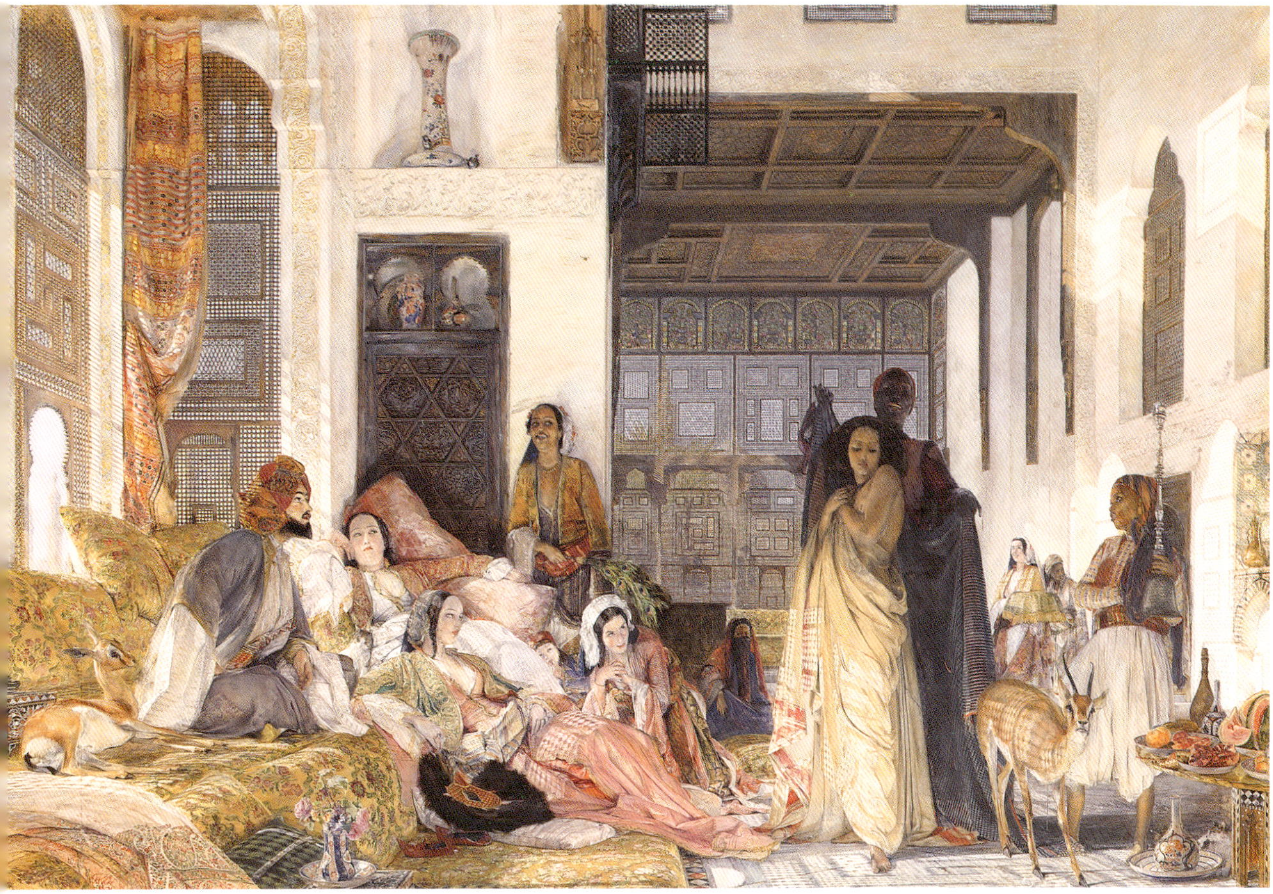

Plate 1. John Frederick Lewis. *Hhareem.* Watercolor and bodycolor. 1850. Private Collection, Osaka.

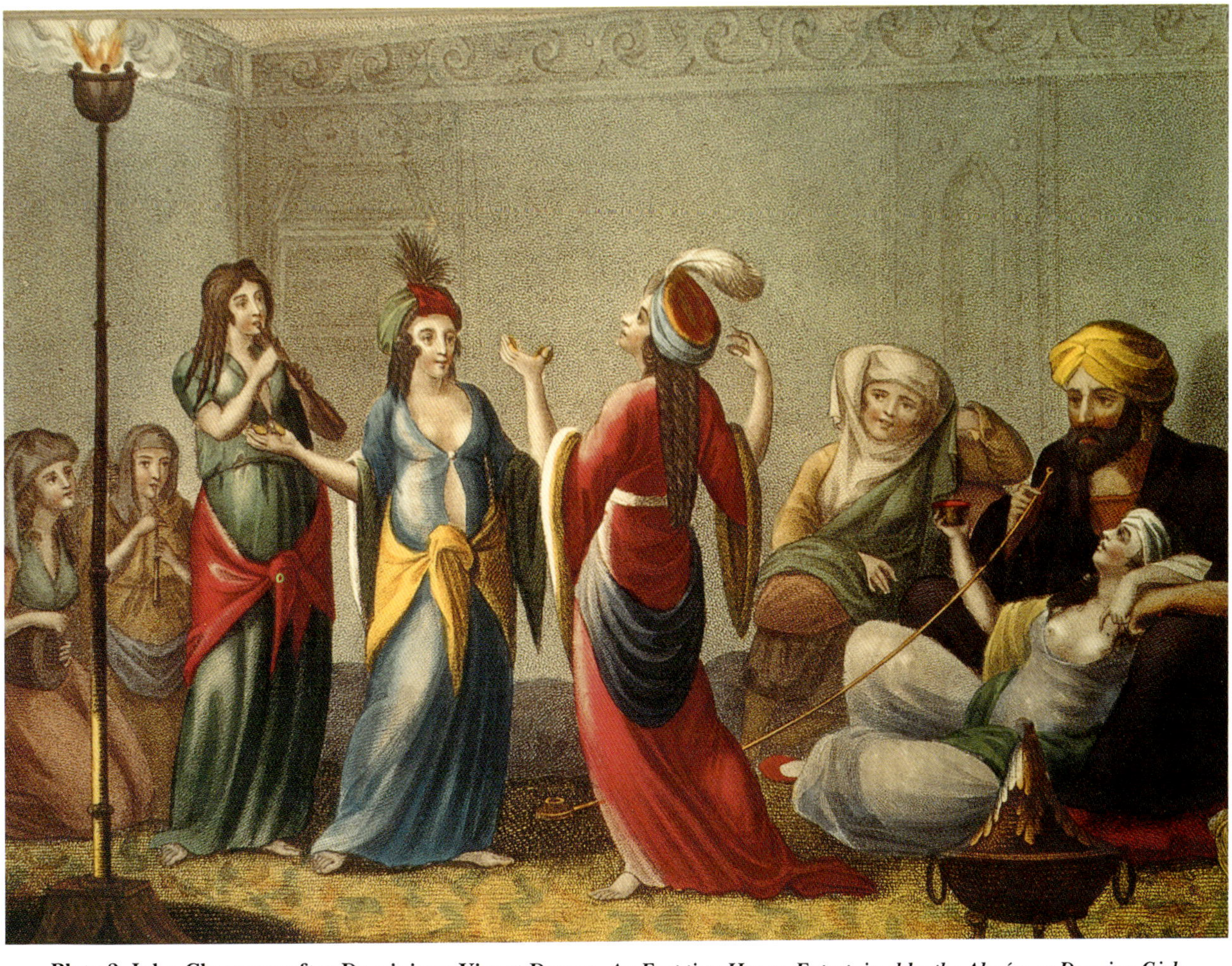

Plate 2. John Chapman after Dominique Vivant Denon. *An Egyptian Harem Entertained by the Almées or Dancing Girls.* Color engraving. *Encyclopedia Londinensis*, 1810–11.

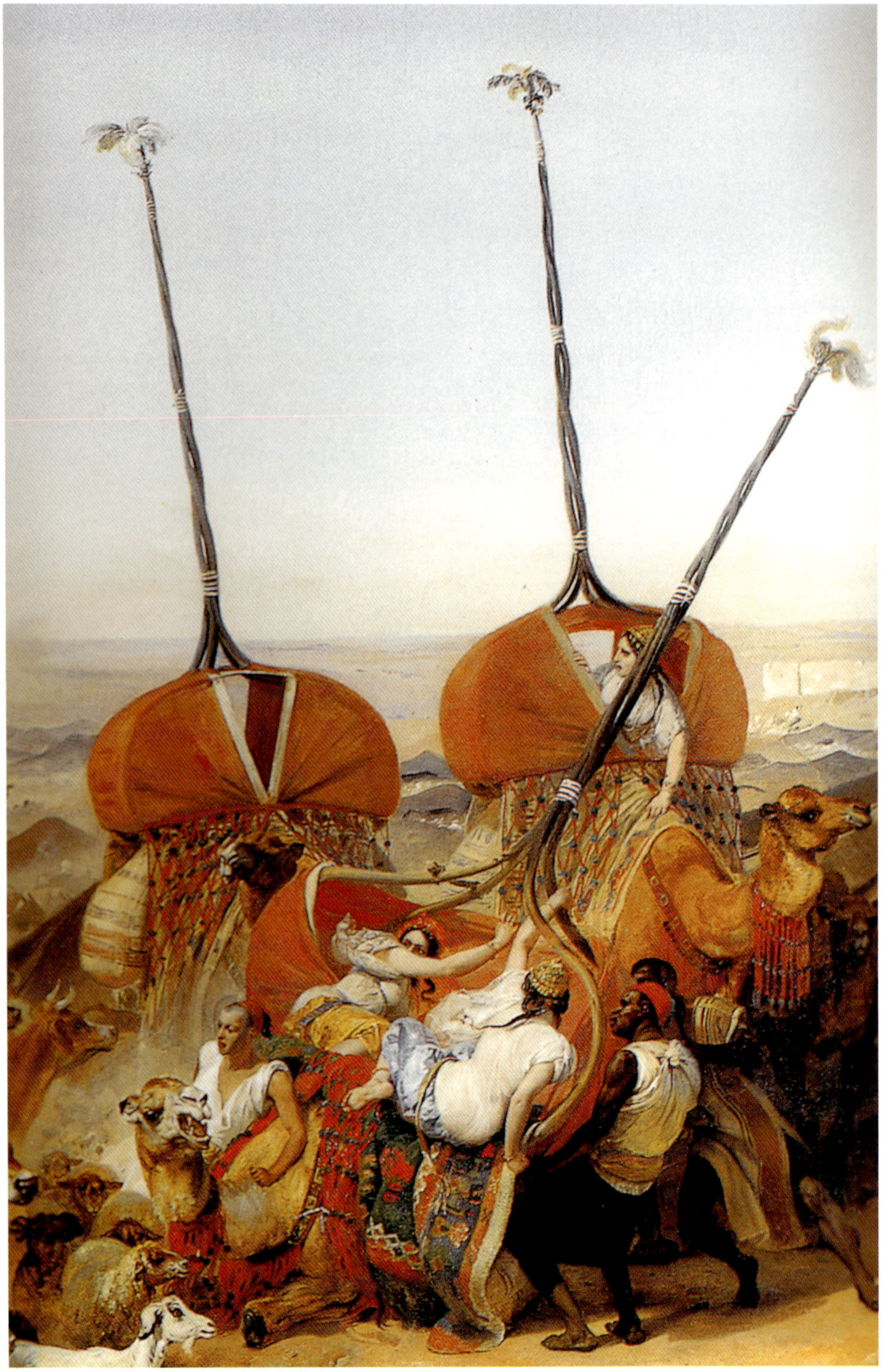

Plate 3. Horace Vernet. Detail, *Capture of the Smala of 'Abd Al-Qadir*. 1845 Salon. Château de Versailles. Photo © Editions Faton.

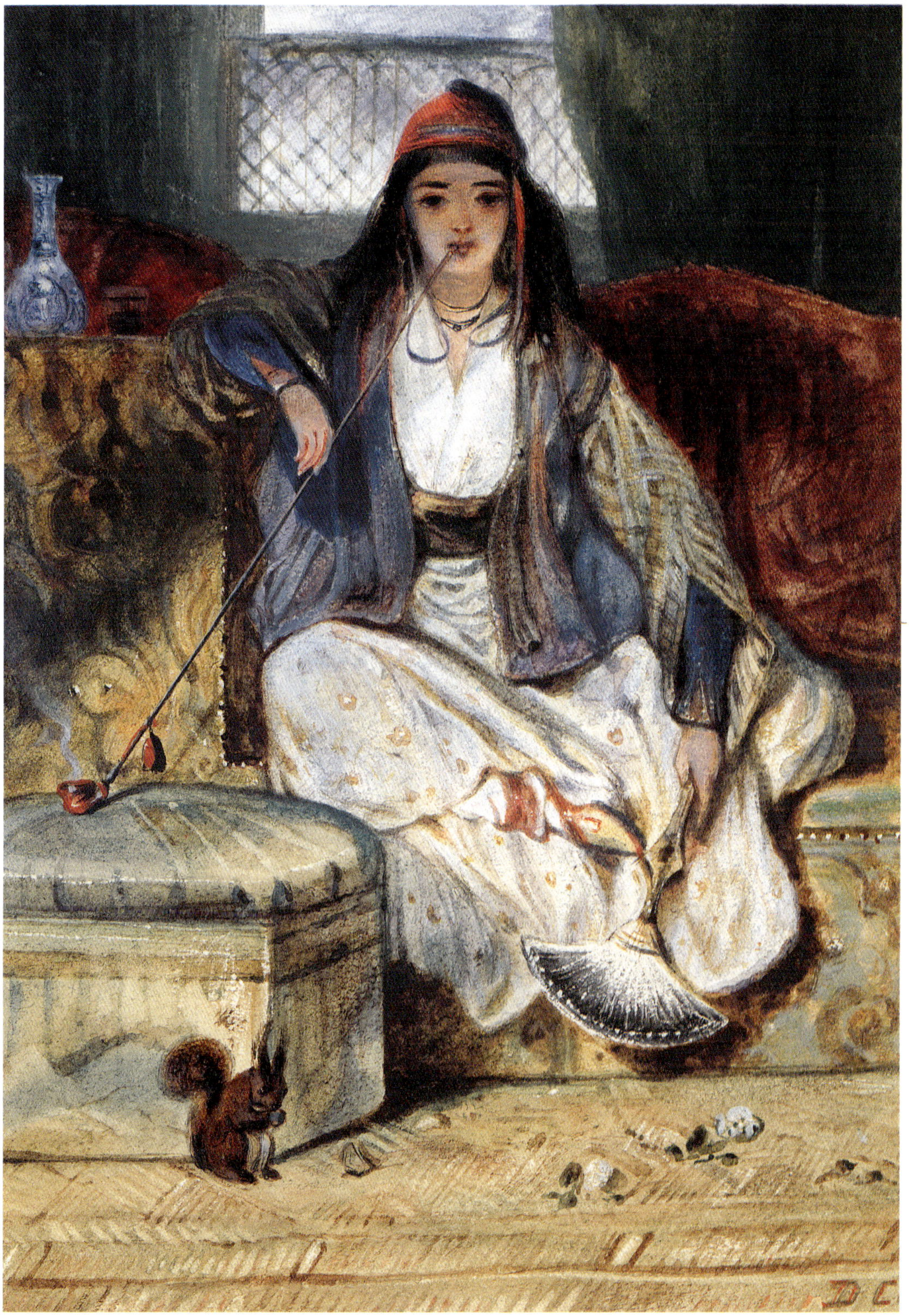

Plate 4. Alexandre Gabriel Decamps. *Turkish Woman Smoking.* N.d. Watercolor, gouache, pen and ink.
© Sterling and Francine Clark Art Institute, Williamstown, Massachusetts.

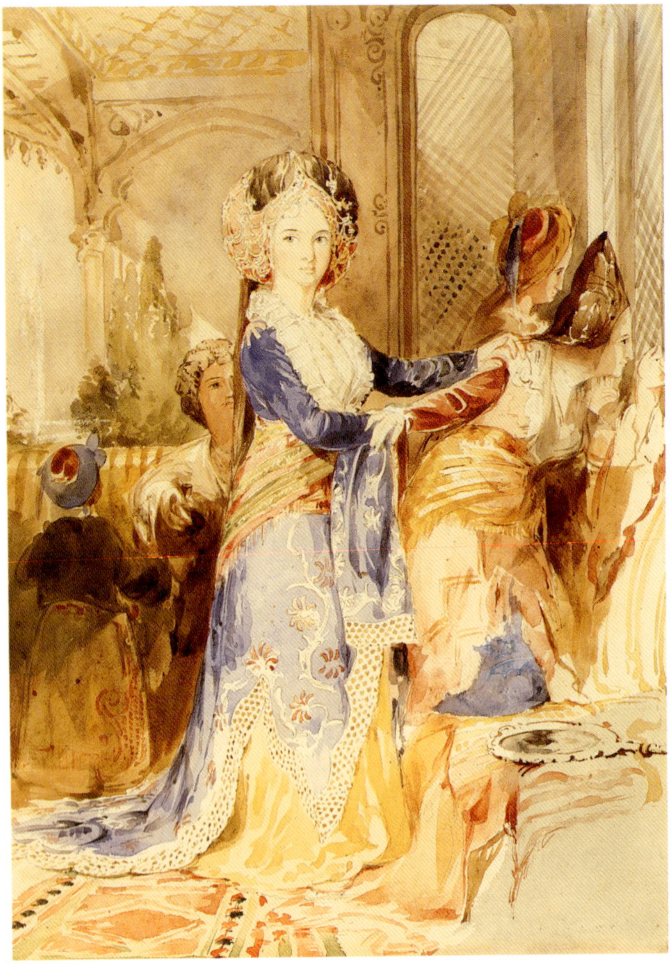

Plate 5. Thomas Allom. *The Favourite Odalisque*. Ca. 1836. Watercolor. Courtesy of the Trustees of the Victoria and Albert. V&A Picture Library.

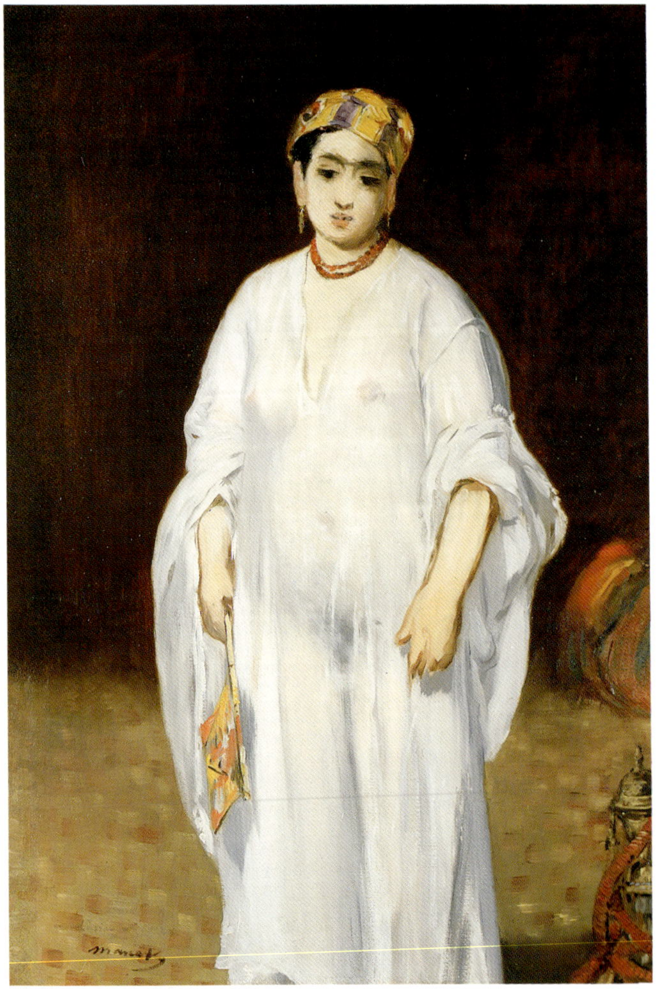

Plate 6. Edouard Manet. *La Sultane*. Ca. 1870. Foundation E. G. Bührle Collection, Zürich.

harem master's role as attentive father and husband; he criticizes European stereotypes of "sloth" and "sensual gratifications."[31]

James MacFarlane, another traveler to Turkey in the 1840s, refuses to grant any mildness to Muslim slavery. He calls the slave trade in Circassians "the most detestable of all slave traffic," because of their white skin; he uses the same word, "detestable," to describe the Turkish harem system.[32] MacFarlane's high moral standards are not consistently humanitarian. In fact, his writing is clearly racist, recalling John Richardson's comments in the *Anti-Slavery Reporter.* Unlike many observers who allow white harem slavery and condemn the crueller black praedial slavery, MacFarlane claims the opposite, because the white race is superior and the black inferior!

> white slave-trade [is] far more horrible in my eyes than the trade in Negroes . . . Must our anti-slavery societies have the warrant of ebony to excite their zeal or kindle their indignation? Is their philanthropy dependent on colour? Have they no sympathy for slaves that are *white*? They have stunned us with the woes of the inferior Negro races and they are mute upon the degradation of the superior race of the Caucasus.[33]

His position demonstrates that the diversity of Victorian rationales for objecting to the harem included a white supremacist one. MacFarlane attacks advocates of the "Circassian mania" like Urquhart whom he claims erroneously portrays the Circassian as a valiant rebel—like the Old Testament David against the Russian giant, Goliath. He links the harem-slavery issue to the arena of international politics, but he is pro-Russian. Russia, he claims, has vastly improved the lot of common people in Poland and elsewhere. Like the statesman and "apostle of free trade" Richard Cobden, he advocates the Russian takeover in Circassia, which would then obliterate the harem system and improve the people's moral standing. He compares Russia's imperialist goals in Circassia to Britain's in India: both are doing good in attempting to "civilize" surrounding areas. His anti-harem stance is pro-imperialist.

Also at midcentury the feminist, activist and traveler Harriet Martineau's comments about slavery and the harem are noteworthy for their lack of ambivalence. She insists that the two institutions be viewed together, that is, that the ease of harem life does not atone for the horror of slavery on which it is based. Martineau claims that she has tried to be open-minded about the subject, as suggested by well-meaning friends before she left. But she radically disagrees with British apologists for the harem who espouse "cosmopolitan philosophy [. . . and] regard [it] complacently." "It has become rather the fashion" to believe that the harem is an improvement over the life of poor and young captives and that it allows them an upward mobility. These arguments she also rejects. Moreover, those who "plea for liberality" are suffering from "some poetical fancy" or are simply ill-informed. The harem has no redeeming quality (*EL* 260, 264–65). To dramatize her view of the Egyptian harem as "hellish" she uses an Old Testament metaphor when she claims that one almost wishes "that the Nile would rise to cover the tops of the hills, and sweep away the whole abomination" (*EL* 265).

After a twenty-year residence in Turkey, Mrs. John Blunt does distinguish harem life from the slave-market experience that often precedes it. In the preface to her book written in 1878 Stanley Lane Poole makes an astounding comment about Turkish women. For him "there is no hope for the Turks so long as Turkish women remain what they are, and home-training is the initiation of vice" (*PT* 1:xxii). Mrs. Blunt reserves similarly negative judgements for Circassian and Armenian women at the seraglio who are called ignorant and barbaric (*PT* 1:250). Slavery is mitigated somewhat, however. White slaves' condition is not bad, even though the principle is "radically wrong, and the initial stage [slave-selling] is full of cruelty" (*PT* 1:126). For black women harem life is much worse (*PT* 1:126), as they are prone to quarreling with their husbands or are separated from them and are miserable. Overall, she decides that humane laws and kind paternalism characterize Turkish slavery (*PT* 1:127). Still, "it is a blot on the country, and so soon as the harem system and polygamy can be got rid of, it [slavery] too must go" (*PT* 1:127). Her condemnatory attitude resembles Martineau's.

Noteworthy about these written comments is their sameness in conceptualization, presentation, and even wording. All claim access to the highest principles and are morally righteous in tone. Often they make judgments that today would strike us as arbitrary or even racist. Though they span forty years they seem to follow the same paradigm of argument: they use chilling examples of "true" events which they claim to have witnessed and craft them into a judgment that presumes mastery as well as truth. Their sameness suggests Bhabha's notion of stereotype: that it requires endless repetition to keep at bay anxiety about difference.

John Ruskin, Art Critic, on "White Slavery," the Slave Market, and Harem Pictures

John Ruskin, the major spokesperson for nineteenth-century British aesthetics, reveals his frustrated desire to comment on the Eastern Question when he writes in November 1876:

> I want to write a long note on Byzantine empire,—Commanders of the Faithful,—Grand Turks,—and the 'Eastern Question.' But can't: and perhaps the reader will be thankful." (*W* 38:738 n)

Ruskin never traveled to the East. Nor did he comment on the issue of the harem *per se* in his writings. But he did address slavery at length. And he directly responded to harem pictures, as will be recounted throughout this study. Moreover, in 1858 Ruskin's father purchased two harem pictures unbeknownst to the son, who had rejoined his parents' household. Examining Ruskin's discourse on slavery in more detail may also help illuminate the often brief and fragmentary writings of other critics who comment on the harem picture. His references to slavery, which change significantly from the 1840s to the 1870s, are scattered and complex. And though in 1878 he chastises western countries, Christian only in name, which had brought Turkey to ruin and profited in the process,[34] indicators are that he was critical of the harem institution.

Ruskin's *Modern Painters* was a panegyric to J. M. W. Turner (1775–1851), painter of *Slave Ship* (1840), a painting which marks the culmination of early nineteenth-century abolitionist sentiment. Turner and Ruskin met in 1840 and became friends. Ruskin's father bought "the Slaver" for his son as a New Year's gift in 1844, a work he calls "the chief Academy picture of the Exhibition of 1840" (*W* 3:571). The son said this:

> I believe, if I were reduced to rest Turner's immortality upon any single work, I should choose this. Its daring conception, ideal in the highest sense of the word, is based on the purest truth [. . .], the whole picture dedicated to the most sublime of subjects. (*W* 3:572–73)

In a lecture ten years later, Ruskin uses the word "genius" to describe the recently-deceased Turner (*W* 12:102).

Ruskin did not endorse all anti-slavery artists, however. The abolitionist painter David Roberts was a friend who attended birthday celebrations staged for the art critic by his doting father. But Ruskin characterized his portrayal of social issues as dreary: "'He was like a kind of grey mirror,'" and he became increasingly critical of Roberts's work in the later 1850s (*W* 3:223 note).

In the 1850s Ruskin reveals a number of stereotypes of easterners within the context of art criticism. He responds to John Lewis's *Hhareem* (see Plate 1) in his 1851 pamphlet on the Pre-Raphaelites and notes eastern indolence, animality and unruliness as part of the essential character of the eastern people represented. He claims that Lewis paints

> portraiture of those European [Spanish] and Asiatic races, among whom the refinements of civilization exist without its laws or its energies, and in whom the fierceness, indolence, and subtlety of animal nature are associated with brilliant imagination and strong affections. (*W* 12:363–64)

And in responding to the 1857 showing of Lewis's *Harem Life—Constantinople* (see Fig. 3.39), Ruskin writes that Lewis will understand how to alter technical imperfections in his painting of one of the harem women "after his eye has been turned for a little while to other subjects" (*W* 14:133). This ambiguous comment is the closest Ruskin gets to criticizing the harem as a subject for high art.

In the 1860s and 1870s Ruskin's focus shifts from art to the abolition of domestic slavery, that is, the abuse of the poor worker by the rich capitalist. In 1872 Ruskin comments on a female worker's testimony that she worked forty-seven and a half hours one week and earned little more than a shilling. "This kind of slavery finds no Abolitionists that I hear of" (*W* 18:551).[35] Ruskin uses the figure of a working-class woman as a way to underscore the vulnerability of all workers and elicit a chivalrous sympathy for her and the class she is called upon to represent. Nonetheless, exploitation of workers is not always clear-cut for Ruskin, as he distinguishes between real abuse of a servant and constructive punishment (*W* 17:550–51). Reinscribing language constructs used in abolitionist discourse, Ruskin advises his readers not to let black foreign slavery distract them from "white slavery" at home (*W* 17:254 n. See also 19:103 and 18:551.) He claims in 1865 that black slavery's evil is surpassed by that of white slavery (*W* 18:551), meaning the mistreatment of lower-class British worker not upper-class Turkish or Egyptian woman.

On the emancipation of slaves Ruskin allies himself in 1862 with Thomas Carlyle's unexpectedly conservative position expressed in the first of his *Latter-Day Pamphlets* written in 1850.[36] In the early 1860s Ruskin writes as part of a lecture on government that slavery was not a political issue but instead "*an inherent natural and eternal inheritance* of a large portion of the human race" (*W* 17:256). Slavery for Ruskin was not inherently evil as long as it was judiciously maintained. He is at pains to distinguish between the acceptable and unacceptable aspects of slavery. For Ruskin the usefulness of slaveholding provides its moral justification.

He condemns only the breaking up of families, common practice among slave scouts.[37] Beyond that, its commonness in history has rendered slavery a "natural" practice. Ruskin sees himself as a spokesperson of his time when he writes of slavery "the dispute seems about the fashion of the thing, rather than the fact of it" (*W* 17:256). In short, Ruskin believed it was fate, not politics, which determined one's enslavement or freedom (*W* 19:124).

Thus Ruskin's early unequivocal abolitionism changed by the 1860s. Nearly twenty-five years later, foreign slavery, previously the "most sublime of subjects," no longer held the same importance for Ruskin, as he shifted his attention to political and social problems closer to home. In 1869 Ruskin sold Turner's *Slave Ship*, reputedly because it had become too "painful" a picture to live with (*W* 3:lv).

Despite his hedging, Ruskin was adamant that one aspect of slavery was absolutely unacceptable—the slave trade. Presumably he would only sanction slavery if one were born into it. He writes in 1867 of the failings of the abolitionists, in particular the Anti-Slavery Society, which by then had abandoned its earlier hope for abolishing slaveholding and instead worked toward closing the slave markets in Egypt and Turkey:

> Parenthetically, may I ask you to observe, that although a fearless defender of some forms of slavery, I am no defender of the slave *trade*. It is by a blundering confusion of ideas between governing men and *trading in* men, and by consequent interference with the restraint, instead of only with the sale, that most of the great errors in action have been caused among the emancipation men.

He continues without a break, writing now as an architect of social systems:

> I am prepared, if the need be clear to my own mind, and if the power is in my hands, to throw men into prison, or any other captivity—to fine them or to beat them—or force them, for such periods as I may judge necessary, to any kind of irksome labour: and on occasion of desperate resistance, to hang or shoot them. But I will not *sell* them. (*W* 17:438)

Selling men (and presumably women) is for Ruskin worse than killing them. This attitude, often expressed by writers of Ruskin's well-educated, upper-middle-class in the 1860s, originates from the high regard placed on individual liberty and dignity, which become sullied when reduced to the "cash nexus," as Carlyle called it. Ruskin was more conservative than John Stuart Mill on the issue of individual liberty.[38] Still, some of Ruskin's loathing of the exchange of people for money can be traced to his critique of capital, part of an increasingly vocal movement in the mid-Victorian era. What was from the Muslim point of view a traditional, age-old process as a way to expand the household—the exchange of harem inhabitants for money—was seen in England as a vile commercial transaction. At other points Ruskin is critical of the distinction between slavery and paid servanthood. Thus Ruskin uses the slave market issue to expose contradictions in Victorian social and economic relations.

As for the artistic use of such a non-Christian theme as the harem, we can make deductions about Ruskin's viewpoint. His preoccupation with the morality of good art was well known even in his own time, as he himself acknowledged (*W* 18:434). Morality, he believed, was grounded in the Bible, which supplies a clear code of ethics. Among other evils it forbids "lasciviousness," as does "every nation of mankind," in Ruskin's view (*W* 17:351). For him non-Christian principles were *de facto* inferior to Christian ideals, which he upheld both morally and artistically. How could the practice of polygyny ever be reconciled with the universal imperative for the Christian family? Presumably, Ruskin could not allow another standard of moral judgment. Indicators are that Ruskin would not approve of the harem as a viable and moral way of life, nor could he allow the harem subject a place in his articulation of the ideals of appropriate subject matter for fine art.[39]

Representing the "Happy Slave" In or Bound for the Harem

At the 1858 Royal Academy the painter John Lewis exhibited a harem picture in which all three figures smile: the privileged inmate in the foreground, the white slave in the middle ground and the black menial slave in the background. It is an extraordinary picture, one whose objects are meticulously rendered in startling color combinations; their subtle intricacy contributes to the work's relaxed and pleasant mood. This work, called *Life in the Harem, Cairo* alternately *Inmate of the Hhareem* (Fig. 3.2), was a resounding critical success. It was quickly purchased by John James Ruskin, though without the knowledge of his son John Ruskin, the art critic.[40] The London *Times* called it "inexpressingly beautiful in feature, sentiment, light and shade" (*T* 1 May 1858:5). The smiles contributed to the work's success, specifically the standing white slave woman's. The *Spectator* admires the slave girl's "winning smile" in this "exquisite" work (*S* 1 May

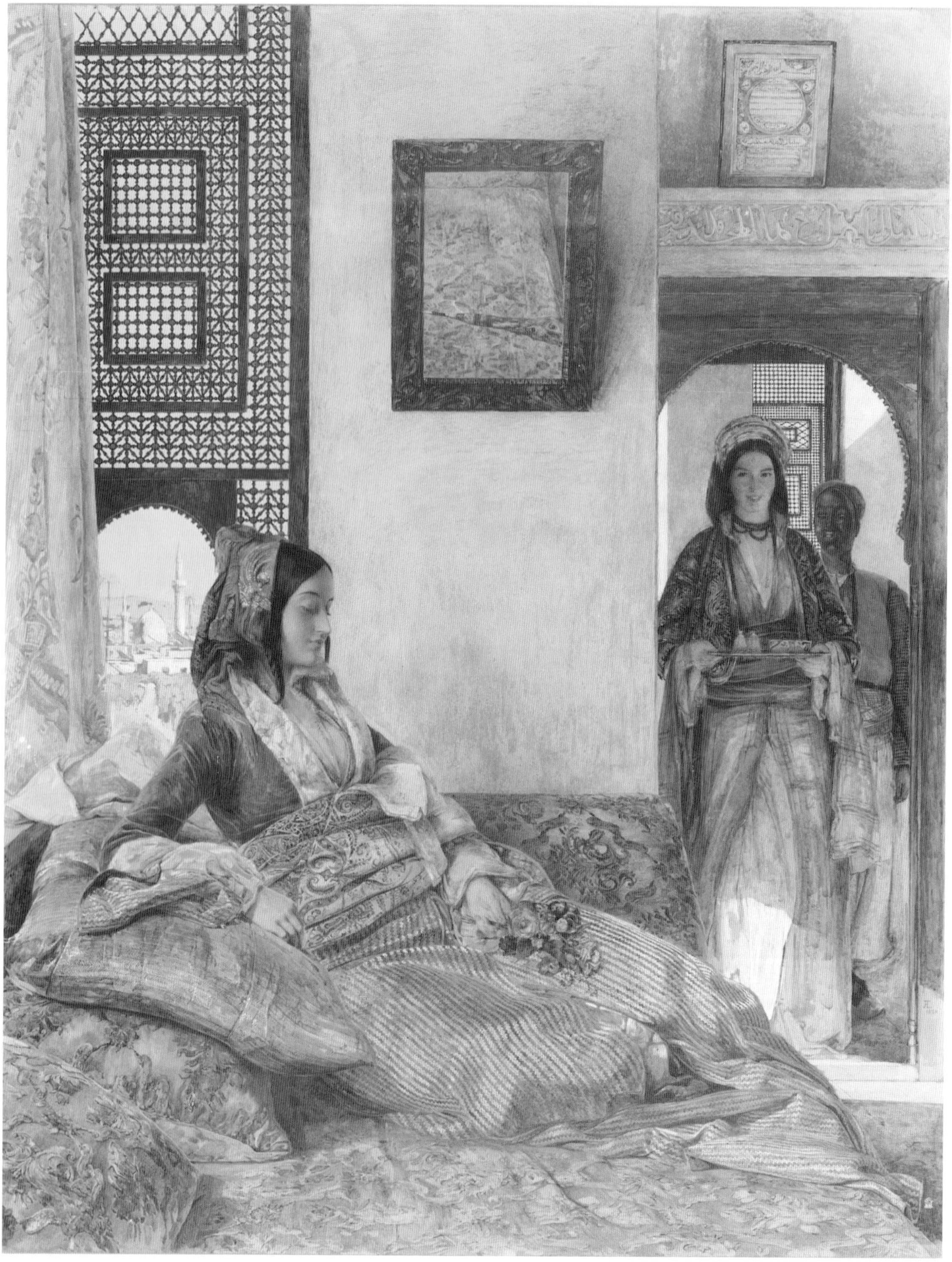

Fig. 3.2. John Frederick Lewis. *Life in the Harem, Cairo,* or *Inmate of the Hhareem.* 1858. Watercolor and bodycolor. Courtesy of the Trustees of the Victoria and Albert. V&A Picture Library.

1858:555). The *Athenaeum* praises Lewis's handling of "the beautiful slave-girl . . . her eyes dancing with love and fun." By extension, that reviewer praises Lewis for his own "sense of humour," while calling his sense of drawing and color "thoroughly Eastern" (*A* 8 May 1858:596). In this case, art succeeded in reconciling happiness with enslavement.

Persian wives generally tend to be somber because of their seclusion, writes Montesquieu's Usbek, in contrast to gay French women (*PL* 104). Indeed the Black Eunuch Solim (accurately) interprets the momentarily happy women of Usbek's harem as adulterous (*PL* 273). This may be one text against which subsequent travelers to the East react when they report that harem women and their attendants whom they encountered smiled and looked "happy." Thackeray, for example, denies outright that they are unhappy as he writes about "a black female slave, grinning as usual." And in a surprisingly explicit passage about the self-referential nature of the understanding of the other, he compares slaves to be bought with English "spinsters" in search of a situation: "once in a family they are kindly treated and well clothed, and fatten [sic] and are the merriest people of the whole community."[41]

On smiling black menials who are pleased with their social station Julia Pardoe claims that if you can "forget" that the slave has been purchased with money, the relationship becomes very much like dedicated servant to kindly lord in Europe "the one so eager and so earnest in his service—the other so gentle and so inexacting in his demands" (*CS* 1:114–15).

As Pardoe implies, the notion that slaves were happy in their confinement was a simple but powerful response to the charge of their enslavement under the Muslim system of "oppression." The argument that slaves were happy serving their masters (and that those masters were easygoing) could deflate avid abolitionist sentiment. Pardoe again supports this. She refers to two children—a Circassian and a Georgian who were the favorites of a high-ranking harem master, Mustafa Effendi. Her first response was to pity them, but she revises that impulse:

> as I looked upon the pleased and happy countenances of these two little girls, and remembered that slavery, in Turkey at least is a mere name, and in nine cases out of ten even voluntary, I felt that here my commiseration would be misplaced. (*CS* 1:114–15)

Pardoe's writing about voluntary slavery, indeed the whole discussion of "happy slaves" suggests the debate over "consent theory," an intellectual development from the Enlightenment that presumed that society is composed of individual beings whose free will would grant them choice (or consent) and personal happiness would follow.[42] From the nineteenth-century observer's viewpoint, the question might be: should a happy slave elicit pity? Or perhaps anger at social injustice that has "duped" this being out of political consciousness and into complacency?

When black slaves (negresses) laugh at the slave market, they are expressing a lack of self-control that is typical of the race, claims Gérard de Nerval. He also believes such laughter is directed at him: "these native natures never hesitate to reveal all their impressions, but I don't know why they should find European clothes so ridiculous." Their laughter is "scornful" or "carefree." Or they laugh "crazily" (*VO* 35, 43–44).

Richard Burton tries to understand why the black women are laughing at the market, "whether from the effect of such unusual splendor, or from the reaction succeeding to their terrible land-joining and sea-voyage" (*PNP* 3:355). For whatever reason, his observation about loudly laughing women moves into a startling assertion of the hierarchy of slave women's "races" to be found at the slave market, a hierarchy based on skin color: from the "pretty Gallas, *douce*-looking Abyssinians," to "Africans of various degrees of hideousness, from the half-Arab Somal to the Baboon-like Swahili" (*PNP* 3:355). Despite his racism, Burton favors the abolition of the slave trade, a paradoxical position we have considered above.

In Istanbul's slave market traveler Albert Smith is approached by a black woman who asks him to purchase her. When he explained his abolitionist stance, he claims that she and her friends laugh in "derision" at the ludicrousness of his elevated response.[43] Smith, Burton, and Nerval reveal an uncomfortability which they project onto the women who laugh at these western men. As such, each writer interprets the women's laughter as an unexpected empowerment of slaves who refuse the role of quiet and pathetic victim up for sale. For all three writers, black slave women's laughter is read as aggression. Indeed, Smith's account suggests his being solicited by a streetwalker. Ironically, the condemnatory tone of their comments erodes any hope for liberation that they themselves may have expressed.

Lord Byron says that black women slaves are not as sad as white female slaves up for sale, and he is more sympathetic to Negroes in his description of a market in canto 5 from *Don Juan* (1819):

> A crowd of shivering slaves of every nation,
> And age, and sex, were in the market ranged;
> Each bevy with the merchant in his station:

Poor creatures! their good looks were sadly changed.
All save the blacks seem'd jaded with vexation,
From friends, and home, and freedom far estranged;
The Negroes more philosophy display'd—
Used to it, no doubt, as eels are to be flay'd.
(*WB* 507)

Here Byron seems to admire black stoicism; his use of the simile of flayed eels to suggest the whipping of slaves is particularly biting abolitionist commentary.

As for the happiness of white harem women, Sophie Lane Poole expresses mixed feelings in 1844. She writes that white harem slave women are frequently happy with their roles, though she implies that much more happiness can be found in British marriage.

> I do not pretend to defend the system of marrying blindfold, as it were; nor do I look for those happy marriages which are most frequently found in England; but I am pleased to find the Eastern women contented, and, without a single exception among my acquaintances, so cheerful, that I naturally conclude they are treated with consideration.[44]

In the same book Poole further qualifies her observation by denying that harem women are truly "happy" since "Christianity is the only medium through which happiness may be attained by any people."[45] David Urquhart judges the "general tenour of the life of the Harem" to be a place of happiness except in the rare event that the wives compete.[46]

This line of argument undermined the abolitionists' absolute condemnation of harem slavery. But when the Anti-Slavery Society admits in 1845 that happy black female slaves can be found along the Nile, its explanation is that smiling was a response learned for survival: "'these slaves are trained, whether by promise or threats, to assume cheerfulness whenever people approach them.'"[47]

By the 1870s when it was obvious to the British that their efforts failed to influence Turkish diplomats to outlaw the harem, the rationale for a *laissez-faire* policy toward the harem became the fact that harem slaves were happy because they led a life of relative ease (especially compared to American praedial slaves). Even under the tenets of Islam, slaveholding was sanctioned only as long as the slaves were happy and not mistreated.

Harem inhabitants of different "races" and stations smile in other pictures by John Lewis. Black menials smile in his *Hhareem* (1850) and *Intercepted Correspondence* (1869). White women smile in *Life in the Harem* (1858) and its sequel, *Eastern Girl Carrying a Tray* (1859). A "brown"-skinned girl smiles broadly in his *Lilium Auratum* (1872). Lewis's painting shows slaves smiling, but they do so without a clear cut rationale. It appears that Lewis paints more subtle facial expressions—relaxed and undisturbed—on the white harem ladies, reserving the broadest grins for the darkest-skinned harem inferiors. That Lewis's harem ladies generally do not smile as broadly as the menials appears to be a sign of their reserve appropriate to their higher rank. Had Lewis painted grinning faces on all his harem figures, it could threaten the serious fine art status of his work. After all, John Ruskin advocates facial stoicism in admiration of the Greek expressionless face (*W* 20:339ff).

An analysis of five critical reactions to Lewis's *Hhareem* (see Plate 1) shown in London in 1850 and Paris in 1855 suggests that the critics were confused over how to come to terms with the smiling slaves in Lewis's pictures. The *Art Journal* claims that the Nubian eunuch who unveils the new arrival receives the harem women's contemptuous glares with a sneer (*AJ* 12 [1850]:179). By this reading, his loyalties lie with the new slave, and his mocking the harem women for their jealousy is a transgression of his role as their protector and guardian.

Secondly, the *Athenaeum* focuses on the smiling black female menial and claims she reacts with "a leer at the new comer, which seems to contemn her pride and confusion" (*A* [4 May 1850], 480). This scenario would be more in keeping with this slave's role, as she was expected to show loyalty to her mistresses, echoing their emotions. But it is difficult to read malice into her expression, especially in comparison to the "favorite" wife seated near her whose expression could more plausibly be considered malicious.

Third, the *Critic* comments that the dark-skinned female attendant "smiles broadly with mouth, teeth and eyes" but offers no direct explanation; it does form its observations about the smiles into what seems to be an objection to Lewis's aesthetic repetition: the smiling figures—eunuch and female attendant—are seen as too much alike in their "national similarity of countenance" (*C* 1850:253). Of the four publications which comment on them, the *Illustrated London News* is the most reluctant to explain the smiles. The journal only briefly notes the fact that the new slave is "unconscious [. . .] of the laughter of the black attendants of the palace" (*ILN* 4 May 1850:300). And at the painting's showing in 1855 the French critic M. E. J. Delécluze admires the way Lewis has expressed "the inquietude, the frivolity or the jealousy of the inferior slaves" with both truth and verve.[48]

These critics notice the smiling faces but are at a loss as to how to account for them. Perhaps these publications are reluctant to voice the incendiary claim that slaves, whether black or white, are happy

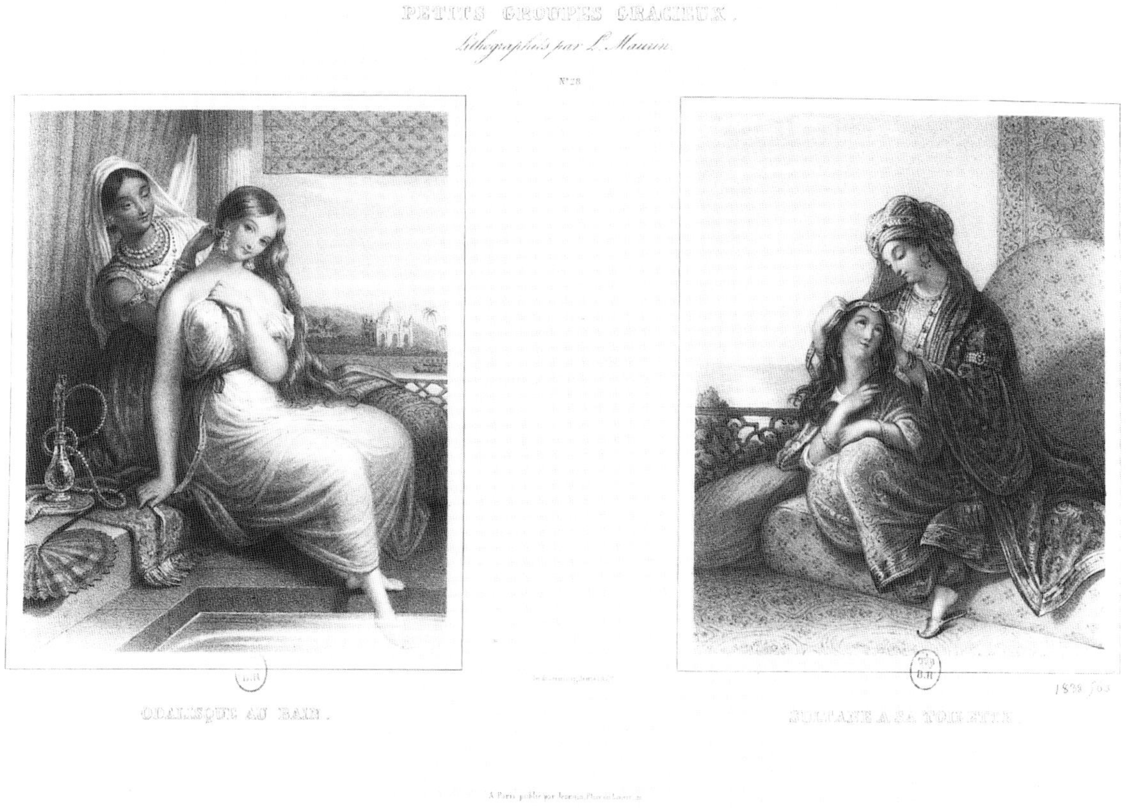

Fig. 3.3. Nicolas Eustache Maurin after Grévedon. *Odalisque au bain* and *Sultane à sa toilette. Petits groupes gracieux.* 1838. Lithographs. Cabinet des Estampes, Cliché Bibliothèque nationale de France, Paris.

with their lot. The British critics instead try to work the smiles into a narrative, while Delécluze simply calls them "the expression of sentiments."[49] For the British critics, inventing a story gives the viewer more distance from a social truth that is presumed to exist and to which the painting refers. Narratives about what is happening in the picture become a tactic for sidestepping the politics of slavery. The critics reveal themselves further in their writing. In reading social antagonism, the *Art Journal*, *Athenaeum*, and Delécluze belie an expectation about the unkind and ultimately immoral behavior of harem inhabitants within its social hierarchy. And in describing the eunuch and attendant the *Critic* expresses a stereotyped notion that the darkest-skinned ethnic, racial, or national groups were prone to foolish grinning. Unlike the later response to Lewis's 1858 *Inmate of the Hareem* (with which I began this section) critics are reluctant to name "happy slaves" in response to this more melodramatic painting shown in 1850 and 1855.

The settings of each of these two harem pictures may help us understand differing reactions to the smiling slaves. Lewis's "quiet" *Inmate* can be read as set in Paradise, a joyous place of good feeling, peace, and social pleasure[50] where inhabitants smile to express that divine bliss. Pictures of a happy harem slave can function on one level as an *apologia* for Islam. In contrast, Lewis's *Hhareem* cannot be heavenly, because it is filled with jealousy and intrigue. The black eunuch's happy countenance recalls Montesquieu's 1721 *Persian Letters* in which the eunuch expresses great joy at trying the women's emotions in the harem of Usbek's brother. The Chief Black Eunuch writes to Usbek that the possibility of unveiling a beautiful new slave in the harem "gives me pleasure" for the consternation it will cause among the women. In his sadistic cruelty he gloats: "I am going to cause a revolution throughout a whole seraglio. What passions I shall instigate! What fears and sorrows are in store!" (*PL* 179). The eunuch's own sense of deprivation at his castrated state provides a partial explanation for his vengeance.

In French harem pictures smiling slaves have other meanings. In one of an 1838 pair of lithographic images by N. Maurin after Henri Grévedon, *Odalisque au bain* (Fig. 3.3), the woman makes eye contact with the viewer, cocks her head demurely, and smiles. These gestures and her long flowing hair are deviations from proper female behaviors: to avert

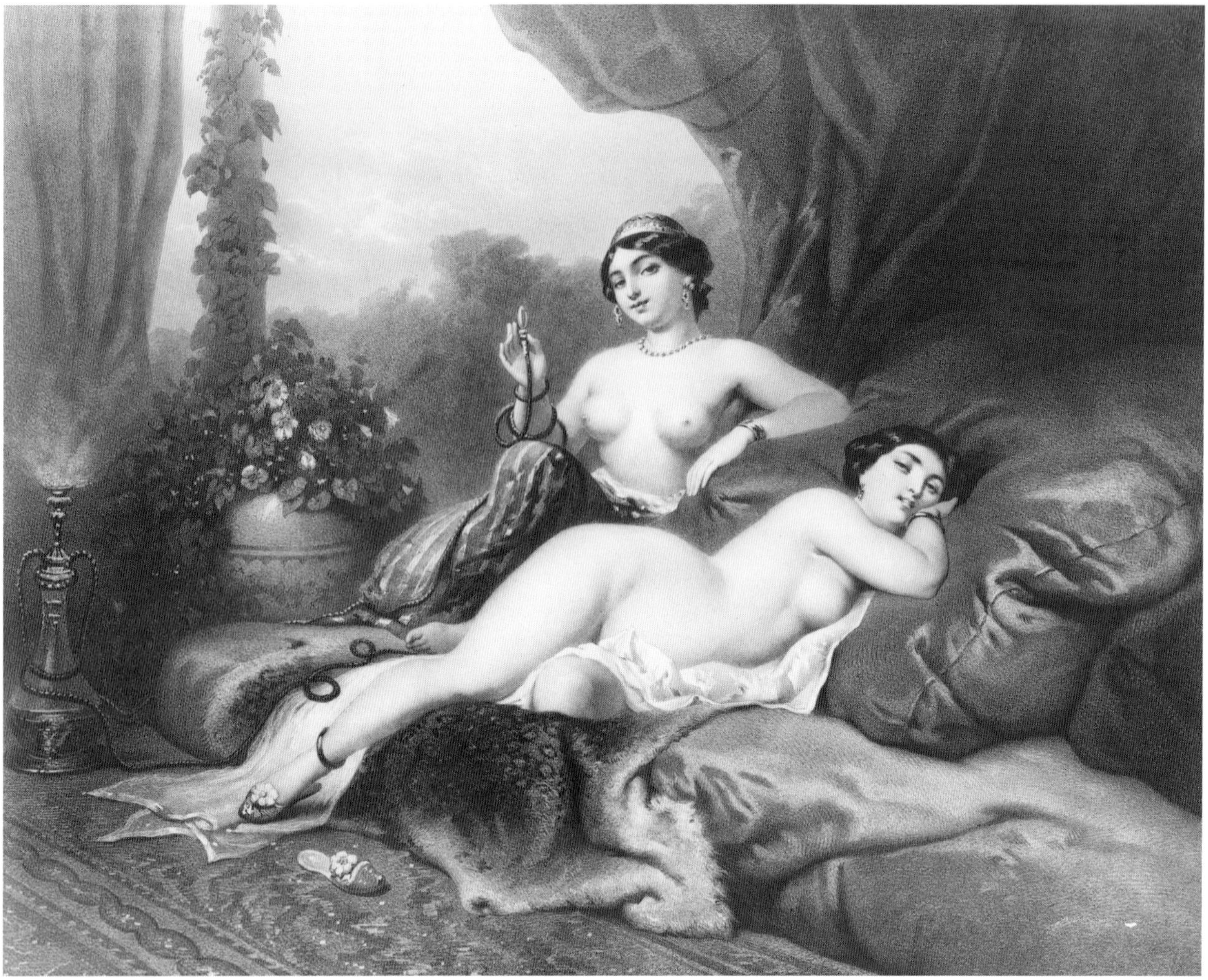

Fig. 3.4. Régnier after Guérard. *La Vie au sérail*, no. 2. 1853. Lithograph. Cliché Bibliothèque nationale de France, Paris. Farwell, *FPLI*, v. 11, 2C6 B79325.

one's eyes, wear the hair up, and maintain a neutral facial expression. Here the bath is the rationale for such a "letting down," and her hand position is the token of modesty. But the smile is undeniably a provocation. It invites the viewer to look and acknowledges her self-consciousness as a sight.

The smile is an indicator less of girlish flirtation than sexual satiation on the face of the recumbent nude harem inmate in Régnier's 1853 lithograph after Guérard's *La vie au sérail* (Fig. 3.4). The smile accompanies half-closed eyes, a crooked elbow, and an undulating body. This figure nestles into satin, fur, and the aroma of smoke, all symbols for the pleasure she has just received—while she offers visual pleasure.

Smiling lips are indistinguishable from a slightly open mouth in a similar work, Ingres's *Odalisque with Slave* of 1842 (see Fig. 2.3), which contains luxurious fabrics, smoke, crooked elbow, and long, loose hair as allusive devices for the abandon of the sexual experience. The whole painting functions to support an excess of femininity, and the odalisque's parted lips, given much formal emphasis, are an analog for her receptive and barely covered genitalia.

Lamartine uses the issue of a slave's happiness to circumvent questions of official politics. For him a person's "misery or happiness" (*PHL* 41) is much more significant than the governmental structure under which he or she lives. And he believes easterners—even slaves—are happy. He goes so far as to claim that eastern slaves are more moral and virtuous than free westerners. In making such claims, Lamartine infantilizes these good people, whom he claims to love (*PHL* 41), for the way he downplays the legitimacy of their political struggles against colonizers such as the French. The assertion of a slave's happiness can function as a cover for political conservatism on the issues of abolition and a subject nation's self-determinism.

Slave Market Pictures and Unveiling Scenes

The veiling of women in Islam is suggested in at least two of the Surahs of the *Qur'an*. The more well-known suggests that veiling is meant to cover women's charms/body parts and that they are to avoid the provocative action of stomping their feet, which might reveal those hidden parts. It also specifies male relatives in front of whom women may remain unveiled:

> And say to the believing women, that they cast down their looks and guard their private parts, and do not display their ornaments except what appears thereof, and let them wear their head-coverings over their bosoms, and not display their ornaments except to their husbands or their fathers, or the fathers of their husbands, or their sons, so the sons of their husband, or their brothers, or their brothers' sons, or their sisters' sons, or their women, or those whom their right hands possess, or the male servants not having need (of women), or the children who have not attained knowledge of what is hidden of women; and let them not strike their feet so that what they hide of ornaments may be known. (24:31)

This Muslim exhortation to veil, constructed by westerners as dramatically different from Christian customs, constitutes a major reason for the great British and French interest in pictures of harem slaves being unveiled.

In this section I analyze together pictures of slave markets and of eastern women being unveiled, because the two narratives are frequently combined. Women are unveiled or sold in the slave market, in private quarters, or in nondescript locations. Women are sometimes inspected by the prospective buyer in the fictional narrative and always by the viewer. When the art critic Théophile Thoré writes "What god or sultan will raise the mysterious curtain?"[51] in response to the 1847 exhibition of Delacroix's *Odalisque with Parrot*, he alludes to both the revealing of the harem and the desire for sexual possession of the woman by a powerful male agent. By virtue of his mastery of language and looking, Thoré becomes that "god or sultan," whose pleasure resides in the act of raising the curtain. Like Thoré's prose, slave market pictures and unveiling scenes are about the act of looking as a promise of possessing exotic women, a promise which is endlessly deferred. Unveiling scenes can bear a strong resemblance to other kinds of visual pornography, as they capture the process whereby public propriety is eschewed for the consumption of private pleasure. In the transition which is the unveiling the boundary is blurred between a neutral, public reality and hyper-sexualized fantasy.

Voyeurism underpins these images more explicitly than any other harem pictures. The unveiling of a single harem slave distills the dynamic at play when the harem is pictured for the eyes of the western viewer; the hidden becomes fetishized and more titillating for its having been covered. The pleasure in being afforded a view is a way to master the threat of sexual and colonial difference. What gives pleasure is the revelation of not only female nakedness but also a spectacle normally hidden from foreign lookers and thinkers. Pleasure is to be had by viewer or reader in having the presumed truth about the harem revealed through representation.

Unveiling and slave market scenes also connote an element of violation/violence. Eastern brothers kill their sister for the mere suspicion of her showing her unveiled face to a stranger in "The Veil" (1828) by Victor Hugo (*SCL* 50). In written accounts, slave women respond to being unveiled with "blushing cheeks" or "lowered eyes." In harem pictures slave women are shown in classic gestures of modesty—bowed heads, hands over breasts and genitals, and eyes lowered. Representations of unveiling that describe the female slave's embarrassment or her desperate displays of modesty can be an analogy for the fantasy of a sadistic deflowering of a virgin.[52] This reaches an apogee in the anonymous *Lustful Turk* (1828), which is constructed as a series of deflowering scenes, all quite violent. Correspondingly, Behdad views the imaginary representation of unveiling a female slave as "a simulacrum for a violent commercial transaction that is being presented as erotic."[53] This observation may also apply to fictionalized scenes of slave-selling and -buying, further linking slave market and unveiling scenes.

Slaves are unveiled in the slave market, sometimes in the harem itself, and sometimes in other, nonspecific environments. The dynamic often implicates: a male purchaser who is made powerful by virtue of his buying ability and/or sexual desire; a neutral (or neutered) displayer or seller whose job is to make available the object of desire; and the passive female, the medium of exchange between male buyer and seller.

In the 1830s Thomas Allom made two images to illustrate the women's slave market in Constantinople, where harem servants and odalisques could be purchased. The images were made into prints. In an

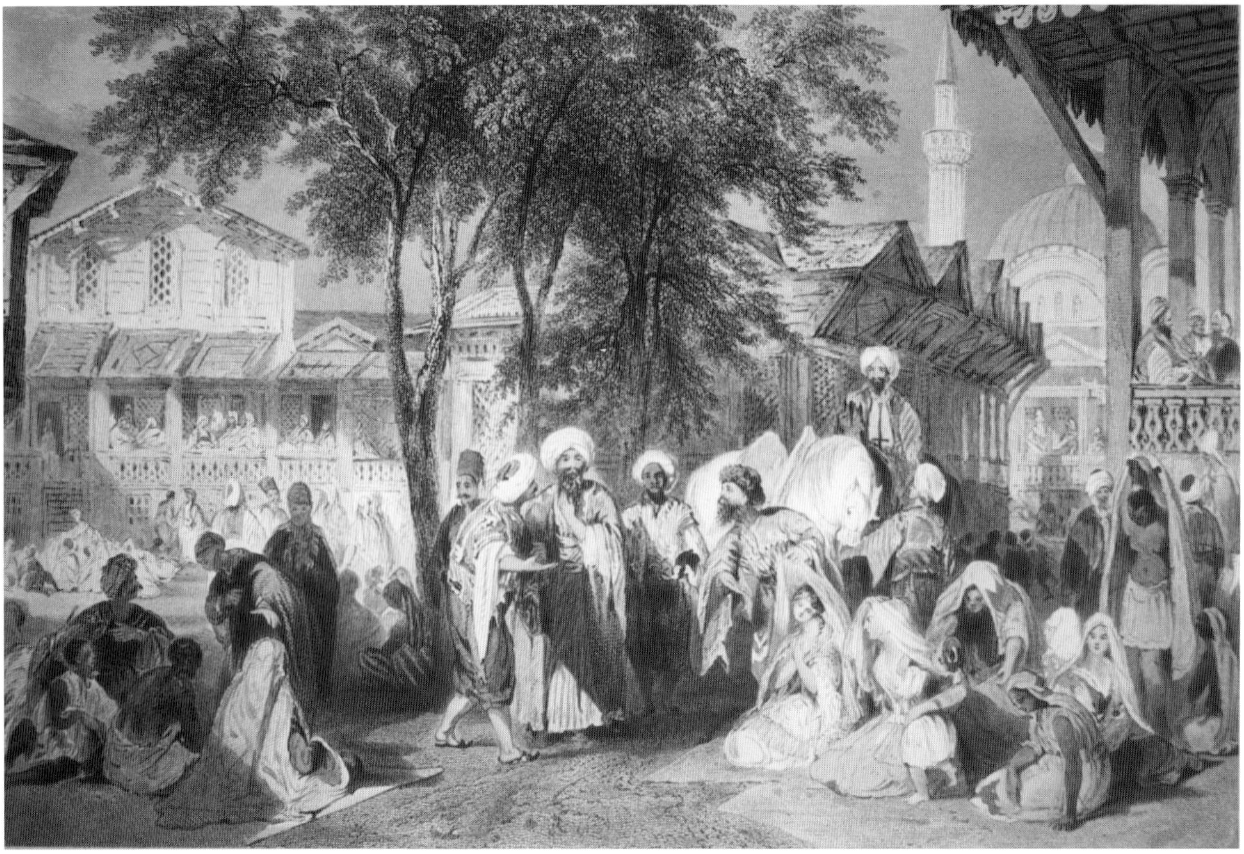

Fig. 3.5. After Thomas Allom. ***The Aurut Bazaar or Slave Market.*** **Ca. 1838. Robert Walsh,** ***Constantinople and the Scenery of the Seven Churches of Asia.*** **Engraving. Photo Michael Mark.**

engraving titled *Aurat Bazaar or Slave Market* (Fig. 3.5) taken from the 1838 book by Reverend Robert Walsh, Allom adapts the popular genre of topography to the slave market subject. Four slaves in the right foreground (Fig. 3.6) demonstrate some degree of resistance to their prospective sale: the two black women, one standing and one seated, hang their heads; a white woman being unveiled crosses her arms in modesty; next to her a mother clutches her veil and her son, anticipating her exposure and the confiscation of her child. Yet the viewer is emotionally distanced from the scene, distracted by the composition's commotion and the architecture. Its antislavery component is thus downplayed.

The tone of the engraving differs from the tone of Walsh's accompanying text, which states that most of the women in the market show "cheerfulness and hilarity" at their prospective sale. Walsh invokes the "happy slave" conception in all its ambiguity. For him the harem is "an amelioration" of the slaves' lives even though they are given little security. He claims that one of the vicissitudes slaves are subject to is the sudden death of their master which could result in exile, "perpetual celibacy" and possibly even "a watery grave."[54]

The second slave market print made after Allom is very different, a two-tone lithograph from Emma Reeve's book published the next year, and it is titled *Slave-Merchant, Constantinople* (Fig. 3.7). The viewer is much closer to the scene, which is more eroticized. Positivist typography gives way to Romantic emotionalism. Allom indicates the seven women's submission to the two men by their postures and nudity. The standing buyer, a turbaned Turk, momentarily stops fingering his worry beads to count out coins from his money bag. The seller, an Arab or Jew dressed in hooded cloak, haggles with the Turk and unveils the slave girl, who modestly draws her hands to her chest, a motif which can also be found in the engraving.

One of Allom's pictorial referents may have been François Boucher's *Marchand d'esclaves* (Fig. 3.8) from the 1746 luxury book *Moeurs et usages des turcs.*[55] Boucher's is also an indoor scene in which a slave-seller gestures toward the female slave while facing a potential buyer who evaluates the terms. In both

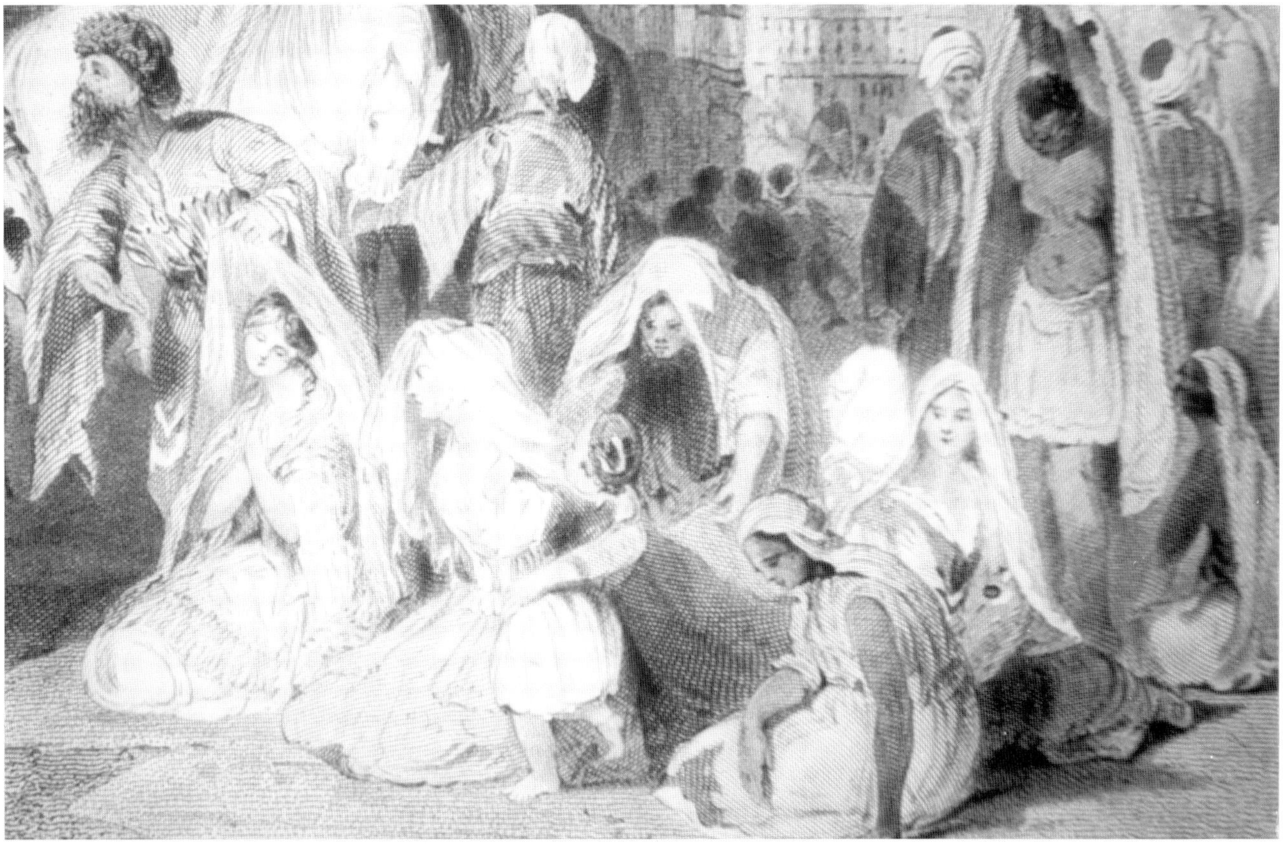

Fig. 3.6. Detail of fig. 3.5. Photo Michael Mark.

scenes a cluster of seated women function as both audience and potential chattel. Allom repeats some additional motifs in the Boucher including the open door at left and one woman's distinctive hand-to-face gesture. Allom's image might be considered rococo-revival.

Here Allom makes explicit the gendered power dynamic of female slaves to the male dealer-owner, but he has quite subtly indicated a range of female emotion. In the background women peer over and around each other to catch glimpses of the transaction. Allom shows each as curious and hopeful about her own fate. In the dyad at left the women shield their faces from the male presence. Allom allows the viewer to see what is denied the buyer at this moment, a bared breast and what the English claimed to be more provocative in Muslim society—the unveiled face, here smiling coquettishly. Allom includes the classic "odalisque pose," well-established by this time in French harem imagery as in for example Eugène Delacroix's 1834 *Women of Algiers* (see Fig. 2.17) or Achille Devéria's *Odalisque* (Fig. 3.9). By intertwining the two iconographies of slave-selling and harem-lounging Allom once again seems to downplay the cruelty of the slave market reported by abolitionists.

Yet Emma Reeve's text is clearly abolitionist and Philhellenic. She uses the authority of English poets to express her abolitionism. Freedom is a "'blest gift' (Roscoe)"; harem life is joyless. She writes that even death is preferable to a life of enslavement under a "'tyrant.'" Like a whole genre of writers, Reeve's Philhellenism is intertwined with a strong antislavery stance. She claims Greek women and children were sold for ten shillings each during the 1822 Massacres of Scio. Reeve and others denounced the harem because it became a repository for women captured during the Greek War of Independence. She relates the fact that Greek males were slaughtered and the women "dragged by the captor, half-dressed, trembling and pale with apprehension and horror."[56]

Rather than collaborating with Reeve's text, ostensibly illustrating it, Allom's lithograph seems instead to contradict it. Was Reeve consciously countering Allom's picture? As the more prestigious and immediate, indeed the more important, of the two media, Allom's imagery predominates over the text. This is confirmed in an 1839 review of Walsh's book which claims that text "is little more than a comment to explain the drawing. It is mostly disregarded as being a trade make-weight to the plates" (*Dublin Universal*

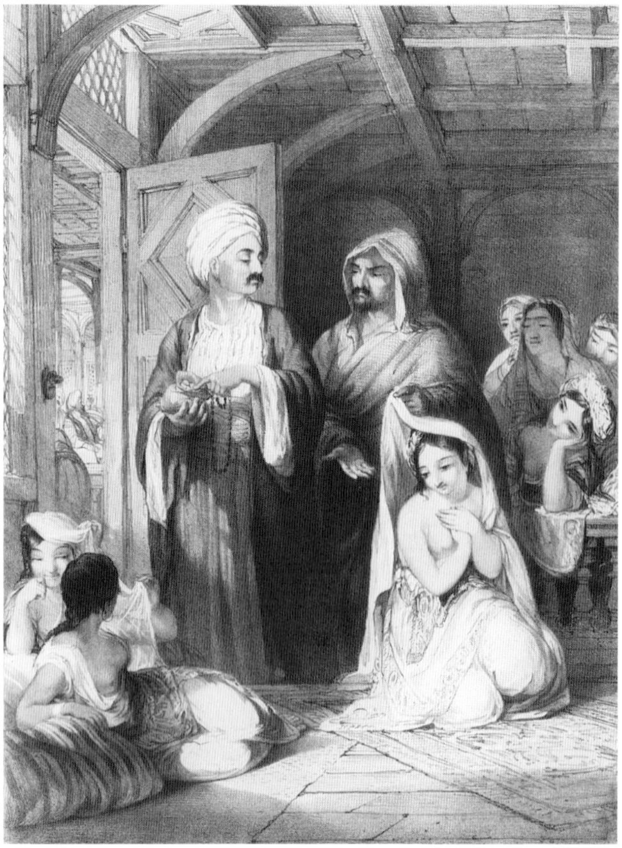

Fig. 3.7. C. Hullmandel after Thomas Allom. *Slave-Merchant, Constantinople.* 1839. Lithograph. Emma Reeve, *Character and Costume in Turkey and Italy.* Yale Center for British Art. Paul Mellon Fund.

Magazine 13 [February 1839]: 140). Such a divergence in the tone of each work is part of the ongoing puzzle of book illustration that remains in this period,[57] a discrepancy that also serves to demonstrate a range of discourses and attitudes about harem slavery.

Such a discrepancy may be attributable to accident, itself a function of the immaturity of the luxury book's technical development. Whatever its causes, the mere appearance of Allom's eroticized slave market scene accompanied by Reeve's token moral protest against it crystallizes the dialectical nature of the early Victorian attitude toward the Muslim harem, for here is self-chastising enjoyment—an expression of cross-cultural ambivalence.

Another slave market picture, this one an unfinished sketch, raises some interesting issues about the topic as artistic subject. John Lewis's so-called *Slave Market in the East* (Fig. 3.10) was acquired in May 1877, the year after his death, by the Victoria and Albert Museum. Done in pencil, watercolor, and gouache, the undated sketch is little documented. There is also some doubt about its setting: Christie's titled it *The Slave Market, Constantinople*[58] before the Victoria and Albert decided to generalize the scene's location. It was probably one of a number of sketches Lewis brought back when he returned to London by 1851 after a twenty-year sojourn in Spain and the Middle East. As far as we know it remained in the artist's possession until his death, as it reached the V and A in the auction authorized by his estate.

There are innumerable reasons why a sketch might remain undone, reasons we can never know. Still

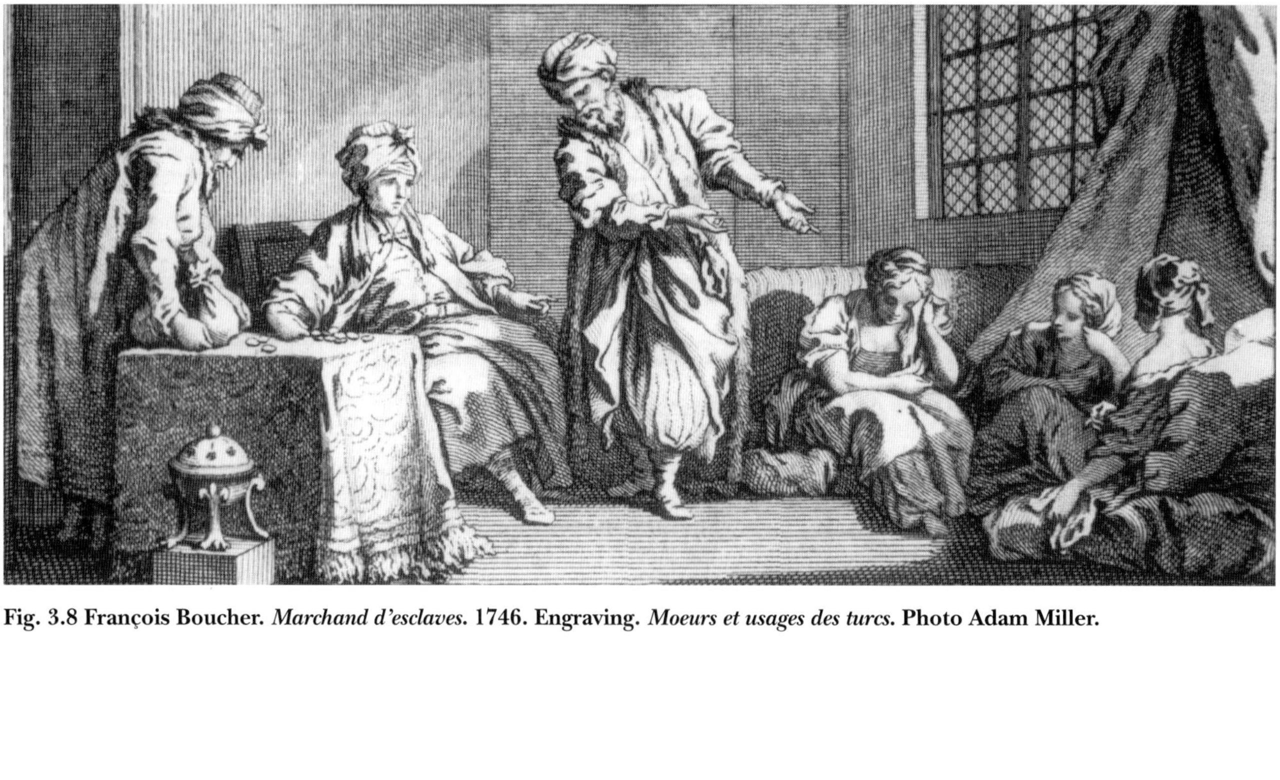

Fig. 3.8 François Boucher. *Marchand d'esclaves.* 1746. Engraving. *Moeurs et usages des turcs.* Photo Adam Miller.

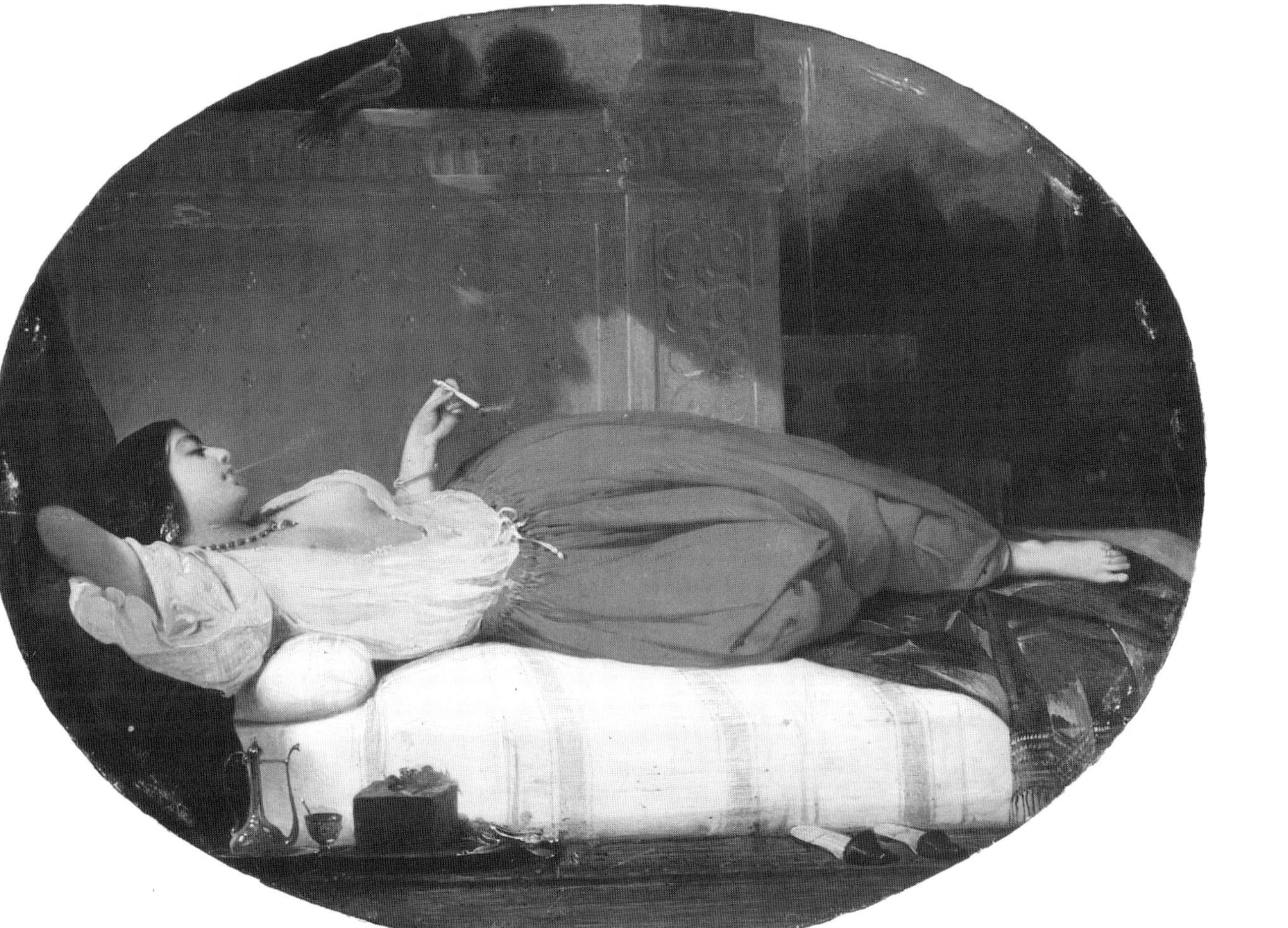

Fig. 3.9. Achille Jacques Jean Marie Devéria. *Odalisque.* 1831? Norton Simon Art Foundation, Pasadena, CA.

I want to focus on one possible explanation that we can document: social and political pressures as they might have affected the artist and interrupted the work's completion. I want to argue that Lewis's intimate familiarity with Egyptian society—gained by his decade-long stay there—would have made it very difficult for him to reconcile opposing attitudes toward the subject of a slave market, making it a challenge for him to finish a picture of one. I maintain that cross-cultural clash of values could be registered at the level of individual artistic production. In some cases, social tension can encourage artistic creativity, while in this case I believe it disrupted it.

The second argument I want to make has to do with how we usually think about the relationship of art to its presumed referent, lived reality. It seems reasonable to ask whether Lewis's *Slave Market* is set in Constantinople as indicated by Christie's 1877 auction catalog. After all, nineteenth-century Constantinople had the largest slave-trading market in the Ottoman Empire.[59] Moreover, British travelers who, like John Frederick Lewis, were in the Middle East in the 1830s and 1840s describe the Constantinople slave market in terms which concur with Lewis's depiction.[60] Or is the sketch situated in another city—Cairo perhaps—where Lewis lived for ten years? There is no hard evidence to definitively establish its locale. And the very question of which city's slave market this represents sidesteps the possibility that the sketch may be a composite, part done at one spot, part at another, part from memory. Even more provocatively, the sketch may record a scene that was never viewed first-hand. The sketch can be closely tied to written texts of eastern slave markets. Indeed, it may very well be derived from them.

In *Slave Market* the figures at left, presumably slave merchants, are drawn in detail. Some of them are made palpable with red watercolor and Chinese white gouache,[61] applied with skillful economy to their turbans and clothing. By contrast, only the barest

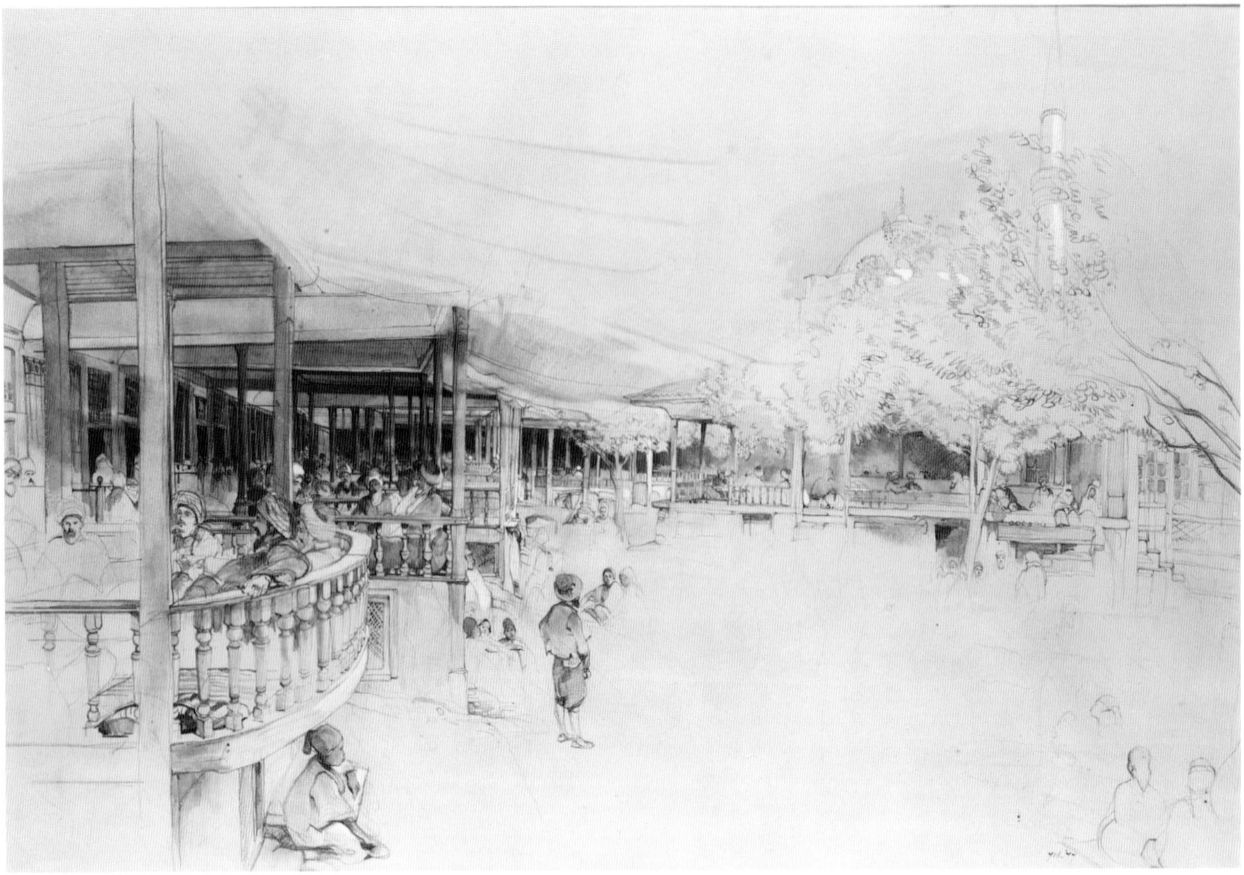

Fig. 3.10. John Frederick Lewis. *Slave Market in the East.* 1840–41. Pencil, watercolor and gouache. Courtesy of the Trustees of the Victoria and Albert. V&A Picture Library

suggestion of figures can be discerned in the center of the sketch. Lewis has, however, taken great pains in describing the architectural setting. At the left colonnaded balconies, washed with a light brown, rise a few feet from the ground. Wooden columns support what may be a striped tent used to protect patrons from a daytime sun. The porches seem connected, and the whole structure winds around to the back of the viewer's field. It may or may not connect with a second structure, partially obscured by some trees, and having a similar colonnaded porch, where additional groups of turbaned patrons sit. This structure appears to terminate at one end with five stairs to the right.

Just as Lewis depicts a central courtyard with colonnaded porches on the periphery, Major George Keppel in 1831 claims about the slave bazaar: "It is a court surrounded by a covered gallery, where the merchants and buyers, seated on their cushions, smoke and transact business."[62] And Edmund Spencer, a traveler to Constantinople in 1836, describes a scene that closely parallels Lewis's: "This building consists of a large quadrangular court, two stories high, surrounded by a portico, with a gallery above: each story contains a range of small cells [where slaves were kept] similar to those in a monastery."[63]

Lewis's sketch of the slave market most closely resembles the description of the traveler Charles White on the Yessir Bazary, which appears in his 1845 travel account, *Three Years in Constantinople.* After providing a brief history of the bazaar he describes the colonnaded portico with patrons, the mosque nearby, even the distinctive steps; Lewis has drawn all of these. Compare his description to Lewis's sketch:

> [The slave market is] open during business hours, that is, from eight a.m. to midday, excepting upon Fridays, when it is closed to purchasers. [. . .] The interior consists of an irregular quadrangle. [. . .] In the center is a detached building, the upper portion serving as lodgings for (*yessirgee*) slave dealers, and underneath are cells for *ajamee* (slaves newly imported). To this is attached a coffee-house, and near to it is a half-ruined mosque. Around the three habitable sides of the court runs an open colonnade, supported by wooden columns, and approached by steps at the angles. Under the colonnade are platforms, separated from each other by low railings

and benches. Upon these dealer and customers may be seen seated during business hours smoking and discussing prices.[64]

White also includes a map of Constantinople to pinpoint the location of the slave market within the city. It shows the slave market located approximately one hundred yards from "the half-ruined mosque" labeled Noory Osmanya.

In the upper right and in the background of the composition Lewis has sketched and highlighted a dome and a minaret, indicating the presence of a nearby mosque. Several writers noted the proximity of the Constantinople slave market to the mosque in 1838 and 1850.[65] Other artists contemporaneous with Lewis indicate a mosque in the background to a slave market scene.[66] William H. Bartlett's engraving published in a book by Julia Pardoe in the same year is actually titled *The Mosque of Osmanié (From the Slave Market)* (Fig. 3.11). There is a formal disjuncture in Bartlett's picture: he emphasizes the mosque over the slave market even though it occurs in the background. While it may be true that the mosque could be seen from the slave market in Constantinople, a pictorial emphasis on it allows for a symbolic reading. It is a foil for contrasting Islamic religiosity with the inhumanity of the slave market system that it presumably sanctions, attesting to the "falsity" of Islam. Thus ostensibly realistic renderings of the slave market can be read as subtle condemnation of Islam.

Besides the slave dealers and the architectural setting, several women are included in Lewis's *Slave Market* sketch. Some can be seen, veiled, on the porches, mingling with the male merchants. Women too sometimes worked as transport and market dealers in both Turkey and Egypt.[67] The figures in the sketch may be these women or upper-class wives, who were often instrumental in examining prospective harem recruits before authorizing their purchase. In the case of the sultan's royal harem at the imperial palace (the Topkapi) in Constantinople, the high-ranking mother of the sultan (*Walide Sultan*)

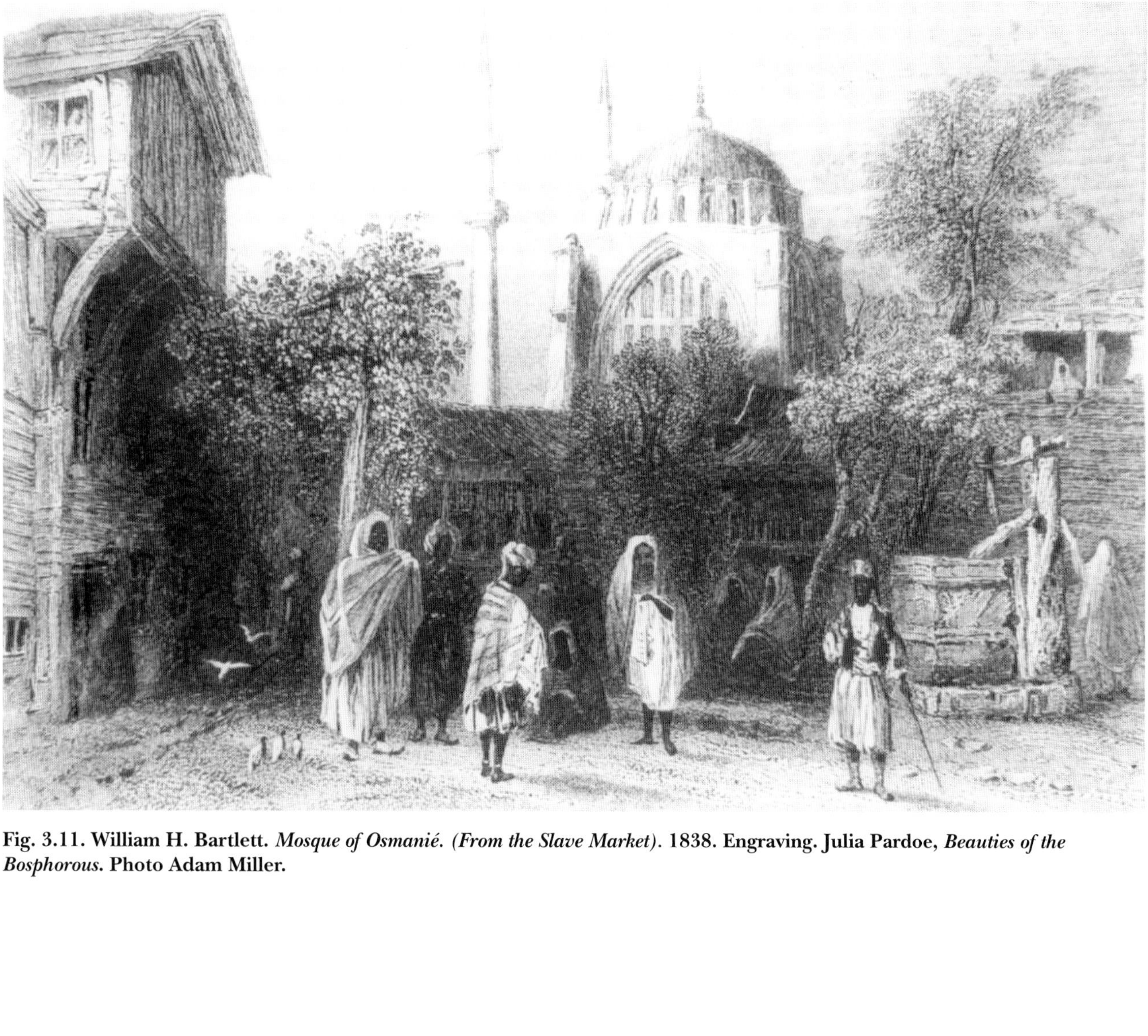

Fig. 3.11. William H. Bartlett. *Mosque of Osmanié. (From the Slave Market).* 1838. Engraving. Julia Pardoe, *Beauties of the Bosphorous.* Photo Adam Miller.

selected for her son healthy and attractive mates who would bear strong progeny, thus guaranteeing proper succession rights.

The women in the sketch may also be the lower-class workers, attendants, and caretakers to the bazaar slaves, which Keppel recounts.[68] The women standing among the men could be intended as slave-sellers, mothers of buyers or lower-class attendants. But other reports are that no woman, regardless of rank or purpose at the market, would be allowed to sit with the male buyers as their peer (*ME* 1:237).

Women appear in another part of Lewis's composition. Clustered around the base of a tree toward the right of the scene is a group of at least five people. Two are turned with their backs to us. Of the remaining three, all of whom appear to be women, one is veiled; the other two are not. One of the unveiled women wears a beaded necklace and a hat or scarf on her head. Lewis has sketched only her head and shoulders. The fact that these two women are unveiled in a public place indicates they are non-Muslims. The only non-Muslim women who would logically be in a slave market are the slaves themselves. Smith's written comment parallels Lewis's drawing. He reports having seen slaves at the market "clustering under the shade of a tree [while] a Turkish woman in her veil was talking to them."[69]

Lewis has taken considerable pains drawing in the auxiliary elements in the composition—the buyers and the architectural setting. But the attention given them is a sort of delay tactic; he has barely gotten to what could be for him the most troubling aspect of the scene, indeed its focus: the slaves. If these tiny figures under the tree are indeed the slaves up for sale, Lewis has spatially distanced himself and his viewer from them. And what of the shadowy palimpsests in the central courtyard? Who is suggested by these outlines?

According to contemporaneous texts (which Lewis may have consulted), the slaves for sale in the outdoor courtyard were probably female, though some male slaves were also sold there.[70] And while patrons on Lewis's balconies seem to be absorbed in their own dealing, oblivious to the display of any slaves, there are at least seven observers on the ground level who focus their attention on the space occupied by the roughly indicated figures. The actual method of bringing slaves into the open courtyard and selling them is described by observers like Keppel, who reports one or two children between the ages of ten and fourteen being sold, and Charles White, describing "newly imported black females [. . .] seated unveiled in groups and lines."[71]

White's mentioning of the women's skin color raises another question about nineteenth-century slave pictures—the racial and ethnic makeup of the female slaves sold at the market. Whether white female slaves ever appeared publicly in the open court of the slave market is a matter of debate. In the 1830s two writers[72] claim white women were not simply kept in the hidden rooms of the market but also publicly sold there. Historians today claim that newly imported white slaves were rarely sold in the public market.[73] Thus, the bulk of the evidence is that mostly blacks were publicly auctioned in the slave market at Constantinople.

Thomas Allom's 1839 luxury book print *Slave Market* (see Fig. 3.7), clearly set indoors, implies that dealing in white Circassians instead took place in settings more private than a slave market. Thus the web of intertextual referents to which Lewis picture is indebted concurs that there were only black women at the Constantinople slave market in the early 1840s, unless they were up for resale, in which case they may have been white women, who rank below the most highly prized Circassian virgins or Muslim-born first wives.

In 1847, however, the public slave market in Constantinople was closed by imperial fermen. Sultan Abdülmecit closed it, Toledano claims, because he was outraged at reports of mistreatment of slaves—and not in any attempt to win approval from European countries. This differs from other legal, military, and industrial reforms, collectively referred to as the *Tanzimat*, which were to some degree attempts to gain the approval of the western political community.[74] Despite the outlawing of the public slave trade in Constantinople, the practice continued clandestinely through the 1870s and beyond. Private trading remained legal. But before mid-century the slave market, one of Constantinople's main tourist attractions, was gone. And representations of the slave market could function to preserve its existence, for better or worse.

Steeped in his impressions of life in the Middle East, convinced of the uniqueness of his opportunity to understand eastern social mores and their points of divergence from British ways, Lewis's artistic sensibility was affected by the ambivalence toward Muslim slavery that he perceived in London society and culture. Judging from his later *oeuvre*, we see that Lewis refrained from describing slave-market slavery, while he achieves his fame in painting harem life, deemphasizing slavery. The artist's slave market sketch shows he was familiar with one of the fundamental processes by which harems were constructed. In the context of the 1850s a "realist" picture of slaves being sold in public markets would be highly provocative, especially when it was clear that Lewis was doing well as a painter of understated and aestheticized harem pictures. His success could have been jeopardized by the appearance of a picture that directly addressed the issue of the slave status of harem inhabitants. It had the potential to undermine the aestheticization which Lewis's harem pictures generally achieve. In the absence of more empirical documentation about the sketch, its unfinished state suggests he was unable—or unwilling—to explore and finally take a stand on the complicated social and political issues such a picture would elicit by virtue of its mere subject.

In another slave-market picture, Jean-Léon Gérôme's *Slave Market* (Fig. 3.12), the narrative centers on clothing and disrobing to which the viewer is privy. The image is organized around the nude body of the female slave under scrutiny, the focal point of the composition. She is nude rather than naked, made more modest by the artistic contrapposto pose and the absence of pubic hair. Clothed women of various ethnicities (read: skin tones), one with a small child, await their fate in the lower right hand corner. Likewise the powerful male buyer is fully and richly clothed with robes and headgear that includes a mouth cover. The nakedness of the slave being considered for purchase is emphasized by such heavily clothed figures around her, by the light cover held by the agent behind her and the pile of now-discarded darker garments at her feet. The shock of the picture is due not only to the stark contrast between the states of dress and undress but also by the quotidian attitudes of the figures, embodied in the child who plays nearby, in the face of so profound a transaction—the selling of a human life. Above all, the composition revolves around the highly charged action of the buyer who forces two very large fingers into her mouth while he manipulates her head, ostensibly to appraise her health. Such treatment of the female slave as chattel (having chilling overtones of sexual violence), is reinforced in the stick held by her agent, in her utterly passive body and animal-like facial expression, and in the echo of the dog in the background made lethargic by the hot sun. Although the picture is undated, Gérôme traveled to Turkey in 1854 and later to Egypt, the Maghreb and elsewhere in the Middle East, collecting ideas and materials for his several images of naked eastern women that are executed with his hallmark polish. In his paintings the discourse on scientific exactitude merges with an imaginary exoticism.

In another version of his *Slave Market* (Fig. 3.13) Gérôme indicates a variety of types of eastern females up for sale based on their varying skin tones and their degrees of moral rectitude, from the lascivious naked woman whose abandon is indicated by her very long unkempt hair, her beckoning pose and her nakedness (she stands on her clothing) to the modest and vulnerable mother. A merchant or his agent keeps close watch from more comfortable quarters, reiterating the fact that the women for sale are subservient to the forces of patriarchy and capital.

The female slave for sale in John Faed's *Bedouin Exchanging a Slave for Armour* c. 1857 (Fig. 3.14) is nearly naked, but the figure is less shocking than Gérôme's. She appears slightly behind her seller, and his heavily clothed body interferes with our visual scrutiny of her nakedness. Though she is the formal and thematic center of the painting, her whole body is in shadow (which acts as a veil of modesty) especially compared to the prospective buyer, his own merchandise and the ruins in the background—all of which are well-lit. The scene takes place somewhere outside an established metropolitan slave market. The principal dynamic is a binary, gendered one: the decorated young female makes eye contact with a somber old male, whose contemplative gesture weighs the equation of warm rounded young flesh with cold metallic (and phallic) weapons. It is a curious clash of female and male worlds. Its profound unease stems from her nakedness and her displacement from a domestic context. The intricate detail of both the arms on display and the "Egyptian" archeological ruins presume the truth of the narrative. But it is unlikely that female slaves would be examined naked. At least in the conventions of the nineteenth-century Cairo market, a prospective male buyer could examine only the hands and feet of a female slave up for sale.[75] Thus the objective/scientific attitude presumed in the slave market pictures of Gérôme and Faed is subject to question.

Unveiling in a more private room adjoining a slave market occurs in Thomas Allom's *Slave-Merchant, Constantinople,* as discussed above. But the slave market is envisioned as a series of tents, and in one of them women are unveiled and emerge to be displayed to a prospective buyer in *L'Asie* (Fig. 3.15). As in Allom's picture, this narrative is fraught with contradiction. The scene itself is not unpleasant, though the merchant's pointing to a bag of coins in the foreground is a direct reference to the exchange of human beings for money. As in Allom's print, the women up for sale appear relaxed and untroubled. The woman on the right might almost be a demure young debutante being introduced to a prospective suitor, her eyes lowered in modesty and her hand extended as her sister slaves look on approvingly. But the caption conveys an abolitionist message:

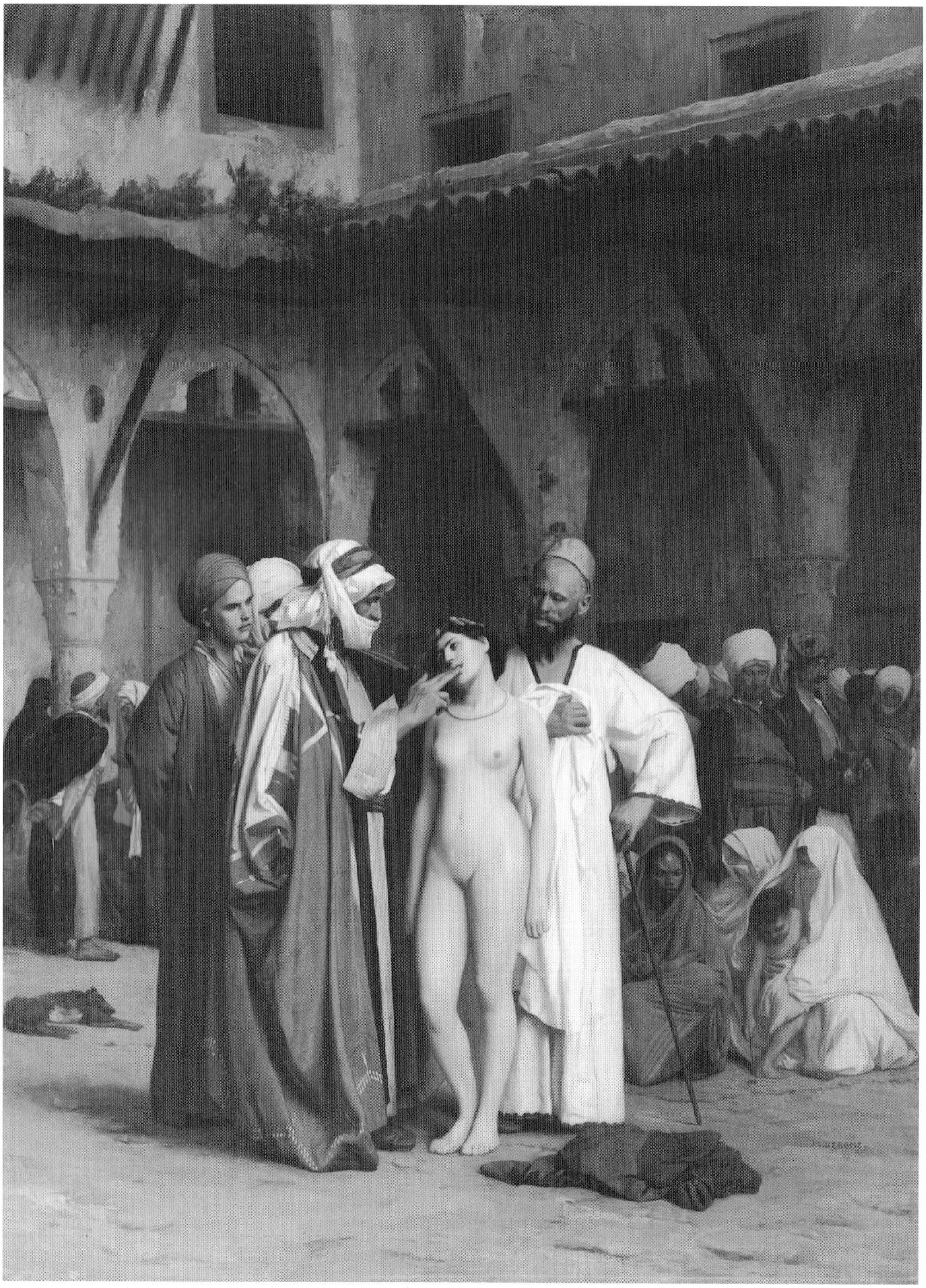

Fig. 3.12. Jean Léon Gérôme. *The Slave Market.* Ca. 1867. Oil on canvas. © Sterling and Francine Clark Art Institute, Williamstown, Massachusetts.

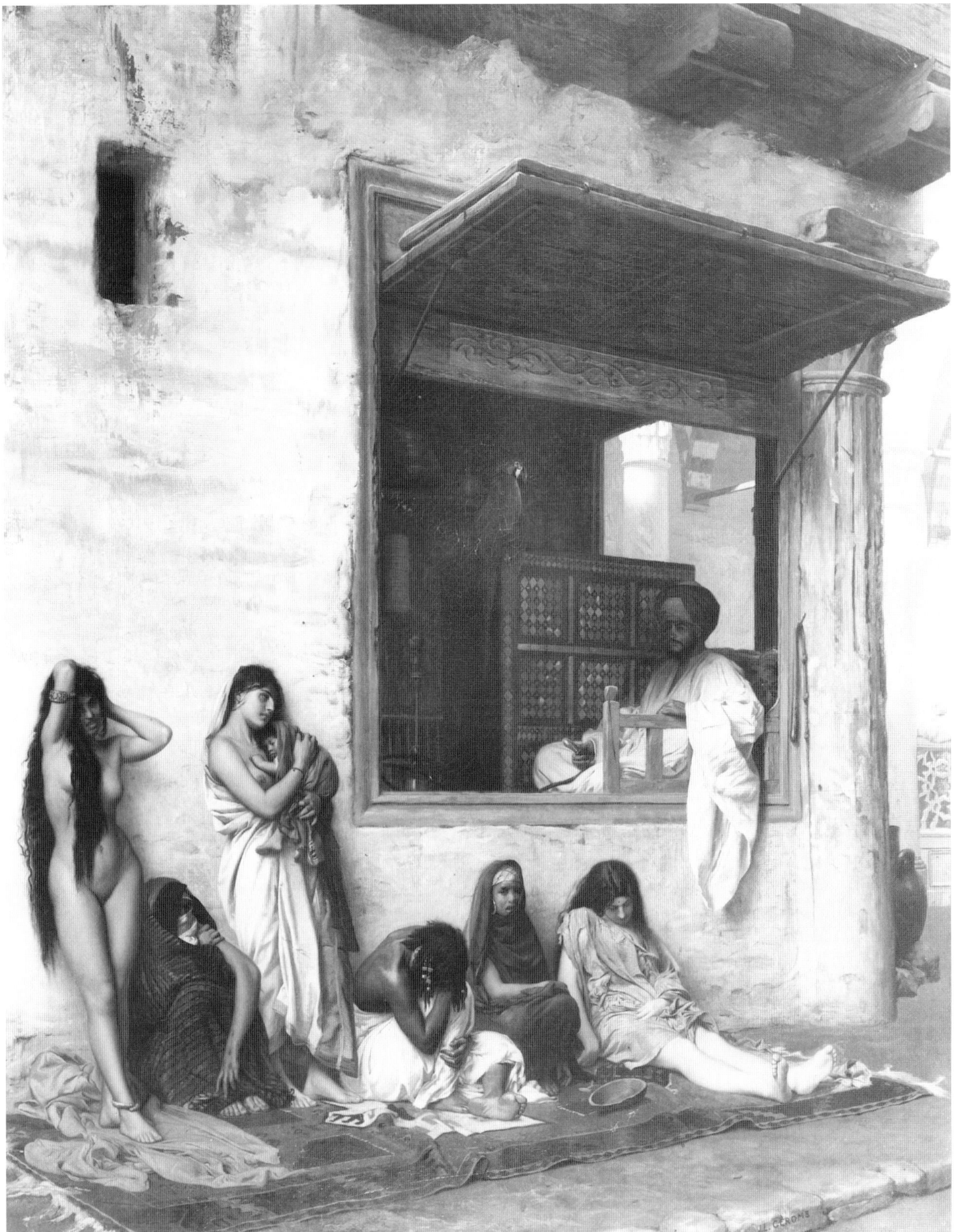

Fig. 3.13. Jean Léon Gérôme. *Slave Market.* 1871. Cincinnati Art Museum, John J. Memory Fund.

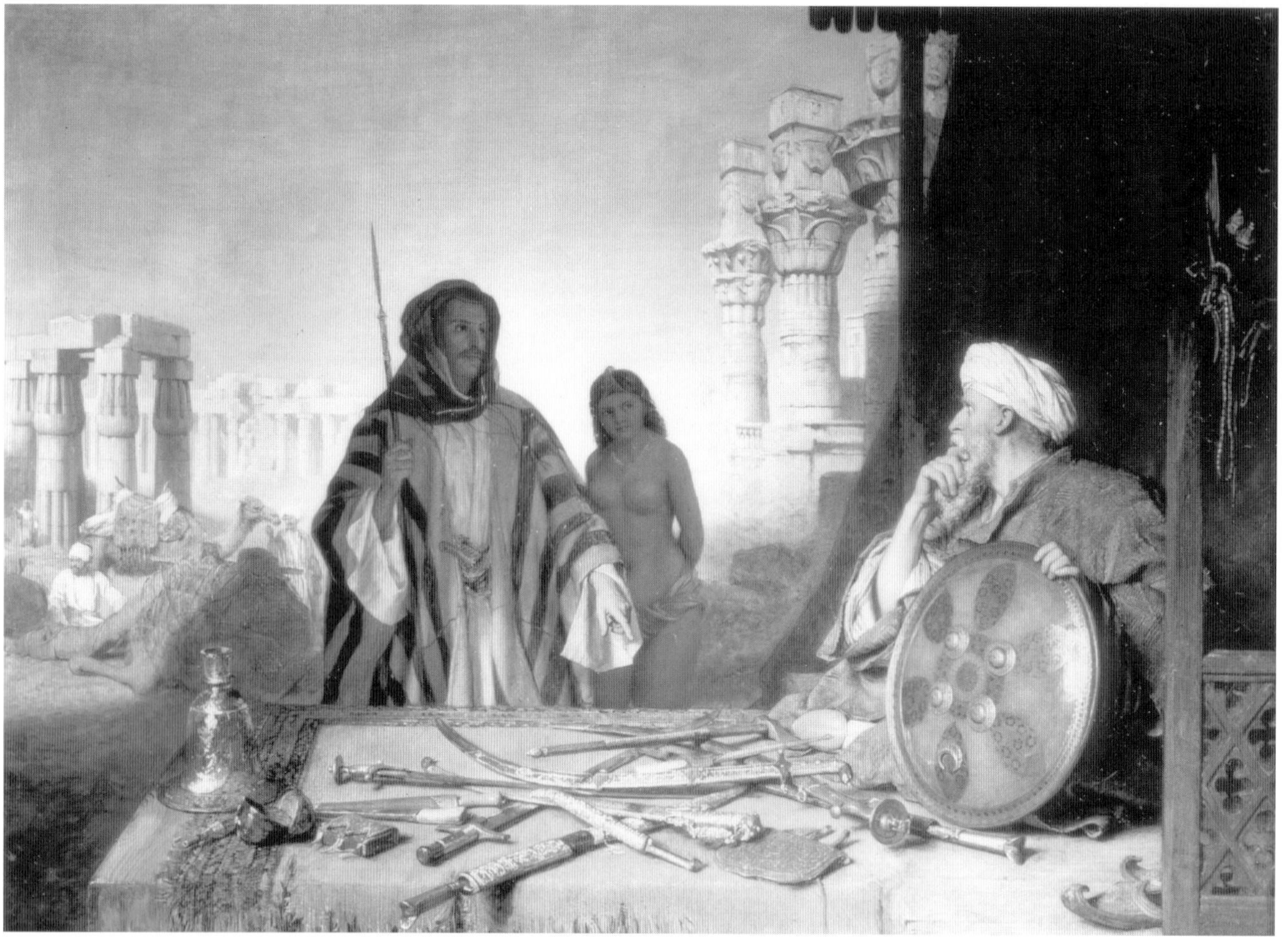

Fig. 3.14. John Faed. *Bedouin Exchanging a Slave for Armour* or *The Arms Dealer*. Ca. 1857. The Fine Arts Society, London, UK/Bridgeman Art Library.

> Love, that pure passion of the heart, has become a vile traffic; woman, in the case of these barbarians, is no longer the companion of man, but a slave subjected to the caprices of a tyrant.

The highly chivalrous presentation of the women who cooperate demurely with their objectification is belied by the critical verbal commentary which accompanies it.

In John Lewis's unveiling scene, *Hhareem* (see Plate 1), the roles of eager buyer, neutral displayer, and passive slave and their related emotions are echoed among the many characters. The work's narrative centers on the introduction of a new slave into the harem. The pasha, his wives, their servants, animals, and even a child are in attendance. A "Nubian eunuch"[76] unveils the new slave. The black-veiled figure seated on the floor behind the new slave is her procuress. She retains her black veil, part of the typical outdoor clothing of Cairene Arab women,[77] in the presence of the harem's owner.[78] She sits awaiting the final approval of the new merchandise.[79] This seems assured, as the master looks on with rapt attention.

Just as Lewis's *Slave Market* seems indebted to written sources, so too his *Hhareem*. It can be considered a pictorial interpretation of Montesquieu's short Letter 79, which is much more explicit in its eroticism for its capturing of the process from dress to undress of the beautiful Circassia slave, being purchased by the eunuch. "I took her to the secret apartments, undressed her and examined her critically. The more I examined her, the more attractions I found." Solim continues "with virginal modesty she seemed to want to conceal [her charms] from my sight. [. . .] she reddened at finding herself naked" (*PL* 157). Writer and painter emphasize the girl's modesty and passivity.[80] Lewis depicts her with eyes lowered and arms crossed over her chest clutching her garb; Montesquieu's eunuch puts a robe around her (*PL* 158). Solim insists on his innocence in admiring the slave and indeed protests too much to his master, given the content of the eunuch's letters of unfulfilled desire written in confidence to

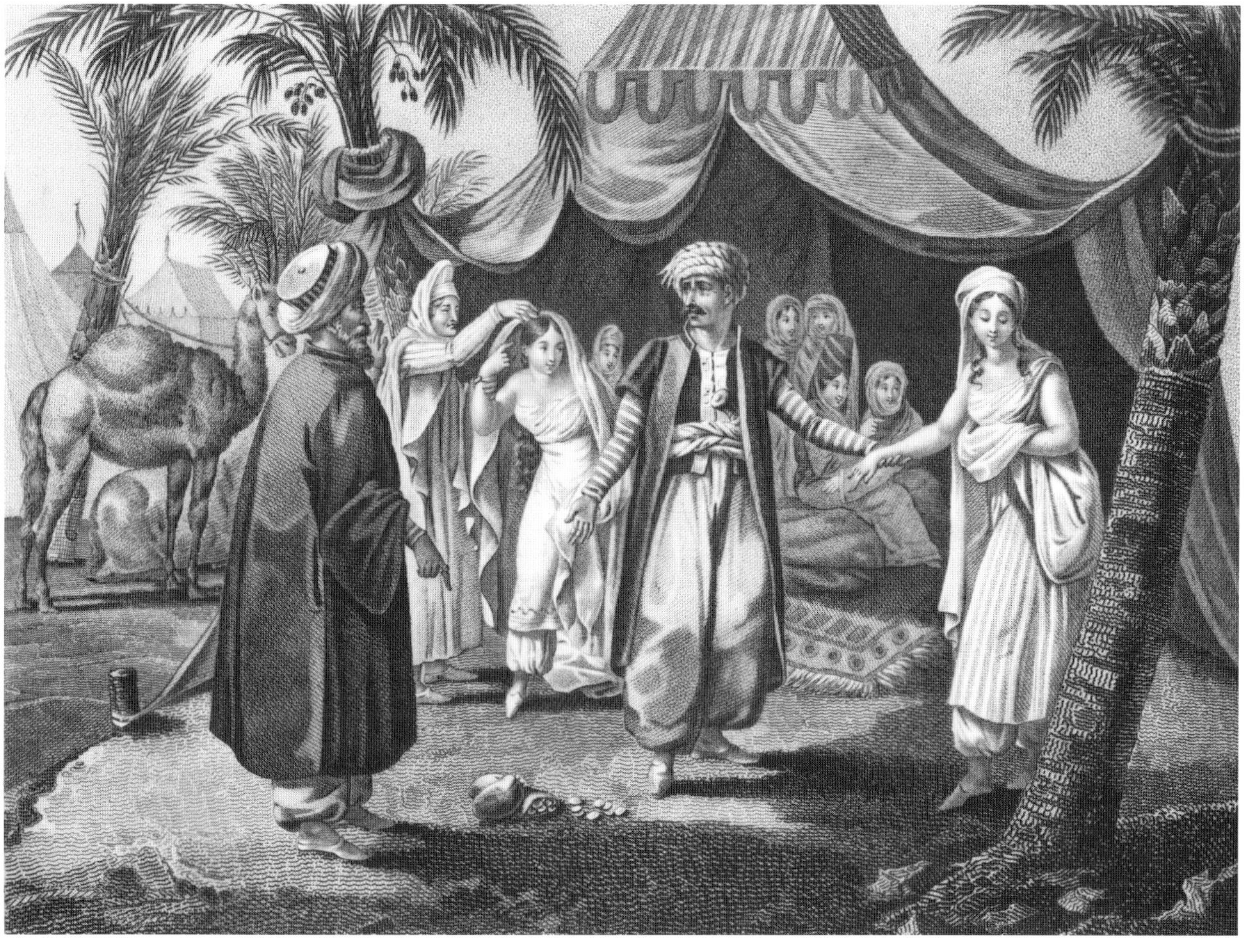

Fig. 3.15. Anonymous. *L'Asie.* Lithograph. Cliché Bibliothèque nationale de France, Paris.

his friend, forming one of the major deceptions of the book. Lewis keeps any desire the eunuch might harbor out of his picture by positioning the woman as a spectacle for the pasha and the viewer; the eunuch, who stands behind her, is a mere medium of that pleasure. Because a eunuch is deemed sexless, his report serves to make mobile and defer the visual pleasure of seeing a naked female body. Though he defers ostensibly to his master Usbek, it is the reader who (vicariously) enjoys the mental visualization of her charms in both Montesquieu's writing and Lewis's picture. In both cases, the slave herself attempts to prevent the unveiling of her body. Her efforts are in vain, contributing to the viewer's heightened pleasure.

The picture was exhibited in 1850 at the Old Water-Colour Society and again in 1855 at the Exposition Universelle in Paris, an era of much public discussion of harem slavery. The year 1855 is a watershed in the history of British interventionism on the issue of Muslim slavery. It is the year the British give up their goal of eliminating Muslim slavery as a whole. Henceforth, they would focus on the more practical goal of restricting the slave trade. Also around this time they learn that black and white slavery would be two separate issues for the Muslims, with two different policies. Simultaneously by 1855 the Ottomans were in the process of prohibiting (temporarily) the slave trade in Circassians and Georgians. The British misinterpreted this action as a victory for their principles when in fact the action was internally motivated. In subsequent years the British reminded the sultan of his own prohibition of the trade, but he promptly ignored such remarks, pointing out the exigencies of war that necessitated such unusual—and temporary—measures.[81]

Like his artistic intentions, Lewis's personal opinions on the harem and slavery are undocumented. Whether he intended his harem ladies to be imprisoned or empowered, whether his genre pictures are meant to be pro-Muslim is unknown. But Lewis's *Hhareem* can have several meanings. The artist has constructed enough ambiguity in his scene that viewers of different persuasions in 1850 could find their viewpoints supported. Lewis's picture of Middle

Eastern slavery offered something to nearly everyone. The Old Water-Colour Society and art critics could applaud the appearance of a subject over which the French had maintained a monopoly, one with a pedigree traceable to the likes of Decamps, Delacroix, Ingres, Vanloo, and Boucher. Here was a work painted in a meticulous technique that appealed to national standards of industry; it was also done in the "British" watercolor medium, one not always considered high art in foreign (French) art circles. The art establishment thus represented the aesthetic attitude. Political views could also be read into the painting. Abolitionists could project their sympathies for the indignation the slave suffers at the abridgement of her personal freedom. Advocates for the toleration of the harem could see here a stunning record of picturesque ethnography. A middle-class viewer with no political interest could enjoy the exotic subject and its pictorial beauty. For all of these viewers Lewis's picture had a lascivious appeal as well. After all, Lewis has chosen to depict a narrative about a slave purchased primarily for her sexuality, and she is shown partially unclothed. One critic claims the theme required the picture to be "voluptuous" (*A* 1850:210).

Thus, at midcentury *Hhareem* combines aspects of two iconographies: the slave market scene and the harem. It takes on many associations of the intertwined subjects, associations which are sometimes contradictory. His work by default enters into the thick of the battle to formulate and correct notions about the harem. Thus Lewis's *Hhareem* does not contain one meaning, or one stance, but acts as a stimulus to provoke widespread and varied notions about the harem and the process of acquiring inmates for it.

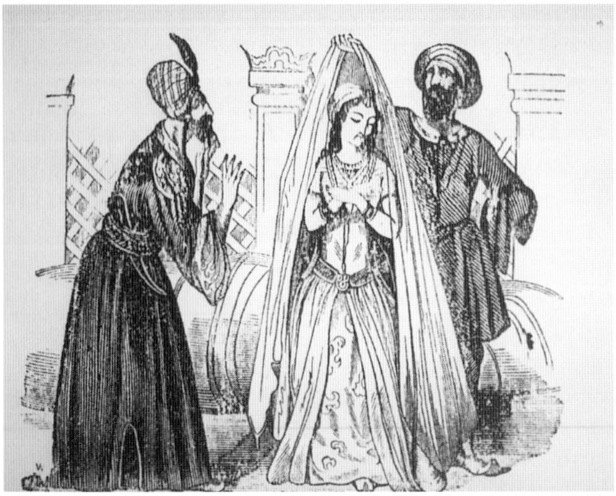

Fig. 3.16. Anonymous. *Beautiful Persian Unveiled by a Merchant. Arabian Nights' Entertainment*, trans. Edward Forster, Ca. 1844. Engraving.

The presumed passivity of the harem slave being unveiled is problematized in two book illustrations viewed alongside their accompanying text, the *Arabian Nights*, deemed in 1839 by the *London and Westminster Review* "'the most popular book in the world at this present writing.'"[82] In one edition c. 1844 the scene shows a merchant unveiling a new slave, named the "Beautiful Persian," to a buyer whose gestures express his great delight (Fig. 3.16). The slave lowers her eyes and crosses her arms over her chest—gestures of modesty and also deference to the eye of the buyer (and the viewer). Yet in the text translated from the Arabic the author refrains from describing an unveiling at all. Instead she is said to possess great beauty, "understanding and knowledge [. . .] there are no books she has not read; [. . .] there never existed till now so accomplished a slave."[83] This slave is an intellectual.

The second unveiling is similar: a full-length figure of a woman with downcast eyes and a hand gesture of modesty signal her beauty and passivity (Fig. 3.17). It may have served as a prototype for other unveilings

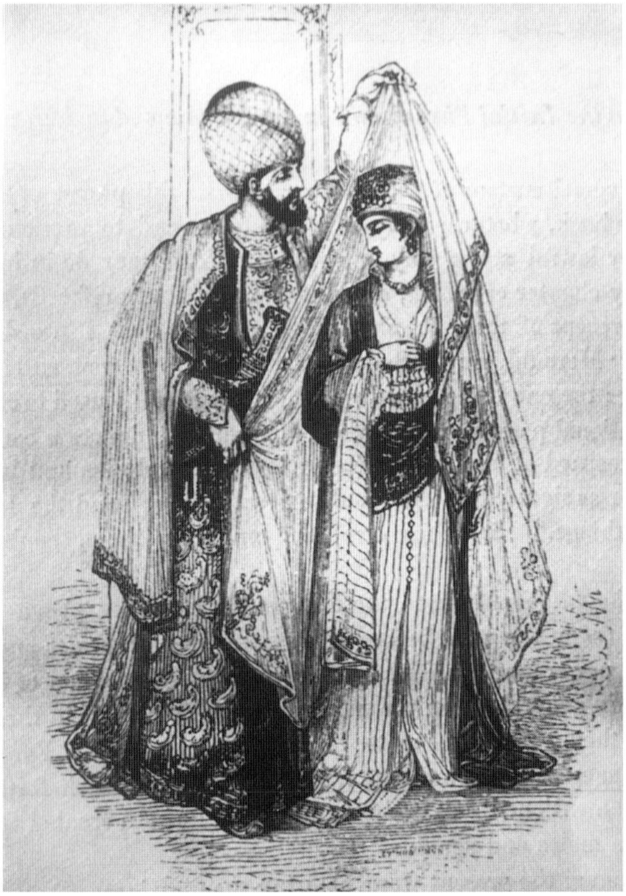

Fig. 3.17. Edward William Lane. *Untitled [Female Slave Being Unveiled]*. Engraving. *1001 Nights*. 1839–41.

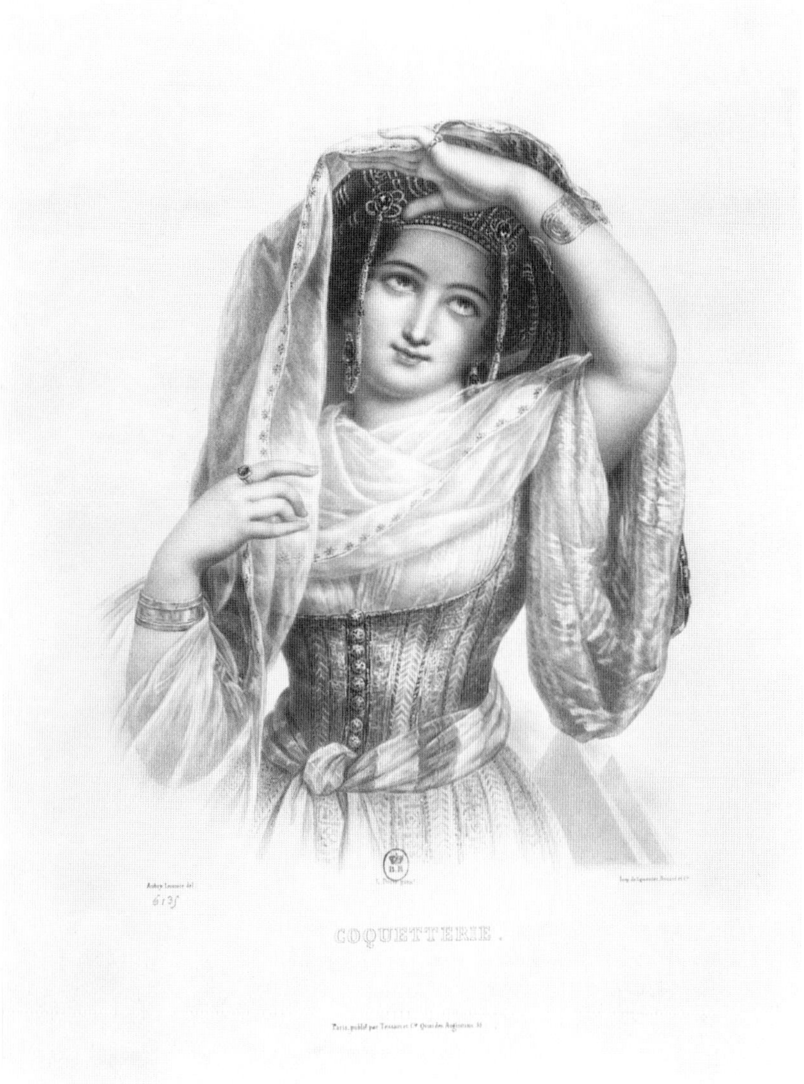

Fig. 3.18. Hyacinthe Aubry-Lecomte after Louis Ducis. *Coquetterie (Portrait de Marie Aubry-Lecomte?)*. 1840. Lithograph. Cliché Bibliothèque nationale de France, Paris. Farwell, *FPLI*, v. 11, 1D5 B84159.

in the harem, as it appeared in 1839–41 in the introduction to the single most renowned English translation of the *1001 Nights*, that by Edward William Lane. But this is no nameless, passive woman. This is Scheherazade, the vizier's intelligent, well-read, and brave daughter who delivers Muslim girls from King Shahriyar's cruel practice of killing at dawn the virgin he has had the night before. By narrating tales for a thousand and one nights, she also prolongs her own life. Thus the texts of both editions of *Nights* describe strong, learned women, while the Victorian artists portray them as passive, self-effacing victims.[84]

The veil can have a very different reading. British artists and writers including Lane recognized that in public Muslim women used the veil as a means of "coquetry" (*ME* 1:225–26). Rather than the symbol of the oppressed woman of the harem, it becomes a means of flirtation. Richard Burton describes the veil as a means of selective concealing and revealing. It is

> the most coquettish article of women's attire [. . .]. It conceals coarse skins, fleshy noses, wide mouths and vanishing chins, while it sets off to best advantage what in these lands is almost always lustrous and liquid—the eye. Who has not remarked this at a masquerade ball? (*PNP* 1:337)

Correspondingly, removing the veil can be a sign of active female seduction in a few French lithographs from the July Monarchy. In the 1840 *Coquetterie* (Fig. 3.18) done by Aubry-Lecomte after L. Ducis,

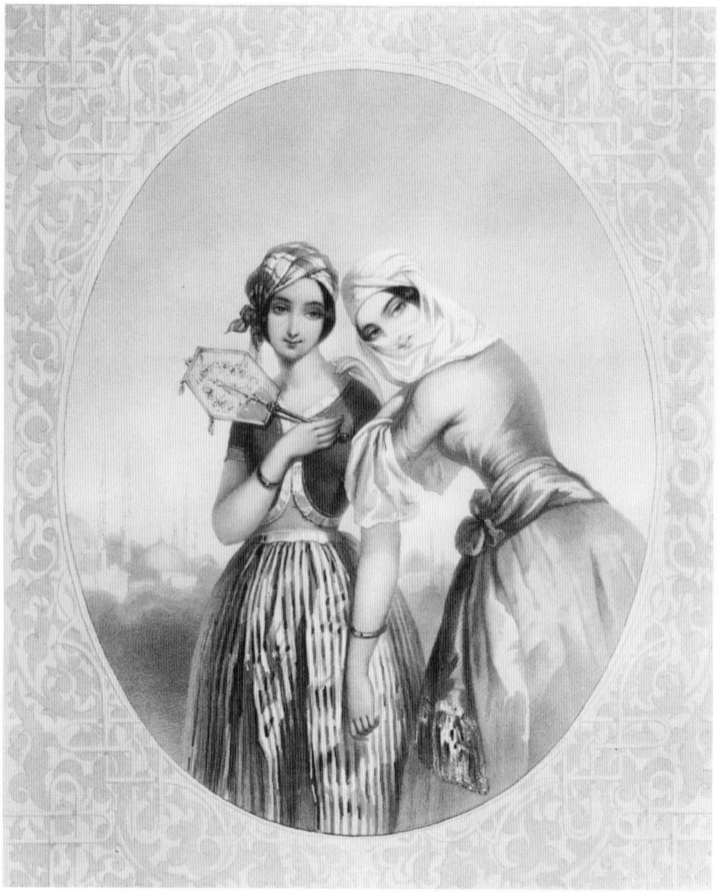

Fig. 3.19. Claude Régnier, J. Bettannier, and/or E. Bettannier after Bouvier. *Le Voile*. 1845. Lithograph. Cliché Bibliothèque nationale de France, Paris. Farwell, *FPLI*, v. 11, 2E2 B81761.

the woman removes her own veil. Two eastern women flirt, one using her veil, in an 1845 print done after Bouvier by Régnier and/or Bettannier and titled *Le Voile* (Fig. 3.19). As a tantalizing prelude, an eastern woman in bed removes her veil, much to the delight of her attentive lover in the untitled, undated lithograph by Adolphe Mouilleron (Fig. 3.20). When eastern women remove their own veils, they are no longer passive victims but sexually assertive women who demonstrate that they are ready for love. Far from the discourse of abolitionism, such a titillating theme was conceivable only within the definition of popular pornographic prints.

In some harem pictures the veil that is removed is not located on the woman's face but across the whole scene, as in Delacroix's *Women of Algiers* (see Fig. 2.17), in which the standing servant pushes aside the curtain, or across the bedchamber on which the woman is located, as in Ingres's *Grande Odalisque* (1819) (Fig. 3.21), where the woman toys with the opened veil/ curtain, that rococo device to suggest the boudoir's privacy. The curtain pushed aside to reveal the whole scene serves to underscore the whole unclothed body that has also been unveiled. Her garb has been removed, very recently, as it lies under her body in wrinkled disarray.

Scholars have long known that Ingres copied portions of Lady Mary Wortley Montagu's *Letters* into Notebook 9 c. 1815–17, specifically her description of a Turkish bath. However, scholars have not developed the possibility that Ingres might have read and used other parts of her letters in his harem painting. In fact, Ingres' rendering of this harem woman's clothing in its color, fabric, and other details corresponds quite closely to parts of her description of Turkish women's dress. A comparison of the two helps define the eroticism of Ingres's painting of an unveiled woman.

The odalisque reclines on a white garment. It is semi-transparent, a texture readable where it covers her skin. It is the article of clothing closest to her body, suggesting an undergarment, one taken off last. In her letter to her sister Lady Mar dated Adrianople 1

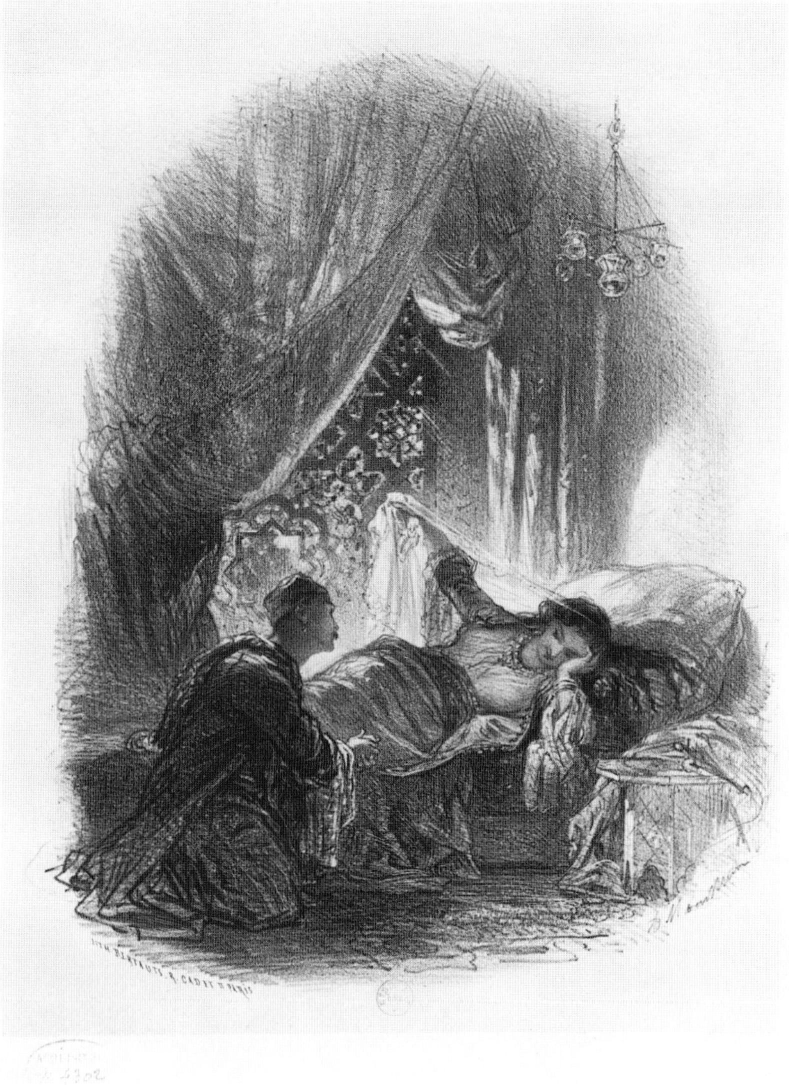

Fig. 3.20. Adolphe Mouilleron. *Untitled [Odalisque].* Lithograph. Cliché Bibliothèque nationale de France, Paris. Farwell, *FPLI*, v. 9, 5F11 B81199.

April 1717, Lady Mary describes the Turkish woman's undergarment as transparent white silk:

> Over this [drawers] hangs my Smock of a fine white silk Gause edg'd with Embrodiery. This smock has wide sleeves hanging halfe way down the Arm and is clos'd at the Neck with a diamond button, but the shape and colour of the bosom very well to be distinguish'd through it (*L* 1:326).

In Ingres's picture, a gold-colored article of clothing is painted to expose a thick white edging, suggesting a garment lining. For this second garment, Ingres may be combining Lady Mary's descriptions of two articles. She writes that the "antery" is a waistcoat made "of white and Gold Damask." But the "Curdée" is the Turkish piece of clothing backed with another fabric: "a loose Robe they throw off or put on according to the Weather, being of a rich Brocade (mine is green and Gold) lined with Ermine or Sables" (*L* 1:326).[85]

Ingres has painted sables as a third garment, especially visible under the odalisque's knees and feather-fan. The fur and feather against skin are fetishes to suggest the exquisite tactile pleasures promised by this odalisque. This suggests that Ingres looked to Lady Mary as an authority on women's issues: clothing and fashion. In painting the clothing under the odalisque instead of having her wear it, Ingres puts Lady Mary's inventory to titillating ends. And he avoids the task of accurately draping the figure.

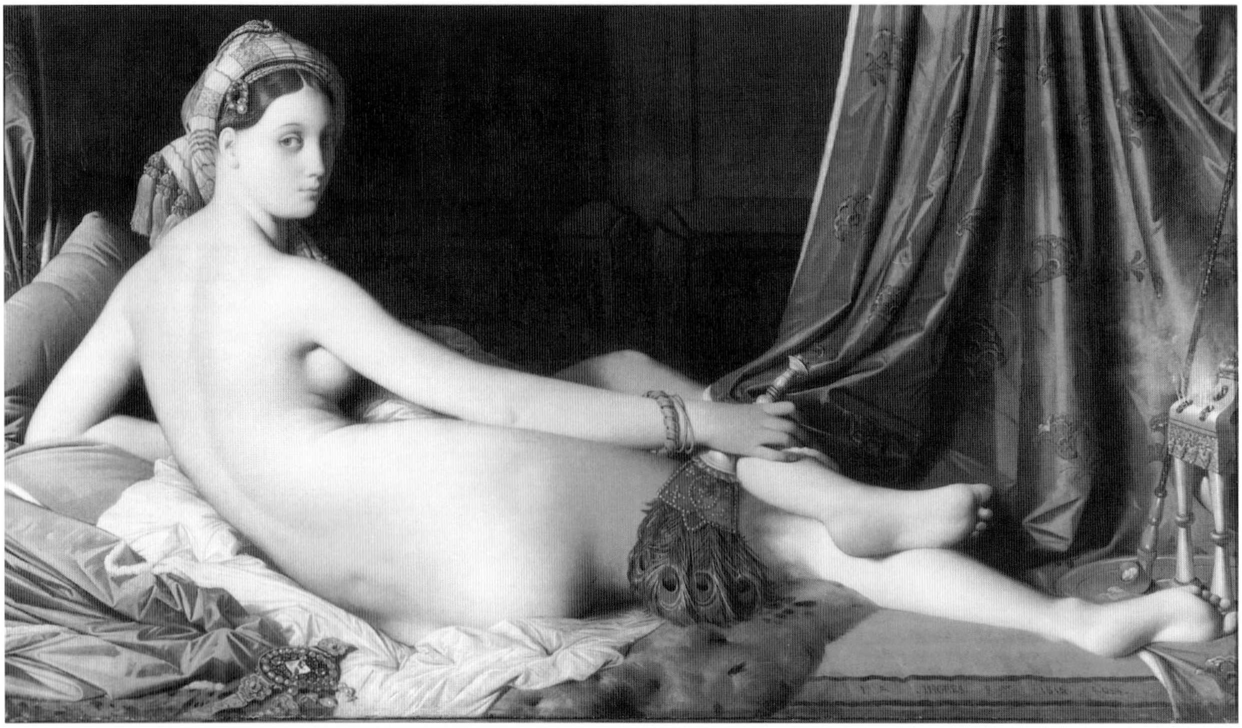

Fig. 3.21. Jean Auguste Dominique Ingres. *Grande Odalisque.* 1814. Musée du Louvre, Paris. © Photo RMN.

The category of representations under the rubric of "slave market pictures and unveiling scenes" includes diverse images. In some of them the women are depicted as sexually exploited victims; in others the women are flirtatious, but self-determining. An appeal to the male element is often built into the fiction of these scenes, whether men are actually there as characters or whether their presence is only implied. But the pictures' primary function is to appeal to the viewer (male and female alike). And the narratives of unveiling and slave-selling are metaphors for the process of the viewer's "mastering"/owning/consuming such pictures.

The Greek War of Independence and Harem Women as War Prisoners

Introduction: The War and Philhellenica

A significant category of harem images in the nineteenth century are those having a reference to the Greek War of Independence, in which Greek women were captured as prisoners and sold as slaves into foreign harems. Because Greeks could be considered westerners, the configuration of the Greek woman in the harem had the potential to make fluid the boundaries between "them" and "us." But for the most part artists and writers chose to represent her as a stranger in a strange land, accenting her suspension between two cultures as she awaited rescue, a representation that might spur political sentiment in favor of the Greeks.

Philhellenic observers were outraged to learn that Islam sanctioned the enslavement of Greeks. But there were restrictions on the use of captured women. Nonbelievers could be enslaved only in war and only with the intention of converting them to Islam, according to recent interpretations.[86] And a Muslim man could not cohabit with a woman who professed a heathen religion. If she converted to Islam, a Christian slave could become part of the harem, and she could also more readily be manumitted.

The years 1825–28 mark a watershed in the history of harem women having Greek origins. In that period Sultan Mahmud II sent Egyptian troops to quell the Greek rebellion. Egyptian forces invaded Greece under the direction of Ali's son, Ibrahim Pasha, who had thousands of Greeks slaughtered. He also brought approximately six thousand captured Greeks into Egypt.[87] News of these developments aroused the sympathies and the wrath of the Philhellenes. Most of the captured Greeks were ransomed by Europeans living in Egypt and by the Viceroy, eager to appease western interests. At the end of the 1830s there were reportedly only six hundred Greek females and three hundred males left in Egypt, most of whom had converted to Islam.[88]

Even before the 1820s, the long history of Ottoman imperialism gave rise to French and British representations of Greek and other Christian women taken by force into the harem. From the seventeenth century travelers claimed harem inmates were mostly virgins. In 1650 Robert Withers claimed harem females in the Grand Seignor's seraglio "are all young virgins taken and stollen from forraign Nations."[89] Moreover, many of them remain virginal, Withers claims, even after they are brought into the harem. In 1675 Paul Rycaut repeats the notion that women in the Grand Segnior's palace are "an Army of Virgins" taken in war, but they are eager to be invited into the master's bed.[90]

It was known in France and England that Greek war captives, male and female alike, were pressed into slavery in harems. So harem pictures produced from the 1820s onward specifying Greek or Greece in their titles are generally war propaganda. These pictures represent a landmark in the history of harem imagery. They no longer provide frivolous titillation; they function as direct political commentary. This challenged artists: a picture about harem-slavery made to support the Greek cause could be open to a salacious reading. Female nudity of a pathetic or heroic kind appeared in visual and verbal Philhellenica describing Greek women captured and sent off to Turkish harems, but nudity of any sort could be read as exploiting female nakedness. A work which used conventions to explicitly titillate would end up a visual exploitation of the very things the Philhellenes would oppose—the expropriation of women from their native country and the imposition of foreign control over their sexuality.

Pictures mainly from the 1820s and 1830s (and beyond) can be grouped to recount the stages in the transformation of free Greek women into harem inmates. The first stage, the most dramatic, pictures Greek women forcibly taken from their homeland. By the mere choice to represent the subject of the actual capture of Greek women, artists and writers are nearly always pro-Greek and anti-Turkish. In the second and third stages in the process of induction into the harem images of Greek women are shown either accepting or rejecting their new home.

Phase I: Scenes of Seizure

The most well-known painting in which a Greek woman is seized for harem slavery is Eugène Delacroix's *Massacres de Scio* (Fig. 3.22), an image rich in intertextuality and emotional content. It is also an image that reuses some Philhellenic formulas for understanding political and personal oppression. At the same time the work's context demonstrates some of the conflicting impulses around which painter and audience formulated the sexuality of Greek women bound for the harem.

The painting was shown at the Salon in 1824, the year Byron's death at Missolonghi fueled Philhellenic sentiment in Delacroix's circle.[91] Purchased for the high sum of six thousand francs by the Restoration for the Luxembourg Palace, *Scio* recalls an actual event that occurred in the fall of 1822 as indicated in its subtitle, noteworthy in that it ensures a contemporary referent: *Greek Families Await Death or Slavery etc. See various accounts and the newspapers of the time.* Under Ottoman Turkish rule since 1566, Christian inhabitants on the island of Chios revolted. Following a defeat of the Christians at Patras, the Ottomans took revenge against the population of one hundred thousand people. The ten thousand troops massacred one-fifth of the populace and abducted many more to be sold as slaves.[92]

Inhumane victimization is the major theme of Delacroix's *Scio.* Most of the Greeks in the painting are extremely passive in accepting their doom—enslavement or death—at the hands of the Turks. Like baroque images of Christian martyrs, this depiction of the classically vulnerable—women, children, and the elderly—raises the scene's emotional pitch. In an example of Philhellenic writing from 1821 Alexander Barginet explicitly identifies these three groups: "The elderly, women and children."[93] And in what may be considered a response to Delacroix's painting the next year Victor Hugo reuses these figures in "The Sacking of the City," from *Les Orientales*: "Died the pale mothers, and the virgins, from their arms, / O Caliph, fiercely torn, bewailed their young years' blight; / With stabs and kisses fouled, all their yet quivering charms [. . .] Some infants yet survived, and the unsated steel / Still drinks the life-blood of each whelp of Christian-kind" (*SCL* 64). In both image and text the overriding emotion is despair and destruction so profound as to ensure that the perpetrators were seen as the barbarian antithesis of civilized nations.

Straddling two of the three categories, women and children, is the trope of a Christian virgin. That she is violated by barbarians, whether her abductor or the pasha who later buys her, constitutes an extremely potent cultural symbol, given its frequency in the Philhellenic literature. This trope itself is not completely desexualized, however, as the Greek harem slave merely sublimates the viewer's desire. And therein lies the fundamental contradiction with which I believe Delacroix's painting struggles.

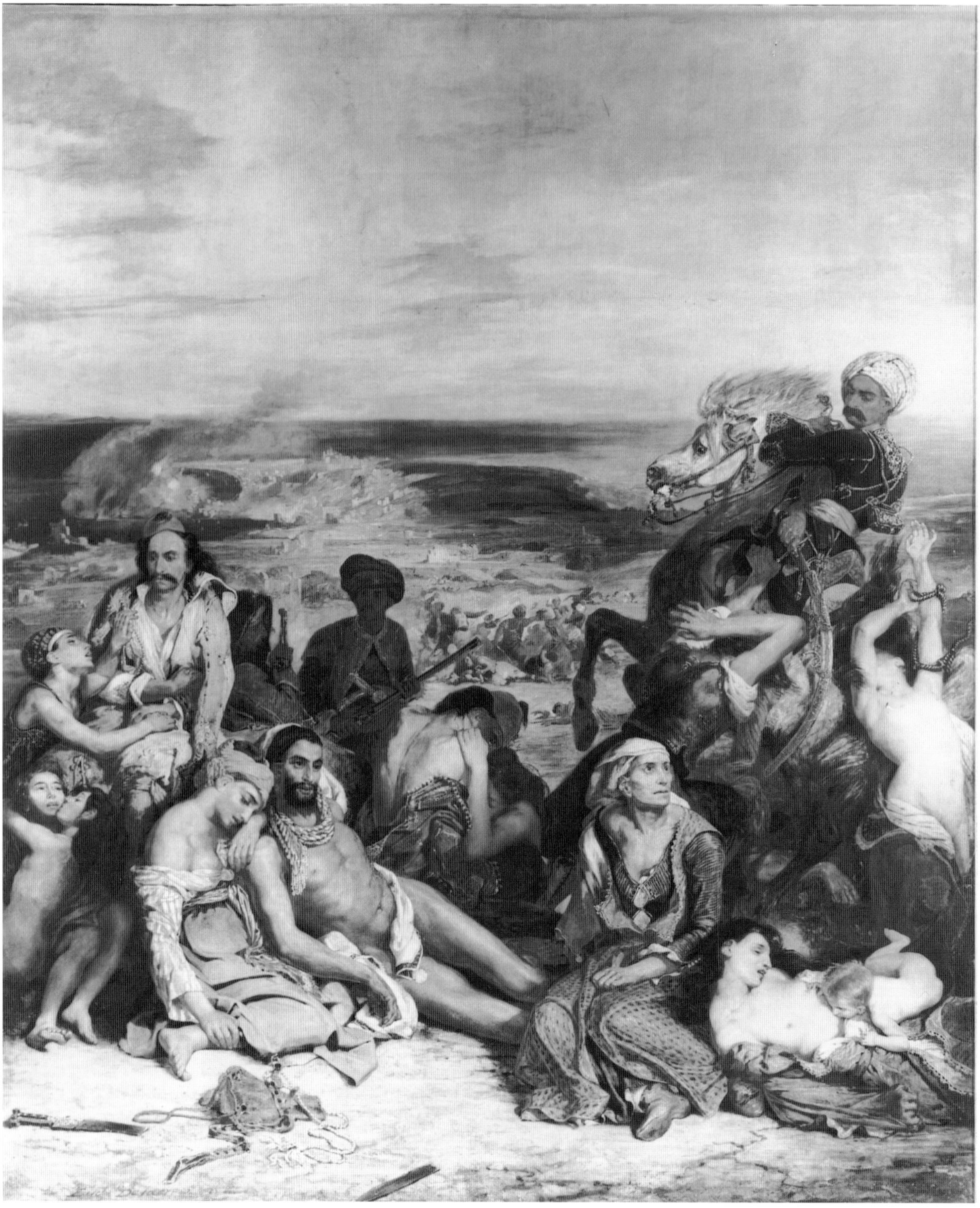

Fig. 3.22. Eugène Delacroix. *Massacres at Scio.* Musée du Louvre, Paris. 1824 Salon. © Photo RMN.

In Delacroix's *Scio* the Greek virgin being abducted is a particularly complex figure, writhing at right attempting to unfasten the ropes which tie her to the Turk's horse. The figure offers a fascinating case study in the way the fear of abduction into the harem was used to provoke Philhellenic sentiment. She is eroticized because of her energized resistance and her exposed torso. In her struggle her clothing has fallen away. Or perhaps it has been stripped from her by the Turk in order to rape her and/or to judge her fit for harem service. She forms an animated contrast to the figure of the pathetically moribund, bare-breasted mother below her: she is eroticized within a field of lethargy and death. And the active segment of the painting to which she belongs is formally odd. She is squeezed into the right margin of the composition, like an afterthought, while the central groupings are the most self-absorbed and inaccessible to the viewer. Having reworked it several times in his preliminary studies for the work over the course of five months,[94] Delacroix had not resolved its odd emotional and compositional tension, one of the complaints of the critics in 1824.[95]

The figure's interaction with the viewer further defines its eroticism. Her drapery functions as a vestige of modesty as it falls over her groin, producing an unbroken expanse of flesh recalling Ingres's minimal use of drapery on his odalisques and bathers as well as the Greek *Venus of Melos*, brought to the Louvre by the secretary of the French embassy in Constantinople in the early 1820s.[96] The woman's averted face allows the viewer her nakedness without the accountability a full face would demand. The body pose is provocative—back arched and arms raised to accentuate the breasts, producing a visual vulnerability that emphasizes the hopelessness of her resistance to both the Turkish equestrian and to our eyes.

Delacroix's pose for this figure was set from early on in his preparatory sketches for the painting, even though some friends were critical. When he began the figure in late January 1824, he records in his *Journal* the negative reactions:

> Today, as I was beginning the woman dragged along by the horse, I was visited by Riesener, Henri Hugue, and Rouget. Imagine how they treated *my poor creation*, which they saw in the most chaotic state, when I alone can guess how it is going to turn out.

Delacroix is defensive about his friends' reactions. He complains

> a lot of mental paupers like those come, even into my den, to nip my inspirations in the bud and measure me with their glasses [. . .] Happily—and I offer you my thanks for this, kind heaven—you give me the presence of mind I need in my poverty to keep at a distance the doubts their stupid criticism often create in me. Even Pierret made some criticism, but they affected me not in the least, for I know what my work needs.[97]

We can only guess at the content of their objections to the female figure. Could it be that they echoed his own doubts about the licentiousness in the eroticized figure within what was ostensibly a political painting? In the 5 March 1824 entry in his journal he claimed to have finished the body and head of the woman attached to the horse.[98] Yet more than a month later, on 10 April, he writes that the painterly problems had not yet been resolved:

> There is still a defect that turns up in what I am doing (the *Massacres at Scio*), especially in the woman bound to the horse; it lacks vigor, the full depth of the paint. The contours are still a wash, and not clean-cut. I must remember this constantly.[99]

Delacroix's formal problems with this figure may be the result of his own struggle over her function: would she be a pathetic victim as understood in Philhellenic discourses ("holy modesty profaned"[100]) or would she be an eroticized object?

When it was shown at the 1824 Salon *Massacres at Scio* caused a furor. The critical consensus was overwhelmingly negative. One of the critics to comment specifically on the nude woman tied to the horse was Stendhal. A member of a small circle of Parisian intellectuals in the 1820s, the *Réunion des dimanches* (held by Etienne Delécluze), Stendhal writing in *Revue de Paris* disliked the painting because he claimed it looked like a plague and was full of clichés: "a fanatical Turk as handsome as Girodet's Turk, slaughtering Greek women of angelic beauty and menacing their fathers, an old man who will in turn succumb to the Turk's blows."[101]

However, the painting was strongly endorsed by the critic Auguste Jal, Delacroix's friend who shared his interest in orientalia. Jal's Philhellenic response includes a critique of harem slavery. He reads the nude female torso not as eroticized but as belonging to a nun! He writes: "the infidel has marked [. . .] for the harem the virgins consecrated to the service of the mother of God."[102] Jal's nun is a variant on the virginal personifications of Greece or Liberty to appear in Philhellenic pamphlets. Whether devoted to God or to Greek liberation, her purity suggests her noble cause. Philhellenic writing is replete with references to virgins, often Minerva or another ancient goddess. Echoing a similar sentiment, one Philhellenic writer complains that young virginal Greek girls were sold into slavery like prostitutes.[103]

To underscore the point that Jal implies, that Delacroix has eliminated lewdness from the woman's naked torso, the critic describes the reaction of a viewer who was a compassionate female (and not a lecherous male):

> the tears which flow from the eyes of this young woman at the painful spectacle of the frightening episode with which the composition on the right ends; there is the most glorious success which the artist could have wished.[104]

Yet even when Jal writes about this figure in the persona of the male Artist, his is a purely aesthetic admiration; he praises Delacroix: "let him never fall below the execution of the woman's torso tied to the tail of the Arabian horse."[105]

Thus the critics disagreed about whether Delacroix's partly naked Greek woman bound for the harem advanced the Greek cause by the artist's use of an effective Philhellenic convention or whether the painter exploited female nudity. The painter's support from Jal must also be attributed to their shared political Liberalism, while criticism for the picture in general and the Greek woman within it needs also to be seen as a conservative assertion of Bourbon politics and the program of aesthetic taste with which the king was associated.

Evidence that the Greek female captive was eroticized—for Delacroix himself—is suggested in his journal where he records his liaisons with the model he used for the figure, Emilie Roberts. From January to March he records their sexual activity, referring to it using the vulgar Italian word *chiavatura*. The painted figure is conflated with his feelings about their sexual encounters on 5 March when he writes: "Did the head and torso of the young girl fastened to the horse. *Dolce chiavatura*."[106]

Thus the problematic nature of the Greek woman in *Massacres de Scio* has several determinants: Delacroix's avid Philhellenism, his political Liberalism and artistic association with other Romantics, his construction of his own masculinity—and his desire to promote his own career by painting a subject having popular appeal, as he himself declares.[107] The work is an awkward attempt to reconcile cliché and political commitment, eroticism and public involvement.

Another French image depicting the first stage in the conversion of a Greek woman into a harem inmate, her capture, is a lithographic print that specifically names the Greek and Turkish identities of the figures, *Jeune grecque sauvée de l'esclavage des Turcs* (Fig. 3.23). It is from an 1827 series by Henri Charles Loeillot, *Combats pour l'indepéndance grecque*. Unlike Delacroix's painting of victimization done three years earlier, the point of this image is salvation. While Delacroix's *Massacres de Scio* was a piece of Philhellenica designed to prompt foreign intervention, Loeillot's series served to acknowledge that intervention by Greece's allies in the Battle of Navarino, a landmark victory for British and French Philhellenes.[108]

In *Jeune grecque* the swooning woman's pose, clothing, and especially the distinctive configuration of her lightly draped thighs owe a formal debt to Delacroix's allegorical figure in *Greece on the Ruins of Missolonghi*, shown the previous year. The print is not high art but popular art, and as such its narrative is formulaic: we see abduction, imminent shackling and transporting to a slave market interrupted by the suggestion of more efficient western troops who are about to rescue her; the three soldiers who emerge from behind a boulder connote the presence of many others. As popular Philhellenica, the representation of this scene is both anecdotal and self-consciously, crudely political.

Like Victor Hugo, Alphonse de Lamartine uses the notion of a Greek virgin, presumably abducted, as a personification of her oppressed people. Incredibly, he claims to have seen her on board a pirate ship, which passes by his own vessel, and that from some distance he can surmise her age (fifteen or sixteen), her emotional state, and her heavenly good looks! She is crying as an old woman combs her long hair. And she is "looking like a celestial figure amongst infernal monsters" (*PHL* 53). Lamartine is writing after the August 1832 battle at Navarino and opines that the Greek government has responded poorly to the cry of help from its people, a cry that European countries have heeded. The pirates themselves are Greek, suggesting that Greece after the official war is "prey to internal ravage" (*PHL* 51). Lamartine uses the trope of the Greek virgin as support for his French nationalistic chauvinism.

Mohja Kahf gives additional levels of interpretation to the motif of the western rescue of a pure harem woman from an oriental despot. She claims that there are Oedipal implications to "a son-like figure contesting the authority of the father-like despot by stealing his women." She also sees it as characterizing one of the rationalizations for Napoleon's Egyptian Campaign. And she identifies it as a construction of Woman that can be readily adapted into the western domestic ideal, as the rescued woman could then give herself freely in gratitude and admire her savior's bravery and generosity.[109]

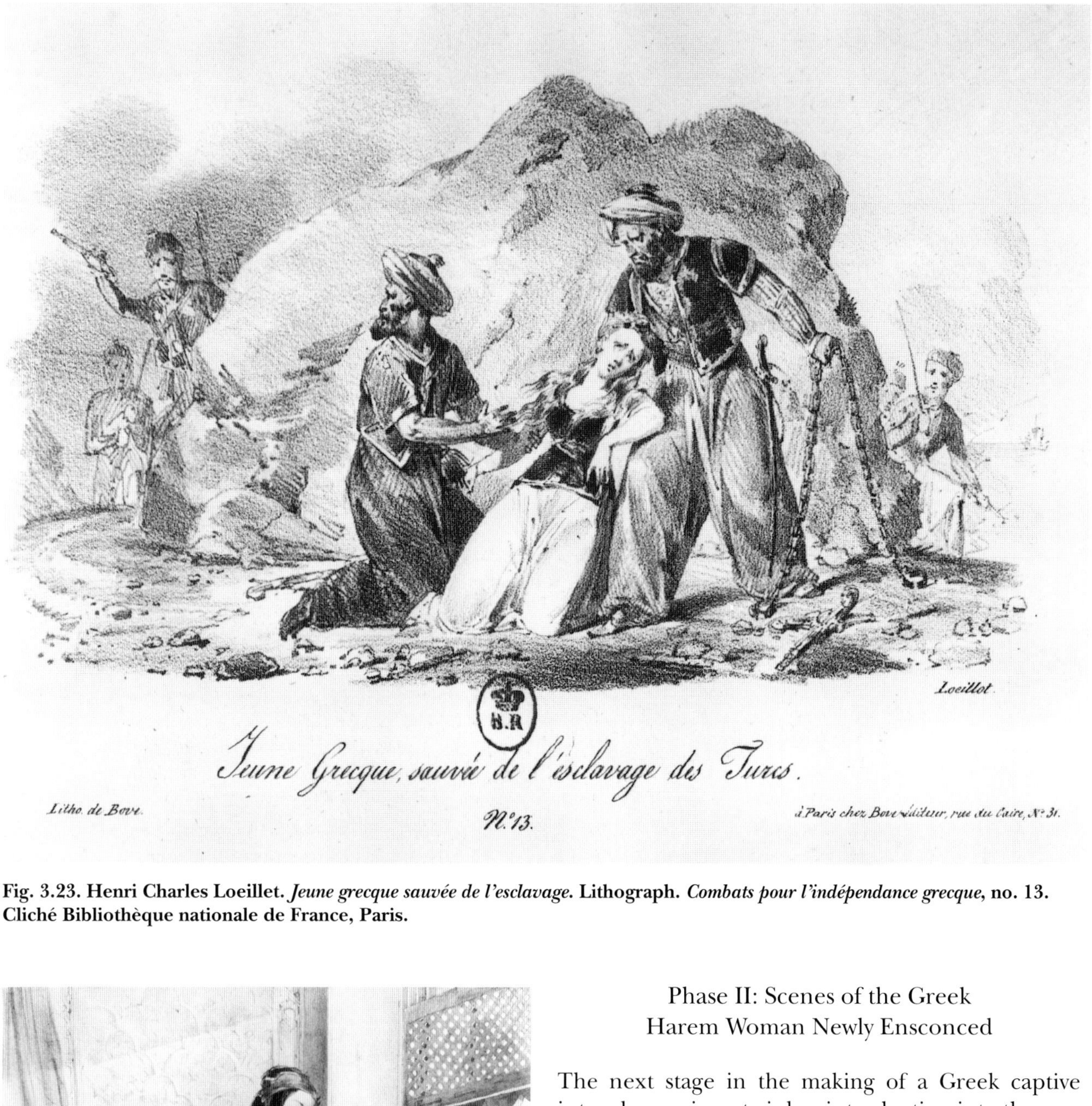

Fig. 3.23. Henri Charles Loeillet. ***Jeune grecque sauvée de l'esclavage.*** **Lithograph.** ***Combats pour l'indépendance grecque,*** **no. 13. Cliché Bibliothèque nationale de France, Paris.**

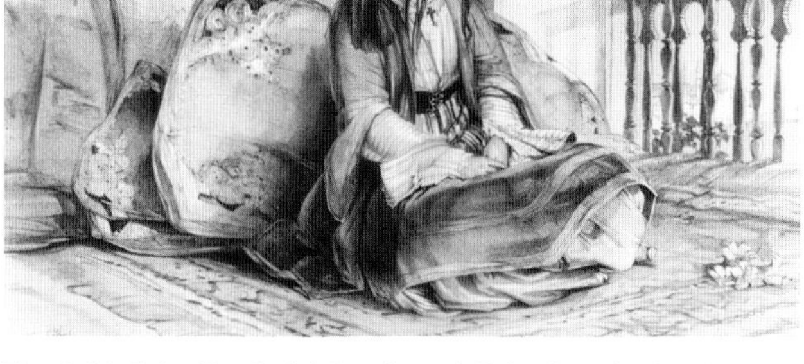

Fig. 3.24. John Frederick Lewis and Coke Smyth. ***Greek Girl/Captive Greek Girl.*** **1837. Lithograph.** ***Lewis's Illustrations of Constantinople,*** **1838. Arts Library, UCLA.**

Phase II: Scenes of the Greek Harem Woman Newly Ensconced

The next stage in the making of a Greek captive into a harem inmate is her introduction into the new eastern environment. Such scenes required that the conflict between the Greek and the Turkish (or the Christian and the Muslim) elements be made explicit. A basic question we can ask of such pictures is whether they support or criticize the Greek woman's new life and how such a viewpoint might be communicated in art. To make political commentary in visual terms, artists utilize both passivity and defiance of the female.

(Captive) Greek Girl (Fig. 3.24) is an illustration of the harem found in the 1838 Coke Smyth-John Lewis *Illustrations of Constantinople* (plate 16).[110] A well-dressed young woman is seated on a carpet

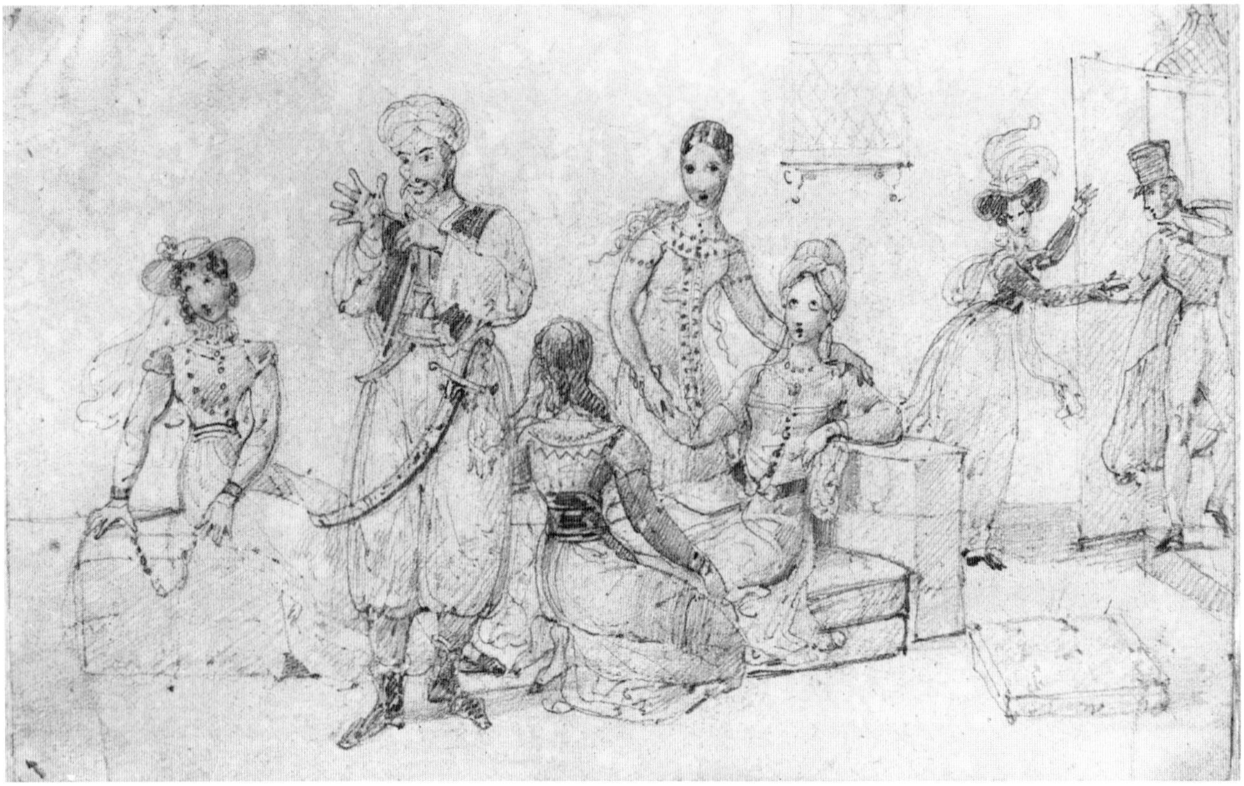

Fig. 3.25. Victor Adam. *Scène Orientale*. Pencil. Musée Grobet-Labadié, Marseille.

and surrounded by pillows. The artistic choice to present one figure underscores her loneliness and melancholy. Her youth is emphasized by the term "girl" in the title, her body proportions, and her long, loose hair. Featured is a group of lilies broken from their stalks, just as this virginal girl has been taken from her native land.[111] The image suggests loss of homeland and family and imminent loss of virginity, for which the elegant material surroundings seem to offer no consolation. And its suggestion of coercion and innocence produces a pained quality.[112] *Greek Girl* implicitly indicts Islam for subjecting children to harem slavery, victimizing them by inducting them too soon into the inherently degraded world of the harem. In Alloula's words, Islam is perceived as demonstrating "a monstrous barbarism that does not even spare childhood."[113] The picture can be considered a piece of nostalgic Philhellenica, as it was done when the Greek cause was *passé*.

Another theme in pictures of women newly arrived in the harem is chivalrous western men providing assistance to helpless female victims as in the pencil sketch, *Scène orientale* (Fig. 3.25) by Victor Adam.[114] The scene takes place in a harem, indicated by the latticework window and the central grouping of three harem women, one of whom reclines on a sofa. Attired in a very different mode of dress are two western women. One sits on a trunk on the left, her wrists shackled, her eyes rolled upward in distress. Next to her stands a turbaned pasha, wearing a long, provocatively placed *yataghan* (sword), alluding both to his cruelty and lust. We know he is greedy, as he smiles and counts out on his fingers the number of slaves he now possesses. He is oblivious to the fact that a Frenchman, the *deus ex machina*, has crossed the harem threshold and is rescuing the other western maiden in distress. There is no explicit reference to the Greek War in this undated sketch. The woman's dress at the left and the clothing trunk beneath her suggest she had been traveling. This sketch may date to the 1820s, as the anti-Muslim hysteria brought on by the war rekindled old fears about Muslim savagery in stealing "our" women (European or Greek); Barbary pirates had kidnapped seafarers in the Maghreb especially before 1815, when British naval supremacy was established.[115] In the sketch these fears are assuaged by the chivalrous intruder who saves the day.

Into this category of harem pictures falls the subject of the harem inmate as a cunning and courageous protector of her own honor as in *L'Odalisque Vertueuse* by B. R. Julien[116] (Fig. 3.26) of 1833, part of a collection of lithographs by A. E. Fragonard[117] entitled

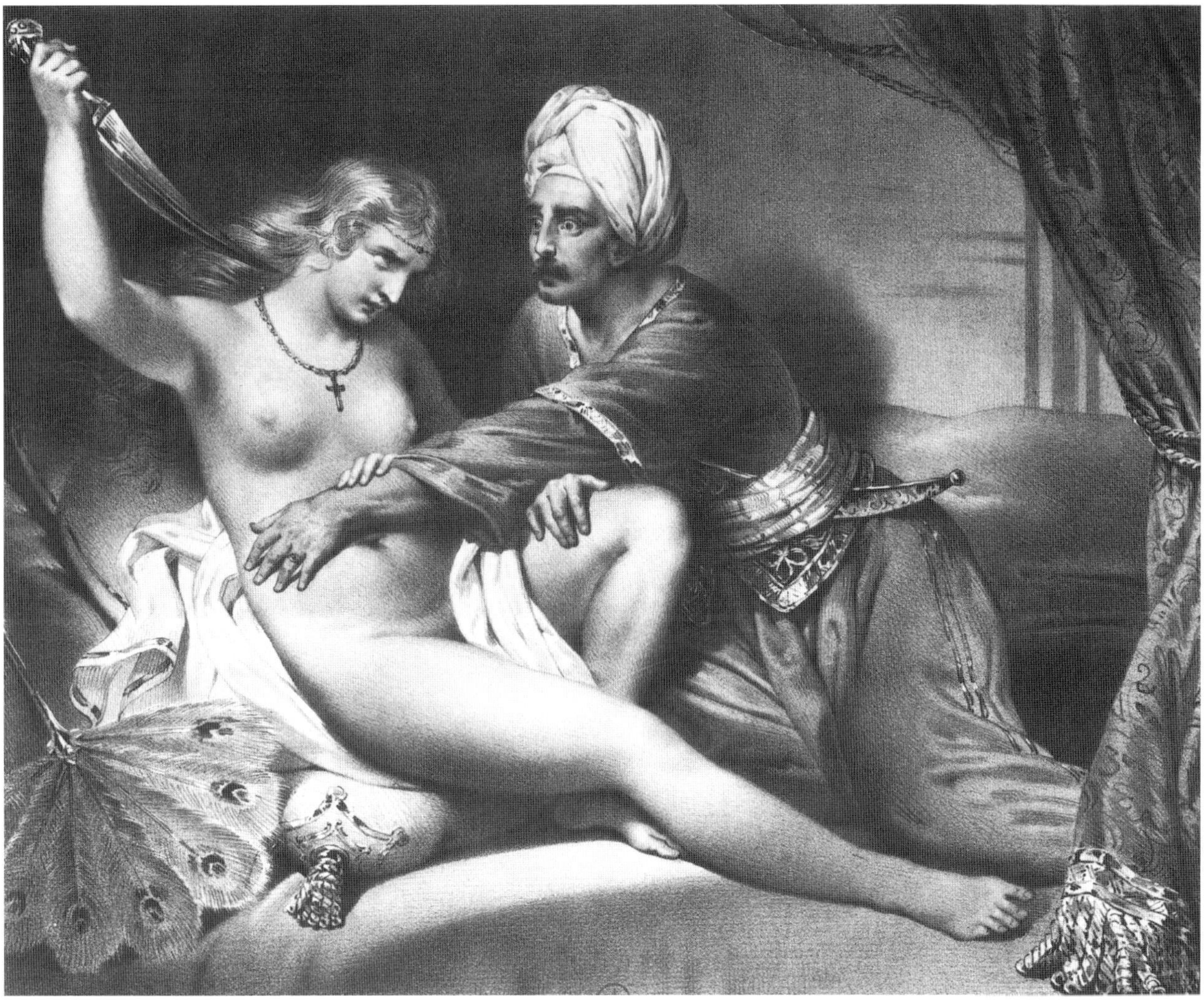

Fig. 3.26. B. R. Julien after Alexandre Evariste Fragonard. *L'Odalisque vertueuse.* 1833. Lithograph. *Moeurs d'un sérail.* Cliché Bibliothèque nationale de France, Paris.

Moeurs d'un sérail. Fragonard has drawn a Christian cross around her neck; this detail and her blond hair[118] clearly indicate a foreign status. One possible identity for the couple in this image is Montesquieu's Usbek and his new wife, Roxana. Usbek writes to Roxana how charming she was as a virginal bride who protected her virginity for two months. Her "last resource" was when she "took a dagger and threatened to destroy the husband who loved" her (*PL* 76). The crucifix around her neck, the sign of her Christianity, is appropriate, given the misconception that Roxana was French.[119] But another possible referent for the image is the Greek War of Independence, even though the conflict had been settled for at least a year with a series of events of 1832. Though Fragonard was interested in antiquity, her profile suggests a heroic Hellenism that relates more to contemporary than ancient Philhellenica. This image is noteworthy for the striking contrast between the woman's fiercely aggressive resistance to the man's advances and her nearly nude body sprawled out in full display. Though Fragonard displays the body across the picture plane, he reverses the traditional power dynamic of gender in French harem pictures. The odalisque has drawn the (symbolic) sword from her master's sheath, making the point that his violent means are his own undoing. The combination of the woman's beauty and effective vengeance constitutes a kind of feminist burlesque. The picture spoofs innumerable scenes of passive harem women on display for their pashas (and their viewers). The pasha is turbaned and mustachioed as always, but here he is wide-eyed with fear and astonishment at the new twist to his amorous advances.

Phase III: Greek Women Absorbed into the Harem and its Pictorial Traditions

The final stage in the life of the Greek slave turned haremite represented by French and British artists is her full integration into the harem. The images in this category suggest no conflict over the induction of Greek women into the harem and instead accept the status quo.[120] In these pictures artists draw upon some of those same conventions used to represent harem inmates of nonspecific ethnicity. Except for the image's title no ethnic distinction is made, and thus the images are relatively depoliticized. Or so it seems at first glance.

The liberation of Greek women from the harem was part of the terms imposed by the allies following the battle of Navarino in October 1827. Despite this victory for Christian Philhellenes, efforts to liberate Greek harem women were obstructed; many had converted to Islam and married Muslims, French consuls reported. And what Philhellenes may have called their Turkish "imprisonment" could also mean freedom from poverty.[121] In effect, a representation of a harem woman comfortably ensconced could be read as a financial success story.

In Achille Devéria's lithograph *Femme grecque* (Fig. 3.27) a fully clothed figure stands in a pose which is a variation on the traditional gesture of both female modesty and display—one hand raised over her breast, the other moving toward the groin. Yet relatively speaking the issues here are less overtly erotic or political. Instead the subject is the charming costume of the exotic woman, the genre of fashion *rapportage* dating from the rococo period. Compare Vanmour's *Dame grecque dans son appartement,* (Fig. 3.28) an image of a mature Greek women who is comfortably adjusted to her foreign but luxurious environment. The only indication of her alien origins is the motif of again a flower broken from its stalk on the background table. Devéria's interest in this theme probably appeared at a time when the Greek cause was won. The Greek woman is merely one more foreigner living in the harem.

High politics is refused and eroticism is reinserted in Régnier's 1843 *La jeune grecque* (Fig. 3.29) done after a work attributed to one of the few known women painters of the harem, Héloïse Suzanne Leloir (1820–73), daughter of Alexandre Marie Colin, who was a friend of Delacroix. This is a scene of the ostensible innocence of childhood, as the girl feeds a pet gazelle. The fact that she is part of a harem is suggested in the costume, the distant palm trees, the exotic animal—and the sleeve that has slipped off her small bared shoulder. The charm of this picture, like French rococo pictures of children, lies in her naivete, though her placement in a harem guarantees that her sexual awakening is not far off. There is no particular tragedy here over the loss of country at the hands of the cruel Turks. Instead the print is about the self-absorption of a child who plays at nurturing. This and her tender age evoke a poignant awareness of imminent change, and her own future role as "pet" to an unknown pasha.

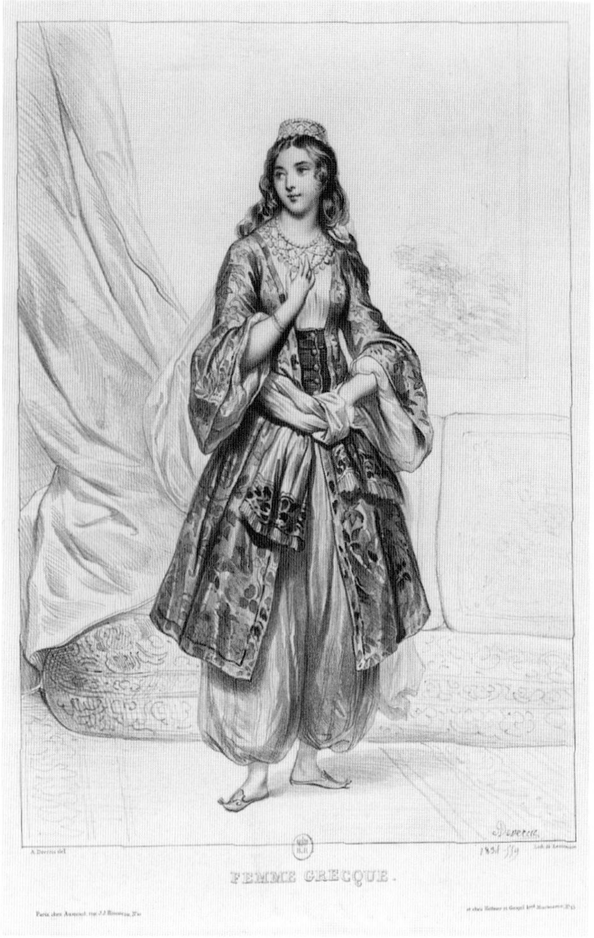

Fig. 3.27. Achille Devéria. *Femme grecque.* 1834. Lithograph. Cliché Bibliothèque nationale de France, Paris. Farwell, *FPLI,* v. 9, 5E3 B82979.

The love of a Greek favorite slave for her master triumphs over political loyalty in Byron's *Sardanapalus.* Despite her proud heritage, Myrrha professes her love for her master Sardanapalus in act 1 as a foreshadowing of her willingness to join the Assyrian king on his funeral pyre at the end of the play.

> —King, I am your subject
> Master, I am your slave! Man, I have loved you—

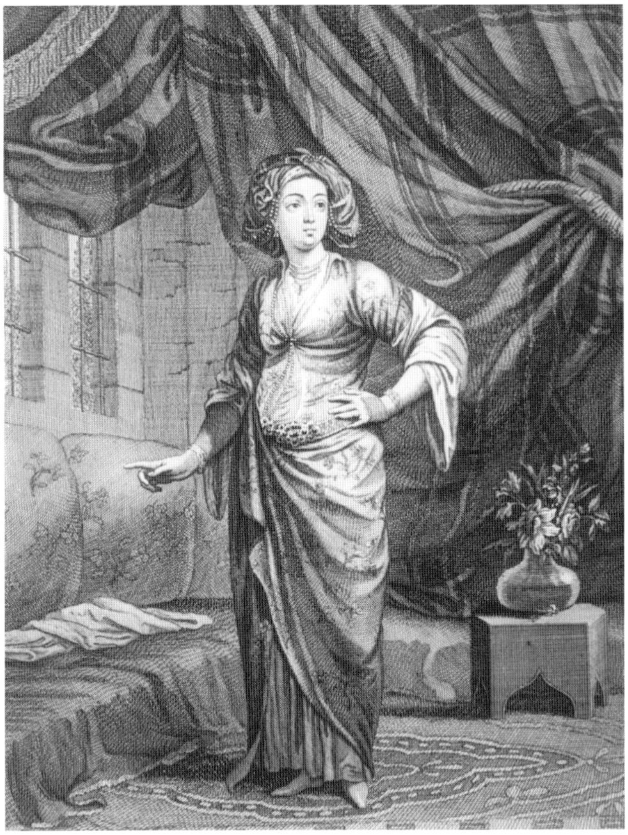

Fig. 3.28. After Vanmour. *Dame grecque dans son appartement.* Ca. 1715. Engraving. *Recueil de cent estampes,* plate 68. Department of Special Collections, Charles E. Young Library, UCLA.

> Loved you, I know not by what fatal weakness,
> Although a Greek, and born a foe to monarchs—
> A slave and hating fetters—An Ionian,
> And, therefore, when I love a stranger more
> Degraded by that passion than by chains!
> Still I have loved you.
>
> (*WB* 200)

Myrrha the slave struggles with her national/racial identity. She is pained when others speak of Greece, yet she announces "I have no country." She believes that as a slave her heaviest chain is to love a man she cannot respect (*WB* 202). She is a Greek slave assimilated, but for Byron the consummate Philhellene the very concept spells her doom.

Grévedon's 1825 lithograph *Odalisque* (Fig. 3.30) is also a serious work. This is an heroic harem woman, indicated by her stance and posture. She can be read as Greek. Her upward glance suggests the high spiritual ideals Philhellenes associated with Greece. She is upright, not lounging; her placement is outdoors, not in a secreted harem. Besides the title, only her partially unbuttoned garment reminds the viewer of her indoor function, as sexual mate to an absent pasha. At the same time her *décolletage* indicates the strength of her inner courage, as in Delacroix's strong female heroines, while her precise delineation and the turban motif recall Ingres's *Grande Odalisque.* The high bridge of her nose is a subtle reference to fourth-century Greek Aphrodites: in his taxonomy of oriental women, Nerval describes "the pure profile which the sculptors of antiquity have made familiar to us"[122] as an indicator of the Greek woman, the fourth "type" to reside within "Byzantine" borders. Like many nineteenth-century artists and writers, Grévedon and Nerval link contemporary Greeks with ancient and do their stereotyping principally through physiognomy and costume.

In strong contrast to Byron's and Grévedon's imagery but similar in spirit to the Régnier print done after Leloir, *The Ionian Captive* (Fig. 3.31) is charmingly picturesque. The 1846 engraving was done by Charles Fox after Henry William Pickersgill's *A Greek Girl* shown at the 1829 Royal Academy (whereabouts unknown). This is far from an impassioned cry for liberation of the Greek slave. Instead the elegance of her jewels, clothing, and perfumes emphasize her life of luxury. The use of the open window convention acts as a foil to her confinement within a spatial corner, but her mundane activity, braiding her hair, recalls so many rococo images of the fair woman preparing her *toilette.*

A volume of poetry gives a very different gloss to this image done after Henry Pickersgill. Titled *Tales of the Harem,* it was published by his wife (known to us only as Mrs. Pickersgill) two years before his picture's showing at the R.A. As in *Ionian Captive,* Mrs. Pickersgill describes a harem girl braiding her hair and focuses on flowers in the first part of her poem:

> And let those bright flowers
> When spangled with dew
> Which hang from our bowers
> Of roseate hue.
> With the champaca sweet,
> To braid our dark hair;
> While their perfumes all meet,
> And are blended there.[123]

And at certain points in her poem there is a resonance with the picture after Pickersgill. She claims that some harem inmates captured as young girls had little recollection or regret about their previous life of freedom:

> Some whom stern War had captives made.
> And to those domes so young were brought,

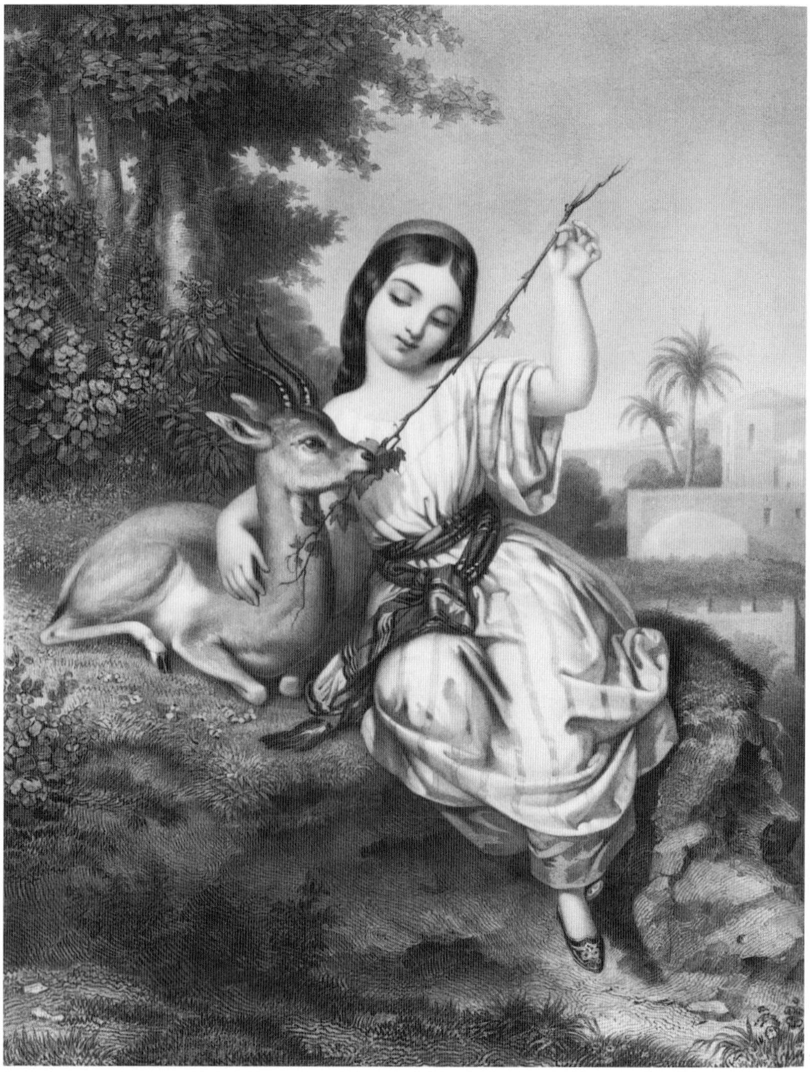

Fig. 3.29. Régnier after Héloïse Leloir (*née* Bouteiller). *La jeune grecque*. 1843. Cliché Bibliothèque nationale de France, Paris. Farwell, *FPLI*, v. 9, 5E4 B81848.

That they amidst their fetters played,
Nor of their gilded cages thought;
Nor dreamed of other years, when free,
Unfettered as the Spring's light gales,
When wandering thru their native vales,
Their sweetest song was Liberty.

(*TH* 9)

Nonetheless, the main thrust of her *Tales of the Harem* is Philhellenic. She compares the melancholy mood of the harem in Constantinople to the mirthful one that reigned before the Turk fought "the giaour." She writes that the elderly and women, even holy ones, are killed or dragged off, recalling the discourses surrounding the reception of Delacroix's *Massacres de Scio*:

And maidens, even from the shrine,
Be borne away, and never more
View the dear plains they loved before.

(*TH* 7)

Mrs. Pickersgill combines her Philhellenism with a kind of early feminism both in her critique of romantic love, "a sorcerer's spell" (*TH* 9), which harem women must overcome to achieve a political consciousness, and in her representation of Greek women not as victims but as active political participants in the resistance against the Turks. At one point, four harem women tell tales to their harem sisters as evening diversion. A captive Greek inmate is described as a "meek girl" who finally vents her sorrow through "her pensive lute." We learn that her parents

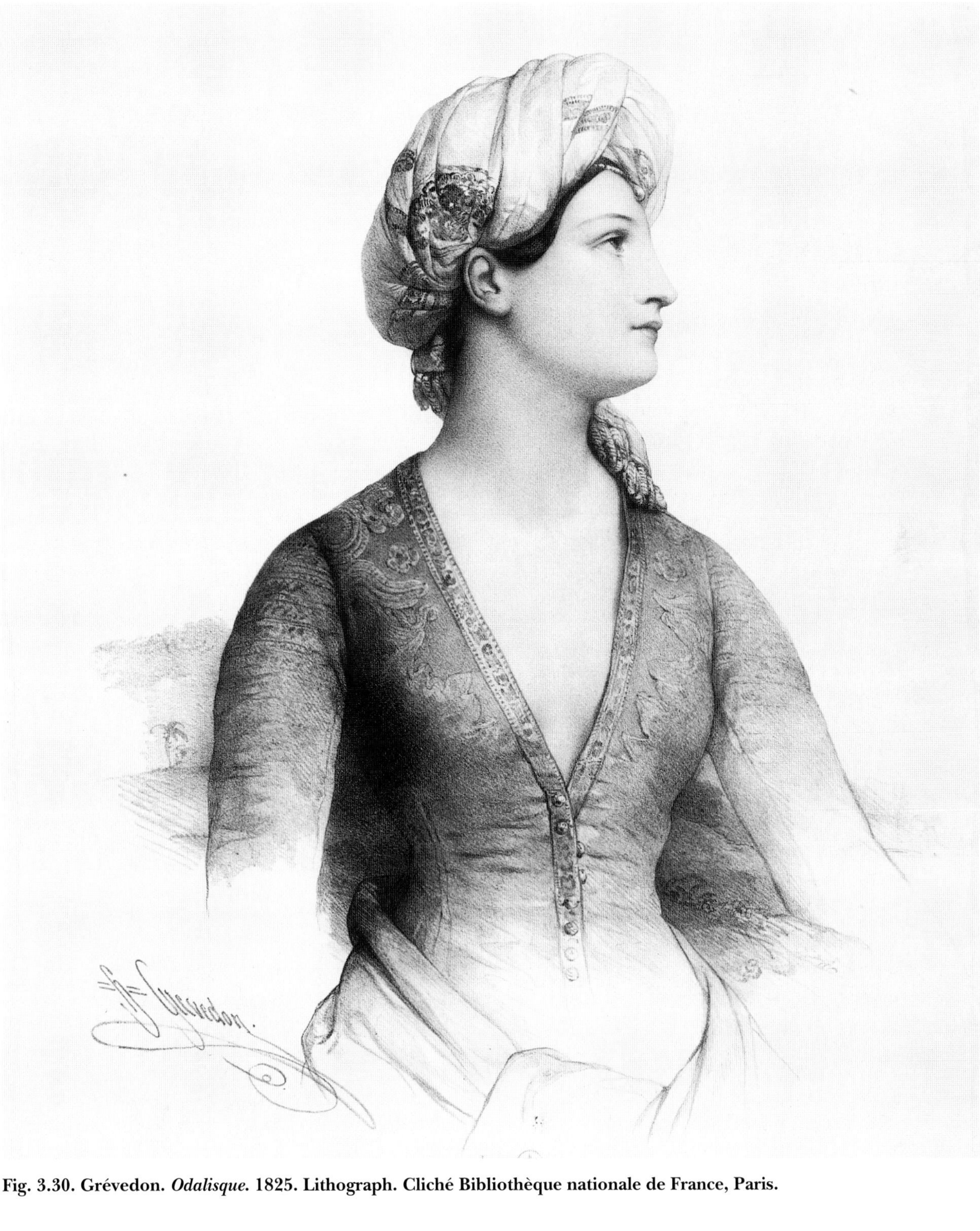

Fig. 3.30. Grévedon. *Odalisque.* 1825. Lithograph. Cliché Bibliothèque nationale de France, Paris.

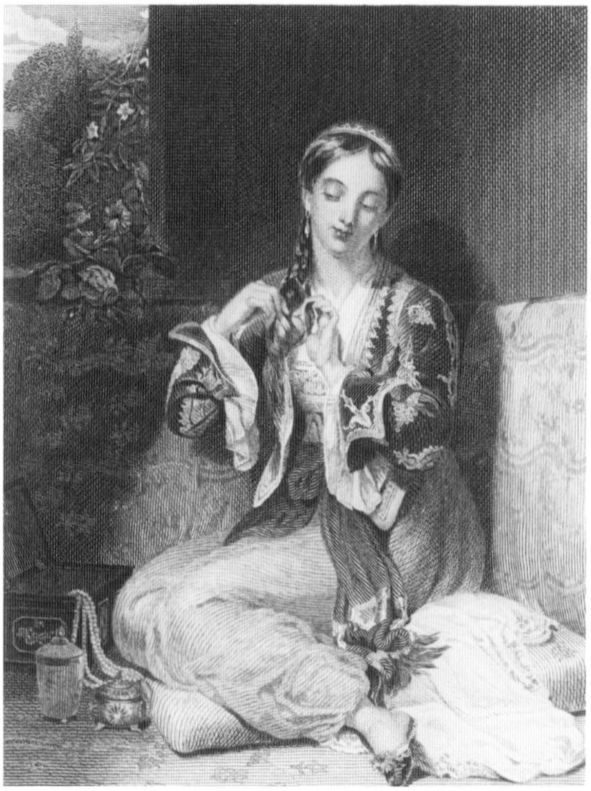

Fig. 3.31. Charles Fox after Henry William Pickersgill. *Ionian Captive.* 1846. Engraving. Witt Library, Courtauld Institute, London.

and lover were killed and that she will never return home. She is forever a captive in the harem.

> While Fancy, in the hovering gloom,
> Now sees again her hapless doom—
> Her lover—parents—kindred slain—
> While she must wear the captive's chain,
> And never—never hope to see
> Her own loved native mountains free.
>
> (*TH* 133)

For the first time in the book Mrs. Pickersgill gives a voice to a Greek woman, captured in war, who recites "The Hetaeria: The Tale of the Greek Slave." (She identifies "Hetaeria" as the underground political society to which Greek women actually belonged, sometimes even serving as leaders.) Through the Greek captive's story within a story, Mrs. Pickersgill heroizes the lives of two cave-dwelling Greek women whom she imagines fought in the resistance. One is "a care-worn matron" (*TH* 138) who had known a free Greece but now dreams of "fierce revenge" (*TH* 141). The other heroine is a "youthful warrior maid" (*TH* 145), barely twenty years old who sings the "Song to Greece" alongside her male comrades, exhorting that nation to "Break—break your chains!—no more be slaves!" (*TH* 147). The young leader's commitment is unswerving: she is courageous and will fight the fiercest battle to the death. At the same time the author seems bent on maintaining the heroine's femininity[124]:

> And yet that slender, fragile form,
> More like a weak, exotic flower,
> Unused to bear the wintry storm,
> Seems fitter for a gentler bower.
>
> (*TH* 149)

In the climax to the tale is the final "vow of the Hetaeria": a promise to end the Muslim foe as long as one Greek remains enslaved and until a new liberated Greece emerges.

Mrs. Pickergill's long poem provides points of comparison and contrast for her husband's later image, as it exists in print form. This case study provides another example of the complex relationship of text and image on the provocative subject of harem slavery as viewed by the British and French especially prevalent in the first half of the century. Moreover, Mrs. Pickersgill spurs a nineteenth-century feminist view of the harem in which the inhabitants are unfree and prevented by love's delusion from achieving a consciousness of their oppression.

One more image of a Greek woman absorbed into a new life as a slave is a drawing done by R. J. Lane of a slave Edward William Lane owned and would finally marry. *Nefeeseh* (Fig. 3.32) is an image whose context is unknown. It does not appear in Lane's *Manners and Customs.* Most likely it was drawn for his personal use. The very young woman depicted had been purchased by the artist Robert Hay and his wife, who was also of Greek ancestry, and given to Lane as a gift when he was in Egypt. Lane did not make Nefeeseh part of a harem, even though she had been his slave. Nonetheless it is interesting that its pictorial devices suggest a harem setting: a woman elaborately dressed presented in profile and seated on a low couch. In the recent biography devoted to Lane, some of his difficulty in owning a slave is spelled out. In 1832 he refuses the suggestion that he marry her, but he also refuses to give her up. About his relationship with her he feels "'topsy turvy and inside out.'"[125] He and his mother set about to "educate" Nefeeseh. She learns reading, writing, and needlework. In July 1840 he finally marries her.

In his *Manners and Customs of the Modern Egyptians,* Lane reports on the historical phenomenon of Greek women rejecting western attempts to liberate them

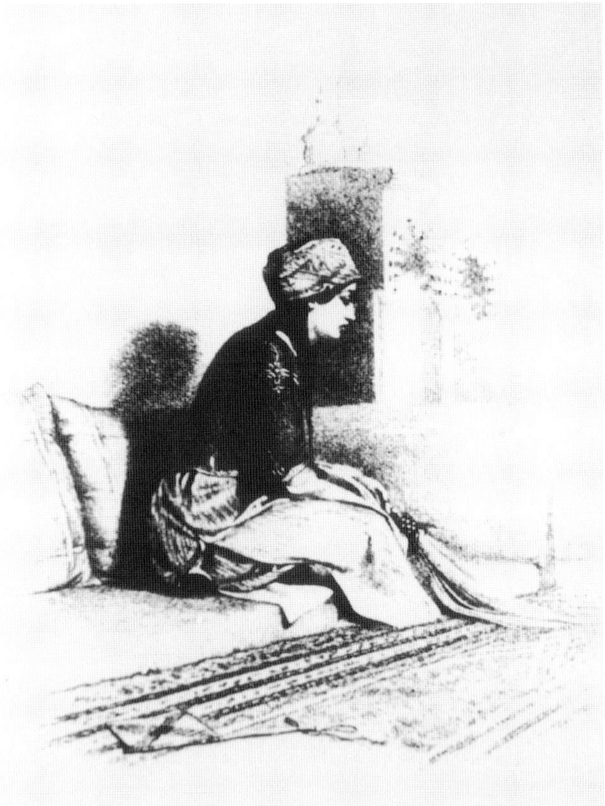

Fig. 3.32. R. J. Lane. *Nefeeseh*. N.d. By permission of Longman, London.

after the war. Lane is pessimistic about their absorption, claiming that only a few Greek women could ever be happy in a foreign home (*ME* 1:234–35). One can only wonder whether Nefeeseh, "liberated" by Lane, was one of those exceptional women who was happy. As the barely literate slave-wife to one of the century's most erudite and prolific Orientalists, her own story was never written.

Freedom, Enslavement, and Domesticity: The Open Window and the Closed Harem

The window (or door) often functioned symbolically in harem representation. As locus for the transition between the outside world and the harem women's life indoors, it provided the opportunity to treat the themes of confinement and freedom metaphorically. Used in reference to female inhabitants, an open door or window in the harem can prompt a reading of the more general theme of domestic confinement.

The open window derives from the convention in baroque and rococo portraiture in both France and England, as in Jean Baptiste Vanmour's *Lady Mary Wortley Montagu and Her Son* (Fig. 3.33), in which the open vista allowed for a pastoral view while also displaying a well-appointed interior, attesting to the sitter's wealth and taste. In her "Turkish Embassy Letters" Lady Mary herself mentioned the garden outside the harem windows, a theme to be explored in a subsequent chapter. Even before it was associated with harem iconography, the open window in a portrait suggested pride in ownership by revealing both interior and exterior commodities. Similarly, the harem window—open or closed—becomes a vehicle to underscore the woman's sexual availability or confinement.

For centuries harem confinement was thought to lead to secret liaisons. In 1733 Aaron Hill writes that the harem women's confinement heightens their sexual desire and makes them "an easy conquest to the first addresses of an advent'rous lover."[126] The shuttered or *moucharabic* window[127] becomes fetishized. And in French and British stories it is often a foreigner who crosses the window to reach his illicit beloved.[128]

Shuttered windows in the East became highly charged symbols in the West. "A Lady" writing in *Chambers's Edinburgh Journal* in 1846 acknowledges the window covers' reputation and implies that suspicious activity takes place behind them when she writes "the windows were all hermetically closed by the fatal screen of which we had heard so much."[129] They are "fatal screens" because they hide dangerous transactions such as trading and abusing slaves. That we have "heard so much" about them suggests the long tradition of their associations. The feminist journal *Englishwoman's Review* in 1878 reveals a suspicion in claiming that despite the Qur'anic injunction against selling Muslims, transgressions occur: "'behind the grated windows of a closed Turkish house, it is easy to be false to such a trust'."[130]

Window shutters not only protect from the scrutiny of the law, they also act like prison bars to keep the harem inmates confined. Florence Nightingale's comments demonstrate this: "The very windows into the garden were wood-worked, so that you could not see out. The cold, the melancholy of that place! I felt inclined to cry" (*LE* 208). A prospective Muslim bride might use the reinforced window to scout out a handsome husband, claims an 1879 writer: "The young lady may catch a glimpse of her future husband from behind the lattice of her prison-like house."[131] The author "Melek-Hanum" claims that harem women in her mother's circle admired a young Frenchman passing by in the street "through the wooden grating of their *djumbaa*,"[132] which acts to restrain their desire. In this case, the author's mother

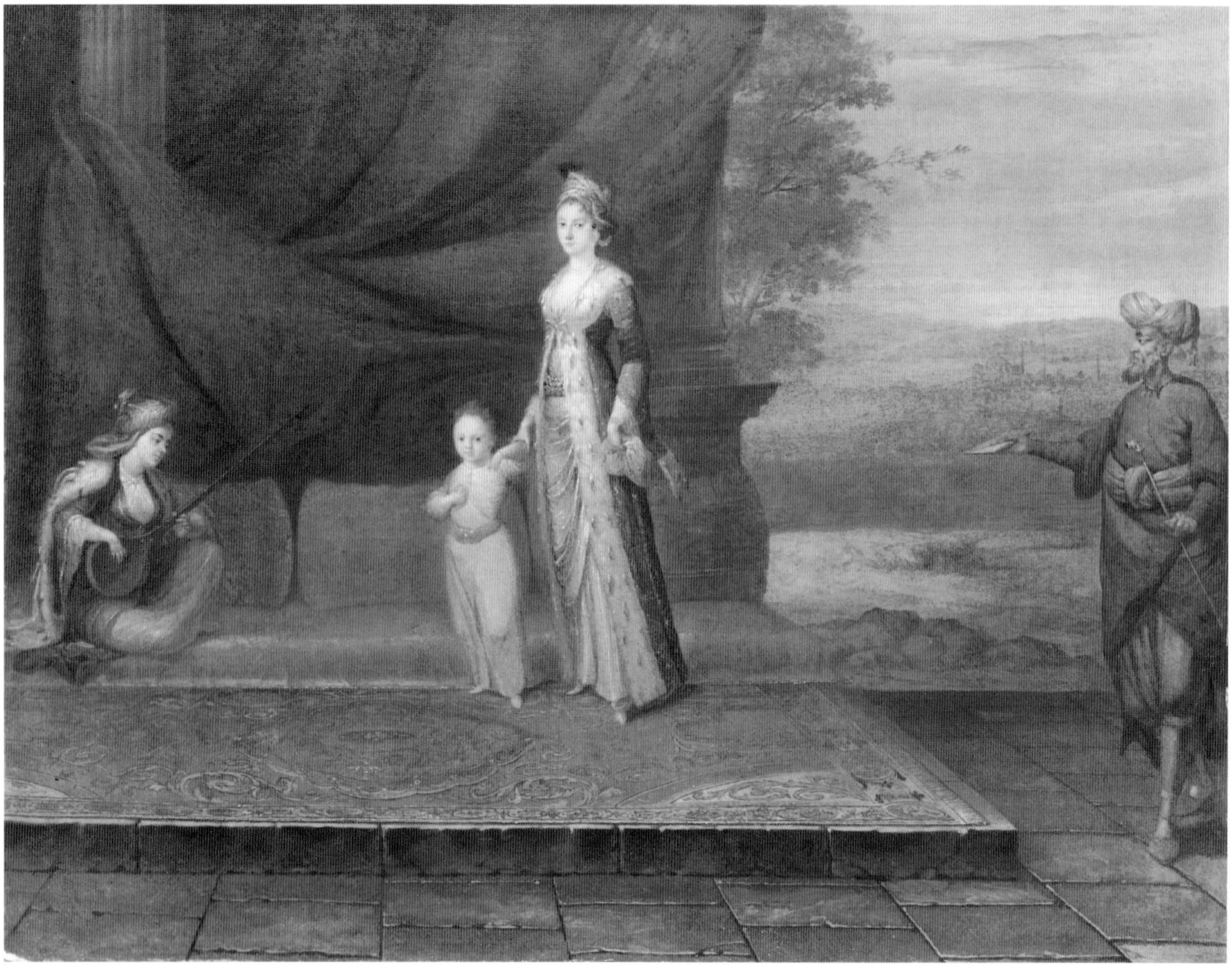

Fig. 3.33. Jean Baptiste Vanmour. *Lady Mary Wortley Montagu and Her Son*. Ca. 1718. By courtesy of the National Portrait Gallery, London.

would marry the Frenchman, who bravely took the initiative to court her.

A newly purchased slave sits on a windowsill watching soldiers on the street "through the lattice-work of the moucharaby" in de Nerval's *Voyage to the Orient* (*VO* 49). The protagonist leads Zetnaybia back to the divan "and indicated that it was more suitable for her to remain there rather than at the window" (*VO* 50). In doing so the male character asserts his ownership of her and interrupts her scopic pleasure, more typically his prerogative, in anticipation of her unhappiness at her inferior status—a theme that forms the central conflict of the story.

As for visual imagery, François Boucher used heavily secured windows to indicate the confinement of harem women in his illustrations to *Moeurs et usages des turcs* (1746). In *Sultana Reading in the Harem* (Fig. 3.34) he combines a baroque open door, through which black eunuch slaves are visible, with a grated window placed behind the sultana's head, referring to her confinement. In three more engravings from the same volume Boucher repeats the theme of a harem woman near a window.

In some cases an open window seems to symbolize a free harem woman, whether free in actuality or in reverie. Baron Dominique Vivant Denon's 1803 engraving, *Egyptian Ladies* (see Fig. 2.1), reputedly an image of Denon's confidante who was having an extramarital affair,[133] is clearly a precedent for an undated engraving by "Stop" [pseudonym of L. P. G. B. Morel-Retz] *Une femme dans son harem* (Fig. 3.35) in which a portly woman presented in profile looks out of her window, seeming to contemplate past the harem's confinement. An escape from the harem is in process in Achille Devéria's[134] *Smirne* (Fig. 3.36), a French lithograph published in 1838, in which a woman steals away from a foreboding fortress at night, assisted by an attentive lover in

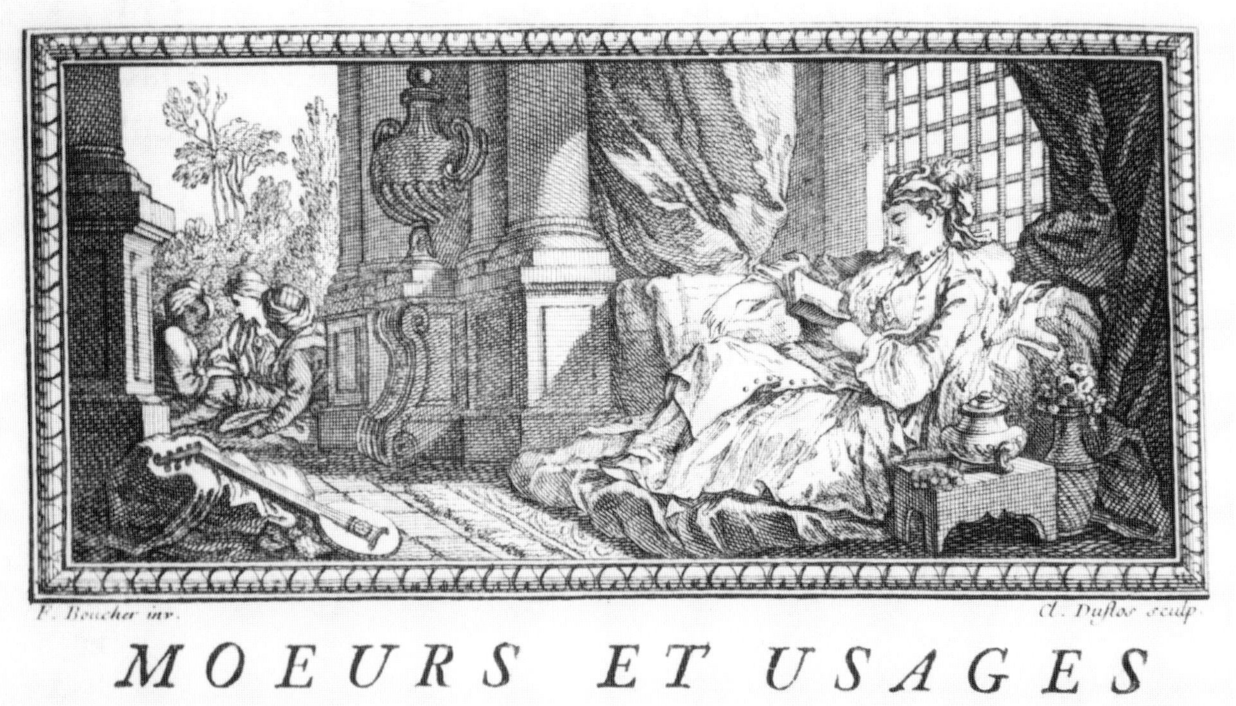

Fig. 3.34. François Boucher. *Sultana Reading in the Harem.* 1746. Engraving. *Moeurs et usages des turcs.* Photo Adam Miller.

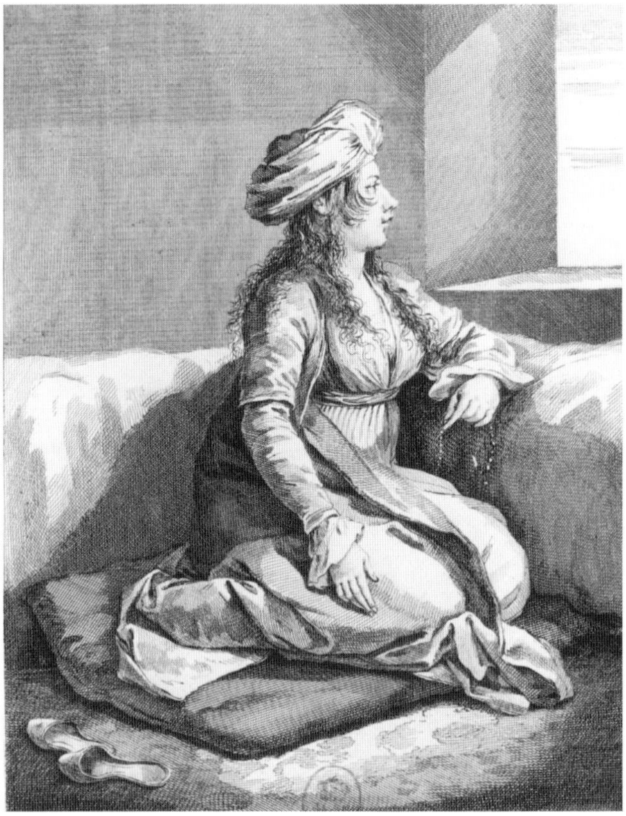

Fig. 3.35. L.P.G.B. Morel Retz ("Stop"). *Une Femme dans son harem.* Engraving. Cliché Bibliothèque nationale de France, Paris.

a boat.[135] Like Byron's *Bride of Abydos* (which also inspired Delacroix), this print is emotionally tense and suggests a short-lived liberation from the harem, one having a tragic ending.

The rococo open door rather than a barred window is used in the frontispiece to the 1838 *Illustrations of Constantinople* by Coke Smyth and John Lewis is a lithograph titled *Harem* (Fig. 3.37). Thus the work has connotations of relaxed elegance and de-emphasizes the women's confinement. The image is more about privileged luxury and less pathetic isolation or confinement than his *(Captive) Greek Girl* in which the open window gives way to a denser, impenetrable grillwork which resembles that in Boucher's *Marchand d'esclaves* (see Fig. 3.8).

In both his 1850 *Hhareem* (see Plate 1) and his 1869 *Intercepted Correspondence* (see Fig. 5.5) John Lewis gives much attention to the colored windows in the harem. In the later image he has repeated many of the elements from *Hhareem* including the poses of the several wives and the vignette of the seated bey,[136] who (like Lewis himself) has aged twenty years, seen in his grey beard and less attenuated pose. But in 1869 Lewis uses more dramatic lighting, which casts deeper shadows, as the French artist Delacroix had done in his second version of *Women of Algiers*, painted fifteen years after his first; Lewis could have seen Delacroix's

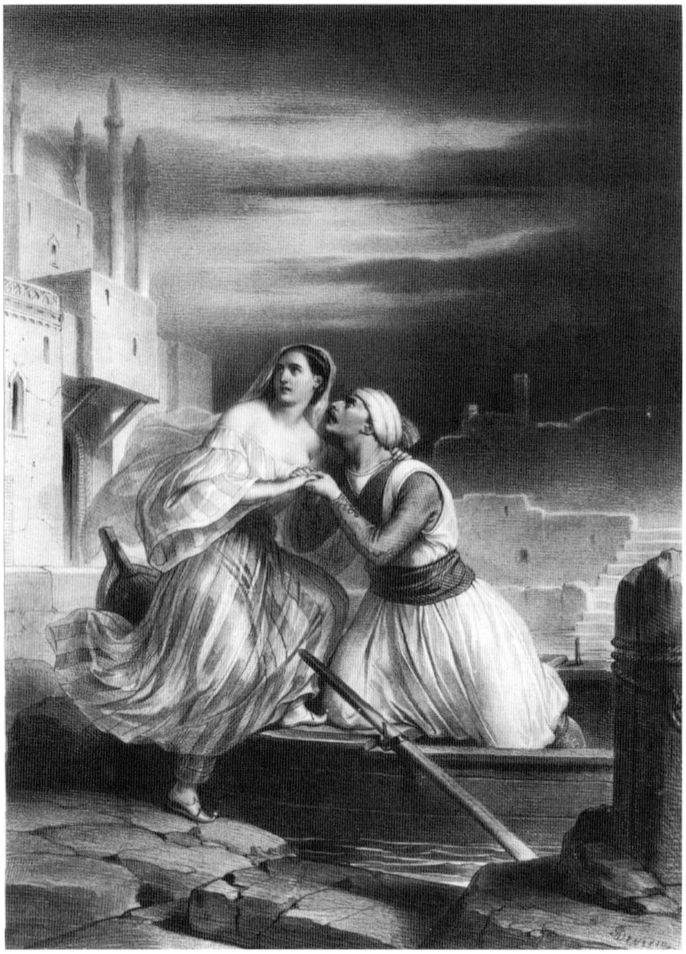

Fig. 3.36. Achille Devéria. *Smirne.* Lithograph. 1835. Cliché Bibliothèque nationale de France, Paris.

first version on his trip to Paris when it appeared in the 1834 Salon. Lewis's use of more pronounced shadow may also be a response to the *Athenaeum*'s suggestion in 1850 about the *Hhareem*: "More force of shadow here would give firmness and consistency to the whole mass" (*A* 80). In this room the colored windows are now more readable. And perhaps their emphasis is more appropriate to this work's theme, the exposure ("illumination"?) of a harem woman's intrigue.

In some pictures there is a division between harem women who are empowered to look out the window and those who are not. In Francis Wyburd's *Xarifa: The Zegri Lady Rose Not* (Fig. 3.38) the seated woman does not join her colleagues in excitedly observing a scene from the outside world, which appears too painful for her. Based on the 1821 poem by Lady Dacre Barbarina Brand,[137] this harem picture is reminiscent of early Victorian scenes by Richard Redgrave of the unhappy sempstress far from home, her eyes swollen from overwork, or relatedly the isolated governess who is left out of the family fun. The image laments the harem woman's loss of liberty, made poignant here by the limited participation possible for her co-inhabitants. Like the ideal of the mournful (but productive) Victorian woman, she sublimates her sadness into her embroidery. Though it recalls British paintings and types, the exotic nature of this scene is emphasized by the use of names beginning with the letters "X" and "Z."[138]

The *Critic* provides a direct comment on the harem as a luxurious prison while it reads the open window as symbolic in John Lewis's 1857 *Harem Life—Constantinople* (Fig. 3.39). The elliptical second sentence, however, leaves some ambiguity about whether the author believes liberty can be fairly traded off with luxury:

> An open window gives a vista of sunny gardens and suggestions of the free breath of heavens, from the full enjoyment of which the inmates of the harem are

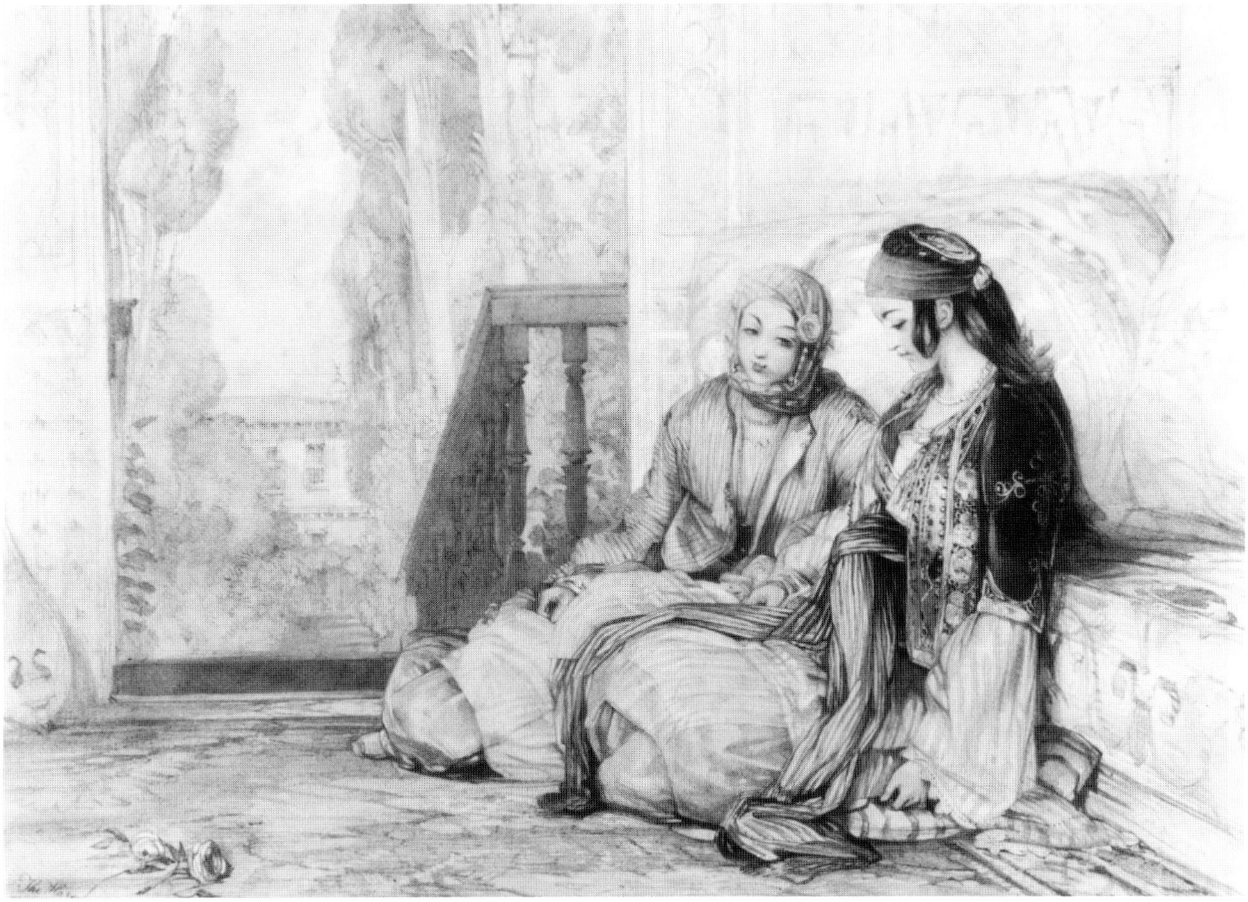

Fig. 3.37. John Frederick Lewis and Coke Smyth. *Harem/Hhareem.* 1837. Lithograph. *Lewis's Illustrations of Constantinople,* 1838. Arts Library, UCLA.

> perhaps debarred. Loss of liberty, however, made up for by the splendour of the interior life. (*C* 209)

Can loss of liberty be made up for by the splendor of the interior life? This typographical error means that the published comment leaves open whether Lewis's picture is thought to depict the harem as a legitimate form of social organization.

The conceptualizing of harem women as confined occurs in a mid-century milieu when one ideal for middle-class women was their confinement at home. Some pictures associate confinement with material luxury and social status, recalling one justification for feminine domesticity: that it is a privilege for the Victorian housewife to stay home and avoid outside paid labor. Logically the harem pictures that associate confinement with tragedy seem not to address the question of woman's domestic restriction *per se* but her loss of a more generalized personal liberty.

In April 1869, the Prince and Princess of Wales journeyed to Egypt and Constantinople for an inspection tour of the newly completed Suez Canal. The *Illustrated London News* carried the following description of some of the changes made in the Imperial Palace at Constantinople to prepare for its royal visitors which included the removing of latticework over the harem windows.

> The lattice-work which is placed on the windows—as usual in Turkish dwellings—to screen the fair inmates from the rude gaze of outsiders, was removed, and the windows all richly hung in magnificent silk hangings. (*ILN* 422)

The implication of this passage, that the harem itself was liberated in celebration of the British monarchs, is undoubtedly false. Still, a major London newspaper perpetuates stereotypes about "fair inmates" and correlates British sovereign presence in Turkey with a reformation of the harem. Such a passage helps shape readings of representations of the harem and reinforces the symbolic meanings of its

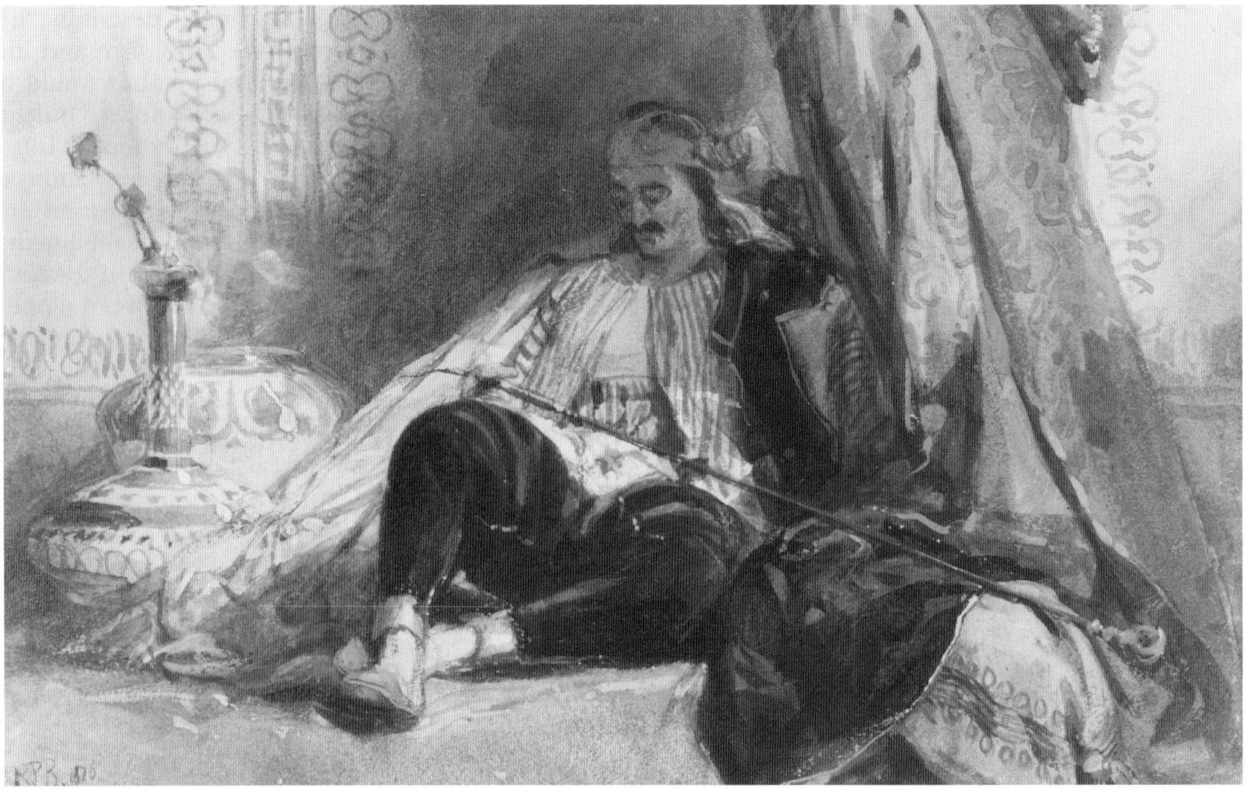

Fig. 4.2. Richard Parkes Bonington. *Turk Reposing.* 1826. Watercolor, Wallace Collection, London.

Men are associated more with the chibouk. Lane describes the *shibuk,* in Turkish *chibook,* as used by men in public. As long as four feet, they are often provided by coffeehouses,[8] though a man might carry his own mouthpiece. The chibouk serves as symbol of masculinity in several works, for example, Bonington's watercolor, *Turk reposing* (Fig. 4.2), in which the chibouk is prominently displayed over his lap. It may have induced his reverie in which he contemplates his absent love, symbolized by the red rose. In the image his loneliness is emphasized, lending a poignant mood.

In several harem pictures the chibouk functions as a scepter to the powerful male as in Decamps's c. 1830 *Seated Sultan with Harem Girl Reposing at His Feet* (Fig. 4.3). In Achille Devéria's *Turcs* (Fig. 4.4) the chibouk is one pleasure he holds in his left hand, the half-naked woman a pleasure in his right. A reclining odalisque offers wine to a huge master puffing on an extraordinarily long, arching chibouk, symbolizing his virility in a color engraving titled *An Egyptian Harem Entertained by the Almées or Dancing Girls* (see Plate 2) by John Chapman (clearly after Denon) which appeared in the *Encyclopaedia Londinensis* published in London in 1810. The phallic referent of the chibouk is made explicit in Rowlandson's bawdy popular print *Harem*

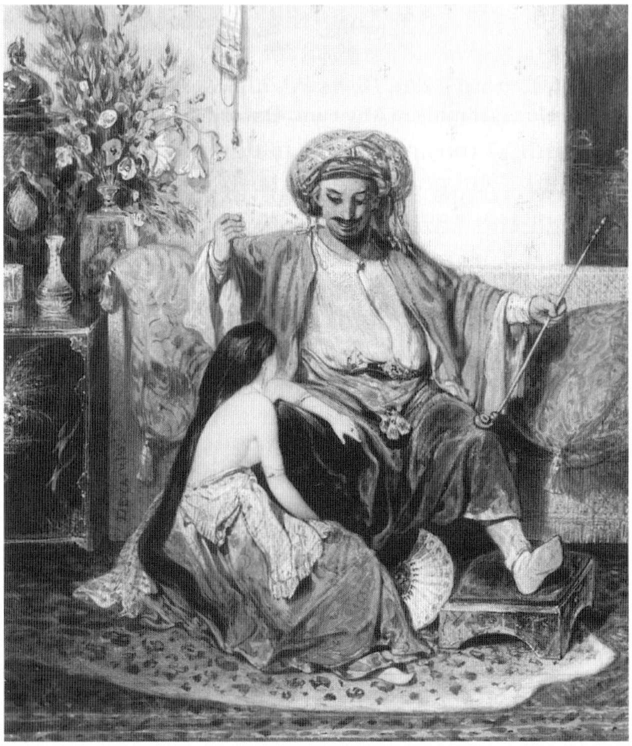

Fig. 4.3. A. G. Decamps. *Seated Sultan with Harem Girl Reposing at his Feet.* Ca. 1830. Watercolor. Reproduced by permission of the Trustees of the Wallace Collection, London.

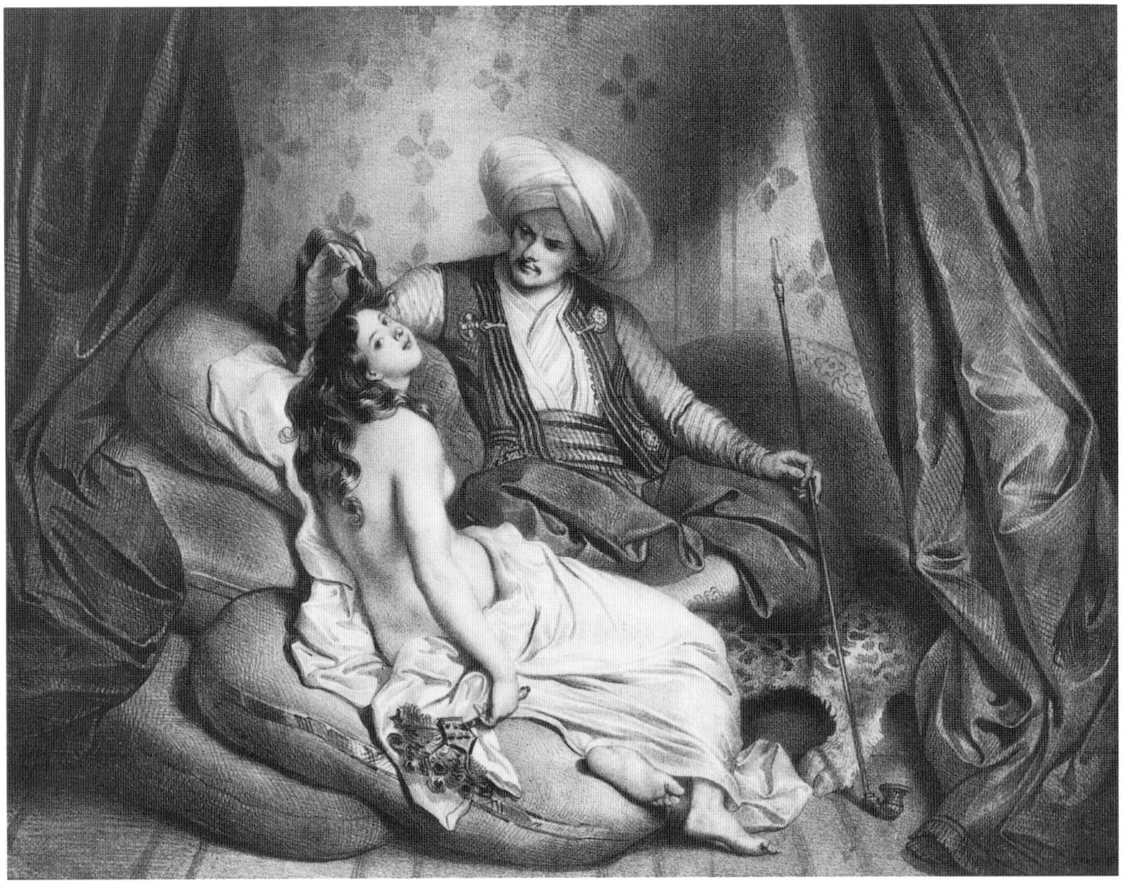

Fig. 4.4. A. Devéria, *Turcs. Les Amants des nations diverses.* Lithograph. 1834–38, reissued 1851. Cliché Bibliothèque nationale de France, Paris. Farwell, *FPLI*, v. 11, 2C1 B64136.

(Fig. 4.5) dated after 1812: one end of the pipe points out the pasha's engorged phallus as he relishes the sight of his many naked women.

Guérard produced several images in which the chibouk is highly sexualized. The old pasha located in the background uses it as postcoital diversion, judging from the disheveled young female companion whose body is displayed for the print's voyeur in the print done by Régnier after him, *Le Pacha, ou la vie dans le sérail* (Fig. 4.6). Secondly, one of two nude women entwines her arms around the chibouk; its straight lines are a masculine foil for the undulations of her body in his libidinous lithography, number 4 from *La vie au sérail* (Fig. 4.7). The chibouk had been similarly juxtaposed against female curves in F. N. Génard's French rococo *Pasha with Odalisque* (Fig. 4.8) (1761–62), a painted decoration on a gold box.

Though it often functions as a male symbol, the chibouk is held or smoked by women in several images beginning at least with Vanmour's 1712 *Fille turque qui fume sur le sopha* (Fig. 4.9). In Ingres's 1814 *Grande Odalisque* (see Fig. 3.21) the chibouk (located on the pipe rack at the right edge of the canvas) can act as a delicate extension of the woman's refinement or as a reminder of the absent man to whom she belongs. The chibouk, a substitute for the pasha, induces the same dreamy delight he could have had he been present in Eugène Giraud's undated *Interior of an Egyptian Harem* (Fig. 4.10), where one of two somnolent women in a darkened interior still holds it. When a harem woman holds the masculine chibouk it can also symbolize her social privilege. In each of two images by Amadeo Preziosi ("Jean Brindisi")[9] a woman holds the chibouk and, correspondingly, is or has been served (Figs. 4.11 and 4.12). Curiously, in Decamps's *Turkish Woman Smoking* (Plate 4) the young woman with a chibouk touching her lips is both compositionally empowered by virtue of her central, triangular, even majestic placement in the scene and disempowered by her drug-induced state, suggested by the shadow over her face and her languorous eyes.

When a man and woman smoke two separate chibouks, their shared domestic power is suggested, as in *A Turkish Family Picture* (see Fig. 3.1), the title

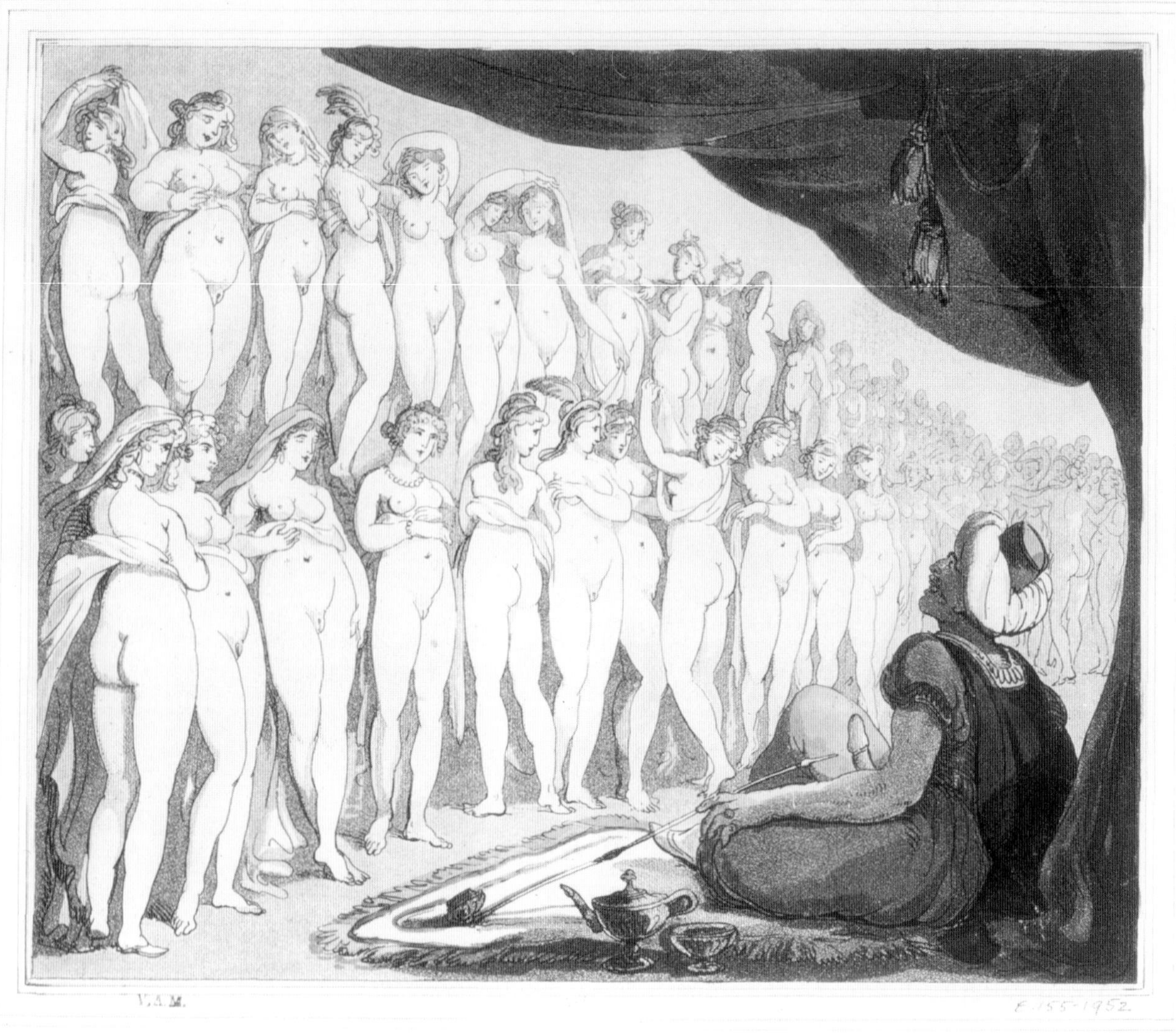

Fig. 4.5. Thomas Rowlandson. *Harem*. 1812. Courtesy of the Trustees of the Victoria and Albert. V&A Picture Library.

page illustration to Edmund Spencer's 1837 book. If this is indeed a family, modeled on British lines, the smoking couple must indeed be Father and Mother, his "companion of equal rank and helper," to quote from an article describing the ideal harem relationships.[10]

More typically when the woman (or women) appears with the hookah, no man is present. In Delacroix's *Women of Algiers* of 1834 (see Fig. 2.17) smoking is the only real activity the women engage in. In response, the critic Théophile Thoré-Bürger, writing in *le Siècle* of 1837, describes the smoke produced and correspondingly the exotic, sensuous nature of the picture. The substance they smoke—tobacco, opium or hashish—becomes a fetish for the female body and merges with it: it works "like a perfume." He writes that the viewer is almost affected by the drug, breathes more slowly, and becomes quiet in the shared space between viewer and viewed.[11]

Another example of a harem woman smoking the narghile without a man present is Lewis's 1876 *Houri* (Fig. 4.13), which is subtitled *Woman with a Hookah*, in which the pipe tube is emphasized by its red coloration. Her provocatively placed red belt tassel links the hookah with her sexual availability, as Lewis's image conflates the discourses of the heavenly houri with that of prostitute. And the narghile becomes the symbol of his powerful *femme fatale* indebted to Manet's *Olympia*.

When a hookah is present with an amorous pair, the woman might hold or smoke it, or it may simply appear close to her. Sometimes it formally echoes the curve of her exposed body, morphologically connecting woman and pipe, as in Régnier and

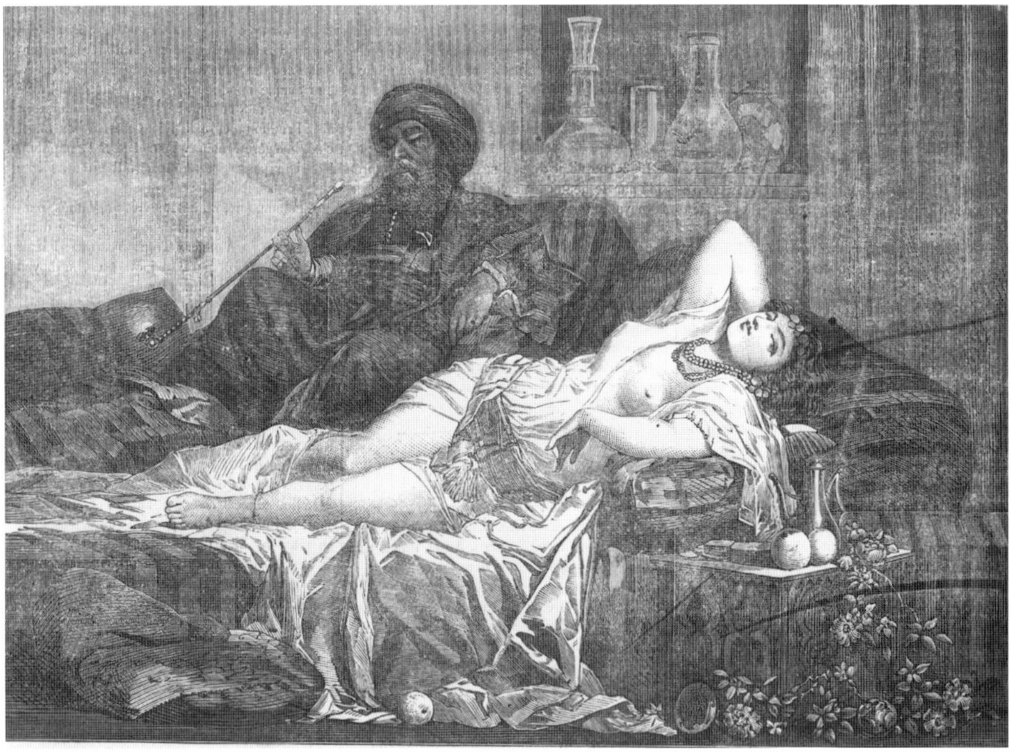

Fig. 4.6. Régnier after Eugène Guérard. ***Le Pacha, ou la vie dans le sérail, d'après le tableau de Guérard.*** **Engraving. Cliché Bibliothèque nationale de France, Paris.**

Bettannier's *Constantinople* (Fig. 4.14) 1855–56 after Morlon or Ernest Hébert's 1843 *Deux Odalisques couchées sur la terrasse* (Fig. 4.15).

A French comic strip parodies the whole phenomenon of representing the harem women and plays with the pipe as allusion to masculine power. In the 1868 caricature entitled *Turcotoquade* the sultan smokes the hookah (Fig. 4.16), while an upstart western artist hired to paint the women puffs on a chibouk, whose length he supports with his foot at a moment in the cartoon's narrative when he tests the sultan's patience.[12] Though the image is exceptional in linking the sultan with the hookah, it is typical in associating the more powerful figure with the masculine chibouk. Here the artist flaunts his power by his irreverent body position, but as the story unfolds, we discover that he is only temporarily in the sultan's good graces.

In a prurient group of French images the tube and mouthpiece of the hookah are phallicized. *Narghillet* (Fig. 4.17), an undated lithograph after Charlemagne Oscar Guet (1801–60/71) by Charles Vogt depicts a blond Circassian wearing a deep *décolletage* and beginning to interact with the long tube. In Manet's aquatint etching titled *Odalisque* (Fig. 4.18) the phallomorphic prop so provocatively placed is more boldly outlined than the very hand that holds it. The tube crosses over the leg and arm of two women, suggesting the male they share in another Régnier and Bettannier lithograph, done after Bouvier and erroneously titled *Le Chibouk* (Fig. 4.19). In Alès's undated engraving, *Odalisque* (Fig. 4.20) the phallic-looking mouthpiece is adorned with two small metallic balls at its base.

The pipe figures prominently in some of the most licentious harem images housed at the Cabinet des estampes. In Charles Bargue's (fl. c. 1850–83) 1852 *Aux bords du Bosphore* (Fig. 4.21) after Henri de Montaut[13] the woman writhes on the bed, her arm raised in the long-standing pose indicating sleepy seduction,[14] as her other hand holds the hookah, from which it appears she has just inhaled. The long tube of the hookah is snakelike in two of Régnier's 1853 lithographs after Guérard from *La vie au sérail* (see Figs. 3.4 and 4.22). In plate number 2 (see Fig. 3.4) it curls over the bed near the reclining woman's ankle, twice repeating the shape of her ankle bracelet, which functions as both adornment and symbol of her slave-status, before it winds up and around the seated woman's forearm, looking much like her bracelet. In plate number 1 (Fig. 4.22) it resembles a snake, as the mouthpiece terminates at her right breast, calling to mind eastern images of Cleopatra just bitten by the deadly asp.[15]

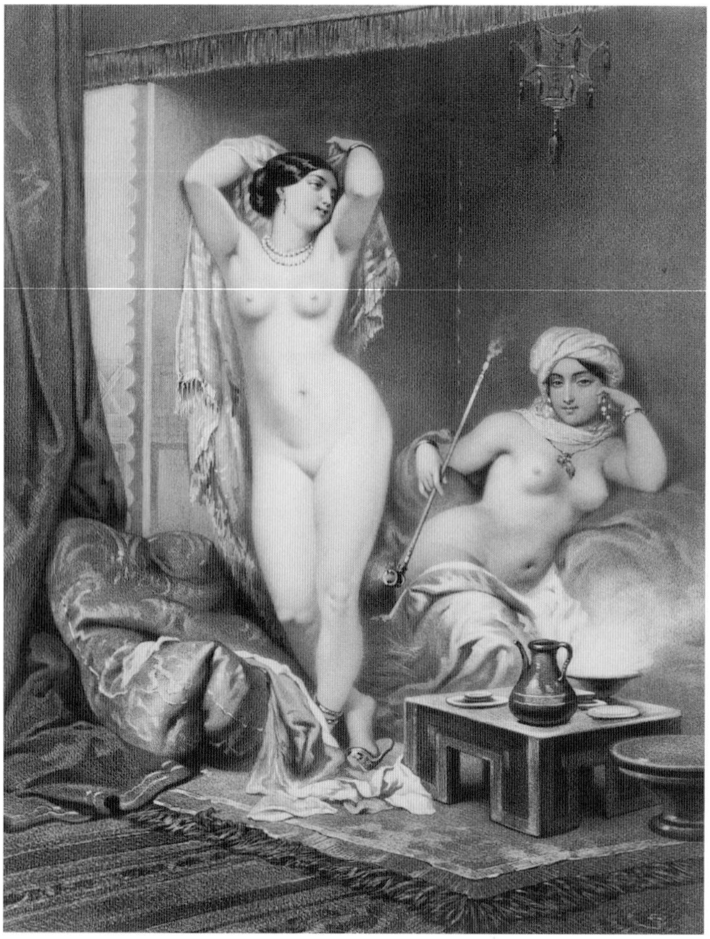

Fig. 4.7. After Eugène Guérard. *La Vie au sérail*, no. 4. 1853. Lithograph. Cliché Bibliothèque nationale de France, Paris. Farwell, *FPLI*, v. 11, 2C8 B79327.

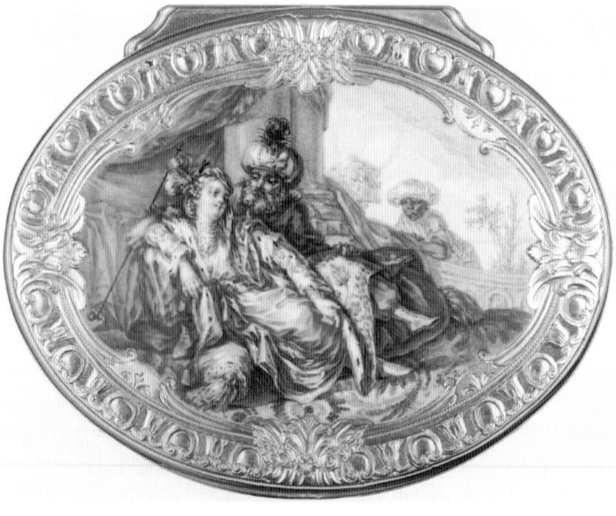

Fig. 4.8. F. N. Génard. *Pasha with Odalisque*. 1761–62. Gold box with painted enamel decoration. Reproduced by permission of the Trustees of the Wallace Collection, London.

Lane himself used the term "snake-like" to describe the hookah tube (*ME* 1:173).

The woman interacts with the hookah tube more than in any other known image in Nicolas Maurin's *Asie: Asia* (Fig. 4.23). The pretext for her movement may be to reposition the pipe for a more comfortable draw, yet in doing so the woman is much more active than the indolent types usually found in popular French pictures of harem. After all, the very purpose of smoking the hookah was to induce a lethargic passivity. This woman's lower body remains passive, but the animated upper half, arms flailing and hair wind blown, implies keen sexual interest and animal energy. To underscore the idea of the male presence, a handsome young man in a turban appears out the window at some distance, dreamlike, as the object of her desire is given form.

An unusually suggestive passage of a harem woman smoking a pipe is Julia Pardoe's 1837 writing, which

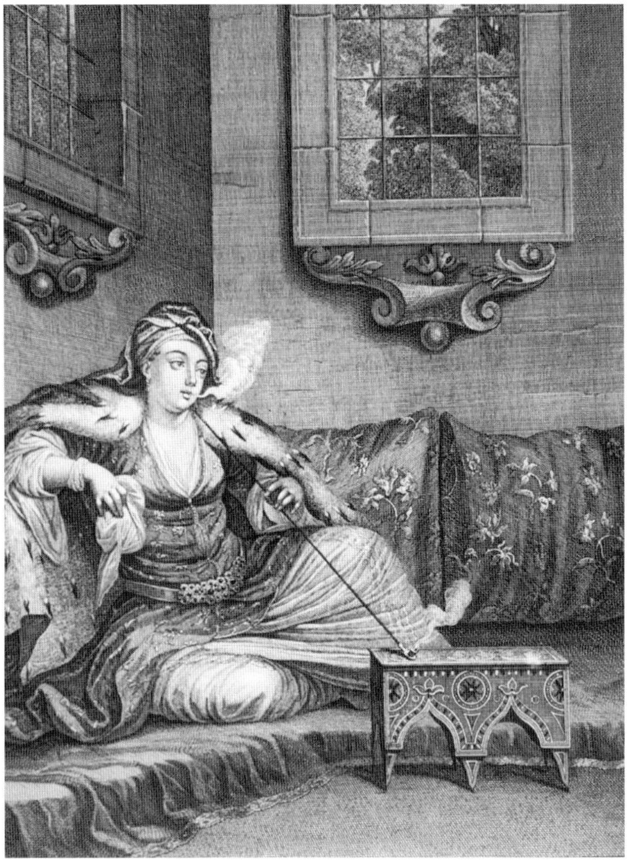

Fig. 4.9. After Vanmour. *Fille turque qui fume sur le sopha*. Ca. 1715. Engraving. *Recueil de cent estampes*, plate 45. Department of Special Collections, Charles E. Young Library, UCLA.

reveals her fascination with smoking in the harem. Pardoe's brief comment is erotically charged and constitutes a verbal parallel to racy French pictures.

> Such soft and studied attitudes—such long and slowly-drawn respiration, having all the sentiment of a sigh without its sadness—such clasping and unclasping of the delicate fingers about the slender tube—no novice should venture to smoke beside a Turkish woman. (*CS* 1:238–39)

An indolent harem woman smoking the hookah personifies Asiatic Turkey in a French animated map of Europe drawn in 1870 (Fig. 4.24). She lies on her side in the "odalisque pose," eyes closed, her head resting on a crooked elbow. By 1870 Turkey is perceived as a sleepy female—doubly passive for her gender and her induced lethargy—when France's real focus is instead the Prussian male giant. Here Turkey is the harem woman smoking.

Thus a survey of representations of the harem woman smoking reveals that the motif was capable of serving several functions. Exotic in itself, smoking also elicited long-standing stereotypes of the harem woman as sensuous, pliant, passive, even lascivious. Artists exploited the phallomorphic potential of the exotic chibouk. Similarly, the hookah/narghile could be used as a device to heighten the picture's prurient appeal and symbolize either the male-as-phallus or the female-as-vessel, composed as it was of both a long flexible tube and a round-bottomed container. Beyond such visual punning, the pipe became a symbol of pleasure and power. One pair of French lithographs from 1854 compares the English custom of taking tea to the eastern custom of smoking the hookah, *Une anglaise romanesque* and *Une persane boudeuse* (see Fig. 1.2) done after Desandré. The point can be deduced from each woman's comparative comportment: smoking the hookah is sexier than drinking tea. Such a cross-cultural contrast provokes ambivalence. But an anonymous British female visitor to a harem in 1838 who tries unsuccessfully to smoke, clearly prefers her "civilized" abstinence to eastern "ignorance" as revealed in this ironic passage:

> the first whiff nearly choked me, and set all the attendants into a titter; and I then explained that my countrywomen not yet being sufficiently civilised to indulge in smoking, I yet remained in ignorance of that accomplishment.[16]

Coffee

> Caught up in an elaborate routine of household tasks, a miniature Versailles where the pouring of coffee took on a sacramental air, the daily monotony of the *harim* slaves stands in marked contrast to visions of wanton luxury.[17]

Serving or drinking coffee in the harem is another activity having a range of meanings. Of course, it is often represented as a ritual of hospitality. But rather than equalizing the server and the served, the serving of coffee, like the pipe in the harem, usually implies a hierarchy. These pictures establish a principle of social deference—whether young to old, slave to mistress, female to male, or hostess to guest. Harem pictures of coffee-serving belong to a fine art tradition, but they also constitute genre scenes of what was still a rather privileged practice in Europe by the mid-nineteenth century, the drinking of coffee.

British and French artists most typically made the server darker skinned and the served lighter. The slave's inferior social status, accented by her skin color, is underscored by her serving coffee in Carle Vanloo's 1755 *Une sultane prenant du café* (Fig. 4.25). Exaggerated facial features as ciphers

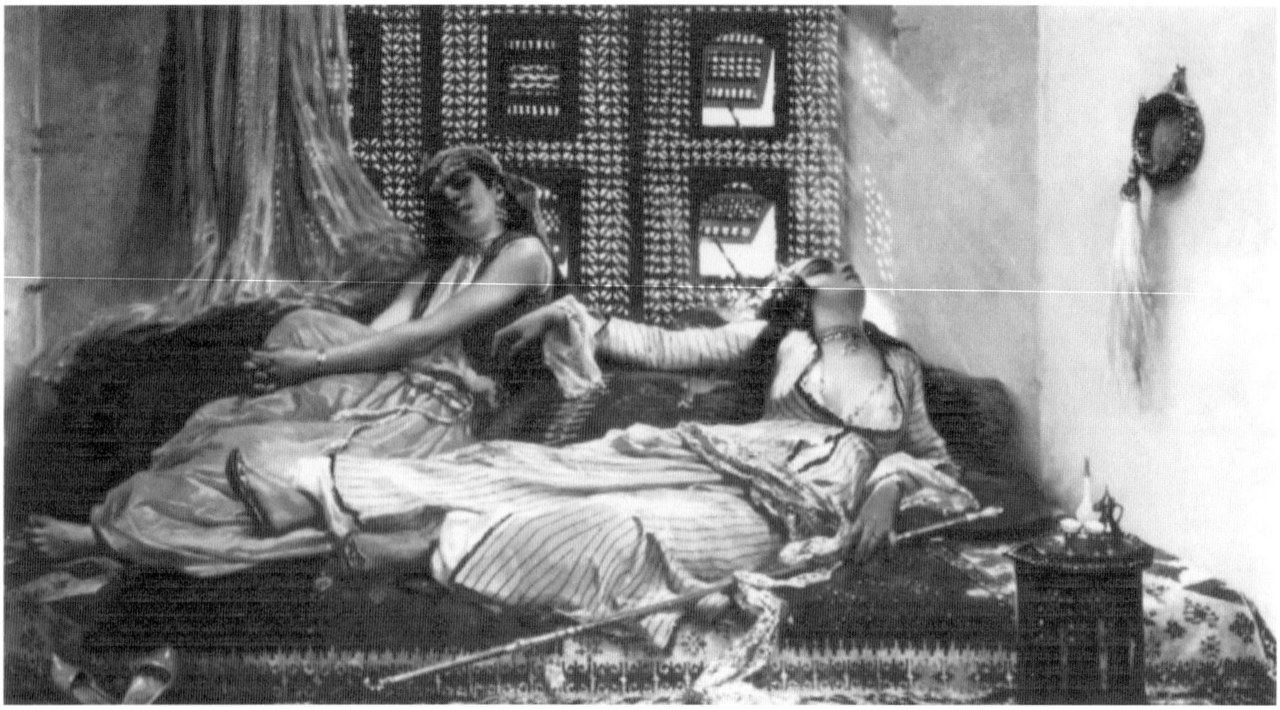

Fig. 4.10. Eugène Giraud. *Femmes au harem/Interior of an Egyptian Harem.* Photo courtesy Mathaf Gallery, Ltd.

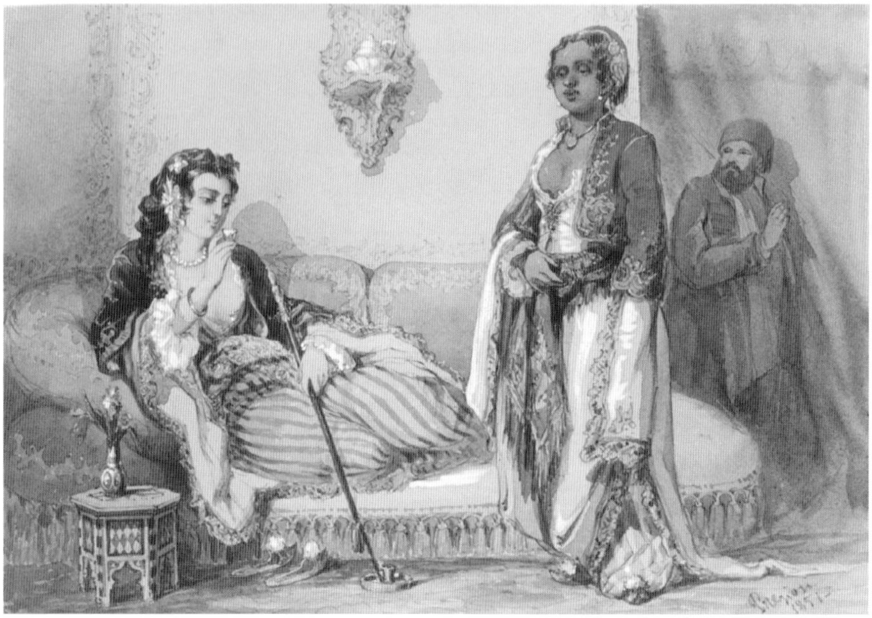

Fig. 4.11. Amadeo Preziosi (Jean Brindisi). *Turkish Woman Holding a Pipe, with a Black Servant at her Side.* 1852. Watercolor gouache on paper. Courtesy of the Trustees of the Victoria and Albert. V&A Picture Library.

of racial difference appear on a slave who serves on the far right edge of Bonington's 1828 *La Siesta* (see Fig. 2.14). "Jean Brindisi" (pseudonym for Amadeo Preziosi) composed *Trois femmes turques* (see Fig. 4.12), an image focused on the black servant who brings coffee to the two women. (Her calico bandana suggests American domestic slavery rather than its eastern counterpart.) Similarly, the standing attendant is brown skinned and carries a vessel containing liquid refreshment to her supine mistress

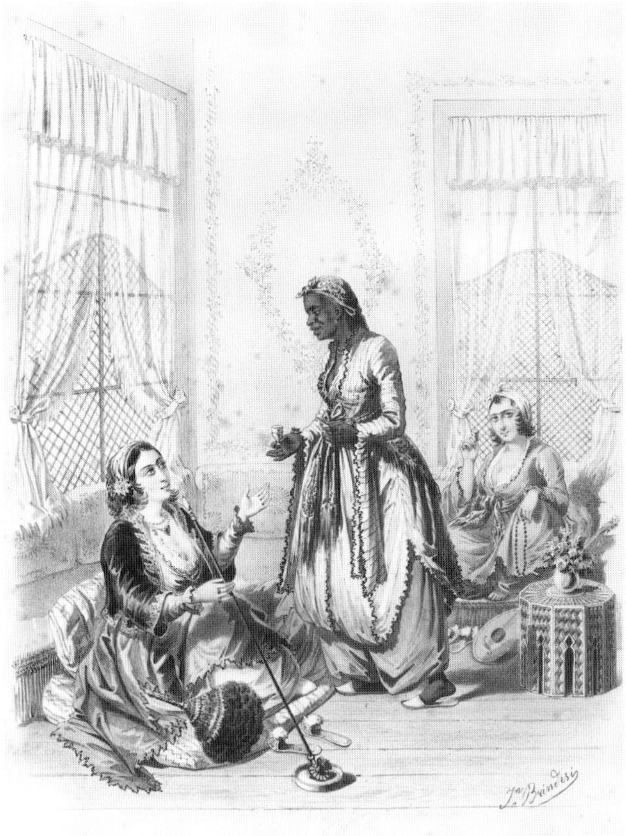

Fig. 4.12. Amadeo Preziosi (Jean Brindisi). *Trois femmes turcs.* Lithograph. Cliché Bibliothèque nationale de France, Paris.

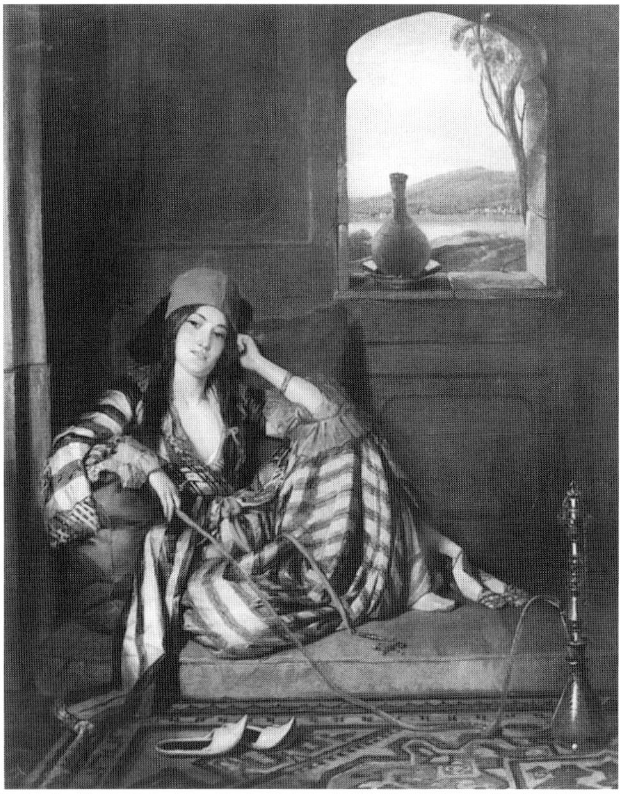

Fig. 4.13. John Frederick Lewis. *Houri, Eastern Woman with a Hookah.* 1876. Private Collection. By permission of Sotheby's. Photo Courtesy Witt Library, Courtauld Institute, London.

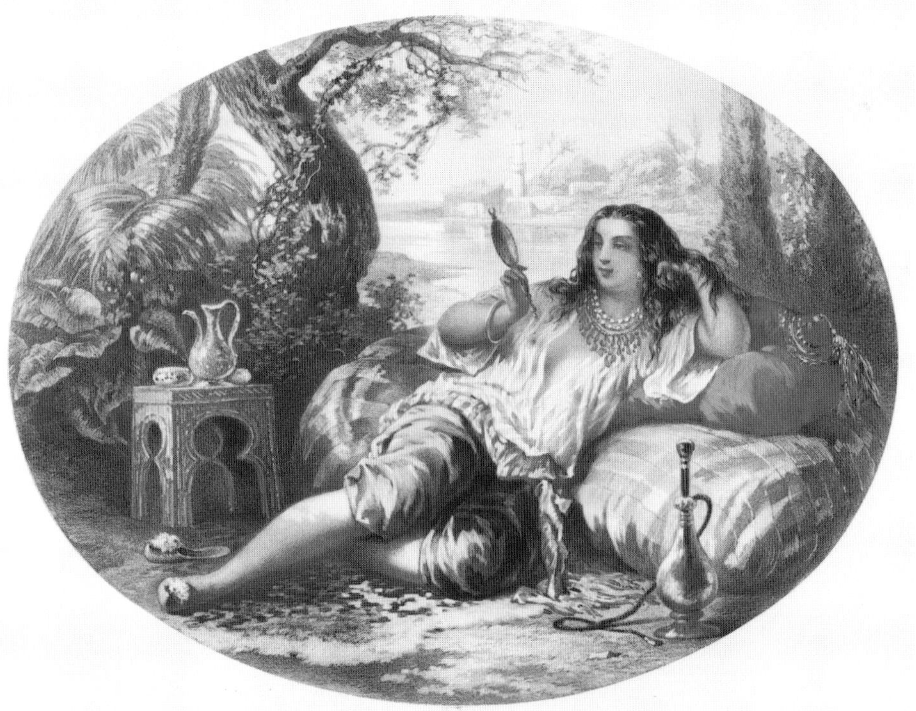

Fig. 4.14. Claude Régnier, Paul Emile Antony Morlon, J. Bettannier, and/or E. Bettannier after Paul Morlon. *Constantinople.* 1855–56. Color lithograph. Cliché Bibliothèque nationale de France, Paris. Farwell, *FPLI*, v.11 2D7 B81997.

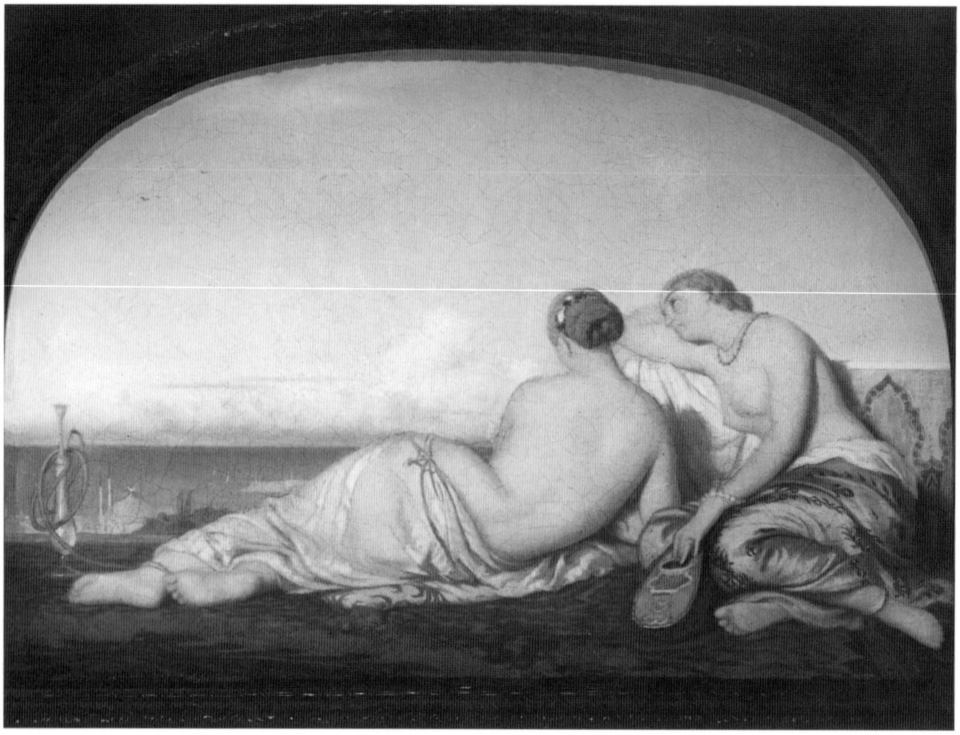

Fig. 4.15. Antoine Auguste Ernest Hébert. *Deux Odalisques couchées sur la terrasse.* 1843 Salon. Butkin Collection, Cleveland. Photo courtesy Shepherd Gallery, New York.

in *Cairene Lady Waited Upon by a Galla Slave Girl* (Fig. 4.26), a lithograph drawn by Mouilleron for Prisse d'Avennes's 1848 album.

In the history of harem pictures, one of the major visual conventions for showing the interdependent ranks of server and served is the standing server viewed from behind, while the served sits or reclines and faces the viewer. Such a back view prevents the reading of the slave as a distinct personality in

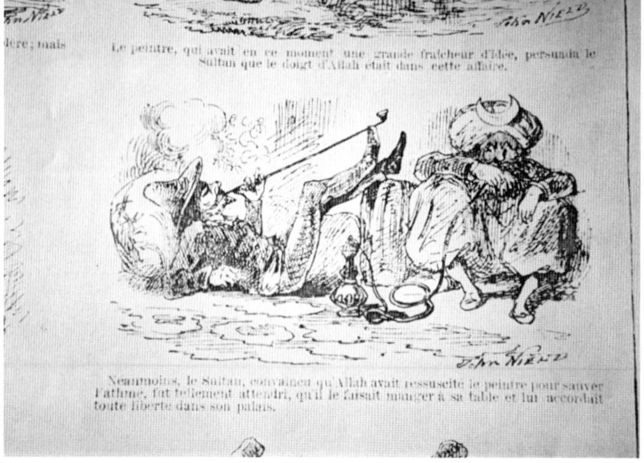

Fig. 4.16. John Nield. "Turcotoquade." *L'Image*, no. 34 (23 August 1868).

Vanmour's c. 1715 *Fille turque prenant le caffé sur le sopha* (Fig. 4.27). That her hair is long and loose suggests her youth and her social inferiority. In his distinctive rococo-revivalist manner, Thomas Allom borrows the convention of presenting the servant's back in *The Odalisque or Favourite of the Harem* (Fig. 4.28 and Plate 5). In Guérard's 1851 *La vie au sérail* (see Fig. 4.22) and the print made after it the harem woman herself, on her knees, serves refreshment to her reclining master. While he is fully clothed, her nudity further indicates her subservience. As suggested in this last image, coffee, especially sweet coffee, can be an allusion to sexual delight.[18] Indeed, the pipe, coffee, and "sweetmeats" are referred to interchangeably in suggesting intense flavors as an analog for sexual pleasure.

In the harem picture purchased by John Ruskin's father, Lewis's 1858 *Life in the Harem, Cairo* (see Fig. 3.2), a white woman brings coffee into another white woman who is seated. But the social hierarchy conventionally indicated by racial difference is much less clear here, especially given the black slave behind the server. By obscuring a strict hierarchy based on race, Lewis's picture is distinctive, because it alludes to a significant convention for showing about harem life and disrupts it.[19]

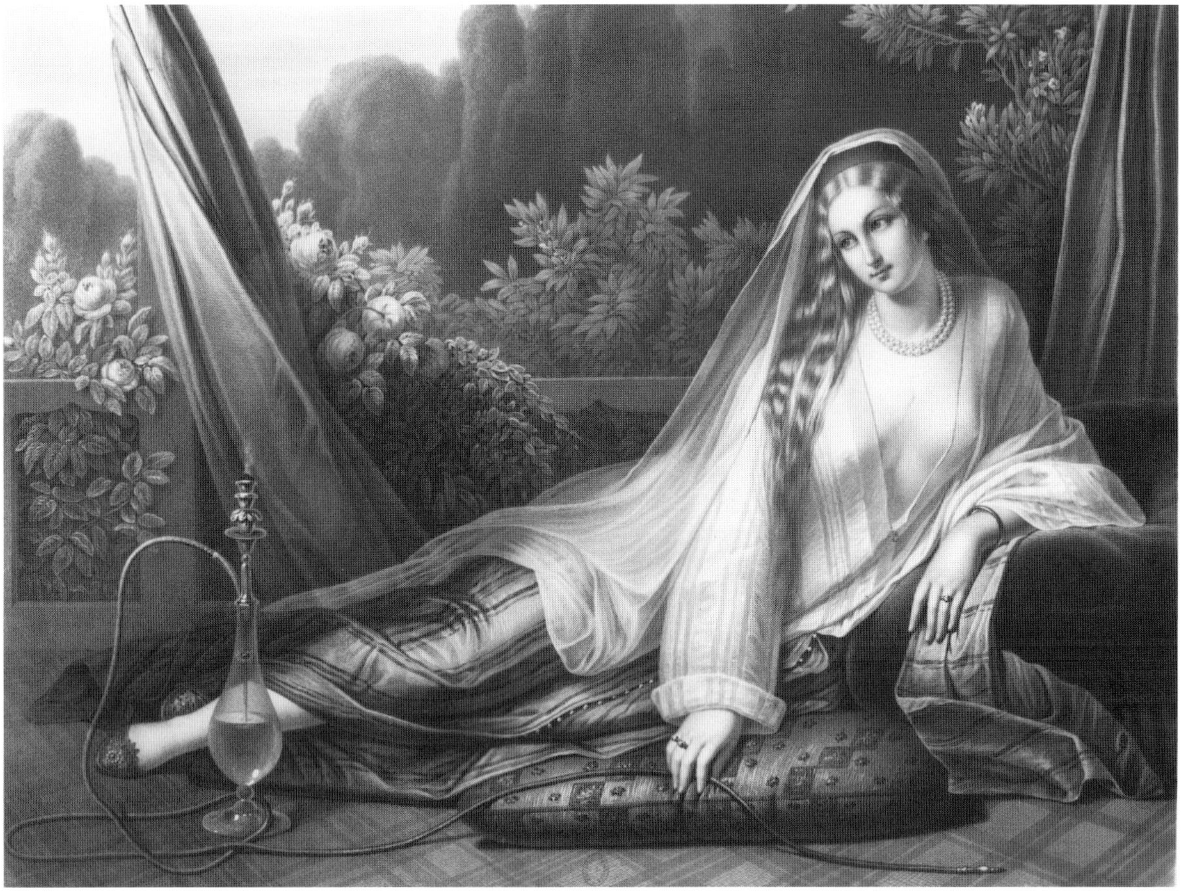

Fig. 4.17. Charles Vogt after Charlemagne Oscar Guet. *Narghillet.* Lithograph. Cliché Bibliothèque nationale de France, Paris.

Harem Animals: Gazelles, Birds, and Cats

Renderings of exotic harem animals, whether in visual or verbal form, link the harem to the natural world. The polygynous harem becomes either a perversion of Nature or an extension of it. Sometimes animals in the harem are represented with a heightened scientific/zoological interest. Other artists and writers depict the animals vaguely or incidentally, but still adding to the picture's dreamy, other-worldly quality. In many of these images the human-animal juxtaposition suggests their interchangeability.

Early on in the nineteenth century Thomas Moore draws a similarity between the animals confined on the grounds of a harem and the imprisoned women: "living things / Of land and wave, whose fate—in bondage thrown / For their weak loveliness—is like her own!" (*LR* 29). In a popular publication harem women are pitied for "their merely animal existence," uneducated and devoid of a spiritual or intellectual life—though they do have "luxuries."[20] By 1877 in a publication of British feminists the attitude toward such an animal existence changes. No longer is the Muslim woman an animal. She is only treated that way by brutish "Moslem" men: "To him she is a mere animal."[21] Just as certain male writers use the harem inmate to comment on the nature of British ladies, so too do some female writers use the harem to express their own fears about the "animality" of western men or the working class, as in the case of Wollstonecraft (*VRW* 249).

Even in twentieth-century scholarship art historians reacting to Delacroix's *Women of Algiers* (see Fig. 2.17) read an animality in the women he renders. Léon Rosenthal in his 1914 classic *Du Romantisme au réalisme* ascribes the women's "animal-like" nature to Delacroix's association with the animal painter Antoine Louis Barye. Germain Bazin in 1933 names one of the women "a beautiful, voluptuous animal." And as late as 1963 Raymond Escholier uncritically refers to the women as having "eyes of a gazelle."[22] The dehumanization of the harem woman in aesthetic discourse is not only a nineteenth-century phenomenon.

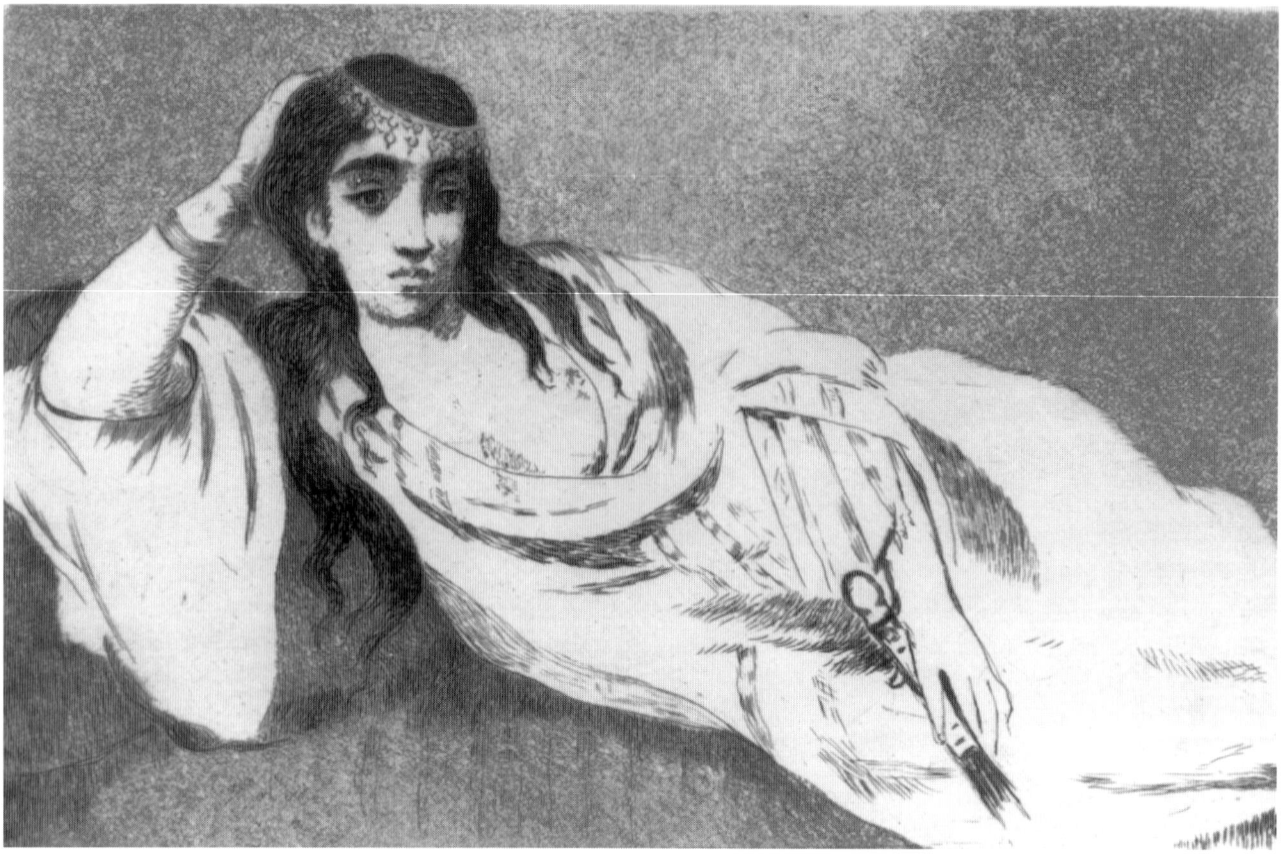

Fig. 4.18. Edouard Manet. *Odalisque.* 1868. Etching and aquatint. Baltimore Museum of Art: George A. Lucas Collection.

Gazelles were indigenous animals, and in the Muslim world they are traditional poetic symbols for eastern women: shy, fleet footed, large eyed, and gentle. That a woman had the eyes of a gazelle was one of the greatest compliments she could receive in the East, claimed Lady Mary Wortley Montagu (*L* 1:355). This was recognized by British and French observers, including Lord Byron, who described beautiful harem women as having the eyes of a gazelle in *Childe Harold* and *The Giaour* (*WB* 2, 54). In an anonymous 1851 article, mention is made of the harem women's "large, gazelle-like eyes," while later in the story the harem master catches a foreigner (the author) in his harem and taunts: "'You would like, then, to run away with my gazelle? tell me, young Nazarene?'" The author plays with the belief that eastern men are fiercely jealous of their women and potentially violent.[23]

Alexandre Dumas describes a beautiful Algerian Jewess whom he sees at the consulate. She was a "magnificent creature" and "her almond eyes emphasized with kohl [. . .] gazed at us with the docile yet untamed look one finds only in gazelles and the women of the Orient" (*AA* 97). Her willingness to "gaze" can be attributable to her primitive state, as civilized women presumably do not stare at men.

French representations of harem gazelles include Théodore Chassériau's undated *Woman and Little Girl of Constantine with a Gazelle* (Fig. 4.29). One function of this image is ethnographic: it documents the fact that North African women, unlike western ladies, sit on the floor and have large animals in their living space. This image's reading can be extended: Muslim women are themselves animalistic in their primitive living habits and in their participation in the animalism of polygyny. A variation on these themes can be seen in one of the few known harem images done by a woman artist, *La Jeune grecque* (see Fig. 3.29), by Régnier after Heloïse Suzanne Leloir. In this 1843 outdoor scene of a Greek girl feeding a gazelle the animal and the distant palm trees tell of a foreign locale. Just as she cares for her little pet, she too will soon become a "pet" at a tender age.

Thackeray reported that the painter John Lewis owned gazelles when he lived in Cairo.[24] In *Hhareem* (see Plate 1) Lewis paints gazelles located to both the right and left of the composition. They are positioned like two of the lounging women: head set back slightly

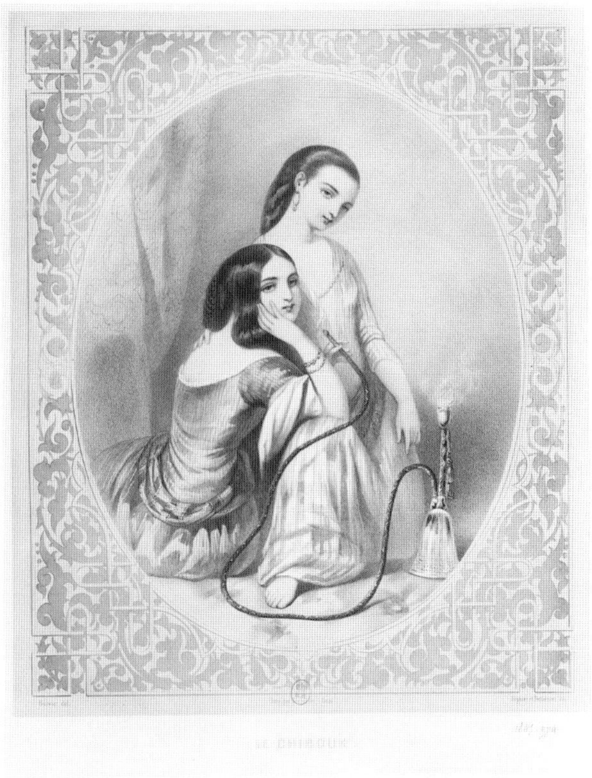

Fig. 4.19. Claude Régnier, J. Bettannier, and/or E. Bettannier after Bouvier. *Le Chibouk.* 1845. Lithograph. Cliché Bibliothèque nationale de France, Paris. Farwell, *FPLI*, v. 11, 2D12 B81766.

and limbs extended. Lewis blurs the distinctions between animals and harem women, and all of them occupy the same living areas. The comparison works both ways. He anthropomorphizes the animals in their poses, and he uses them to comment on the harem inmate's animal nature, tamed only minimally by the constraints of the harem.[25]

Birds are a frequent motif in representations of the harem. In the early eighteenth century Lady Mary Wortley Montagu writes of the special regard birds are given in eastern harems, "Here are some birds held in a sort of religious Reverence and for that reason Multiply prodigiously" (*L* 1:341). Her comment suggests a parallel between the birds and harem women who are expected to bear many children. Caged birds appear in Mary Wollstonecraft's lament on the status of women's rights. Women "everywhere" are sheltered from the truth and purposely kept "ignorant," though she claims it is euphemistically called "innocence." Women's bodies may look like gilt cages, but they can be veritable prisons: "Taught from their infancy that beauty is woman's scepter, the mind shapes itself to the body, and roaming round its gilt cage, only seeks to adore its prison" (*VRW* 130–31). In her analysis the female body itself is a beautiful trap that holds an animalistic spirit which lacks proper education. She continues that women so pent up are idle and preen themselves like birds. But there is a price for such a free ride; women forfeit their liberty, their virtue, and their health.

> Confined, then, in cages like the feathered race, [women] have nothing to do but to plume themselves, and stalk with mock majesty from perch to perch. It is true they are provided with food and raiment, for which they neither toil nor spin; but health, liberty, and virtue are given in exchange. (*VRW* 146)

In the early nineteenth century Lane describes an Egyptian and Arab belief in which birds and beasts communicate and praise God (*ME* 1:311). Several species of harem pet birds, including parrots and minahs, reportedly served another useful function: by screeching and squawking they could detect potentially poisonous snakes that had managed to find their way indoors, claims a later twentieth-century chronicler of the harem.[26] In a story about birds called "The Merchant and the Parrot" written by the famous thirteenth-century Persian author, Jelal-ud-Din Rumi, and reissued in the Victorian period[27] the merchant keeps a beautiful parrot in a cage. He loves his talking bird, who longs to be freed. In *Tales of a Parrot* a jealous husband uses a parrot to distract his wife from her unfaithfulness by telling her stories.[28] (In Arabic the second wife is called *durrah*, meaning parrot.)[29]

In eastern written traditions white doves symbolize the beautiful women of Paradise. Houris/peris appear as four white doves in the Persian romance, "King Baturan Ghur and Husn Banu." The story "How Hassan Captured the Bird Maidens," included in Lane's translation of *Arabian Nights* (1839–41), is a variation on the basic myth in which a man wins an unearthly maiden by first stealing her headdress. In these traditions other birds are sometimes substituted for the doves: swans, geese, or pigeons. Thus, in both eastern and western traditions a parallel is drawn between harem women and birds.

Caged birds, like gazelles, are often described as harem pets.[30] Like her compatriot Mary Wollstonecraft who claims that harem women have nowhere to go and nothing to do, Julia Pardoe in 1837 writes that when they take their periodic outings, harem women are at a loss as to how to use their time constructively: "Like caged birds, occasionally set free, they do not know how to use their liberty" (*CS* 1:35). But curiously in a book written in the next

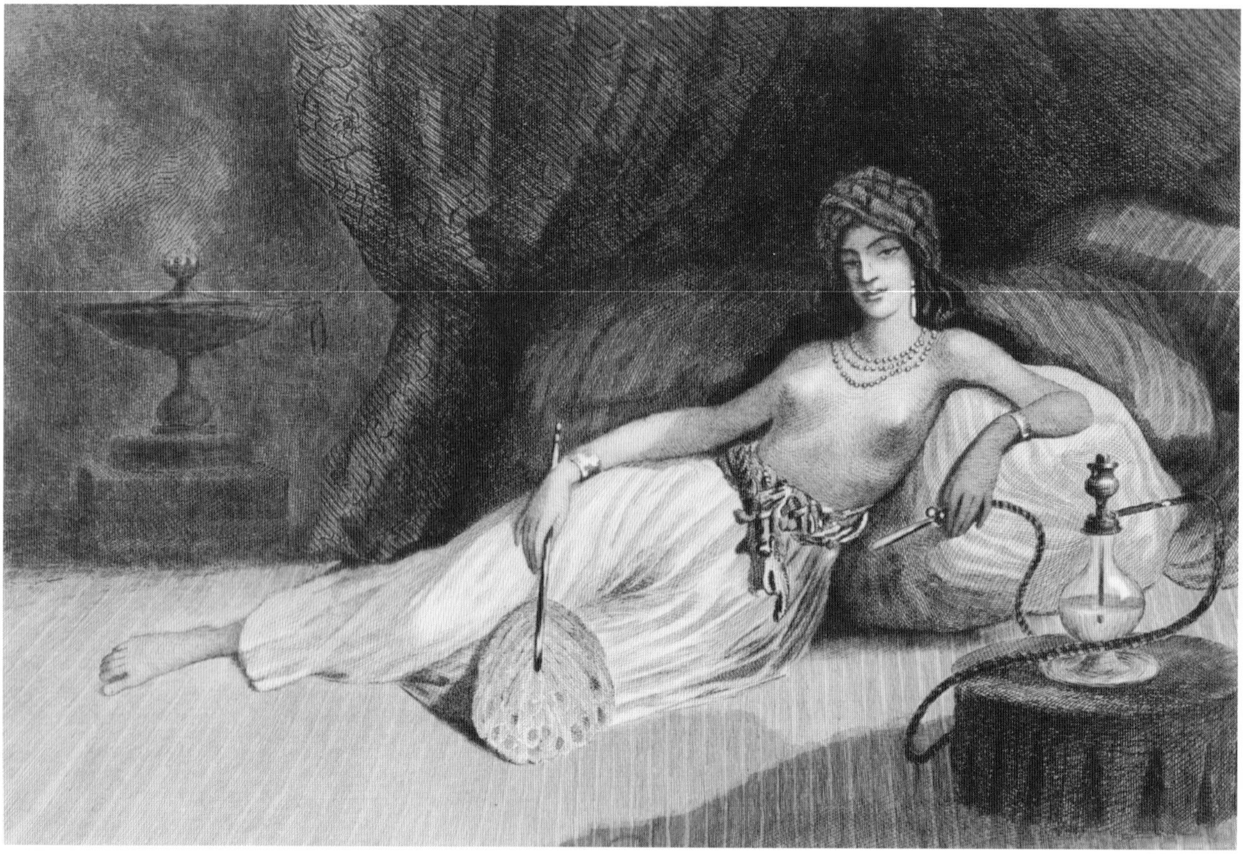

Fig. 4.20. Auguste François Alès. *Odalisque.* Engraving. *L'Espérance album de gravures.* 1838. Cliché Bibliothèque nationale de France, Paris.

year Pardoe denies this metaphor: "it is a great fallacy to imagine that Turkish females are like birds in a cage, or captives in a cell;—far from it."[31] William Makepeace Thackeray too connects harem women with birds in 1844 when he refers to them as "these birds of Paradise" confined to "the interior of the cage."[32] An anonymous female writer in 1846 mixes the old metaphor with another: Christian women are the birds who fly freely, compared to the molelike existence of harem women forced to take part in this "atrocious system."[33] Four years later another traveler who supposedly witnessed the revolt of an Indian harem records her or his impression of its women in a courtyard: it was like "entering a large aviary in which the birds, stricken with terror, fly madly to and fro against the walls."[34] One of Nerval's first impressions of his newly purchased slave is that she was "a magnificent bird in a cage" (*VO* 48). And in his account of his visit through the seraglio another traveler writes in 1866: "So far, the cage is sufficiently fine, if somewhat incongruous; but we follow in search of the birds, and find one, the Princess Epouse."[35] As late as 1878 Mrs. Blunt compares harem women freed for the day to have a picnic or take a country drive to "flock of strange birds let loose from their cages, not knowing what to make of their new freedom" (*PT* 1:114). She reminds us that these "birds" inevitably return by sunset.

More generally, birds are symbolic in French and British art, where they belong to an old tradition which alludes to female sexual activity, the empty cage symbolizing the loss of virginity.[36] By the mid-nineteenth century in France birds of indeterminate species proliferate in harem pictures sometimes representing freedom, and caged birds, confinement.

In several nineteenth-century pictures, the harem woman does not acknowledge the bird, which is merely one more kind of eastern bric-brac. In Colin's *L'Odalisque* (Fig. 4.30) it is located in the upper-right corner, but it is nearly lost in the profusion of harem stuff, which contrasts dramatically with the nudity of the woman abed offering her unencumbered body to the viewer, here, a reader of the *Bulletin de l'ami des arts* in which the image appeared. Though there is no real interaction between woman and bird in this or other images, an affinity between them is sometimes drawn by the similar coloration in the bird's plumage and the woman's clothing. In Bonington's 1827 watercolor

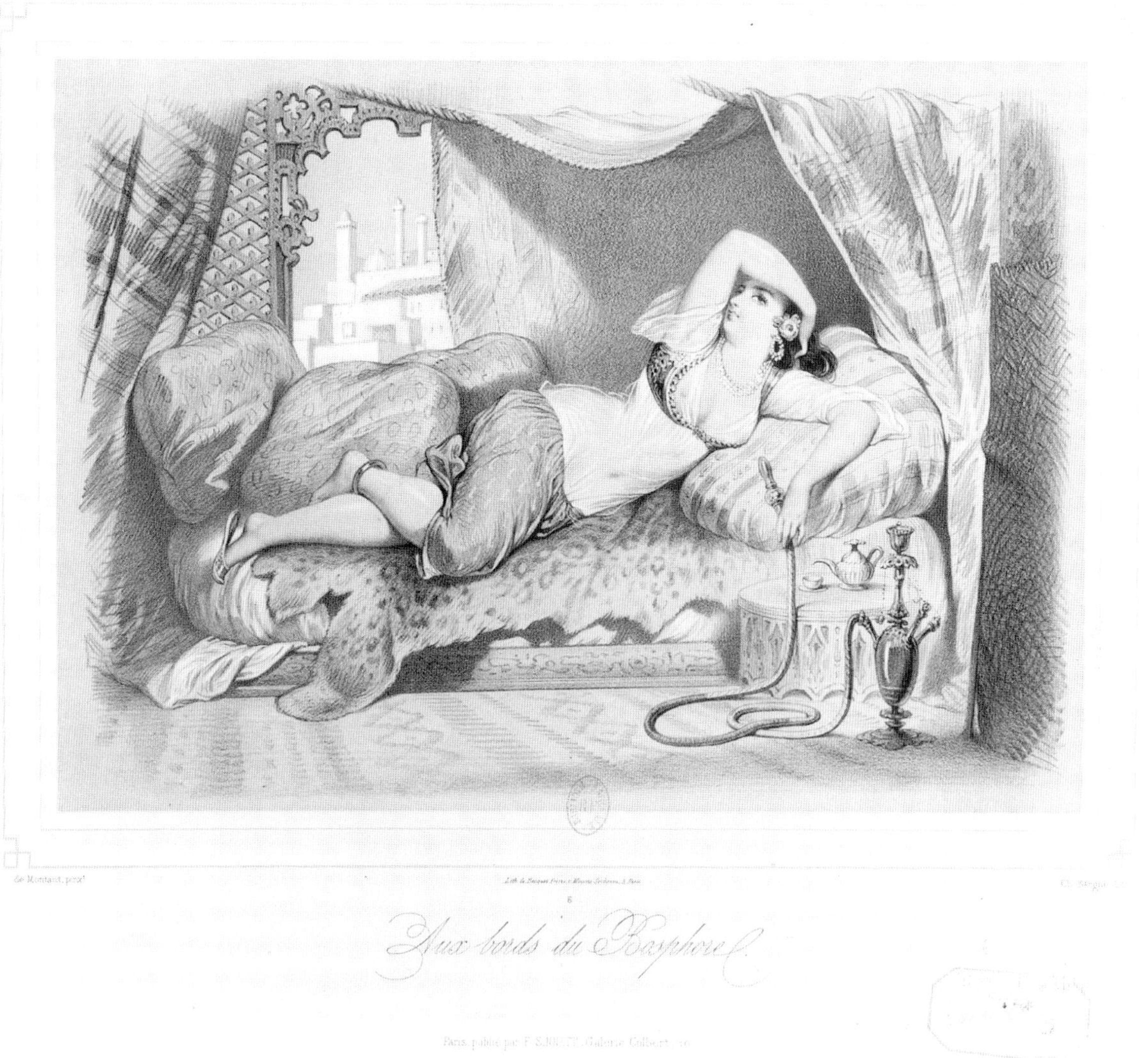

Fig. 4.21. Charles Bargue after Henri de Montaut. *Aux bords du Bosphore*. 1852. Lithograph. Cliché Bibliothèque nationale de France, Paris. Farwell, *FPLI*, v. 11, 2B5 B83905.

Odalisque (with Red Parrot) (Fig. 4.31) and Devéria's painting *Odalisque* c. 1831 (see Fig. 3.9) the bird and the woman are accented with the same red color. A metaphorical meaning for the harem bird is even more apparent when the harem woman interacts with it. In Decamps's watercolor *An Algerian Woman* (Fig. 4.32) c. 1830–32 the bird's freedom contrasts with the woman's confinement; however, like the woman a monkey remains confined and chained to the interior. An elaborately dressed woman plays with a bird in Lacambrie's lithograph *Costumes turcs* (Fig. 4.33). Nude women play with split-tail parrots in the 1850 *Le harem* (Fig. 4.34) by Joseph Félon and the 1856 *Fatime* (Fig. 4.35) after Désondré by Régnier. These last two female figures are posed provocatively: legs crossed, one elbow crooked, the other arm extended to serve as perch for the pet.

In John Lewis's 1864 *Caged Doves, Cairo* (Fig. 4.36), animals again form a significant part of the whole. Two doves, one perched on the finger of the woman's left hand, the other about to alight on the table in front of her, allude to the harem inmate in what is Lewis's most transparent use of symbolism in a harem picture. In 1878 the *Art Journal* would name John Lewis the painter of "latticed harems with their caged doves" (*AJ* 40 [1878]:200), implying that the women are doves, as none of his harem pictures contains an actual cage.

The birds are not caged in any of these French or British images; instead the harem interior itself acts

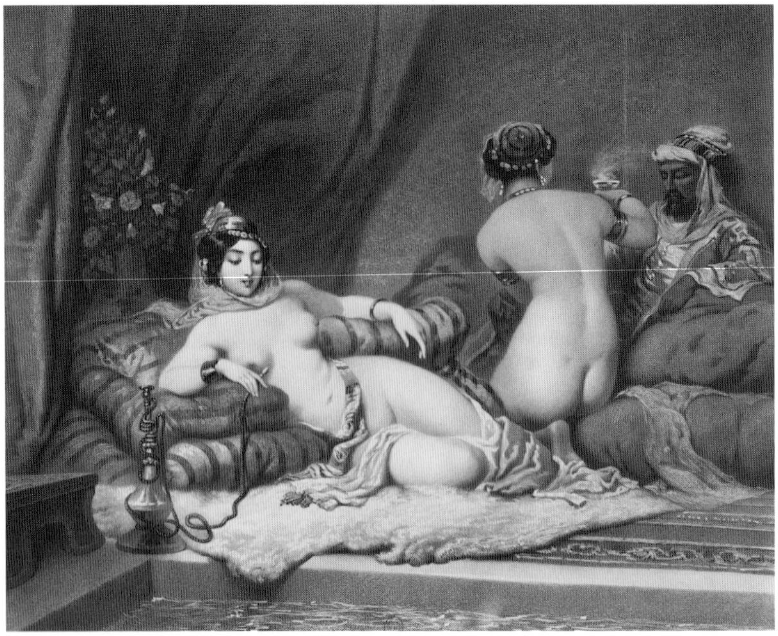

Fig. 4.22. Régnier after Eugène Guérard. *La Vie au sérail*, no. 1. 1853. Lithograph. Cliché Bibliothèque nationale de France, Paris. Farwell, *FPLI*, v. 1, 2C9 B58971; v. 11, 2C5 B64031.

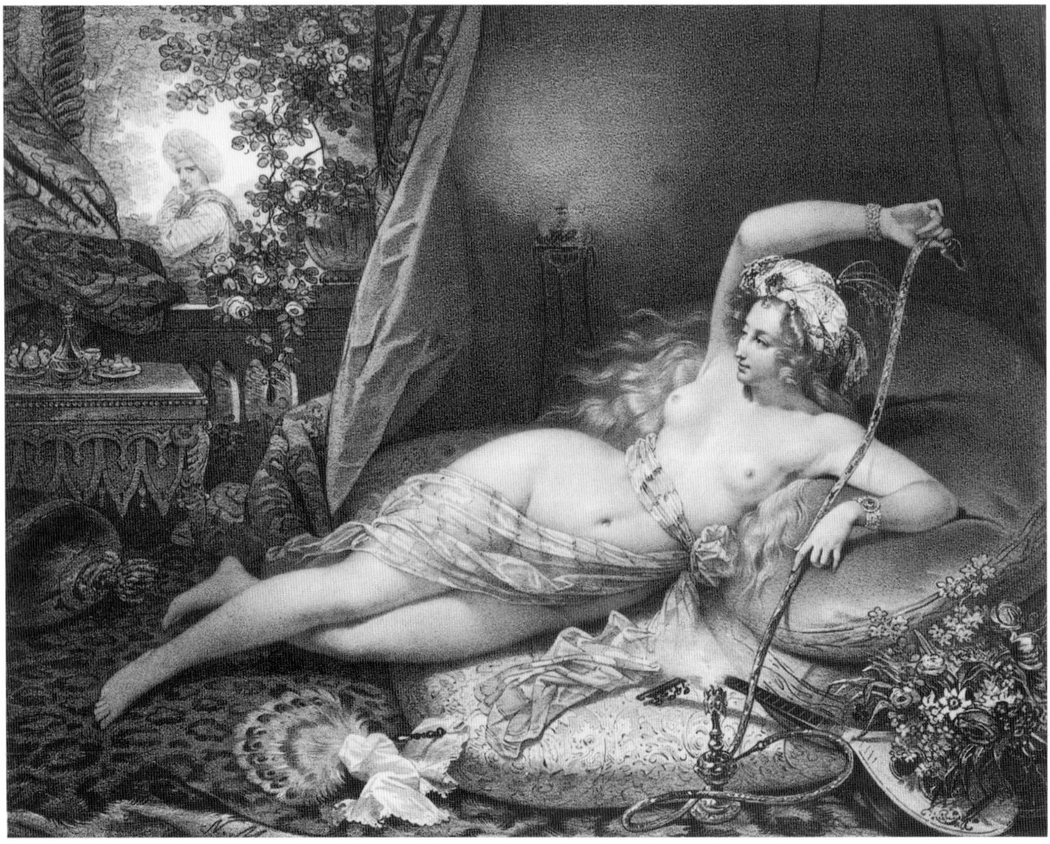

Fig. 4.23. Nicolas Eustache Maurin. *Asie: Asia*. Ca. 1830. Lithograph. Cliché Bibliothèque nationale de France, Paris. Farwell, *FPLI*, v. 11, 2A7 B82446.

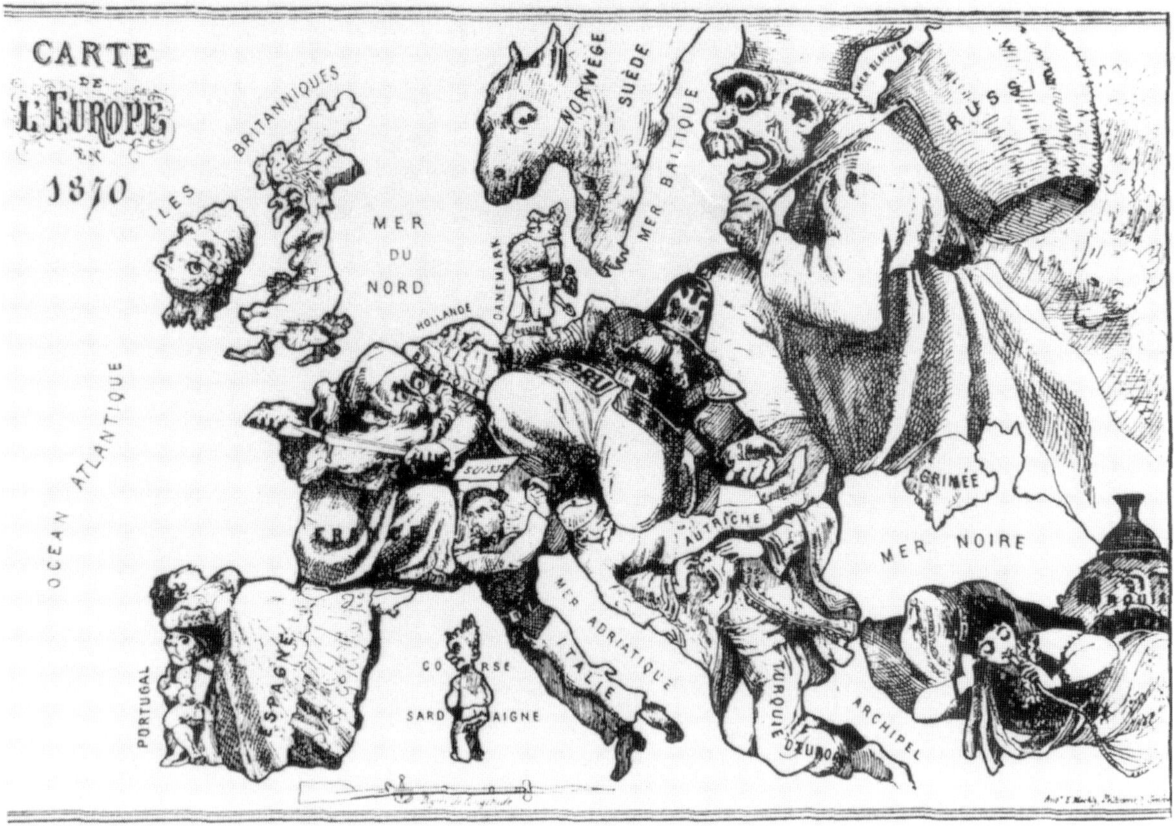

Fig. 4.24. ***Carte de l'Europe en 1870. French animated map of Europe.*** **1870. Used with Permission, Harcourt Publishers.**

as a means of restraining the birds—and the women. In the interrelationships of Persian, Latin, Italian, and French language similar words have been conflated in associating the harem with animal cages. Even today the Italian word *serraglio* (compare the French *sérail*) refers to the royal buildings in Constantinople, the women's apartments there, and notably "'a cage for wild animals.'"[37]

Caged birds do occur in Régnier's 1843 lithograph, *La marchande d'oiseaux des tropiques: georgienne* (see Fig. 2.7); though it has a French title, it is a British-looking image of a harem woman fully clothed and surrounded by eastern birds done after "Barker."[38] Small finches are caged to the right, but larger exotic birds surround this rare and exotic Georgian creature, who is herself confined by the grating over the window.[39]

The white dove serves as docile ornament to an elegant lady in John Brett's[40] *Lady with a Dove: Madame Loeser* (Fig. 4.37) of 1864. In this portrait commissioned by her husband the greying hair of Mathilde Dinkelsbühl indicates that this is an individual and not simply a female type. The dove alights on her shoulder, one wing forming a graceful line to accent the outline of the woman's face. In this interior there is nothing to indicate imprisonment. The dove suggests Christian conversion, claims Mike Hickox.

An earlier full-length picture of a woman in profile with a caged bird of indeterminate species and others uncaged around her is *A Pet* (Fig. 4.38) by the Pre-Raphaelite, Walter Howell Deverell, exhibited at the Liverpool Academy in 1853.[41] Again the title refers to the woman as well as the bird with which she plays. In the exhibition catalog the Deverell entry includes a quotation from the contemporary poet, W. J. Broderip: "'But after all, it is very questionable kindness to make a pet of a creature so essentially volatile'"; again the term "pet" is used to refer to either the animal or the woman. The poet William Rossetti drew out the erotic undertones in the subject of the woman and the bird in his sonnet "The Bullfinch" (1869), in which the woman feeds the bird with her tongue "'which rosily / Peeped as a piercing bud between her lips.'"[42]

An even earlier British work related to Deverell's, Brett's, and Lewis's is Edwin Henry Landseer's chalk portrait, *Miss Ellen ("Nellie") Power* (Fig. 4.39), a half-length view of a young woman seen in a partial profile; she plays with a single uncaged white dove. Reflecting the type of beauties popular in the *Keepsake* annuals,

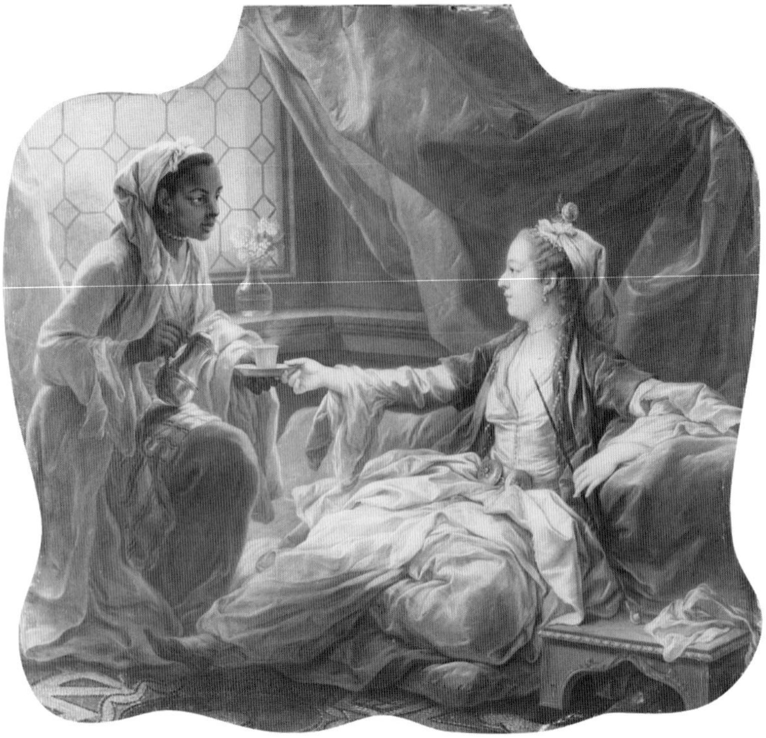

Fig. 4.25. Carle Vanloo. *Une sultane prenant du café, réprésentée sous les traits de Mme. de Pompadour.* 1755 Salon. State Hermitage Museum, St. Petersburg.

this picture's sitter lived from 1831–49 with Lady Marguerite Gardiner, Countess of Blessington (*née* Power) (1789–1849), prolific *salonnière* and editor of the *Keepsake.*

In part birds occur in harem pictures because they were actually pets there. Increasingly birds were also pets in the Victorian middle-class home.[43] But the bird-woman theme can also be traced to several literary and pictorial traditions: the classical literary tradition of the East; French erotic images—popular and high art alike, where they were already a symbol of the libertine woman; and British portraiture. Sometimes the bird is an erotic allusion to the woman, however subtle; sometimes it is merely an exotic touch. When they are seen symbolically, birds can be correlated to a range of readings about the degree of (sexual) freedom harem women have.

In French and British iconography, cats have a number of meanings. Occasionally the cat is conflated with a dog,[44] as when it suggests fidelity or when it indicates the wanton woman, as it does in the French rococo boudoir scene. In the early eighteenth century Vanmour claimed that the cat is revered in the East.[45] In the mid-nineteenth century one commentator claims they are quite rare.[46] In Indian harems they were reputedly used to kill poisonous snakes.[47]

Conversely, the harem woman herself is considered a feline—and a dangerous one at that—in an article from an 1862 periodical published by Charles Dickens's son: "it is to be more than suspected that the deep inner nature of the Persian Khanum [*sic*] is that of the panther or the tigress."[48] Here the image provoked by the harem woman as cat is that of wild (oversexed?) beast.

In three of John Lewis's harem pictures cats appear, and they bear some relationship to human inhabitants.[49] In his *Hhareem* (see Plate 1) two cats can be identified, as Lewis draws upon his youthful experience as an animal painter to represent several kinds of animals here including birds and even bees (*C* 1850:253). (At least from Thomas Moore's 1817 poem bees near a hive were another harem symbol.[50]) One cat is nestled in the cushions between the pasha and the "indolent" wife, another under the small fruit table at right. Cats are used by Lewis in a Hogarthian way: to reflect on the reclining women. His cats look less like wild beasts and more like sleepy kittens, suggesting the notion of the indolent harem woman. Responding to *Hhareem*, the *Athenaeum* finds parallels between people and the cats. The animals indicate the somnolent mood of the composition. The women are "just around from their enjoyment of luxurious

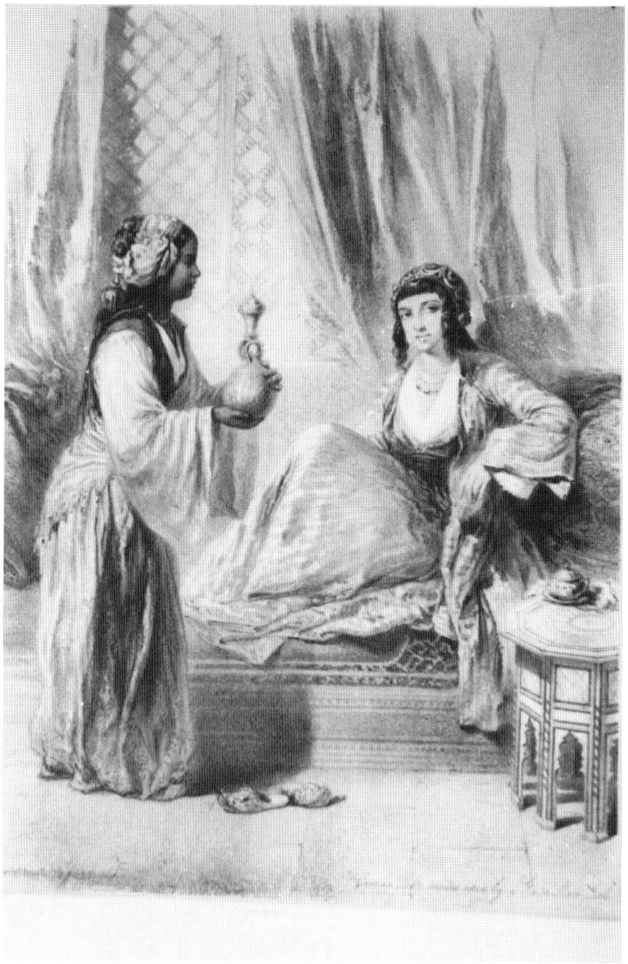

Fig. 4.26. Adolphe Mouilleron after Prisse d'Avennes. *Cairene Lady Waited Upon by a Galla Servant.* 1848. Lithograph. *Oriental Album,* plate 10.

repose." And "a cat in a similar state of somnolency [as the child] fills in and gives richness to this mass of Oriental luxury, with its sleepy suggestion" (*A* 4 May 1850:480).

Secondly, in Lewis's 1857 watercolor *Harem Life—Constantinople* (see Fig. 3.39) the reclining woman plays with a household cat, "holding over it a feather-fan, from which the animal has torn portions of the feathers" (*AJ* 1857:178). The cat's luxurious coat and lounging pose serve here, as in the 1850 *Hhareem,* as analogy for the sumptuously dressed reclining woman. Ruskin likens cat to harem woman when he injects an element of ambiguity in his response to the showing of this painting. Does he refer in this comment to the cat or the woman as dangerous feline? "but Van Eyck could not . . . have given all her tigerish strength and cruel waywardness to the couchant cat" (*W* 14:132). In a fascinating flip-flop of the stereotype of the dangerous harem woman, a cruel eastern boy, one of the "embryo pashas," beats and tortures girls who no longer are the aggressor but the meek submissive victims, "a whole [N.B.:] flock of little girls."[51] This comment appears in an article published within a year of Lewis's painting.

Thirdly, in the right foreground of Lewis's 1872 *Prayer of Faith* (Fig. 4.40) a cat lies quietly below the black eunuch who half-reclines, his hands folded. Curiously, the cat's coloration matches that of the sick woman's dress, black and white with a pink accent, paralleling the harem woman with that animal. The eunuch's awkward pose is rather unusual. Half-sitting, half-reclining, he is crouching like an animal.

This odd pairing of a eunuch with a cat appears in a French harem picture showing a sick harem woman. In Georg Opiz's *El Hashim, ou le Médecin* (Fig. 4.41) the gentleness (emasculation?) of one of two attentive eunuchs is suggested by his subservient placement at the woman's feet and by the fact that he holds the cat, perhaps caring for it, because she

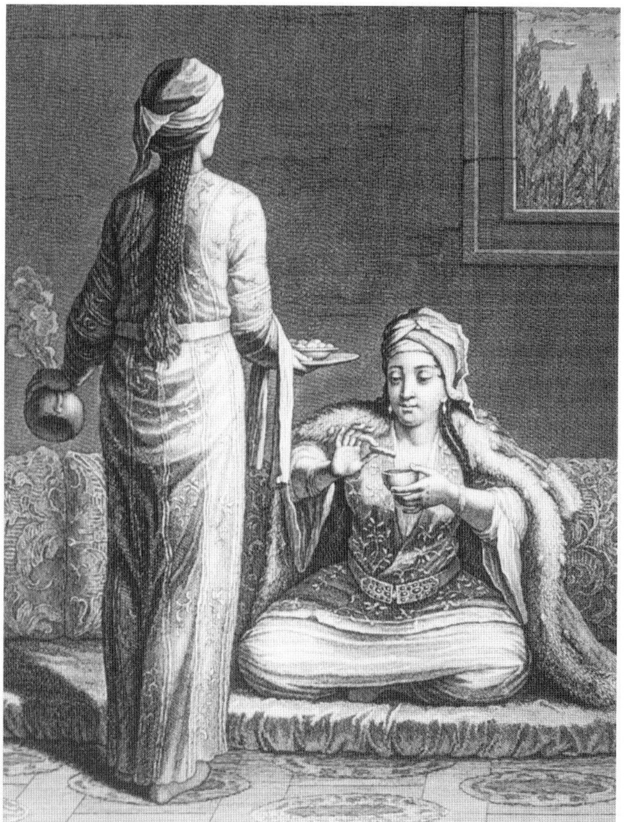

Fig. 4.27. After Vanmour. *Fille turque prenant le caffé sur le sopha.* Ca. 1715. Engraving. *Recueil de cent estampes,* plate 48. Department of Special Collections, Charles E. Young Library, UCLA.

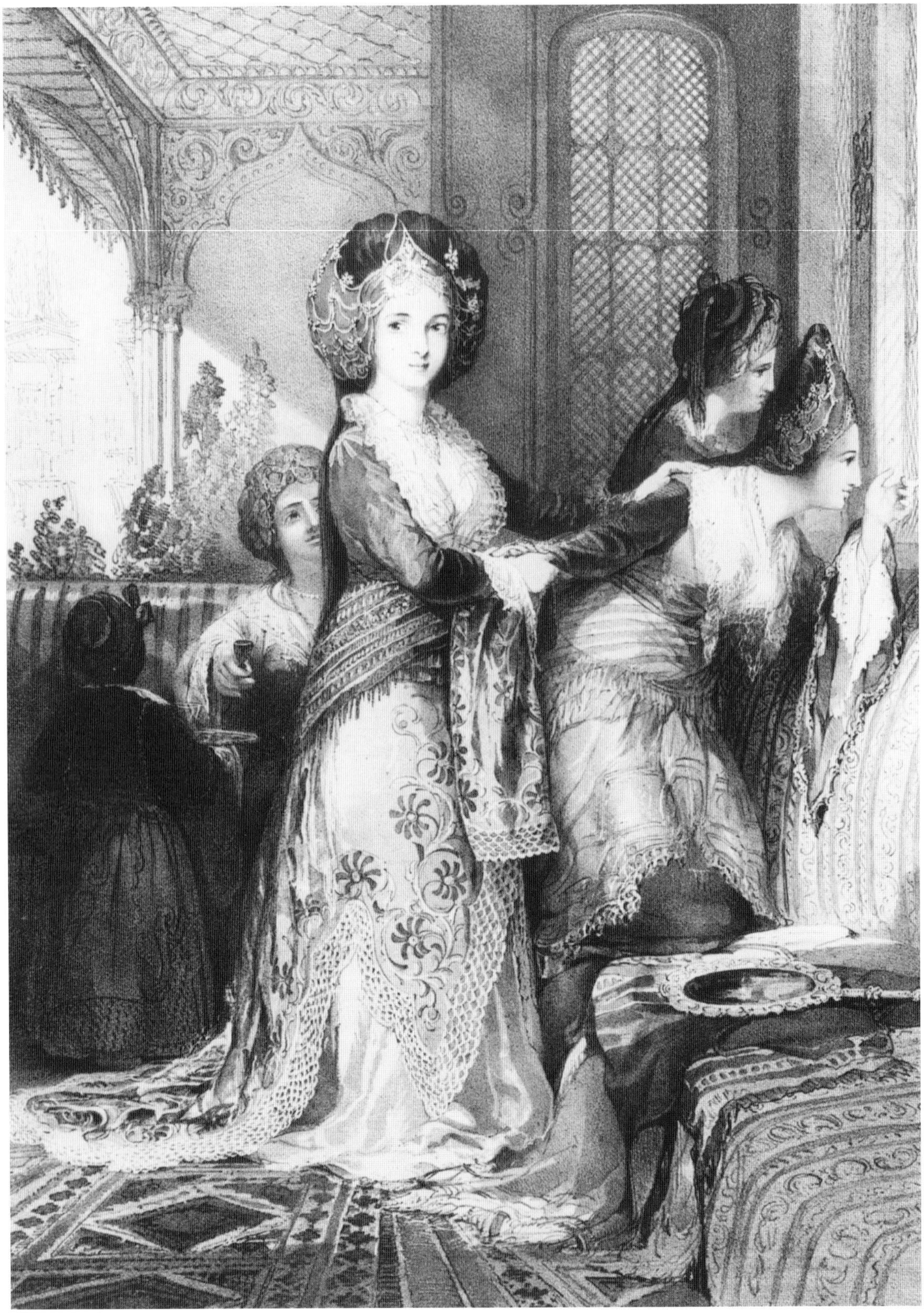

Fig. 4.28. C. Hullmandel after Thomas Allom. *The Odalique* [*sic*] *or Favourite of the Harem, Constantinople.* Lithograph, 1839. Yale Center for British Art, Paul Mellon Fund.

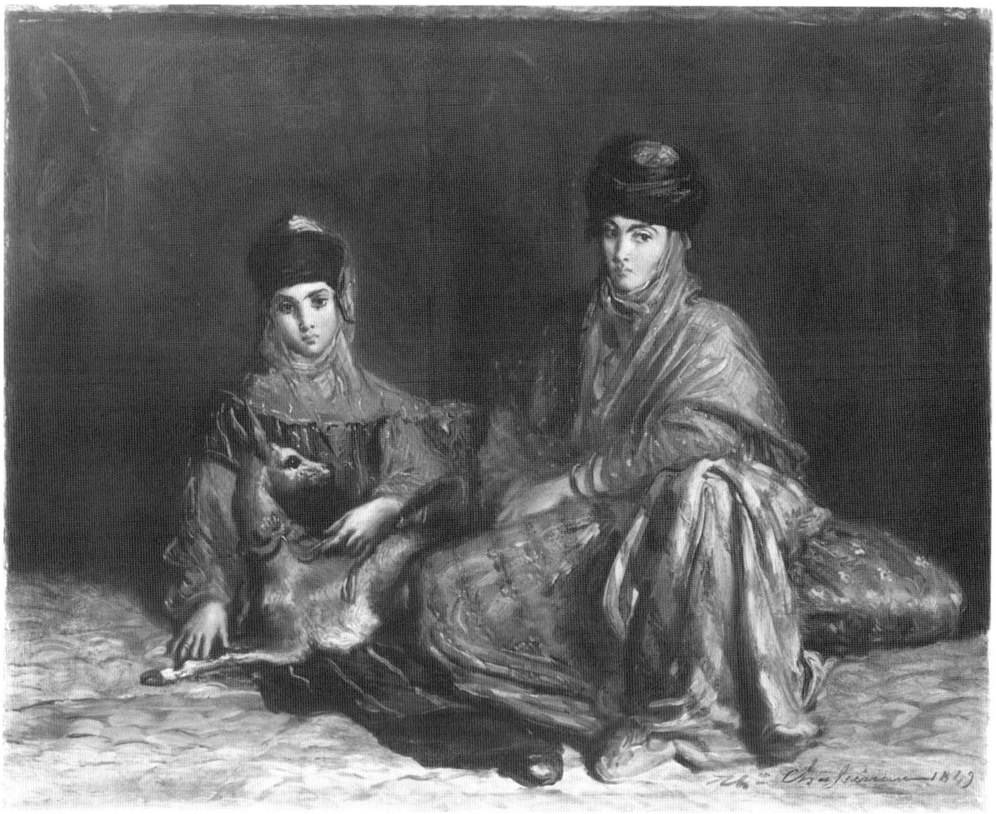

Fig. 4.29. Théodore Chassériau. *Woman and Little Girl of Constantine with a Gazelle.* 1849. Oil on wood. The Museum of Fine Arts, Houston; Museum purchase with funds provided by the Agnes Cullen Arnold Endowment Fund.

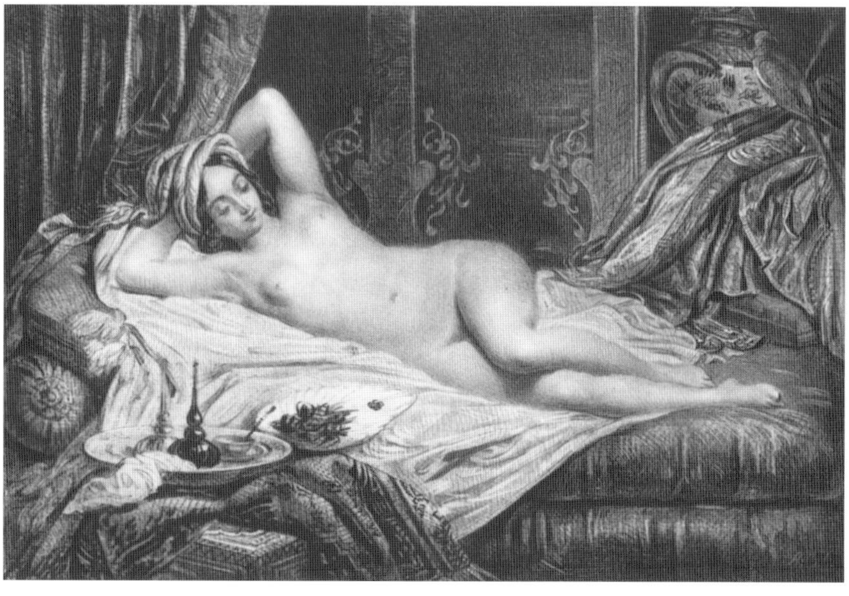

Fig. 4.30. Colin. *L'Odalisque.* Lithograph. *Bulletin de l'ami des arts.* Cliché Bibliothèque nationale de France, Paris.

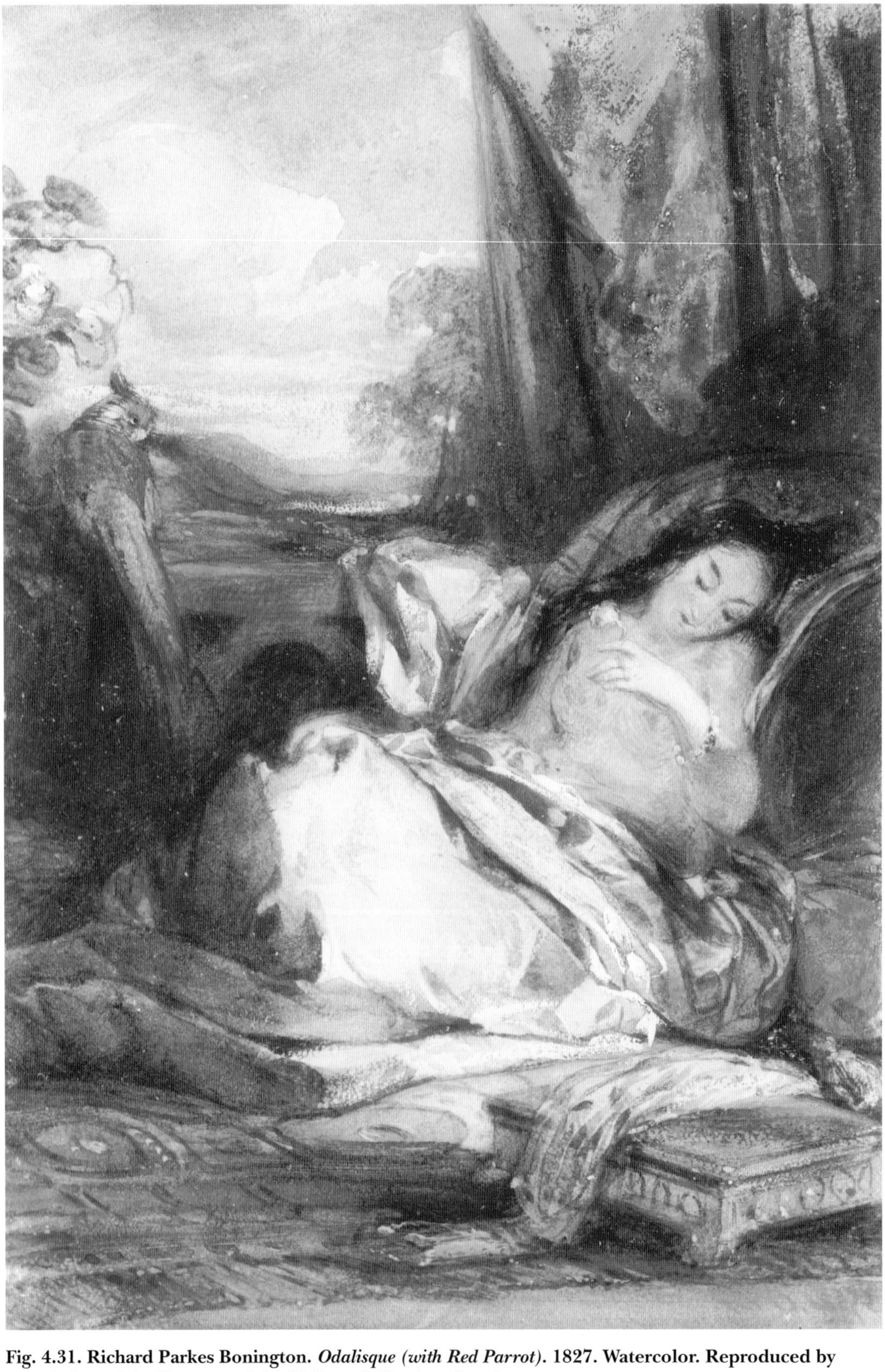

Fig. 4.31. Richard Parkes Bonington. *Odalisque (with Red Parrot)*. 1827. Watercolor. Reproduced by permission of the Trustees of the Wallace Collection, London.

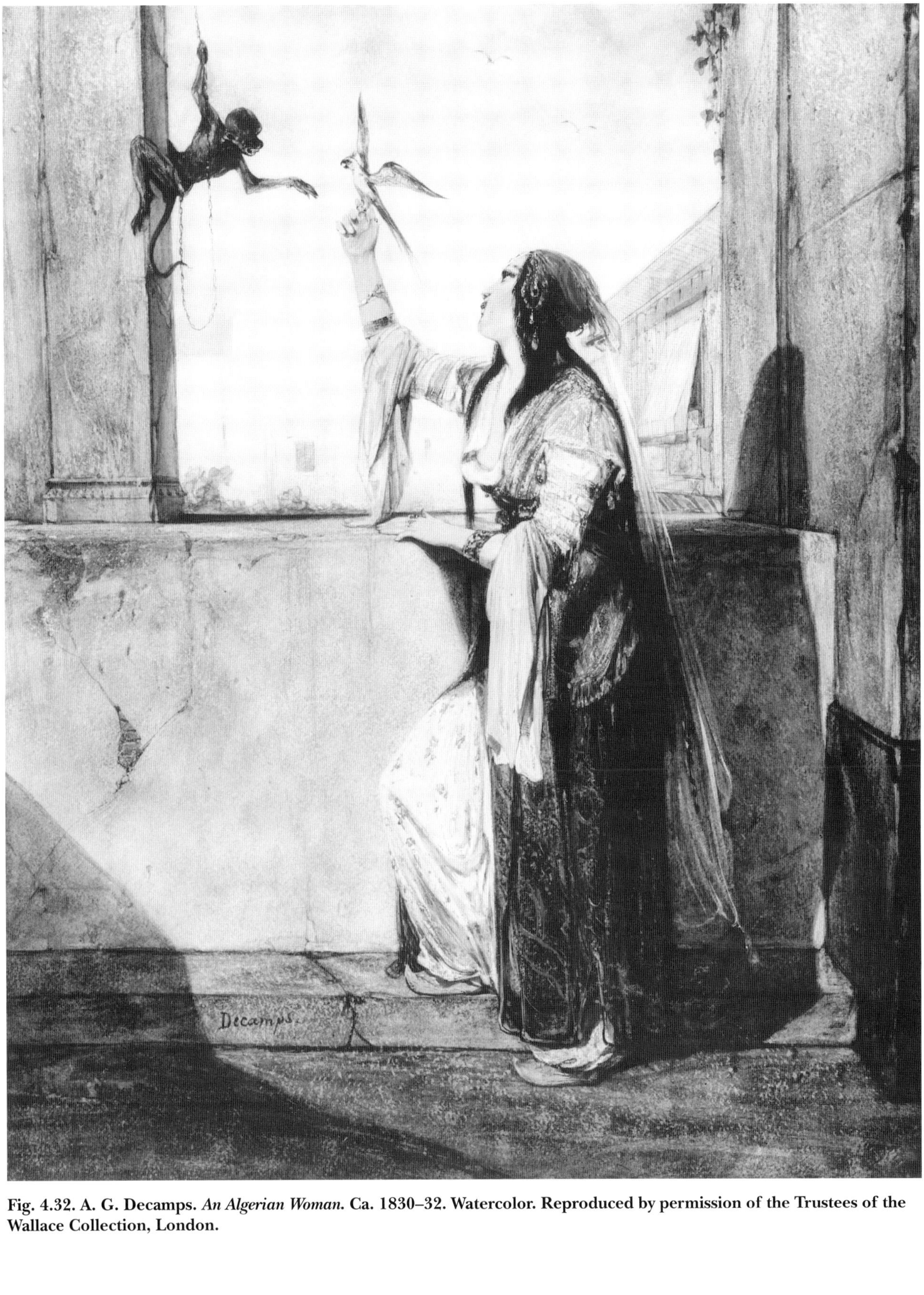

Fig. 4.32. A. G. Decamps. *An Algerian Woman.* Ca. 1830–32. Watercolor. Reproduced by permission of the Trustees of the Wallace Collection, London.

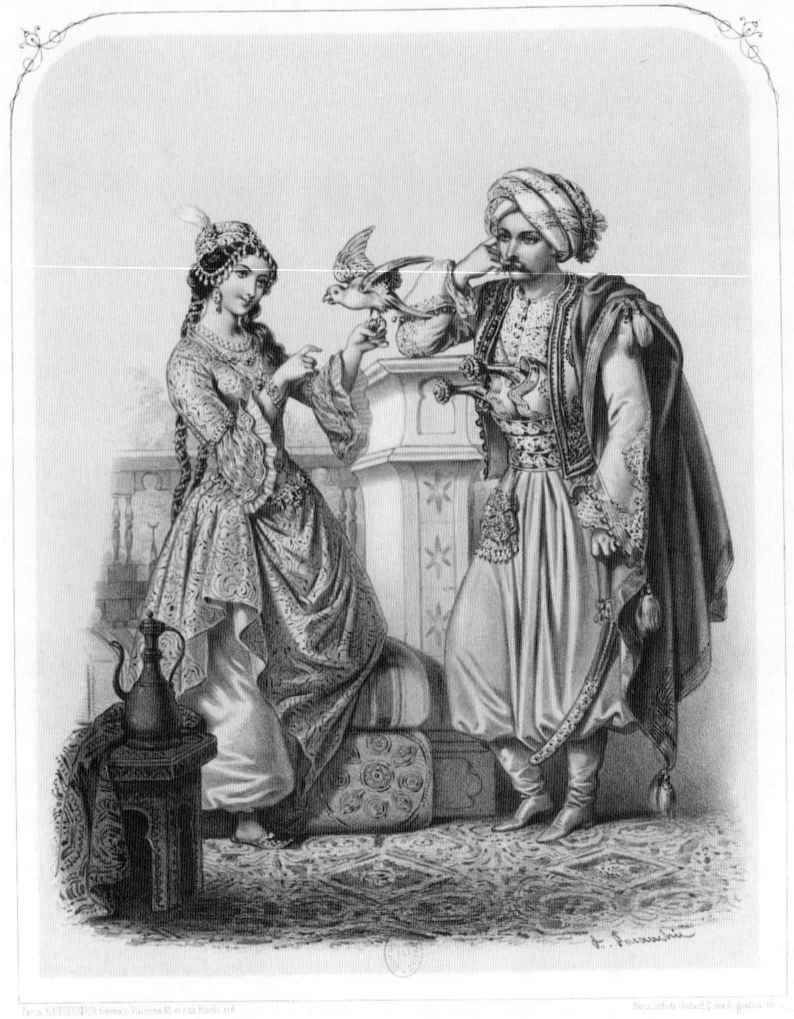

Fig. 4.33. Lacambrie. *Costumes Turcs.* Lithograph. Cliché Bibliothèque nationale de France, Paris.

is too ill to do so. Here the artist has placed the tail rather incongruously near the eunuch's knee where it gets more formal emphasis, perhaps alluding to his castrated phallus.

Lute Music

British and French travelers reported women singing and playing musical instruments in the harem primarily to entertain each other in their long hours of leisure and sometimes to entertain their master. Music can be the Romantic expression of the state of their (confined) soul or the prelude to seduction. In the ongoing parallel that can be developed between the harem and Paradise, music is one of the attributes of both locales. Music in heaven, according to some Muslim traditions, is the sound of the heavenly doors creaking or the greetings of the gatekeeper to those who enter.[52]

Occasionally, the instrument is simply an ethnographic oddity. Eighteenth-century images of harem women playing stringed musical instruments include the engraving after Vanmour entitled *Fille turque jouant du tehegour* (his plate 51) (Fig. 4.42) and its derivation, his portrait of *Lady Mary Wortley Montagu and Her Son* c. 1717 (see Fig. 3.33).[53] And in the early nineteenth century Edward William Lane's concerns seem largely documentary as he illustrates both an *'Ood* (Fig. 4.43), an instrument which is wider in the body and shorter in the neck than the instrument Vanmour showed, and then *A Performer on the 'Ood* (*ME* 2:67–68). He writes that it is a forerunner of

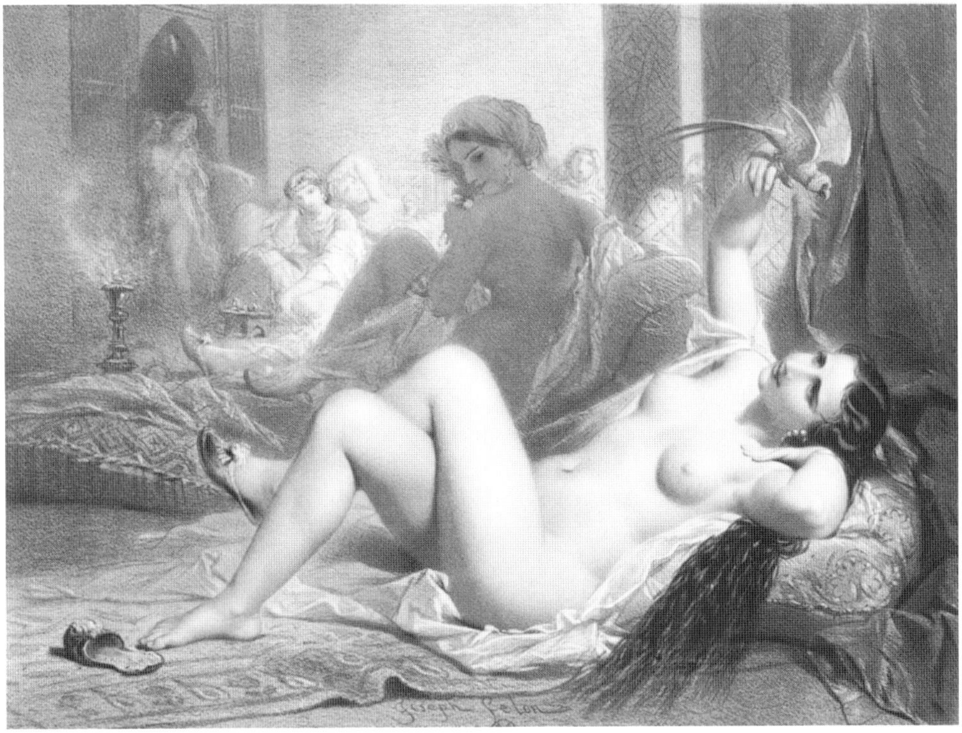

Fig. 4.34. Joseph Félon. *Le Harem.* 1850. Lithograph. Cliché Bibliothèque nationale de France, Paris. Farwell, *FPLI*, v. 11, 2C4 B78483.

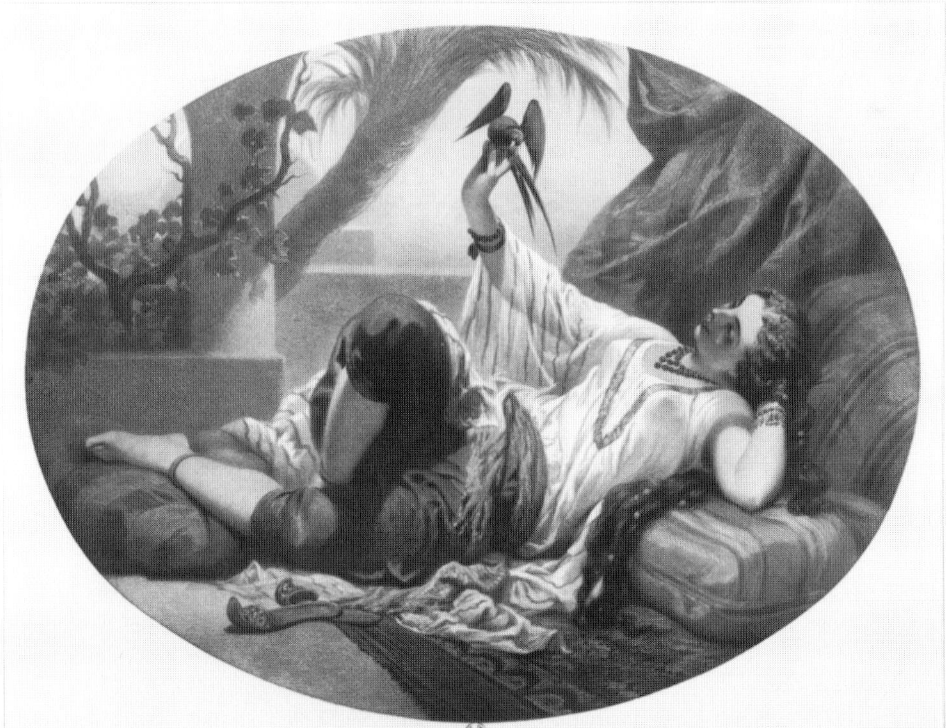

Fig. 4.35. Régnier after Désondré. *Fatime.* 1856. Lithograph. Cliché Bibliothèque nationale de France, Paris. Farwell, *FPLI*, v. 11, 2D6 B64029.

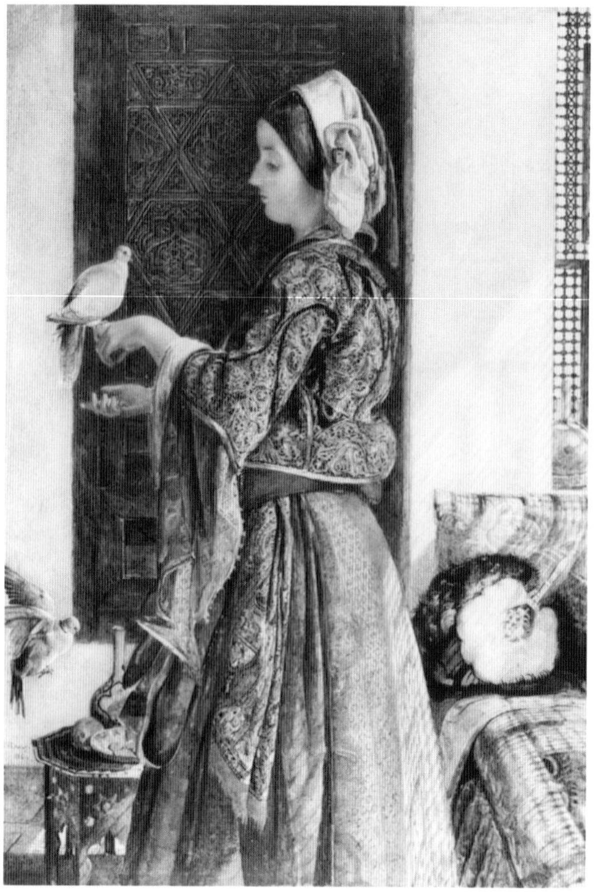

Fig. 4.36. John Frederick Lewis. *Caged Doves, Cairo.* 1864. Watercolor and bodycolor. Reproduction by permission of the Syndics of the Fitzwilliam Museum, Cambridge.

the Italian lute, describing in detail its double chording and how it is played with a plectrum. He claims that Arab musicians and poets have used it for centuries. His ethnographic drawing seems to have been a model for Thomas Allom in his 1838 lithograph *Circassian Slaves* (see Fig. 2.4). In Allom's narrative, part of the Circassian's charm is her musical ability, which in combination with the pipe is the means of seduction.

Sometimes it is a servant who plays the *'ood* for the harem woman, as in Bonington's 1828 *La Siesta* (see Fig. 2.14) and lulls her into the somnolence that is so crucial to defining this image's eroticism. Similarly, in Ingres's *Odalisque with Slave* (1842) (see Fig. 2.3), the servant's music combined with her mistress's having indulged in the hookah brings her to a state of indolence. Ready for love, she has removed her garments and now raises her arms in a gesture of abandon thus exposing her body in anticipation of her master's arrival. (Is his virility symbolized by the massive red column so prominent in the background?) In Ernest Hébert's 1843 *Deux Odalisques* (see Fig. 4.15) one of the women fingers the stringed instrument, but seems too languid to make music given her heavy posture and supported head.[54] A more playful rendering of the servant making music to arouse the female occurs in *La musique* (Fig. 4.44), an 1845 lithograph done by Régnier and Bettannier after Charles Auguste Bouvier, in which loose hair and *déshabillé* distinguish the affected listener from the musician.

In all four of these images, the servant not only provides music to arouse the woman for an unseen master, but there is the piquancy of a sexual interest between them. This theme of harem music leading to lesbian love[55] is perhaps most fully developed in Ingres's famous *Turkish Bath* of 1863 (Fig. 4.45), though here the locale is the bath and not the harem. Like a servant who offers coffee, this attendant who "serves" music has her back to the spectator.

In striking contrast to these images, the harem woman playing the *'ood* provides wholesome family entertainment in *A Turkish Family Picture* (see Fig. 3.1), illustrating Edmund Spencer's 1837 book. Like the Victorian ideal of the daughter playing the piano, this woman's interests are meant to be read as pleasant diversion and ladylike accomplishment rather than the entree to seduction.

Sometimes the stringed instrument is present but is not played in a harem interior. In Boucher's 1746 *Sultana Reading in the Harem* (see Fig. 3.34) the "tehegour," though still prominently displayed in the foreground, has been set aside. The sultana is reading, an intellectual pursuit; the instrument she has abandoned symbolizes its perceived opposite: erotic pleasures. The lute set aside suggests the potential for sexual activity in Bonington's so-called *Medora* of 1826 (Fig. 4.46), a work whose subject is based on Byron's *Corsair* of 1814. In the tiny watercolor a brown-skinned Medora has abandoned her lute, though it is draped with a silk scarf. This and the metal curass she holds serve as reminders of the absent Conrad. The couple's mutual "music-making" must await his return.

In Thomas Moore's 1817 poem the harem woman Zelica plays "a small lute of gold and sandal-wood," and it is music that draws her old lover Azim to rediscover her and seal the fate of their illicit love (*LR* 33). For Lamartine, the nonverbal communication of silent love affairs in the East is "the highest and most divine language of love" comparable to music (*PHL* 40). Lord Byron offers a particularly rich few lines in the opening scene of *Sardanapalus* which link the sounds of musical instruments to relaxation, to the harem women, to lovemaking, and to the harem

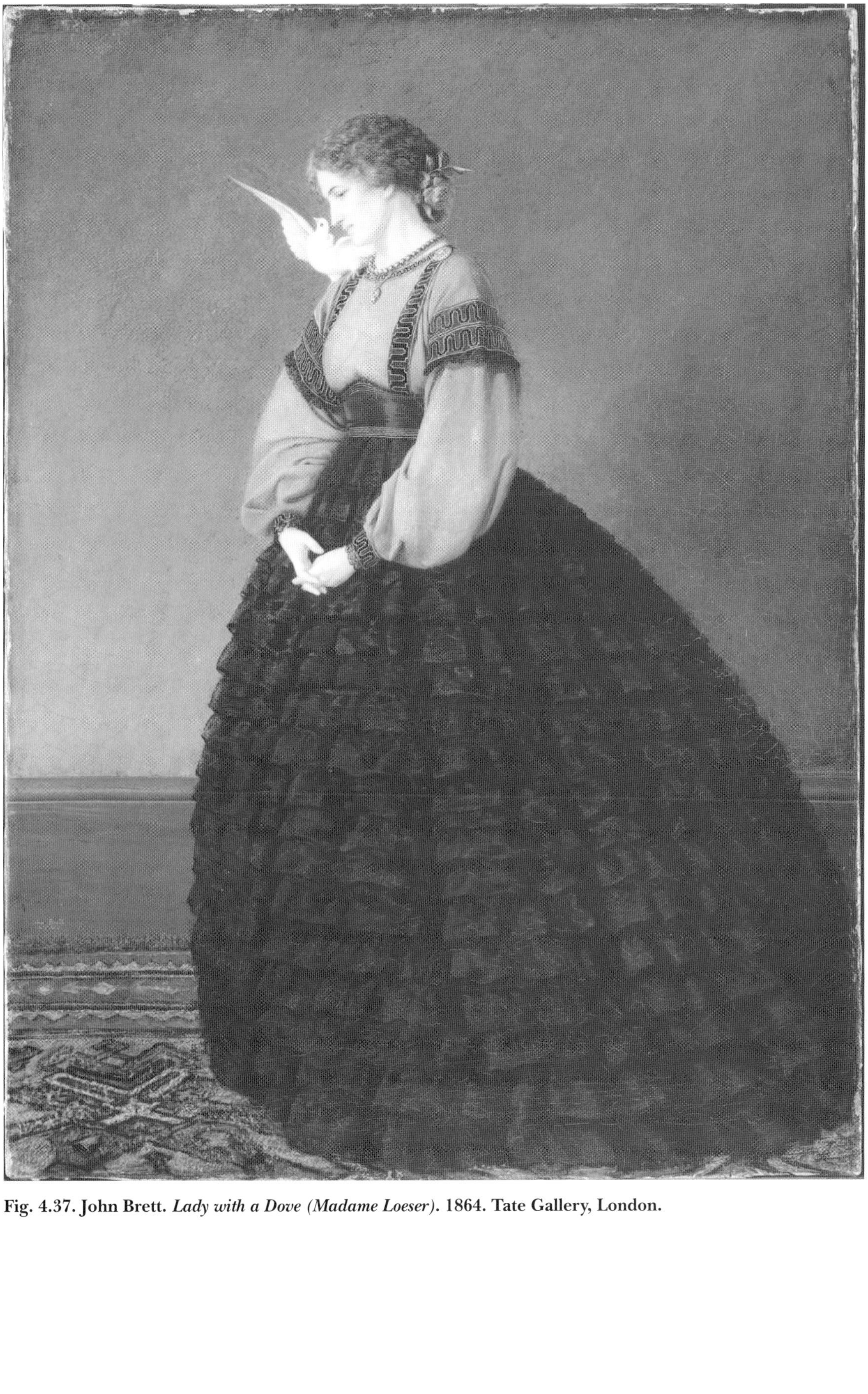

Fig. 4.37. John Brett. *Lady with a Dove (Madame Loeser)*. 1864. Tate Gallery, London.

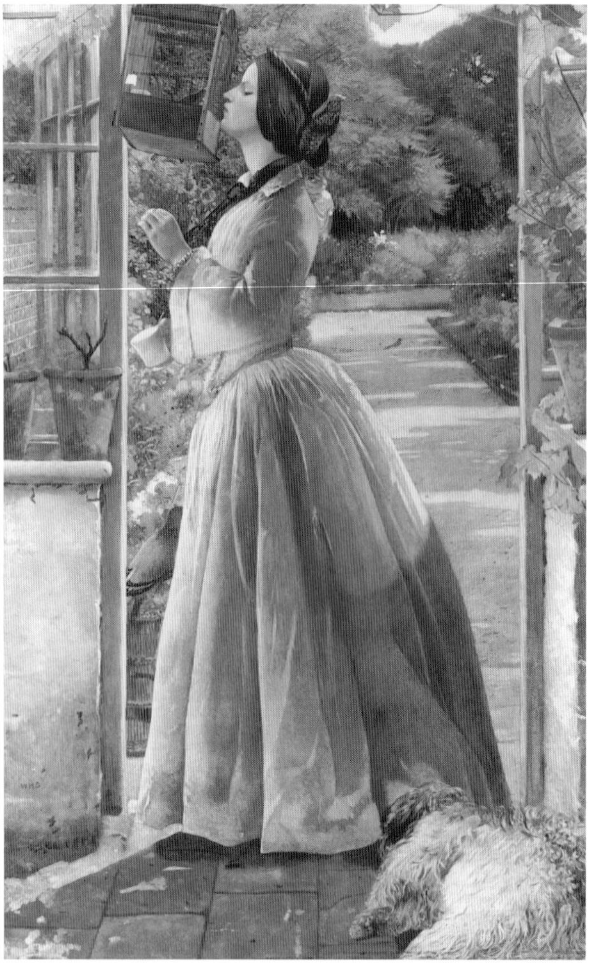

Fig. 4.38. Walter Howell Deverell. *A Pet.* 1853 Liverpool Academy. Tate Gallery, London 1999.

eunuchs: "Hark! The lute / The lyre, the timbrel; the lascivious tinklings / Of lulling instruments, the softening voices / Of women, and of beings less than women" (*WB* 196). The music Salemenes hears evokes the narcotic pleasures of the harem at a moment when he laments his brother-in-law's obliviousness to problems in the land.

Moore, Byron, and Lamartine help solidify the Romantic use of musical motifs in harem pictures to suggest eastern love, an association that continues throughout the rest of the nineteenth century.

Symbolic Flowers

The flower has been perhaps the most frequent symbol of femininity in European pictorial traditions. When it appears in harem pictures, its meanings become even richer. Flowers have particular significance in the context of late Georgian/early Victorian garden history, where the flower-female connection recalls gentility, social ease, and privilege. Garden flower symbolism used in a context of harem pictures has its own conventions, considered in a subsequent chapter. This section concerns flowers used symbolically within the harem interior.

Roses are a common metaphor in eastern literary traditions. They are strewn over the floor in a harem described in *Arabian Nights.*[56] Floral-patterned carpets often follow the architectural scheme of outdoor gardens[57] and symbolize the celestial garden in Paradise, inhabited by the houri, beautiful companions in the afterlife. According to Prophetic tradition, the rose, symbol of spirituality, sprang from the perspiration of Muhammad's forehead as he journeyed to Heaven. Its perfume reminds believers of the Prophet, who loved roses. The rose can also symbolize Divine perfection and beauty. According to Islamic tradition, then, the beautiful women of Paradise resemble the rose.[58]

Paradise, Muhammad, the rose, and its pleasing odor are linked in a French lithograph from 1851 by Nicolas Maurin, *L'Odorat* (Fig. 4.47) from the series *Paradise de Mahomet.* Visually the image is indebted to playful French rococo love imagery, replete with *putti,* flower garlands and a frontal, lightly clad female, set outdoors and visually exposed to the viewer. Muhammad is almost incidental to the attention given to the beautiful houri, whose waist his large hand encircles. He has reached Paradise, shown as a sylvan environment but really embodied in the woman and, by extension, the perfume of the rose. The harem woman's aroma is likened to a flower's in Thoré's response to Delacroix's *Odalisque with Parrot*: "A tepid perfume like the exhalation of a flower or of a woman dominates this tranquil interior."[59]

The earliest reporters claimed that harem women, who were often thought illiterate, communicated by means of flower symbolism with their outside lovers. In 1718 Lady Mary Wortley Montagu sent a sample of a Turkish loveletter to a female friend; it included flowers, fruit, spices, and other small objects—all with specific, detailed meanings, which she explained. Popular nineteenth-century guidebooks on flower symbolism referred to the Turkish tradition of symbolic readings of flowers. A later Victorian book on flower symbolism verifies this in quoting a verse from Percival:

> In Eastern lands they talk in flowers,
> And tell in a garland their loves and cares,
> Each blossom that blooms in their garden bowers,
> On its leaves a mystic language bears.[60]

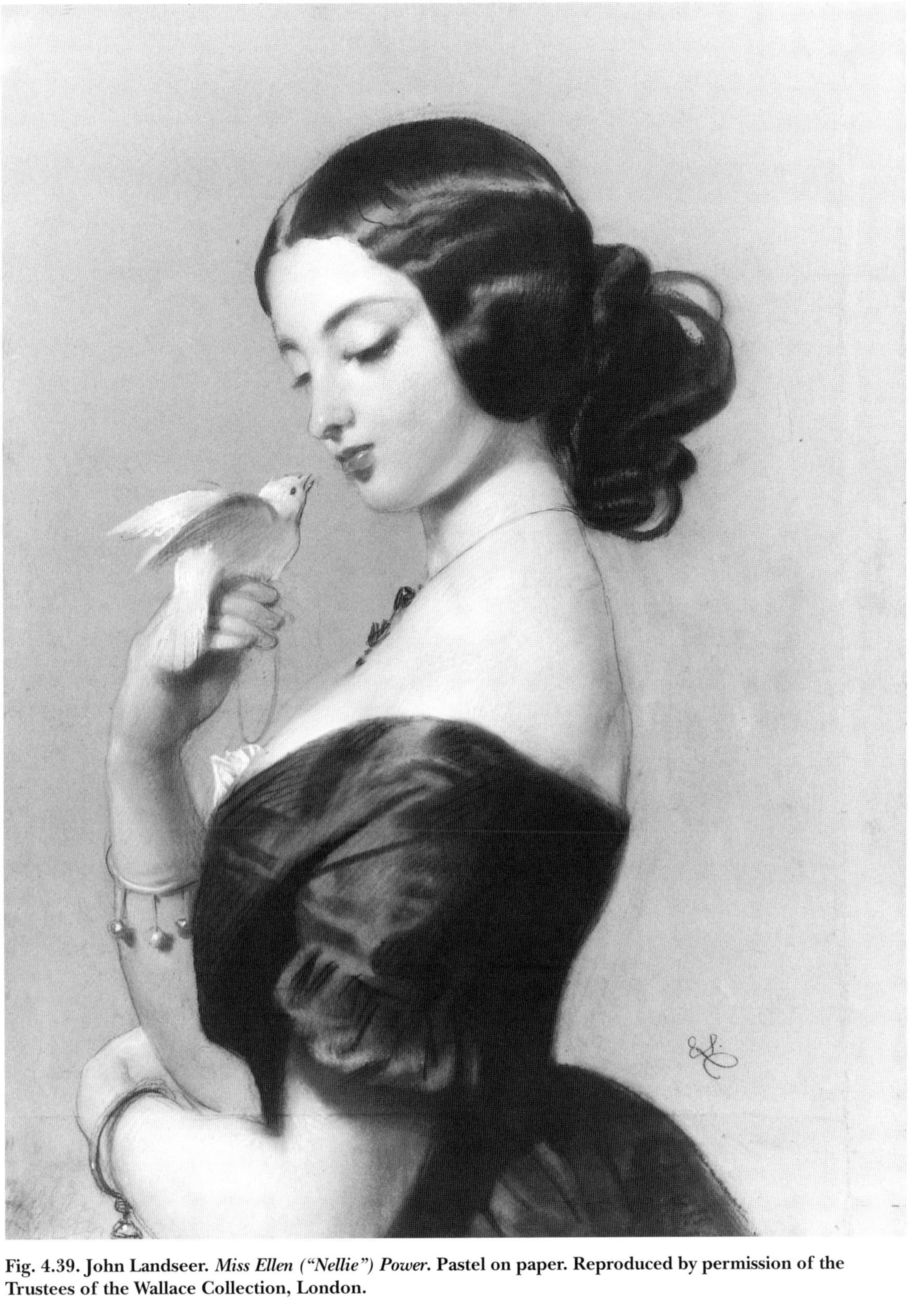

Fig. 4.39. John Landseer. *Miss Ellen ("Nellie") Power.* Pastel on paper. Reproduced by permission of the Trustees of the Wallace Collection, London.

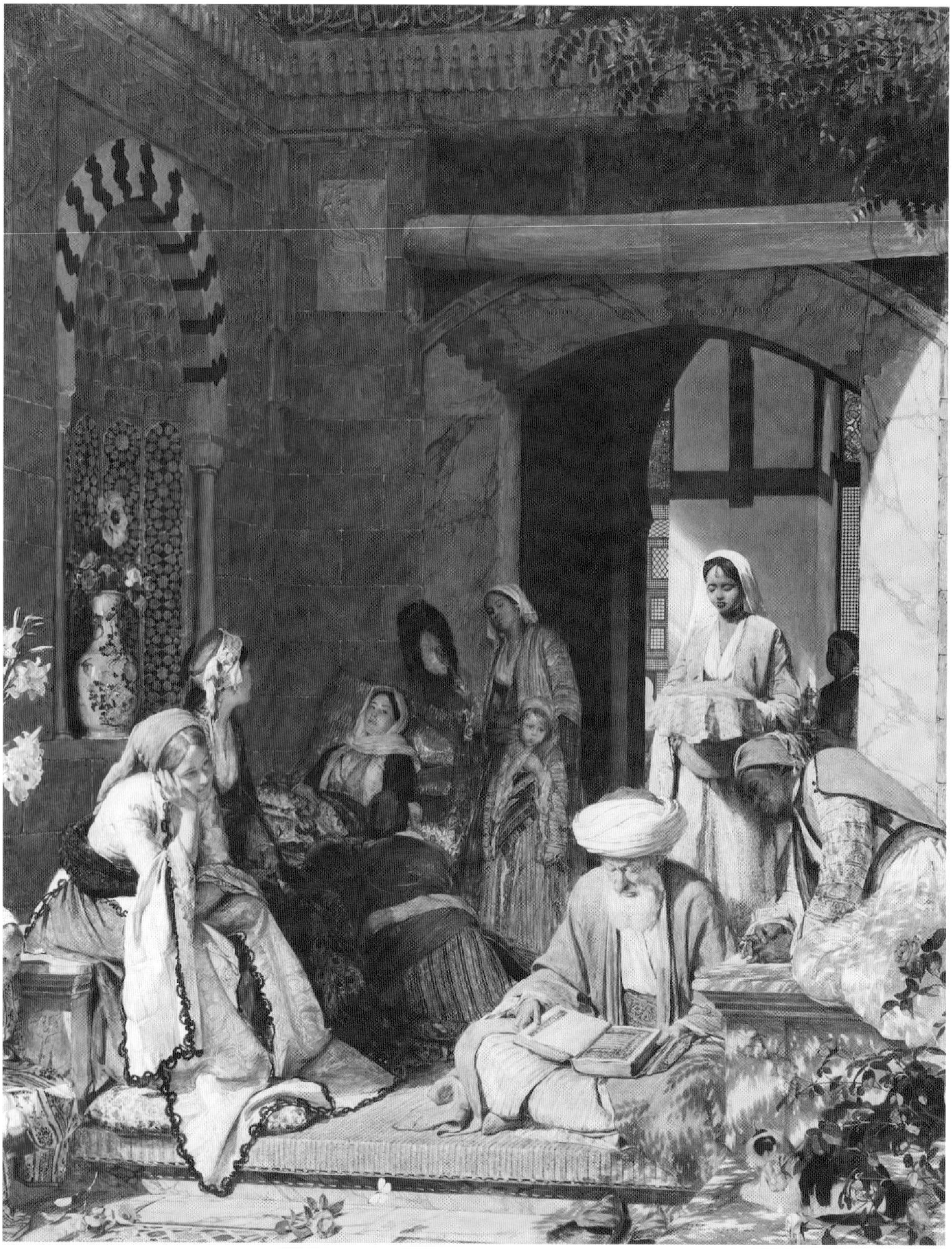

Fig. 4.40. John Frederick Lewis. "*And the Prayer of Faith Shall Save the Sick*" *(James 5:15)*. 1872. Watercolor. Yale Center for British Art, Paul Mellon Collection.

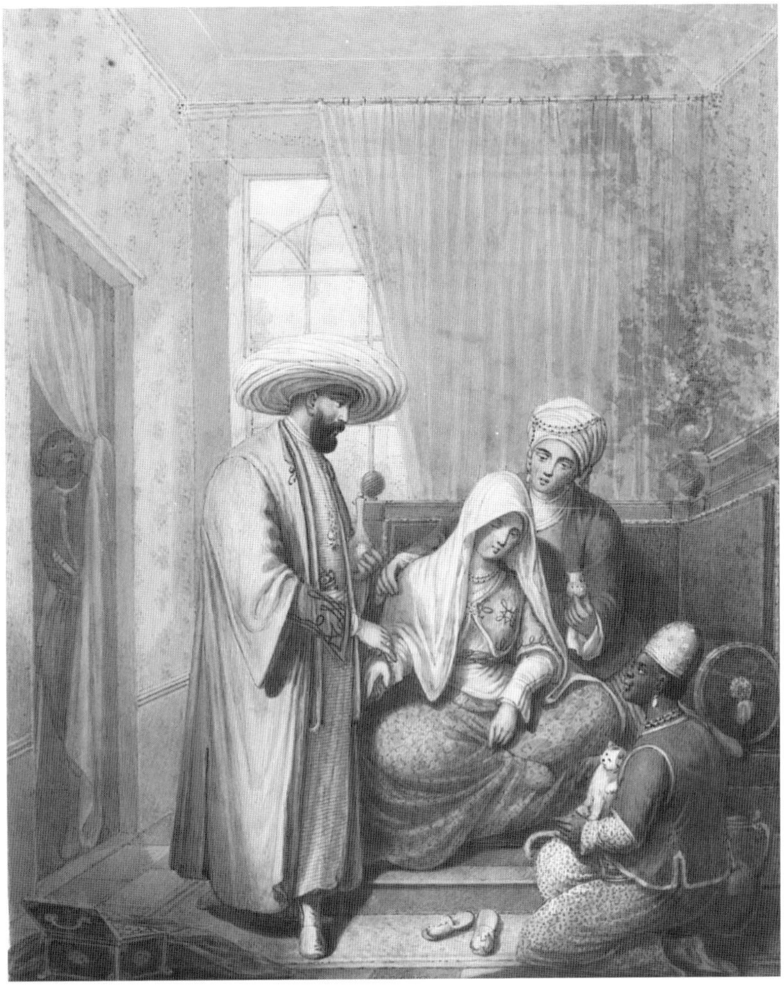

Fig. 4.41. Georg Emmanuel Opiz. *El Hashim ou le Médecin*. Lithograph. Cliché Bibliothèque nationale de France, Paris.

In the rococo harem tradition, flowers served as symbols for the women. An engraving after Vanmour is one of the earliest harem images in which flowers are included. In his plate 68, *Dame grecque dans son appartement* (see Fig. 3.28) a vase of flowers is prominently displayed in the room; they are rendered in careful detail, so that their stems are visible through the glass vase suggesting a symbolic value. One flower has fallen from the bouquet and lies on the table outside the vase, a possible allusion to the Greek woman's displaced status as foreigner. In two of the three harem images which Madame de Pompadour purchased from Carle Vanloo c.1755 to be hung in her Bellevue boudoir[61] a case could be made for the flowers as allusion to the women. In one of them, *Une sultane prenant du café* (see Fig. 4.25) the glass vase of flowers on the window sill are unobtrusive, except that "Madame de Pompadour" wears the same type of pink rose in her turban. Such symbolism continues in Richard Parkes Bonington's 1827 rococo-revival *Odalisque (with Red Parrot)* (see Fig. 4.31) in which a bare-breasted odalisque muses upon the single blue and white flower in her hand, a metaphor for love.

At first glance the harem woman might pass for Shakespeare's Ophelia in Henry William Pickersgill's 1824 painting of a privileged woman who focuses intently on arranging symbolic flowers. But the painting's title, *Oriental Love-Letter* (Fig. 4.48) makes explicit that these are flowers arranged in a harem. If she is composing an illicit love letter, her passion would need to be powerful indeed to break her confinement, suggested by the great volumes of rich, embroidered silk curtain that all but cover her window in this scene and shield her from the outside world. Pickersgill paints a "luxurious prison," from which a pathetically meager floral arrangement offers only the slimmest hope of escape.

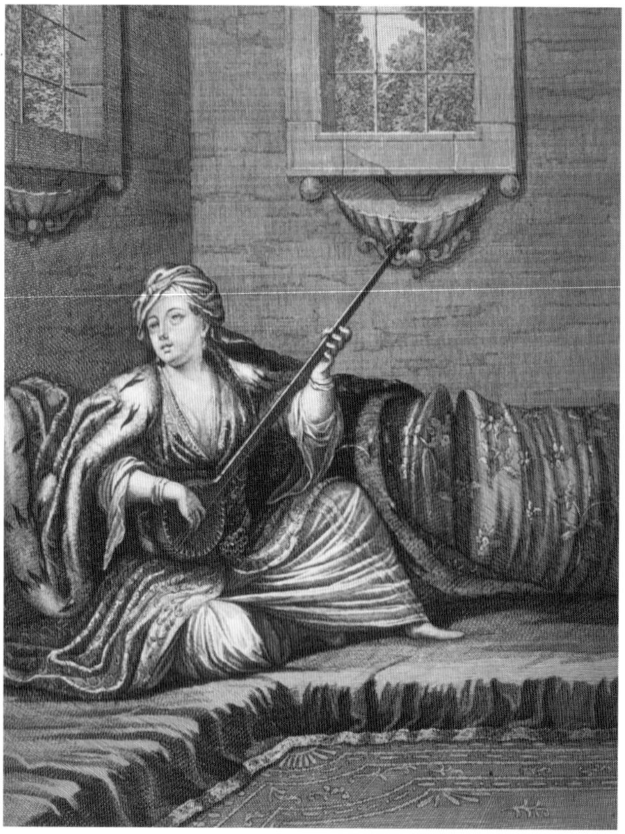

Fig. 4.42. After Vanmour. *Fille Turque jouant du tehegour*. Ca. 1715. Engraving. *Recueil de cent estampes*, pl. 51. Department of Special Collections, Charles E. Young Library, UCLA.

In several lithographs from the July Monarchy flowers are clearly symbols for harem women. There is an extravagant bouquet in Maurin's unrestrained lithograph from 1830 *Asie: Asia* (see Fig. 4.23); even more flowers are visible in the rose bush seen through the window. The Turkish woman's bust portrait (which resembles Ingres's 1814 *Grande Odalisque* in its headdress) is encircled by the narcissus, an apt symbol for the reputedly self-absorbed harem woman[62] in Devéria's 1831 *Le narcisse de la Turquie: The Narcissus of Turkey* (Fig. 4.49), number 21 from the series significantly titled *Les fleurs et les femmes.* According to Islamic traditions, the narcissus looks like the eye but is blind.[63] Two roses appear prominently in the foreground referring to a couple seated on the ground in Eugène Delacroix's 1832 watercolor, *Moorish Conversation* (Fig. 4.50), done on his visit to Morocco.

In a more sexually explicit picture, the 1836 lithograph, *La femme esclave,* (Fig. 4.51) done after Jules Joseph Guillaume Bourdet (1799–1869), roses are strewn over the bed of a nude slave. Again the flowers allude to the woman within the composition—the spherical rose echoes the shape of her breasts; even the "casual" placement of the flower draped over the edge of the rug in the right foreground echoes the woman's left arm hung over the bed.

Latent sexuality is a theme in Smyth and Lewis's lithograph *Harem* (see Fig. 3.37). Two roses on the floor, one fully open, the other only partially are located in front of the women. Small as this detail may be, the roses are emphasized by their placement and their positioning, much like the two women, one older and more experienced (she wears yet another open rose in her hair), the other a younger newcomer, her hair not yet pinned up. The roses are not simply decorative details or filler but a continuation of a textual tradition, one that sexualizes the image by suggesting a host of sensual pleasures. Still, by foregoing nudity or other explicit devices Smyth and

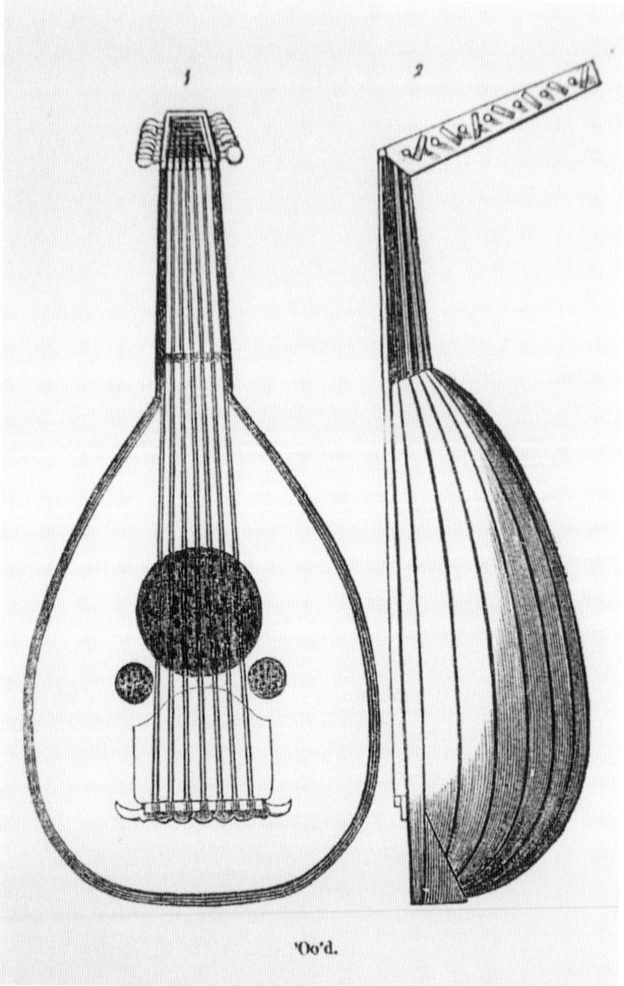

Fig. 4.43. After Edward William Lane. *'Ood.* Engraving. *Manners and Customs of the Modern Egyptians*, 1836. Photo Adam Miller.

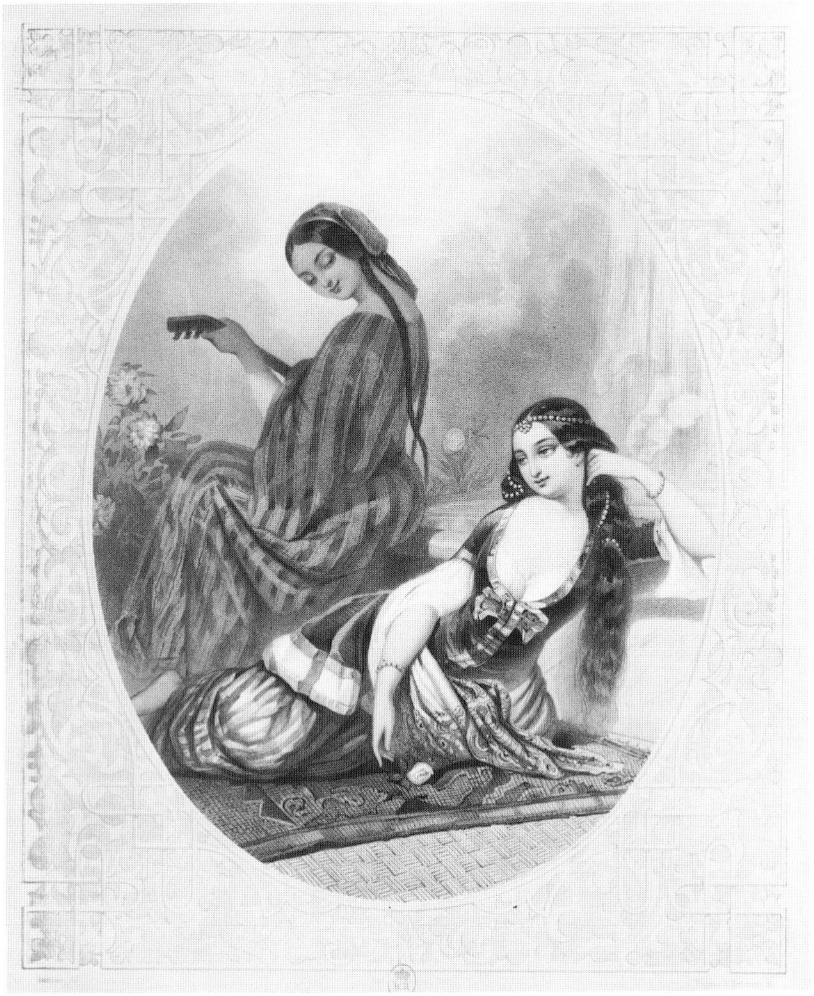

Fig. 4.44. Claude Régnier, J. Bettannier, and/or E. Bettannier after Charles Auguste Bouvier. *La Musique*. 1845. Lithograph. Cliché Bibliothèque nationale de France, Paris. Farwell, *FPLI*, v. 11, 2D9 B81763.

Lewis keep their picture tasteful and mollify titillation.

Roses in the harem are not always titillating. Harriet Martineau keeps as a memento roses given to her by the chief lady of the harem she visited. For her they are associated ironically with women who are "injured, [. . .] depressed and corrupted" by the Muslim harem (*EL* 270).

Jewelry and Slippers

Two more types of fetishized objects often found in harem representations are elaborate jewelry and slippers. Harem slippers (babooshes, in French *les babouches*) are distinctive: backless with a pointed, curled toe, they are often embroidered. Such footwear takes on significance as the more casual, comfortable, and "natural" alternative to the laced, tight-fitting ankle- or calf-high footwear popular in England and France (see Fig. 1.2). Like western footwear in nineteenth-century pictures, they are typically very small, a sign of leisure-class refinement.[64] Slippers are located in a number of places in harem images. Occasionally they are simply part of eastern garb as depicted rather dispassionately, for example, in Lacambrie's *Costumes Turcs* (see Fig. 4.33)

Though occasionally they belong to a man, harem slippers more typically are a woman's. Often they are placed in the foreground of the composition and on the floor near her (see Fig. 3.9). And when they remain on the floor they presume that the harem woman is barefoot and located in a relaxed, private interior. As such, particular representations of harem slippers constitute a sexual provocation.

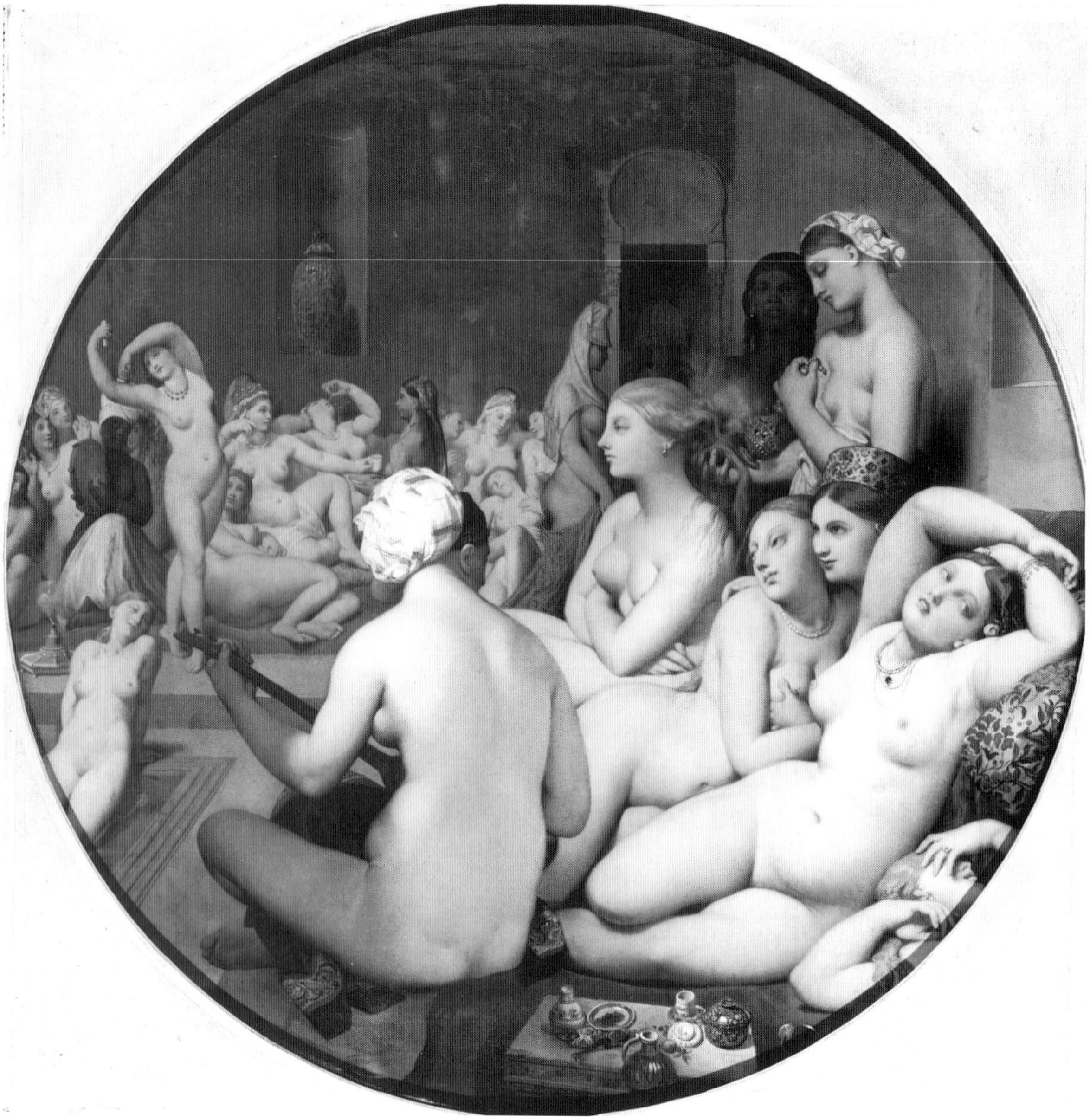

Fig. 4.45. J. A. D. Ingres. ***Bain turc.*** **1863. Musée du Louvre, Paris. © Photo RMN.**

When they are deliberately emphasized as in Lewis's *Houri* (see Fig. 4.13) or Delacroix's *Femmes d'Alger* (see Fig. 2.17) they are fetishized as a female receptacle for the male presence. This is especially noteworthy in such relatively nonexplicit works. The fitting of the foot into a shoe has been associated with sexual union, according to David Kunzle writing on the history of proverbs.[65] Like the long-standing association of femininity with flowers or fruit, the shoe in the West can be sexualized. And when its context is the harem, it must have eroticized meanings. In both their form and place within a narrative, harem slippers function as an invitation to the viewer to become the male presence.

Like a sheath awaiting its sword, the empty slipper alludes to a foot to fill it. Such an analogy has particular resonance for John Faed's *Arms Dealer* (see Fig. 3.14), where an elaborately decorated pair of harem slippers can be found in the foreground to the far right of the composition alongside a collection of weapons which are soon to be traded for the naked female slave. As the dealer already wears his shoes, these slippers might simply be more valuable booty to be swapped. Or they might well function symbolically,

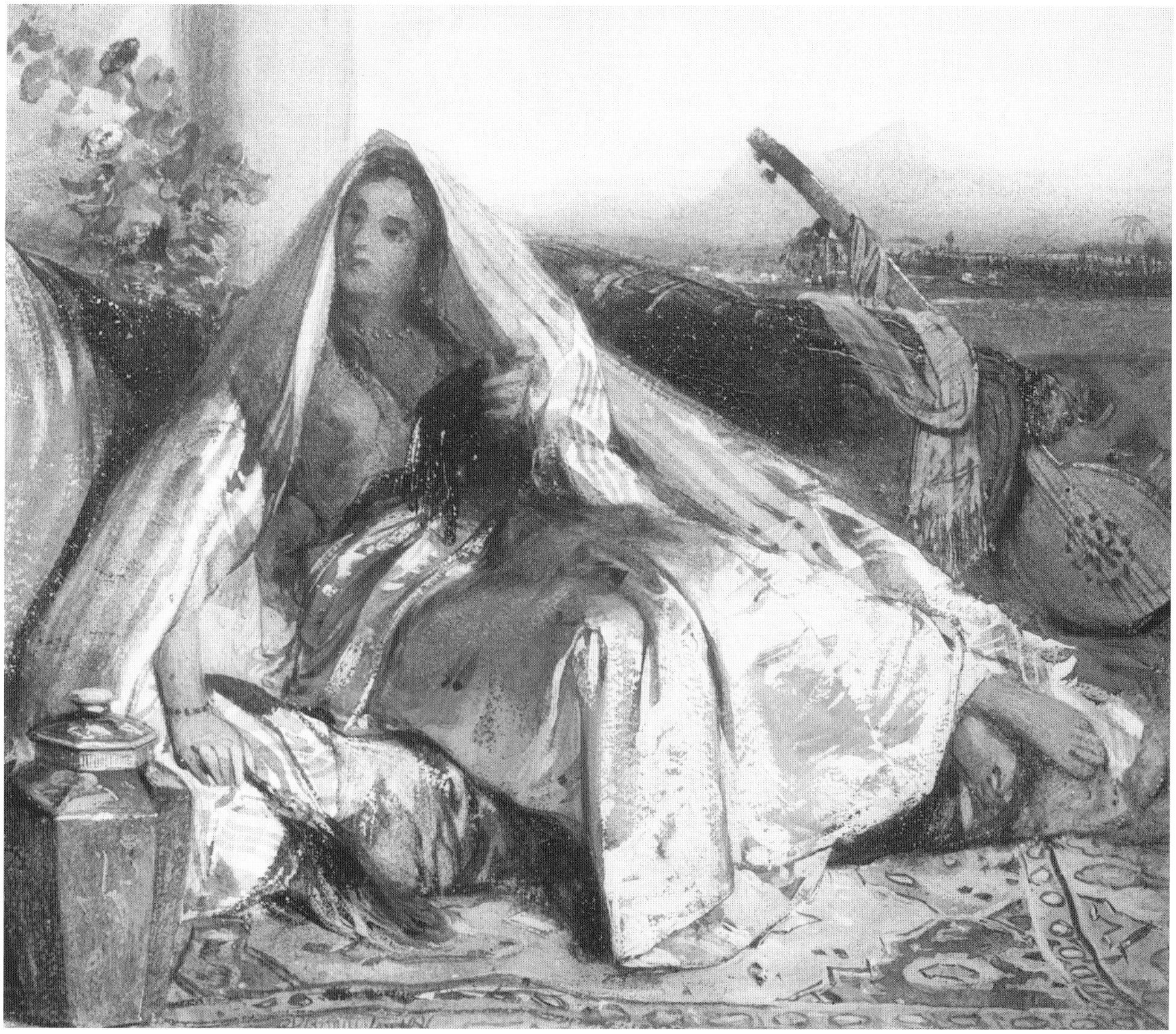

Fig. 4.46. R. P. Bonington. *Medora.* (*Odalisque in Yellow*). 1826. Watercolor. Reproduced by permission of the Trustees of the Wallace Collection, London.

alluding to the eminent sexual activity between the new slave and this buyer or another in the near future.

In several of the more lascivious popular French lithographs from mid-century one of the slippers has been removed or is being slipped off the foot, referring to the process of undressing, as in *Aux Bords du Bosphore* (see Fig. 4.21) by Bargue after de Montaut or especially Félon's *Le Harem* (see Fig. 4.34). In one of Guérard's prints from the series *La Vie au sérail*, the slipper and a shawl are removed simultaneously (see Fig. 4.7).

Harem slippers are described in British and French sources too numerous to recount. One example may suffice to illustrate the interest surrounding this exotic artifact. While visiting a consulate in Algeria, Alexandre Dumas claims to have seen a wife who appears before an arbitrator to complain about a husband. She communicates his crime nonverbally by inverting her slipper and then handing it to the consul. In naming this transgression a primitive "wickedness" (*AA* 97), Dumas hints that at issue was the practice of sodomy.[66]

Jewelry too can function as a fetish object in the harem. Jewels are a means by which the material values of the outside world infiltrate the domestic world of love and sex. In western judgments about the harem social dynamic, when a master gives extravagant jewels to one or several of his beloved women, it is a useless expenditure. If he is a high-ranking official the complaint is that he drains public

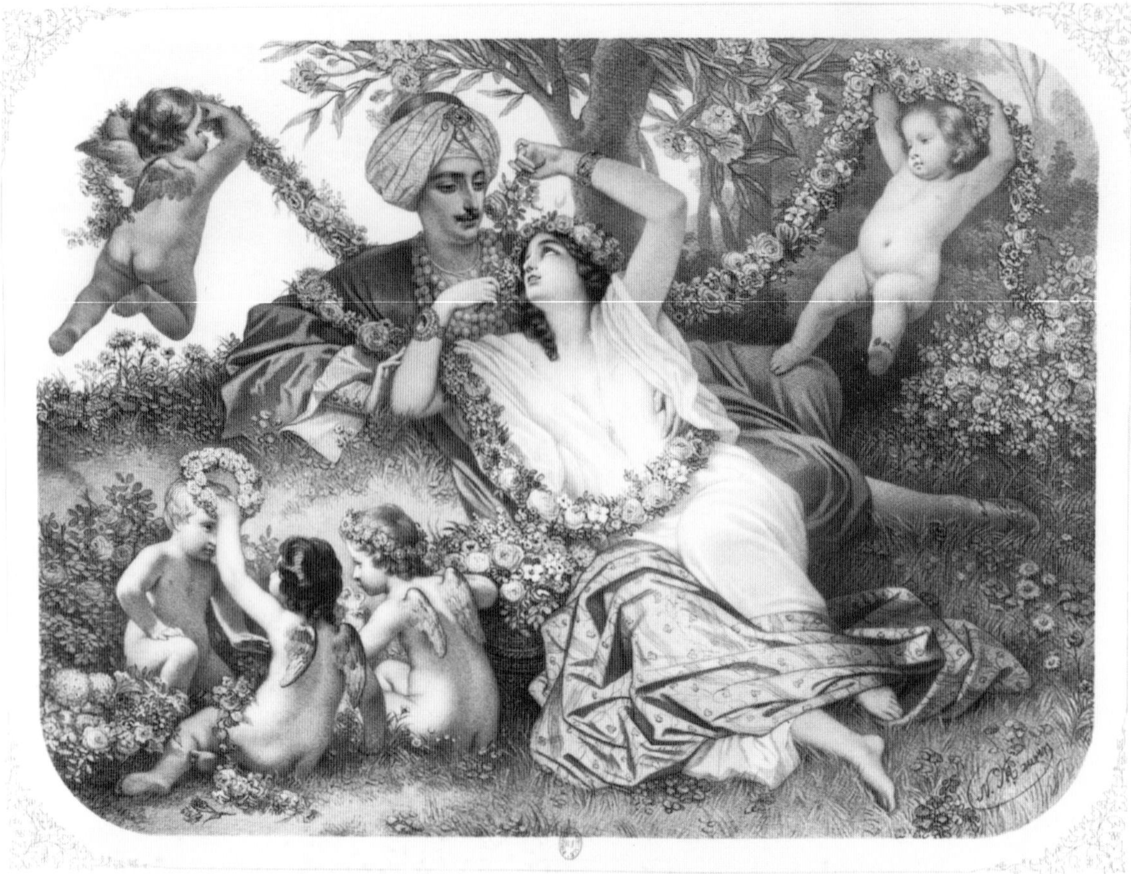

Fig. 4.47. N. Maurin. *L'Odorat, Paradis de Mahomet.* 1851. Lithograph. Cliché Bibliothèque nationale de France, Paris. Farwell, *FPLI*, v. 9, 5F9 B82692.

monies. As the moral values of the Muslim world are seen as suspect, jewels are evidence of the corruption of private and public resources. Representations of jewelry could also serve to describe the perceived power imbalance between a pasha and his women or between the pasha and the outside world.

The jewelry owned by harem women is described in innumerable accounts of harem life. Lady Mary Wortley Montagu mentions jewelry in several sections of the Turkish Embassy Letters (*L* 1:326, 381–82, 384). Lane provides seven drawings illustrating typical harem women's jewelry in Egypt (*ME* 1:313, 315–18, 320–21). Both Lady Mary and Lane are part of a scientific/ethnographic paradigm in the even-handed description they provide in discussing harem jewelry.

However, in some writing expensive jewelry functions to make more explicit the exotic nature of the wearer, her distance from European norms of taste and discretion. In this 1863 excerpt the writer slips readily from Turkish harem women's supercilious laziness to their unreasonable indulgence in gems: "the ladies . . . expect to be waited on from morn till night, and reckon pearls and diamonds as the first of their wants."[67] Writers are simultaneously fascinated and repelled by jewels, especially diamonds, for all their associations. For example, one author in 1866 uses the word "diamond" in her or his description of harem wives' clothing no less than seven times, revealing an obsession with the gem. At the same time the author criticizes it, claiming that the modest golden wedding band of Christians serves the same symbolic purpose much better.[68]

Harem jewels could be interpreted by nineteenth-century artists and writers as a reflection of the power of the men who give them. In one written account we learn that harem women who are daughters of rich men have the most magnificent display of jewels on their persons as they in effect wear "their entire dowry."[69] Another harem woman wore a diamond ring bought by her father-in-law, Mehemet Ali of Egypt, and it cost £2000 (*HTT* 112). We are reminded who owns whom and who purchased the young girl's necklace, bejeweled crown, and her gauzy clothing

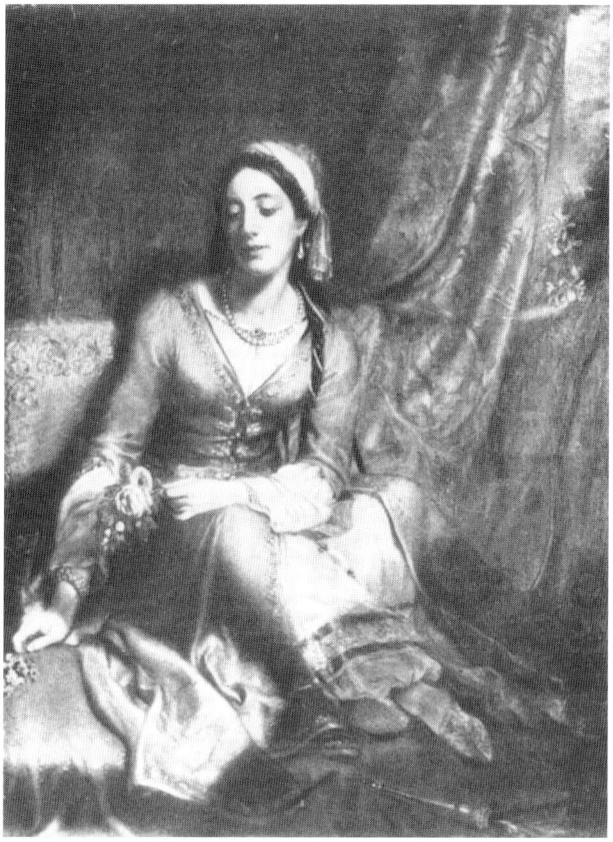

Fig. 4.48. Henry William Pickersgill. *Oriental Love-Letter.* 1824. Royal Academy of Arts. Photo courtesy Witt Library, Courtauld Institute, London.

by the layout of Jean Baptiste LePrince's *Harem Scene* (Fig. 4.52): he reaches for what are his "possessions," animate and inanimate alike. The material treasures are the woman's reward for her beauty and charm, and also what confers her status as prize.

This elision between harem stuff and a pasha's power is given a sadistic charge in the most chilling picture of a harem in nineteenth-century art, Delacroix's 1827 *Sardanapalus* (Fig. 4.53). Rather than be taken captive, the Assyrian king Sardanapalus has all his property destroyed—jewels, horses, and women. To increase the tension in this interpretation of the story, we are shown women about to be slaughtered or else now dying. Chaotic carnage, flailing limbs, female nudity are watched (and enjoyed?) by a calm master, scopically powerful, who acts as a stand-in for the viewer overwhelmed by the sex and gore. Originating from him a torrent of red tapestry hemorrhages throughout the composition. His double-suicide with his favorite slave Myrrha is imminent, judging from the 1821 play by Byron, which inspired Delacroix.

Jewels change what is simply a woman into an exotic object. They can also indicate a hierarchy among the women, as in Delacroix's *Women of Algiers* (see Fig. 2.17), where the black slave-attendant wears noticeably less jewelry than the seated women whom she serves. Without the depiction of those things Delacroix's painting would be thematically incomprehensible: the painting *is* that exotic stuff. Without her jewels (and fan, pipe, and turban) Ingres's *Grande Odalisque* (see Fig. 3.21) would be merely an academic study.

Again consulting the letters of Lady Mary Wortley Montagu proves profitable for understanding a nineteenth-century harem picture. I believe that the garb on which this odalisque lies, her turban and jewelry suggests that Ingres has drawn from Lady Mary's description of eastern women's clothing. Beginning with a close look at the metal belt which Ingres so prominently displays in the left foreground, it is jewel-encrusted with pearls and a large diamond in the center. Lady Mary describes the "Girdle" which is made of precious gems or embroidered satin and "fasten'd before with a clasp of Di'monds" (*L* 1:326). In describing the haremite's bejewelled turbaned headdress Lady Mary is quite detailed, and the correspondence to Ingres's painting is most compelling. Ingres illustrates the headgear carefully described by Lady Mary: asymmetrical summer turban, made of shiny silver material, and decorated with gold tassels. He also paints the hair bauble that resembles a "Bouquet of Jewels" and composed of pearls and various other jewels, here, the ruby which is the color of the rose and "so well set and enammell'd tis hard to imagine anything of that kind so beautifull." He parts the hair of his odalisque so that it is "divided into tresses braided" as she specifies (*L* 1:327).[70]

The jewels can be read in relation to the erogenous zones of the woman's body. The bejeweled belt, located at the base of the odalisque's infamous attenuated spine, substitutes for the cleavage in her buttocks that is denied to our view by Ingres's careful covering of it. Similarly in his 1842 *Odalisque with Slave* (see Fig. 2.34) the single darkened pearl within a necklace of white ones around her neck echoes her navel and especially her left nipple. In their polish and tactility, beauty and clarity, the jewels evoke the skin of each odalisque, while the jewels' hard, cold inanimateness accentuates the fiction of the woman's warm and vital pliancy. The jewels fetishize the women's bodies by their formal placement and narrative interaction with them.

Not surprisingly, some writers juxtapose descriptions of jewels, specifically diamonds, with a moral objection about the wearer. For example, a woman

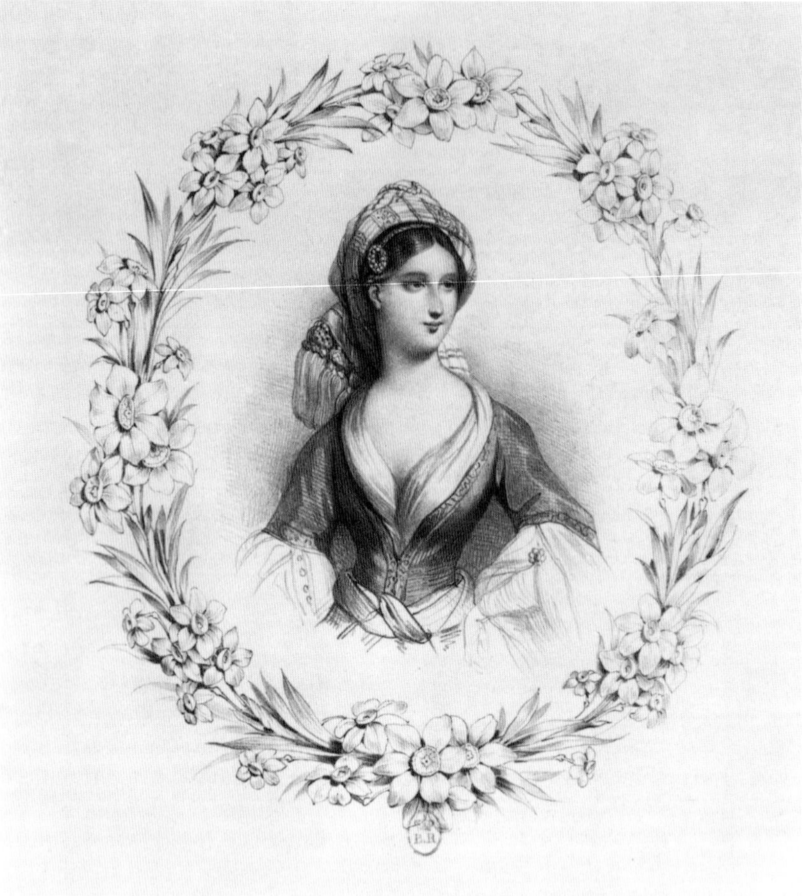

Fig. 4.49. A. Devéria. *Le Narcisse de la Turquie (The Narcissus of Turkey)*, number 21. *Les Fleurs et les femmes de tous les pays*. 1831. Lithograph. Cliché Bibliothèque nationale de France, Paris. Farwell, *FPLI*, v. 11, 2A11 B83089.

author in 1838 mentions the "diamonds and pearls . . . in profusion" on harem women but laments their wearers' ignorance, confinement and "melancholy . . . moral position."[71] Similarly, in an 1846 article also written by "A Lady" a stately sultana is dressed in extravagant clothing: silk, fur, gold embroidery, cashmere, and satin, and "to complete her costume, she was literally covered with diamonds." But again, she was "far from handsome" and "nothing could be more splendid than her dress, or more perfectly ungraceful."[72] One Persian child bride, age eleven or twelve, is described as knowing no limits to decorating herself with jewels, gold coins, and trinkets. She especially likes pearls and diamonds but is indiscriminate, inattentive to their flaws, cut or color. This illustrates the author's conclusions about her personality as uneducated, unaccomplished, "inelegant," "uncultivated" and given to "a good deal of flowery talk about roses and nightingales."[73] She is a woman-child whose acquaintance with life is unnatural, almost aberrant: "She knows a great many things which she ought not to know and [. . .] she would outwit the wisest man who ever wore a grey beard."[74] Her jewelry could not be simply beautiful; when the Good is a criterion for the Beautiful, jewelry on a harem inmate can only be falsely beautiful.

In two additional examples from British writing at midcentury the contrast between the proliferation of jewels and moral/physical health is articulated quite clearly. Harriet Martineau describes a twelve-year-old wife who wears jewels and flowers in her hair, creating the illusion of "a bouquet sprinkled with diamonds," while her facial complexion was sallow; she missed the exercise girls of her age ought to have, and harem jewels fail to compensate for such a deprivation (*EL* 267–68). And in 1850 the Indian harem inmate who is forced to revolt laments to a British male rescuer the poor treatment inflicted on the women by their cruel master: "'The splendor which surrounds us is only a mockery . . . His attendants deprive us even of our food and we sit in the beautiful palace loaded with jewels, and suffer from the hunger not felt even

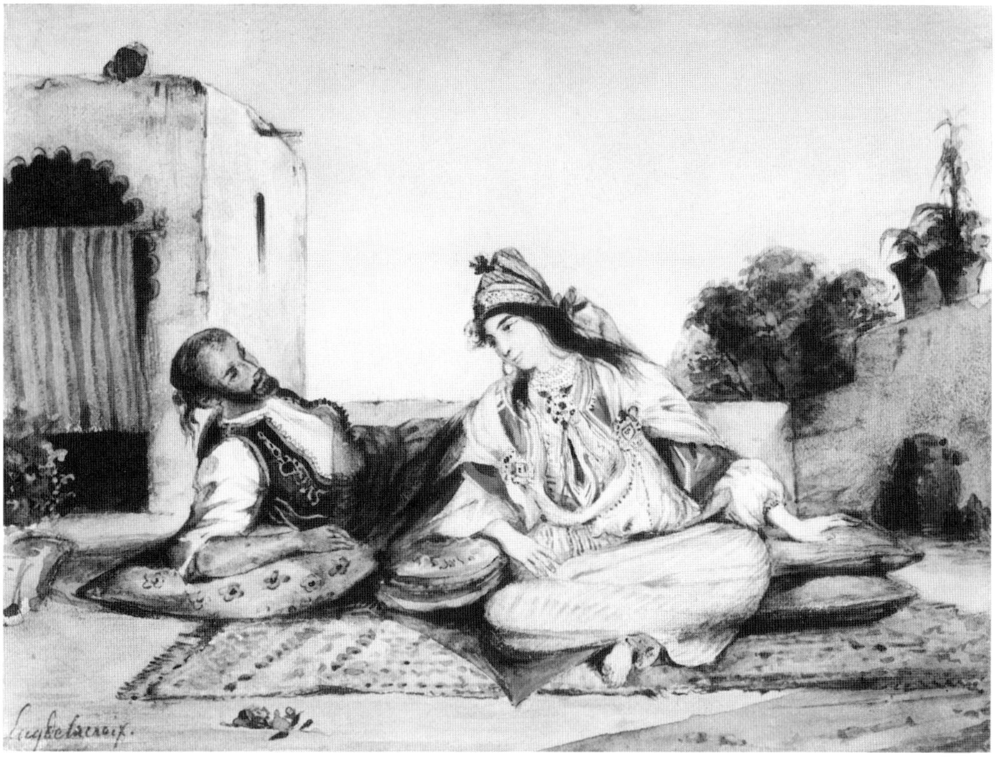

Fig. 4.50. Eugène Delacroix. *Moorish Conversation.* Watercolor and pencil. 1833. All rights reserved, The Metropolitan Museum of Art.

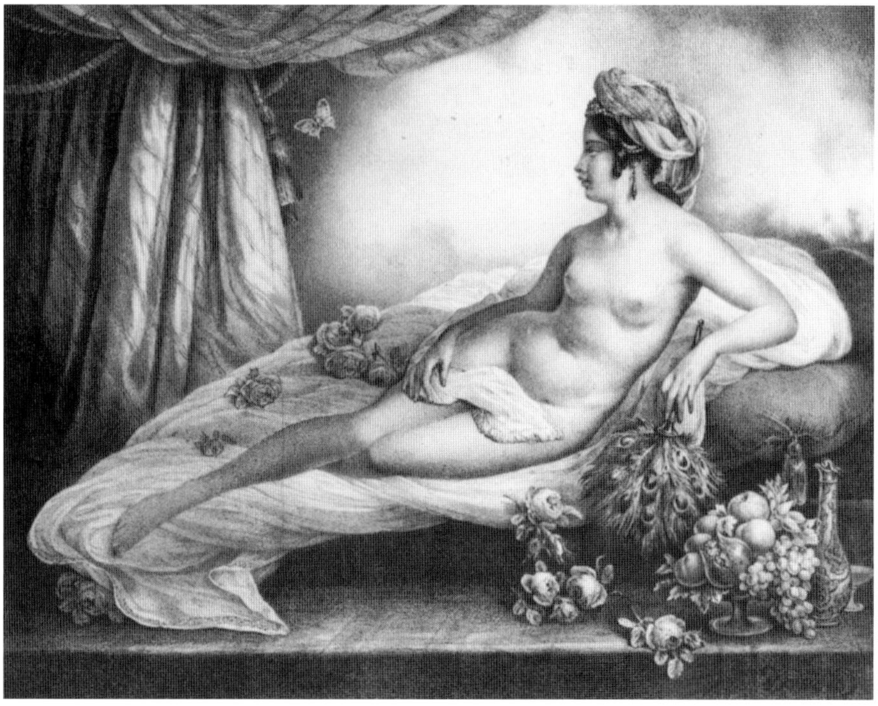

Fig. 4.51. After Jules Joseph Guillaume Bourdet. *La Femme esclave.* 1836. Lithograph. Cliché Bibliothèque nationale de France, Paris. Farwell, *FPLI*, v. 11, 2C2 B83459.

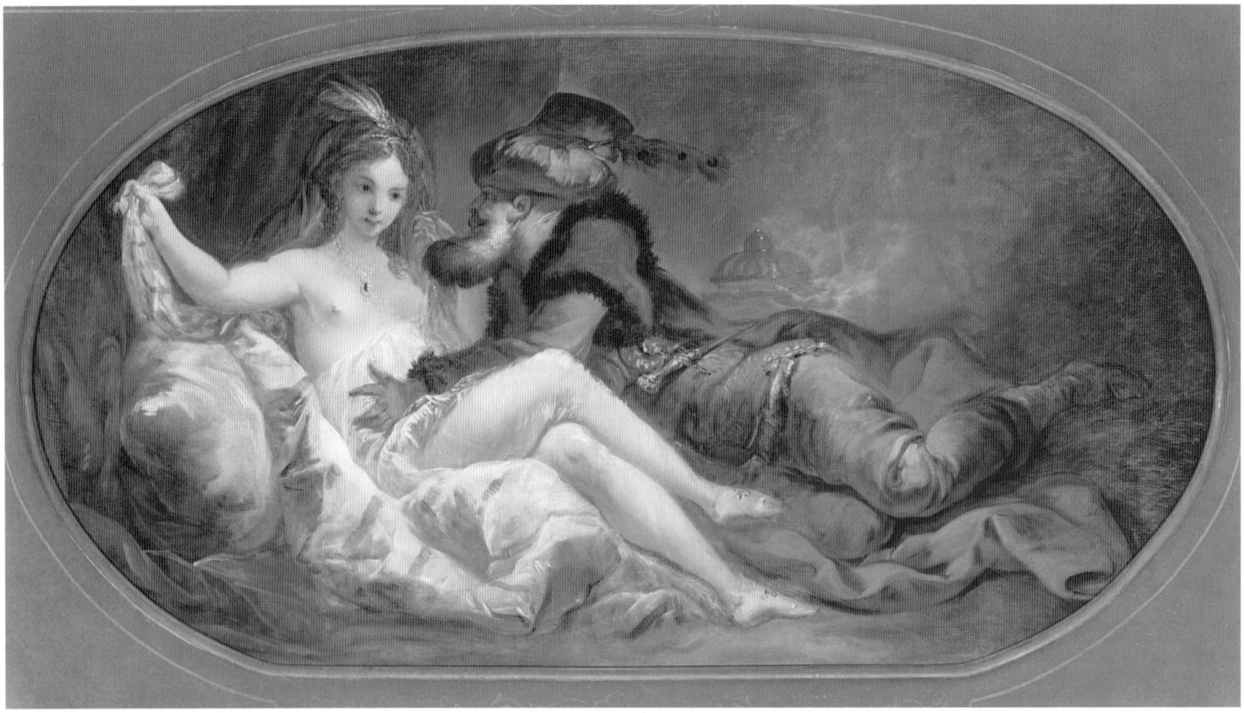

Fig. 4.52. Jean Baptiste LePrince. *Harem Scene.* N.d. Oil on canvas. Private collection on extended loan to the University of New Mexico Art Museum.

by the poor Pariah'."[75] In both of these writings the mounds of jewels suggest the failure of a polygynous social system, which promotes ill-health.

Some of this negative response to the easterner's abundant use of jewelry can be explained by different standards of taste and fashion. Yet the criticism is not just about these divergences. Morals are also at stake. Lamartine's observations about jewelry which he sees at the bazaar prompts his negative value judgments about eastern tasteless extravagance. In his writing the artless use of pearls and other precious jewels appeals to an essential oriental nature marked by "erratic and unsettled habits" (*PHL* 349). In the Judeo-Christian tradition it is sinful to be materially extravagant: *luxuria* is a sin of both material luxury and sexual promiscuity. Victor Hugo's Spanish Juana (in "The Obdurate Beauty") asks her pasha master to exchange his pearl necklace for a rosary in response to his question of how he may win her love.[76]

Some French lithographs suggests a relationship between diamonds and concupiscence, for example, Achille Devéria's 1829 *La Coquetterie* (Fig. 4.54). The woman embodies physical luxury indicated by her nudity, her pose, and the eye contact she makes with the spectator. She displays her jewels and offers her sex, another *bijou indiscret.* Is this a harem woman or a wealthy French aristocrat? A courtesan? The discourses merge in this image, as they do in Denis Diderot's 1748 *Les bijoux indiscrets,* a racy novel about an African sultan who, to counteract his boredom, uses his magic ring to force women of the court (not quite harem women) to describe their amorous escapades by talking not through their mouths but their genitals. The novel spoofed Louis XV, Mme. de Pompadour, and the fad within their court for stories of intimate encounters.

Jewels, love, and luxury are linked in other French popular prints. In Hollier's 1848 *L'Odalisque* (Fig. 4.55) a diadem, bracelets, and necklace serve as metaphors for her lightly draped "jewels." They are the ciphers of excess that are reiterated in the plethora of fabric patterns (and the fan's pseudo-inscription)—all rendered precisely in this lithograph. And in Grévedon's *Sultane à sa Toilette* (see Fig. 3.3) from 1838 set in a luxurious harem the older woman fastens a bejeweled diadem on the younger woman's forehead. Is this an adoring mother sending her daughter out with all her best wishes to meet the pasha? Or is this a pairing of unrelated women who wear jewels to please each other as part of their lesbian romance?

The wearing of jewelry in the harem is the ostensible subject of Lewis's 1873 *In-door Gossip, (Hareem) Cairo* (Fig. 4.56). One woman helps prepare the toilet of a standing woman and hands her a string of pearls emphasized by their placement at

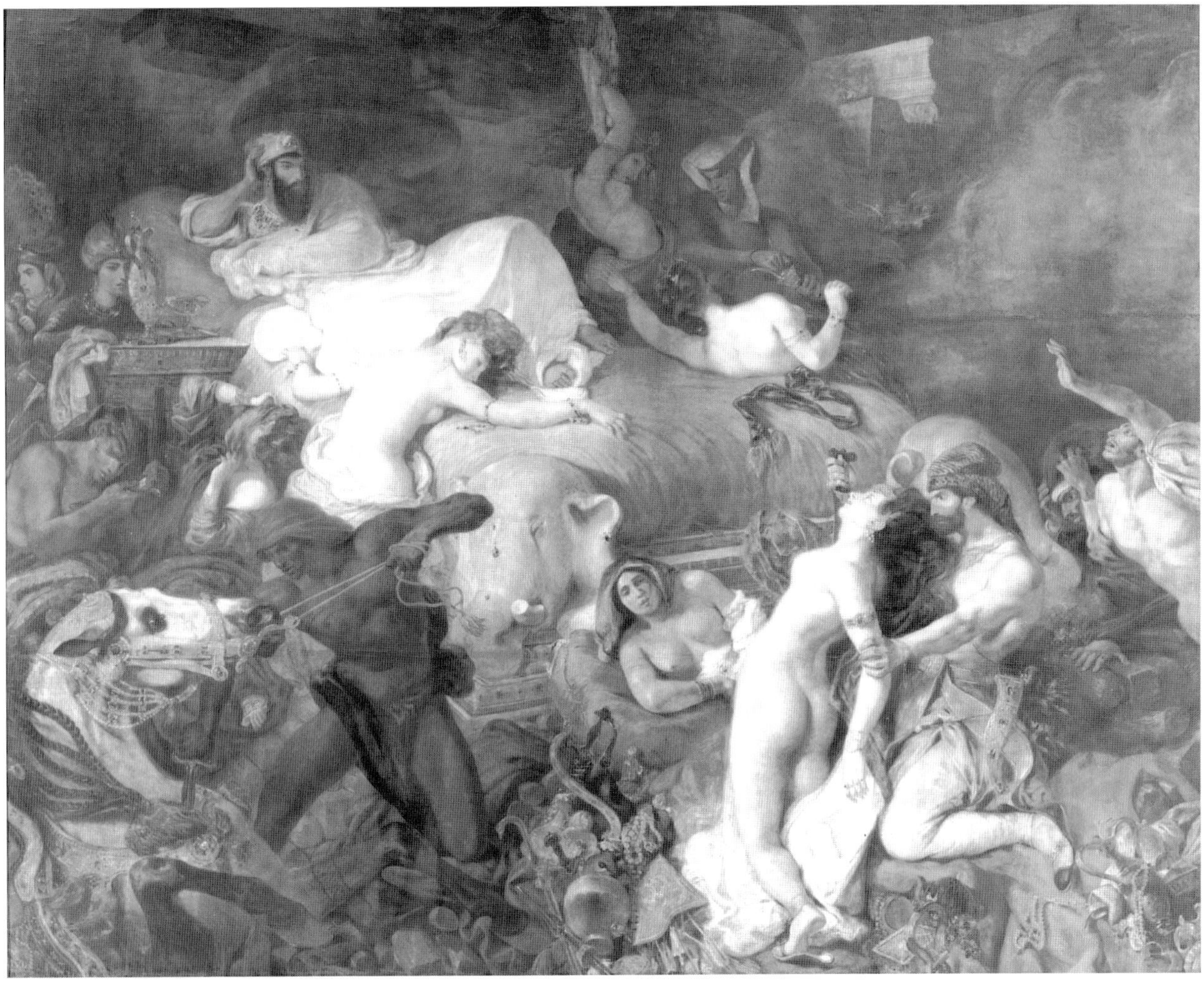

Fig. 4.53. Eugène Delacroix. *Death of Sardanapalus.* Musée du Louvre, Paris. 1827 Salon. © Photo RMN.

the center of the composition as the other adjusts the headdress over her unseen left earring, her dangling pearl earring visible on her right ear. The jewel box from which they have been taken appears at the lower right, cut off *à la japonaise.* One possible narrative for this picture is provided again by the letters of Lady Mary Wortley Montagu, who relates the grand event of the master having chosen from his collection one woman with whom he would spend the night. Her competitors now play the role of "bridesmaids," helping her dress for the occasion: "She is immediately complemented upon it by the others, and lead to the bath where she is perfum'd and dress'd in the most magnificent and becoming Manner" (*L* 1:383). Lewis includes only one instead of several attendants who function as bridesmaids. He has again inverted the usual standing attendant/seated mistress configuration used in the serving of coffee, for example, from at least the early eighteenth century. As a result, there is a conflation of the harem hierarchy.

The narrative of a harem woman preparing to cohabit with her master is itself inverted in an article ironically entitled "An Abode of Bliss" (1866), and the extravagant use of jewelry to mark the occasion is a sham. Note especially the development of associations in this passage from the pasha's visit to preparing the toilet to dirt to jewelry:

> The grand event is a visit from the pasha, and the toilets made on those occasions are very gorgeous, but very incongruous. Fine robes are put on over dirty, tumbled muslin dresses, which have been worn day and night—for the ladies of the harem sleep fully attired—and quantities of superb jewellery are worn on unwashed necks and arms. [. . .] the tresses so adorned [with the jeweled head-dress] are unbrushed and infested with vermin.[77]

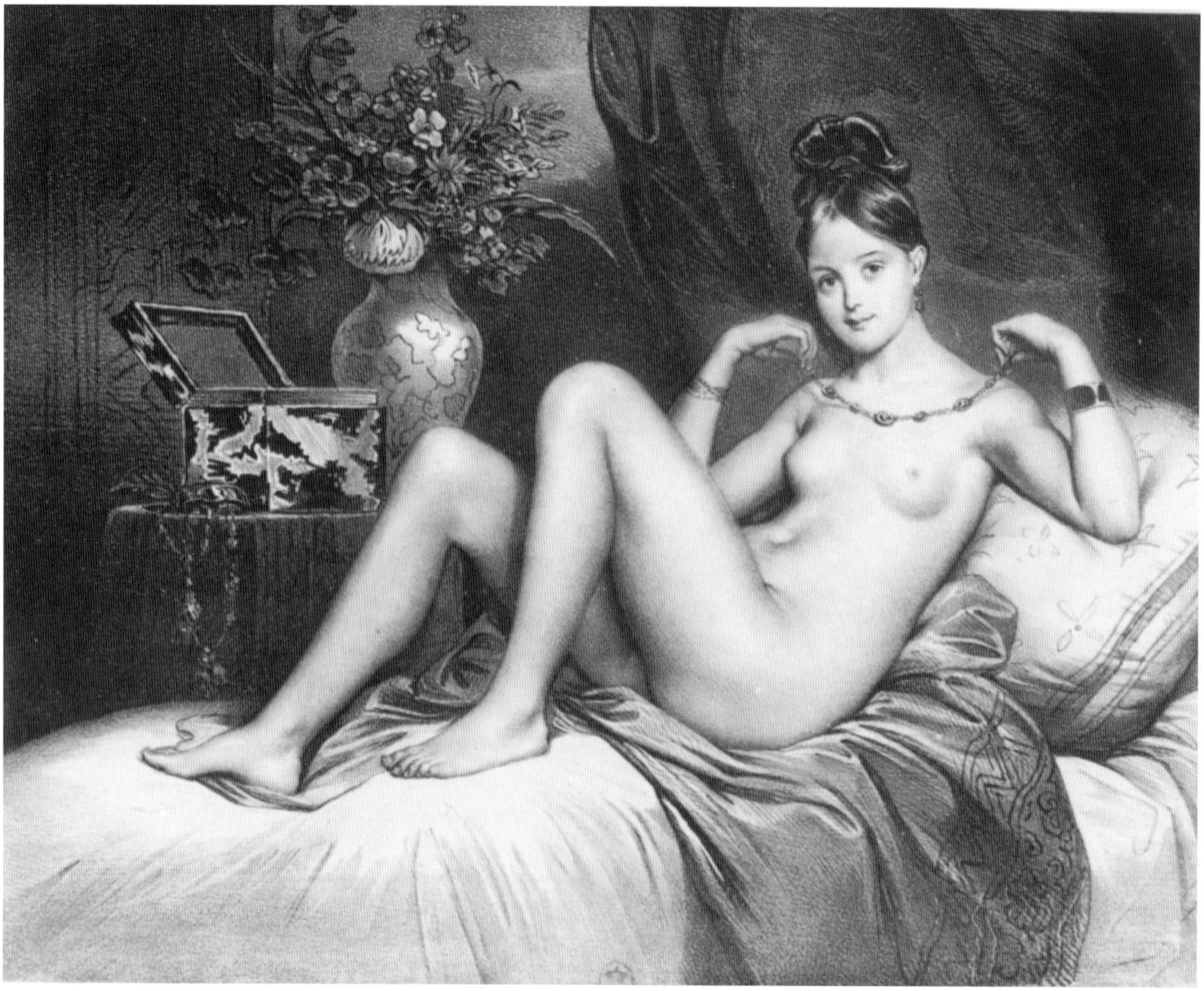

Fig. 4.54. After Achille Devéria. *La Coquetterie.* 1829. Lithograph. *Six sujets des femmes nues d'après nature.* Cliché Bibliothèque nationale de France, Paris. Farwell, *FPLI,* v. 11, 3C7 B64084.

Another possible reading for the narrative in Lewis's *In-door Gossip* is a variation on the first. Given the fact that the harem is an analogue for Paradise, the *Qur'an* promises that each man will have two wives—though, as might be expected, each woman will have only one husband.[78] So this might be a scene of the chosen wife being dressed by her peer, both of whom belong not to an earthly pasha but to the faithful Muslim soul in Paradise. On another level Lewis obscures the heavenly reading, however, by specifying Cairo as the harem's locale in the work's title and by assuring the viewer that the women "gossip," a practice which is nonexistent in Paradise.

Why popular writers so criticized the bejeweled harem woman may be illuminated by analyzing Ruskin's writing on the subject, writing that constitutes high literature. Ruskin eloquently disdained jewels, especially diamonds. In the process of elevating his personal opinions to the realm of aesthetic principles, he disparages any perceived beauty of these gems. As early as 1849 ("The Seven Lamps of Architecture") he militates with admitted excess against "decorated women" urging them to direct their wealth to community projects:

> most women would, in the end, prefer the pleasure of having built a church, or contributed to the adornment of a cathedral, to the pride of bearing a certain quantity of adamant on their foreheads. I could pursue this subject willingly but I have some strong notions about it which it is perhaps wiser not loosely to set down. (*W* 8:265)

Ruskin explains his strong feeling in terms of a moral economist: the diamond required great effort to mine and cut, true "slavery" of labor (*W* 8:82) for an aesthetic effect which is ultimately indistinguishable from that produced by cut glass. His objection to diamonds rests largely on the fact of the social inequity

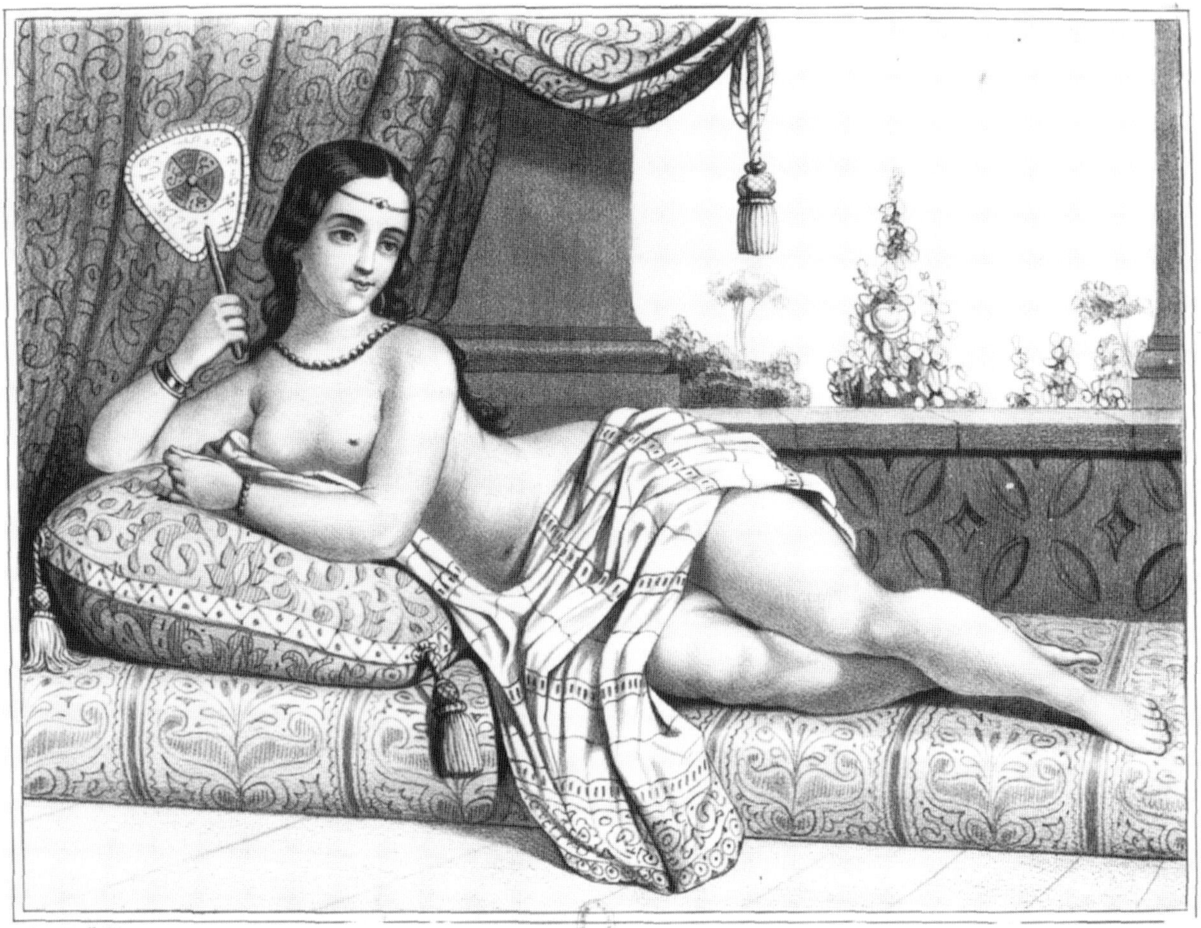

Fig. 4.55. Hollier. *L'Odalisque*. 1848. Lithograph. Cliché Bibliothèque nationale de France, Paris.

which they require to be produced. He expresses his concern for artisans and workers "wasting" time and effort in "A Joy For Ever" (*W* 16:38). This is in 1857, the same year he criticizes John Lewis for wasting his time and effort making pictures of the harem subject. The next year Ruskin lectures on "Education in Art" at the Social Science Congress about artistic challenges. He claims art cannot affect significant changes when "ill-wrought though costly trinkets [are] the principal entertainment of the boudoir" (*W* 16:148). In 1865 by which time his critique of capitalism had become more pointed he advises well-dressed ladies in his lecture audience to first dress the poor and only then indulge their interest in fashion (*W* 18:407). He implies that if the working class is oppressed, it is due in part to the extravagant taste of leisure-class women.

Ruskin kept up his diatribe against jewelry into the 1870s. He had mentioned the evil of jewelry in two lectures in 1870; in one he sees jewelry as the pastime of the wealthy to relieve their "indolence."[79] He directed his fulmination against the "esthetes" of the 1870s and their bejewelled patrons who, ignoring his fire and brimstone, revived the fashion of elaborate jewelry.

But Ruskin was inconsistent in his disdain for diamonds. In a personal letter written in April 1871 he confesses that he had purchased a diamond necklace for himself for £30. He explains why he bought it: "because I was a Fool, and wanted it"; still he admits the gem is completely "useless" (*W* 27:66). Moreover by 1875 Ruskin received a South African diamond as a gift from the Bishop of Natal. Ironically, the same bishop, named Colenso, was a well-known defender of polygyny: according to the famous orientalist Sir Richard Burton (1821–1890), Colenso "'not only tolerates polygamy in converts but defends it on the ground of religion and humanity'."[80] By this time (October 1875) Ruskin would mollify his criticism of gems by allowing uncut ones (which did not require "slave labour") to be used in making art objects, but only in furniture or architecture and not in dress (*W* 28:434). Later Ruskin would purchase the large "Colenso Diamond" (*W* 26:lv).

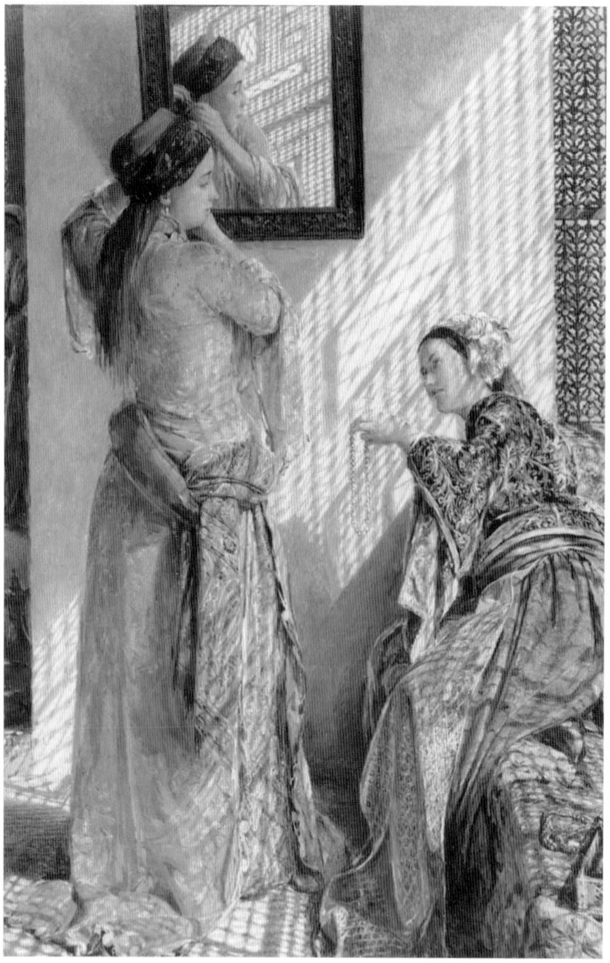

Fig. 4.56. John Frederick Lewis. *In-door Gossip, Cairo* or *A Scene in a Hareem.* 1873. The Whitworth Art Gallery, The University of Manchester.

The impassioned intensity of Ruskin's discourse on these subjects suggests his inner conflicts over them. Like popular writers on the harem, he was simultaneously attracted and repelled by ostentatious jewelry. His public, moral objections appear to have been too rigid to serve as guiding principles for his private life.

Ruskin's feelings may be relevant to Lewis's harem pictures which depict several types of jewelry over time. Lewis's 1850 *Hhareem,* painted in the late 1840s when he was still in Egypt and probably before Ruskin's objections to jewels, which are recorded by 1849. Over the next twenty-four years Lewis does not paint jewels on his harem women. Their necks are bare, their earlobes covered by hair. A few wear braided necklaces without gems as in his 1858 *Life in the Harem* (see Fig. 3.2).[81] For unknown reasons in the 1874 *In-door Gossip* Lewis breaks with his practice of representing harem women gemless. Ruskin was still publicly railing against jewelry in the 1870s. And he would repeat both the jewelry and *vanitas* theme in *Harem* two years later. Perhaps it is worth noting that Ruskin had eliminated praise, indeed any mention of John Lewis in the 1873 edition of *Modern Painters.*

The Harem Space

What distinguishes us is exoticism. There are two senses of the exotic: the first gives you the taste for exoticism in space, the taste for America, for women, yellow ones, green ones, etc. . . . [the other is] the taste for exoticism across time . . .

—Charles Baudelaire[82]

(Social) space is a (social) product.

—Henri Lefebvre[83]

In a history of harem pictures the question of how artists conceive of the harem space is perhaps so fundamental as to be overlooked. The conventional questions art historical might be: In envisioning harem space, how much did the artist follow earlier prototypes? What changes did he or she make? How has the artist created the fiction of space within the illusion of the composition? But newer questions need to be raised, questions which consider space as more than the neutral "container" for a collection of individual (albeit fetishized) objects and figures. At stake are more complex questions of the gender-based power politics of colonial representation.

Scholars of postcolonial studies maintain that "place" (the harem, the East) is composed of language, history, and environment. Colonial space is constructed by a two-pronged process: displacement and "an immense investment of culture."[84] Inventing the harem space meant emptying its indigenous content and filling it with the self-referential. The sheer number of British and French reactions to the harem support the observation that the harem signals an enormous investment—financially, psychically, and culturally.

Creating a harem space inhabited by a lone woman of the harem seemed the most common formula for conceptualizing a harem woman in space. But in avoiding the explicit depiction of multiple wives, the artist was compelled to find other means for communicating the harem subject. When an artist chose to depict a second wife or female slave, he risked diluting the erotic intimacy of the scene. Various resolutions to the dilemma of balancing harem recognizability with erotic intensity are set forth in popular French imagery done before 1850, in which segmented pictorial space preserves the privacy

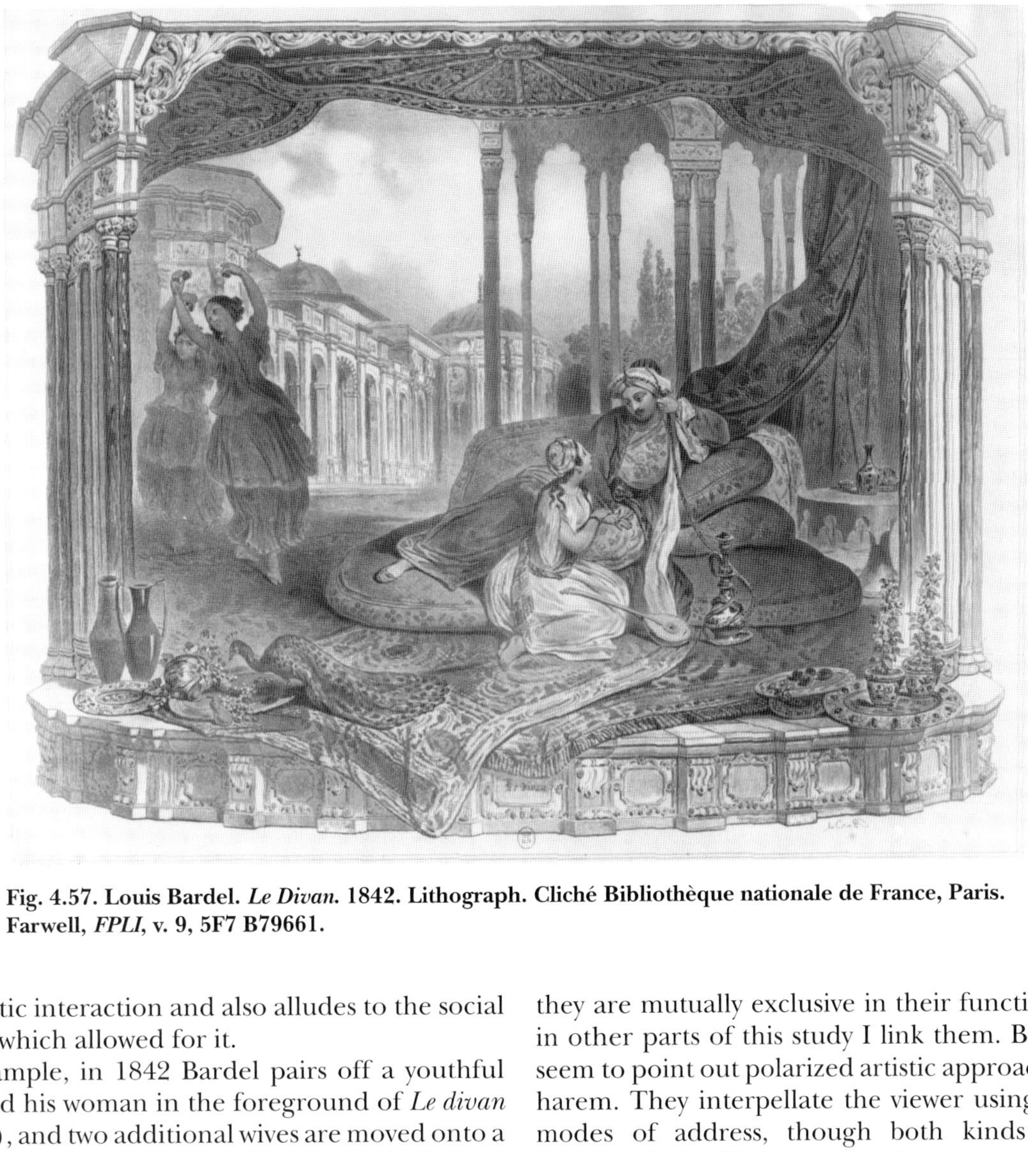

Fig. 4.57. Louis Bardel. *Le Divan.* 1842. Lithograph. Cliché Bibliothèque nationale de France, Paris. Farwell, *FPLI*, v. 9, 5F7 B79661.

of the erotic interaction and also alludes to the social structure which allowed for it.

For example, in 1842 Bardel pairs off a youthful master and his woman in the foreground of *Le divan* (Fig. 4.57), and two additional wives are moved onto a stagelike setting. N. Maurin finds a solution in *Le songe* (Fig. 4.58) from his 1851 series *Paradis de Mahomet*: Muhammad communes with a primary houri, while the others are transformed into ethereal musicians and attendants in the space allotted to his dream. And in one of the lithographs based on Eugène Guerard's paintings in the series *La vie au sérail* (see Fig. 4.22) the harem space has been bifurcated. A couple, consisting of the master and his nearly nude woman, is placed in the background; a second woman is on display in the foreground and is offered to the viewer whose fictive presence completes the second coupling.

Harem artists generally employ one of two spatial forms: the closed, darkened, and thus "eroticized" space, on the one hand, or the open, light, and thus "scientific" harem space, on the other. I am opposing the terms erotic and scientific not because I believe they are mutually exclusive in their function; in fact in other parts of this study I link them. But they do seem to point out polarized artistic approaches to the harem. They interpellate the viewer using different modes of address, though both kinds of space "unleash desire,"[85] the desire to know the unknowable harem woman and the land she is called upon to represent.

Dark "Erotic" Space

Occasionally the out-of-doors provides a dark, verdant cover for the secluded happenings, as in Auguste's rococo-revival *Deux odalisques* (Fig. 4.59). More frequently, however, a dark indoor space is created by divan, bed curtain, mounds of pillows, and other bedding. Tactile female flesh emerging from an obscure environment defines an eroticism of fantasy. Perhaps the best example of this is Ingres's prototypical *Grande Odalisque* (see Fig. 3.21) in which shallow space and dark pillowed background heighten the immediacy of exposed flesh.

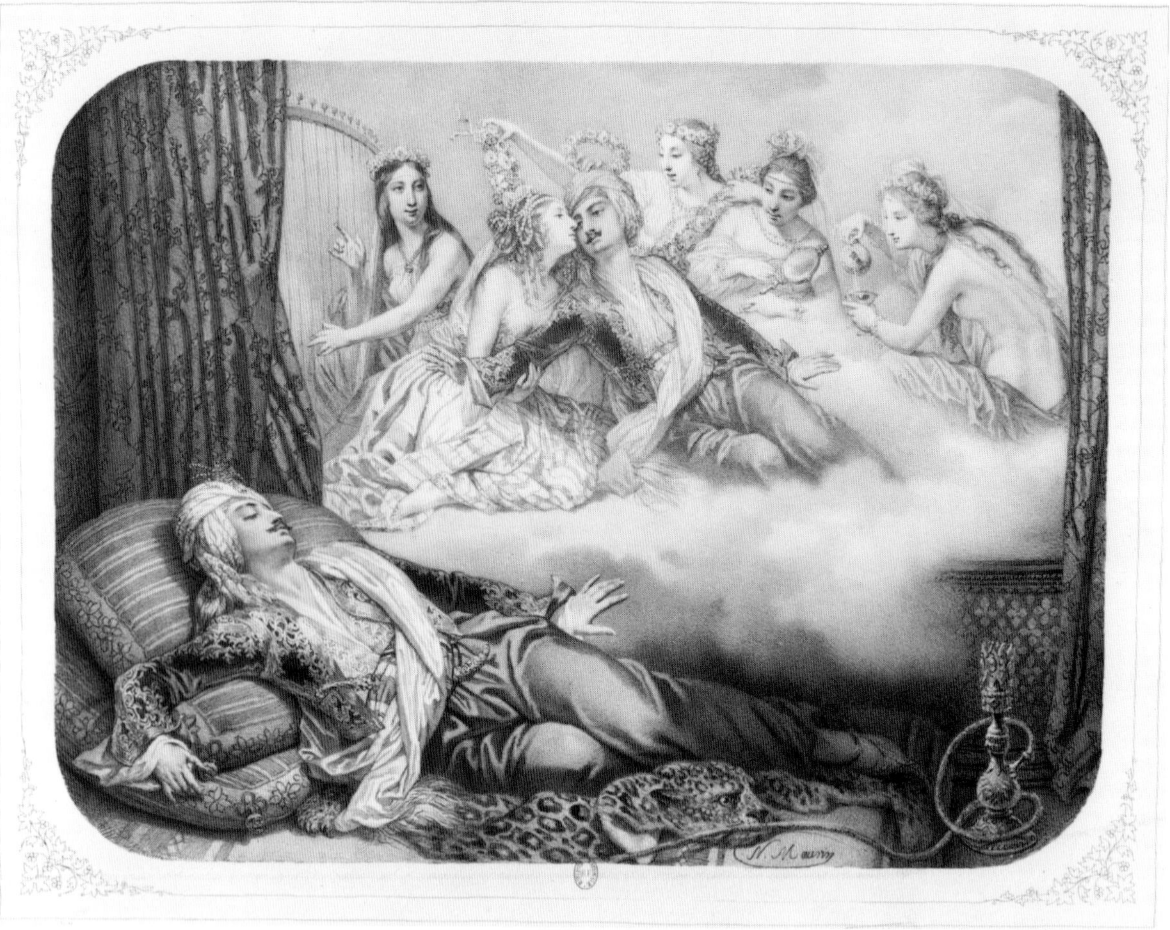

Fig. 4.58. Nicolas Eustache Maurin. *Le Songe. Paradis de Mahomet.* 1851. Lithograph. Cliché Bibliothèque nationale de France, Paris. Farwell, *FPLI*, v. 9, 5F8 B82694.

A late French painting that conflates the harem with its dark, eroticized space is Renoir's 1870 *Odalisque* (Fig. 4.60) (reputedly inspired by Delacroix's *Femmes d'Algers*). Here the woman appears enormous, as she is forced into the forefront of the picture plane. The edges of the canvas are cropped tightly around her, and the viewer's vantage point is very low. There is little depth behind her; beyond the dividing wall there is darkness. The spotlighting of the odalisque's body further discourages a reading of the space that presumably contains her. Instead, she *is* the harem space. Visually entering the dark, cramped space means penetrating her. Perhaps more so than in any other harem picture the space of the *haremlik* is a vaginal analogue, even though the figure is clothed. Yet the work's effect totters between seduction and claustrophobia. We are offered the odalisque's bedroom eyes, parted lips, and ample body, but her lethargy seems pernicious, her large body overwhelming in its relationship to its surroundings. In the painting's narrative the inescapable, darkened, and cramped space she occupies and defines might be an opium den. Here is harem woman as *femme fatale.*

Light "Scientific" Space

In sharp contrast to the lubricity of a darkened, enclosed bedchamber and a close-up view of the woman are harem spaces that are open and well-lit offering the viewer a means of visual escape. Whether ethnographic or theatrical, these pictures seem to be reactions against the melodramatic harem representation. Lighter in both formal tonality and mood, they can be correlated to a rational approach to the harem. A light background does much to remove the heavy, insistent eroticism of the darkened harem space. In Delacroix's 1833 watercolor *Moorish Conversation* (see Fig. 4.50) (from a book of watercolors the artist gave to Charles Edgar de Mornay as a souvenir of the diplomatic trip to Morocco on which Delacroix accompanied him) the daylight makes this a friendly—not a

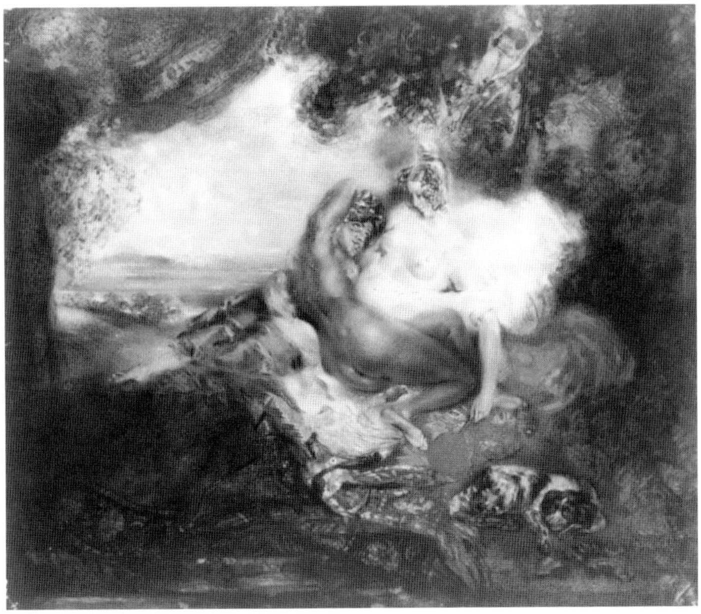

Fig. 4.59. Jules Robert Auguste. *Deux odalisques dans un paysage* or *The Girlfriends.* Musée du Louvre, Cabinet des Dessins, Paris. Gouache. Ca. 1820. © Photo RMN.

passionate—scene, even though a man and a woman occupy the same "forbidden" space.

As part of a scientificizing tendency toward understanding the harem, some artists chose to describe the "Islamic" architecture that delimits its space. The emphasis on harem interiors begins at least with Vanmour's and Boucher's scenes where the room constitutes a significant part of the image (see Figs. 3.33, 3.34), creating a sense of spacious opulence. Similarly in A. Vanloo's *La Sultane et ses domestiques* (Fig. 4.61) the distant view of the women and the spacious interior with high ceilings function as symbol for the freedom of the privileged—not the confinement of the enslaved.

A basic model for an Islamic architectural interior for pictures after 1836 was Lane's wood engraving of *A Ka'ah* (Fig. 4.62), the harem's largest room having the highest ceiling, which he illustrates in this wide-angle manner to reveal the architectural details of an Egyptian home (*ME* 1:21–22). Thomas Allom, who was trained as an architect, included ceiling details in his 1838 harem picture where architectural style seems to correlate to meaning: as with his use of the window, the stark, heavy ceiling beams in his somber *Slave-Merchant* (see Fig. 3.7) contrast with the elaborate, rococo architectural detail in his more carefree subject of musical entertainment in *Circassian Slaves* (see Fig. 2.4).

Lane's ethnographic-scientific engraving seems to have affected Lewis's 1850 *Hhareem* (see Plate 1). Lewis shows an elaborate architectural setting that commands nearly half of the pictorial space, wide-angle and stagelike. In constructing the spatial environment of a harem Lewis drew in part from his own firsthand experience of Egyptian domestic architecture, as in an image of the courtyard of his Egyptian home (Fig. 4.63). The room itself in *Hhareem* functions symbolically. It contains several references to the harem inhabitants. The vase of flowers on the floor near the pasha and the tables of fruit, both of which were described by Lady Mary Wortley Montagu (*L* 1: 414), located at the far right can be read as symbols of the beautiful women, artificially confined and here displayed in a lavish "container" which is the room itself.[86] Lewis's focus on wealthy ostentation acts to detract the viewer from the polemics of the harem. Followers after Lewis borrowed his particular type of wide-angle, high ceiling harem interior most notably Frank Dillon, for example, in his *A Turkish Interior in Cairo* (Fig. 4.64).

In both English and French traditions a more distant, architectural view of the harem interior serves to undermine both erotic intensity and abolitionist content. An illustration of the Pavillon du Bosphore (Fig. 4.65) erected at the 1867 Exposition universelle in Paris is similarly "scientificized": the viewer, at some remove from the scene, is given a sweeping view of the pavilion's main room containing built-in couches, tapestries, and a running fountain scented with jasmine. Five of six sides which form the "box" of

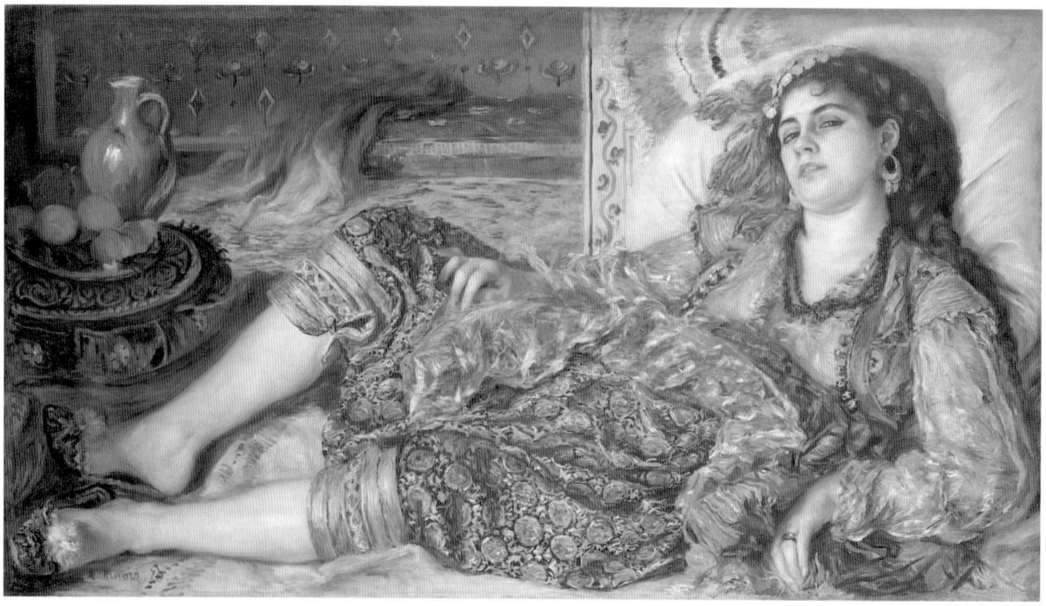

Fig. 4.60. Pierre Auguste Renoir. *Woman of Algiers* or *Odalisque*. 1870. Chester Dale Collection, National Gallery of Art, Washington, DC © 1999 Board of Trustees.

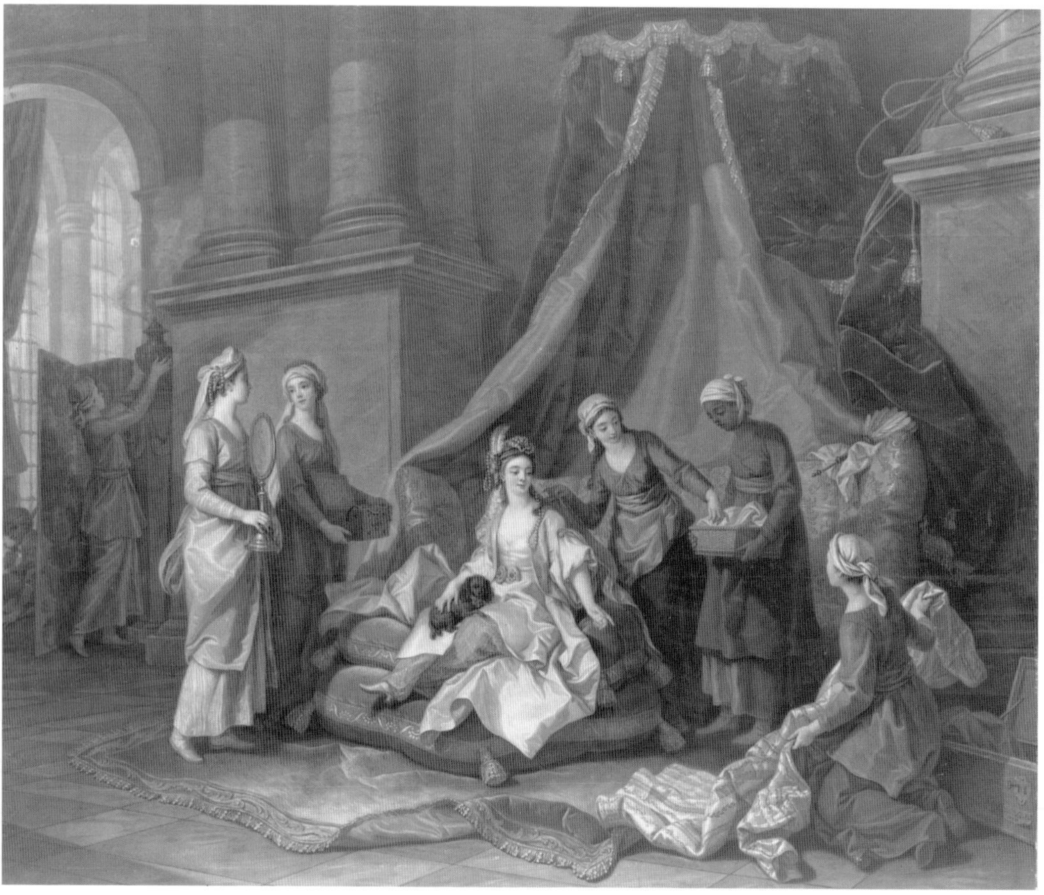

Fig. 4.61. Amédée Vanloo. *La Sultane et ses domestiques* or *La Sultane commandant des ouvrages au odalisques*. Musée du Louvre. © Photo RMN.

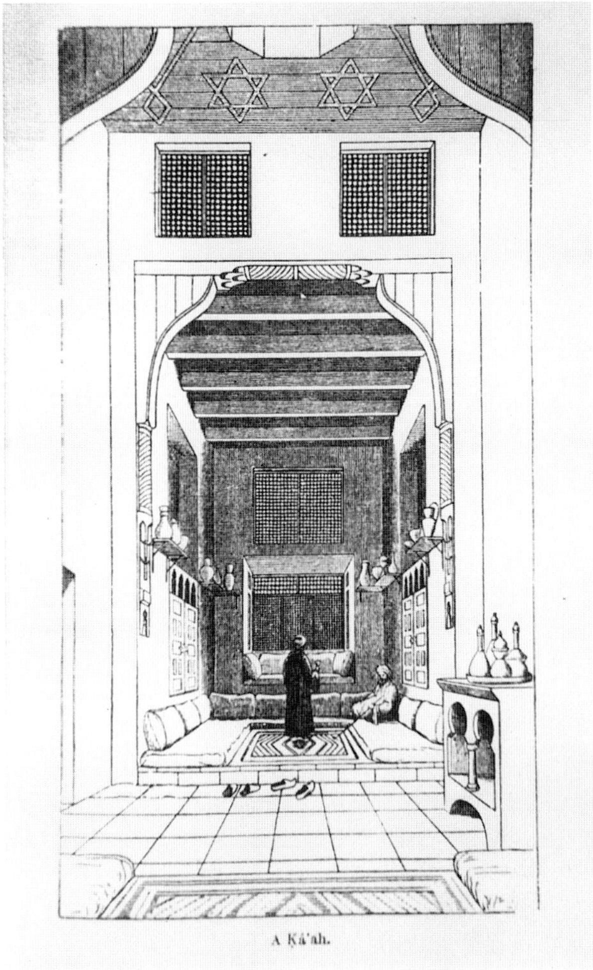

Fig. 4.62. Edward William Lane. ***A Ka'ah.*** **Engraving.** ***Manners and Customs of the Modern Egyptians,*** **1836. Photo Adam Miller.**

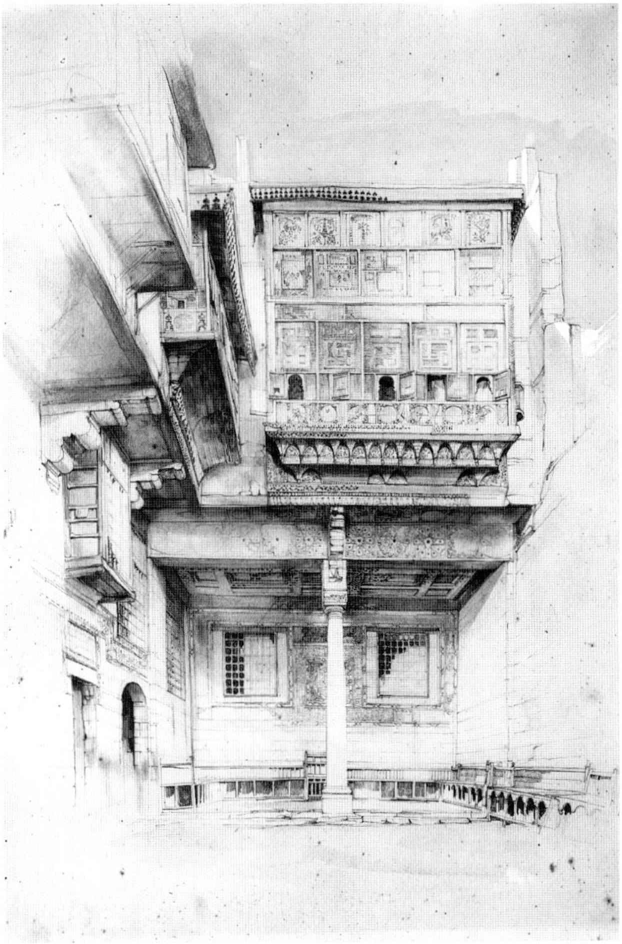

Fig. 4.63. John Frederick Lewis. ***Courtyard of the Painter's House, Cairo.*** **Pencil. Courtesy of the Trustees of the Victoria and Albert. V&A Picture Library.**

the room, its walls, ceiling, and floor, are painstakingly described. Sunlight floods the room and allows for such detailed scrutiny. Most surprising about the illustration is the artist's inclusion of four women in the lower left. This is not merely a pavilion; it is a "harem"! The print appeared in the illustrated catalog to the exhibition. Whether the image in fact depicted actresses who actually occupied the pavilion during the exhibition (creating a *tableau vivant* of the harem picture) or whether these figures were added to enliven an otherwise dry architectural study, the print is unique among harem pictures in its additional remove from representing the truth of a "real" harem: the print simulates what is already an architectural simulacrum of the harem. As such the image is in keeping with the goal of the whole exposition, indeed, the phenomenon of the modern world's fair in general: to provide a means of "'self-congratulation'" for the achievements of science and industry in capitalist countries, a role to which imperialism contributes.[87] And this picture's rational space facilitates that attitude. Through the pavilion and its pictorial representation the exotic harem space is brought home to Paris, thus enframing and taming the unruly, primitive harem.

In the art and literature of the postcolonial period space is thought of in new ways, according to Fredric Jameson, who calls the representation of space a "new and historically original problem." Because the economic system depends on colonies located far from daily (western) routine, suffering, exploitation and life in the colonies can never be comprehended within the culture of the metropolis. Space is conceived of differently and always includes a lack, a "spatial disjuncture." Nonetheless, artists, writers, and patrons continue the search for a total spatial understanding. In doing so they contribute to what Jameson calls a central dilemma of modernism.[88]

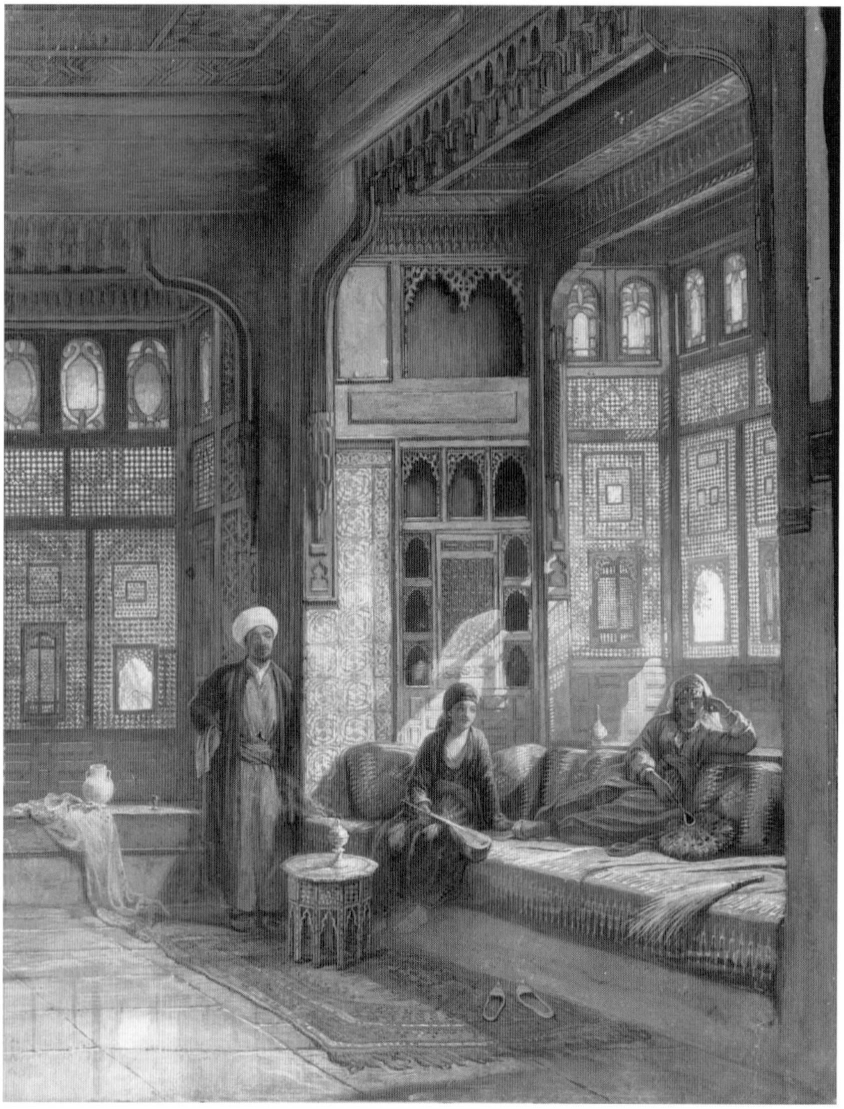

Fig. 4.64. Frank Dillon. *A Turkish Interior in Cairo.* Courtesy of the Trustees of the Victoria and Albert. V&A Picture Library.

Harem images in the nineteenth century seem to concretize this dilemma by envisioning one aspect of that colonial space—the *haremlik*—that can never be known in the West. It is significant that the poles around which harem artists and writers work are those of fantasy and science. In the attempt to know the harem puzzle, polygamy is set in an imagined, fantastic space that is itself the extension of what is perceived as the primary function of the harem, sexual titillation. Thus in several harem pictures the harem space is eroticized. Conversely, in other pictures the harem is represented scientifically, open to the close scrutiny of positivism and presumably devoid of emotion and value judgment. But Jameson is rightly skeptical about science's ability to know "this radical otherness of colonial life," in part because it is based on "the internal evidence of First World data."[89] In the end, what is pictured within harem space, whether ostensibly erotic or scientific, is the curiously insatiable desire to know the unknowable.

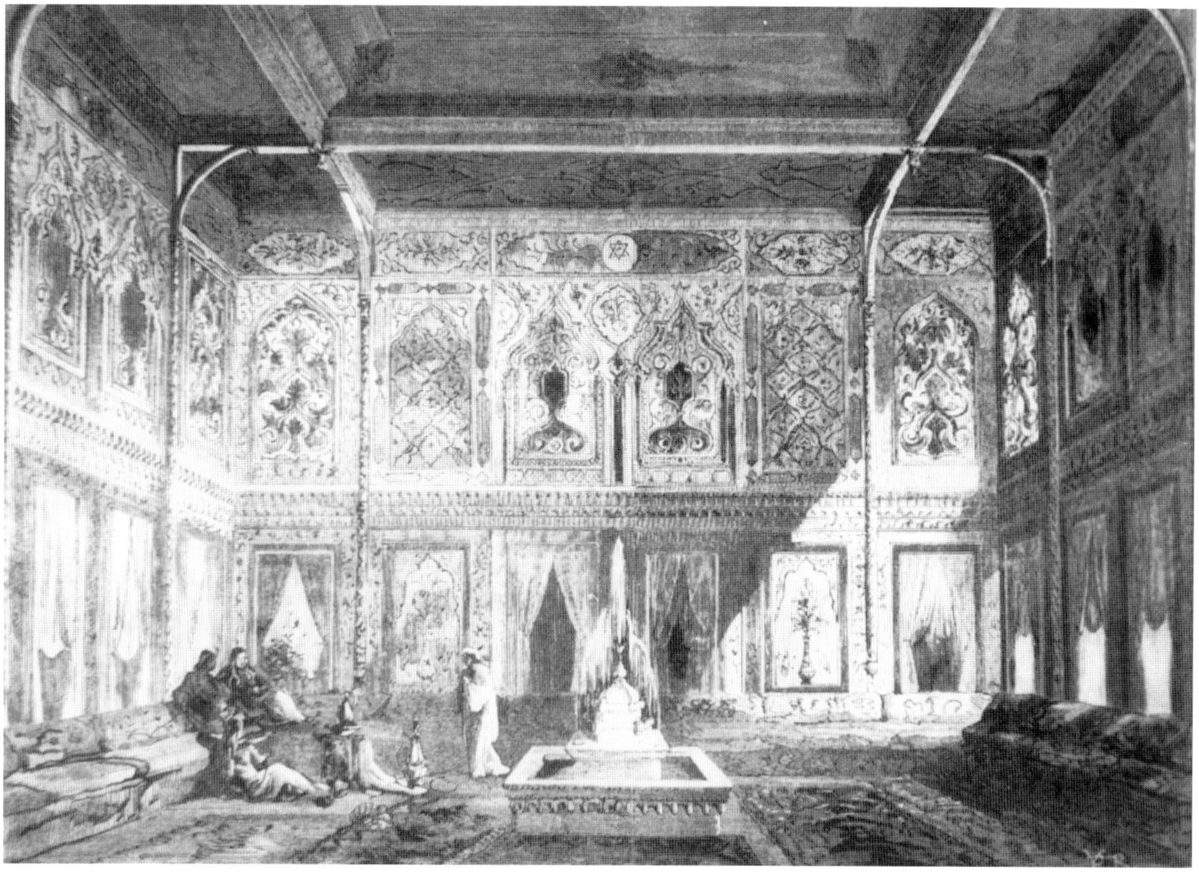

Fig. 4.65. *Interior of the Pavillon du Bosphore, Paris, 1867, L'Exposition universelle de 1867 illustrée.* (Zeynep Çelik, *Displaying the Orient*, Berkeley: University California Press, 1992, 104). By Permission of author and publisher.

5
The Harem Fetishized: Harem Women as Immoral

Introduction

the first figure to be invested by the deployment of sexuality, one of the first to be "sexualized," was the "idle" woman.

—Michel Foucault[1]

Besides slavery, the major British and French objection to the harem was that its polygyny had ill effects on the morality of women, children and eastern nations as a whole. Images of the immoral harem woman abound in print and pictures, as she is transformed into any one of a number of undesirable female stereotypes. These include: the adulterous wife, the negligent mother, the perverse lesbian, the gossip, the indolent sensualist, the narcissistic prostitute, the jealous rival, the extravagant consumer, and the sexually precocious child. These stereotypes often overlap, so that a lesbian in the harem might also be seen as a sensualist or a harem mother is negligent because she is distracted by her jealousy toward a rival.

These shorthand descriptors—whether visual formulas or verbal epithets—cut off deeper thinking about how the harem might provide a viable alternative to bourgeois and Christian monogamous marriage. Islam is indicted as the corrupter of Woman provoking her worst, most primitive animal instincts. While the outsider is always constructed as lacking control over the passions,[2] the harem woman is simultaneously the most natural woman and the most unnatural: one for whom layers of civilizing influence (read: restraint) have not been imposed and one ruled by the basest of human impulses—sexual desire, constructed as a fundamental and inescapable impulse. Demonizing the female practitioners of an already suspect eastern religion, a feminizing of the feminine, is a way to reassert the moral superiority of Christian bourgeois ethics. Occasionally a pasha is implicated in the critique, but he is typically seen as reactive, that is, becoming vengeful in response to the woman's outrageous deviance. His violent, supposedly deadly response to domestic conflict is constructed by western viewers as tyrannical, arbitrary, and overall a farcical system of justice, another arena for the corruption thought to characterize Islamic society.

There is an ironic reversal in logic (and power) of a harem's dynamic here: strictly speaking, the master was polygamous and not the woman, who would have him as her single, often infrequent, sex partner. Yet the master's harem women are implicated in his "promiscuity." In fact, the woman is made the polygamous culprit. Artists stack the deck against her by often portraying her alone; thus, she functions both visually and conceptually as the representative of the harem system's immorality. But the impulse to blame the woman in matters of a couple's sexual misconduct appears in other discourses on bourgeois morality. Paragons of virtue and guardians of morality within the family structure, women were expected to know better than the "naturally" more wayward man. Thus the image of the harem woman as a sexual deviant is partly a projection of a western double standard onto Muslim cultures.

The notion of the harem woman as sexually excessive is harshly ironic, as local customs sometimes caused the permanent sexual dysfunction of actual harem women. Her preparation for marriage could include total or partial circumcision of the clitoris or a more radical removal of the inner labia. Clitoridectomy, also called female circumcision, is a custom which continues to the present day in some countries, though it was outlawed in Egypt in 1959.[3]

I focus on stereotypes in this chapter. I may disappoint readers who expect this study to describe how stereotypes about harem women deviate from the ways in which such women actually lived and what really characterized their personalities. I believe these "facts" cannot be fully ascertained. At first it may appear that scholars are trapped by such a theory of representation in which critiques of representation have access only to other representations as reference points. But we are in fact freed to shift our focus to examining the more dynamic means by which pseudo-information about harem women's lives and personalities held such an importance for artists, writers, and audience. Instead of contrasting stereotypes with the truth about harem women, I want to explore how stereotypes worked and what purposes they might have served, in other words, what Gayatri Chakravorty Spivak calls the "*mechanics* of the constitution of the Other,"[4] a tactic that can offer a more effective critique of representation.

Morality and Art: Examining the Argument that the Faces of Harem Women Can Not Be Beautiful

In Muslim theological traditions the beauty of heavenly houris provides pleasure that is God-given.[5] In Persian literature the beauty of one's beloved gives rise to complex imagery involving the flowers and gardens of Paradise.[6] By extension, the beauty of harem women, the beloved of the faithful, provides an earthly pleasure sanctioned by God. In light of the deeply spiritual understanding of female facial beauty in Islam, it is revealing to contrast western comments (mostly British) about the "unbeautiful" harem woman. The art criticism written about John Lewis's harem pictures yields a recurrent theme: that the faces of the women he paints were not beautiful. This is an odd comment, because the faces found in those painted images are exquisite, in my opinion. I maintain that this comment evolves from another, unnamed attitude that warrants exploration, namely, harem women's inherent immorality which makes them an inappropriate subject for high art.

Sometimes this complaint is couched in technical criticism. Ruskin initiates the objection in response to Lewis's 1850 *Hhareem* (see Plate 1). There "the faces were the worst painted portions of the whole" (*W* 12:326). This criticism would follow Lewis's harem pictures for the next seven years. When Lewis shows *An Armenian Lady, Cairo* at the 1855 Royal Academy exhibition, Ruskin claims that Lewis has overworked his canvas in search of "impossible delicacy" in the flesh tones and again criticizes the face of the harem woman as "too blue" (*W* 14:12–13). The *Art Journal* takes issue with Ruskin's criticisms: "In the colour of the flesh there is nothing blue: the tint is the natural brown complexion of an Oriental" (*AJ* 1855:238).

In 1857 the *Critic* finds fault with Lewis's *Harem Life—Constantinople* (see Fig. 3.39) in "the face of the principal figure, which is a little subdued by the splendour of the surrounding colours" (*C* 1857:209). Likewise, the *Illustrated London News* takes exception "to the opaque leaden tone of the face of the lady reclining" (*ILN* 9 May 1857:444). A slightly different spin is offered by the *Spectator* which admires Lewis's treatment of the women's faces, "painted with astonishing delicacy of manipulation," despite the fact that they are "neither very beautiful nor exalted by depth of expression [. . .]." A key phrase follows: "[. . .] which would, indeed, be out of character in such a subject" (*S* 2 May 1857:463). Here the press explicitly articulates the connection between its formal criticism and the underlying bone of contention: the moral decrepitude of harem women.

Ruskin had admired Lewis's meticulous technique but seems to advise him to think about painting subjects other than the harem in this comment from 1857 where he criticizes the rendering of the harem woman's face: "at all events, I am quite sure the master will see cause for altering [imperfections in the seated woman's face] after his eye has been turned for a little while to other subjects" (*W* 14:133). Ruskin implies that Lewis's virtuoso technique is used on a disreputable subject, thus he is wasting his time and effort.

Nineteenth-century publications on the subject of harems provide a fuller explanation as to why the representation of a harem woman's face could not convey "beauty" or "depth of expression." Writers enjoy dwelling on harem women's facial beauty, yet they rarely leave it at that. If writers admit that the women are beautiful, it is usually qualified in some way—intellectual or moral. For example, St. John writes in 1848: "Occasionally they are possessed of much beauty, though there is frequently a want of expression caused, perhaps, by the dormancy of the intellectual faculties."[7] Harriet Martineau describes the chief lady of the harem. Her face "had no beauty in it, nor traces of former beauty" only "waywardness and peevishness" around her mouth (*EL* 261).

The discourse that distinguishes kinds of beauty is indebted to writers like Mary Wollstonecraft who discusses weak and strong beauty in women. Instead of "soft bewitching beauty," "relaxed beauty [. . .] or the graces of helplessness" that indicated moral delinquence in traditional women, Wollstonecraft advocates a new definition of female beauty as "strength of body and mind" which she believes will define a "dignified beauty and true grace." She reveals the reigning neoclassical paradigm when she advocates a "noble" beauty that resembles that prevalent in "antiquity"(*VRW* 290). In decrying the attitude that women were made to serve men's appetites, she claims that society has developed "mistaken notions of beauty and female excellence"; we choose to elevate women's defects into virtues when they are not (*VRW* 126).

A fundamental premise of the argument is this: that as a window on the soul the face could be truly beautiful only when the soul was radiant. And a frequent French and British misconception, documentable at least since the eighteenth century, was that Islam failed to grant women souls. Lady Mary takes issue with "our Vulgar Notion" in a 1717 letter to the Abbé Conti (*VRW* 1:363). Her friend Alexander Pope was undoubtedly familiar with Lady Mary's attitude, as he spoofs the idea in a rather risqué letter to her at the point in their friendship when he was still flirting with her:

> "I shall hear how the very first night you lay in Pera you had a Vision of Mahomet's Paradise, and happily awaked without a soul. For which blessed instant the beautiful Body was left at full liberty to perform all the agreeable functions it was made for."[8]

Mary Wollstonecraft writes that Muslim women are thought to have no souls, but she implies that this is a cultural construction that needs changing (*VRW* 100, 311). Byron writes in *The Giaour* (1813): "Oh! who young Leila's glance could read / And keep that portion of his creed, / Which saith that woman is but dust, / A soulless toy for tyrant's lust?" (*WB* 54).[9] Sir Richard Burton also believes that Europe is mistaken in the belief that Muslims consider women soulless, as he claims to have heard pilgrims praying for the souls of their deceased male and female brethren while visiting the Prophet's tomb at Ziyarat (*PNP* 244).

For the critics of the 1850s influenced by Ruskin, genuine beauty could only emanate from high moral standing. In *Modern Painters* Ruskin advises artists, when painting faces, to eliminate "signs of sensuality and sloth" and instead to "substitute energy and intensity for vacancy and insipidity" in facial features. The face's function is to reflect "the operation of the moral feelings conjointly with the intellectual powers" (*W* 4:179). By both eighteenth- and nineteenth-century accounts, an immoral woman could not be truly beautiful. Apparently, neither could the harem woman, representative of an immoral (polygynous) institution.

This notion—that physical beauty had to be matched by high spiritual worth (impossible when Muslim women were considered spiritless)—helps explain the otherwise perplexing comment of the *Illustrated London News* that the harem woman's face in Lewis's 1857 *Harem Life* suffered from a "lack of beauty." The influential Ruskin may have set the tone and content for the criticisms of Lewis, to be echoed by the press. The formal discourse of art criticism gets used in 1851, 1855, and 1857 to express moral reservations about the harem. Some critics couched their hostility toward the harem in the guise of unfavorable but still elevated art criticism.

For Ruskin, successful art expressed the moral truth of nature. The painted subject of a harem woman simply had no place in the discourse on aesthetic values when art was to reflect Morality and Beauty. But Ruskin's expectations about art and sexual morality were not unanimously endorsed by other critics nor presumably by Lewis. Their apparent disagreement signals an important site for the conflict over whether harem women could be good women and whether the harem could be a legitimate means of social-sexual organization.

The stereotype of the "unbeautiful" harem woman has interesting implications. It seems to be an elevated corrective to the (French?) claim that the harem was full of beauties. Alphonse de Lamartine for one expresses such a Romantic view that primitive peoples are more beautiful than civilized in the context of comparing eastern women to European (*PHL* 77). The conception of the "unbeautiful" harem woman stems from a belief that a healthy environment and true beauty are inextricable. Lamartine's view of beautiful eastern women (those who inhabitant the harem as well as those who do not) is consistent with this premise, as he sees Islam as a legitimate religion. Melman summarizes the nineteenth-century belief this way: that a life characterized by indulgence in physicality—appetites and the flesh—cannot be rewarded.[10]

A final comment by Martineau clinches the hypothesis that harem women's faces are considered "unbeautiful" because the inmates are, in a word, oversexed. She claims to have examined closely all the faces of the women in the harem she visited and none revealed a "mind" except for that of an old crone. The young women were dull-looking and "soulless." Exercising a ladylike tact, she refers to their sexual desire euphemistically:

> How could it be otherwise, when the only idea of their whole lives is that which, with all our interests and engagements, we consider too prominent with us? There cannot be a woman of them all who is not dwarfed and withered in mind and soul by being kept whollng engrossed with that one interest,—detailed at that stage in existence which, though most important in its place, is so as a means to ulterior ends. The ignorance is fearful enough; but the grossness is revolting. (*EL* 263–64)

Whether in England or the Orient, the expression of female desire is undesirable, claims this feminist and abolitionist.

An extremely provocative section of Montesquieu's *Persian Letters*, Letter 141, deals with the theme of the Muslim controversy over women's souls and whether they too would experience a sensual Paradise. A harem inmate named Anais is murdered by her master and goes to Paradise, where she is greeted by a palace full of "celestial men intended for her pleasures" who bathe, perfume, dress, and feed her. She enjoys music and dancing before the two of them take her to bed where "her ecstasies surpassed even her desires" (*PL* 249). Montesquieu addresses the formal difficulties of getting this story into the structure of a letter in an ingenious way. The events are presented as a tale from an unnamed Arab book, which is told by an intelligent harem inmate named Zulema, who uses it to dispute the claim that women have no souls. Zulema's story is called a Persian tale, which is retold by a beautiful western woman at court whom Rica meets and whose retelling he integrates into his own letter. Thus Montesquieu presents a story within a story within a story within a letter! The effect of this play with form is to suggest the esoteric nature of an exotic truth. The unnamed western woman at court who begins the chain of information is an intellectual feminist, whom Montesquieu has appropriating the tale of female sexual pleasure in Paradise for her own ends: the empowerment of the female sex.[11] At the end of *Persian Letters* the harem is liberated. The point of this letter is that the harem is untenable precisely because its structure fails to allow for the satisfying of female desire, a position that is born out at the end of the *Letters* when the harem falls apart and Roxana asserts that Usbek's flaw has been "to thwart my desires."

Negative Stereotypes of Harem Women

The many critical stereotypes of harem women produced by British and French writers and artists stem from a fundamental belief that the harem was a place of chaos, noise, and social disorder. Such comments suggest that, by contrast, the ideal bourgeois home was to be run in a quiet and orderly manner. This statement of ideals is anticipated in Wollstonecraft's writing in which the poor education of French and British women is to blame in part for their "disregard of order" which leads to their enslavement (*VRW* 104). The idea that the quality of one's environment affects one's morality is a relatively new one, in contrast to the belief that people are innately good or bad, a less frequent analysis for the negative stereotypes of harem women. To look to environment for understanding one's nature is the basis of the argument that harem women's beauty is determined by the health of their environment.

In Montesquieu's *Persian Letters* the Chief Black Eunuch informs Usbek that in his absence the harem has fallen into "appalling disorder and confusion" (*PL* 130). "The chaos of interior existence" disheartens a young girl of the harem who grows into consciousness, claims Harriet Martineau (*EL* 262). Harem women are out of control, and by implication the social system is chaotic and ineffective in Murray's 1871 guidebook for travelers, which quotes an unnamed woman writer:

> 'They seized brass shields and short swords, clashing them furiously as they whirled about like young Furies. They threw away their arms and began to romp like hoydens, tumbling over each other, rolling on the floor, throwing pillows at those that fell, laughing and screaming, more as maniacs than as the well-behaved, demure young damsels we took them for.' (*HTT* 113)

The harem environment is simply a "hell" for Florence Nightingale (*LE* 208). Similarly, in Harriet Martineau's opinion, the harem makes the whole country of Egypt the lowest depths of hell (*EL* 260).[12]

Influenced by Foucault's writing on modern societies' imperative for order and control, Timothy Mitchell names general Egyptian "disorder" as one of the justifications for colonialism. The urban space of cities such as Cairo, the old methods of teaching, the military—were considered in need of rational, western methods. In his view "space, minds, and bodies" were seen as contiguous; all required "a common economy of order and discipline."[13] How that "disorder" was thought to be manifested in the harem representation is the topic of this chapter.

Adulterous Wives

> [F]aithless husbands will make faithless wives. (*VRW* 88)

The harem woman was blamed for her involvement in a polygynous social system that was also culpable. Did a flawed social system which rarely gave female inmates the intimacy they craved force a woman's adulterous behavior? Or did her adulterous "nature" weaken the system making it chaotic and untenable? These questions arise from reading both pictures and written reports of the adulterous harem woman. The themes of the several representations examined in this section plot out important points in a dire narrative: the cause, exposure, and punishment of a harem woman's infidelity.

The subject of the harem violated by an adulterous woman and her young lover becomes especially popular in the French romantic period: in several lithographs from the July Monarchy illicit sex and the avenging master's violence are combined into titillating drama. For example, in Nicolas Maurin's

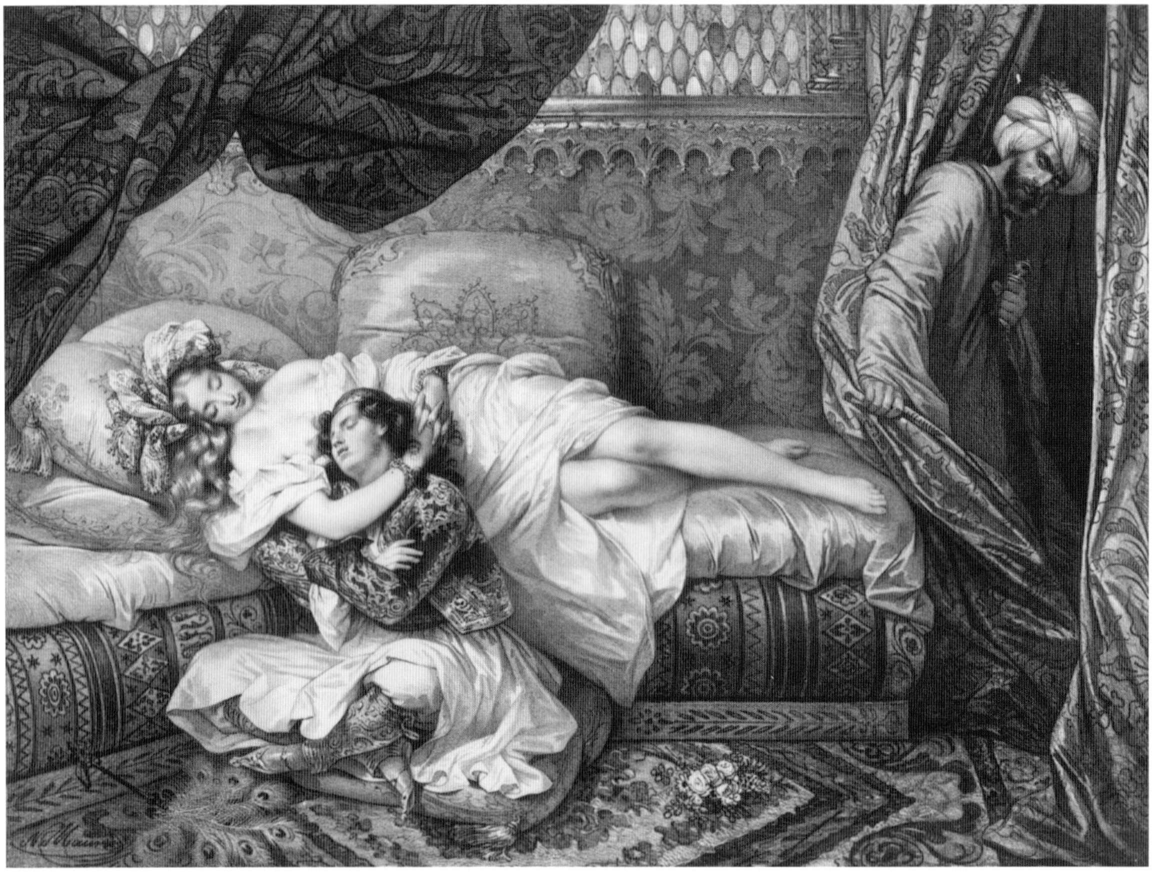

Fig. 5.1. Nicolas Eustache Maurin. *Constantinople*. Lithograph, 1833. Cliché Bibliothèque nationale de France, Paris.

beautifully rendered 1833 *Constantinople* (Fig. 5.1) a vengeful pasha, dagger[14] secreted close to him, opens a curtain and comes upon a slumbering couple, composed of one of his women—presumably Circassian because of her blond hair—and her lover, whose cleanly-shaven young countenance forms a striking contrast to the owner's bearded and lined one. The whole room is lush with exotic finery including the lover's nosegay on the floor, composed primarily of roses, the symbol of love. The intruder is too late to prevent their lovemaking, as indicated by the woman's sheet-draped body and their postcoital bliss. Reminiscent of Ingres's paintings of Dante's *Paolo and Francesca* the poignancy of the scene is the impending doom of the young and beautiful couple in love, whose serenity here belies their imminent danger. While both men remain (partially) upright in posture, the woman's recumbent body is made the contested territory. In this print titled *Constantinople*, a whole city, indeed a whole culture, is condemned. The intransigence of established male ownership is considered the law of the land.

In the similarly titled *Tunis* (Fig. 5.2) by Devéria the entwined couple is awake and startled by the armed intruder. Visually indebted to Ingres's *Grande Odalisque* (see Fig. 3.21), the nude female figure is on display and forms the centerpiece of the whole scene. In the male-female couple, the woman's averted gaze bespeaks her submission. She is the powerless property over which the men will fight. Her lover is dominant by virtue of his clothing and his visual confrontation of the intruder. But his power is about to be challenged, as the harem master is armed and the caption reiterates the theme of pleasure paid for by imminent pain: "Tunis / Youssouf and Rabboura daughter of the Dey, surprised in the seraglio / What excess of pleasures which love excites in us, / (And) sometimes misfortune follows." Ostensibly advocating restraint, the scene is constructed so that the viewer can enjoy the salacious content, located in the contestation over the female body. This image is one in a 1834–38 suite of thirty images, *Les Amants des différents pays*, reissued in 1851, in which the generalized category "Tunisian Lovers" is represented by this triad.

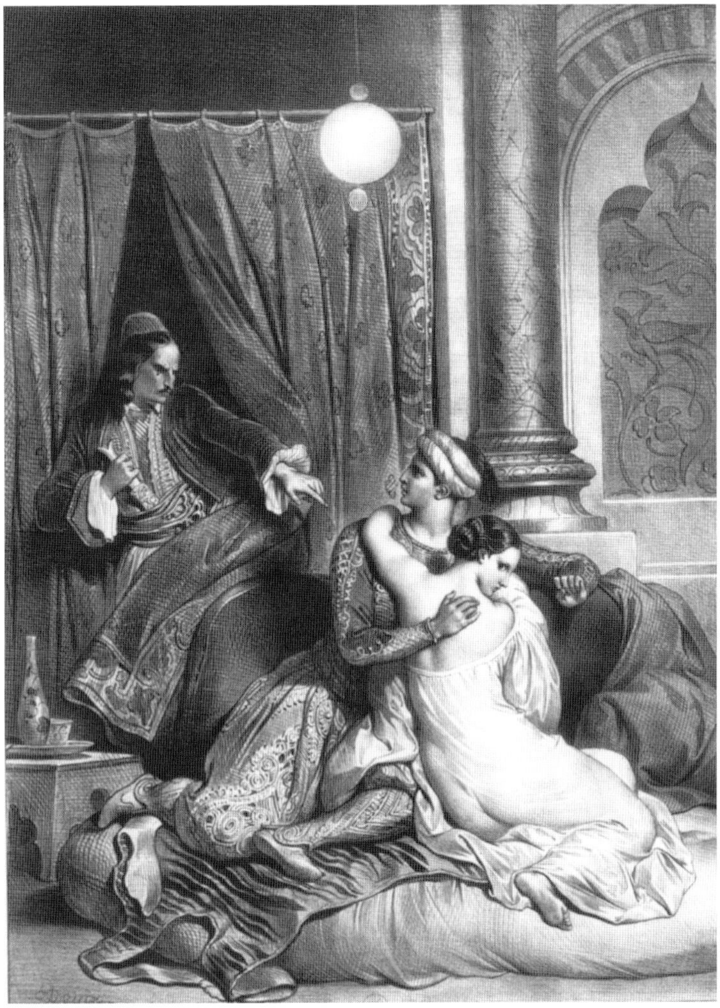

Fig. 5.2. A. Devéria. *Tunis*. Lithograph. *Les amants des différents pays*, 1834–38, reissued in 1851. Cliché Bibliothèque nationale de France, Paris. Farwell, *FPLI*, v. 9, 5C12 B80827.

In each of these images the harem woman plots to violate the harem sanctity with what appears to be a native man. But in a pair of lithographs called *Moeurs d'un sérail* (1829–30) done after Fragonard it is a Frenchman who corrupts the harem woman. In the first, *La Musulmane imprudente* (Fig. 5.3), drawn by Mendouze, the subcaption explains the presence of the uniformed French soldier in the harem, toasting wine goblets with a nude inebriated odalisque:

> After the defeat of the Mamelukes in Egypt,[15] the harem of Mourad-bey was liberated by the French. The young slaves learned to transgress the law of Muhammad which prohibits the drinking of wine.

Paradoxically, the print's caption blames the French presence for corrupting the harem, while its French viewer is expected to enjoy the sight of a naked woman on display. In the sequel to this image, *La Vengeance* (Fig. 5.4) drawn by Barathier, the woman sprawled out naked for the viewer has once more become property of the pasha, who watches her gasp her last few breaths, a stab wound eliciting a single, rather neat drop of blood. The French soldier, meanwhile, is visible in the background; he struggles in vain against the strangulation administered by three of the pasha's henchmen. The link between sex and violence is heightened by the woman's undulating pose and half-closed eyes, which suggest sexual abandon as much as death.[16]

Adultery in the harem is a theme in two of John Lewis's harem pictures, though it is handled quite differently than in these French images. The title of his 1869 *Intercepted Correspondence* (Fig. 5.5) indicates its focus is a correspondence, presumably from a lover, making this a scene of an adulteress discovered.

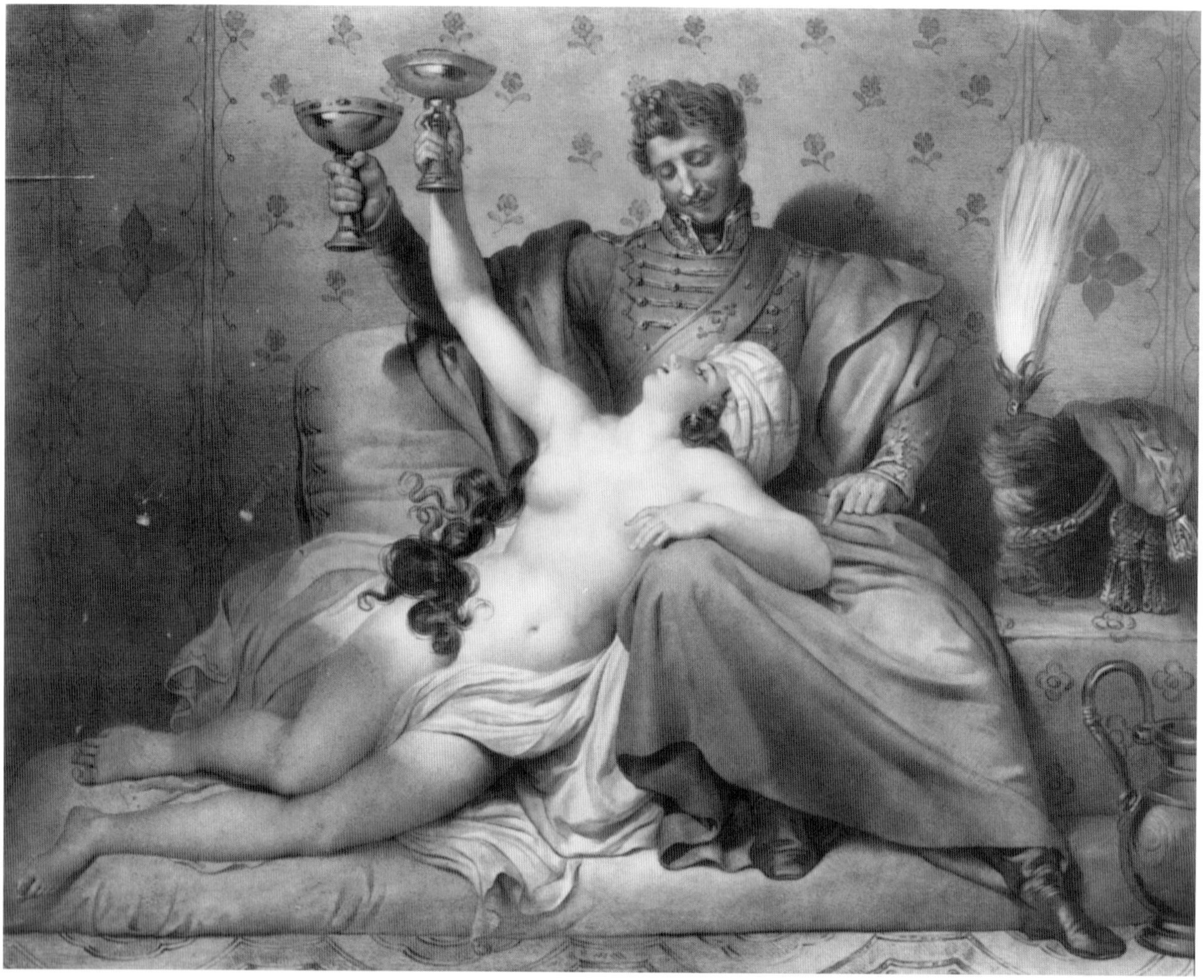

Fig. 5.3. Mendouze after A. E. Fragonard. *La Musulmane imprudente.* 1829–30. Lithograph. *Moeurs d'un sérail.* Cliché Bibliothèque nationale de France, Paris.

There is no letter, only a nosegay, thought to be a common method of communication between lovers. Details of Lewis's somewhat ambiguous narrative are read by the *Illustrated London News.* In the scene "a whimpering girl receiving an apparently mild admonition from her patriarchal lord for having been detected . . . conducting an illicit intrigue through the medium of the nosegay produced in evidence." Presuming a competition among harem women of all ranks, it is the "slave at her side" who exposed the affair "while the ladies of the seraglio indulge in varied expressions of mischievous enjoyment, jealous triumph or shocked propriety, real or assumed" (*ILN* 8 May 1868:471).[17] To the right of the composition, news of the exposed intrigue ripples through the rest of the harem, reaching another group of four women, the servant boy (now cut off at the right edge), the tall black eunuch, and the particularly amused woman in the lower right-hand corner of the composition, whose pose recalls a similar coquettish observer portrayed from an unusual perspective in Thomas Allom's 1838 *Slave-Merchant* (see Fig. 3.7). The young woman implicated in the plot is a vulnerable sinner about to incur her master's condemnation—and a possible death sentence. The cut melon on a tandour in the foreground and "pointed" in her direction is an allusion to her transgression. In reviewing this painting the *Illustrated London News* writes that the girl receives only a "mild admonition" from her master, that is to say, "mild," relative to the western belief that her exposure could warrant, under Islam, her drowning and the killing of her paramour. (Strictly speaking, the *Qur'an* does not sanction capital punishment for *zina* [adultery] if the offender is a slave, but in practice a master's killing a slave may or may not be a punishable offense.[18])

Lewis's narrative might be based loosely on Letter 147 from Montesquieu's *Persian Letters,* in which the

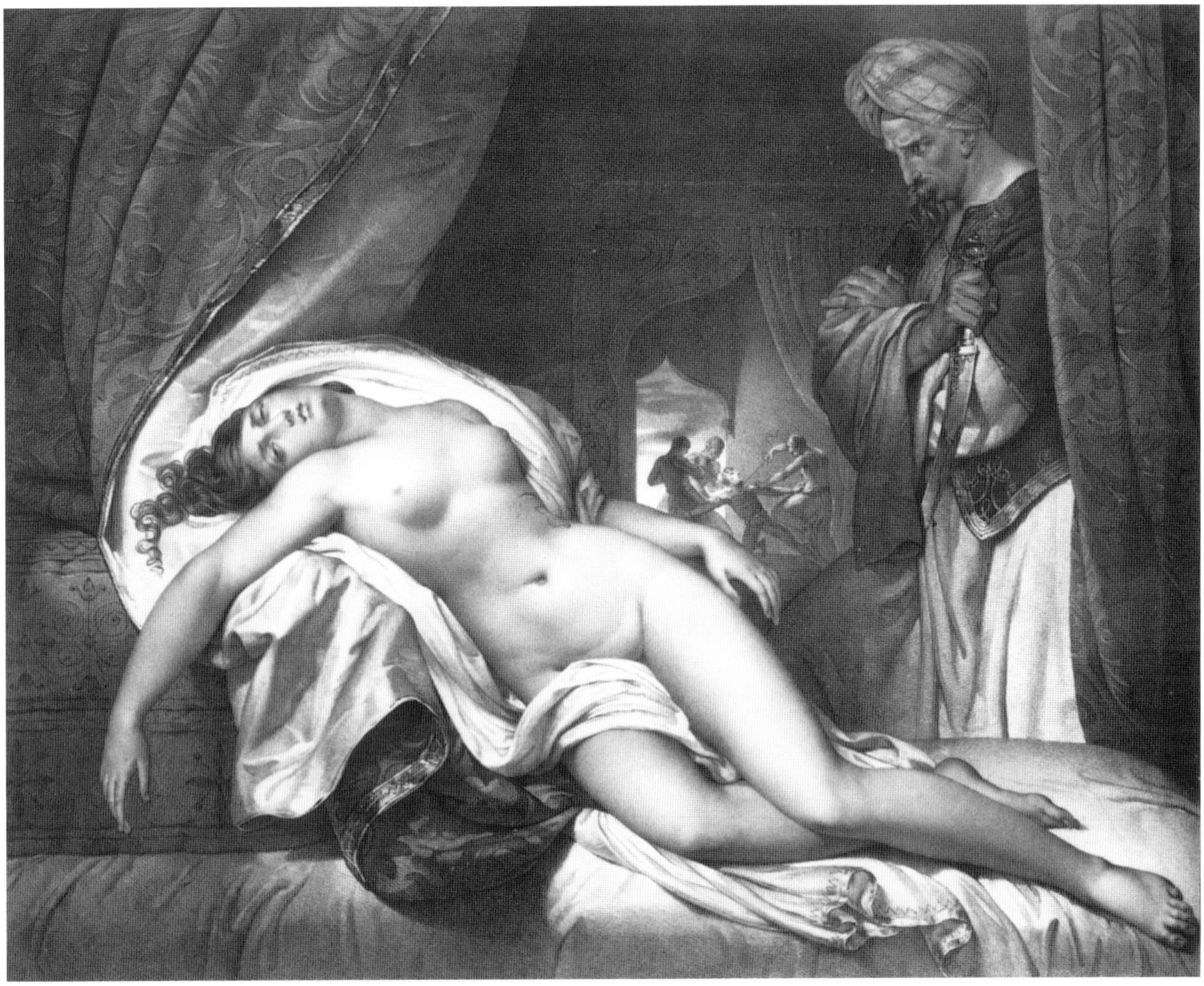

Fig. 5.4. Barathier after A. E. Fragonard. *La Vengeance*. 1829–30. Lithograph. *Moeurs d'un sérail*. Cliché Bibliothèque nationale de France, Paris.

Chief Black Eunuch intercepts a correspondence, and Usbek suspects the wrong wife, a sign of his ineffectuality as head of the harem. By the end of the book Roxana is discovered to be the adulteress. One possible reading of Roxana's consequent suicide is that it is essential for the novel's narrative to show the failure of the harem, poorly led by women in the absence of the despot Usbek; the story chronicles women's pseudo-liberation. Alternatively, the story is feminist in that his wives are powerful enough to destroy the harem that confines them.[19] And though she was a slave Roxana proclaims: "I have always been free [. . .] my mind has always remained independent" (*PL* 280). Roxana's victory is her death.

For offending women who refused to punish themselves, retribution is administered by the master or his emissary, in British and French reports. As early as 1650 Robert Withers relates the horrible fate awaiting criminal harem women. Insolence and disobedience are punished by beating and isolation in the old seraglio, while witchcraft "or any such like abomination" is punished by being "bound hand and foot, and put into a sack, and in the night cast into the sea."[20] In the early eighteenth century Lady Mary Wortley Montagu wrote that Turkish women "suffer sometimes for their Indiscretions in a very severe manner" and reports that "Murder is never persu'd by the King's officers as with us." Still she assures her readers that tragedies in the harem are quite rare (*L* 1:407–8).

Death for the harem woman and her lover at the hands of the husband is cited as punishment for adultery in several articles and books in nineteenth-century England and France. In 1828 Victor Hugo's poem "Moonlight on the Bosphorus" begins with a sultana enjoying the vision of "merry moonbeams" reflecting on the water outside her window as she

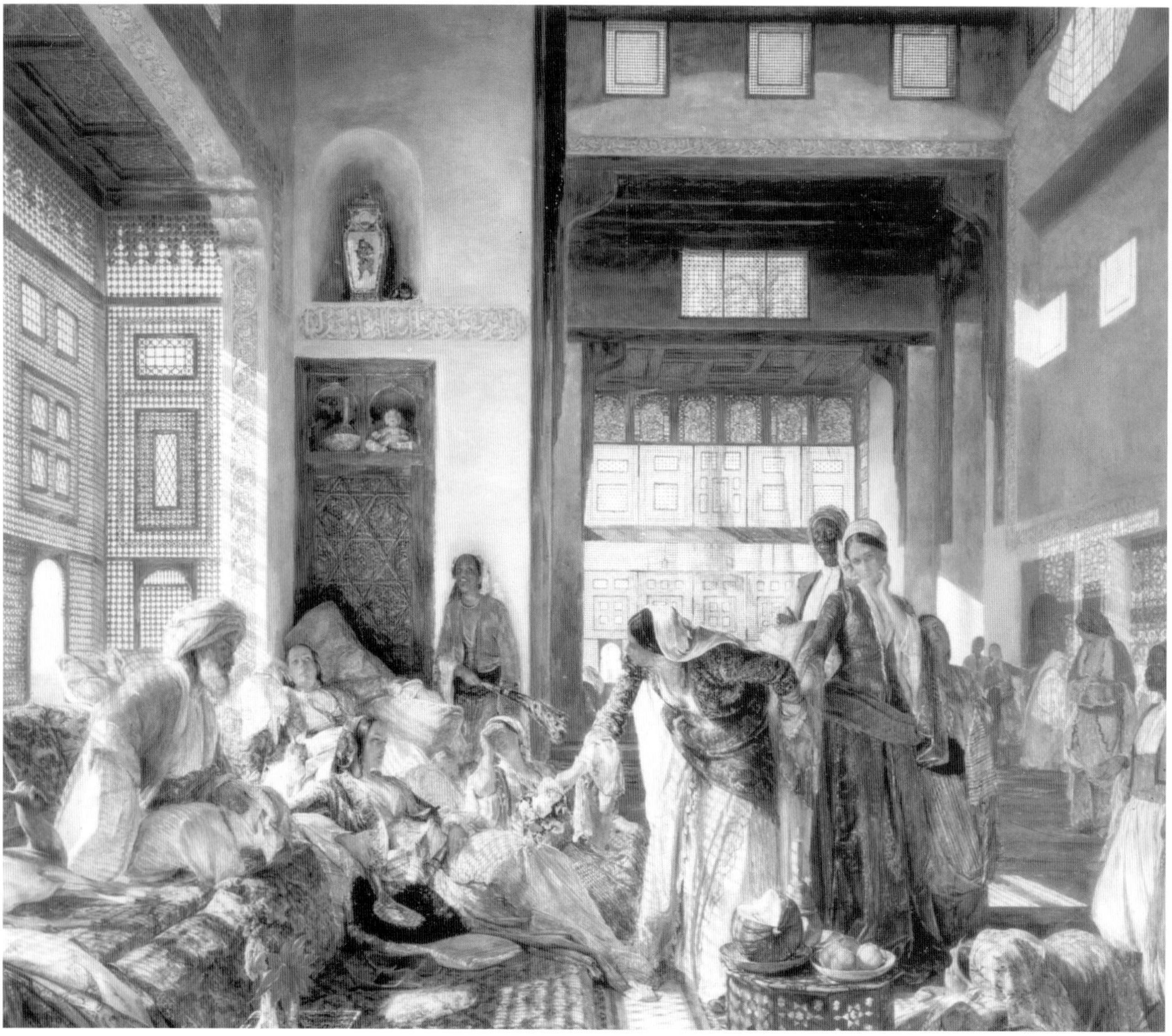

Fig. 5.5. John Frederick Lewis. *Intercepted Correspondence*. 1869. Watercolor. The Fine Art Society, London, UK/Bridgeman Art Library.

plays her guitar. She hears a sound and finally ascertains it to be "heavy sacks, borne each by voiceless dusky slaves" that have washed ashore. They contain, of course, bodies of harem women, a chilling revelation which Hugo juxtaposes with the repeated image of "merry moonbeams" at the end of the poem (*SCL* 47–48). Julia Pardoe in 1837 may have had in mind texts such as Victor Hugo's poem when she describes the long-standing notion of the condemned woman forced into a sack and thrown into the Bosphorus Sea. She also gives a perspective on its history:

> A vast deal of very romantic and affecting sentiment has been from time to time committed to paper, on the subject of the Turkish female drowned in the Bosphorus; and some tale-writer has even gone so far as to describe, in the character of the witnesses, the extreme beauty and the heart-rending tears of the victims. (*CS* 2:183)

What Pardoe objects to is not the falsity of such accounts, but the romanticization of what is such a horrible act. She claims that drowning is much harsher and more inhumane than romantics admit, though the punishment is not about adultery per se.

Lane writes that an adulterous woman is publicly drowned unless she is from a respectable family, in which case she is put to death in private (*ME* 1:379). Thackeray too mentions the Bosphorus "into which some luckless beauty is plunged occasionally."[21] With tongue in cheek he advises his reader to avoid any sacks they might spot floating on eastern seas. In 1850 James MacFarlane repeats the rumor that Muhammad Ali killed both "his fair Circassian and then her paramour the Georgian slave"—crimes for which he was never properly tried.[22] In 1871 Annie Harvey alludes to rumors on the subject when she writes "C——Pasha supposedly killed one of his odalisques for her flirtation with a young secretary [. . .] let us hope it is only a story and not a truth." She contends that guilty odalisques used to be put into sacks and thrown into the Bosphorus, while in later years they were strangled in the fortress of Roumel. To her credit she cautions that the frequency of any punishment, done in private, can never be known.[23] As late as 1872 writers maintain the myth: one harem inmate becomes enamored of a Greek merchant at the bazaar and in selecting a Christian lover she risks "being thrown into the Bosporus [*sic*] in a sack weighted with shot."[24]

Fun is poked at this long-held notion of an untimely death for the offenders in an 1863 review of a new publication. In the process the anonymous author provides a glimpse into the range of texts with which any writer on the harem had to contend. The adulteress belonged to the harem of the magnanimous Sultan Abdul-Medjid, and

> her love did not have the tragic ending which harem adventures assume in romances. No band of Bostandjis broke into the general's house at night, and brought an executioner with them, who laid the lady's head at the feet of her lover; no mysterious bark pushed out in the dark into the Bosphorus and discharged a sack from which, ere it sank in the waves a voice gasped: "Soon united with thee eternally."[25]

Instead, the general's punishment comes in a more humorous form. In an era when middle-class women were becoming the main commodity consumers in England and France, he is bankrupted by the spending habits of his new wife.

This long tradition of detailing horrifying punishments for an unfaithful harem wife is one Alexandre Dumas contributes to when he describes a former method of execution for an adultress in Tunis. The custom was to sew her "into a leather sack with a cock, a cat and a viper, and throw her in the lake," a punishment he claims was outlawed by the much more civilized French people, specifically the father of Ferdinand de Lesseps, who worked for the Suez Canal project (*AA* 112). Dumas corrects that mistaken belief but nonetheless maintains an essentialist evaluation that "adultery is more common among the Arabs than anywhere else in the world." And if a husband finds his wife and her lover together, he "would instantly slay them both" (*AA* 117–18). He relates a principle of Muslim law based on the double standard: a cuckolded man is obliged to kill both his wife and her lover, but a cuckolded man who spares his wife in his vengeance-taking is executed as a murderer (*AA* 190–91). His comparison of "Arab" justice and "our own" is ambiguous. Whether his point is to make his reader sympathize with a principle of eastern jurisprudence or declare it barbaric is left unclear.

In the second of Lewis's harem pictures having adultery as a theme, his 1872 watercolor "*And the Prayer of Faith Shall Save the Sick*" (see Fig. 4.40), an ill woman lies abed, members of the Egyptian[26] household around her. A dark-skinned female servant brings in a covered vessel, and behind her another slave bears a covered urn to be used for ablutions, commonly performed when the ill feels death is near (*ME* 2:251).[27] The nature of the woman's illness needs exploration. She is obviously not dying of old age, given her rich hair color and the age of the (her?) child close by. The extension of the biblical verse which Lewis uses in his title reads "any sins he may have committed will be forgiven." The most common sin of a harem woman mentioned in the written English texts is adultery. I propose that this as an image of the unfaithful and thus doomed harem woman, whether "sick" with remorse or "sick" at heart over her now-lost lover or even sick because she has been poisoned as punishment from her cuckolded husband. By this interpretation the woman might be the same character accused in *Intercepted Correspondence* (see Fig. 5.5) exhibited three years earlier, making this work a sequel to it.

The harem institution, rife with scheming women and tyrannical masters, wreaks destruction and social havoc. Yet some of these pictures might also be read as pathetic images of female deviance, desperate women whose infidelity is forced upon them by a cruel social system. And while the harem is filled with amoral people committing desperate and despicable acts, representing them produces great pleasure for nineteenth-century viewers and readers who were both horrified and delighted in imagining the adulterous woman.[28]

Negligent Mothers

Motherhood was touted as the ultimate expression of feminine fulfillment in British and French bourgeois ideology about gender roles. Conversely, the neglect of children was thought to be symptomatic of the disease called polygyny that fails to answer women's emotional needs. Harem women were thought negligent toward their offspring because of a selfish obsession with establishing their love life with the master. Their success in pleasing (or defying) him indicated their power struggles within and sometimes beyond the harem, which were thought to distract them from effective mothering. The roles of mother and active lover could not merge in these representations.

That a woman neglects her children indicates she has a poor relationship with her husband, according to Wollstonecraft, who writes: "the mother will not neglect her children to practise the arts of coquetry, when sense and modesty secure her the friendship of her husband" (*VRW* 89). First mention of the seraglio in *Vindication* occurs when she claims that aristocratic women, like harem inmates, are not good mothers because they are shallow and have poor judgment:

> they dress, they paint, and nickname God's creatures. Surely these weak beings are only fit for a seraglio! Can they be expected to govern a family with judgement, or take care of the poor babes whom they bring into the world? (*VRW* 83)

High-class women are not inherently inferior in their nature, she says. Rather society fails to encourage women's moral development. Because woman—especially French woman—is a "slave" to prejudice and simply isn't taught "enlightened maternal affection," she either neglects or indulges her children (*VRW* 265).

Based on what she claims is her own experience with a woman of this type, Wollstonecraft is appalled by "the lady who sheds tears for the bird starved in a snare" or other animals in pain, while she is insensitive to her own servants' hardships or the woman who coddles her dogs but ignores her own children's need for moral guidance. Such a woman was considered by her circle of friends "feminine." For Wollstonecraft and many nineteenth-century observers, the spiritual generosity of motherhood could not be achieved in the context of a vain self-love. Because harem women were considered vain they *de facto* could not be proper mothers.

VanLoo's *La Sultane et ses domestiques* (see Fig. 4.61) might illustrate Wollstonecraft's criticism of the harem. Six servants fawn over an enthroned sultana, offering a mirror, jewels, and fine fabrics, which are being tailored to fit her. An important detail in the painting disrupts a reading of it as a celebration of aristocratic women's power. At the far left a seated boy hides behind a screen. The window behind him helps indicate his turbaned head, sullen countenance—and the sword he holds menacingly over his right shoulder. This sultana's obvious affection for her lap dog is an inappropriate substitute for the moral educating her vanity prevents her from undertaking. Similarly, the aristocrat Wollstonecraft describes mistakenly loved her pets, "spoiled brutes that filled the place which her children ought to have occupied," and a poor education limited her interests to a "selfish vanity of beauty" (*VRW* 292–93).

Into the nineteenth century, the literature contains mostly unfavorable judgments about harem women's mothering abilities. For example, Lane says upper-class mothers are indulgent and that a son is "an effeminate prisoner" in the harem. However, he also claims that the boy's harem training is valuable, because there he learns loyalty and respect for his father (*ME* 1:67–68). MacFarlane also does not approve of harem mothers as the first teachers for their sons. He asks "what are the lessons he gets there, from ignorant, indolent and sensual women."[29] Mothers show no modesty or restraint in front of their male children, claims an anonymous author at midcentury: "all these women dress and undress before their youngest sons, and the most improper remarks are made in their presence."[30] The sexual innuendo of romping eunuchs and insensitive lusty women seen by a boy raised in the harem until age ten will "brutalize him for life," claims Martineau (*EL* 262). Muslim mothers are even described as child abusers: "Imagine the chance of any clear moral perception on the part of a boy whose mother, watched like a thief, and locked up like a chattel herself, punishes his childish faults by tearing his flesh with her gold pins, and orders her own slaves to torture his (who are his own relatives), for his amusement!"[31] Some writers claim that the mother corrupts her son, who continues the cycle of abuse. Young pashas are said to be cruel to their mothers and their female playmates.[32]

Some French pictures showing the Muslim household as a family make a point of its contrast with the Christian nuclear family. Achille Devéria's 1836 lithograph, *Intérieur d'un harem* (Fig. 5.6), resembles an extended western family, albeit in a more disorderly form. There are several groupings of female figures; two of them encircle infants. A black wetnurse suckles a white baby, receiving advice from a plump, grandmother type at right. The baby's mother may be the central woman who adjusts her coiffure and lowers her lute. Devéria shows mothers preoccupied with their own persons and not their children, a criticism of both harem inmates and western aristocrats traceable to Mary Wollstonecraft. Overall, the relations of people to each other are not clear-cut based on blood but on servitude.

Nuclear family distinctions are blurred in Pierre François Lehoux's undated pencil sketch *Scène de*

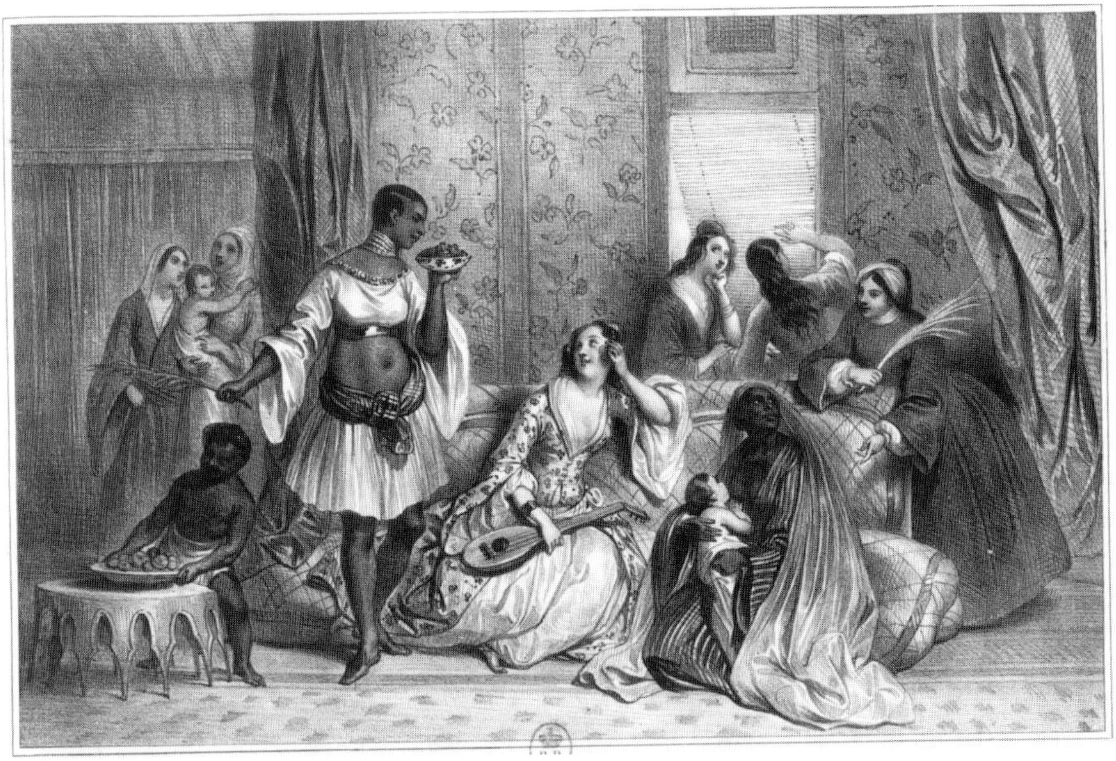

Fig. 5.6. Achille Devéria. *Intérieur d'un harem.* 1836. Lithograph. Cliché Bibliothèque nationale de France, Paris. Farwell, *FPLI*, v. 9, 5F6 B80853.

harem (Fig. 5.7) in which one harem inmate attempts to quiet two children as her friend (and co-wife/concubine?) naps, resting her head on her lap. Social roles are flexible here, and the sleeping woman becomes childlike herself, protected by the other mother. Perhaps the sleeping woman has spent the night with the harem master, whose presence is suggested by the pipe.[33] Though her night life has made her unfit for the daytime responsibilities of mothering, the social structure of shared mothering among women can accommodate that disruption.

For some observers the harem, locale for disorderly sexual activity, could hardly encourage a healthy family dynamic. In both texts and images a moral Muslim family arrangement is allowed only when the configuration of an orderly (western) nuclear triad takes shape. The tendency to project this conception of the family onto the East as its "exotic . . . replica" is developed further in the early twentieth-century harem image found in picture postcards, as Alloula observes.[34]

Tucked in the mass of veils and pillows in Lewis's 1850 *Hhareem* (see Plate 1 and Fig. 1.2) is the head of a small male child with a finger to his mouth. His headdress indicates his gender.[35] He clings to the skirts of what the press named as "the favorite" harem woman, presumably his mother. In having borne a male child, she earns a superior social status in the harem hierarchy (*CS* 1:214).[36] In the narrative of the painting the wife's unhappy facial expression is thus more understandable: a new addition to the harem means another potential son-producer to usurp her favored status. In this painting and two others (*Intercepted Correspondence*, 1879, and *And the Prayer of Faith*, 1872) Lewis paints the child somewhat removed from his mother, who totally ignores him in each case. This suggests a view of Muslim motherhood at variance with British ideals for effective mothering.

Another picture dealing with the theme of the "flawed" system of motherhood in the East is the lithograph after E. Prisse d'Avennes showing an eastern mother and child with their darker-skinned domestic from the 1848 *Oriental Album*. Titled *Habesh, or Abyssinian Slave, Cairo* (see Fig. 2.16), it shows a harem mother holding her child, while an Abyssinian slave in the center of the composition looks wistfully at and rocks the empty cradle, her hand over her own flat, barren abdomen. The image recounts the pain of motherhood denied harem menials. Is the image a criticism of the slave institution that "unnaturally" prevents a beautiful and healthy woman from bearing a child, diverting her own mothering skills to care for another woman's baby? If harem slaves were thought to bear the master's children without the

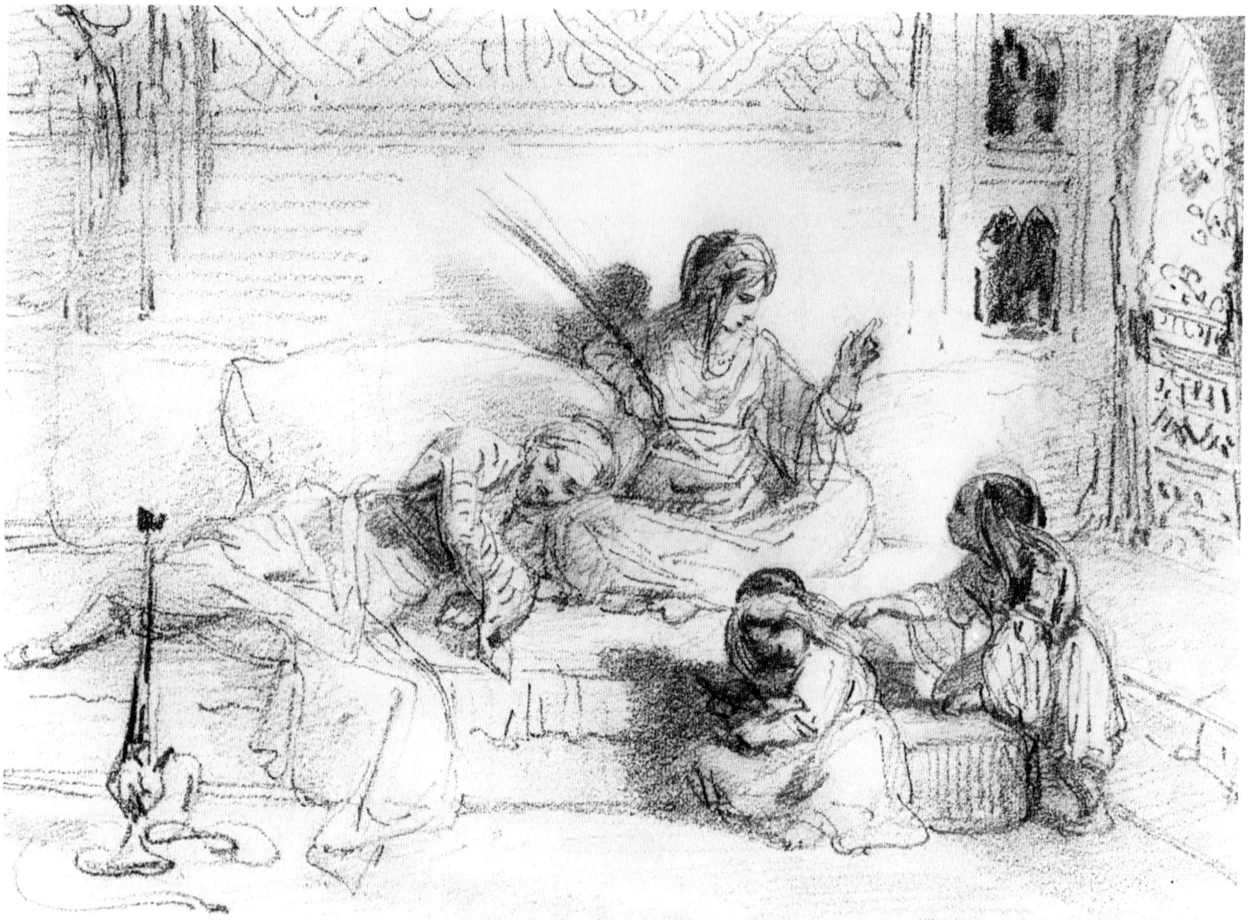

Fig. 5.7. Pierre François Lehoux. ***Scène de harem.*** **1837–38. Pencil. Musée Grobet-Labadié, Marseille.**

crippling stigma of illegitimacy as in the West, as Urquhart describes, this image may be read instead as a projection of the impossibility of motherhood for western female servants who abandon hopes for motherhood in order to keep their employment. As such, it can be read as an expression of working-class sympathy.

The conception of harem women as inadequate mothers did not stop there. They were sometimes called child murderers. Harem women were notorious practitioners of infanticide (the outcome of the harem's supposed intrigues), and female newborns were most vulnerable. The sisters of sultans were reputedly obliged to have killed not only their newborn sons, who threatened the line of ascendency, but also sometimes their lovers/husbands as a further sign of their perverse power.[37] Even a healthy baby born into a large harem "always dies—killed with kindness" by having too many indulgent women eager to mother, claims Martineau. And a woman mourns inappropriately, in her opinion, when a child dies there, for an offspring that may not even be her own (*EL* 261–62). It is no surprise that in western understandings, a child is poorly raised when "correct" channels of desire and gratification are disrupted[38] threatening the western nuclear family's function.

One explanation advanced for the "fact" that harem women were bad mothers is that they themselves supposedly had "unnatural," "semi-barbarous" parent-models, who sold them into slavery (*PT* 1:146, 250). Historically, parents of the slave class in Circassia did sell their children to slave dealers, but this could have been considered a rite of passage done in hopes of improving the girls' material lot.[39] Also the separation was not necessarily lifelong, as women who joined wealthy harems could often send for their parents. Moreover, the British criticism of Circassian parenting can be linked to Russophilia as a way to counter the contention that Circassians were loyal citizens who loved family and homeland, as discussed in chapter 2.

The notion that harem women were bad mothers was extended into the political realm to explain the degeneration of the whole Ottoman Empire, crumbling because its leaders, having been raised in the harem, lacked the proper moral fiber to govern effectively.[40] Stanley Lane Poole, writing the introduction to Mrs. Blunt's book, uses some of the same terminology: the Turkish potential for greatness will not develop because of "the pernicious social system which destroys the moral force of the women and thereafter the men of the empire" (*PT* 1:xxii). This criticism of Muslim women sounds remarkably like Mary Wollstonecraft's late eighteenth-century bourgeois critique of the aristocracy; to her mind French aristocrats made bad mothers because of their faulty education, which allowed the development of the skills of coquetry over childcare (*VRW* 89).

Overall, harem women were considered poor mothers because they were too indulgent both in their own habits and in disciplining their children. In turn their offspring were thought to become lax in their education, manners, and sensitivity to others' needs. Inappropriate mothering is one more manifestation of harem women's disorderliness.

Perverse Lesbians and Gossiping Sisters

When two (or more) harem women are depicted together, they inevitably stand for polygyny, whether they are meant to be read as two wives, a wife and a concubine, or a servant and her mistress. They are often shown making physical contact, arms interlocked. The perception that a plethora of female sex partners were awaiting a single master gave rise to the notion that women turned to other women for emotional and sexual sustenance. There were a range of readings given scenes of women shown together in the harem in nineteenth-century England and France, when the lines were blurred between female-female friendship and romance, according to one study on women's relationships in Victorian America.[41] "Sisterly" affection included several kinds of socially acceptable physical contact. In contrast, a woman's sexual (genital) activity with another woman, though it was still deviant and immoral to most observers, was not categorized as lesbian until the last third of the nineteenth century. Harem "lesbianism" would likewise be considered an unnatural separation of sexual intimacy from pregnancy and childbearing.

In this section I also consider the subject of gossiping women, that is, women who turned their talk to malicious ends. The themes of lesbianism and womanly gossip are similar when two women are pictured together in that they are each other's solace, and their interaction can act to divert an inmate's loyalty from the harem master. Whether their relationship was read as involving sexual intimacy or just spiritual communion, female connections were thought unnaturally close because the harem put several women in extended contact with each other mediated only by the rare appearance of a man. Both lesbianism and gossip were considered consequences of "too much" female closeness.

I want to widen my consideration to further include those harem images in which the two women pictured are either twinned or formally complementary; these figures may not exhibit sexual interest in each other. Schick develops this theme of harem women who are not considered individuals but as multiply occurring groups.[42] Such imagery of a pair or a plurality of women in the absence of the male owner could serve as erotic spectacle, as the assertion of affection among harem inmates or simply as an indicator of harem polygyny.

At least from the seventeenth century two or more women in a harem prompted writers to suggest lesbian activity takes place there as one more manifestation of the harem's reputed "polysexuality."[43] On harem women's sexual appetite and autoeroticism which need to be kept in check, Robert Withers writes in euphemistic language in 1650:

> Now it is not lawfull for any one to bring ought in unto them, with which they may commit the deeds of beastly, and unnaturall uncleanesse; so that if they have a will to eat, radishes, cucumbers, gourds, or such like meats; they are sent in unto them sliced, to deprive them of the means of playing the wanton: for they being all young, lusty, and lascivious wenches, and wanting the society of men (which would better instruct them, and questionlesse far better employ them) are doubtless of themselves inclined to that which is naught, and will often be possest with unchast thoughts.[44]

For similar reasons harem women were reputedly prohibited from keeping monkeys and male dogs as pets, and they were denied uncut phallic-shaped gourds and cucumbers, as Alexander Pope reminds Lady Mary Wortley Montagu in teasing her about her trip to Turkey.[45] Mozart's burlesque character Osmin in the third aria of *Abduction from the Seraglio* complains about the morals of the harem women he must guard by calling them "lazy women chasing monkeys" (*AS* 22). And early on in Montesquieu's highly influential *Persian Letters* lesbianism is suggested. Usbek's wife Zephis writes to him protesting that the eunuch has misjudged her relationship with her female slave. In claiming their relationship has been "innocent," she raises suspicion about Zelid, a slave "who serves me so faithfully, whose deft hands create beauty and grace wherever they go" (*PL* 44).

Vanmour's *Recueil* provides an early example of relevance to the pictorial tradition of harem women's mutual affection. Two white women in a harem interior modestly amuse themselves with a board game in *Filles turques qui jouent au mangala* (Fig. 5.8), plate 53 from his 1712 volume. In Carle Vanloo's 1755 *Deux sultanes travaillant à la tapisserie* (Fig. 5.9) the sultanas "work," although the earnest arching of the sultana's torso at right suggests livelier conversation—perhaps gossip. Her posture contrasts with the composure of the sultana at left and suggests a relationship of mentor and protégé.

"Lesbian" imagery appeared long before the rococo period, but Boucher's pornographic works (not set in the harem at all but out-of-doors) seem to serve as a model for rococo-revival imagery such as that by Jules Robert Auguste dating from the 1820s.[46] Auguste merges the theme of the harem with the lesbian pastoral in his rococo-revival gouache, *Deux odalisques dans un paysage* (see Fig. 4.59).

Various kinds of complementarity between women of the harem are offered the viewer in harem pictures: white and black skin tones, seated and standing postures, views of the women from front and back. All three of these binaries are subtly presented in J. L. Gérôme's *Moorish Bath* (1870) (Fig. 5.10). Though the presumption of their different social ranks can prevent the viewer from drawing too close a similarity between them, the artist juxtaposes tonalities of naked female flesh to appeal to a range of taste for the exotic. A woman slave's dark skin may serve to exaggerate the lightness of a white slave's and vice versa. And yet at the very center of the composition, Gérôme has highlighted the black woman's left forearm and darkened the same arm of the white woman by placing it in shadow, thus correlating their skin tones more closely than they appear at first. In establishing such a complementarity the artist may be hinting at their intimacy. In contrast, Auguste's black-white pairing of odalisques is more overtly about sexual intimacy between women, as in *Deux Odalisques/"Girlfriends"* (see Fig. 4.59).

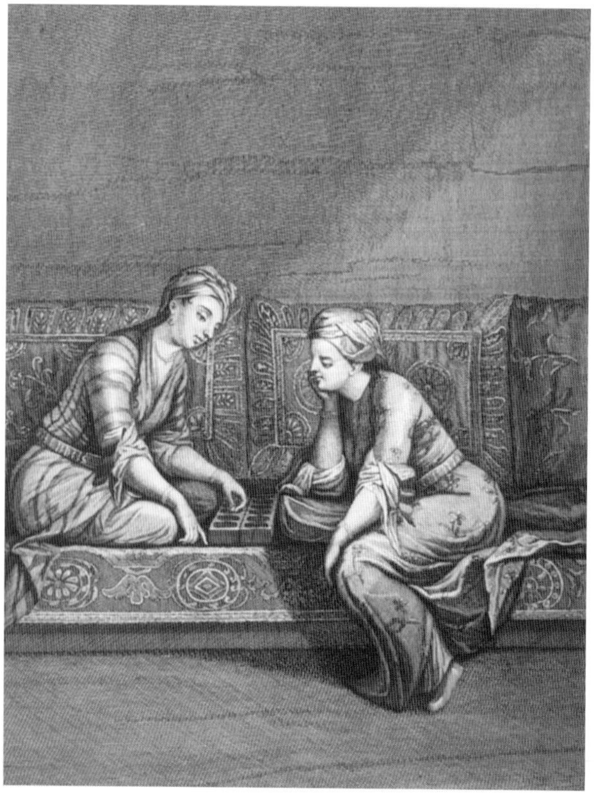

Fig. 5.8. After Vanmour. *Filles turques qui jouent au mangala*. Ca. 1715. Engraving. *Recueil de cent estampes*, plate 53. Department of Special Collections, Charles E. Young Library, UCLA.

The convention of the front-back pairing of harem women functions in more salacious imagery to heighten visual titillation by doubling the amount of bare flesh exposed. Like the mirror, it allows for all three dimensions of female charms to be displayed on the painted surface. This fact is exaggerated in Rowlandson's ribald print, *Harem* (see Fig. 4.5), done after 1812, where the women are arranged to afford multiple views of female nakedness. However, this print points out the difficulty of reconciling the fantasies of intimacy and group sex, and this image ends up as humorous pornography. For all its crudity, Rowlandson's print still includes at the extreme right the configuration of the antique aesthetic convention of Three Graces that also allowed a more complete view of womanliness. Philipon also varied the Three Graces theme by clothing eastern women in a relatively innocent lithograph c. 1837, *Palanquins d'Isfahan* (Fig. 5.11) in which the viewer has only a frontal view of the three women. Judging from the title referring to a Persian city in Montesquieu's *Persian Letters* they may be Usbek's wives.

The "total view" afforded by the front and back images of harem women provides artists with a manageable formula to imply a much greater number of women. Thus it could serve a viewer's fantasy for group sex. Yet the doubling or twinning of the same female type does not necessarily represent two separate women but could be one ideal woman free of individuality. For example, the two figures in Ernest Hébert's 1843 *Deux Odalisques couchées sur la terrasse* (see Fig. 4.15) who share a hairdo and body type can be seen as either two distinct women or two views of the same odalisque. In either case, the back and side views offer more titillation than

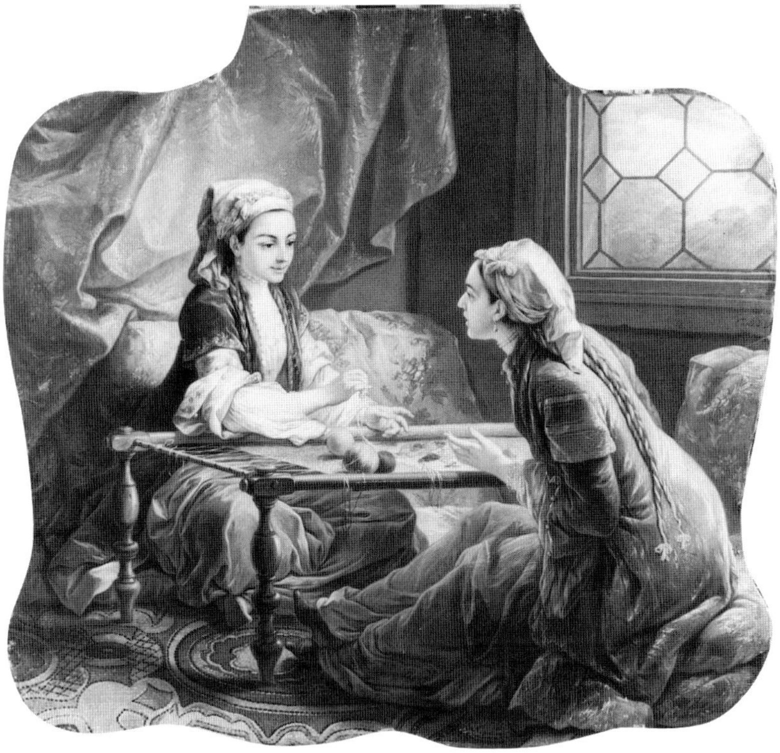

Fig. 5.9. Carle Vanloo. *Deux sultanes travaillant à la tapisserie.* 1755 Salon. State Hermitage Museum, St. Petersburg.

the single two-dimensional represented figure can. Such images can be read as less about polygyny than idealized monogamy, each woman replicating the ideal qualities of Woman without introducing any imperfections that a second, real woman might present. Needless to say, these are unidimensional, fantastic fabrications.[47]

One French and one British picture from the late 1830s are curiously alike in their ambiguity about harem lesbianism. In the lithograph by Henri Grévedon, *Sultane à sa toilette* (see Fig. 3.3) done before 1838 an older woman, her hair covered, adjusts the diadem of the younger with dark, flowing hair, presumably the sultana referred to in the title. If so, the older woman may be her mother, her servant—or her older lover. There is an erotic piquancy in the picture due to the "passionate," upward glance of the younger woman and the amount of physical contact between the two women. The second image again shows an older woman with her head covered; it is John Lewis's earliest harem picture, a collaborative effort done with Coke Smyth titled *Harem* (see Fig. 3.37) from 1837. The two white women at first seem to be peers rather than slave and mistress. The younger woman closer to the viewer has long, loose hair; she looks down modestly. The lesbian component is subtle: the older woman's eyelids are languorous and heavy as she looks sidelong at her younger and larger-featured friend. Flower symbolism further suggests this theme of the sexually initiated and the virginal; one rose is in full bloom, the other only partially open. A third rose, this one also fully opened, is placed atop the kerchief of the experienced mentor. Meanwhile, the lute stands silently by, an allusion to their forthcoming pleasures, to be shared with the master and/or with each other.

Ingres's *Bain Turc* (see Fig. 4.45) is the most famous harem scene in the history of nineteenth-century French art to suggest lesbianism. In the configuration of female bodies to the right of the composition does one woman fondle the breasts of another, or does one harem inmate cross her arms over her own breasts? In this image lesbianism is again made ambiguous; it is both "affirmed and denied."[48]

What significance might there be for oblique references to lesbian practices within the harem? If polygyny was thought to be an exotic deviation from proper sexual relations, then harem lesbianism is the extreme oddity within that exoticism, the Other within the Other in which woman's need for female friendship and physical intimacy are unnaturally combined. Harem lesbians recall the British and French conception of "female redundancy" in which old maids lacked the amorous attention of a man.

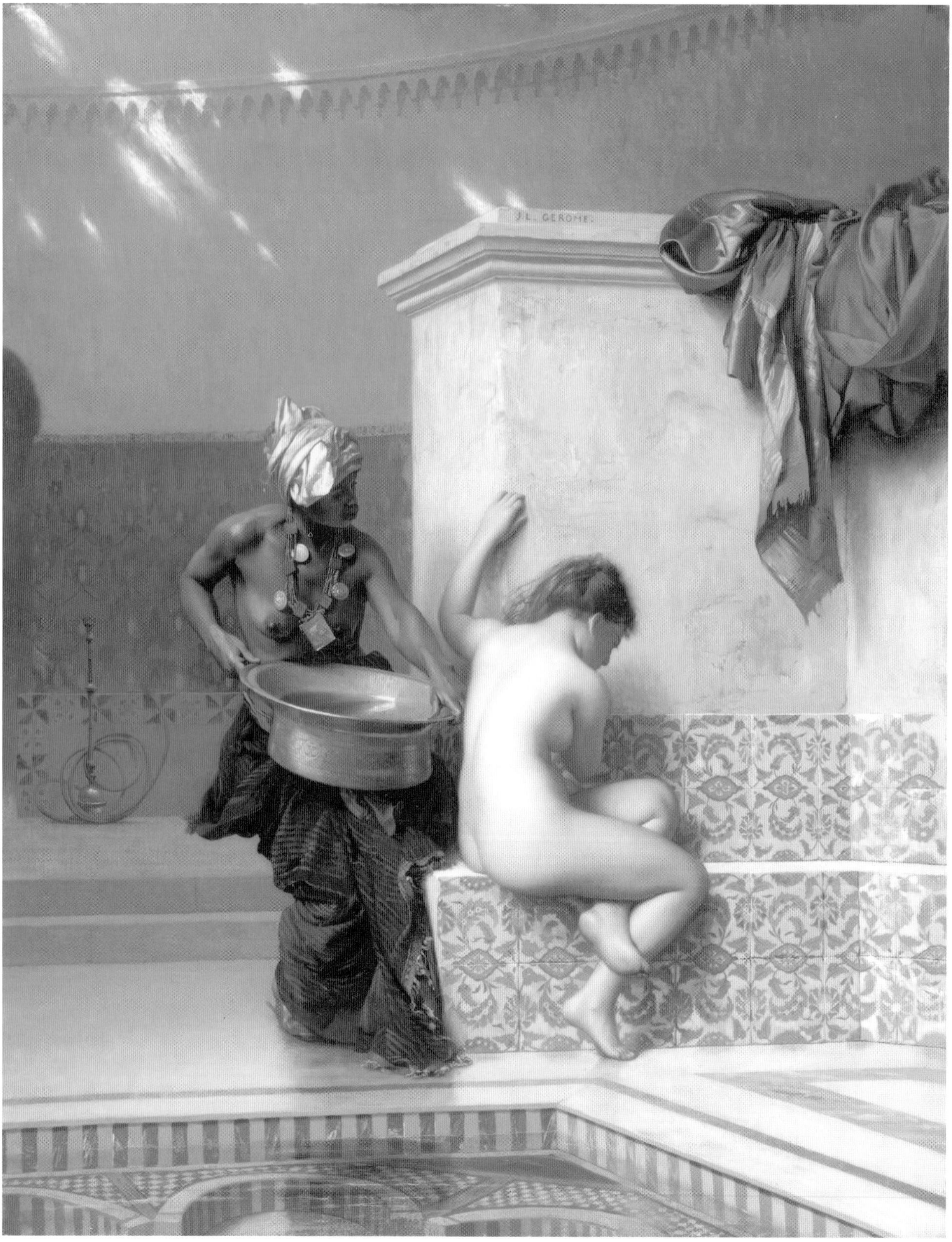

Fig. 5.10. Jean Léon Gérôme. *Moorish Bath*. 1870. Oil on canvas. Courtesy, Museum of Fine Arts, Boston. Reproduced with Permission. © 1999 Museum of Fine Arts, Boston. All rights reserved.

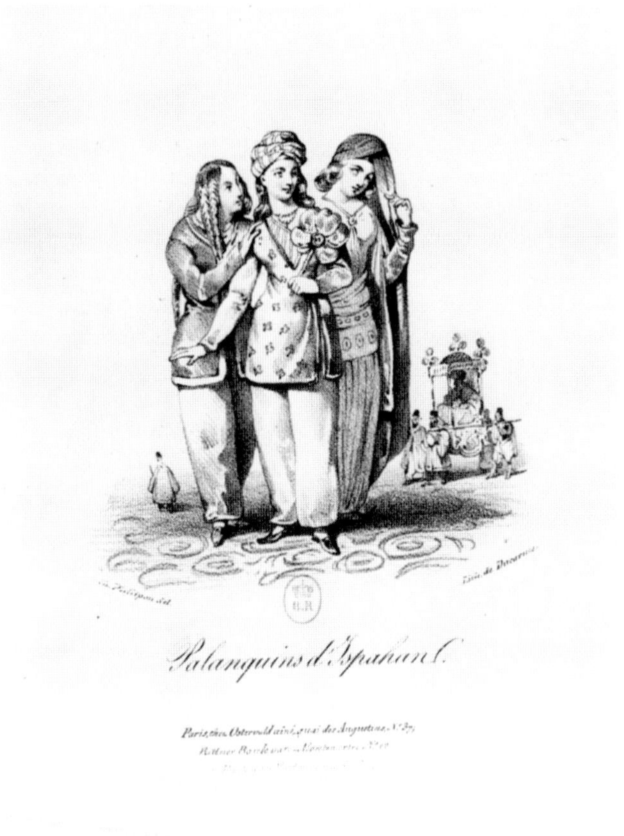

Fig. 5.11. Charles Philipon. *Palanquins d'Isfahan*. Ca. 1837. Lithograph. Cliché Bibliothèque nationale de France, Paris. Farwell, *FPLI*, v. 9, 5F3 B78131.

Both the eastern harem lesbian and the western spinster were deviants who were threatening in their independence from male-defined sexual and social standards. As for pictures of harem lesbianism, their suggestiveness is intended to fascinate and titillate.

Indolent Narcissists

In the history of harem imagery, one of the most pervasive stereotypes is that the harem woman is indolent, spoiled by inactivity and self-absorption. Her indolence is reputed even in Elizabethan England.[49] The *Oxford English Dictionary* traces the etymology of "indolence" from the early eighteenth century, when it meant insensibility to pain and referred to medical pathology, to the early nineteenth, when it took on the sense of laziness. The latter is the usage many nineteenth-century commentators imply in describing harem women. The evolution of the word's nuance toward moral value judgment may also be related to the critique of the idle wealthy, a more prevalent position in public discourse in the Revolutionary and post-Revolutionary period. The expanded meaning of the English word indolence is intertwined with the explosion of harem representations in the nineteenth century, which is itself inseparable from the critique of aristocratic privilege.[50]

In visual art, indolence can be registered in two ways: in pictorial representations of harem women who are in a reclining pose and in the reactions made by art critics, who frequently use the term itself. In Lewis's 1850 *Hhareem* (see Plate 1) the women lie about the harem, rather than stand or work. The woman to the pasha's left is described by three art critics as "indolent" and by one as "pampered."[51] The *Art Journal* rather impatiently comments that "the khanum, odalisque, or what you will reclines [. . .] in the profound listlessness of oriental life" in Lewis's 1857 *Harem Life* (see Fig. 3.39) (*AJ* 1857:178).

The motif of a woman lying on a couch or bed was provocative. These pictures were not interpreted as narratives on a woman at rest after a long day of work. Instead relaxation was thought to be a perpetual posture, the way harem women spent their nights—and days. Slaves were thought to do the housework and raise the children. Florence Nightingale compares harem life to "a circle of hell"; it was she who felt trapped by the *ennui* of the inhabitants, who failed to understand the value of her busy life (*LE* 208).

If the harem woman could ignore child-rearing and housework, she was presumed to exert herself only to partake in pleasure. Images of women at rest were read as living a life of endless indulgence. The imagery alone of course did not convey these notions, but because it participated in stereotypes about the harem women as lazy, it provoked more of the same. The mythology was developed at some length. The inevitable result of the harem woman's leisure, especially when she was shown on a couch or bed, was that she turned her attention to love. Such a focus was thought to evolve both from her vanity and her shirking of work responsibilities. Relaxing was considered an extreme disposition of the body and therefore immoral. She was not simply lying available to the master, an interpretation that might provoke pity for her as victim, but she actively desired sexual relations. To this end, she is shown primping and admiring herself in a mirror as a prelude to sexual activity. A laxity in morals was thought to result from physical indolence.

The harem woman's reputed indolence was believed to result in part from the enervating effects of the bath. Harem inmates use the women's public baths (*hammam*), made famous by Mary Wortley Montagu's description in her *Turkish Embassy Letters*. Again, bathing is considered an extreme indulgence, if taken too frequently and for prolonged periods of time.[52]

The harem women's inherent indolence was seen as the cause for her corpulence, or conversely her corpulence was thought to lead to laziness.[53] One of the women Lewis paints in *Hhareem* is called plump—"large and voluminous in form," says the *Athenaeum* (*A* 4 May 1850:480); "full and voluptuous in form," says the *Critic* (*C* 1850:253). (Her plumpness can be debated, but the figure is uncorseted.) In responding to Lewis's 1857 image *Harem Life—Constantinople* (see Fig. 3.39) the *Art Journal* implies that harem indolence produces women who are heavier, a more desirable characteristic than in England: "The lady is not old, but already *enbonpointée* [sic]—the most charming characteristic in the eyes of a Turk" (*AJ* 302 1857:178).

A harem woman's indolence slips into somnolence in Bonington's *La Siesta* (see Fig. 2.14) (1828). Given the title, her sleep is not for the night, but for a nap. The focus on a harem woman sleeping evokes the judgment that her life was one of *dolce far niente.* John Lewis, who painted a *Siesta* (see Fig. 2.13) in 1876, might have seen Bonington's work, acquired by the Wallace Collection by 1874.[54] In Lewis's picture the harem woman's sleeping state and the whiteness of her partially exposed breast heighten her vulnerability. Like a swooning woman in a stage production, the figure is artfully draped (and displayed) over a divan. In Delacroix's *Reclining Odalisque* (see Fig. 2.15) of 1827–28 the eastern woman is also asleep, but unlike the woman in Bonington's or Lewis's images, she is nearly nude and invites more visual penetration. All glimpses into the harem, visual or literal, assure the artist-viewer's status as a voyeur. But the theme of the sleeping woman emphasizes her powerlessness in resisting the probing eyes of the voyeur.

A harem woman, asleep and ill and thus doubly vulnerable, is described in the 1824 account told by "an eastern physician" named Meerza Ahmed Tubeeb. The woman is alone, and the author has fetishized the surrounding accouterments—colored brocades, henna-stained nails, and a fan. The first-person narrative, the up-close description, and the narrator's self-consciousness heighten the immediacy of the passage's visual eroticism. His visual intensity bespeaks ardent desire in terms that recall Jacques Lacan's critical theories of the gaze as phallic: "all this, and ten thousand other beauties, riveted me to the spot. I gazed and gazed, and scarcely dared to draw my breath—and strained my sight till my eyes grew dim."[55] In both pictures and texts the harem woman is the passive spectacle; the reader/viewer plays the role of the powerful (male) presence creating the total environment through his privileged gaze.

But women too watched (or claimed to have watched) harem women asleep. In 1837 Julia Pardoe's playful description of sleepy harem girls had less of the physician's intense scrutiny. But she too fetishizes the "bevy of fair girls" in focusing on fragmented body parts: "What eyes, and lips, and teeth, were grouped together." And she too makes the transition from the women's idleness to sleep: "with their delicate fingers clasped together, and almost making their idleness look graceful. Here and there one lay fast asleep, with her cheek pillowed upon her hand, and a smile upon her lips" (*CS* 1:312–13). Again indolence leads to somnolence, as Pardoe describes the Circassian slave girl, who has the

> softest sleepiest expression—the lowest voice—and the most indolently graceful movements [. . .] As she pillows her pure, pale cheek upon her small dimpled hands, you feel no inclination to arouse her into exertion. (*CS* 2:212)

The harem woman, indolent or finally asleep, embodies certain feminine ideals: malleability, dependence, helplessness, and passivity. She is the object of the spectacle offered by her slumber.[56] She is less morally culpable asleep than awake.

Besides their sleepiness, another indicator of harem women's reputed self-absorption was the mirror. Harem women gaze upon their own images in a silver-mounted mirror, and this is their last thought before falling asleep, claims Julia Pardoe (*CS* 1:313).[57] The mirror, to be found in Renaissance pictures on the *vanitas* theme, was often included in rococo scenes of harem women, usually preparing her toilet as in Boucher's *La Sultane (à la toilette)* (Fig. 5.12). A harem woman vainly gazes into a handheld mirror in the color lithograph done after Morlon titled *Constantinople* (see Fig. 4.14) of 1855–1856. Thomas Allom includes a mirror on the sofa in the foreground of his watercolor drawing *Favourite Odalisque* c. 1836 (Plate 5), though the harem ladies have set it aside for what must be a more interesting sight out the window.

Whether reclining or standing the harem woman was idle, and if idle she was interested primarily in herself. The narcissistic harem woman is another part of this stereotype. It appears for example in Devéria's *The Narcissus of Turkey* of 1831 (see Fig. 4.49), a *Keepsake*-like image in which the narcissus is both the woman and the garland of flowers that enframe her.

That the harem woman was narcissistic, overly concerned with her toilette and body, is anticipated in the writing of Wollstonecraft, who uses a

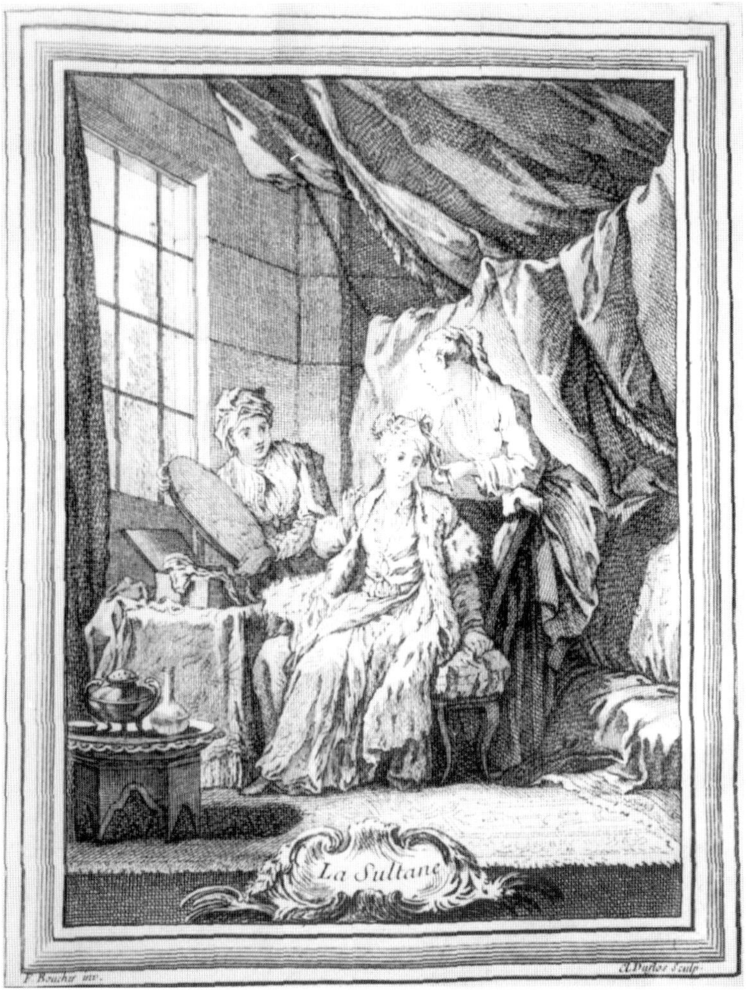

Fig. 5.12. François Boucher. *La Sultane (à la toilette)*. 1746. Engraving. *Moeurs et usages des turcs*. Photo Adam Miller.

comparison between western women and the uncivilized as a rhetorical device in her writing about the value of women's education. For her a woman's self-absorption becomes compensation for an inactive mind: "When the mind is not sufficiently opened to take pleasure in reflection, the body will be adorned with sedulous care; and ambition will appear in tattooing or painting it" (*VRW* 310). This characterizes women as well as "savages" whom she believes are incapable of devising a moral code, preoccupied as they are with "pleasure" (*VRW* 311).

Wollstonecraft makes a rather startling rhetorical comment about the "indolence" of all women, not just those living in the harem. Women's indolence is enforced by an unfair society: "As a sex, women are habitually indolent; and everything tends to make them so" (*VRW* 237). She describes one of her own acquaintances, a woman of high society who ate little and "recline[d] with self-complacency on a sofa;" she was "weak and depraved" and "dissolved in luxury." Wollstonecraft constructs this unnamed acquaintance in binary opposition to a person of virtue whose mind is cultivated. This woman is compared to the Roman emperors who were "irrational monster[s] . . . depraved by lawless power" (*VRW* 130). For Wollstonecraft, women are not allowed to be virtuous or even respected for fear that they might look unwomanly. She compares this mistreatment of women in the West to the Muslim treatment of harem slaves who are neither property nor human. Wollstonecraft implies that the harem is the locale for the most degraded state of womanhood. She paraphrases "the vulgar tale of Mahomet's coffin; they have neither the unerring instinct of brutes, not are allowed to fix the eye of reason on a perfect model" (*VRW* 118). Again the concept of an indolent woman arises. She asks rhetorically: "Do passive indolent women make the best wives?" (*VRW* 119).

In the history of colonization, the terms indolent and lazy have often been used to disparage local, usually male resistance to imperialism in Southeast Asia as well as the Middle East.[58] Lazy natives might also refer to men who are not fully employed in the public sphere. Whether referring to men on the street or women in the harem, its implications are similar: easterners are idle—and thus prone to evil deeds. The stereotype served as justification for imperialist intervention and the introduction of capitalism, which would properly employ men and also replace life in the harem with a lifestyle that resembled the French or British bourgeois home.

Thus the harem woman is constructed in opposition to a western self-image of its women as busy, centered on children and home, morally—as well as physically—"upright." British and French representations about idleness bespeak much about its binary opposition: (house)work and/or the care of children fill a void that would otherwise give rise to vice. As such, they assuage western anxiety about what lies beyond the practice of social norms. In art and in written discourse the eastern woman recumbent was a trope for submission that could only imply western moral superiority.

Exotic Prostitutes

The conception of the harem woman as prostitute had a long history. It was based on one obvious point of similarity. Like a brothel, the harem houses an assortment of sexually available women. The French or British observer carried the analogy further by implying that the harem woman had a nature similar to the prostitute's: each actively desired sex. One longstanding explanation for this is tautological. If the eastern woman is imprisoned within the harem, so goes the argument, it must be because she has the lascivious disposition that requires it.[59] Relatedly, the harem woman's moral standing is considered so low and her preoccupation with sex so great that she slips into the same life of wantonness as a prostitute. Simile then becomes fact. Prostitution merges with harem life as in this portion of an 1855 article which quotes an unnamed source:

> Frequently have we heard stories of the liaisons between Turkish women and Europeans; but they are generally fictitious . . . [In one case we are told] 'The heroine was merely the common-place girl of the too-celebrated Stamboolina. Egyptian women are, according to all accounts, licentious and prone to intrigue; and many of them have had affairs with Franks even during the months of Ramadhan.'[60]

This view of the harem woman, that she is immoral and oversexed, drawn to prostitution because she is unable to find fulfilment in monogamy, appeared a few years later in misogynist terms: "There are no fiercer viragoes in the world than some of these dyed and painted Orientals."[61]

A critical analysis of the stereotype of harem women as prostitutes must also consider a popular debate about the role of heavenly beings, houris, in Paradise. The term houri is derived from the Persian *hour* meaning "white" or an Arabic word describing eyes in which black and white are strongly contrasted.[62] It is used in the Qur'anic description of Paradise, where (male) believers who have led good lives are to be rewarded in Heaven by virginal houris to answer their every desire. The good man could in effect obtain his "harem" in the afterlife.

Lane quotes the *Qur'an* and interjects his own commentary in recounting the bounty of Paradise, in which even the lowest ranking man will have his own collection of houris. Paradise will consist of

> "the indulgence of the appetites [. . .] in the pleasures afforded by the company of the girls of Paradise, whose eyes will be very large and entirely black [. . .]. [T]he very meanest" believer will have "72 wives of the girls of Paradise ('hooreeyehs') besides the wives he had in this world," if he desire to have the latter (and the good will doubtless desire the good). (*ME* 1:82–83)

Scholars on Islam have debated whether Paradise would be the locale for sexual expression or bliss of a pure sort.[63] Whether justifiably or not, some nineteenth-century texts perpetuated the notion of the houri as offering sexual indulgence. For example, Alexandre Dumas claims that the Muslim paradise Muhammad envisioned was "entirely sensual" in keeping with the inherent nature of the people he hoped to convert (*AA* 113). Dumas may have gotten this impression from the famous poem by Thomas Moore, *Lalla Rookh*, first published in 1817. Moore writes

> A Heaven too ye must have, ye lords of dust, -
> A splendid Paradise, - pure souls, ye must:
> That Prophet ill sustains his holy call,
> Who finds not heavens to suit the tastes of all;
> Houris for boys, omniscience for sages,
> And wings and glories for all ranks and ages.
> Vain things! - as lust or vanity inspires,
> The heaven of each is but what each desires,
> And, soul or sense, whate'er the object be,
> man would be man to all eternity!
>
> (*LR* 20)

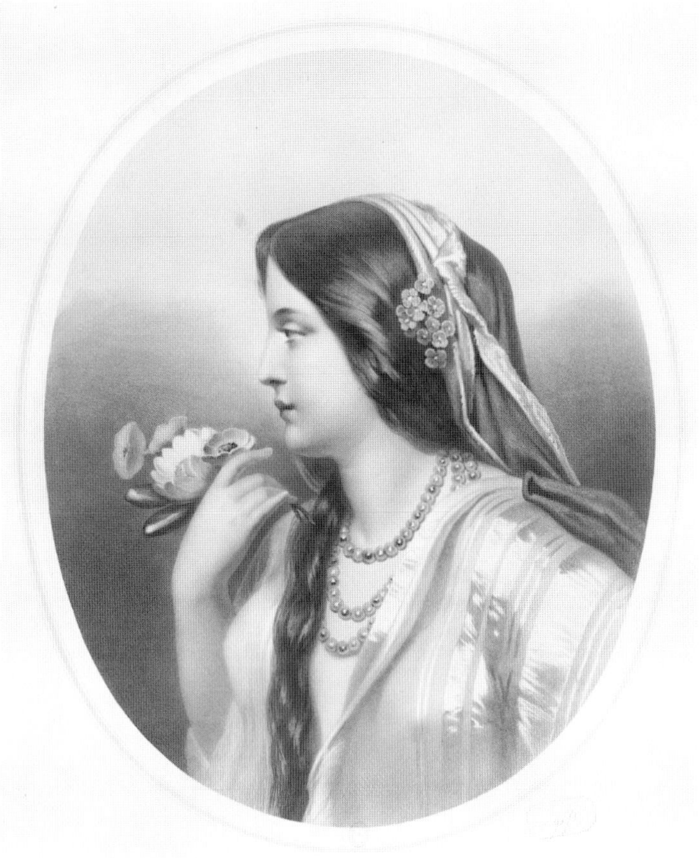

Fig. 5.13. Régnier after Constant Joseph Brochart. *Séraphita*. 1854. Lithograph. Cliché Bibliothèque nationale de France, Paris. Farwell, *FPLI*, v. 9, 5F1 B82019.

Because houris were popularly thought to be available for sex, they (like harem women) were compared to prostitutes. (The belief that the houri provided a nonsexual reward will be examined in greater detail in the next chapter.)

A second debate over the houris of Paradise concerned the nature of Paradise for women. Would deceased Muslim females be entitled to a life of companionship with male houris to answer their needs? Lady Mary Wortley Montagu has an opinion on this. She writes that good women will occupy a Paradise of a lower order than men. While men are to be "entertain'd by Celestial Beautys," women will reside in a kind of asexual "Eternal bliss," a conception that agrees with Robert Withers (1650) and Jean de Thévenot (1687) (*L* 1:363). But the nineteenth-century press entertained the opposite possibility: that good women who died would indeed be rewarded in the same lascivious way as men, an observation that was sometimes made with tongue in cheek.

A pair of pictures that suggests these popular debates about the nature of the rewards in Paradise are *Séraphita* and *Saidah* (Figs. 5.13 and 5.14) done by Régnier after Constant Joseph Brochart from 1854. In Balzac's novel of the same name, "Séraphita" is an androgynous angel who appears to both female and male lovers as a member of the opposite sex.[64] The androgynous and eastern Séraphita depicted in the print may be the virgin to whom faithful men will have access. Her alter ego Saidah does not appear in Balzac's story. In the pendant print this eastern invention is shown as an "experienced" woman: hair crimped and *décolletage* exposed, she blows apart a spent dandelion gone to seed. As the binary opposite of Séraphita, does Saidah embody the faithful Muslim *woman* thought by some to be entitled to a paradisiacal life of sexual pleasure? If so, the good and faithful Muslim woman goes on to become the "heavenly whore" embodied in Brochart's *Saidah*. By this reading, Brochart's print implies a criticism of Islam as a false religion for promising suspect

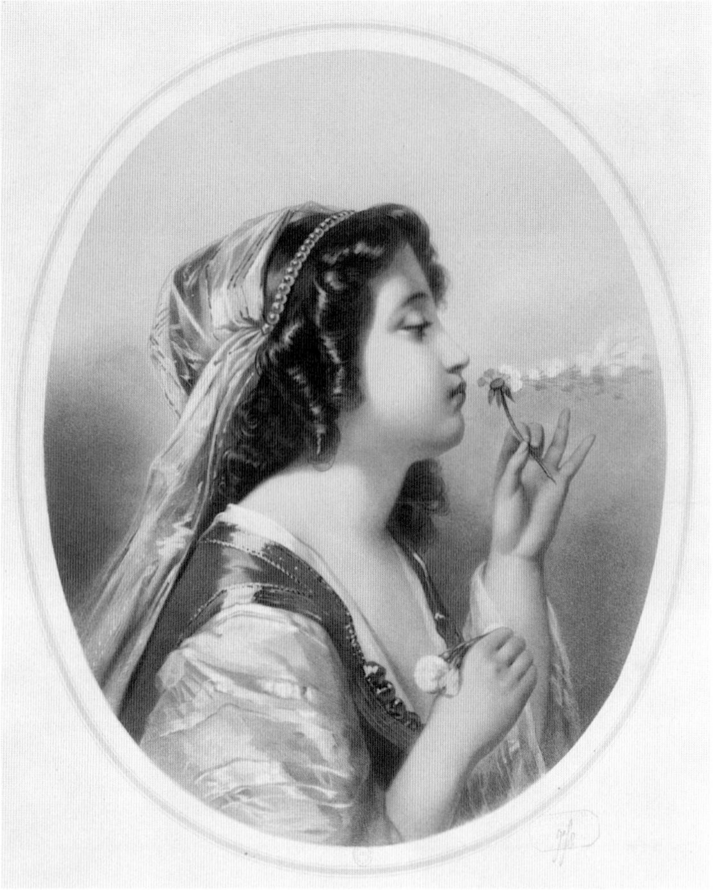

Fig. 5.14. Régnier after Constant Joseph Brochart. *Saidah.* 1854. Lithograph. Cliché Bibliothèque nationale de France, Paris. Farwell, *FPLI*, v. 9, 5F2 B82020.

pleasure in the afterlife. If such a reading would be too recondite for most French viewers, they could instead enjoy the spectacle of beautiful and youthful women shown in a familiar binary: as "good" and "bad" participants in an exotic moral system.

A picture representing the *houri* as prostitute is Lewis's 1876 *Houri, Eastern Woman with a Hookah* (see Fig. 4.13). Besides the title, other indicators that the woman represented here is a houri are the river of Paradise visible outside an open window and the houri's silken garb colored in shades of green.[65] Two years earlier the *Art Journal* made a biting comment about Lewis's pretty and "pure" harem pictures as containing the same type of "stupid houris"; this one is of a very different type of female. As an image of a prostitute, *Houri* is the most radical departure from all his earlier, aestheticized harem pictures. Instead of a good, virginal woman, Lewis paints a lascivious one. Here is the coquettish gesture of hand-to-head seen in slaves up for sale in slave market pictures; this prostitute too is for sale. Lewis has eliminated the chemise, that sheer white cover of modesty so consistent in his earlier, publicly exhibited pictures of women.[66] Her red belt is suggestively placed. The salaciousness of *Houri* is due mostly, however, to the way she challenges the gaze of the spectator. Her direct eye contact, rouged face, and shorter body type, even her bracelet, recall Manet's provocative and anti-bourgeois *Olympia,* a painting exhibited in Paris in 1865 and thereafter known in London and elsewhere through the medium of popular prints. Thus the woman's challenging gaze, her clothing and body posture, and the prominently placed hookah, symbol of sensual delight and also painted red—all point to this picture of the harem woman as a prostitute.

Another indicator that Lewis's *Houri* is a prostitute is her too-large scarlet fez tipped at an angle, a style not worn in any other known harem picture either French or British. Usually worn by men, the fez was identified with modern Egypt after Sultan Mahmud II mandated a change of the national dress to frockcoat and fez in1828. Muslim women did not wear the fez,

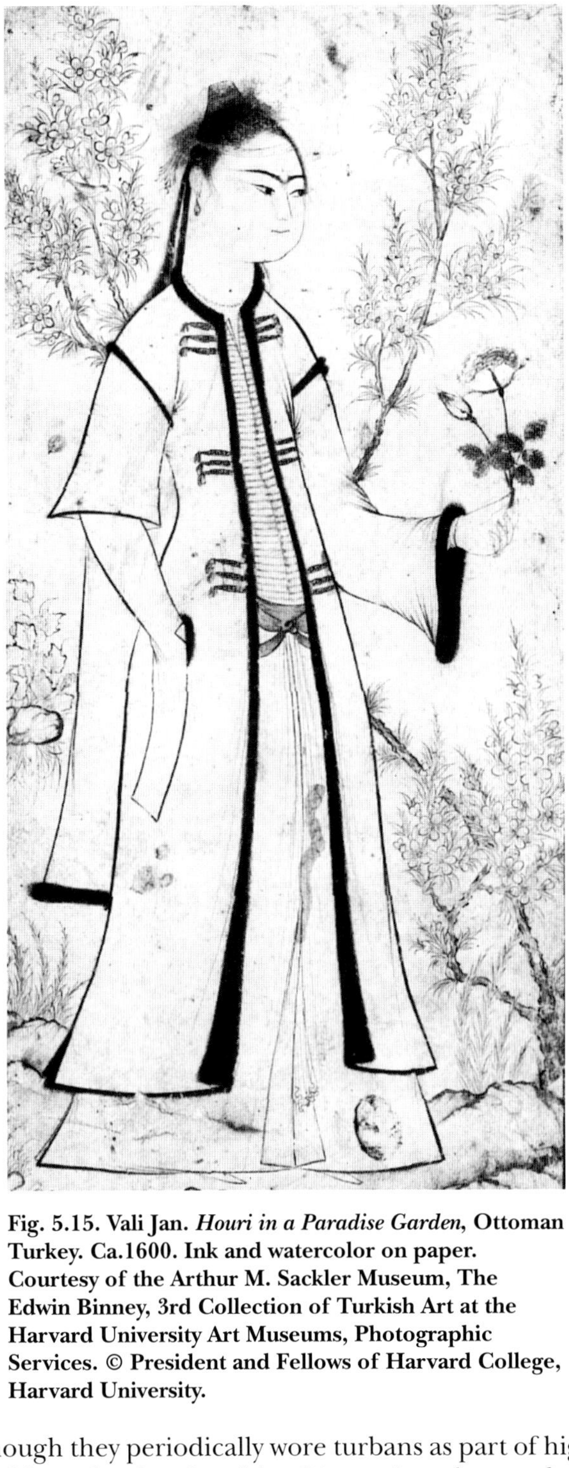

Fig. 5.15. Vali Jan. *Houri in a Paradise Garden*, Ottoman Turkey. Ca.1600. Ink and watercolor on paper. Courtesy of the Arthur M. Sackler Museum, The Edwin Binney, 3rd Collection of Turkish Art at the Harvard University Art Museums, Photographic Services. © President and Fellows of Harvard College, Harvard University.

though they periodically wore turbans as part of high fashion, despite the risk of incurring the wrath of religious leaders.[67] A much smaller hat does appear in two Ottoman Turkish depictions of houris, including the ink and watercolor by Vali Jan, *Houri in a Paradise Garden* c. 1600 (Fig. 5.15).[68] According to Islamic apocryphal tradition, the Prophet "'with his silken cap awry'" beheld Allah.[69] Islamic poets also describe a graceful youth wearing his cap this way.

Eastern women do wear other types of headgear in French and British pictures that constitute scenes of moral transgression, if not outright prostitution. With their backs towards us, a man courting the French "odalisque" wears a fez in the center of *L'Amour, le vin et le tabac* (Fig. 5.16). The woman wears an old-fashioned turban, tipped at an angle showing it is too large for her and may belong to her husband in the lithograph after A. E. Fragonard from c. 1830, *La musulmane imprudente* (Fig. 5.3).[70] In Benjamin Roubaud's[71] lithograph *Mauresque* (Fig. 5.17) of 1846 a woman with legs splayed wears an unusual hat that looks more French than eastern; perhaps it is a client's gift. The connection between a prostitute and the hat of a male client is clinched in Eugène Guérard's *Le lendemain de victoire* (Fig. 5.18), from a series of prints about French courtesans.[72] The top hat left behind by a wealthy client thus becomes a symbol of her "conquest." Like the bouquet in Manet's 1865 *Olympia*, it is a souvenir of the client who has just visited this woman.

Cigarettes are another indicator that a harem woman represented is being compared to a prostitute. As early as 1834 Devéria had painted a sultry *Odalisque* (see Fig. 3.9) blatantly smoking a cigarette. A harem woman also poses with a cigarette in Roubaud's *Mauresque* (see Fig. 5.17). These two images convey the sense—in the aloof profile view of the Devéria *Odalisque*, the challenging gaze of Roubaud's Moorish woman and in the deep *décolletage* of both—that these "harem women" are really prostitutes. Indeed, women who smoked were often identified with prostitutes in the first half of the nineteenth century. In 1858 Maxime du Camp writes that respectable French women smoked cigarettes to imitate the prostitute's luxurious life.[73] Moorish dancers who entertain Dumas and his party doubled as prostitutes. They offered the French champagne and "cigarettes that they rolled with amazing dexterity" (*AA* 170).[74]

As the century progressed, writers reported that cigarettes became more popular in the harem (*HTT* 111). In France smoking Turkish tobacco became a fad, as illustrated in a lithograph by Régnier and/or Bettannier after Eugène Guérard, *L'Amour, le vin et le tabac*, (see Fig. 5.16) dated 1848, number 24 in a suite, *Le Musée des rieurs*. The party, which has degenerated into an orgy, is probably given by a student or other bohemian-type.[75] Noteworthy are the two long-stemmed chibouks, one straight, the other arching and especially the "pasha-odalisque" configuration in the center of the composition. Though seen from behind, it is still clear the woman has both her bent knee and elbow raised in the "odalisque pose." Though the female guests are not smoking, this print

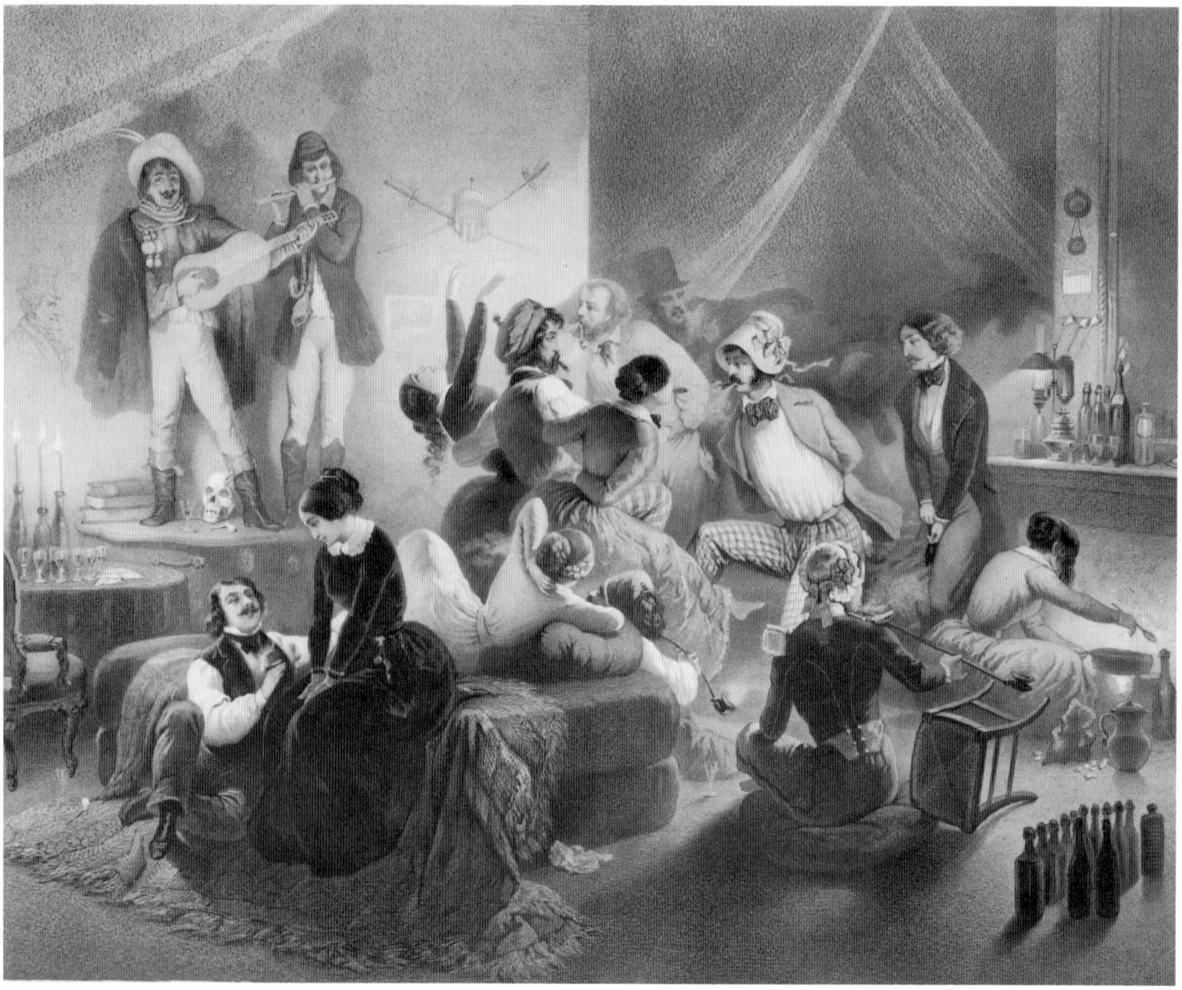

Fig. 5.16. Claude Régnier and E. Bettannier after Guérard. ***L'Amour, le vin et le tabac.*** **1848. Lithograph.** ***Le Musée des rieurs,*** **no. 24. Cliché Bibliothèque nationale de France, Paris. Farwell,** ***FPLI,*** **v. 3, 4E5 B81988.**

shows the "Turkish" style of relaxing (on the floor) and lovemaking, surrounded by willing "odalisques." In bohemian circles the Turkish style appealed to anti-bourgeois sentiments, and could have had political overtones in 1848.

Harem women are likened to prostitutes not only in their common love of sex and cigarettes but also in the accusation that they are "dirty." Despite all their primping, the inmates were unwashed under the layers of cosmetics, authors claimed. According to this point of view, preparing the toilet was futile, even a sham. Authors argue over whether and to what extent Turkish women and their homes were clean. The following is a typical description of dirty harem women, ironically entitled "An Abode of Bliss" (1866):

> Fine robes are put on over dirty, tumbled muslin dresses, which have been worn day and night [. . .] and quantities of superb jewellery are worn on unwashed necks and arms. [. . .] the tresses so adorned are unbrushed and infested with vermin.[76]

Vermin and fleas appear in the *haremlik* in Mrs. Blunt's account of a slave scalding the floor. The women were distressed at the loss of their "pets." But thirteen pages later the Turks are described as fans of the bath and regular ablutions which prevent several diseases (*PT* 1:221, 234). Paradoxically, harem women were considered both too dirty and too preoccupied with bathing, which was said to induce lethargy and indolence. Perhaps it was thought, by a twist of logic, that harem women bathed a lot because they were inherently dirty?

The concept of a "dirty woman" was highly charged. By disparaging "unclean" harem women British writers imply their own superior, civilized cultural standards. Moreover, physical and moral cleanliness are intimately linked. Yet the distinctions being drawn

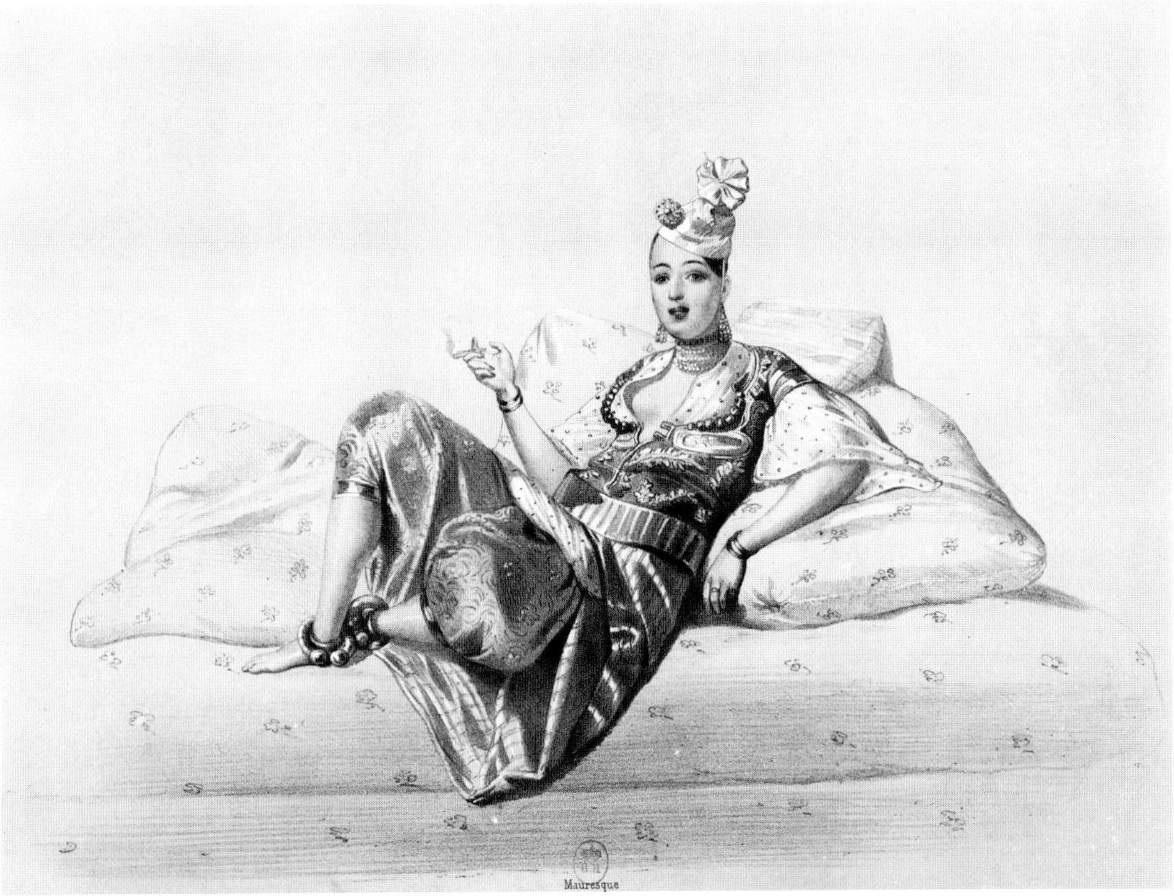

Fig. 5.17. After Benjamin Roubaud. *Mauresque.* 1846. Lithograph. Cliché Bibliothèque nationale de France, Paris. Farwell, *FPLI*, v. 9, 5G8 B85397.

are not only cultural and moral but also sociological. In nineteenth-century England "dirty" women also meant working-class women, more specifically prostitutes, from whom the respectable bourgeoise had to be distanced.

The stereotypical link between prostitutes and harem women had some basis in the changes induced by colonialist practices. Though the history of Egyptian prostitution in the first half of the nineteenth century is difficult to reconstruct, we know that some women were forced into prostitution in part due to the "reforms" in Egyptian society made under Muhammad Ali—with French assistance.[77] Wives of men conscripted into his recently upgraded army became a new group of prostitutes, some only until their men returned, some permanently. These changes affected not only the former harem woman but also the Egyptian man of status who, in the wake of the breakup of the harem, frequented the modern prostitute as a sign of his reform.

A few British writers recognized that hard times forced some former harem inhabitants to become prostitutes. In 1850 one anonymous author predicted that women who revolt against their harem confinement (with the assistance of British travelers) would "sink into vice." The harem would gradually dissolve, claimed James C. McCoan in 1877, who also believed Muslim slavery is preferable to European prostitution.[78] By the last decade of the nineteenth century, when harems in both Egypt and Turkey did break down (due to different factors in each country), prostitution became necessary for many former inmates left with few marketable skills and little access to job training.[79]

Some harem women who had been concubine-slaves or menials became prostitutes from the late 1870s because of partially successful attempts by British consuls to free slaves. The Convention between the British and Egyptian Governments for the Suppression of the Slave-Trade, held on 4 August 1877, authorized manumission for black and "brown" slaves of both genders.[80] This action ran against the grain of some pious Egyptians, who viewed it as an attempt to deprive Muslims of their religious traditions

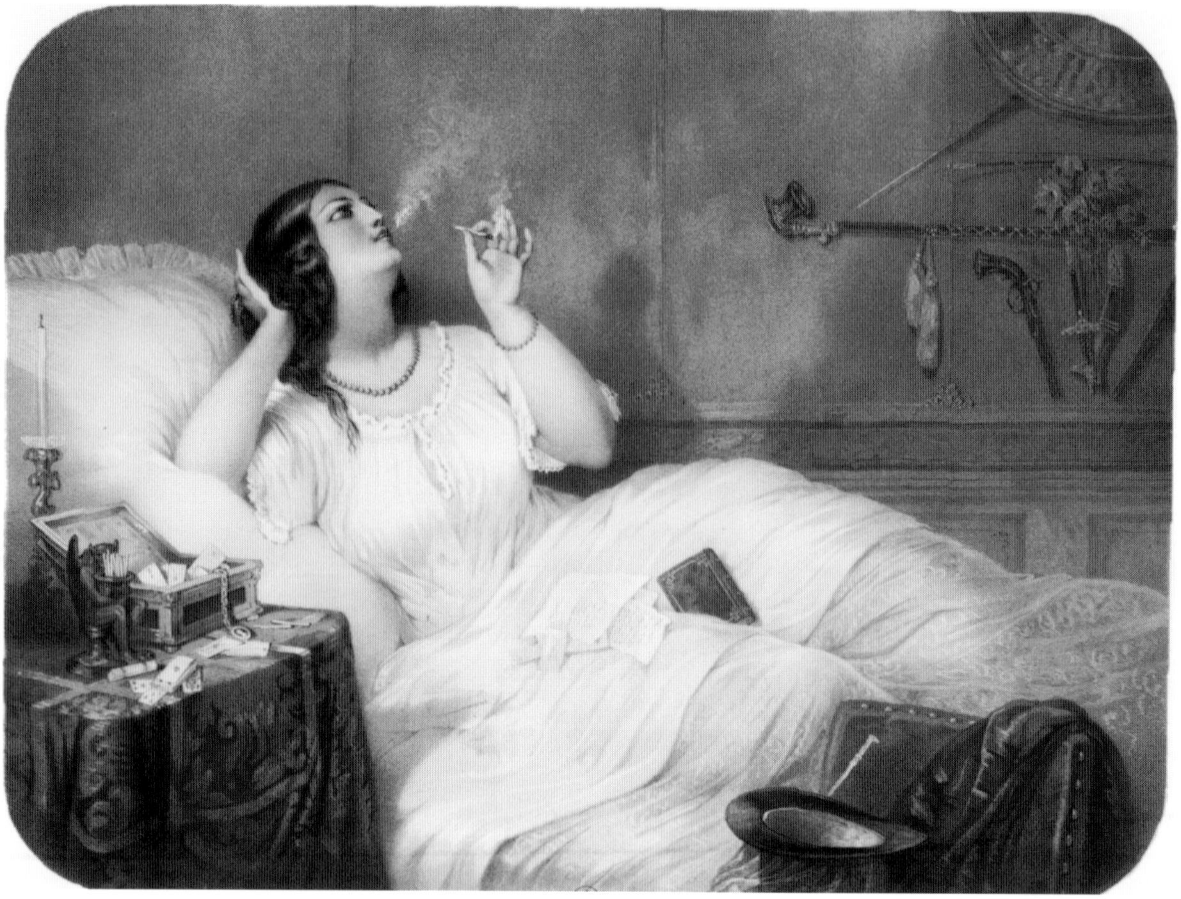

Fig. 5.18. Scultz after E. Guérard. *Le lendemain de victoire. Les Lionnes,* no. 3. 1846. Lithograph. Cliché Bibliothèque nationale de France, Paris. Farwell, *FPLI,* v. 1, 2B11 B87504.

and indeed their identity. Dislocated women, and men too, could not be absorbed into the workforce of a Cairean society which lacked a free market system at least until the 1880s. As a result, prostitution was the only option for many black and Abyssinian women and most of the Circassian women who were also freed from harems.[81] The trade in all white slaves would also be prohibited seven years later. Not until 1895 would the white slave trade be specifically mentioned and enforced in an 1895 agreement between Britain and Egypt to suppress both the slave trade and the practice of slavery.[82]

The historical development of Algerian prostitution Alexandre Dumas claims to have learned from local people. He ascribes its development to the "sheer grinding poverty" (*AA* 185) brought about by the French, whose presence disrupted the indigenous economic system, forcing "Moors" to sell their daughters. But rather than excoriate the French, Dumas sees this as the fulfillment of a sixteenth-century prophecy given to Algiers by a Muslim seer (*AA*184). And Dumas frequents those prostitutes (and Jewish ones in Tunis). By Dumas's account, poverty and prostitution are only nominally caused by the French. The more profound explanation is that the phenomena are inevitable and thus natural. He harbors no illusions about the interpersonal dynamics of the situation: Algerian prostitutes entertain the French but fundamentally hate them (*AA* 186).

That some former harem women were forced into prostitution is only a partial explanation for the recurrence of the conflation of harem women and prostitutes. By the third quarter of the nineteenth century the discourse of the eastern harem woman overlapped with that of British domestic prostitution. "White slaves," a highly charged term used to refer to the plight of harem women, becomes a rallying cry used by reformers and philanthropists like Josephine Butler to evoke sympathy for English prostitutes smuggled against their will into Paris or Geneva. The feminist publication *Englishwoman's Review* reports in 1877 on the International Congress on Public Morality held in Geneva in September that year, which attempted to end this practice of forcing women into foreign prostitution. The journal's rhetoric resembles that used to describe imprisoned harem inmates. The women are said to live in homes which are

> veritable prisons from which escape is impossible: that when a girl is once entrapped there [. . .] she never stirs from its walls, except when once a month the inmates are taken out for a day in the country in closed carriages.[83]

"White slavery" would also become the rallying cry for the repeal of the Contagious Diseases (C.D.) Acts, sounded particularly vociferously in the 1860s.[84]

A curious, circular process takes place here. The rhetoric of white female enslavement, advanced in the early nineteenth century by abolitionist groups and already rich in associations, is appropriated by a domestic reformist group to oppose government regulation of prostitution. It then gets reabsorbed in its mutated and even more highly charged form to refer to harem women, who are likened to prostitutes. The discourse on harem women is intertwined with moral crusades to rescue female victims of other sorts.

Jealous Rivals

From the seventeenth century jealousy among wives and concubines had been one of the most persistent notions about the harem.[85] Both Edward Lane and even David Urquhart, otherwise "pro-harem," agree that polygyny is a difficult emotional experience for the wives. For most observers harem polygyny is understood not as a viable alternative to monogamy in which women might live cooperatively and happily but rather as a kind of monogamy gone askew, a form of institutionalized adultery, which can evoke the worst in human emotions, scarring children along the way.

In the eighteenth century Alexander Pope calls Turkey "the land of Jealousy" in a letter to Lady Mary Wortley Montagu.[86] By the nineteenth century the entire race of "Orientals" was considered rivalrous in temperament, even though the harem was an institution of the elite in Egyptian society.[87] "Jealousy," claims Nerval, "is only too well appreciated in the Orient, and when it comes to women reserve, even caution, is [. . .] natural and habitual" (*VO* 49). It is true that a wife's future share in her husband's estate was halved when a second wife appeared on the scene,[88] but whether that caused female rivalry is no more certain than shared family resources causing sibling rivalry in western families.

How rivalry in the harem supposedly leads to inappropriate, sometimes outrageous or even deadly behavior is illustrated by anecdotes told by one Melek-Hanum. The author begins to feel jealous of a young fourteen-year-old Circassian whom she had educated and who served as governess to her own five-year-old daughter. Seeing the girl's beauty deepen, she marries her off without her husband's knowledge to obviate a potential rival. Or again, when another master thanked a servant girl for pouring his water, calling her "my lamb" his wife had the servant decapitated, her head stuffed and served to him like lamb.[89] Similarly in Victor Hugo's "The Favourite Sultana" (1828) the sultan thins out his harem in order "to please you, Jewess, jewel!" Even though "in jealousy so zealous, / Never was there woman worse," he is in effect her slave, who is compelled to submit to her deadly requests, as he himself recognizes: "beauties sultans must adorn / As dagger-hilts the pearls" (*SCL* 51–52). In the cases illustrated here the rivalry takes place between a rightful or favorite wife and her perceived threat across class lines. As such, each can serve as a projection of anxiety at home about working-class servants' potential to disrupt social order and break through their station.

Competition among the women is read by the critics when Lewis's *Hhareem* (see Plate 1) was shown at the 1850 OWCS and the 1855 Paris Exposition Universelle. The master is interested in the new slave because of her "newer charms" (*S* 4 May 1850:427). One of the slaves seated on the ground is abandoned, according to French critic Delécluze viewing this at that Parisian exhibition.[90] This wife, seen in fullface view, sits with her head still leaning slightly on one of the huge pillows around her. The fact that she is reclining so fully also demonstrates her disrespect for the new slave, whom she eyes suspiciously. Critics read her as the "favorite"[91] until this moment, when the potential usurper arrives on the scene. As for the other female figures in the picture, they are called the bey's wives. The British press does not use the word concubine or odalisque, as French critic Théophile Gautier would do at its 1855 showing in Paris.[92] Counting from the left, the second wife is called "a younger beauty—exceedingly graceful and seemingly more tender" (*A* 4 May 1850:480). She sits in a more relaxed and composed posture and watches the new arrival with more equanimity and directness than the so-called favorite, presumably because she is less threatened by the introduction of the new slave. The *Critic*, however, has a slightly different interpretation: as "the one most likely to be supplanted" she "looks wistfully but with a touch of scorn, at the newcomer" (*C* 1850, 253).

The third wife is the most intriguing. She is also

the least interested in the unveiling. The *Athenaeum* sees in her "features of a European cast, intelligent, curious, and *espiègle,* the Roxana of the group."[93] Roxana (d. 1558) was the favorite wife of Sultan Sulieman I, who reigned when the Ottoman Empire reached its apogee. A Circassian, she was known to Renaissance scholars as the Russian[94] or sometimes the French harem inmate.[95] Roxana is also the name of Usbek's favorite wife in Montesquieu's 1721 *Persian Letters,* where she proves to be unfaithful despite Usbek's trust in her. The mischievous quality noted by both the *Athenaeum* and the *Critic* characterized the historical Roxana, who instigated the murder of Sulieman's son Mustafa in hopes of instating her own son, Selim II. Indeed, this woman's hunched pose and her hands held close to her breast suggest she is secreting something.

What she is hiding is revealed in this painting's thematic sequel, *An Intercepted Correspondence* (see Fig. 5.5) exhibited at the Royal Academy in 1869. Lewis may have felt the detail of a "mischievous" wife was significant enough to bear developing, as the critics did not make much of it the first time around. Also Lewis repeats earlier harem motifs in part because their reworkings continued to sell. *Intercepted Correspondence,* like his 1850 *Hhareem,* fetched a good price.[96] In painting a melodramatic scene focused on harem rivalry, Lewis might also have been responding to the criticism of John Ruskin, who in 1858 claimed that his two harem pictures that year were "not dramatic enough" (*W* 14:159):

> I hardly know what is the matter with me this year, for I find Mr. [J.N.] Paton's pictures too dramatic, and Mr. Lewis's not dramatic enough. He has 31 figures in all upon the walls, and all the drama to be got out of the whole number is the arrangement of a nosegay [a reference to *The Bouquet* discussed in the next chapter] and the presentation of a cup of coffee. Perhaps those who delight in the gloomier pictures of the present exhibition may be able to excite themselves into some interest in the last event, by supposing the coffee to be poisoned. (*W* 14:159)[97]

Ruskin's sardonic comment also demonstrates his familiarity with the conception of the harem as a place of scheming and intrigue. "Poisoned coffee" was another old line about how "jealous" harem women might deal with their rivals. It is an effective metaphor, as it inverts the usual association of serving coffee with hospitality. "Poisoned coffee" is a trope that corrupts feminine decorum and service, making it deadly. In 1837 Pardoe blames an unnamed modern French traveler for having invented this method of disposal and adds "this assertion . . . would be comic were it not wicked" (*CS* 1:120). The cliché surfaces as late as 1880.[98]

The major theme of Lewis's *Hhareem,* the wives' various reactions to the unveiling of a new slave by a eunuch, may be drawn from Montesquieu's *Persian Letters* (1721). The First Eunuch writes to Usbek that he takes great pleasure in anticipating the range of women's feelings when a beautiful "yellow-skinned" woman, his latest find, is unveiled in the harem of Usbek's brother:

> it gives me pleasure to foresee how taken aback his wives will be, some of them majestic in their affliction, and others mute but more distressed; the malicious satisfaction of those who have nothing left to hope for, and the stimulus given to the ambition of those whose hopes still remain. (*PL* 179)

"Taken aback," "majestic in their affliction," "mute but more distressed," "malicious satisfaction"—such an emotional collage has a parallel in the range of reactions of figures whom Lewis paints and in the tessellated colors and fabrics of his composition. In both Lewis's work and Montesquieu's, serious rivalry among the harem inmates is presumed in the complex narrative each text offers.

Extravagant Consumers

An obvious facet of the harem was that it was expensive to maintain more than one wife. Nearly any French or British representation of harem objects—jewels, large floral bouquets, tobacco or pipes, coffee, exotic animals, rarefied musical instruments, luxurious fabrics, and silverware (not to mention slaves themselves)—presumes an economy of material extravagance. And material lavishness could serve as indicator of the moral extravagance of polygyny itself, which many writers felt compelled to attack. The keeping of multiple wives was cited as proof of the harem's extravagance.

A curious tactic is used by some writers to critique the monetary extravagance of the harem. They make virtuous either a modest harem or the eastern peasant who cannot afford to maintain a harem. Harem women are thus "like us" when their husbands are frugal. Sometimes the poor Muslim is compared to the British proletarian, who shares his meager but honest means with one wife, his lifelong friend. The implications of this kind of comment are that monetary extravagance is immoral and that harem women cannot be longtime companions to their husbands. Monogamy and thrift are intertwined ideals in such moral pronouncements.

Florence Nightingale writes that she has no interest in seeing a wealthy harem for its superficiality. "But," she enthuses, "I do want to see the common hareems" (*LE* 165). She is thrilled to note the picturesque quality of the poor harem's mud floor and lack of furniture. The wife makes do with a single good dress. For Nightingale authentic cultural life is that of the poor.

Harems showing different degrees of wealth are evaluated in 1858; while the middle- and upper-class harems are dirty and disgusting, the female author concludes that the peasant marriage in the East is "the least strange of all, and bear[s] the nearest affinity to the Christian menage." And because the kind peasant husband does not imprison his wife, who works hard, in contradistinction to harem women, his life not only "resembles that of a Christian peasant, [but also serves as] a model to the latter."[99] Another author laments the sale of a female slave to "some khan, rich enough to afford himself such a luxury, and to give the broker a handsome profit on the transaction," while at the other end of the social spectrum there are poor easterners, and "poverty, far from bringing contempt on a man in the East, seems even to be invested with a kind of majesty."[100] Similarly, Mrs. Blunt claims that Turkish peasants rarely practice polygyny, and "they do not often indulge in the luxury of divorce" (*PT* 1:91). For her wealth necessarily leads to an immoral life.

For these authors, eastern society provides a point of contrast to western society in two ways. The Muslim upper-class harem provides a model for how British society should not conduct itself, a concept that recalls Wollstonecraft's analysis. And, conversely, the poor monogamous Muslim who humbly accepts his lot in life illustrates the ideal attitude to be adopted by those in the lower rungs of English society. Though commenting ostensibly on eastern mores, each writer provides a rationale about the inevitability and permanence of the British class structure. Sympathy for the poor may seem a progressive attitude, but in these contexts it is a position that serves the status quo.

Sexually Precocious Children

The comparison of harem women to children reflects preexisting thought about women in general. Nineteenth-century British and French observers compared "their own" women to children. Generally smaller in physique and thought to be more governed by emotion, women were considered more fundamentally like children than men. Both women and children were thought primitives, who could be either revered or dismissed. Harem women formed yet another category of primitive, a conception that was reinforced by reports that harem women were sometimes betrothed as children and married in their early to mid-teens. This describes first wives from reputable families, who arranged their children's marriages. In nineteenth-century "anthropological" studies, early marriage itself was considered a characteristic of uncivilized societies. Observers could have known that the Prophet Muhammad reputedly married his favorite wife Aisha when she was six and still played with dolls; he was nine.[101]

Harem women are girls in several accounts from the British periodical press at midcentury.[102] As late as 1878 harem women on an outing are noisy and disorderly as they roam at will "like a troop of schoolgirls during recreation hours"; their "screams of laughter and wild frolic" would shock "any European garden party," claims Mrs. Blunt (*PT* 1:246). For her, harem women's inherent lack of self-control, a microcosm of the polygynous system's disorderliness, manifests itself in rude, uncivilized behaviors. That such women act as schoolgirls further blurs the line between the two groups.

The notion that harem women were children (or childlike) of course discredits the institution for exploiting "girls." It can also reflect poorly on the master, who is considered inappropriately forceful or immoral in robbing the cradle. A young harem woman can be shown pictorially if she appears much smaller than the master as in A. G. Decamps's c. 1830 watercolor, *Seated Sultan with Harem Girl Reposing at His Feet* (see Fig. 4.3); or A. Devéria's 1837 lithograph, *Arabes du désert* (Fig. 5.19). The woman is significantly younger than the master as indicated by his grey beard in both the undated lithograph after Eugène Guérard entitled *Le pacha ou la vie dans le sérail* (see Fig. 4.6) and J. B. LePrince's[103] much earlier rococo *Harem Scene* (see Fig. 4.52).

A dramatic differential in scale or age can imply that the harem women are childlike. In a parallel vein, Wollstonecraft compares French and British aristocratic women to children on the basis that society discourages their learning of real values and instead encourages "their childish attachment to toys" (*VRW* 285). She writes that women are educated to behave as children. These women-children are thus incapable of being good mothers themselves.

Some readings of young Greek girls as harem inmates can now be deepened. John Lewis's *Greek Girl* (see Fig. 3.24) is an image of an unhappily confined girl wearing her hair long and unpinned. Her imminent fate is that of violation by a much older and powerful man, a realization that makes the scene poignant to a viewing public which valued

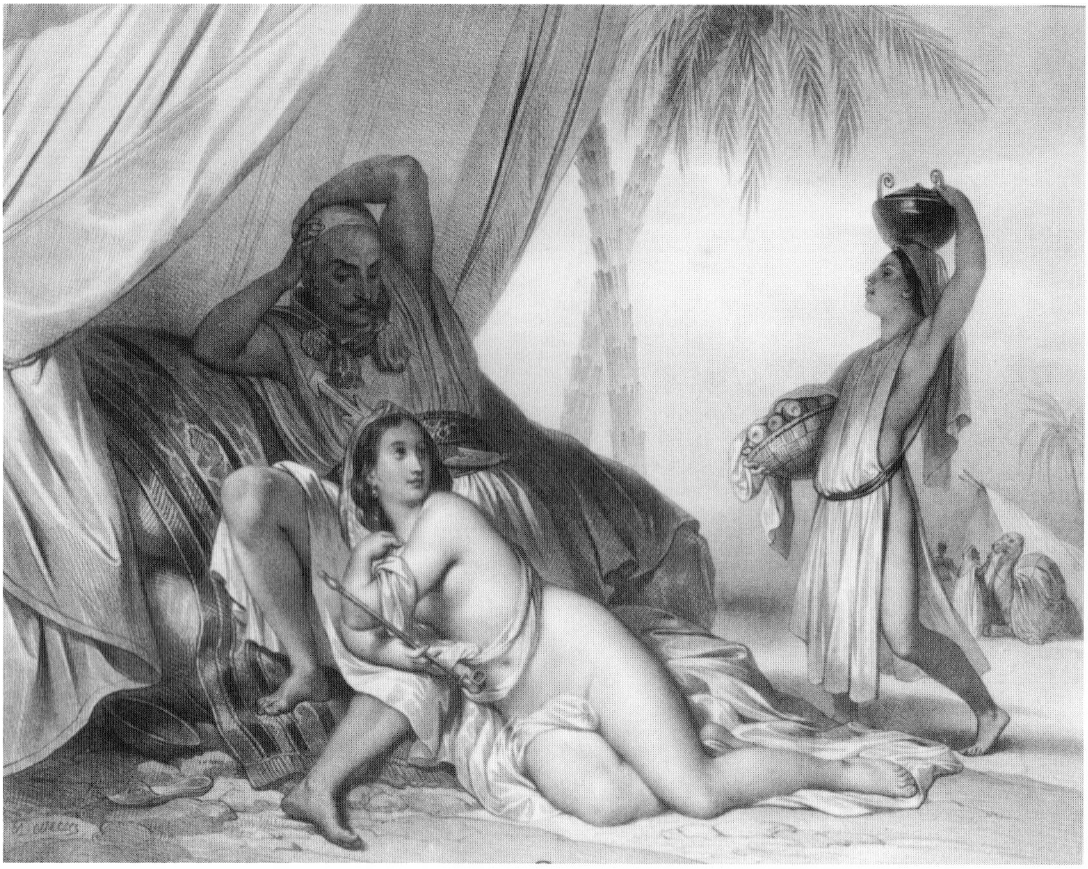

Fig. 5.19. A. Devéria. *Arabes du désert.* 1837. Lithograph. Cliché Bibliothèque nationale de France, Paris. Farwell, *FPLI*, v. 7, 5C10 B83009.

protracted childhood innocence. *La jeune grecque,* a print after Leloir (see Fig. 3.29) could evoke a similar knowledge for the viewer especially given her bared shoulder, though this child seems innocent of her fate. Similarly, the servile child depicted in the undated lithograph after Charles de Chassiron, *Jeune Fille Moresque (Tunis)* (Fig. 5.20) may have been read as either a servant (given her skin tone) or a very young sex partner to the absent master. Large hoop earrings and remarkable facial beauty suggest an unchildlike role for her within the harem.[104]

In the illustration to Byron's *Childe Harold,* a print after Pickersgill, the mother is seated with her two children (Fig. 5.21). Her position on the floor suggests both her affinity for her children, which Byron describes, and her affinity to them. The writing of Byron is ambivalent as to whether the childishness of harem women is desirable or even accurate. In his play *Sardanapalus* the Assyrian king says to Myrrha, his favorite concubine: "I thought you were exempt from this [fear] as from the childish helplessness of Asian women" (*WB* 207). Though the king claims this as a truth, Myrrha's personality defies it (perhaps because she is Greek and not Asian at all). Similarly, Byron dedicates his 1812 *Childe Harold's Pilgrimage* to "Ianthe," a Hellenic pseudonym for the eleven-year-old Lady Charlotte Harley (later Bacon), to whom he refers as a "Young Peri of the West!" (*WB* 2).

Very young eastern women are described by the Catholic Alphonse de Lamartine in a 1832–33 travelog account characterized by restrained desire. He claims that his hostesses' two daughters, who offer him sweetmeats and orange flower water, are personifications of the East itself in their innocence and primitivism. Born of a Greek mother and a father (then deceased) who had been a rich Frank merchant, the daughters' physical beauty as vehicle for their spirituality is described at great length in prose redolent with longing. One of the two daughters is on the cusp of adolescence,

> when delicacy of contour, virginal purity of outline, suppleness and elegance of form reveal to the eye the voluptuous characteristic of a being who is born for pure and virtuous love. (*PHL* 173)

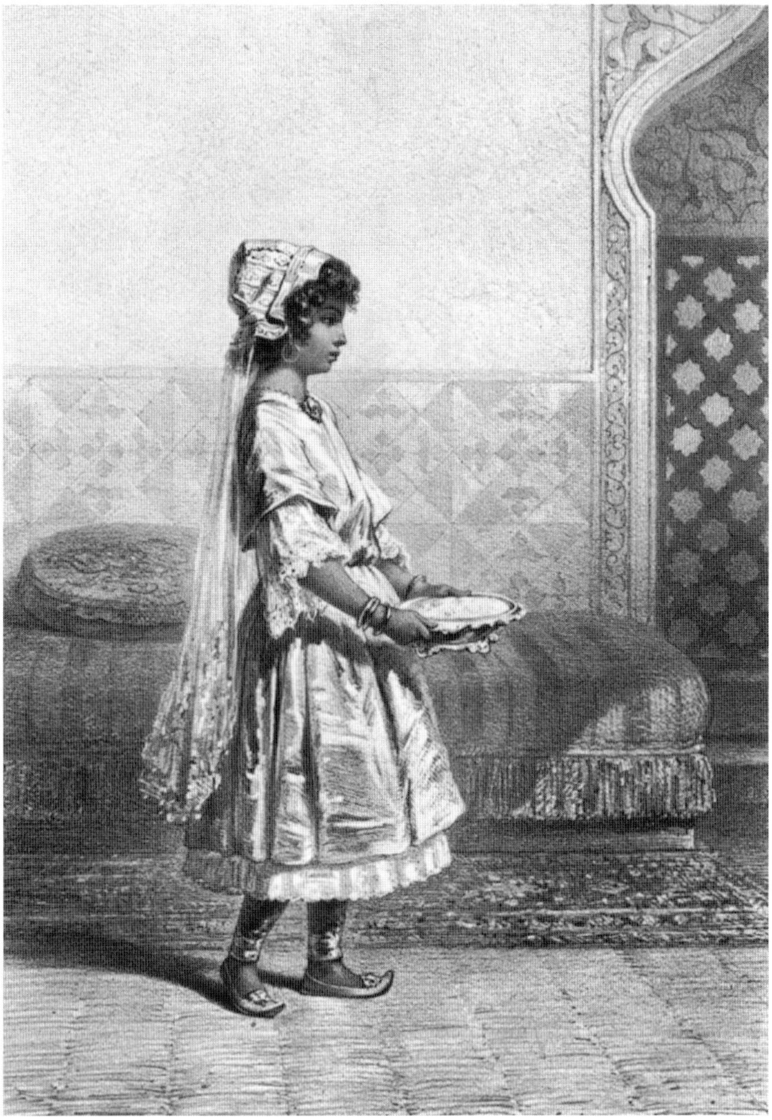

Fig. 5.20. Mouilleron after Charles de Chassiron. ***Jeune Fille Moresque [sic] (Tunis).*** **Lithograph.** ***Régence de Tunis,*** **no. 8. Cliché Bibliothèque nationale de France, Paris. Farwell,** ***FPLI,*** **v. 9, 5G5 B81191.**

Lamartine's desire is framed in a context of speechlessness. The girls don't speak, forming a crucial component of their primitive nature, and he is unable to express verbally their extraordinary and youthful beauty. Here he appeals to the "genius" of the wordless painter, whom he believes can more accurately capture beauty by reproducing it visually. The writer's admiration is all the more ardent for his inability to have the desired object, in reality due to her age and even in representation due to his meager art form.

Alexandre Dumas is less respectful of the eleven-year-old eastern girl he encounters (poor but "tidy and clean") whom he tests by asking whether she would be willing to return to France with him. She readily agrees in a decision that illustrates to Dumas her immature judgment and the dangerousness of her position. Dumas gives her some coins and leaves her behind. He remains affected by the memory of her and asks Giraud, one of the two artists who accompanied him on the trip, to produce a sketch of her. Like Lamartine, Dumas invokes visual art as a substitute, however weak, for the fulfillment of impossible sexual desire (*AA*122–23) provoked by an eastern woman-child. In Dumas's travelog the frozen desire of painting needs only real life to revitalize it: he hopes to find the actual oriental woman painted by his friend Delacroix (*AA* 29). The

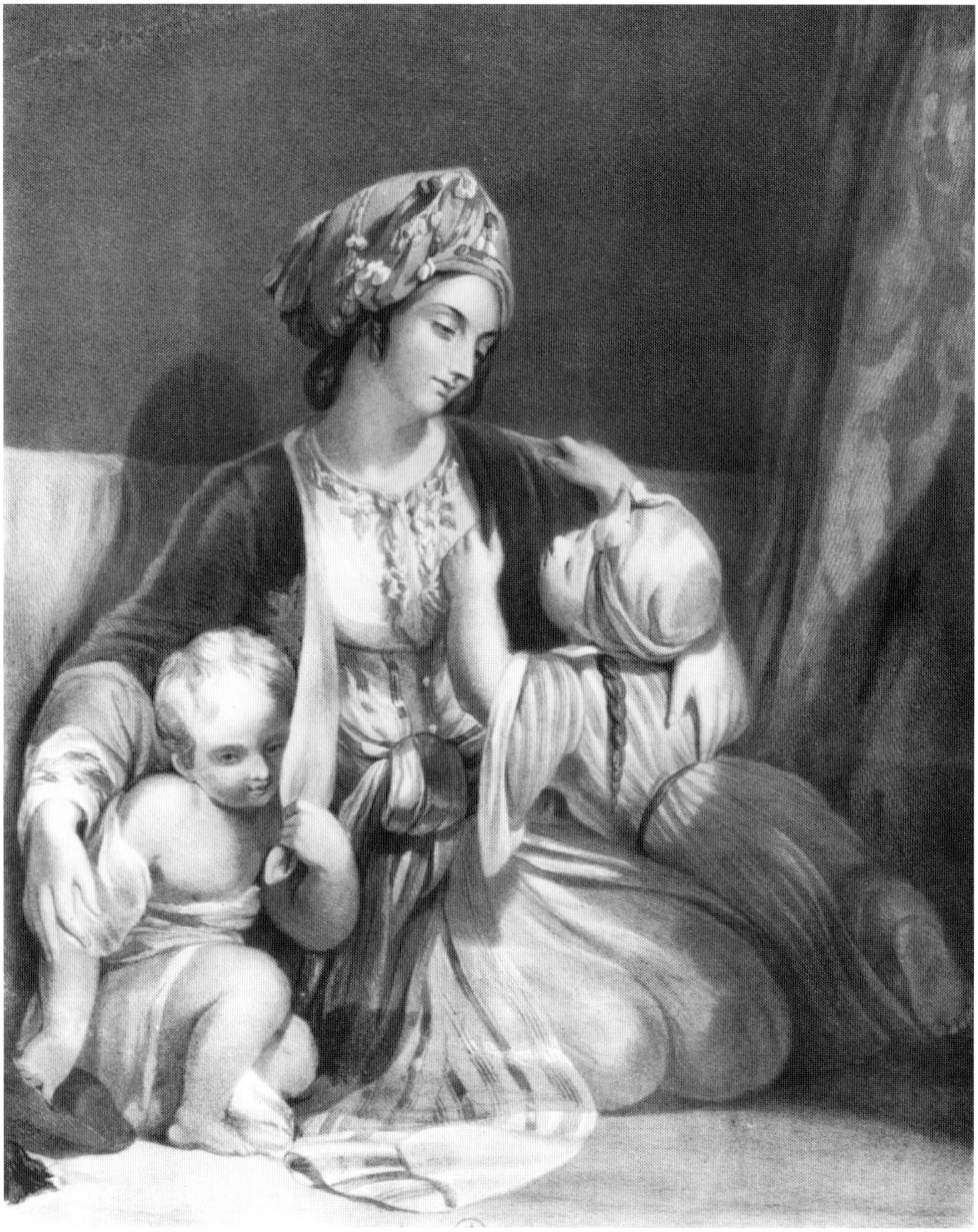

Fig. 5.21. After Pickersgill. *Femme d'Orient: Childe Harold (Lord Byron)*. 1839. Lithograph. Witt Library, Courtauld Institute, London.

girl Dumas seeks is not a woman in the harem, but his description of her draws from stereotypes found in other accounts of the harem inhabitant forced to grow up too soon, one of the travesties of the harem system which held great interest for French and British observers. Such cultural ambivalence toward sexualized children, whether in the harem or at home, contributed to the milieu in which John Ruskin's "deviant" pedophilia developed by age forty.

Rococo-Revival Harem Imagery and the Critique of Tyranny as an Enlightenment Inheritance

On 10 October 1843, the leftist sculptor David d'Angers wrote to his former pupil, A. A. Ernest Hébert, responding to the success received by Hébert's harem picture *Deux odalisques couchées sur la terrasse* (see Fig. 4.15) at the Salon that year. In that letter he contrasts "serious art" with art whose subject is the seraglio urging Hébert to end the continuation of the "licentious productions" of Boucher, whom he refers to as one of the painters of "the most shameful era" in French history.[105] For nineteenth-century critics and artists like d'Angers, the harem maintained its pre-Revolutionary rococo associations—frivolity, slavery, and domination, and luxury in both senses of the word: material wealth and sexual debauchery. For d'Angers writing in the July Monarchy, the critique of the harem was a rejection of aristocratic politics and an assertion of Republicanism. In addition to evoking colonial politics, the harem, as understood by French and British observers, could function as a vehicle for expressing anti-aristocratic class antagonism[106] at the same time that it could provoke the question of the desirability of male domination over women.

Pictorially, two groups of rococo-revival harem pictures elicit these issues. They are images in which the female harem inmate and her master are physically present. Because the master is not usually represented in the harem, his inclusion in these pictures is significant. In plotting out their spatial relationships, artists respond in part to preexisting discourses over whether the man or the woman is to be dominant. In formal terms, artists react to received notions about the power dynamic between men and women in the harem. A basic question is whether the man's comportment is "gallant" or "despotic" toward the woman. The (binary) terms are actually Mary Wollstonecraft's, written not about art at all but which are quite relevant here. I want to explore how her 1792 manifesto, *Vindication of the Rights of Women*, along with Montesquieu's 1721 *Persian Letters* and the libretto to Mozart's 1782 *Abduction from the Seraglio* help elucidate the two groups of harem pictures made as late as the middle of the nineteenth century. All three written texts consider the harem as an extreme expression of tyranny, both sexual and political, thus constructing the domestic as contiguous with the political. In all three texts the harem's tyranny is denigrated if not destroyed. These Enlightenment ideas have a continuing impact on the meaning of harem representation in the nineteenth century.

I have no evidence to be able to claim that any of these three texts directly influenced nineteenth-century harem artists working in a rococo-revivalist manner. Rather these written texts are part of a dense web of referents suggested by the harem pictures I present. And they can be correlated to later pictures, because they are interdependent for their meanings. Examining other writings helps establish conventions for picturing the harem and articulates new interpretations for them.

Political and Sexual Tyranny in the East and at Home: The Eighteenth-Century Critique of the Excesses of the Harem and the *Ancien régime*

> [. . .] the unlimited authority which the Turks usurp, as a right of nature, over their submissive wives, extends its force to the remotest borders of the unmeasur'd empire.[107]

The eighteenth-century discourse on the harem gives a new twist to the "battle of the sexes" by raising the ante. Conflict between the genders (man versus woman) is conflated with the clash between types of government (monarchy versus the people). To complicate things even further, both debates overlap with discussion about East versus West.

In her introduction to the *Vindication* Mary Wollstonecraft addresses women of the middle class "because they appear to be in the most natural state" (*VRW* 81) in contrast to the aristocracy which is "immoral," "vain," "weak," "artificial," and "unnatural," who live only in order to while away time with "barren amusement" (*VRW* 81). Her analysis of middle-class and aristocratic women is one of several binary oppositions she uses to establish the polemical nature of her tract, written in the thick of the French Revolution. From early on in the *Vindication* it is clear that she uses nonwestern cultures in order to critique the West. The work is an excellent example of how the harem Other is constructed for its relevance to the western European Self. In the first chapter she problematizes the idea that Europeans are civilized. She questions whether Europeans have become more virtuous as they have given up their innocence, and she draws a parallel to other cultures' "freedom which has been bartered for splendid slavery" (*VRW* 92). She continues, alluding to both the wealthy aristocrat and, I believe, the eastern pasha both of whom own luxury objects and can command "flattering sycophants," examples of "doting self-love." With Republican fervor, she critiques absolutist notions of patriotism, implying that the true patriot is the Enlightened revolutionary. Importantly, she likens women in general to "the rich of both sexes" when she claims that they have taken on "all the follies and vices" that culture has to offer, while ignoring its real value (*VRW* 151).

Revealing an organicist conception of the development of society and government, she describes the "infancy of society" that came out of "barbarism." Civilization dawns with an aristocratically based monarchy and despotism, characteristics of both French history until the time she writes and presumably eastern society (*VRW* 98). Her conception of society posits that improved social development requires a new form of enlightened government.

At certain points in *Vindication* Wollstonecraft rails specifically against Turkey and the harem. Turkey is an extreme example in having produced unnatural despotism, which obliterates nascent "virtue and genius" and "desolates" the country, making the men and the country's output "unfruitful." Her discussion of Turkey is a rhetorical device used to return to her point about women's inadequate education in Europe. The hold societies have over their women is likened to Turkish tyranny, because they are not trusted to be educated with the truth. And women everywhere are condemned to "this deplorable state." Women are allowed only the power of their beauty, and their minds suffer from lack of use (*VRW* 131).

Women of the European aristocracy are likened to Muslim women in that they seem to be without souls, that is, they are not fully human, yet they are not quite animals. As Wollstonecraft puts it, "according to the vulgar tale of Mahomet's coffin [. . .] they have neither the unerring instinct of brutes, nor are allowed to fix the eye of reason on a perfect model" (*VRW* 118). In Turkey women are thought to have no souls, she claims, but in France and England aristocratic women are treated as such in that their "captivity" produces a weak soul (*VRW* 311). Wollstonecraft may be recalling her personal pain as a feminist derided as unwomanly when she writes that women are viewed as beings thought to contribute nothing but love to society. They "must not aim at respect, lest they should be hunted out of society as masculine" (*VRW* 119). Part of the effectiveness of her argument is her appeal to seriously consider the distinction between what truly benefits society in contrast to what is merely socially sanctioned. She asks rhetorically, "Do passive indolent women make the best wives?" (*VRW* 119).

As for polygyny, Wollstonecraft sees it as a "natural" phenomenon—but an unfair and degraded one. It is natural in that it springs from a culture in which there are more women than men. In those societies, however, women are considered "inferior to man, and made for him" (*VRW* 164). It also has injurious effects on men, who become "enervated by the use of so many women," while women on the other hand are "of a hotter constitution" because "they are deprived in their matrimony of that share of physical love which, in a monogamous condition, would be all theirs." Her construction of enervated men and unsatisfied females also helps explain why there are more females born (*VRW* 164). The harem is made into a metaphor for a restricted tyrannical government and a patriarchal home, dominated by a suspicious husband. She claims that women can never be made "virtuous by authority," an oxymoron embodied in the seraglio, where they are "watched with a jealous eye."

Like Wollstonecraft, Montesquieu uses the harem to investigate "the natural state" of the sexes and of political life. Like her, he works within binary concepts, as in Letter 38 when he comments on whether men should give women personal freedom (as in monogamy) or take it away (as in polygyny). Curiously, a clash between men and women mutates into a disagreement between European men and Asian men and how each weighs the marriage customs of their own culture. At that point "men" become a unified group who consider how to handle "women." In a series of letters describing the impressions of two Persian tourists' gradual understanding of French culture, *Persian Letters* is an investigation into the inner workings of political tyranny characterizing eastern rule and its relationship to the monarchical principles of the *ancien régime* in the chaos of French society during the rule of the regent following the death of Louis XIV (*PL* 114 n. 12). But it is also an investigation into the fluctuating power relationships between men and women.[108] The eastern view is ostensibly that men and women respect each other, but men—without apology—maintain a natural superiority over women. This is called into question in that Usbek's wives become powerful in his absence and revolt against his confinement of them. The western view of male-female power relations is also questioned in the course of the book, as the two cultures continue to compare their customs. Male superiority is most explicitly criticized by an unnamed French philosopher who argues that women only allow men to dominate them because they are naturally more gentle and agreeable. Women are superior in their rational nonviolence, he continues, while men use physical coercion against women and each other. Anticipating Wollstonecraft's comments written at the end of the century, this philosopher claims that men's rule over women using their physical strength is "absolutely tyrannical [and] completely unjust" (*VRW* 93).

The libretto Mozart draws upon in his three-act opera has none of the depth or complexity of argument that Montesquieu and Wollstonecraft marshal in their protracted analyses. It is a comic opera, and it has been called "one of the weakest Mozart ever set."[109] All the more reason why similar underlying patterns between it and "serious" writing are significant. In the opera these binary opposites can be readily detected: male versus female, political tyranny versus freedom, monogamy versus polygyny. As in Montesquieu, the harem is dissolved and political tyranny broken. The feminine principle proves victorious here as well—twice, in that Constanza's fight to protect her virtue has won out over Pasha Selim, and that she and her servant Blonde are vindicated in the eyes of their suspicious male rescuers. Selim is dissuaded from his male tyranny and praised as "noble" for his decision to free the westerners based on an ethical principle. He lets them go: "It is a far greater pleasure for me to right a suffered injustice through a good deed, than to repay wickedness in kind" (*AS* 162). By his own admission, keeping Constanza and disposing of Belmonte would not be a right sanctioned by his culture but an act of "wickedness," from which he recoils.

Eighteenth-century English and French cultural texts share an ambivalence toward the harem's "tyranny," perceived to be one of its organizing principles. Critique accompanies fascination for the antidemocratic nature of the institution. While European viewers might have struggled with their own impulses to dominate within monogamous marriage, the idea that those impulses were allowed to reign produces disgust and intrigue. Likewise, given the increasingly unpopular nature of a philosophy of political domination, a culture which was thought to unabashedly maintain it was met with skepticism and delight.

Cluster 1: "Despotism": The Man "On Top"

In some eighteenth-century rococo harem pictures the presentation of a dominant harem master serves to embody the concept of tyrannical power over women and "the people." These pictures would come to serve as the prototype for nineteenth-century rococo-revival harem pictures of this same type. When d'Angers criticizes Hébert's choice of harem subject with a reference to François Boucher, he may have had in mind a work like Boucher's 1747 *Marchand d'esclaves* (see Fig. 3.8), a fantasy of unjust male ownership. The center of a pyramidal shape, the sultan is surrounded by three women whom he owns and who adore him, as indicated by their physical contact with him. The woman on our right reveals her bodice to him and looks at him with eyes of longing. His bejeweled turban, ermine-lined robe, and aloof gaze are ciphers for his political authority.

One cluster of rococo-revival nineteenth-century pictures shows the harem master reigning over one or more vulnerable women, emphasizing his power and authority rather than his tenderness as a lover. According to this view, the harem is the locale for one man's tyranny, a position observers could either accept as natural or criticize as unenlightened. We have already seen how male superiority (and female inferiority) are indicated pictorially in works such as Decamps' *Seated Sultan with Harem Girl* (see Fig. 4.3) or Devéria's 1837 *Arabes du désert* (see Fig. 5.19), namely, by strongly contrasting size or age. Another way artists underscore the harem power differential is to depict the woman naked or partially naked, while the man remains fully clothed, as in Guérard's 1851 *Le pacha, ou la vie au harem* (see Fig. 4.6) or Achille Devéria's *Turcs* of 1851 (see Fig. 4.4). A master who is clothed while in an intimate setting maintains his connection to an outside, public world, where his clothing functions as a symbol of wealth, fashion and status. Clothed he is the foil for the undressed and therefore sexualized woman. Using Wollstonecraft's binary, she is "body" (*VRW* 171). She further argues that women are the private manifestation of men's public status: "Riches and hereditary honours have made cyphers of women to give consequence to the numerical figure" (*VRW* 106).

The greater the harem master's physical involvement with his female partner, the less she is visually available for the viewer. Aware of this, some of these artists struggled to represent female nudity as part of an internal narrative and as spectacle pitched to the voyeuristic spectator. The images with the greatest eye-catching appeal are those in which the woman is laid out for the delectation of the viewer and simply placed near her lover, a mere adjunct in the background, as in the first scene in Guérard's 1853 series *La vie au sérail* (see Fig. 4.22). Conversely, the strongest expression of the authority of the harem master requires his physical presence. Montesquieu deals with this same concept when Usbek warns him that the integrity of his harem depends on his imminent return. The masculine aura he emanates cannot be effectively transferred to the eunuchs. It is his attenuated absence that is blamed for the women's turning to other means of gratification. Similarly, the explicit presence of the pasha in harem pictures threatens their erotic appeal to the interloper who is the viewer.

Another hierarchizing device used in harem pictures, often in combination with others, is to position the master spatially higher, occupying the upper half of the composition and usually seated upright, while the woman is both supine and occupying the lower space. Particularly relevant are Wollstonecraft's spatial metaphors in describing the political tyrant's behavior in personal and political affairs. Although he seems to be "above his fellows," external advantages "sink him in reality below them" (*VRW* 131). Similarly, the reclining female in the harem, sometimes thought to be soulless and preoccupied with languorous pleasure, is an apt parallel to the wealthy European woman whose life is aimless. Here Wollstonecraft condemns political tyrants through the extended metaphor of the seraglio. Again her spatial terms relate to the harem images of pashas and concubines in this cluster: "supinely," "the lap of pleasure," "languor," "sink," "loiter life away" (*VRW* 112–13). Succinctly put, for Wollstonecraft the problem of sensualist male tyrants is their expectation of "blind obedience" to their wills, whether women in question are actual eastern slaves or French playthings (*VRW* 107). Writing in England in 1733 Aaron Hill claims that even proud eastern harem women admit they are inferior to their husbands and obey them with great humility.[110]

The pasha is spatially and psychologically dominant in the print after Guérard's painting, *Le pacha* (see Fig. 4.6). And in Lewis's *Hhareem* (see Plate 1) the mameluke's[111] placement within a space is also "despotic." His social dominance in the picture is indicated by his physical position as he sits above his supine women. He leans toward the spectacle of the unveiling while his wives and concubines lean back.

But viewers of these harem pictures might well have seen the pictorial assertion of male power as false. Importantly, the harem master's power is false in all three eighteenth-century texts under analysis. In both Mozart and Montesquieu the despot who imprisons women is himself named as imprisoned by his lustful extravagance. Usbek is so-named by Zelis (*PL* 129) and Selim by Constanza. Wollstonecraft calls such despots weak (*VRW* 131). In each case it is a woman who makes this observation about male power, which is given an immoral spin: tyranny is considered evil. Representative of moral conscience in cultural texts, women level the critique against male tyrants. Usbek as much as admits his moral corruption when he provides a revealing explanation for his *wanderlust*: "In the crowded seraglio in which I lived I forestalled and destroyed love by love itself; but from my very lack of feeling has come a secret jealousy which is devouring me" (*PL* 46). His sentiment, expressed early on in the book, dooms his role as harem master and makes the continuation of the institution untenable.

Rarely articulated outright but always understood in harem pictures where the pasha is shown as pictorially dominant is the expectation that he forces sexual relations on the woman pictured with him. "Male tyranny" in the harem can be a euphemism for the rape that was thought to occur there. In Mozart's *Abduction* Selim gives Constanza an ultimatum: she is to give him her love the next day—or else (*AS* 75).[112] Good and "constant" woman that she is, betrothed to Belmonte, Constanza is willing to refuse him to the death. She pleas with him to kill her. Nonetheless, her lover Belmonte later suspects her of being unfaithful to him, and Blonde's boyfriend Pedrillo guesses the same of her. This late eighteenth-century assumption is paradoxical: a good woman was somehow expected to protect her virtue even when it was thought she was coerced to submit.[113]

This expectation is upended in the most explicitly prurient representation of the harem in all the nineteenth-century writing examined, namely, the anonymous *Lustful Turk* first published in 1828. Abducted by pirates, the British virgin Emily Barstow who finds herself in the harem of Ali, the bey of Algiers, vehemently and repeatedly fights off her new owner, as we learn in her "private letters" sent to her best friend, the sister of her betrothed. The titillation of the book, however, is the transformation of initial female disgust into feminine arousal and sexual ecstacy. Perhaps this change was as much the book's scandal as its graphically violent descriptions of the deflowering of virgins: it suggested that behind every respectable young Englishwomen was a sexually hungry creature.

Female enjoyment of sex in the harem appears in other texts from both the eighteenth and nineteenth centuries. In rococo-revival images the harem inmates often are pictured enjoying the luxurious display of their bodies, judging from their languorous poses and softened faces. And Wollstonecraft's outraged criticisms of aristocratic women implies that they enjoy sex under improper circumstances. She writes: "genteel women are, literally speaking, slaves to their bodies, and glory in their subjection" (*VRW* 130), her analysis of the only agency she believes woman is accorded. Therein lies the appeal and the scandal of harem images depicting dominant men and happily submissive happy women: they represent people who choose to operate according to the laws of Nature.

Cluster 2: "Gallantry": The Woman "On Top"[114]

In some nineteenth-century harem pictures the woman is shown as more dominant than her master.

These images are indebted to the rococo tradition of courtship pictures in which the woman is superior, both compositionally and as the moral agent who determines the degree of the couple's intimacy, while the suitor is submissively genteel and adoring as in Jean Honoré Fragonard's well-known *Happy Lovers*, c. 1760. Compositionally, this gallant dynamic is indicated by a woman's placement in the central-upper part of the composition, while the man is located off to one side and lower on the picture plane. An example of a rococo harem painting where the woman is more dominant is Jean Baptiste LePrince's undated *Harem Scene* (see Fig. 4.52). Though she is younger than the greying pasha and her diaphanous clothing reveals her body, she is relatively more powerful than he. His infatuation with her is indicated by his supine and attentive pose, and he surrenders to her will, indicated by her raised arm and her seated body pose. Though gallant in this interaction, his sexual potency is unquestionable given the phallomorphic attenuation of his grisly beard and his intense, clawlike groping of her body. Here is an eighteenth-century visualization of the magic of female charms in the face of which the usually despotic male is made helpless.

In the nineteenth-century Delacroix's 1832 watercolor *Moorish Conversation* (see Fig. 4.50) is structured so that the woman seems to control the interaction. Her clothed body is directed to the spectator rather than toward the darker-skinned male lover supine and located to her lower right. She appears as the more dominant figure. Her voluminous clothing, the outdoor setting, and their lack of physical contact help to de-eroticize the scene, suggesting friendship and conversation rather than love and passion—at least for the moment. Perhaps the relative restraint of the scene indicates the dominance of her will, as Woman holds in check Man's wayward passion.

A similar theme appears in Mouilleron's untitled lithograph of an odalisque (see Fig. 3.20). The setting of a bedchamber, however, suggests the couple's intimacy is imminent. But the moment represented is when the man is still at a distance from the woman abed; indeed he is on his knees and clasps his hands in supplication. She is in the process of removing her own veil and seems to be very much in charge of the sexual dynamic.

We are less certain about the outcome of the flirtation in Allom's rococo-inspired *Circassian Slaves* (see Figs. 2.4 and 2.5) from 1838 where there is a lack of significant contact between master and female slave, and her clothed body and his positioning lower than hers suggest gentlemanly restraint as a part of his admiration for the female slave who dominates by virtue of her beauty. The mere one-quarter-profile presentation of the pasha deemphasizes him. Her empowerment is constructed in relation to the master's disempowerment. She is in effect Woman put on a pedestal.

Love and beauty are aspects of Woman that grant her power over Man, according to the characters in Mozart's comic opera. Belmonte's aria cedes great power to Constanza. Following the reconciliation of the distrusting men and their faithful women, he vows to her: "I build my faith upon your power, oh love, confiding in your might. Through you my hope began to flower, you lead my way as guiding light" (*AS* 129–30). Love of woman exerts a spiritual effect on man; she becomes a moral beacon for him. This declaration sets the stage for Belmonte's request for pity from the pasha to grant Constanza her freedom from harem life, thus allowing Selim to act virtuously. Monogamous romantic love is the epicenter from which the opera's redemption emanates.

The powerful harem woman appears in Montesquieu as well. Usbek *de facto* empowers his wives by his reminder that he is not only their master but also their husband. In other words, he uses their mutual love as the basis for his exhortation to them to "behave" (*PL* 133) at a point in the *Letters* when they are reported to be quarreling with each other. His strategy backfires, however; in the unspoken rules of the harem, tender love is read as an abdication of power.

In Allom's two pictures the slave woman is admired for her musical talent as well as her beauty. Similarly, Montesquieu's Anais is talented and beautiful. She is admired by male lovers while in Paradise, where she experiences innumerable other sensuous pleasures (*PL* 251). Moreover, she and the other two women who participate in the active construction of the story of women's sexual reward in Paradise are distinguished by Montesquieu as intellectually gifted. Anais possesses "the mind of a true philosopher" (*PL* 251) wanting to share the pleasures of Paradise with her harem sisters, in the story told by Zulema (*PL* 248), who is herself highly learned about Islam, as recounted by the European woman at court who "is fond of reading [and is] curious" (*PL* 247). Montesquieu seems to imply that the most profound pleasures are to be had by women learned enough to expect them and then enjoy them judiciously. Likewise Allom's pictures might be read as an ode to the ideal qualities justifying women's social predominance and power: beauty, talent, and education even though she may be a slave.

Both Montesquieu and Wollstonecraft suggest that women's improved education offers a way out of her oppression. *Vindication* calls for the reform of female education, which in its current sorry state excludes women from participating as equal partners in the making of a truly enlightened nation. In forming a nation "men of genius and talent" (*VRW* 172) expect no significant help from poorly educated women—and they do not get any. Wollstonecraft is outraged when Rousseau writes that "educational reform" for British women about to be married should be modeled on that of a young Circassian trained in the harem to fulfill the sexual needs of "the eastern bashaw" (*VRW* 183). To refute his argument, she asserts that it is children, rather than sex ("love," "beauty," "coquetry," or "artificial graces") that keep couples together.

Montesquieu also addresses women's comparative education in France and the East. His French philosopher character opines that society interferes with the development of women's courage. He makes a startlingly feminist comment that flies in the face of the dictates of nature: "'If our upbringing were similar, our strength would be also. Test them [women] on the kinds of ability that their upbringing has not impaired, and we shall soon see if we are so superior'" (*PL* 93). And in the letter on the heavenly rewards for females, all three women are feminist in having integrated their mental and bodily pleasures.

Ever wary, Wollstonecraft offers a biting analysis of how the presentation of women's dominance is in fact illusory. First of all, because women are so poorly educated, when they rule they do so without virtue. Theirs is thus an "illicit" power, necessarily short-lived (*VRW* 125–26), as they are unprepared to accept it. She compares women to despots: both have too much power and forgo the appropriate use of reason. Both women and despots are "degraded" even though they may be highly influential. Their model of life infiltrates all society. Elevating women or despots, unnatural as the process is, has injurious effects throughout (*VRW* 107, 126). Correspondingly, when Wollstonecraft critiques Milton's view of idealized womanhood—that she is "formed for softness and sweet attractive grace"(*VRW* 100)—she claims it is based on the premise that women do not own themselves and are mere sex objects for a man ruled by appetites, that is, they are soulless, as she borrows a stereotype about Islam infusing it with a feminist gloss:

> I cannot comprehend his meaning, unless, in the true Mahometan strain, he meant to deprive us of souls, and insinuate that we were beings only designed by sweet attractive grace, and docile blind obedience, to gratify the senses of man when he can no longer soar on the wing of contemplation. (*VRW* 100–101)

She argues that unless women have their own validity as human beings they cannot be credited with "virtue," as Rousseau defined it. Baldly she rails that "trifling employments have rendered woman a trifler" (*VRW* 171).

Beauty and seduction, in a word, "vice" (*VRW* 132) must have been the means of women's power. What they have lost is "reason," "all simplicity, all dignity of mind" as they "act as men are observed to act when they have been exalted by the same means" (*VRW* 132). Woman has not had the moderating effect of reason: "it is sufficient to allow that she [woman] has always been either a slave or a despot, and to remark that each of these situations equally retards the progress of reason" (*VRW* 144). Thus the idealization of women is "a curse," a use of "illegitimate power which they obtain by degrading themselves." Beauty grants them only "hollow respect" (*VRW* 146). She hopes for a time when kings will step down from power so that, relatedly, women will "resign the arbitrary power of beauty" (*VRW* 103).

With Wollstonecraft in mind, the logic of the harem woman "on top" as understood in French and British representation makes woman's dominance illusory. Woman is "despot" only as long as the master consents to it. The "dominant" woman is a curiosity, a carefully controlled disruption in the overarching narrative of the master's power. Ironically, the harem picture's articulation (or visualization) of her playacting at "power" serves to emphasize his silent authority.

For Wollstonecraft "gallantry" and "despotism" are two sides of the same coin. Each results from a society based in "idleness," the kind of leisure bought by the aristocracy at the price of the exploitive treatment of the poor. "Gallantry" emanates from the relationship of a man to his mistress, not his wife. It is a poor way of interacting with women, as it leads to male resentment of women's unnatural power, which encourages male tyranny over women. She writes:

> idleness has produced a mixture of gallantry and despotism into society, which leads the very men who are the slaves of their mistresses to tyrannize over their sisters, wives and daughters. (*VRW* 106–7)

Women's inappropriate exercising of power over men leads full circle to men's inappropriate display of power over women. What she wants for the relationship of the sexes is not female dominance but equal partnership. She says clearly: "I do not wish them [women] to have power over men; but over themselves" (*VRW* 154).

Though Wollstonecraft was independent thinking and courageous in her willingness to critique revered thinkers such as Rousseau and Milton, she still advocated the male model of experience for women's improvement: "reason" and a vague "virtue," which she thought characterized male heroes and should be adopted as universal values for both genders and all cultures. While her focus on environment as a crucial component of gender-formation and education as a powerful tool to change its undesirable effects may seem very timely to us today, her use of the harem metaphor to critique the immoral western aristocracy again fetishizes and simplifies it as the locale for unbridled sexuality and sloth. The construction of harem woman as despot or slave is a caricature that again serves western ends: her own. Wollstonecraft's method of argument is to critique existing thought and not to explicitly state ideals, though she does advocate men and women as equal partners who do not coerce one another. But in that social ideal, there is no parity with Others who remain outside "enlightened" society and in fact whose very existence gives rise to its articulation. When she advocates the dissolution of patriarchy and monarchy, trusting that Enlightenment reason will eliminate both, it is the western European modes of these institutions that interest her: "The *divine right* of husbands, like the divine right of kings, may, it is to be hoped, in this enlightened age, be contested without danger" (*VRW* 127). When she links tyrannical husbands with tyrannical rulers, both injurious to women's well-being, her primary interest is England and France, and less so Turkey and Egypt.

Thus given the intellectual and political inheritance of these images, harem pictures cannot but provoke discussion about the inappropriateness of the tyranny of both men over women and women over men. The critique of harem tyranny having overtones of political and sexual liberation was well-developed by the nineteenth century.

Summary

Condemnation of the harem woman allowed for the construction of the moral superiority of western womanhood and monogamous marriage, whether articulated by defenders of the status quo on gender relations (writers in the mainstream press) or attackers of it (Mary Wollstonecraft). Many of these negative stereotypes evolve from a belief in the harem woman's sexual excess. Just as the harem institution exceeds British and French expectations for the number of wives necessary in marriage, the women themselves are thought to lack restraint, leading to general disorder and immorality. Harem women are saddled with the function of moral barometer of the East. As woman goes, so goes the culture. That the unknowable harem woman be made known in pictures and verbal accounts as the familiar, negative stereotypes of woman defuses her potential to truly subvert the perceived truth of British and French religions, customs, beliefs, and knowledge. What is ultimately at stake in negative stereotyping of harem women is anxiety about the desire and power of women/Other.

6

The Harem Fetishized: Muslim Women as Moral: Angels in Heaven and the House

Introduction

A favorable judgment about the harem—that it was a familial institution marked by conjugal love, duty, and respect where children could be raised to an ethical adulthood—is part of a more widespread softening of attitudes toward Islam discernible in nineteenth-century England and France. In the late 1830s Alphonse de Lamartine has warm relationships with several Muslim contacts on his trip to the East, prompting his admiration for Islam: "The Mohammedan worship has many virtues, and I love this people, for it is the people of prayer!" (*PHL* 74). In matters of philosophy and religion, he sees Muslims as "a people of heroes and martyrs" (*PHL* 491). One of the same terms, hero, appears in a reappraisal of Islam marked by Thomas Carlyle's 1840 lecture, "The Hero as Prophet" written on the subject of Muhammad.[1] This is a significant document in the history of nineteenth-century orientalism for its desire—however problematic—to legitimize Islam. Two aspects of Carlyle's line of argument are relevant here.

First, he disputes Muhammad's reputation as "a scheming Impostor, a Falsehood incarnate" (*H* 43). Instead, he claims Muhammad was a thoughtful, true, and faithful man much like Jesus (*H* 52–53). Carlyle takes the argumentative tact of likening Islam to Christianity; for him Islam is a kind of Christianity (*H* 76). Both religions have a genuine holy book (*H* 64); both have conquered with the sword; both have survived because of their fundamentally sound principles and their dedication to a single God, "that great, central Law" (*H* 56). Carlyle also likens the eastern races to the western: the Persians are "the French of the East"; the Arabs are the "Oriental Italians," while they possess a "Jewish quality"—namely, religiosity (*H* 47–48). The Arabs, the people among whom Muhammad was born, are called "agile, active, and yet most meditative [and] enthusiastic" (*H* 47). Carlyle's racial analogies, like his claims of similarity between the religions, are intended as complimentary.

Secondly, Carlyle addresses the idea that Islam is a sensual and indulgent religion. Undoubtedly, Carlyle is thinking of polygyny here, as he points out Muhammad's own longtime love for Kadijah, his elder by fifteen years, and claims that he began to found Islam when he was an older man, "the prurient heat of his life all burnt out" (*H* 54). Carlyle describes Muhammad as rather ascetic: "We shall err widely if we consider this man as a common voluptuary, intent mainly on base enjoyments,—nay, on enjoyments of any kind" (*H* 71). And surely his subject is polygyny when he writes of Islam's "indulgences, criminal to us" (*H* 70). He claims these were not of the Prophet's own choosing but characterize long-standing Arabian practices. He in fact curtailed or restricted them.

Having said this, Carlyle asserts that the Paradise of Muhammad *is* sensual, as is his Hell, a fact which "shocks all spiritual feeling in us" (*H* 74). But his qualification of this is threefold: that such sensual conceptions preceded Muhammad's influence; that his followers are worse culprits for advocating a Paradise of pleasure; that for the Prophet the spiritual joy of peace is the most profound.

Carlyle acknowledges the sensual nature of Islamic Paradise (i.e., that houris offer a sexual reward) and that the historical personage of Muhammad constitute "the sorest chapter of all for us" (*H* 74), but offers a modulating observation: that enjoying pleasures in themselves is not evil; what is reprehensible is "the reducing of our moral self to slavery by them" (*H* 74–75). Still, the unconventional content of Carlyle's lecture shocked its initial audience.

Each of Carlyle's two argumentative strategies has a parallel in the positive harem representations to be explored in this chapter: sometimes the inmate is shown to be much like a French or British woman (usually bourgeois); sometimes she is shown as a chaste embodiment of pleasure. Often these are combined in positive harem representations.

The notion of harem women as virtuous can be reactive: it counters the casting of them as immoral. One writer to refute the stereotype was David Urquhart, also one of the most prolific British writers on Turkey in the first half of the nineteenth century. He acknowledges in 1838 the "idea so universally established in Europe [. . .], that of the licentiousness of the Harem" (*SE* 2:393) and disagrees with it and its corollary, that the harem woman sits idle all day. Instead he describes her active life: she embroiders[2] and makes dresses, spins cotton and silk,[3] prepares dyes, works the loom, grinds coffee and corn, performs religious duties, cleans the house, visits friends, shops, and takes drives in her carriage (*SE* 2:395–400). In effect he dignifies the harem woman's life by correlating her industriousness, productivity, and civility to similar attributes of the bourgeois lady of the house.

Representations of "good" harem women correlate her roles to those British and French women were expected to play: loving wives and mothers, cordial hostesses, selfless nuns, obedient servants, often silent females, and always "natural" women. These types often overlap in the images, though they will be analyzed separately here. Artists can depict a harem woman positively by having her engage in a desirable activity. But much subtler is an artist's use of compositional or thematic structuring devices borrowed from images of respectable ladies found throughout the western European pictorial traditions. This use of positive pictorial prototypes is an intertextual referencing that exploits vestigial meanings from earlier texts in order to lend respectability to the harem picture at hand. When nineteenth-century viewers were familiar with the fine arts tradition, their readings were deeper than viewers for whom the associations were not as clear. But even for viewers unfamiliar with such referents, these harem pictures were mostly positive.

Pure Creatures in Heavenly and Earthly Gardens

> Every good harem has [. . .] a garden gay with flowers and fountains attached to it, where the women may wander at will among the leaves and birds, or dream away the sultry hours in their pretty kiosks overhanging the Bosphorus.[4]
>
> 'Within the gay kiosk reclined
> Above the scent of lemon groves,
> Where bubbling fountains kiss the wind,
> And birds make music to their loves,—
> She lives a kind of faery life,
> In sisterhood of fruits and flowers,
> Unconscious of the outer strife.
> That wears the palpitating hours.'
> —"The Hareem," Richard Monckton Milnes[5]
>
> Although this conception is poetical, to one who has lived many years in the East, it appears a conception, not a description of the real hareem life, even among the noble and wealthy of those lands.[6]

> What impious tongue, ye blushing saints, would dare
> To hint that aught but Heaven hath placed you there?
> Or that the loves of this light world could bind,
> In their gross chain, your Prophet's soaring mind?
> No - wrongful thought! - commissioned from above
> To people Eden's bowers with shapes of love,
> (Creatures so bright, that the same lips and eyes
> They wear on earth will serve in Paradise,)
> There to recline among Heaven's native maids
> And crown the' Elect with bliss that never fades.
> (*LR* 6)

Virgins in the Muslim and Christian Paradise

We have seen how French and British representations of the harem showed the women housed there as voraciously sexual. But opposing images show them as admirably passionless. The theme of a girl at prayer is a double embodiment of purity. This is the subject of Lord Leighton's *At a Reading Desk* (Fig. 6.1) of 1877. One of the latest pictures addressed in this study, it is tantamount to a refusal of the notion of the lascivious harem found in innumerable pictures that preceded it. Utterly absorbed in her religious study and folded into herself, the girl arches earnestly into her devotion, her body posture a human variation on the shape of the *Qur'an* atop its stand. Disciplined, devout, and well-schooled, she is the female body molded to Victorian ideals of restraint and industry. Still the partially visible, bared foot is a reminder that she belongs to a "primitive" society. By Victorian standards, she is too young to be wearing her hair up, suggesting the early maturation forced on Muslim girls in the harem. Nonetheless, Leighton's image is an unusual representation in nineteenth-century representations of the harem in presuming that female literacy can take place there from an early age.

Sometimes a positive representation of the harem woman can also be read as a depiction of a houri, the youth promised as reward to souls who had been faithful followers of the Prophet. But there are differing representations of the houri. Sometimes the pleasure she is thought to offer is pure; other times it is interpreted as sexual. This bifurcation is traceable

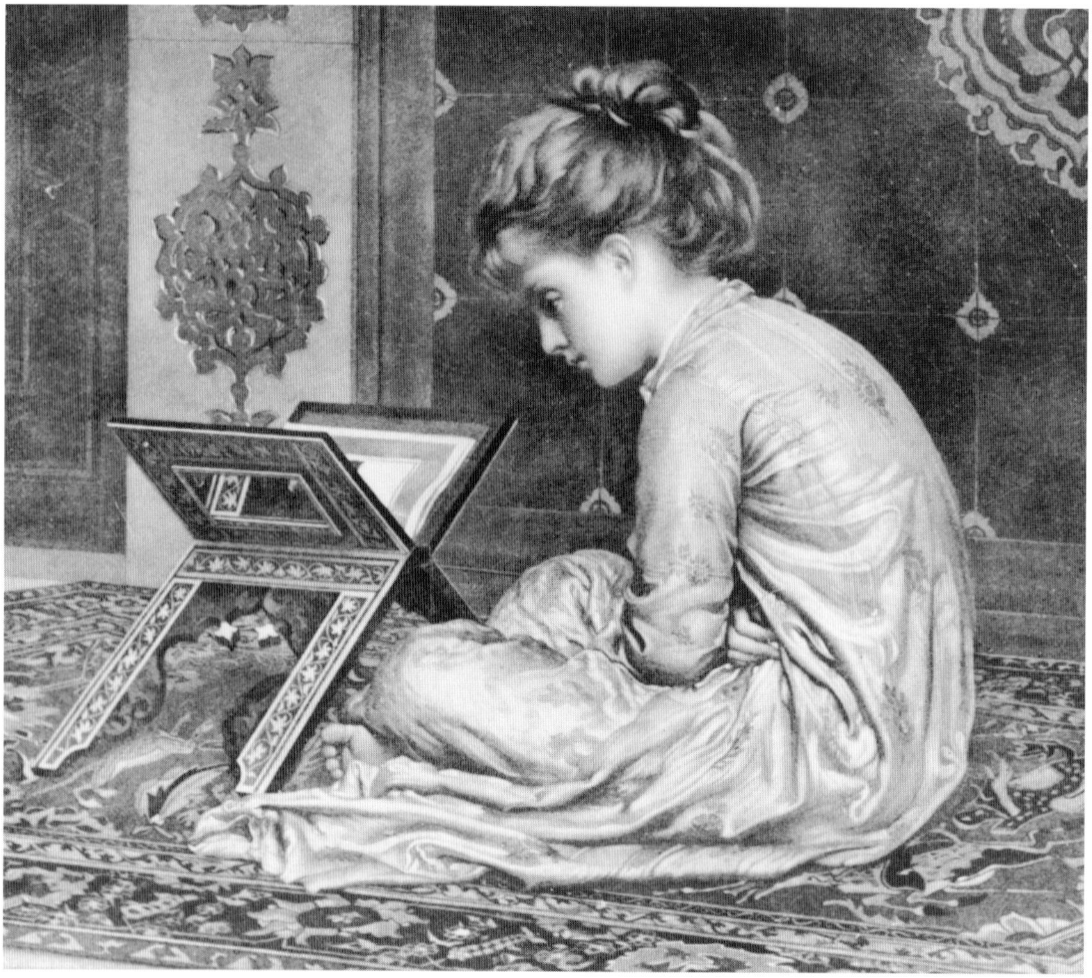

Fig. 6.1. Lord Frederick Leighton. *At a Reading Desk.* 1877. Sudley House, Walker Art Gallery. The Board of Trustees of the National Museums and Galleries on Merseyside. Photo courtesy Witt Library, Courtauld Institute, London.

in part to the debate within Islam itself about whether Paradise would offer not only spiritual but also physical pleasure to the deceased. Both Islam and Christianity drew distinctions between body and mind, between the pleasure of the flesh, which is degraded, and the pleasure of the spirit, which is elevated. Though she is rarely depicted in Islamic art,[7] the houri is described in popular interpretations of Islam in which limitless sexual indulgence with her is one of the paradisiacal rewards for the believer. Yet in conceptions of Heaven described by theologians, she and the pleasure she brings serve as a reflection of divine love.[8] The purity of houris in Paradise is made explicit in the *Qur'an*: they are called "maiden" or "virgin."[9]

More so than visual images done by any other single artist, French or British, John Lewis's pictures of harem women suggest heavenly houris. In a retrospective judgment made after Lewis had exhibited harem pictures for nearly a quarter of a century (and two years before his death), the collective subject of his harem paintings is called "Mr. Lewis's Oriental paradise" (*A* 31 May 1874:740). A comparison of his harem *oeuvre* and descriptions of Paradise in the *Qur'an* yields some significant findings. The following *Qur'anic* passage is especially relevant to his paintings:

> O which of your Lord's bounties will you and you deny?
> reclining upon couches lined with brocade,
> the fruits of the gardens nigh to gather—
> O which of your Lord's bounties will you and you deny?
> therein maidens restraining their glances,
> untouched before them by any man or jinn—.[10]

That holy book refers to Paradise as "a lofty Garden";[11] Lewis paints an elevated setting for his harem, as seen through the window in his 1857 *Harem Life—Constantinople* (see Fig. 3.39). Houris are to be found reclining on couches in at least four parts of

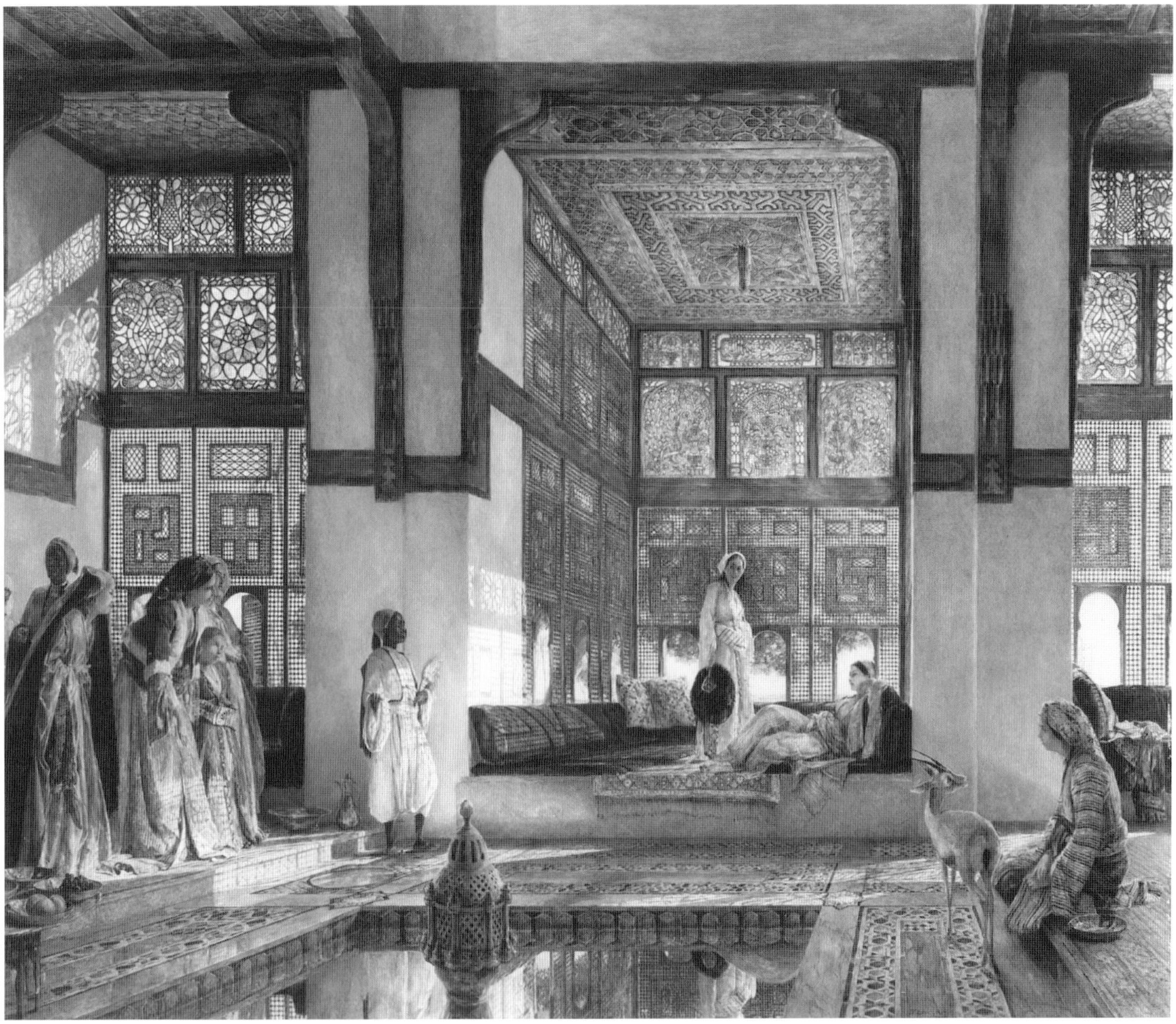

Fig. 6.2. John Frederick Lewis. *Reception.* 1873. Oil on panel. Yale Center for British Art, Paul Mellon Collection.

the holy book;[12] harem women are on couches in nearly all of Lewis's publicly exhibited harem pictures. Green is the color most frequently associated with Paradise in the *Qur'an,* since it is the ultimate spiritual oasis in contrast to the dessication of death; it is also the color of the greatest mystical experiences.[13] It is either worn by the immortal youths, or it decorates the large cushions against which the houris recline.[14] Harem women wear green (often a short green jacket with fur edging) in Lewis's *Harem Life—Constantinople,* 1857 (see Fig. 3.39); *In the Bey's Garden, Asia Minor,* 1865 (see Fig. 6.13); *Life in the Harem, Cairo,* 1858 (see Fig. 3.2); *Reception,* 1873 (Fig. 6.2); *Siesta,* 1876 (see Fig. 2.13) and others. Silk and brocade dress are mentioned in descriptions of the immortal youths and the "godfearing" souls who join them in the afterlife, and brocade lines the couches on which the maidens await him.[15] Lewis uses silk and brocade throughout his pictures. Also relevant is the Qur'anic description of the afterlife in which the faithful resides in peace and quiet: "Therein they shall hear no idle talk, no cause of sin, only the saying 'Peace, Peace!'" (56:25–26). Silence is suggested in several of Lewis's pictures, as discussed more fully below. Qur'anic descriptions of houris in the celestial garden are "cloistered in cool pavilions";[16] two females in Lewis's *Lilium Auratum* (Fig. 6.3) (1872) enter a kiosk according to one observer of the time (*ILN* 25 May 1872:502).[17] In many of his harem pictures there is a sharp contrast between the blazing light seen outside windows and the darkened, cooler interiors.

Several more complex details in Lewis's harem pictures indicate they are depictions of *houris* in Paradise. In his *Harem Life—Constantinople* (see Fig. 3.39)

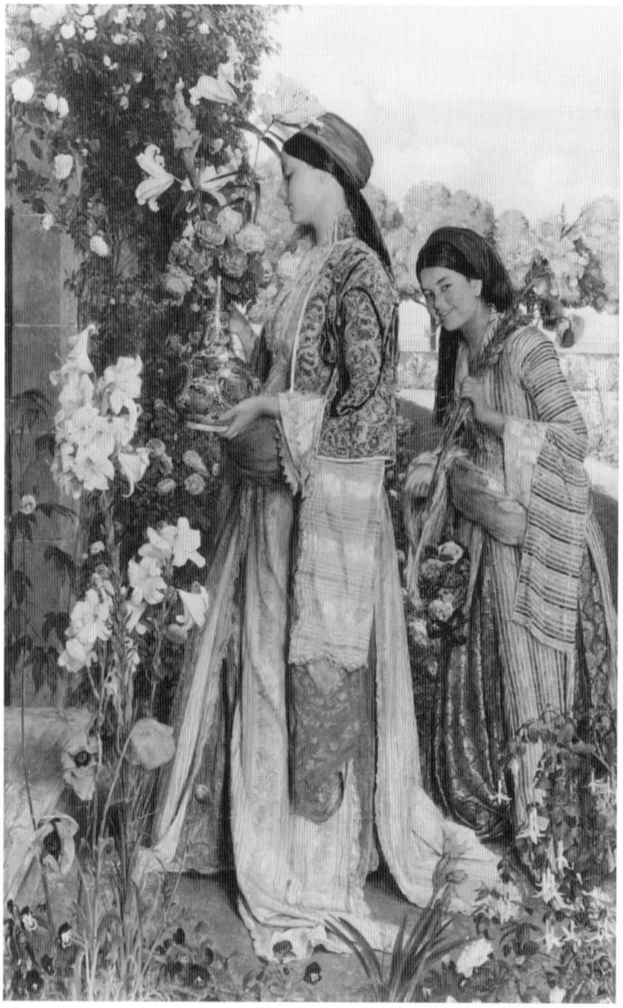

Fig. 6.3. John Frederick Lewis. *Lilium Auratum*. 1871. Birmingham Museums & Art Gallery.

a mirror shows the feet and trousered legs of a third figure. Are we looking at the feet of a deceased soul just entering Paradise and approaching his houri reward?[18] In the popular Islamic conception of Paradise a type of butterfly called *rafraf* would transport the faithful soul to the heavenly garden.[19] In his *In the Bey's Garden* (see Fig. 6.13) Lewis paints a butterfly alighting on the edge of a vase and a pot to either side of the woman; another is dead on the ground at her feet. Is this butterfly dead because it has accomplished its task of transporting the viewer to Paradise?

In Paradise the faithful may recline and call for refreshment and be accompanied by pure houris who keep their eyes lowered in modesty (38:50–52). We have described several scenes of service in the harem. Many of the women in Lewis's harem pictures have their eyes lowered, as in *Hhareem* 1850, *Armenian Lady* 1855, *Harem Life—Constantinople* 1857, and *Harem Life, Cairo* 1858.

In nineteenth-century French and British harem pictures there are far fewer representations of the outdoor harem scene than the indoor. At first it seems that images of the harem woman outdoors function less as erotic art and more as a scientific documentation of harem women's clothing and environment, images granted a high degree of realism and truth value. Noteworthy in this regard is a Boucher engraving in which appears a full-length single eastern woman standing among foliage: *Dame de Constantinople* (Fig. 6.4).[20] Conversely, the harem subject seemingly has more titillating potential when it is set indoors, within a secretive, closed-off and private interior, which might serve as metaphor for the female sexual "space." However, I want to argue that the garden scenes are also eroticized, though in different ways from harem interiors: the intensification of the female body, echoed by feminine flora and fabric set within a context of upper-class leisure constitute a kind of eroticized discourse that bespeaks rarefied

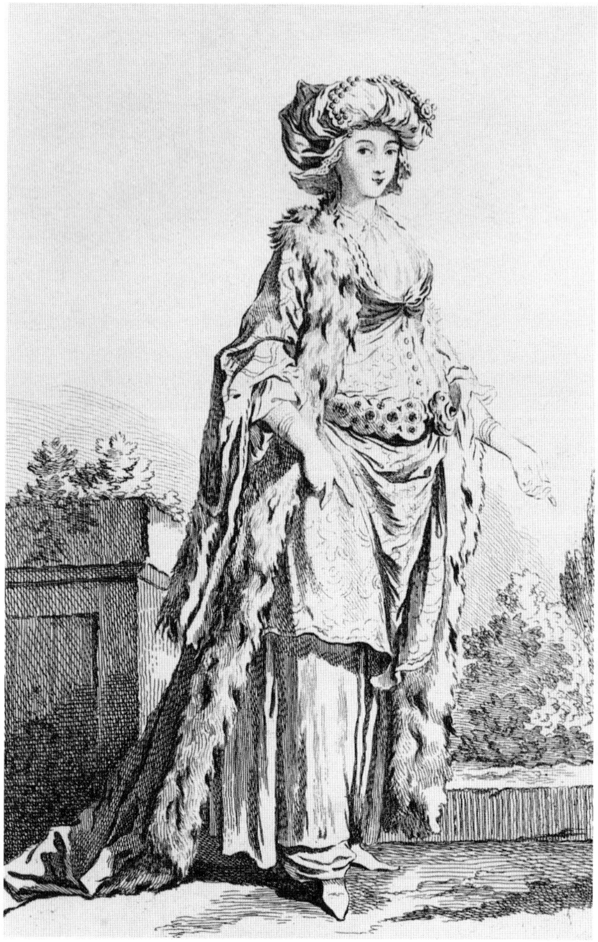

Fig. 6.4. Ravenet after François Boucher. *Dame de Constantinople*. Engraving. *Recueil de diverses figures étrangères*. Cliché Bibliothèque nationale de France, Paris.

refinement rather than low-class explicitness. Schick makes an interesting point in this regard by his observation that conventions of botanical classification are extended in the eighteenth and nineteenth centuries to refer to nations, races, and regions.[21] Thus associating types of garden flowers with types of harem women has a long history. *Eros* and science merge in these pictures.

Victorian travel literature about the harem woman outdoors is also eroticized in a new way. One historian reports a type of "aesthetically charming lady" seen outdoors who replaced the "lascivious odalisque" indoors.[22] Unlike imagery of harem women hidden from public view, these descriptions have as their subject the woman who could be viewed as a public spectacle. The Victorian traveler frequently described harem women going for a drive in the *araba* or picnicking outdoors in the well-known leisure spot outside Constantinople, the Valley of the Sweet Waters. But the artist encounters a logistical problem: how to represent the harem woman, if not through the props of the traditional erotic interior. Artists rely primarily on two devices, a title indicating a harem scene and an enclosed garden as analogue for the heavenly garden inhabited by houris.

In the early eighteenth century Lady Mary Wortley Montagu provides a written precedent for describing harem women in their gardens which contains several elements used in nineteenth-century harem garden scenes:

> It [the harem] has also a Gallery running round it towards the Garden to which all the Windows are Turned [. . .] the Women's Apartments are all built backwards, remov'd from sight, and have no other prospect than the Gardens, which are enclosed with very high Walls. [. . .] In the midst of the Garden is the Chiosk, that is, a large room, commonly beautify'd with a fine fountain in the midst of it. It is rais'd 9 or 10 steps, and enclos'd with Gilded Lattices, round which vines, jess'mines, and Honey suckles twineing make a sort of Green Wall. Large Trees are planted round this place, which is the Scene of their greatest Pleasures, and where the Ladys spend most of their Hours, employ'd by their Music or Embroidery. (*L* 1:342–43)

As Lady Mary undoubtedly observed on her travels to Turkey and elsewhere, the Islamic garden was indeed popular with divergent social classes and in various locales throughout the Middle East.[23] It functioned aesthetically and religiously: to refresh and delight the weary desert traveler, providing an oasis within an oasis, as well as to remind the believer of the ultimate paradisiacal garden awaiting him or her in the afterlife (*janna*).[24]

The garden of Paradise is mentioned more than 130 times in the *Qur'an*, and the more general references to heaven are innumerable.[25] The promised garden is described as very large but enclosed by walls, while the gates to it are open. Paradise consists of two gardens and two kinds of every fruit and tree. These gardens are filled with flowers, each having individual holy significance but all meant as praises to Allah, the water- and life-giver: the plants and flowers in Paradise are as the faithful who are "free and happy like the cyprus and the lily singing their glories in different tongues."[26] Correspondingly, the women in a harem garden are "free and happy" like the flowers surrounding them.

There are also images from Islamic art traditions showing young women standing in a garden, who are understood as houris in the celestial garden. A pen and watercolor drawing from Ottoman Turkey dating to around 1600 and titled *Houri in a Paradise Garden* (see Fig. 5.15) depicts a houri wearing a full and elaborately layered costume with an open outer robe standing against flowering trees; in her left hand she holds a rose, "a poetic metaphor for the beloved."[27] An image like this has several meanings within the tradition of Islamic lyric poetry: the beloved for whom the poet writes is often compared to a houri, and so the earthly is correlated to the heavenly.

According to Islamic tradition, the rose is the predominant flower and symbol in the garden. The rose and the rose garden symbolize all things beautiful, above all, God's love. Moreover, the rose petals gathered around its center symbolize the community surrounding the Prophet Muhammad.[28] The earthly paradise is the main source for nature imagery in Persian literature.[29] And just as the heavenly garden contains manifestations of God, the earthly garden—its flowers and trees—"are all used to describe and celebrate the beloved."[30] As in the courtly love tradition shared by Muslim and Christian cultures, the human lover from whom the mate is separated serves as analogy to God from whom the human soul is separated during this life. And images of a woman alone with a rose refer both to her absent lover and to God.

Again, John Lewis provides the most developed pictures on the subject of the harem woman in a garden, images that can double as depictions of houris in heavenly gardens. Three of his works can be read this way: *The Bouquet* (Fig. 6.5) 1858, *In the Bey's Garden, Asia Minor* (see Fig. 6.13) 1865, and *Lilium Auratum* (see Fig. 6.3) 1871. All are beautiful renderings of the "good" harem woman set in a pleasant and peaceful locale. The images are thus positive and, I maintain, eroticized, though in

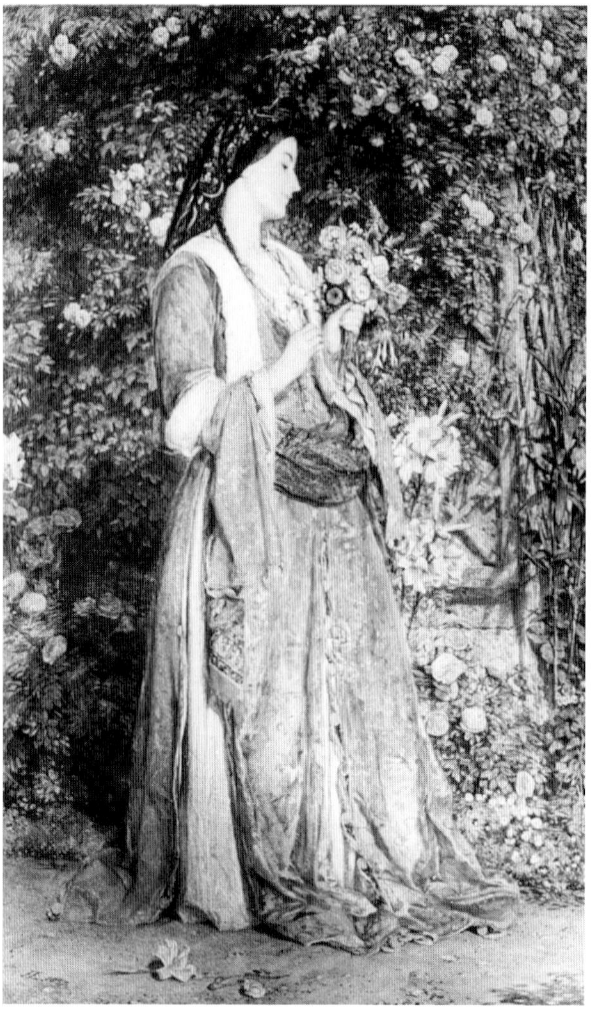

Fig. 6.5. John Frederick Lewis. *Bouquet/Lilies and Roses, Constantinople.* 1857. Oil on wood. Used by permission of Dunedin Public Art Gallery.

a very different way and much more subtly than in the typical French harem pictures. Lewis here uses a plethora of flowers and an abundance of luxurious materials, lovingly, even obsessively described, as analogy for and indeed ciphers of the women's femininity. In *Bey's Garden* the flowers take at least half of the pictorial space and as much painterly attention as the woman herself. And she is defined mostly by luxurious fabrics. Woman *is* the organic growth, decorated vessels, and yards of tactile cloth enveloping her. Such stuffs are fetishized objects that intensify her body, endlessly reiterating her sex. Rather than revealing any universal feminine, however, Lewis's work unabashedly admires the feminine body within a position of social privilege of the leisured class.

If harem women were likened to the pure houris of the Muslim Paradise, they might also be compared to that archetypically pure woman of Christianity, the Virgin Mary, in a kind of mistranslation of the houri. Harem women are comparable to the Virgin herself in two of John Lewis's harem pictures because of his use of Flemish Renaissance pictures as intertextual referents. These pictures date from the late 1850s: *Harem Life—Constantinople* (see Fig. 3.39) of 1857 and *Bouquet/Lilies and Roses, Constantinople* (1857, 1858 R.A.)[31] (see Fig. 6.5) of 1858.

Critic John Ruskin responds to Lewis's 1857 watercolor *Harem Life—Constantinople* by writing that the artist "takes Van Eyck for his model" (*W* 14:94).[32] The *Athenaeum* echoes the reference to Van Eyck that year and like Ruskin exhorts Lewis to abandon watercolor in favor of the more durable medium of oil painting (*A* 2 May 1857:571),[33] whose invention is credited to Van Eyck. Certainly in its remarkable detailing and vivid coloration, *Harem Life* recalls Van Eyck. And indeed in its theme, composition, and configuration of the seated woman Lewis's watercolor recalls the central panel of the *Mérode Altarpiece*[34] (Fig. 6.6), a work now attributed to the earlier painter Robert Campin and featuring the Virgin of the Annunciation.

Both Lewis's picture and Campin's are interiors containing two figures set in similar relationship to each other. In each a seated woman with a markedly oval face and surrounded by elaborate drapery folds has her eyes modestly averted. Like Campin, Lewis has used a narrowing perspective for his couch, whose right angles are repeated in the rear wall. The resemblance is striking in latticeworked windows, that crucial architectural symbol of harem scenes. Both have high ceilings and a miniaturized view of the outside world seen through open windows. But the similarities are also thematic. The elevated perspective seen through the window in *Harem Life—Constantinople* recalls the Qur'anic Paradise referred to as "a lofty Garden."[35] While Islam does not admit saints, there are some theological similarities between the Virgin Mary and the houri: the purpose of each of these pure and modest females is to serve men, and as such each represents the pinnacle of holy femininity. While the femininity of each is the basis of her identity, her sexuality is subordinated to her theological definition as a symbol of the emptying of desire.

Lewis's merging of the Muslim houri with the Christian Virgin Mary is a search for legitimation of the harem subject. Lewis's seated harem woman unlike her prototype, the Virgin herself, does not read or pray. She is called merely a "portly lady" (*T* 28 April 1857:7); that particular critic failed to read her as a holy figure. Lewis's intertextual references are not necessarily consciously understood by his audience.

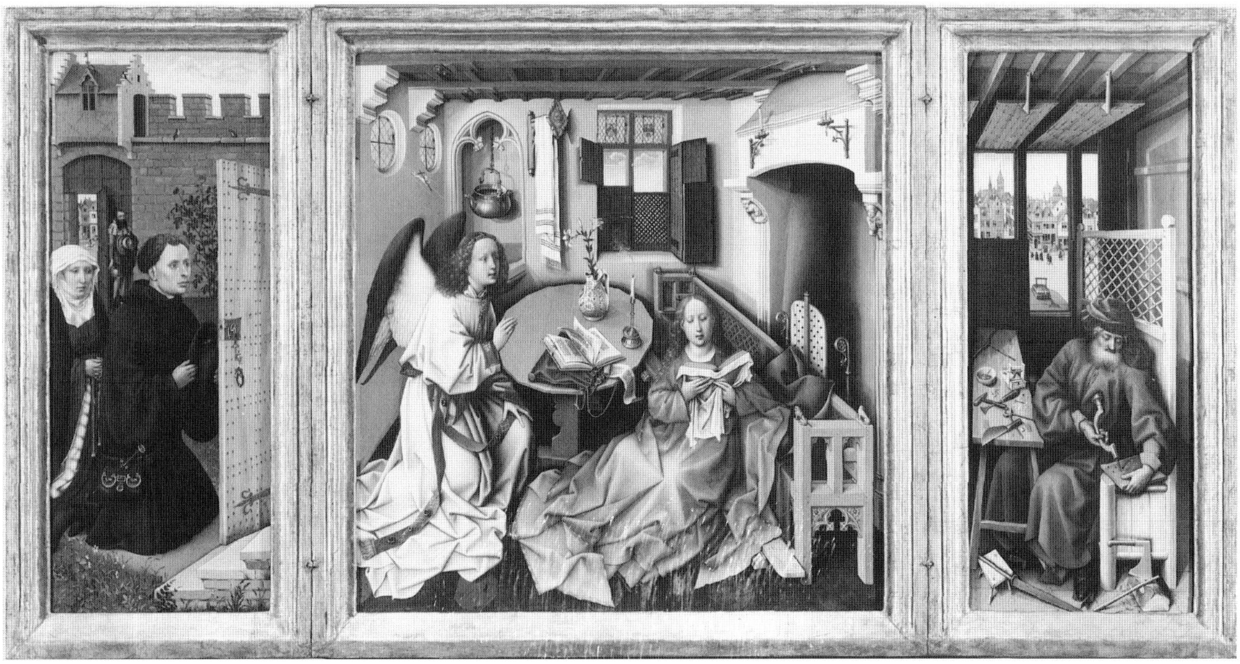

Fig. 6.6. Robert Campin. *Mérode Altarpiece*. Early 15th century. All rights reserved, The Metropolitan Museum of Art.

Secondly, Lewis's *The Bouquet/Lilies and Roses, Constantinople* recalls the *Madonna of Humility* (Fig. 6.7) by Robert Campin. In both images a female figure clothed in voluminous robes dominates the flattened picture plane, and the garden foliage, partially covering a wall, closes off the visual escape from the main subject.

Lewis uses a single haremite, accentuated by a dark background of foliage, to elicit a range of constructions on female sexuality and class privilege. In Flemish art this "garden enclosed" served as a metaphor for the Madonna's virginity. Like the flowers and fabrics in Lewis's three harem woman/houri pictures discussed above, the garden overdetermines her femininity, here registered as virginity. There is a tension in the picture between what we know to be her inaccessibility (a parallel to Mary's virginity) and what Lewis provides us as the scopic intruders—namely, her vulnerability to our gaze. In Lewis's painting we are given the privilege of sight normally reserved for the harem master.

The contact of the Virgin's holy garment with the earth (*humus*) attests to a new view of Mary as a humble mother of a more human Christ in the fifteenth century. Campin has even allowed the foliage to go untended: it grows beyond the wall's edge and through its cracks. Like Campin, Lewis uses a cipher for class, but he shows privileged instead of lowly women. In place of seeded dandelions, he paints roses and lilies, which require laborious cultivation.

This small work, only 12 by 8 inches, is Lewis's first attempt to exhibit in oil since his youth. The *Art Journal* sees "a certain infirmity" (*AJ* 1858:162) in the work and blames this on his transition to a new medium, one in which Ruskin in 1856 had urged Lewis to work exclusively. He writes: "*Are* you sure of your material—If one of those bits of white hairstroke fade—where are you?—*Why* don't you paint in oil only, now?"[36]

Lewis's religious referent, even if invisible to his viewers in the 1850s, serves to rehabilitate both the harem subject and his move from watercolor into oil painting. Perhaps it is no coincidence that his harem pictures evoke a religiosity as he moves from making genre pictures to making fine art that draws from high art traditions.

Good Mothers

> The chaste wife and serious mother should only consider her power to please as the polish of her virtues and the affection of her husband as one of the comforts that render her task less difficult, and her life happier. (*VRW* 111)

As compared to the great number of representations of mothers in western painting, there are relatively few images of eastern women as mothers, as Judy Mabro has observed.[37] Occasionally harem women

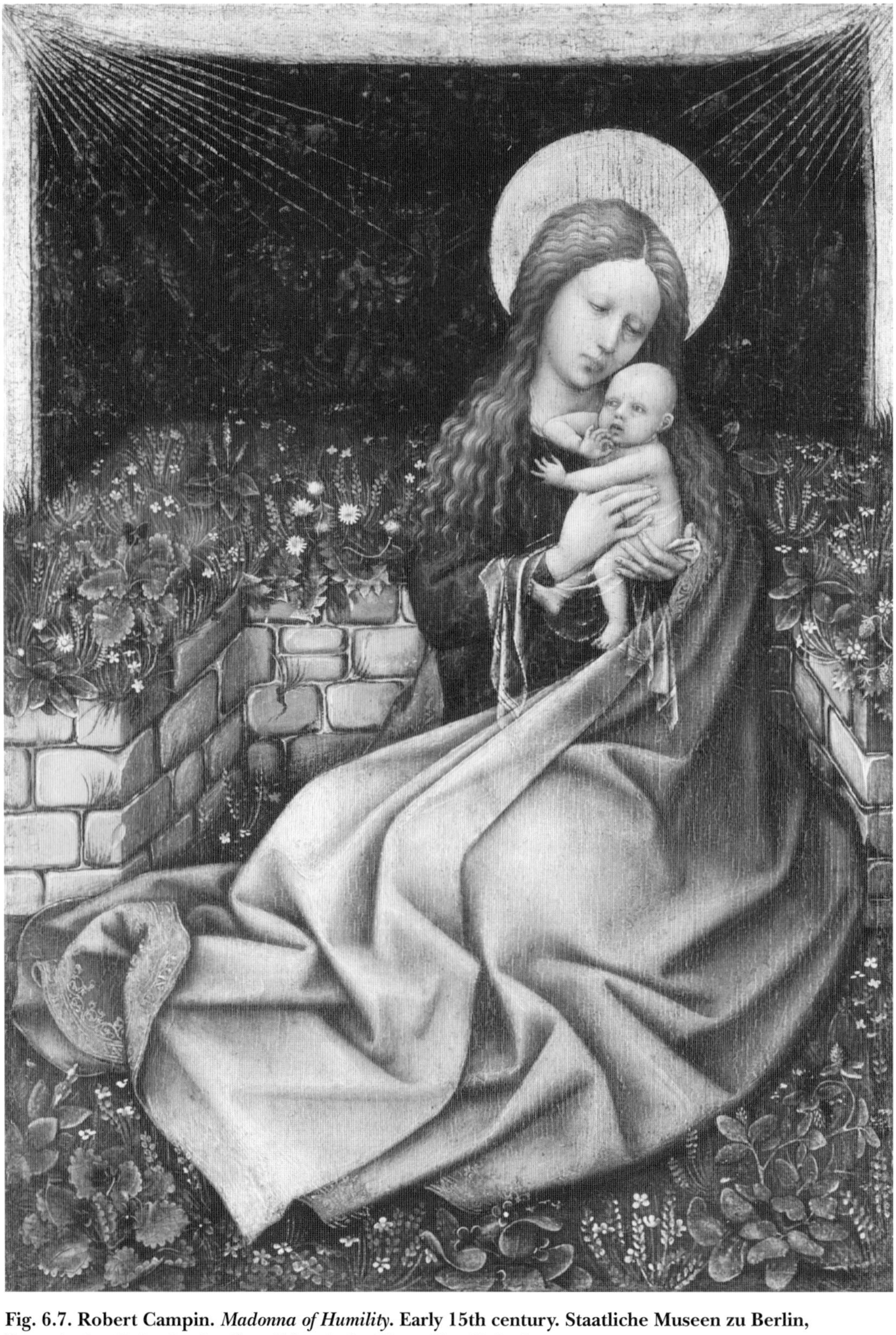

Fig. 6.7. Robert Campin. *Madonna of Humility*. Early 15th century. Staatliche Museen zu Berlin, Preussischer Kulturbesitz, Gemäldegalerie. Photo Jörg P. Anders.

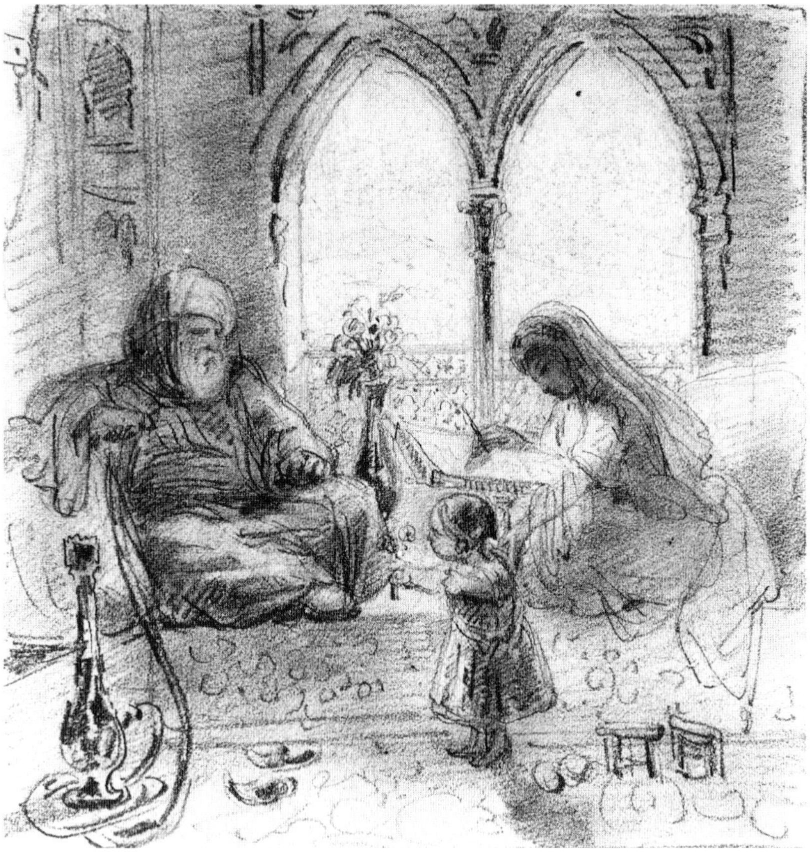

Fig. 6.8. Pierre François Lehoux. *Scène familiale en Orient.* 1837–38. Pencil. Musée Grobet-Labadié, Marseille.

are judged as good and attentive mothers, rather than negligent ones. Lady Augusta Hamilton writes "few [harem] mothers neglect the care of their infants." Charles White claims Muslim women are devoted but not very good mothers. Annie Harvey says Turkish women are kind mothers, though somewhat overindulgent.[38] The unpopularity of the belief that harem women can be capable mothers must be attributable to the presumption that polygyny sexualizes women in a way that monogamy does not, and that a sexualized woman *de facto* cannot be a good mother: the perpetual focus on flirtation considered fundamental to polygyny is thought to interfere with good child care. Only in a monogamous (read: sexually orderly) condition can women mother well, functioning as an appropriate role model to her children, who are presumed to be sexually naive. Polygyny is the sexualized Other to monogamy's sexual restraint.

The belief that harem mothers cannot be sexually interested is precisely the belief Montesquieu at first seems to oppose in his *Persian Letters* using the personage of his wife Zelis. She is an attentive mother who calls upon the common sense of "habit" in raising her seven-year-old daughter. But Zelis is also a mother who has desire and claims to experience "the heat of passion." She defiantly and rather cryptically informs Usbek that she has been enjoying pleasures he can never experience (*PL* 128–29). Thus Zelis too is punished at the end of the book by the tyrannical eunuch, who strikes the women in an attempt to reestablish order in the harem, a mandate issued by Usbek from afar. Nonetheless Zelis emerges powerful in proudly renouncing her love for Usbek.

An undated sketch by P. F. Lehoux is a notable exception in its refusal to condemn the Muslim harem mother. An analogy is drawn between the eastern harem family and the western monogamous family in *Scène familiale en Orient* (Fig. 6.8). And the family relationships are familiar to French viewers: the young mother takes a moment from her needlework to encourage the toddler—her hand on its back—to present a small bouquet to the old patriarch in a touching gesture. Love masks the subordination of woman and child to the classic family hierarchy determined by gender and age. This is the western monogamous ideal in eastern masquerade.

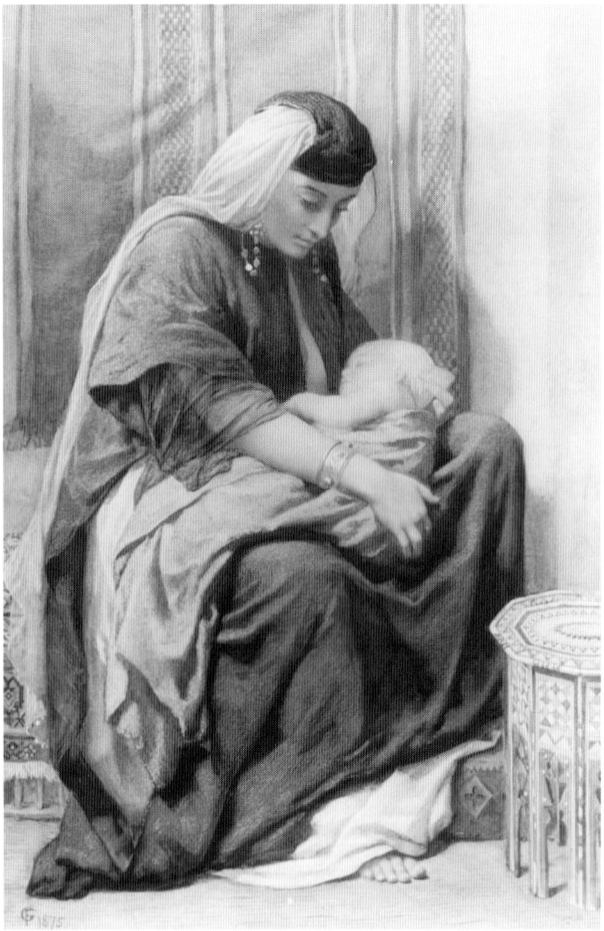

Fig. 6.9. Frederick Goodall. *Eastern Mother and Child.* 1875. Watercolor. Courtesy of the Trustees of the Victoria and Albert. V&A Picture Library.

Frederick Goodall's 1875 *Eastern Mother and Child* (Fig. 6.9) is another positive view of motherhood in the harem. The large, comforting body proportions of the mother, which fill up much of the picture plane; the intensity of the woman's focus on the sleeping baby; the tenderness of her hand gestures; the peaceful simplicity of the scene—all contribute to the effect of an idealization of motherhood. The clothing and surroundings are eastern: jewelry, headdress, table, and carpet wall hanging. This is in effect an easternized adaptation of a monumental, psychologically intense Giottesque Madonna and Child. But is it indeed a harem scene? The absence of any additional female figures interrupts a reading of this picture as a polygynous harem. New research at the V&A reveals it was titled *Copt Mother* at the Grosvenor Gallery in winter 1878–79. The point is simply that this is a good and happy eastern mother precisely because she is not part of a harem. A positive view of motherhood is expressed insofar as it reveals Christian, indeed, christological, ideals.

Pickersgill's good mother appears in the 1839 *Femme de l'Orient: Childe Harold (Lord Byron)* (see Fig. 5.21), a lithograph which is both French and British. She is described in the first Canto of *Childe Harold's Pilgrimage* (1812). There we read that Childe Harold, a young debauched rake, had a sister and a mother whom he dearly loved. Before beginning his journey Harold could not bear to say goodbye to them because

> Ye, who have known what 't is to dote upon
> A few dear objects, will in sadness feel
> Such partings break the heart they fondly hope to heal.
> (I, x) (*WB* 3)

The mother of Childe Harold pictured here is, appropriately, a good (and therefore beautiful) eastern mother because she manages to be attentive to her children demonstrating her exclusive devotion to them. Childe Harold at left who receives physical comfort already has a darkened brow, emphasizing his heroic nature. The mother occupies the same ground level as her children, whether on a harem couch or floor, and in doing so her social status is closer to theirs than could be expected from a bourgeois French or British mother. Her ground-level positioning suggests she is herself childlike, another stereotyping of eastern women. Yet, Childe Harold was Greek. Is she good because she is Greek and not a mother in the harem?

"Silent" Women Waiting in Paradise and at Home: Earthly "Angels in the House"

The intertextual references for harem pictures includes images in which a woman waits for a man. These women are "silent," perhaps an odd term to use in referring to visual art, which is of course soundless. In written accounts of the harem noise (and silence) are explicitly at issue. Some harem pictures do suggest silence more than others. The portrayal of the silent woman who awaits a man has been of great interest to feminist scholarship as a type that fundamentally denies female agency and reiterates her subservient role. It is true that the theme of "waiting for a man" can also suggest active, anticipatory preparation for sexual activity which a woman chooses. Though the theme of waiting is not inherently retrograde, in the contexts of these representations the harem woman's waiting makes her feminine, because it implies related virtues of patient restraint and self-sacrifice.

Similarly, the "silent colonial" is a desirable type in imperial discourse, one that strongly contrasted with noisy, disorderly, threatening types at home—working-class types like Chartists, trade unionists and socialists.[39] The silent harem woman is doubly dominated; she accepts restrictions placed on her because of her gender and her colonialized status. She is good.

Again characterizations of the harem parallel understandings of Muslim heaven. As the faithful soul enters Paradise, he is greeted by houris—who have been awaiting his arrival. Also the afterlife in which the faithful resides is characterized by quiet according to the *Qur'an*. To a busy world filled with noise and distraction, Heaven as a place of peaceful silence provides the ultimate respite. Similarly, in nineteenth-century European society, especially in the burgeoning cities of London or Paris, the ideal bourgeois home offered a relaxing and quiet antidote to the bustle of urban sounds and sights. Such a home was tended by the "Angel in the House," to quote the title of Coventry Patmore's 1854–56 poem idealizing the bourgeois mother and wife, one of the best-selling poems in the Victorian era. Richard Burton compares the harem to a western home, while he cautions that the latter doesn't guarantee happiness:

> It very much resembles a European home composed of a man, his wife, and his mother. And I have seen in the West many a "happy fire-side" fitter to make Miss Martineau's heart ache than any harem in Grand Cairo. (*PNP* 52)

A sense of silence is achieved in some of John Lewis's images of harem women waiting. His uncluttered space and orderly composition have as their intertextual references other "quiet" paintings, specifically those done by the seventeenth-century Dutch artist Johannes Vermeer.

Victorian art is replete with imitations after Dutch masters. The *Art Journal* comments in 1864: "The Dutch School has gained in England, at least since the days of [the artist John] Wilkie [1785–1841], numerous and arduous disciples" (*AJ* 1 June 1864:164). John Ruskin's *Modern Painters* contains several references to the importance of Dutch painting as a model to British artists.

Lewis consciously responded to the Dutch tradition throughout his working life. As a youth he copied Van Ostade and other Dutch masters. While in Spain from 1832 to 1840 he copied the Dutch masters in the Prado.[40] At his death he had seventy-five engravings after Dutch and Flemish masters in his possession.[41] Lewis is also linked to the Dutch by contemporary sources. *Athenaeum* comments about the *Hhareem* (see Plate 1) in 1850: "No interior of Neefs or Steenwyk surpasses the skill with which it is wrought" (*A* 4 May 1850:480). One of his few surviving conversation fragments is reported by the Pre-Raphaelite artist Holman Hunt. Though it is apocryphal, Lewis—portrayed as an irascible, cigar-smoking eccentric—advises that John Millais use the Dutch as a source of inspiration:

> "I intend to take to oil colours myself, and damme, I'll show you how it ought to be done. The illusion of all modern painting is destroyed by its inequality of surface. Hang if this cigar won't draw," and he stopped to give it attention with his penknife. "Holbein's and Janet's paintings are as smooth as plate glass. Why should not yours be equally even?"[42]

Vermeer is recalled in a quiet scene of women waiting, Lewis's 1857 *Harem Life—Constantinople* (see Fig. 3.39), because of the even side lighting, few-figured interior and geometricized room interior. Similarly, in Vermeer's *Girl Reading a Letter at an Open Window* (Fig. 6.10) (c. 1655–60) a woman seen in profile stands facing an open window that reflects her presence. Both scenes are quiet because of the sedentary activity in which the women take part and their relaxed demeanor.

A contradiction arises between the pleasing look of this Lewis painting and a snide critical reaction to it. The *Critic* sees the standing woman as an attendant who "appears to be regaling her mistress's ears with compliment or scandal" (*C* 1857:209). The remark indicates a familiarity with the belief that a harem woman and her (presumed) slave frequently became confidantes.[43] The *Qur'an* promises a double reward in Paradise to the loyal servant who performs her usual duties and also gives good advice to her mistress.[44] However, "compliment or scandal" is hardly the same as good advice, and the *Critic*'s comment serves to trivialize the domestic, whether eastern or western.

Lewis's 1873 harem picture in which the seated woman helps the standing woman put on her jewelry, *In-door Gossip, Cairo, A Scene in a Hareem* (see Fig. 4.56) formally and thematically evokes a work such as Vermeer's *Woman with a Pearl Necklace* (c. 1664) (Fig. 6.11) in which a single standing figure, wearing an ermine-lined yellow jacket, ties the end ribbons of her pearl choker. Even though the title of Lewis's work denotes "gossip," the scene, like Vermeer's, is quiet by virtue of its simple geometricized composition, the women's informal poses and placid facial expressions, and the genre-like activity in which they are involved. This may be a scene of a woman preparing her toilette

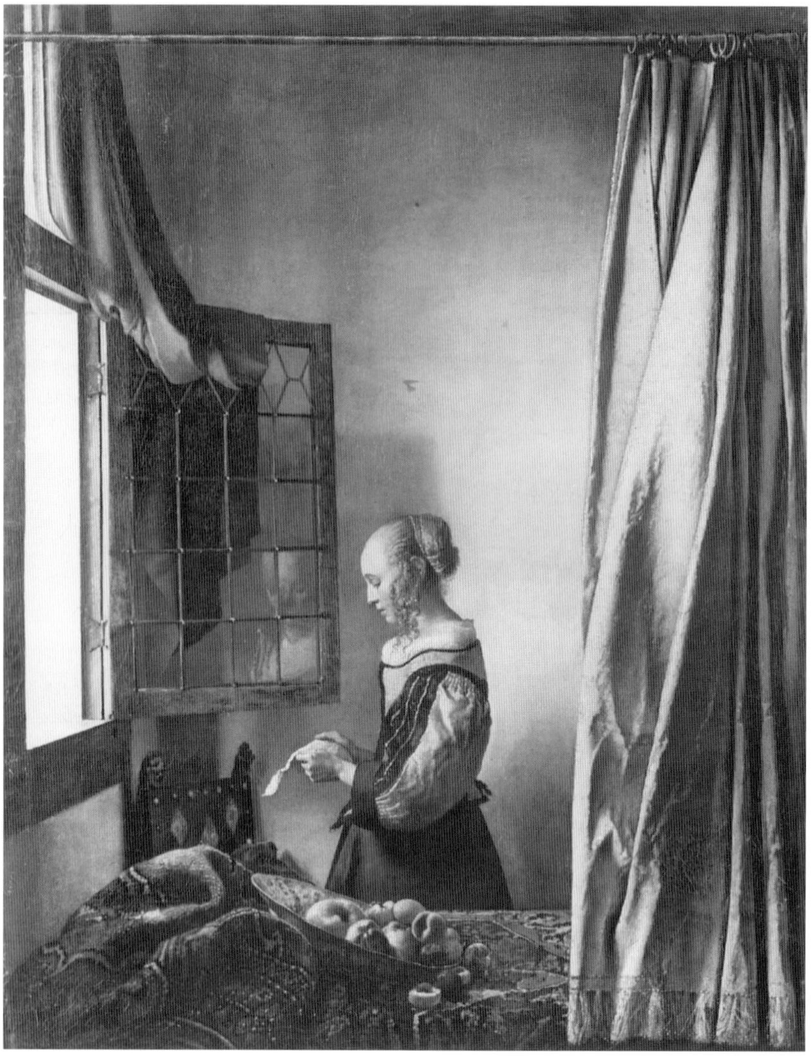

Fig. 6.10. Johannes Vermeer. *Girl Reading a Letter at an Open Window.* Ca. 1657. Gemäldegalerie Alte Meister, Staatliche Kunstsammlungen, Dresden.

before her rendezvous with her master, in which case she awaits his arrival.

Like the Vermeer, another of *In-door Gossip*'s intertextual referents can be found in examining an artistic movement that by 1874 had been inculcated into a respectable tradition, this one indigenously British: the Pre-Raphaelites. The standing woman's body shape echoes that in Millais's *Mariana* (Fig. 6.12), a work fervently attacked by critics in 1851, the year Lewis returned to London eager to absorb the contemporary art scene, and defended by Ruskin in both his letters to the editor of *The Times* that year. Lewis has reversed the woman's direction and changed the color of her dress from blue to red. (Ruskin had called her "the lady in blue" in 1851.) Mariana too awaits her man. The painting *Mariana* was accompanied by four lines from Tennyson's poem of the same title printed in the R.A. catalog. Shakespeare's Mariana in *Measure for Measure* lives isolated in a moated grange for five years pining for an absent Angelo, who broke their engagement after her dowry was lost in a shipwreck. Harem women lived in isolation from other men and were thought to pine away if separated from lost lovers.

Lewis's harem women are well-mannered and composed; their behavior and their lives, like Lewis's compositions, are orderly. His are indeed "well-behaved, demure young damsels," a type of harem woman which reflects one kind of ideal for moral British and French women as well.

Cordial Hostesses

In representations the harem was legitimized by excluding direct reference to the master or sexual

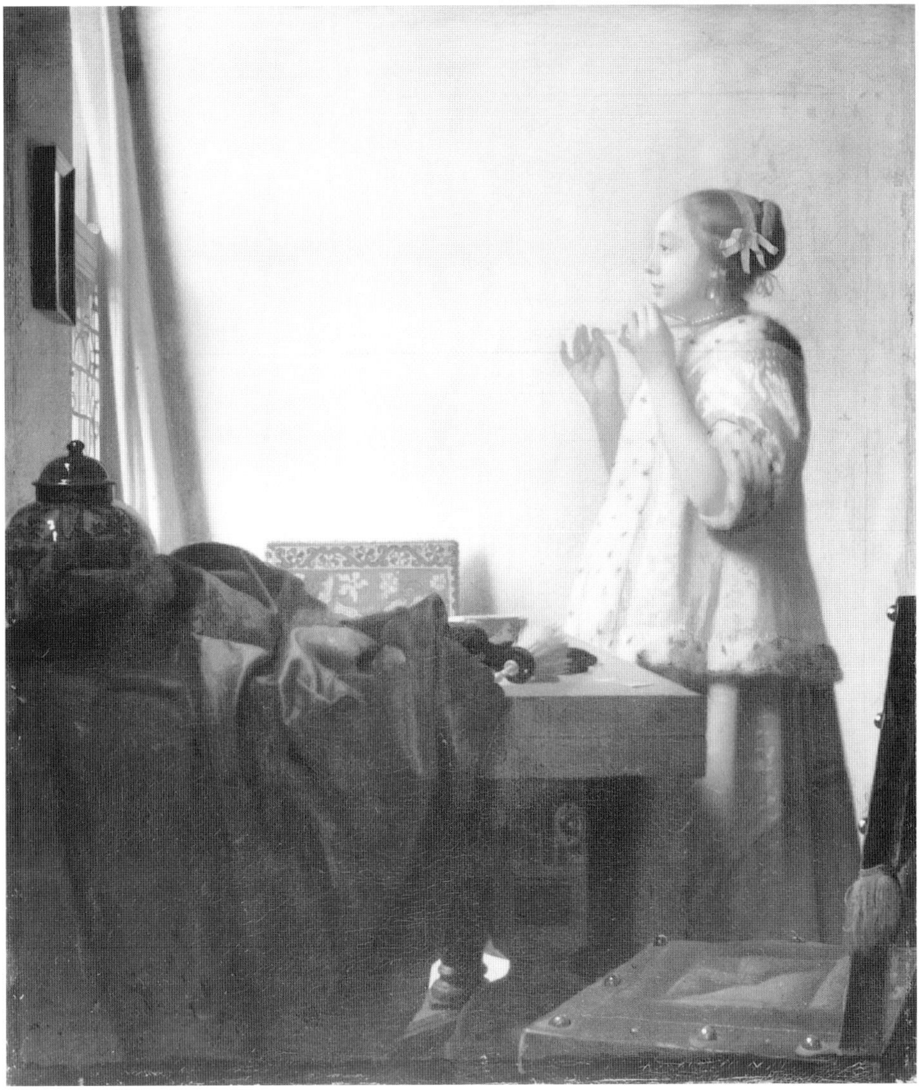

Fig. 6.11. Johannes Vermeer. *Woman with a Pearl Necklace.* Ca. 1664. Staatliche Museen zu Berlin, Preussischer Kulturbesitz, Gemäldegalerie. Photo Jörg P. Anders.

activity. Images of harem hospitality downplay the institution's polygyny and emphasize female civility.[45] The harem woman becomes kindly and solicitous toward her guest, who is a stand-in for the reader-viewer.

For Lady Mary Wortley Montagu the fact that harem women visit each other is proof of their civility. She argues that they are not shut up in a harem, as writers before her had claimed, but they enjoy social intercourse as much as British ladies.[46] In her letters Lady Mary uses the theme of a reception to introduce her description of the Turkish bath, a section made famous by Ingres's having copied them into his Notebook 9. There at the bath Turkish ladies also visit and develop friendships. However, for French nineteenth-century artists the theme of harem women at the bath[47] was much more popular than in-home receptions, as it presented the opportunity to portray harem women nude and on display for the viewer.

The subtitle of Lewis's *Reception* (see Fig. 6.2) reads *A Lady Receiving Visitors: the apartment is the mandarah, the lower floor of the house, Cairo.* Lewis's portrayal of such a civilized subject allows British viewers to witness similarities between their own social conventions and those of harem women. Like Lady Mary, he draws parallels between eastern and western customs. Here harem women are relaxed, well-mannered, and governed by standards of etiquette, as two guests, now unveiled, bow slightly to greet their friend. The main hostess is couched in the central sector of the large, airy gallery. The fountain is turned off, the reflecting

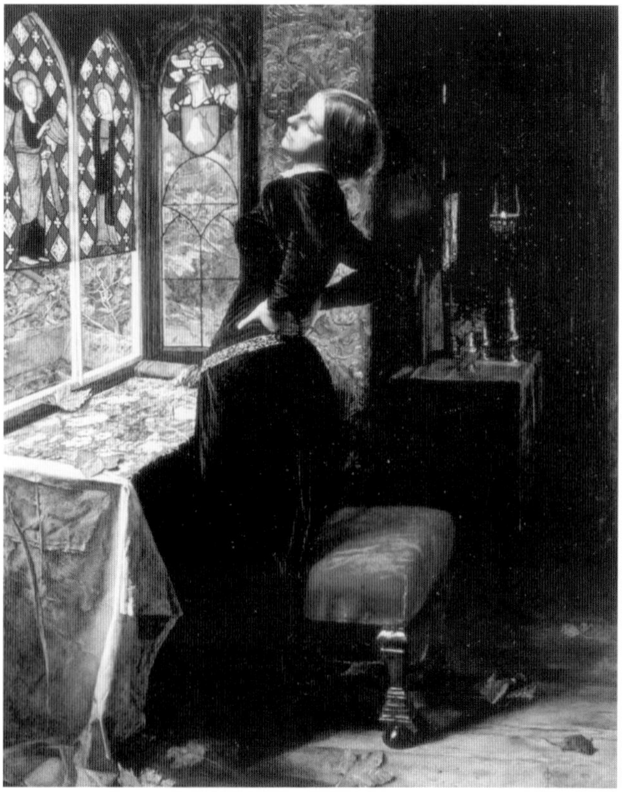

Fig. 6.12. John Everett Millais. *Mariana in the Moated Grange*. 1851. Oil on panel. The Makins Collection/Bridgeman Art Library.

pool calm and inviting. Overall, the environment of the room is a cipher for the women's social privilege. And in portraying visitors to the harem Lewis develops a new parallel for the spectator's position: the viewer can comfortably identify with a friendly female—instead of a lecherous male voyeur, as in the French tradition of harem imagery. Just as the harem has been opened up to the visitors in the picture's narrative, Lewis opens the harem up to light, air—and the beholder.

Critical reaction to Lewis's work was positive. *Athenaeum* favorably compared it to his other work, the very different-looking harem picture, *In-door Gossip* (see Fig. 4.56), also shown at the 1874 R.A., and praised his handling of the figures:

> The figures are capitally painted. Mr. Lewis has produced a much more valuable picture than "In-door Gossip" in the not dissimilar work, *A Lady receiving Visitors, Cairo* (354). The materials are, as usual, the women, their dresses, the sunlight diaper [. . .] and other characteristic features. [. . .] [T]he picture [. . .] is, like all the others, intensely solid. (*A* 30 May 1874:740)

Similarly the *Times* describes the largest picture, *Reception*, at some length while barely mentioning the two smaller indoor and outdoor gossip pictures. Why the critics preferred *Reception* to *In-door Gossip* is not spelled out. Perhaps its expansive, stagelike setting afforded the viewer a pleasant distraction from Lewis's usual "close up" presentation of harem women. The detailed fountain and the panoramic interior are motifs which allowed Lewis to display his astounding technique and allowed the reviewers more distance from the social issues suggested by the harem theme, issues that must have been outdated by the mid-1870s.

Appearing two years before Lewis's picture, a description of a reception in the harem (written, we are told, by a woman whose husband was a high-ranking eastern official) might serve as caption to it:

> During those fetes I remained in the palace, where the ladies of the principal dignitaries of the city came to call on me; it is usual in the East to do so at the time of the chief solemnities of the year. My fair visitors belonged to the most diverse nationalities: Moors, with light hair and fair complexions; Arabs, with their expression full of pride; Georgians and Circassians, with regular and pleasing features. All brought their narghiles, or pipes; they seated themselves in a circle round me, and we passed out time agreeably, chatting together with the utmost freedom; for all etiquette is banished from conversations among women.[48]

This scene she describes seems pleasant enough—and it parallels the relaxed atmosphere of Lewis's painting. But the comment that etiquette is ignored is a sign that all is not well. The female visitors try to cajole their hostess to do favors for them and their male relatives, even offering bribes. No such portent interferes with the pleasantness of Lewis's scene.

Obedient Servants of God: Nuns

Drawing on reports from the seventeenth century,[49] Lady Mary Wortley Montagu compares harem women's quarters to nunneries (*L* 1:342). Vivant Denon, observing eastern women fully veiled, compares their dress to "the dismal costume of a nun of the order of penitents."[50] In the early Victorian era Sophie Lane Poole writes that harem discipline "can only be compared to that which is established in the convent."[51] Several other Victorian writers draw the comparison between harem women and nuns, countering the erroneous notion of rampant sexuality in the harem and in effect advocating a set of ideals for proper female behavior in the period.[52]

In its theme and compositional structure Lewis's *In the Bey's Garden, Asia Minor* (Fig. 6.13) shown at

material stuff found there. In this context as well some gorgeous pictures by John Lewis require scrutiny; their narratives allow for an analysis of class conflict. And these harem pictures provided the opportunity for art critics within highly stratified British society to express rather conservative attitudes toward class.

"[P]urely natural without the intervention of the expedients of art." This is how the *Art Journal* compliments Lewis's *In the Bey's Garden* (see Fig. 6.13) (*AJ* July 1865:156).[65] This intriguing comment has multilayered implications. Most obviously, this is an aesthetic judgment related to Lewis's technique. This "natural" work has a high degree of verisimilitude and is evenly handled: the artist has used a comparable amount of detailing throughout. The work's "natural" quality may also refer to its subject. The woman is surrounded by foliage, potted on our right but still relatively natural on our left. Moreover, Wollstonecraft distinguished the ethical ("natural") middle class from the corrupt ("artificial") aristocracy (*VRW* 81). Does this woman, wealthy but still "natural," serve to defy the class-based condemnation of the harem issued by the likes of Wollstonecraft?

In the debate on harem slavery the natural/artificial issue can be stated in this way: Is harem polygyny natural—a legitimate form of social organization? Or is it unnatural—aberrant and morally reprehensible? Nineteenth-century thinkers wrestled with freshly articulated and related binary categories of normal and pathological, licit and illicit sexuality.[66] If this kind of discourse relates here, then of course the critic's comment about the picture's "natural" quality suggests the harem's legitimacy as a social system.

In *Bouquet/Lilies and Roses* (see Fig. 6.5) Lewis's harem woman is unequivocally of the privileged class. The pose of the statuesque woman, her small hands and fussy dress are ciphers for the elegant refinement of the privileged. The *Art Journal* confirms this presentation of an upper-class woman: the picture "represent[s] one of the most distinguished inmates of the harem of some wealthy pacha" (*AJ* 1858:162). She is not a "wild"[67] beauty, as we saw in Lewis's *Circassian* (see Fig. 2.6), but a composed woman whose body proportions suggest slow and measured movements appropriate to her social station.

In *Bey's Garden* the woman cuts flowers, cultivated in the artificial Nature of a garden. She puts them into a tall vase, decorated (simulacrum-like) with an image of one of the same flowers it holds, a large red poppy. The vase in itself is an artificial means of sustenance; it serves, like the harem woman, as an indoor ornament. Thus the woman here does to the flowers what has been done to her: severed from her origins, she is carefully selected on the basis of her beauty and expected to survive in an artificially created environment (the harem) as an object for display. The woman is a flower that has been carefully selected early in life, well-tended, isolated, and guarded until bloom/consummation—characteristic of the stages of female protection among the most privileged classes. She is a flower, and with the other ladies of the harem—other flowers—they comprise a "bouquet," one of the titles of Fig. 6.5.

Elite class associations are also suggested by the flowers in the title, lilies and roses, both of which are rare and can require cultivation. The rose is named a symbol for gentility in two dictionaries of flower language dating from the 1870s.[68] As for the white lilies, Forbes Watson (1840–69), the artist and naturalist noted by Ruskin, calls them "large queenly flowers."[69] Alternately, the lily, the old Christian symbol of Mary's virginity, is mixed with the metaphor of roses in full bloom, the symbol of ripe female sexuality.[70] If this picture is considered a portrayal of a houri, then the combination of lilies and roses can have symbolic meaning: the ethical purity of the deceased soul is rewarded by sexual fulfilment in Paradise (according to one interpretation of the nature of heaven).[71] The houri embodies purity (lilies) and love (roses).

The woman's aristocratic elegance is a theme in *Bey's Garden*'s form and content. She works at tending her garden, but her labor is only that of a hobbyist.[72] The slight bow of her head and hunch of her shoulders indicate that she stoops just enough to do her job but not enough to disturb her turban or dress, which resembles the costume worn in Lewis's earlier harem pictures *Life in the Harem, Cairo* (1858) (see Fig. 3.2) and Lane's illustration, *A Lady in the Dress Worn in Private* (Fig. 6.16) (*ME* 1:52).[73] Despite her labor, she is still an elegant lady. Paradoxically, her refinement is heightened by her manual effort. Elegance is clearly Lewis's concern in carefully indicating the thick folds of her finery, as her hem drags along the dirt path. *Athenaeum* confirms this graceful—and courtly—reading calling her "a Circassian damsel, fair after her fashion, a model of grace in action" (*A* 6 May 1865:626). The *Times*'s use of the word "stately" is also a cipher for high-class standing, as the newspaper correlates the woman to the flower in Lewis' *Lilium Auratum* (see Fig. 6.3): "a stately golden lily" in the center of the composition is carried by "a stately Eastern lady" (*T* 21 May 1872:7).

As in *Bouquet/Lilies and Roses* those two types of flowers are prominent in *Bey's Garden*.[74] Other flowers featured in the latter painting have upper-class symbolic readings. Fuchsias, visible to the right of the woman's gown, indicate "taste," more specifically,

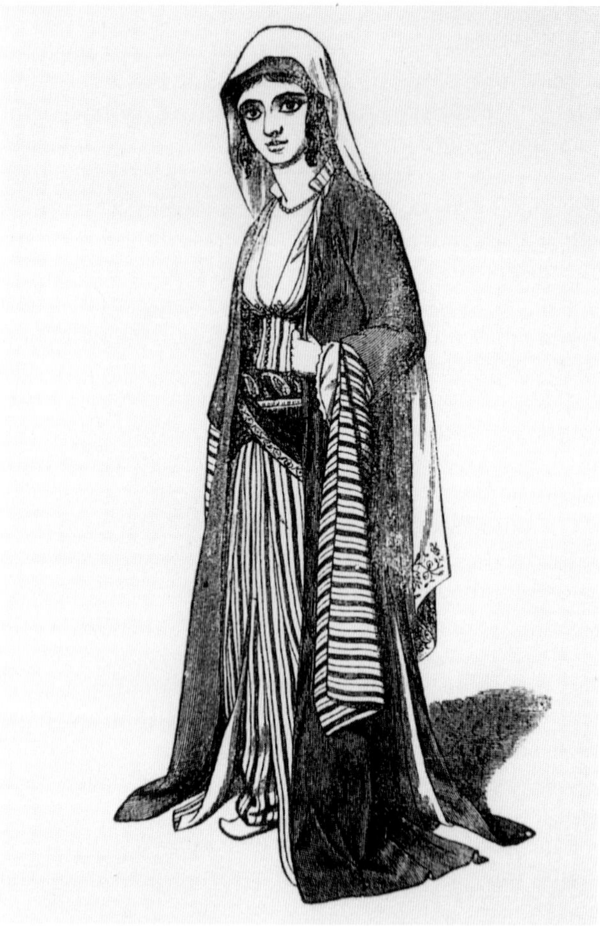

Fig. 6.16. Edward William Lane. *A Lady in the Dress Worn in Private.* Engraving. *Manners and Customs of the Modern Egyptians*, 1836. Photo Adam Miller.

"elegan[ce], with ease," according to the same two nineteenth-century flower dictionaries mentioned above. Similarly, the single geranium placed on a step close to the front of the picture plane indicates "preference." The flower that is arguably the most prominent, placed to the left of the woman's head, is the red poppy. An 1877 flower dictionary declares the scarlet poppy symbolizes "fantastic extravagance,"[75] an apt description for both the array of garden flowers shown and, by reputation, the harem itself.

The meticulous—indeed loving—rendering of the harem women's clothing and the formal emphasis given it in nearly all of Lewis's pictures encourage the viewer's admiration of the harem lifestyle which allows such lavish outlay of resources. Lewis returned to England in 1851 with Egyptian costumes that were used in harem pictures until 1876. The exoticism of the dress is assured by the articulation of the complex layering of the clothing system and by the unusual color schemes and fabrics. Such ethnic dress suggests unchanging tradition and an underlying cultural essentialism.[76] But are these clothes authentically eastern? Turkish and Egyptian raw materials exported to Britain included silk and wool, valonia (an acorn extract), and madder root. The latter two substances were used to produce dyes. And Britain used eastern markets to sell manufactured goods, including textiles. Thus whether the clothing was eastern or English is an open question.

The effect of such voluminous clothing is also an endorsement of conspicuous consumption (both eastern and western). Like the advertising in early Victorian fashion plates, these pictures offer the promise of pleasure to potential consumers. Here the pleasure of looking at beautiful women in stunning garb can also substitute for the pleasure of owning either. That these pictures name the natural entitlement of the wealthy can reflect positively onto the women depicted. Like well-to-do families who have "shopped around" for a well-placed man who could take good care of their eligible daughters in marriage, these women have done well. Lewis's pictures can be viewed as a congratulations on the successful marriage of the wealthy—whether eastern or western.

Alternatively, the woman Lewis paints in *Bouquet/Lilies and Roses* is restrained by the boundaries of the harem and its garden. The latticework gate at right subtly reminds the viewer that a walk in the garden is only a temporary freedom. In the related *Lilium Auratum* (see Fig. 6.3) the two females leave the bright sunlight, seen in the upper right corner, and are about to ascend the step leading into the shaded interior. The high, impregnable wall, visible at the left, is a reminder to the viewer of the relentless pattern of return following each outing. Their facial expressions indicate the equanimity with which they accept their life of confinement. Or perhaps they entirely defy the conception of confinement as loss of freedom. In Lewis's "luxurious prisons" the emphasis is on luxury; that they happen to be confined can be forgotten.

These pictures of harem women by Lewis seem to suggest the acceptability of harem life, because it is rarefied and extravagant. Unlike Wollstonecraft's text that rails against aristocratic privilege, these elegant images display social privilege as the highest ideal of feminine desirability. And as such the women portrayed—whether harem ladies or houris—are "good" in their complicity with a system that rewards the deserving. These are the social winners. This group of Lewis's paintings provoke a rationale for eastern material success that sounds a lot like western capitalism's.

Things Are Not What They Seem: "Good" Harem Women and Readings of *Memento mori*

Up to this point, the images of harem women presented in this chapter have been considered positive depictions of the eastern Other. That view gets complicated when the possibility arises that some of the seemingly pleasant pictures may contain a *memento mori*, reminder of death. Then a pleasing image about feminine desirability evolves into a frightening morality tale about the moral corruption of the beauty and pleasure of the harem institution over time.[77] Such an interpretation affects a number of harem pictures. Whether such a gloss registered with some nineteenth-century viewers is only tentatively suggested in the works' documentation.

The *memento mori* is relevant to nineteenth-century ideas about harem women in a number of ways. First of all, in Islam and Christianity heaven and hell are opposites, and each is necessary for the construction of the other. As the *Qur'an* promises, a component of the pleasure of Paradise is the knowledge that the pain of hell has been averted. Correspondingly, every detail of the joy of the Muslim garden prompts a reminder of the specter of hell's flames.[78] That paradisiacal images would have horrific overtones is in keeping with perceptions about the interconnections of pleasure and pain which characterize both Muslim and Christian theology.

Secondly, visitors to the harem often returned to England to comment on the early age at which high-ranking Turkish or Egyptian girls were betrothed. Promised as young as age seven, they were married at the onset of puberty. Travelers reported that harem women are "used up" at an early age and that their beauty fades early (*ME* 1:44), often by age thirty. Relatedly, observers lamented what they perceived as the absence of a lifelong love and sex commitment to a single woman, who stood being abandoned as a result of the pasha's mercurial tastes.

Wollstonecraft applied this same conception to western women of leisure. She warned them of the fleeting nature of men's adoration and women's hollow-based power:

> And why do they [women] not discover, when "in the noon of beauty's power," that they are treated like queens only to be deluded by hollow respect, till they are led to resign, or not assume, their natural prerogatives. [. . .] They will smile—yes, they will smile, though told that: "In beauty's empire is no mean,/And woman, either slave or queen,/Is quickly scorned when not adored." But the adoration comes first, and the scorn is not anticipated. (*VRW* 145–46)

This theme of present favor and future abandonment in the harem is explicitly presented in Achille Devéria's 1834–38 *Turcs* (see Fig. 4.4).[79] To a scene of a half-nude harem woman (*à la* Ingres's *Grande Odalisque*) seated with a very interested pasha the caption reads: "Adored today and left tomorrow." The print offers several readings. Apart from its title, the image offers the visual pleasure of a naked female body being appreciated in the work's narrative, and by us, as the work's viewer. Yet its caption seems to contend that beauty offers only fleeting pleasure and a woman should not rely on her physical charms to catch a man she cannot hold. Moreover, only monogamous marriage guarantees a woman protection against abandonment and the loneliness of old age. But the print suggests that it is more divorce and less polygyny that is of interest to the West. Indeed, while polygyny was rare in the East, divorce was relatively easy and commonplace.[80] This print can be read as a criticism of European divorce by comparing the harsh pasha to the rich bourgeois who could afford to divorce his wife in England.

Often images that function as *memento mori* about the harem's pleasures rely on flower symbolism such as the 1854 pendants done by Régnier after Constant Joseph Brochart, *Séraphita* and *Saidah* (see Figs. 5.13 and 5.14). Séraphita, who strikes a classical pose, is the young virgin, fresh as the blooming flower decorating her unpinned hair, symbol of her maidenhood. Saidah, on the other hand, carries spent flowers. She playfully blows one gone to seed while two more have withered in her hands. She has a low-cut *décolletage*, and her hair has been artificially crimped. These are not individuals but types of eastern women, akin to the foolish and wise virgins. The prints may be alluding to the loss of girlish innocence that reputedly occurs at an early age in the harem. The virgin and the woman can be read as the before and after stages in the life of a haremite who is forced to mate too soon.

In some harem pictures the butterfly functions as a *memento mori*, a symbol used (again) in the seventeenth- and eighteenth-century Dutch still life tradition, for example, at the lower left in Rachel Ruysch's undated *Flowers in a Vase* (Fig. 6.17), where it suggests the rebirth or freeing of the Christian soul following death and decay.[81] But in other harem pictures it simply suggests freedom that harem women do not have. A live butterfly appears in a lithograph done after Bourdet, the 1836 *La femme esclave* (see Fig. 4.51) where it functions like the harem bird, as a foil for the slave, equally pretty but quite unfree. Lewis used butterflies to symbolize the temporary freedom of the women in *An Arab Scribe, Cairo*, shown at the OWCS in 1852 and illustrated

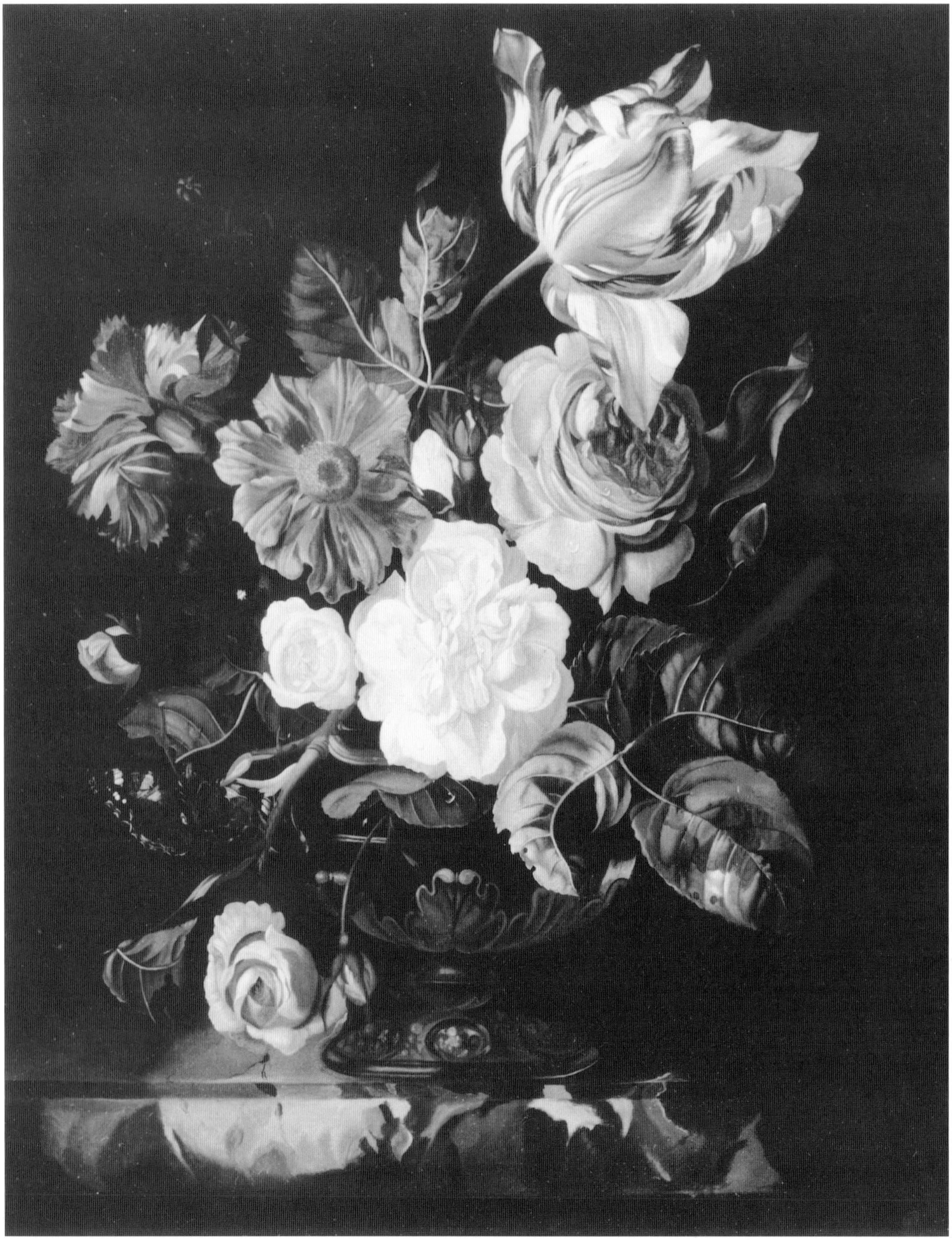

Fig. 6.17. Rachel Ruysch. *Flowers in a Vase*. N.d. The National Museum of Women in the Arts, Gift of Wallace and Wilhelmina Holladay.

in the *Art Journal* in 1858, a picture of an Egyptian lady and a slave girl on an outing from their usual confinement.

The butterfly is a *memento mori* in several of Lewis's other works. As mentioned above, there is a popular Islamic belief that the butterfly transports the faithful to heaven; this may be the significance of the butterflies, dead and alive, in Lewis's *In the Bey's Garden* (see Fig. 6.13). Another butterfly functions symbolically in Lewis' *"And the Prayer of Faith Shall Save the Sick"* (see Fig. 4.40) 1872. Fluttering very close to the ground in the center of the composition, it is a harbinger of the sick harem woman's death. At the same time, of course, it functions as a charming curiosity and as a *tour de force* of Lewis's astounding mimetic painting technique.

The *memento mori* of Lewis's *Lilium Auratum* (see Fig. 6.3) centers around its unusual title. In botany *lilium auratum* is a species of lily streaked with golden rays which Lewis has included in a vase in the picture. The title refers to both the flowers and the centrally placed woman. The title's English translation, "golden lily," can be a reference to the expression "to gild the lily," meaning to adorn unnecessarily something that nature has already made beautiful. This harem woman is so lovely that the luxury heaped upon her by doting, wealthy masters is needless extravagance. So in this picture the floral surroundings and rich robes are superfluous.

But the painting *Lilium Auratum* is not titled *Golden Lily*. Lewis's use of an archaic language elicits the older, archaic meaning of "gild" provided in the *Oxford English Dictionary*, that is, to gloss over or attempt to beautify the appearance of something basically corrupt. Given the largely negative view of the harem in Victorian society, this painting gilds "the lily"—the harem woman—by improving her image. This does not necessarily mean that Lewis agrees that harem women are basically corrupt; we have no hard documentation of his attitudes toward the harem. It could mean that his picture acknowledges their unfortunate reputation. His translation of the English phrase into Latin is an affectation, as the expression did not exist in that ancient language.[82] By latinizing the title Lewis lends an erudition and a sophistication to his painting, a verbal aestheticizing.

Additional levels of significance for Lewis's *Lilium Auratum* are suggested by the writings of John Ruskin, which are full of references to lilies. In *Stones of Venice* (1st edition 1851) he remarks on the beauty and the uselessness of the lily (*W* 9:72); both are qualities commonly attributed to harem women in nineteenth-century texts. Ruskin mentions the word *lilium* several times in his writing, most notably in *Prosperina*, which contains his botanical classification and study of flowers. In the genealogy section of that piece Ruskin proposes an odd association of evil with eschatology for the Latin form of *lilium* in his system of plant nomenclature:

> (iii) The neuter names terminating in 'um' will always indicate some power either of active or suggestive evil (Conium, Salanum, Satyrium), or a relation, more or less definite, to death; but this relation to death may sometimes be noble, or pathetic,—'which to-day is, and to-morrow is cast into the oven,'—Lilium. (*W* 25:345)

In light of Ruskin's text,[83] Lewis's title *Lilium Auratum* suggests that despite its shadowy reputation, the harem had a noble side personified by "stately" harem ladies.

Ruskin here links the word *lilium* to death, prompting again a reading of Lewis's picture which has the word in its title as a *memento mori*. This reading can be developed still further by examining the fuller citation from the gospel, which Ruskin partially quotes, also a lily metaphor (Matthew 6:28–30):

> Consider how the lilies grow in the fields; they do not work, they do not spin; and yet, I tell you, even Solomon in all his splendour was not attired like one of these. But if that is how God clothes grass in the fields, which is there today, and tomorrow is thrown on the stove, will he not all the more clothe you? How little faith you have!

The lessons of the passage are that faith is more important than labor and that (spiritual) beauty is God-given. But Ruskin's extrapolation of the word *lilium* based on this passage interprets it from another angle: not only is the beauty of lilies short-lived, but their profound beauty is essentially a *memento mori*.

The same biblical passage is obliquely integrated into Mary Wollstonecraft's *Vindication* in reference to the aristocratic woman. Her conclusion is likewise negative: that a life of complete leisure is no life at all and is akin to selling one's soul: "It is true they are provided with food and raiment, for which they neither toil nor spin; but health, liberty, and virtue are given in exchange" (*VRW* 146).

In *Lilium Auratum* is Lewis commenting that harem women are "used" only until their beauty fades? And that the woman pictured here would later be abandoned? Does this pattern of neglecting harem women reflect a failure of the harem institution? If one locus for the work's meanings is in the critical reaction to this work, *Lilium Auratum* may indeed be about the pointlessness of physical beauty. The *Times* gives a slightly different twist to this issue by applying it not to the ideas in the paintings but to Lewis's work practices. That critic believes that aesthetic diligence was put into a picture which fails to make any substantive point (or perhaps have a narrative): "But except brightness and finish, what fruit is here of all this patience and labour?" (*T* 21 May 1872:7). Lewis's title subtly acknowledges some of the critical conceptions of harem women, while the pleasantness of the picture itself counters those ideas.

The Interdependence of Positive and Negative Stereotyping

In these pictures of the good harem woman, the bad press she is often given is countered, in effect. The jealous, indolent, intriguing female is replaced by the happy, well-groomed, respectable lady. The intertextual referents of these works lend a modest purity to the women represented; the pictures only obliquely allude to their sexuality (though critics may bring a disapproving reading to the works). "Good" harem women are incorporated into Christian (and occasionally Islamic) traditions that have been granted artistic authority and religious respectability, a correlation which some critics did recognize. The result is a view of the harem in which a rarified femininity is removed from social or political strife. The pleasure she brings for the master and the viewer lies in the *promise* of erotic delights. The pictures recount in careful detail the presumed knowledge of that good femininity. Yet I maintain that even the notion of the good harem woman is inherently ambivalent.

Pictures of immoral and moral harem women can be understood apart from this strict diametrical opposition. Other kinds of difference interfere with a reading of the good-bad dichotomy. Even within the same category of harem women as evil / actively desirous / disorderly (the more plentiful images), the pictures are stylistically different from each other ranging from precise mimesis to a Romantic sketchiness. Correspondingly, representations of "bad" harem women may be philosophically different (spanning positivist rationality to exotic antirationality). There may be differences between the British and French schools. Harem pictures of "evil" women may differ from each other in format (book illustration, single-leaf popular "girlie pin-up" or Royal Academy submission). And such images may differ in the conditions of reception. Internal factors that affect reception include artistic conscious and unconscious choices and can be located in the final picture. External factors derive from the historical moment (regarding abolition, colonialism, servant-master relations, "the women question") which contribute to the way of looking shared by an audience or particular to an individual viewer.

Still, negative and positive representations of the harem represent flip sides of the same coin of objectification minted by cultural condescension. Whether the judgment is positive or negative, it originates in the western-based values and thinking of the evaluator. That the harem is even considered fair game for inquiry is part of a more generalized colonial intrusiveness. The private is opened and becomes revealed as the stuff of public discourse and critical dissection. The harem becomes a newsy commodity in nineteenth-century England and France, a trendy topic of conversation and cultural production having great entertainment value, even though that moment of newness has a long history. Whether the harem is represented positively or negatively, western European mores are left intact by comparison. A recognition of difference fails to dislodge any perceived truths about the status quo; attitudes towards race, gender, class, colonialism—power in many of its manifestations at home or abroad—is unmitigated and in fact reasserted, buttressed by representations of an inherently inferior social structure that cannot compare favorably to the West.

Perhaps positive representations of harem women act as legitimation of the harem institution, proof that it is as good as Christian monogamy? Even these relativist images presume a frame of reference, an approach, that is not Muslim. Granted, to attempt to understand the Other in terms of the Self is inevitable, but it is inevitably flawed. For all their beauty, ease, and sensory appeal, positive images construct harem women according to the constraints and roles afforded western women. These pictures represent women whose agency is subordinated to methods of western repression and excision. They are slim fragments indeed of uncountable numbers of women reduced to innocuous types which are given servile, decorative functions. The attempt to know, and produce a knowledge about, the overwhelming complexity of other human societies is deeply problematic. Whether positive or negative, conclusions about "the Turkish woman," "the Algerian woman," "the Egyptian woman," or "the harem woman" serve to express a power of discipline and surveillance that typifies colonialism.[84]

Basic theoretical formulations of Self and Other are interdependent. But how could the harem woman be both desired and feared? What accounts for the pairing of the harem women *Séraphita*, the modest virgin, and *Saidah*, the loose prostitute? At a deeper level, the positive and negative stereotypes of the colonial Other are also interdependent, as Homi Bhabha has argued.[85] This is based on Freud's contribution to understanding the dynamics of fetishism. The defining subject experiences a "double attitude" toward the fetish object, having reactions that involve both worship and castration. That the fetishist worships the fetish object is understandable, since it protects him from acknowledging his castration anxiety. The fetish object makes him feel good and thus is good. That the fetishist is also antagonistic towards the fetish object is more difficult to comprehend. This Freud explains by the little boy's belief that his father has violently caused his mother's "castrated" (penisless) state, and if he strongly identifies with his father, he replicates that violent castration on fetishes, "either actually or in phantasy." The woman *whom he constructs* as actively desirous rather than a nurturing mother reminds him of his own potential castration, and she must be disempowered. I propose that the "double attitude" of fetishists described by Freud and further developed by Homi Bhabha to describe colonialist stereotyping provides at least a partial explanatory model for the profound ambivalence of nineteenth-century French and British culture toward harem representations.

One last comment of Freud's is useful in understanding the admixture of positive and negative stereotypes about the harem woman, sometimes one more than the other, depending on how it is framed—by artist, country, medium, and historical moment—but occurring simultaneously: "Tender and hostile treatment of fetishes is mixed in unequal degrees—like the denial and the recognition of castration—in different cases, so that the one or the other is more evident."[86] Here he recognizes that there is "great tenacity" in the struggle between two attitudes, a tension that produces movement and meaning. That Freud uses the term "tenacity" in describing the fetishist's process suggests his acknowledgment of the subject's inventiveness and ability to accommodate his needs within the world. In this critical study, I want to encourage appreciation for the profundity, the complexity, and the necessity of practices of viewer identification—of self and other, of male and female, of Christian and Muslim—provoked by the harem representation, without endorsing the racism and misogyny they imply. This energized movement ("motility"[87]) between the stereotypes or attitudes of tenderness and hostility toward the harem woman is an extremely productive tension, as it contributes to the construction of an historical phenomenon evident in arenas of culture, art, politics, and society as well as psychology.

7
Conclusions

The End of the Phenomenon of the Harem Representation

In the first three-quarters of the nineteenth century many of the structures of the harem representation identified in this study remained in place, as the preceding chapters have hopefully demonstrated. At the same time, variations on these themes occurred in response to social and political events. Around 1870 the harem representation undergoes a paradigmatic shift marked by a skepticism[1] on the part of artists and critics. By this year the harem institution itself has declined, as has Ottoman slavery more broadly. The harem picture is read as formulaic and hollow in the very era when the colonialist process intensifies.

In Egypt in the 1870s polygyny suffered, as there was a loss of rationale for slavery generally in light of broad social and political changes.[2] As for the harem, Tucker's judgment is that it had mostly a vestigial, symbolic function in nineteenth-century Egypt; its loss in economic significance parallels the decline in power of the private household, as the state apparatus strengthens first under Muhammed Ali and then under the British. Slaves provided physical niceties and pleasures in the nineteenth-century elite home in Egypt, but they were hardly a source of significant political power for their owners.[3] Tucker writes that the surprise is that harem slavery continued as long as it did into the nineteenth century and attributes this to a view of female service and inferiority which coincided with notions of women's place imported from Europe.[4] In Turkey and the vestiges of the Ottoman Empire, polygamy and the male prerogative in divorce were officially ended in 1924,[5] though in some parts of the world the harem continues as a highly rarefied institution even today.[6]

In British diplomacy there is a final sputter of British activism in 1874, an attempt to intervene on behalf of white harem women in a departure from England's noninterventionist policy. From about 1872 to 1874 the British government hears cries of protest from male Circassians against harem masters. When the ambassador in Constantinople, Sir Henry Elliot, learns in 1873 that slave families were being broken up at their sale, he demands that Turkey's foreign minister, Halil Pasha, reconsider the issue. Once again the Turks reassert that how they kept their women was not the business of foreign diplomats. And no significant policy changes result from Elliot's initiative.[7]

How much of the historical events in British diplomacy and whether the changes in the institutions of the harem and slavery directly affected the artists, writers, and their consumers cannot be documented. Still in the art worlds centered around London and Paris the new critique of mimesis called for a rethinking of stylistic precision with a more personal and subjective vision. In London a distrust of the mimetic agenda surfaces in examining the highlights of the critical reaction to John Lewis's harem pictures of the 1870s, responses which suggest a waning public interest in the harem picture. In the new Parisian art of Courbet, Manet, and the early Impressionists mimesis was being questioned for its ability to promote natural expression. This occurs in a period on the cusp of the Franco-Prussian War and the Commune, events which had a profound effect on the nature of subsequent French art, as Albert Boime has demonstrated.[8] There is a group of proto-Impressionist paintings of the harem made in Paris around 1870, which have never been considered as a whole until now. They were done by some of the artists who would become the Impressionists whose first exhibition dates to 1874, artists whom Albert Boime has defined as "moderate republicans."[9] Because the harem implied social privilege in the East and could be supported only by the wealthiest men, it could also serve as a reminder of French class privilege, which was itself under scrutiny in the public discourses in 1870–71.

Britain: The Critical Reaction to Lewis's Late Harem Painting

Given the uneasy relationship to the truth which the harem picture had always had in England and

France, this new crisis of representation had serious implications for the viability of the harem picture. The positivist aesthetic is empty by 1872 as articulated by the *Illustrated London News* in response to Lewis's *Lilium Auratum* (see Fig. 6.3). The reviewer wants more than technical fidelity to nature, an ideal that had been considered inherently truthful. Now the newspaper is ambivalent about verisimilitude as an end in itself. The flowers and other details create "the extreme of possible decoration" that is "ornamental," and an effect which is true. But the reviewer "cannot accept" the principles the artist has adopted. "Fine art" requires more "artistic interpretation" and a grasping of "the more central or generalized facts of relative aspect and impression." What Lewis's technique provides is "little more than hard, toilsome, piecemeal copyism." This harem picture appeals only to the sense of wonder we experience as children playing with visual illusions and color in a mirror, a kaleidoscope, or a camera (*ILN* 25 May 1872:502). According to this critic, the aesthetic positivism of Lewis's harem picture is superficial.

The *Times*'s review of this picture makes some of the same points. After praising Lewis's "carefulness and eye-deceiving effect" it asks "But except brightness and finish, what fruit is there of all this patience and labour?" (*T* 21 May 1872:7). Both critics expect that art be less descriptive and more interpretive, generalized, and subjective. And that mimesis be put in the service of an end goal.

Two years later the critics claimed to be bored with Lewis's type of harem picture when he exhibited *In-door Gossip* (see Fig. 4.56) with two others at the R.A. that year—its pendant, *Outdoor Gossip, Cairo*, which is not a harem scene, and *Reception* (see Fig. 6.2), which is. The *Art Journal* complains about *In-door Gossip*'s sameness: the artist's "narrow range of subject" and his willingness "to reproduce each time with fresh care and more studious labour" patterns of sunlight in an "eastern" interior. It continues that the titles of his harem pictures change but the effects of light on the canvas are "well-known." More bitingly, "Figures are introduced, but they have no more significance than is afforded by the colour of the garments they wear" (*AJ* 13 1874:200). This impatience with his harem subject's lack of real "significance" is noteworthy. It says, in essence, that Lewis no longer communicates anything about harem women. Now they are viewed only as mannequins on which he displays his technique. Such commentary suggests a saturation with pictorial and verbal impressions about harem women. This is confirmed in the scathing commentary by the *Athenaeum* regarding *In-door Gossip*:

> [It] shows women chattering, with the usual harem accompaniments, dazzling effects, plump, rosy female faces and exuberant forms, with the apparently inexhaustible wardrobe of the artist's *atelier*. The effect of sunlight falling on the room, chequered by shadows of lattice, is given with the painter's usual felicity. We enjoy the other picture *Outdoor Gossip, Cairo* much more heartily. It is something like a novelty to have nothing to do with the plump women of that rather tiresome hareem, the glitter of the everlasting sunlight dispersed by trellis shadows, and lying on the brocade, silks, satins, pavements and what not, of Mr. Lewis's Oriental paradise. Here we are out of scents, away from the stupid houris. (*A* 31 May 1874:740)

The *Athenaeum* no longer objects just to the subject of the harem, the "stupid houris," but also to Lewis's hackneyed treatment of it. Exotic clothing is no longer a cipher of race but an artist's prop. Worn thin by repetition and pitched to an audience whose expectations have changed, the positivist-based harem representation is no longer considered successful.

Lewis painted three more harem pictures before his death in 1876, itself another landmark in the periodization of the harem picture phenomenon. One of the three, *Houri* (see Fig. 4.13) is not like his usual kind of few-figured harem scene; he has eliminated the "plump" type of woman, the sunlight effects, even the "felicity" in this relatively harsh image. As explored earlier, this is hardly a heavenly figure but a representation of a harem woman as prostitute which is indebted to Manet's 1865 *Olympia*. The harem woman has become a prostitute in English painting.

France: Pre-Impressionist "Modern" Harem Painting

Likewise in France there is a crisis in representing the harem, judging by the rash of images produced from 1868–70 by three artists in particular: Jean Frédéric Bazille, Pierre Auguste Renoir, and Edouard Manet. The class politics which surfaced in the upheavals of 1870–71 made the representation of the harem, a subject grounded in a privileged society, highly problematic for these young artists with interest in republican politics.[10] Their central dilemma seems to have been how to paint a new harem picture, one which acknowledged the Romantic tradition but reworked it in a way that was contemporary. By the late 1860s the harem was a traditional subject painted by revered masters of the past including Ingres and Delacroix. But conservative defenders of the academic status quo such as Gérôme also painted harem scenes, including *Moorish Bath* in 1870 (see Fig. 5.10) and *Slave Market* in 1871 (see Fig. 3.12). In addition, a new view of the painting of the nude female body had been advanced by the incendiary artist and anarchist, Gustave Courbet, at least one of whose works from the 1860s has, arguably, "harem" overtones.[11] Manet's *Olympia* of 1865, a work which T. J. Clark has called "the founding monument of modern art,"[12] elicited a scandal among art critics and had reverberations for any artist painting a female nude for at least the next decade. Caught between such competing art-politics, these proto-Impressionist painters of the harem had to tread carefully, attentive to nuance in the subject and its manner of representation in a complex dance of selecting certain harem motifs, alluding to and rejecting other.[13] Around 1870 the harem was once again a subject for contestation among artistic factions.

It is well-known in the history of art that Delacroix influenced early Impressionists who admired his handling of color, his erudition, and his freedom from academic rules. Delacroix's death in 1863 ushered in a reappraisal of the once-radical artist and a rewriting of his legacy as a source of inspiration for the artists of modernity. But this affinity for the old master is rather remarkable given his political conservatism especially later in his life. Fantin-Latour's famous studio scene of modern painters *Homage to Delacroix* (1864) was followed six years later by a similar *Studio of the Batignolles* (exhibited at the 1870 Salon), which featured Manet at the easel painting the portrait of a seated Zacharie Astruc and surrounded by other advocates and practitioners of the new art, including Renoir (wearing a hat and enframed by the picture hung behind him), a tall Bazille standing at right in Scottish plaid pants, and Emile Zola facing him.[14] Bazille, Renoir, and Manet were part of an unofficial group of young artists who lived together or close by, shared models, and painted works in response to each other.

Bazille wrote of his admiration for Delacroix, having seen several of his paintings as a child. The master's second version of *Women of Algiers* (see Fig. 2.18) was purchased in 1868 by the Musée Fabre located in Montpellier, where Bazille grew up in an *haute-bourgeois* family who appreciated art. The young painter produced several works inspired by Delacroix. Bazille's *Studio on the Rue de la Condamine* 1870 (Fig. 7.1), a depiction of his own studio, which presented an opportunity for self-reflexivity, has its roots in Fantin-Latour's 1864 tribute to Delacroix, while it anticipates Fantin's *Studio of the Batignolles*, done later in the month of January and shown in the April Salon that year. Still it deviates significantly from both darker canvases and his two versions of earlier studios painted in 1865 and 1867. More distant, full of blank spaces, and asymmetrical, its visual language like the interior it describes is fresh, airy, sketchy, and thus modern. The distance between the viewer and the figures and the indistinct means by which they are portrayed deemphasize the men's identities. Bazille, Manet, and Renoir have been identified,[15] three artists on whose harem-orientalist pictures I want to focus. Noteworthy in the painting is the inclusion of three painted canvases. Two had been rejected by the Salon, and the third was an early version of Bazille's own harem bath scene, *La Toilette* (Fig. 7.2). Its inclusion was prophetic, as it too would be rejected from the Salon that year.[16]

La Toilette gets much painterly attention in *Studio* by virtue of its placement on the rear wall to the right of the window and over the light-colored sofa. It is one of at least three nude pictures in a sparsely furnished studio occupied by male artists, having hardly the suggestion of a female presence. These pictures of nudes act as another kind of shared male interest. In *Studio*, a painted manifesto of the group solidarity of the new painters on 1 January 1870, the first day of the new decade, this painting within a painting is a flag of the new vision of the harem.

A harem setting for the activity of *La Toilette* itself is suggested by its luxurious fabrics, eastern wall decoration, and the bright green coloration of the Turkish slippers. Harem lesbianism is suggested by the physical interconnection of black servant and white served figures, particularly the white hand on the black skin, the proximity of the servant's precisely chiseled profile to her lady's right breast, and their juxtaposed limbs.[17] Bazille had high hopes for *La Toilette*, and when it was rejected by the jury he wrote to his mother that the jury was at fault. Bazille acknowledges the harem tradition here. His placement of the foreground slippers; the standing figure at right; and the servant whose delicate facial profile, turban, exaggeratedly wide hips seen from the back, and exposed sole of the foot recall such details in Delacroix's now-classic 1834 *Femmes d'Alger* (see Fig. 2.17). Ingres's 1814 *Grande Odalisque* (Fig. 3.21) is also suggested in Bazille's interest in bare skin against animal fur and the tension between exposure and revelation in the motif of the woman's hair covering one breast.[18] Paradoxically, Bazille's theme of black service to a white nude body can be seen as both an appeasement to the taste of Gérôme in his bid for inclusion by conservative members of the jury as some scholars have suggested based on a reading of Bazille's letters,[19] and an indication of his loyalty to the more radical strain of nudes indicated by Manet's *Olympia*, in which a black servant also attends to a naked white

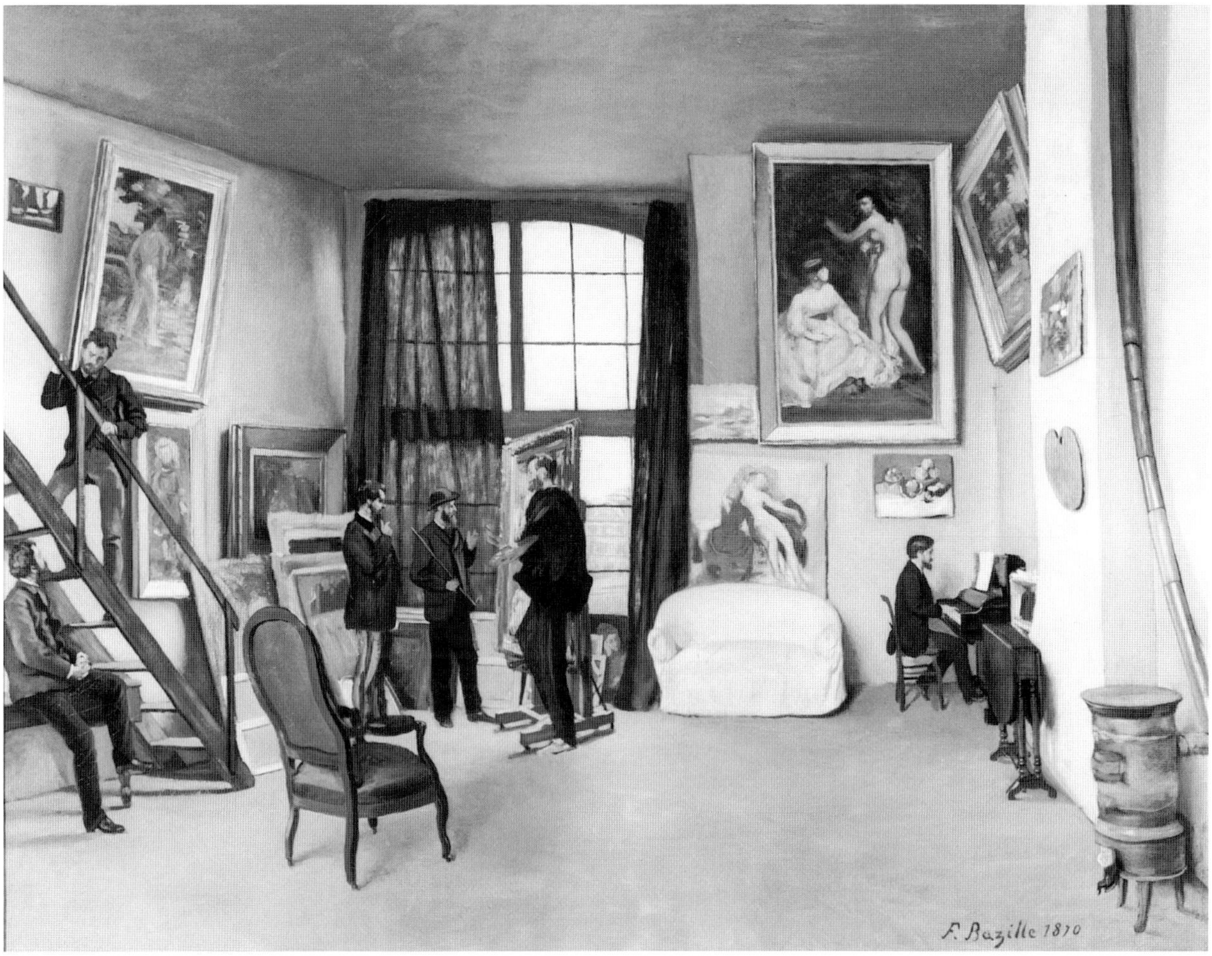

Fig. 7.1. Jean Frédéric Bazille. *Studio on the Rue de la Condamine.* 1870. Musée d'Orsay, Paris. © Photo RMN.

woman; in face and petite body type Bazille's woman resembles Manet's model Victorine Meurent. Such an eclectic tradition is reworked here in a canvas which aims to be more "natural" than its predecessors, using Zola's description of the ideals of the new painting as both true on the one hand and "personal and live" on the other.[20] This appears most noticeably in the flattening out of the body against the backdrop, the shallow space, the tentative presentation of the co-wife who is hunched and cut-off at right.

Bazille's more explicitly orientalist work, *Woman in Moorish Costume (Mauresque)* of 1869 (Fig. 7.3) depicts an eastern dancer adjusting her multicolored sash. Here he more self-consciously constructs a modern picture of an oriental woman, judging from his title. The work owes much to Manet's several full-length portraits of women from the 1860s, in particular, a portrait of another "primitive" dancer at rest but still "on stage," *Lola de Valence* (1862, reworked 1867). Both works show a female entertainer dressed in colorful exotic costume standing against a plain, neutral background.[21] Both artists play with the erotic effects of skin seen through sheer white fabric. Bazille includes a few crucial indicators of the Orient: striped caftan and sheathed sword hanging on the wall behind the dancer, a tambourine at her feet. This is, however, an eastern dancer-entertainer, which falls somewhat outside the domain of the polygynous harem tradition as I have established it here. Still, it is useful to consider, as it suggests that Bazille's *La Toilette* was conceived within an orientalist context and the degree to which these early modern artists' images can be interrelated.

The harem pictorial tradition is squarely addressed in Renoir's 1870 *Femme d'Algers/Odalisque* (see Fig. 4.60), whose title has been considered an acknowledgment of Delacroix's famous work of 1834. Both this work and Bazille's *Mauresque* reputedly are painted after the model Renoir favored in this period, twenty-two-year-old Lise Tréhot. Renoir's painting was accepted for the very Salon from which Bazille's orientalized *La Toilette* was rejected. In response

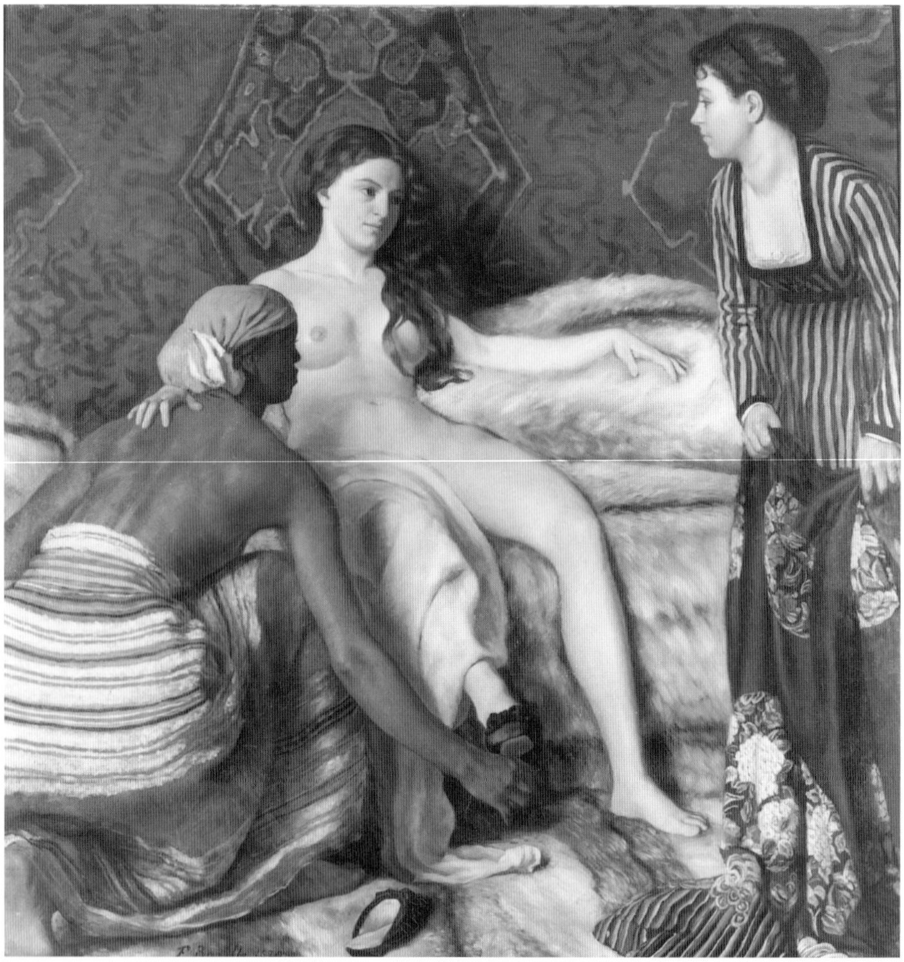

Fig. 7.2. Jean Frédéric Bazille. *La Toilette.* Musée Fabre, Montpellier © Photo RMN.

to its showing the critic Marius Chaumelin named Delacroix the master whom Renoir was evoking: it is "in all regards" that Renoir's work "is reminiscent of Delacroix."[22] And, it is true, similarities exist in intricately rendered knee pants and full body type. If Renoir has been looking at Delacroix, the younger artist's new composition is formally more compressed and has a lower vantage point. Renoir goes even further than Delacroix in fragmenting light into tessellated colors. (Like the painter Renoir, the art critic Charles Blanc in 1876 makes timely Delacroix's *Femmes d'Alger* done over thirty years earlier by calling it a striking example of an early work of "an optical mixture."[23])

What was latent in Delacroix's *Women of Algiers* is exaggerated here. Renoir exceeds Delacroix in overdetermining the female body: besides the fleshy face, Renoir gives much attention to billowing fabrics and gauzy scarfs; one appears in the background, and another, which she fingers, snakes over her body. Delacroix's three seated women are transformed into Renoir's single woman abed, her legs open provocatively, her head thrust back, her bedroom eyes defiant, her face painted and harsh—ciphers of a dangerous femininity. Delacroix's silent, nonchalant, indeed, passive women are reworked into Renoir's single, aggressive *femme fatale*.

Though Renoir also deeply appreciated the influence of Delacroix's work, his reference to Edouard Manet's *Olympia* is even more convincing here, on the bases of the shallow space and half-paneled background, both figures' supine posture, the fact that they are pushed into the forefront of the picture plane, and the provocative eye contact each makes with the spectator. Renoir's modern reinterpretation of the harem tradition is, like John Lewis's *Houri* six years later, a presentation of the harem woman as a prostitute, though the analogy had a long history, as we have explored.

Besides *Olympia*, Renoir may have seen Manet's 1868 etching *Odalisque* (see Fig. 4.18), which at first glance seems a fairly traditional rendering of the

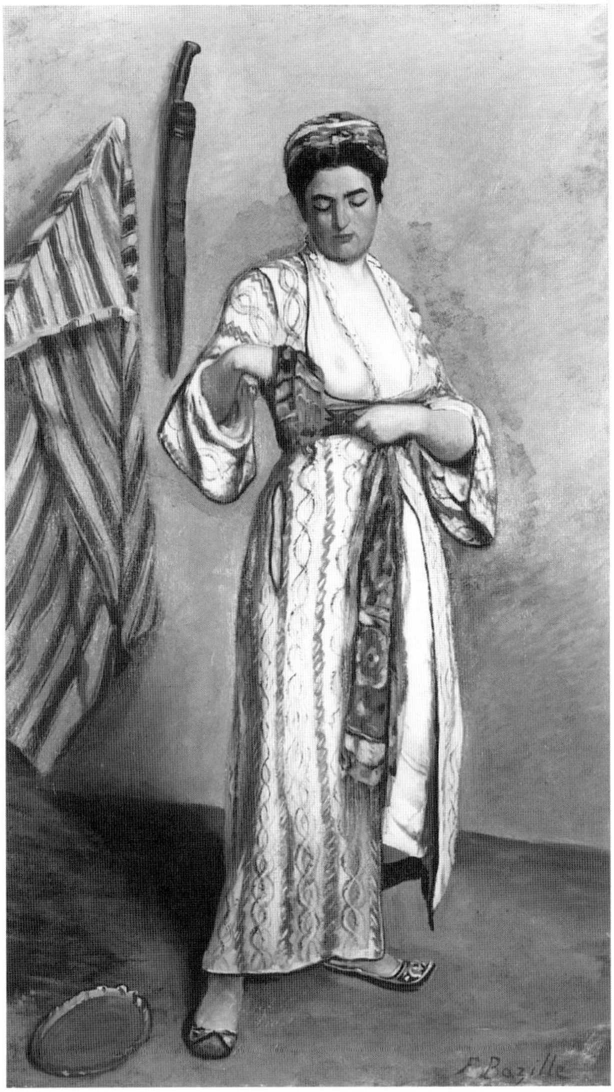

Fig. 7.3. Jean Frédéric Bazille. *Woman in Moorish Costume (Mauresque)*. 1869. Norton Simon Foundation, Pasadena, CA.

harem woman, iconographically speaking. But spatially the print is marked by significant disjunctures: the head is supported by a too-thick arm that hardly seems connected to the right shoulder, especially weighed against the unfinished, nearly atrophied left arm. Rather than being invitingly curvaceous, the overall shape of the woman's body is ovoid and muffled by course clothing. The absence of feet dislocates her and interrupts the viewer's relationship to her as an object of desire, especially as Manet hollows out spaces arbitrarily around the phallomorphic mouthpiece of the narghile. The interaction of the phallic and the feminine is matter-of-fact, neutralized, joyless. The minimal jewelry suggests an impoverished eastern woman, a low-ranking prostitute rather than a coddled woman. Already by 1868 Manet is experimenting with a modern, anti-odalisque odalisque.

Manet's *La Sultane* (Plate 6) c. 1870 is a picture whose extraordinary visual radicalism has never been adequately addressed by scholars. When the British critics complain about the "rather tiresome hareem" picture of John Lewis in 1874, they could be describing the very attitude of the woman represented in this French picture. This is an image of refusal. It refuses the formula of reclining woman flirting with the spectator that characterized so many French harem pictures of odalisques from Ingres to Renoir. It refuses the highly descriptive and fetishized luxury objects of the harem. This woman too wears minimal jewelry, and only the vaguest suggestion is given of a cushion in the background and a tapestry carpet. This is hardly an eroticized environment. Instead the figure is awkwardly placed in the harem space: forced into the front of the picture plane, she is cut off just below the knees. Rather than reclining in a relaxed manner, she is standing and faces the spectator in an ungainly pose, her arms strangely defined appendages like those in his 1865 *Olympia* or 1868 *Odalisque*. The body seen through the clothing, consisting of only the sheer, light-colored muslin undergarment as Lady Mary described it in her Turkish Embassy Letters, is broad in breasts and belly, the maternal body widened by childbearing. Excessive cloth at the sleeves gives the figure the look of even more girth. There is no coy presentation of oblique body curves. The body is frank, planar, unflattering. A carelessly placed cap prevents the viewer from seeing the long sleek hair that appears in so many pictures of harem women. The pipe at the lower right is her body's morphological parallel.

Unlike the vast majority of painters of nudes in the nineteenth century, Manet indicates pubic hair in *La Sultana*, visible through the sheer drapery. Though lightly covered, it is unmistakable here, and marks this figure as even more radical than his scandalous *Olympia* painted five years earlier.[24] Harem women were reputed to remove all extraneous body hair in the numerous accounts of their depilatory practice which appeared over the centuries.[25] And in indicating body hair Manet breaks a major convention of the category of nude paintings and their subgenre, harem pictures. If the convention to omit pubic hair can be read as a cipher of social control over the power of the female body, a desire to keep desire out of the nude,[26] Manet's reference to it functions to alert the viewer to the futility of his desire for a mere representation. The erotic harem picture's unnamed prurience is named and undermined. This contributes fundamentally to the picture's mood of poignancy.

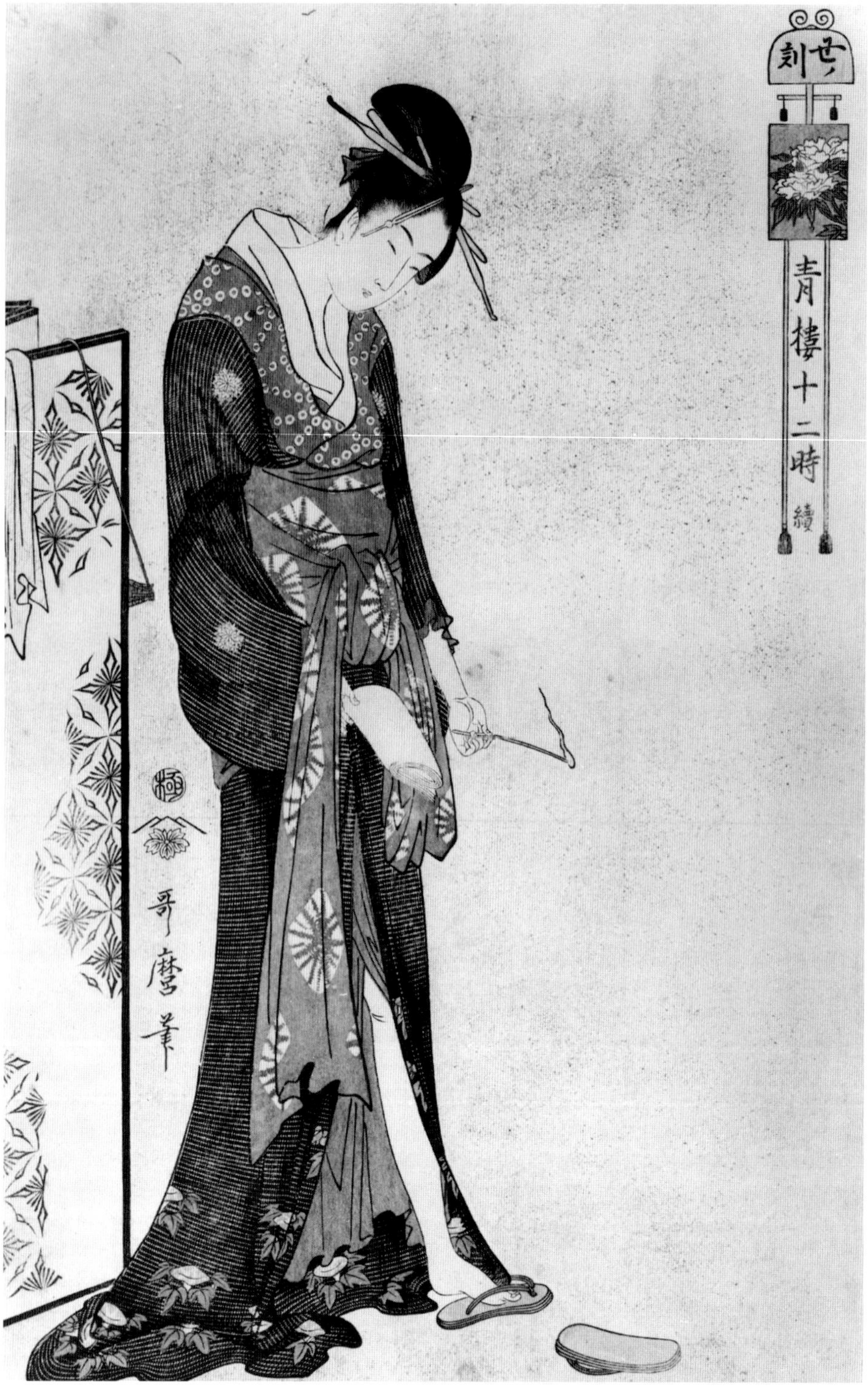

Fig. 7.4. Kitagawa Utamaro. *Hour of the Ox [Midnight]/Courtesan with Lit Taper.* Tokyo National Museum. Kyoryokukai.

Psychologically the painting refuses as well. Its darkness frames and isolates a lone figure whose weariness—depression even—is forced upon the spectator, with whom eye contact is refused. Her connected eyebrows (also referred to frequently in travel accounts of harem women's grooming habits) weight and age the face. This sultana lives in a luxurious prison. Her identity as an unhappy wife of a fabulously wealthy sultan means that her sexual exploitation is grounded in an economic arrangement, one which is tantamount to a kind of prostitution. The work's ambivalence is to be located in the gap between the erotic expectations the viewer holds for a picture of a sultana and the minimal degree to which Manet's painting allows participation in visual titillation.

Another image of a reluctant "eastern" lady-of-love has a strikingly similar composition and mood, Kitagawa Utamaro's *Hour of the Ox [Midnight]/Courtesan with Lit Taper* (Fig. 7.4), an *ukiyo-e* of a courtesan in a private moment alone who slips off her tatami, one of a series of twelve woodblock prints, *Twelve Lunar Hours in the Pleasure Quarters*. Both figures hold a long stick-like object in their lowered right hand. The courtesan is almost too weary to light a lamp with this taper. The object in the sultana's hand is probably a fan. Manet the *japoniste* had access to this kind of print in his haunts of Parisian stores that sold Japanese curios, as suggested by his 1868 *Portrait of Zola*.[27] Each image shows the "down time" of a woman whose ostensible function was to entertain a man with her wiles. And each functions as a critique of the genre of exotic glamor to which it belongs.

The tensions in Manet's unusual picture between the public persona of the sultana/prostitute and the suggestions of her private angst has a literary parallel in the travel notes and letters of Gustave Flaubert written on his trip to Egypt. Both painter and writer dispense with the euphemisms and romanticized trappings of eastern sex. In fact, Flaubert barely mentions the harem, as if a reference to it cannot but be infused with both mystery and convention. Instead he relates innumerable encounters with Egyptian prostitutes—his own trysts and those of native men. In these abrupt descriptions written in 1849–50 there is a flat affect, in which he asserts the subjectivity of his/the male narrator's casual experience. For example:

> A litter of kittens had to be removed from my bed. Hadely did not undo her jacket, making signs to show me she had a pain in her chest. Effect: she is front of me, the rustle of her clothes, the sound made by the gold piastres of her snood—a clear, slow sound. Moonlight. She carried a torch. On the matting: firm flesh, bronze arse, shaven cunt, dry though fatty; the whole thing gave me effect of a plague victim or a leperhouse.[28]

Flaubert's jaded writing forms a literary correlative to Manet's somber image. But when Flaubert describes so matter-of-factly public couplings (sometimes rapes) perpetrated by Egyptian men, there is an awareness of the negation of the woman's perspective, and he both delights in and is pained by it:

> That day, a few soldiers and women were smoking at the foot of the arches and eating oranges; one of them was keeping a look-out on top of the aqueduct. I shall never forget the brutal movement of my old donkey-driver as he came down on the girl, taking her in his right arm, caressing her breasts with his left hand, dragging her down, all in one movement, laughing with his great white teeth. His little black wooden *chibouk* attached to his back; the rags wrapped around the lower part of his diseased legs.[29]

Another shocking effect of both of these descriptions is Flaubert's intermingling of desire and disease. His abbreviated prose approaches Manet's minimalist style. And both are highly ambivalent representations of the alienated female role within the eastern sexual experience. Both Flaubert and Manet build into their texts a slippage between the eastern and western male protagonist. Sometimes Flaubert's active sexual agent is French, sometimes Egyptian. Manet's male protagonist (though absent from the painting) is presumably an eastern pasha, but the shallow placement of the female figure on the picture plane forces a self-conscious encounter with the "male" French viewer. Finally both painter and writer in effect epitomize the eastern experience in terms of male sexual opportunity (and opportunism). That Flaubert's writing from this trip barely mentioned harem women is significant. As in early Impressionist visual imagery and John Lewis's last harem picture, any harem woman in Flaubert's writing is supplanted by the figure of the eastern prostitute.

Affected by the mood in a postwar Paris still stunned by deprivation and the horror of a bloody military repression of the Commune, Renoir produced a rather strained response to the harem theme. His *Parisian Women in Algerian Costume (Harem)* (Fig. 7.5) was offered to the 1872 Salon, which rejected it. The painting is a garish mixture of old harem themes updated. The subject here is again preparing the toilette. The picture's three main women are arranged on a diagonal, and Renoir utilizes complementary principles to organize them. The servant holding a mirror at lower right is clothed and in shadow, while the two "harem women" are highlighted and partially nude; one helps dress the central figure by handing her a piece of jewelry. The work's oblique angle and high perspective suggest Renoir's use of some basic principles of *japonisme* as his nod to the new modernist vocabulary. The heavily painted blonde with exposed thighs elicits the modern discourse on the courtesan. But even more obviously, Renoir's title reveals the collapse of the harem subject into that of Parisian prostitutes' costuming. Here there are no pretenses toward

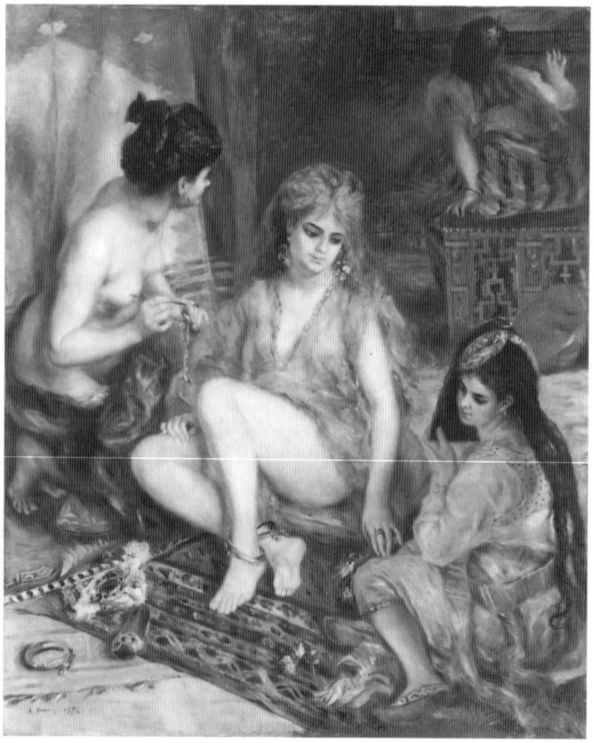

Fig. 7.5. Pierre Auguste Renoir. *Parisian Women in Algerian Costume (Harem)*. 1872. Matsukata Collection, National Museum of Western Art, Tokyo.

authenticity of the harem experience, in itself a loss of confidence in the harem subject to which it alludes. As in the case of Lewis's *Houri* of 1876, only purchased artifice, commodified love, is possible. Such reworking of the harem woman confirms Clark's observation that the courtesan was "a main representative of modernity" by the 1860s and beyond.[30]

Historical circumstances surrounding the Franco-Prussian War, in which all three artists served, and the fall of the Commune, necessitated the obsolescence of the harem theme for artists increasingly eager to pursue subjects of modern life (often set in Paris and environs, with a focus on leisure and spectacle). Bazille lived long enough only to raise some of the issues of the harem picture and the "modernized exotic." It is a cruel historical irony that this orientalist was killed in battle in Algeria in November 1870 wearing the uniform of a Zouave as the last great Kabylic uprising began to take form.[31] Renoir reverted to retrogressive harem conventions and failed to produce a thoroughly modern picture, a theme to which he would return more than once, particularly after his trip to Algeria in 1881. Only Manet produced a truly radical rethinking of the harem picture and its traditions, one which is avant-garde in both its stylistic rhetoric and its substance, as a subject which is on the one hand grounded in the same kind of economic principles which oppress French women and on the other hand deeply alienated from western understanding.

Given its old associations, the harem subject could not play a central role in the development of the Impressionist aesthetic. The boredom with harems and harem pictures critics express indicates that the *cause célèbre* of the 1850s was a *cause morte* into the 1870s—in both diplomatic and artistic circles. Harem representations continued to be made in England and France after the mid-1870s, but they were no longer a subject as grounded in cultural conviction. Later harem representations of the 1880s and 1890s may have attempted to retain a formal hold on stylistic mimesis, but the perception of an unproblematic link to a transparent reality lived by real harem women in the East evaporated. In painting the theme of the harem woman is subsumed by representations of the dangerous eastern woman, Salomé, popularized by Oscar Wilde's 1891 play.

Conclusion

The harem was a rich, unfixed symbol which functioned in many ways. It was nearly always a discourse on male superiority, whether European or eastern. A recurrent notion in the mythology of the harem is that the women who occupied it represent a truer, more fundamental natural womanhood than their western counterparts, whose essential nature has been obscured by artificial layers of civilization. Whether a more natural woman was positive or negative was at issue. The harem *was* Woman whether the commentator be French or British, male or female, bourgeois or aristocrat. Perhaps the ladies at the 1850 Old Water-colour Society who "passed rapidly by" Lewis's *Hhareem* (see Plate 1) did so because they sensed that this picture exposed them as much as the fictional harem slave. The *Illustrated London News* nearly says as much in trying to understand women's refusal to look closely at it when it claims

> There is nothing in the picture, indeed, to offend the finest female delicacy: it is all purity of appearance; but, at the same time, *it exhibits woman, to a woman's mind in her least attractive qualities.* (*ILN* 4 May 1850:300, my emphasis)

The wide range of readings of the harem examined in this study has been possible precisely because "fact" about the harem could not be known, all the more so given its exotic nature. A representation of the harem freed of myth and value judgment—entirely objective—could not be produced by the West, given its relationship of political and economic dominance over the East. In the final analysis harem paintings, like the art critics' reactions to them, stockpile additional layers of preconception, myth, and their own situatedness onto the view of harem women's lives. These representations constitute additional readings of the lives of eastern and western women. This study, necessarily implicated in the processes it critiques, is one more reading of those lives.

If previous thinking about the harem woman has been based on stereotyping, fearful projection and defense, identity-formation and colonialism, how might she be re-conceived? Perhaps more fundamentally we can ask why she needs to be conceptualized at all. What positive purposes might such a rethinking serve? A resonant comment is that of Julia Kristeva, who in 1974 asserted: "In 'woman' I see something that cannot be represented, something that is not said, something above and beyond nomenclatures and ideologies."[32] At first her comment might seem nihilistic. After all, if the conclusion of a scholarly study is that we can't know its subject, scholarship cannot but fail. But hopefully this book has revealed that the ostensible subject of the harem representation is not its real subject. And it responds to Kristeva's implication that scholarship needs to eschew a closed epistemological product and provide a critique of previous patterns of thinking.

Her comment allows us to think more expansively. It implies that no matter how much ink (or paint) is spilled in an attempt to capture the truth about the harem woman, lived reality will always exceed it, because it is always fuller and richer, forever beyond the grasp of western thinking. "The harem woman," disempowered within so many French and British representations in the nineteenth century, remains by virtue of her historical existence defiant, elusive, potent.

Notes

In citing works in the notes, short titles have generally been used. Works frequently cited have been identified by the following abbreviations:

A *Athenaeum.*

AA Dumas, Alexandre. *Adventures in Algeria.* Trans. Alma Elizabeth Murch. 1848–51. Reprint, Philadelphia and New York: Chilton Co., 1959.

AJ *Art Journal.*

AS Wolfgang Amadeus Mozart. *Abduction from the Seraglio.* Trans. Ruth Martin and Thomas Martin. 1782. Reprint, n.p.: Boosey and Hawkes, Inc., 1962.

ASR *Anti-Slavery Reporter.*

C *Critic.*

CS Julia Pardoe. *The City of the Sultan and Domestic Manners of the Turks in 1836.* 2 Vols. London: Henry Colburn, 1837.

E Dominique Vivant Denon. *Travels in Upper and Lower Egypt: In Company with Several Divisions of the French Army, during the Campaign of General Bonaparte in that Country.* 2 Vols. Trans. Arthur Aikin. London: T. N. Longman and O. Rees, 1803.

EL Harriet Martineau. *Eastern Life, Present and Past.* Philadelphia: Lea and Blanchard, 1848.

FPLI Beatrice Farwell. *French Popular Lithographic Imagery, 1815–70.* 12 Vols. Chicago: University of Chicago Press, 1981–97.

H Thomas Carlyle. *On Heroes, Hero-Worship and the Heroic in History.* Ed. Carl Niemeyer. Lincoln: University of Nebraska Press, 1966.

HTT *Handbook for Travellers in Turkey in Asia including Constantinople, the Bosphorus, Dardanelles, Brousa . . . and the Plain of Troy.* 4th ed. London: John Murray, 1871.

ILN *Illustrated London News.*

L Lady Mary Wortley Montagu. *The Complete Letters of Lady Mary Wortley Montagu.* 3 Vols. Ed. Robert Halsband. Oxford: Clarendon Press, 1965.

LE Florence Nightingale. *Letters from Egypt: A Journey on the Nile 1849–1850.* New York: Weidenfeld and Nicholson, 1987.

LR Thomas Moore. *Lalla Rookh: An Oriental Romance.* 1817. Reprint, New York: Lincoln Macveagh, The Dial Press, Longmans Green and Co., 1930.

ME Edward William Lane. *An Account of the Manners and Customs of the Modern Egyptians, Written in Egypt During the Years 1833, –34 and –35.* 5th ed. London: John Murray, 1871.

PHL Alphonse de Lamartine. *A Pilgrimage to the Holy Land (Voyage en Orient).* 1838. Reprint, Delmar, NY: Scholars' Facsimiles and Reprints, 1978.

PL Montesquieu. *Persian Letters.* Ed. and trans. C. J. Betts. London: Penguin, 1973.

PNP Richard F. Burton. *Personal Narrative of a Pilgrimage to El-Medinah and Meccah.* 3 Vols. London: Longman, Brown, and Longmans, 1855.

PT Mrs. [John Elijah] Blunt. *The People of Turkey: Twenty Years' Residence Among Bulgarians, Greeks, Albanians, Turks and Armenians.* 2 vols. Ed. Stanley Lane Poole. London: John Murray, 1878.

S *Spectator.*

SCL Hugo, Victor. *Selections Chiefly Lyrical from the Poetical Works of Victor Hugo.* Ed. Henry Llewellyn Williams. London: George Bell and Sons, 1885.

SE Urquhart, David. *Spirit of the East Illustrated in a Journal of Travels through Roumeli during an Eventful Period.* London: Henry Colburn, 1838.

T *(London) Times.*

V Edmond About. *Voyage à travers l'exposition des beaux-arts.* Paris: Hachette, 1855.

VO Gérard de Nerval. *Voyage to the Orient.* Ed. and trans. Norman Glass. 1851. Reprint, New York: New York University Press, 1972.

VRW Mary Wollstonecraft. *Vindication of the Rights of Women.* 1792. Ed. Miriam Brody. Reprint, London: Penguin Books, 1988.

W John Ruskin. *Works of John Ruskin.* London: George Allen, 1904.

WB Lord (George Gordon Noel) Byron. *Complete Works of Lord Byron.* Philadelphia: David McKay, 1883.

Preface

1. See my "Passivity and Politics in Delacroix's 1834 *Women of Algiers*," in Amy Tucker, *Visual Literacy* (New York: McGraw-Hill, 2002), 244–51.

2. N. M. Penzer, *The Harem* (London: George G. Harrap, 1936), 15; Edward William Lane, *An Account of the Manners and Customs of the Modern Egyptians*, 5th ed. (London: John Murray, 1871), 1:197 note (hereafter cited as *ME*.) On the difficulties of defining the harem see Fatima Mernissi, *Dreams of Trespass: Tales of a Harem Girlhood* (Reading, MA: Addison-Wesley, 1994), 150–55.

3. Penzer, *Harem*, 15.

4. Leila Ahmed, *Women and Gender in Islam* (New Haven: Yale, 1992), 55–56.

5. Judith E. Tucker, *Women in Nineteenth-Century Egypt* (Cambridge: Cambridge University Press, 1985), 3.

6. Ahmed, *Women and Gender in Islam*, 63–64.

7. Tucker, *Women*, 5.

8. Fatima Mernissi, *Beyond the Veil: Male-Female Dynamics in a Modern Muslim Society* (New York: John Wiley and Sons, 1975): 3ff. See also her more recent *The Veil and the Male Elite: A Feminist Interpretation of Women's Rights in Islam* (Reading, MA: Perseus Books, 1991) on the historical roots of veiling and seclusion.

9. Henri Lefebvre, *Production of Space* (London: Basil Blackwell, 1994), 92, 293.

10. This schema is loosely indebted to Henri Lefebvre, *Production of Space*, 33, 38–39. He provides specific terms for this schema but gives them rather ambiguous meanings: spatial practice, representations of space, and representational spaces. His intellectual biographer confirms the lack of clarity in Lefebvre's three-part dialectic (Rob Shields, *Lefebvre, Love and Struggle: Spatial Dialectics* [London and New York: Routledge, 1999], 144). I explore the value of his schema for understanding harem pictures in my article, "Lefebvre's Critique of Space as Interdisciplinary Paradigm: Desire and Colonialism in Three Harem Paintings by Delacroix, Renoir and Lewis," in *Gendered Space: An Interdisciplinary Exploration of Past Place and Space*, ed. Bonj Szczygiel, Josephine Carubia, and Lorraine Dowler (University Park: The Pennsylvania State University, 2000), 68–81.

11. Bill Ashcroft, Gareth Griffiths, and Helen Tiffin, *The Post-Colonial Studies Reader* (London and New York: Routledge, 1995), 391.

12. Timothy Mitchell, *Colonising Egypt* (Cambridge and New York: Cambridge University Press, 1988), 31.

13. Rushad Rushdi, "English Travellers in Egypt During the Reign of Mohammed Ali," *Bulletin of the Faculty of Arts Fouad I. University* (Cairo) 14, Part 2 (1952), 1.

14. Beatrice Farwell, *French Popular Lithographic Imagery, 1815–70*, 12 vols. (Chicago: University of Chicago Press, 1981–97), 1:vii.

15. This is the harem picture *Turkish Woman Holding a Pipe, with a Black Servant at her Side*, 1852, done by Count Amadeo Preziosi ("Jean Brindisi"). See Philippe Jullian, *The Orientalists: European Painters of Eastern Scenes* (Oxford: Phaidon, 1977), 95. I illustrate a very similar Preziosi, fig. 4.12

16. Marcia Pointon, *The Bonington Circle: English Watercolour and Anglo-French Landscape*, (Sussex: Hendon Press, 1985), 1.

17. On the sameness of colonialist texts see Edward Said quoted in Mitchell, *Colonising Egypt*, 31.

18. Homi K. Bhabha, "The Other Question . . ." *Screen* 24, no. 6 (November-December 1983), 18–36.

19. Malek Alloula, *The Colonial Harem*, trans. Myrna and Wlad Godzich (Minneapolis: University of Minnesota Press, 1986), 67.

20. Edward Said, *Culture and Imperialism* (New York: Vintage [Random House], 1993), xxi. I have chosen not to include Indian harems specifically in this study.

21. Farwell, *French Popular Lithographic Imagery*, 9:22.

22. Harriet Martineau, *Eastern Life, Present and Past* (Philadelphia: Lea and Blanchard 1848), 259 (hereafter cited as *EL*).

23. Noted by Chandra Talpade Mohanty, "Under Western Eyes: Feminist Scholarship and Colonialist Discourses," in *The Post-Colonial Studies Reader*, ed. Bill Ashcroft, Gareth Griffiths, and Helen Tiffin (London and New York: Routledge, 1995), 261.

24. Michel Foucault, *The History of Sexuality*, vol. 1, trans. Robert Hurley (New York: Pantheon, 1990), 11.

25. Said, *Culture and Imperialism*, 66.

26. Gayatri Chakravorty Spivak, "Can the Subaltern Speak?" in *Marxism and the Interpretation of Culture*, ed. Cary Nelson and Lawrence Grossberg (Urbana-Champaign: University of Illinois, 1988), 283, 306, 308.

27. Marilyn Brown, "The Harem De-historicized: Ingres' *Bain turc*," *Arts Magazine* 61, no. 10 (summer 1987), 59.

28. Terry Eagleton, *Literary Theory: An Introduction* (Minneapolis: University of Minnesota Press, 1983), 128.

29. Edward Said, *Orientalism* (New York: Pantheon, 1978). I will use the two terms, but I want to remind my reader that I have put them "under erasure": they are necessary in order to communicate, though they are seriously flawed.

30. Said, *Culture and Imperialism*, 9.

31. Ibid., xiii.

32. Homi K. Bhabha, "Signs Taken for Wonders: Questions of Ambivalent Authority Under a Tree Outside Delhi, May 1817," in *"Race," Writing and Difference*, ed. Henry Louis Gates, Jr. (Chicago: University of Chicago Press, 1986), 170.

33. Even before the eighteenth century, travelers report the deadly consequences awaiting the viewer of a harem woman. Montesquieu develops this idea more fully in several passages of his *Persian Letters*, which would become a source of information for many painters and writers in the nineteenth century (Montesquieu, *Persian Letters*, ed. and trans. C. J. Betts [London: Penguin, 1973], 75, 179, 271, 274).

34. Julia V. Douthwaite, *Exotic Women: Literary Heroines and Cultural Strategies in Ancien Régime France* (Philadelphia: University of Pennsylvania Press, 1992), 3.

35. Douthwaite, *Exotic Women*, 21.

36. Note the following example: "a *séjour* in the East . . . had . . . been one of my favourite contemplations. I wished to visit Turkey *while it yet contained Turks*, and before every *prestige* attached to that once noble race, the descendants of Othman, had vanished beneath the encroachments of reform; and as I knew that Russian intrigue had rendered the duration of the first state of things problematical, and that the well meant but ill directed efforts of Sultan Mahmud had almost effected the latter, I felt that no further time was to be lost" ("A Visit to the Harem of the Pasha of Widdin," *Fraser Magazine* 18, no. 108 [December 1838], 679).

Chapter 1. Introduction

1. Homi K. Bhabha, "Signs Taken for Wonders," 173.
2. Michel Foucault, *History of Sexuality*, 1:18.
3. Ibid., 1:25.
4. Mary Wollstonecraft, *Vindication of the Rights of Women*, ed. Miriam Brody (London: Penguin Books, 1988), 131, 164 (hereafter cited as *VRW*).
5. Montesquieu, *Persian Letters*, ed. and trans. C. J. Betts (London: Penguin, 1973), 206–7 (hereafter cited as *PL*).
6. Gayatri Chakravorty Spivak, "Can the Subaltern Speak?" 299.
7. Alain Grosrichard, *Structure du sérail: La Fiction du despotisme asiatique dans l'occident classique* (Paris: Editions du Seuil, 1979), 144.
8. Ibid., 223.
9. Ibid., 178.
10. Joan DelPlato, "An English Feminist in the Turkish Harem: A Portrait of Lady Mary Wortley Montagu," *Eighteenth-Century Women and the Arts*, ed. Frederick M. Keener and Susan E. Lorsch (New York: Greenwood Press, 1988), 173; and Lady Mary Wortley Montagu, *The Complete Letters of Lady Mary Wortley Montagu*, 3 vols., ed. Robert Halsband (Oxford: Clarendon Press, 1965), 1:327–30 (hereafter cited as *L*).
11. See, for example, Robyn Cooper, "Millais' *The Rescue*: A Painting of a 'Dreadful Interruption of Domestic Peace,'" *Art History* 9, no. 4 (December 1986): 471–86.
12. The claim that the harem was home could serve ideological, pro-Turkish ends, as I will describe in the next chapter.
13. Grosrichard, *Structure du sérail*, 176.
14. Lefebvre, *Production of Space*, 310.
15. Ibid., 353.
16. Douthwaite, *Exotic Women*, 20.
17. Quoted in ibid., 186.
18. In making this point Doreen Massey cites the work of feminist essayist Luce Irigaray (1978) and art historians Craig Owens (1988) and Griselda Pollock (1988) (Doreen Massey, *Space, Place and Gender* [Minneapolis: University of Minnesota Press, 1994], 232).
19. "A Visit to the Harem of the Pasha of Widdin," 679.
20. For a close study of the role of the harem as part of "feminist orientalism" in Charlotte Brontë's *Jane Eyre* (1847), see Joyce Zonana, "The Sultan and the Slave: Feminist Orientalism and the Structure of *Jane Eyre*," *Signs* 18, no. 3 (spring 1993): 592–617.
21. Carol Ockman, *Ingres's Eroticized Bodies: Retracing the Serpentine Line* (New Haven: Yale University Press, 1995), 48–51.
22. The comment continues: "There is nothing in the picture, indeed, to offend the finest female delicacy: it is all purity of appearance; but, at the same time, it exhibits woman, to a woman's mind in her least attractive qualities" (*Illustrated London News* [14 May 1850]: 300) (hereafter cited as *ILN*).
23. *PL* 1:63 quoted in Douthwaite, *Exotic Women*, 98.
24. I choose to use the term "aesthetic positivism," while Said calls Orientalism "a form of radical realism" (Said, *Orientalism*, 72). Bhabha makes the point that Orientalism "employs a system of representation, a regime of truth, that is structurally similar to Realism" (Bhabha, "The Other Question . . ." *Screen* 24, no. 6 [November-December 1983]: 23); his terminology is broader than mine, though he described a phenomenon not limited to the nineteenth century.
25. Irvin Cemil Schick, "Representing Middle Eastern Women: Feminism and Colonial Discourse," *Feminist Studies* 16, no. 2 (summer 1990): 356.
26. See Sarah Graham-Browne, *Images of Women: The Portrayal of Women in Photography of the Middle East, 1860–1950* (New York: Columbia University Press, 1988).
27. *Art Journal* new series 8 (1869): 469 (hereafter cited as *AJ*).
28. Edmond About, *Voyage à travers l'exposition des beaux-arts* (Paris: Hachette, 1855), 32 (hereafter cited as *V*).
29. Billie Melman, *Women's Orients: English Women and the Middle East, 1718–1918: Sexuality, Religion and Work* (Ann Arbor: University of Michigan Press, 1992), 122.
30. In analyzing the presentation of the Orient at Paris World's Fairs from 1867 to 1900, Çelik sees the exhibitions as having a scientific aura in their attempt to display as many of the "races" as possible. And the critical reaction to them was also scientific (Zeynep Çelik, *Displaying the Orient: Architecture of Islam at the Nineteenth-Century World's Fairs* [Berkeley: University of California Press, 1992], 30).
31. Said, *Culture and Imperialism*, 1993, 35.
32. Schick has a similar goal in his recent study of literary pornography ("works of xenological erotica") set in the East: "I attempt to formulate a taxonomy of the sexual tropes" (Irvin C. Schick, *The Erotic Margin: Sexuality and Spatiality in Alteritist Discourse* [London and New York: Verso, 1999], 12–13).
33. Bhabha, "Signs Taken for Wonders,"170.
34. Ibid., 171.
35. Ibid.
36. Foucault, *History of Sexuality*, 1:71.
37. Ibid., 65–66.
38. Ibid., 73.
39. Mitchell, *Colonising Egypt*, 112.
40. Alison Blunt and Gillian Rose, *Writing Women and Space: Colonial and Postcolonial Geographies* (New York: Guilford Press, 1994), 12.
41. See Bonnie G. Smith, *Ladies of the Leisure Class* (Princeton: Princeton University Press, 1981).
42. Gérard de Nerval, *Voyage to the Orient*, ed. and trans. Norman Glass (1851; reprint, New York: New York University Press, 1972), 48 (hereafter cited as *VO*).
43. Alphonse de Lamartine, *A Pilgrimage to the Holy Land (Voyage en Orient)* (1838; reprint, Delmar, NY: Scholars' Facsimiles and Reprints, 1978), 38 (hereafter cited as *PHL*).
44. Alexandre Dumas, *Adventures in Algeria*, trans. Alma Elizabeth Murch (1848–51; reprint, Philadelphia and New York: Chilton Co., 1959), 186 (hereafter cited as *AA*).
45. Similarly, the *Art Journal* says that John Lewis's picture of a "harem woman" looks too English (as noted above), which "injures the uniformity of his composition," suggesting a longing for ethnic purity in visual representations of the eastern other (*AJ* new series 8 [1869]: 469).
46. Nancy Tapper, "Mysteries of the Harem? An Anthropological Perspective on Recent Studies of Women of the Muslim Middle East," *Women's Studies International Quarterly* 2 (1979): 481.
47. Bhabha, "Signs Taken for Wonders," 172.
48. The metaphor is Behdad's (Ali Behdad, "The Eroticized Orient: Images of the Harem in Montesquieu and His

Precursors," *Stanford French Review* 13, nos. 2–3 [fall-winter 1989]: 126).

Chapter 2. The Colonial Contexts for the Harem Representation

1. Joan Wallach Scott, "Gender: A Useful Category of Historical Analysis," *Gender and the Politics of History* (New York: Columbia University Press, 1988), 46.

2. Henri Lefebvre quoted in Blunt and Rose, *Writing, Women and Space*, 15.

3. Montesquieu's character Rica compares the consummation of Persian and French marriage. Virginal wives "guarding their territory" finally "surrender" in "the moment of their defeat" (*PL* 118).

4. Kumari Jayawardena, *Feminism and Nationalism in the Third World* (London: Zea Books, Inc., 1986), 43.

5. Tucker, *Women*, 165–66.

6. Ibid., 192.

7. Ibid., 166, 187.

8. Ibid., 192.

9. Ibid., 165.

10. Jayawardena, *Feminism and Nationalism*, 49–50.

11. Ibid., 30.

12. Wolfgang Amadeus Mozart, *Abduction from the Seraglio*, trans. Ruth Martin and Thomas Martin (1782; reprint, n.p.: Boosey and Hawkes, Inc., 1962), 173 (hereafter cited as *AS*).

13. Lord Byron [George Gordon Noel], *Sardanapalus*, in *The Complete Works of Lord Byron* (Philadelphia: David McKay, 1883), 215 (hereafter cited as *WB*).

14. Pointon, *Bonington Circle*, 118–20.

15. Napoleon Bonaparte, *Dictionnaire-Napoléon ou recueil alphabétique des opinions et jugements de l'empereur Napoléon Ier* including *Mémoires pour servir à l'histoire de France sous le règne de Napoléon.*, 2d ed., ed. Damas Hinard (Paris: Plon Frères, 1854), 185.

16. For example, in 1826 Britain finally sided with France to help the Greek insurgents against Turkey not because of any warm feelings towards France but in an attempt to hold off a Russo-Turkish War. Likewise the "entente cordiale" Palmerston established with King Louis-Philippe in the early 1830s was a move to unite in the face of the alliance pledged by Russia and Turkey at the 1833 Treaty of Unkiar Skelessi. Great Britain had in fact strongly disapproved of the French takeover of Algiers in 1830. By the late 1830s France and England took opposite sides on whether Mohammed Ali should be forced to leave the Syrian soil Egypt had just occupied.

In July 1840 the Treaty of London was signed in France's absence in an attempt to pressure that country to reconsider its support of the viceroy's interventionism. In the late 1840s the conservative Palmerston approved of Louis-Napoleon's election and even his subsequent *coup d'état* in 1851, but a British alliance with France over Crimea in the mid-1850s was short lived. British foreign policy in the late 1850s was determined in part by fear of France especially over the Italian Question. In the 1860s British lawmakers were absorbed by the question of Parliamentary reform. By the Franco-Prussian War, England saw Bismarck's foreign policy as a useful check on both France and Russia. The early 1870s marked a new age in British foreign policy, one in which French influence had been seriously undermined (Frederick S. Rodkey, *The Turco-Egyptian Question in the Relations of England, France and Russia, 1832–1841* [University of Illinois Studies in Social Science, 11, nos. 3–4 (September-December 1923)], 28–42 and 100–23).

17. In Victor Hugo, *Selections Chiefly Lyrical from the Poetical Works of Victor Hugo*, ed. Henry Llewellyn Williams (London: George Bell and Sons, 1885), 76 (hereafter cited as *SCL*).

18. Dominique Vivant Denon, *Travels in Upper and Lower Egypt: In Company with Several Divisions of the French Army, during the Campaign of General Bonaparte in that Country*, 2 vols., trans. Arthur Aikin (London: T.N. Longman and O. Rees, 1803) (hereafter cited as *E*). The title page credits Napoleon as patron.

19. He was also a member of the Académie de Peinture from 1787. Denon had been protected by the artist Jacques-Louis David during the Revolution. He became the minister of arts under the Consulate and the Empire and the general director of museums under the Empire. After his trip to Egypt he would become one of the first artists to introduce lithography into France. His first lithograph is dated 15 September 1809.

20. Bonaparte, s.v. "Esclavage," from *Mémoires de Napoléon*, in *Dictionnaire-Napoléon*, 200. Translations are mine unless indicated otherwise.

21. Bonaparte, s.v. "Orientaux," from *Mémorial de Ste.-Hélène*, in *Dictionnaire-Napoléon*, 396.

22. Ibid.

23. Quoted in John Cairncross, *After Polygamy Was Made a Sin: The Social History of Christian Polygamy* (London: Routledge and Kegan Paul, 1974), 122.

24. Ibid., 123–24. The French wording can be found in Bonaparte, s.v. "Orientaux," from *Mémorial de Ste.-Hélène*, in *Dictionnaire-Napoléon*, 396.

25. Bonaparte, s.v. "Orientaux," from *Mémorial de Ste.-Hélène*, in *Dictionnaire-Napoléon*, 396.

26. Bonaparte, s.v. "Femmes," from *Mémorial de Ste.-Hélène*, in *Dictionnaire-Napoléon*, 214.

27. In his campaign Napoleon announced the French presence as "friends" who had come to liberate Islam from the tyranny of the mamelukes, his principal opposition. He encountered and defeated them in his takeover of Cairo, and recounts their large but disorderly management.

28. Bonaparte, s.v. "Egypte," from *Mémoires de Napoléon*, in *Dictionnaire-Napoléon*, 181.

29. See, for example, Lynne Thornton, *Women as Portrayed in Orientalist Painting* (Paris: ACR, 1993) 98ff; Alloula, *Colonial Harem*, 85–93.

30. Bonaparte, s.v. "Femmes," from *Mémorial de Ste.-Hélène*, in *Dictionnaire-Napoléon*, 213.

31. Ibid.

32. Ibid., 214.

33. Napoleon distinguishes between European and Oriental types and offers several justifications for Muslim slavery. One is that it allows greater social mobility ("A female servant marries the master" [Bonaparte, s.v. "Esclavage," from *Mémoires de Napoléon*, in *Dictionnaire-Napoléon*, 200]), a social concept to which this Corsican, who was not a pure aristocrat, might be especially sensitive. He claims two famous Muslim leaders, Mourad-Bey and Ali-Bey, had been purchased in Circassia and sold by merchants to adoptive families (and presumably raised in the harem). It was then because of "their handsome faces,

their attitude for drilling, their bravery or their intelligence, they gradually achieved the highest ranks" (Bonaparte, s.v. "Esclavage," from *Mémoires de Napoléon*, in *Dictionnaire-Napoléon*, 200). Again Napoleon seems to use an autobiographical voice in recounting a rags-to-riches story, which parallels his progressive ideals for a French civil and military bureaucracy based on merit. He contrasts eastern slavery with European where slaves remain "in the lowest rank of domestic service" (Ibid.). And Napoleon admires the color-blind system of Muslim slavery, which contrasts so markedly with the system in the French colonies—one that is more "rigid" and "debasing" than the Muslim (Ibid.).

Napoleon assigns polygyny another rather unusual social function. He claims that in the East the population is represented by a greater heterogeneity of races than at home in the West, a fact which could engender disunity and conflict. He believes the harem is valuable because it allows members of "the four races" (white, black, copper, and mixed) to be unified within the same household. He claims this was Mohammed's reason for limiting the number of allowable wives to four. Napoleon also said that the upper-class harem owner who adhered to this guideline in choosing his mates would serve as an example to encourage social harmony. Napoleon even hoped to introduce polygyny in the West Indies, where slaves were needed to work the sugar plantations. He claimed this would create a more industrious workforce. Approving polygyny on "eastern" soil, he even went so far as to approach Catholic theologians about changing Church doctrine to allow its introduction into the West Indies. Still he would never have allowed it in France, where he advocated monogamy in the *Code Napoléon*. See also Bonaparte, s.v. "Noirs," from *Mémoires de Napoléon*, in *Dictionnaire-Napoléon*, 392.

34. Stewart writes of the "confused relationship" between the double purposes of documenting and allegorizing in eighteenth-century book illustration. In representing ethnographic or geographic difference, "Racial attributes are supposed to be 'real' [. . .] yet they are [. . .] stylized by iconological convention" (Philip Stewart, "On the 'Iconology' of Literary Illustration," in *Dilemmes du roman: Essays in Honor of Georges May*, ed. Catherine Lafarge [Saratoga CA: Anma Libri and Company, 1989], 261).

35. On this point see George L. Mosse, *Nationalism and Sexuality: Middle-Class Morality and Sexual Norms in Modern Europe* (Madison: University of Wisconsin Press, 1988), chapter 7.

36. Grosrichard, *Structure du sérail*, 214.

37. Thomas Moore, *Lalla Rookh: An Oriental Romance* (1817; reprint, New York: Lincoln Macveagh, The Dial Press, Longmans Green and Co., 1930), 7 (hereafter cited as *LR*).

38. Homi K. Bhabha, "The Other Question . . ." *Screen* (24, no. 6 [November-December 1983]), 23.

39. Henry Louis Gates, Jr. *"Race," Writing and Difference* (Chicago: University of Chicago Press, 1986), 4–5.

40. Homi K. Bhabha, "Other Question," 30.

41. Another "fetish of difference" for Nerval is the slaves' feet made long and wide by "their practice at climbing trees, [which] made them bear a close resemblance to the monkey" (*VO* 35). Note that the First Eunuch in *Persian Letters* is wildly enthusiastic about a "yellow-skinned" slave from Bijapur whom he purchases for Usbek's brother: she has "the quality of a complexion which could eclipse all the splendors of Circassia" (*PL* 178–79).

42. Montesquieu had satirized the French fascination with eastern clothing in his *Persian Letters*. Rica writes that when he is introduced to French society, he is fawned over, receiving it as an honour. But he is crushed to recognize that when he dresses as the French do, he is ignored (*PL* 83). More than mere entertainment, clothing is constructed as an indicator of identity, indeed, a fetish of difference (Lisa Lowe, *Critical Terrains: French and British Orientalisms* [Ithaca: Cornell University Press, 1991], 57).

43. Tucker, *Women*, 170.

44. Joanna de Groot, "'Sex' and 'Race': the Construction of Language and Image in the Nineteenth Century," in *Sexuality and Subordination: Interdisciplinary Studies of Gender in the Nineteenth Century*, ed. Susan Mendus and Jane Rendall (London: Routledge, 1989), 100.

45. Emma Reeve, *Character and Costume in Turkey and Italy: A Description of Eight Turkish and Twelve Italian Plates, Designed and Drawn from Nature by Thomas Allom, Esq.* (London: Fisher, Son and Co., 1839), 29.

46. Florence Nightingale, *Letters from Egypt: A Journey on the Nile 1849–1850* (New York: Weidenfeld and Nicholson, 1987), 208 (hereafter cited as *LE*).

47. Bonaparte, s.v. "Egypte," from *Mémoires de Napoléon*, in *Dictionnaire-Napoléon*, 181.

48. Mrs. John Elijah Blunt, *The People of Turkey: Twenty Years' Residence Among Bulgarians, Greeks, Albanians, Turks and Armenians*, 2 vols., ed. Stanley Lane Poole (London: John Murray, 1878), 1:150–54 (hereafter cited as *PT*).

49. Compare the comment from Murray's 1871 travel guidebook to Turkey, which quotes an earlier female traveler writing of music in the harem: "The band next struck up a war-tune, and the savage instinct of the Circassian mountaineers seemed to awaken" (*A Handbook for Travellers in Turkey in Asia including Constantinople, the Bosphorus, Dardanelles, Brousa . . . and the Plain of Troy*, 4th ed. [London: John Murray, 1871], 112–13) (hereafter cited as *HTT*).

50. Victorian foreign policy towards Circassia remained fairly consistent. As early as 1836 Palmerston expressed the desire to aid Circassians resisting Russia's attempts to open the trade route from the Caucasus into Central Asia. In effect this would be a retaliation against Russia. Prime Minister Melbourne convinced Palmerston not to act on his sympathies, which would have meant a major financial commitment for Britain. When in December 1836 the British ship *Vixen* attempted to run the blockade off the coast of Circassia, David Urquhart and his supporters excoriated Palmerston. His opposition to the then-British policy of support with Russia and his lack of cooperation with Ponsonby lead to the Vixen Affair, culminating in his removal in 1837 from the office of first secretary to the Constantinople embassy.

In a memorandum of 20 June 1853 Palmerston echoed Urquhart's anti-Russian sentiment by supporting the rebellious Circassian subjects. Again in 1854 Palmerston's "beau ideal" of the Russian map was sketched out in his correspondence:

> The Crimea, Circassia, and Georgia [would be] wrested from Russia, the Crimea and Georgia given to Turkey, and Circassia either independent or connected with the Sultan as Suzerain. (Quoted in Kenneth Bourne, *The Foreign Policy of Victorian England 1830–1902* [Oxford: Clarendon Press, 1970], 78).

Unwilling to risk the cost of direct intervention, the British failed to enter Circassian territory. After losing the Crimean War and other diplomatic failures, Russia became alarmed and strengthened its efforts to quell resistance in the Caucasus. In fact by 1864 Russia had succeeded in subduing Circassian resistance. After Palmerston's handling of the 1839–41 Eastern Question with Nicholas of Russia, Urquhart accused Palmerston of high treason "and devoted the rest of his colorful career to the unmasking and defeat of this supposed Russian agent" (ibid., 45).

51. David Urquhart, *Spirit of the East Illustrated in a Journal of Travels through Roumeli during an Eventful Period* (London: Henry Colburn, 1838), (hereafter cited as *SE*). Urquhart's pro-Turkish vehemence had already been expressed in his 1833 *Turkey and its Resources,* commissioned by Lord Palmerston, Foreign Secretary from 1830–41.

52. Urquhart wrote a curious little book entitled *The Turkish Bath, with a View to its Introduction into the British Dominions* (London: D. Bryce, 1856). References to him are scattered through the nineteenth-century British travel literature, for example, James MacFarlane, *Turkey and Its Destiny: the Results of Journeys . . . in 1847 and 1848,* 2 vols. (London: John Murray, 1850), 2:420. Even Edward Lane acknowledged a debt to Urquhart, who provided comments and corrections to the third edition of his *Manners and Customs of the Modern Egyptians* (*ME* xxi). From the earlier twentieth century see G. H. Bolsover, "David Urquhart and the Eastern Question, 1833–37," *Journal of Modern History* (December 1936). Today there is a website on Urquhart and the Turkish bath in London.

53. On his "conversion," see C. M. Woodhouse, *The Philhellenes* (London: Hodder and Stoughton, 1969), 149–51.

54. Urquhart was not only anti-Russian; he was also vehemently anti-French. In *Spirit of the East* he criticizes the conduct of French merchants in Egypt since the days of the Directory, the government which often provoked minor conflicts with local authorities and then overreacted by recalling the French Consul and forbidding those merchants to trade (*SE* 2:323). He chastises not only French merchants but also the French military imperialist invasions in Egypt and Algiers. As a retort to anti-British remarks he says the French have demonstrated their "duplicity" and "design" on Middle Eastern territory, while Britain has been honest about its motives in the bombing of Algiers, a retaliatory measure for its piracy. He criticized Britain's Turkish policy under Palmerston, calling it "contemptible," yet he claimed it is not as bad as France's.

55. Urquhart quoted in Lane (*ME* 1:69, n. 2).

56. Urquhart quoted in Frank Edgar Bailey, *British Policy and the Turkish Reform Movement: A Study in Anglo-Turkish Relations, 1826–1853,* Harvard Historical Studies (New York: Howard Fertig, 1970), 164.

57. In his publicly exhibited, finished works on the harem which I will examine in detail, Lewis always wraps the bodices of his harem women modestly, but here he exposes much of one breast. Lewis is usually so precise in his oils and watercolors of the harem beginning in the 1850s and this work is so atypical of them that its attribution to him is questionable.

58. Wiebke Walther, *Woman in Islam,* translated by C. S. V. Salt (Montclair, NJ: Abner Schram, 1981), 71.

59. One of the earliest depictions of an Armenian woman belongs to Jean-Baptiste Vanmour's *Recueil de cent estampes représentant différentes nations du Levant tirées sur les tableaux peints d'après nature . . .* ([Paris: Le Hay, 1714], pl. 87). This woman is not residing in the harem but rather being led to her marriage ceremony, her whole body, head and eyes completely covered by a veil. Lady Mary Wortley Montagu provides an unintended commentary on this image when she writes that the Armenian bride is covered head to toe and married unseen by the bridegroom, "Deformitys" and all and that "her vail [is] never lifted up, not even by her husband, till she has been 3 days marry'd" (*L* 1:412, 411). Here the exaggeration of her veiling is undercut in the naming of her as Armenian; it is in effect "explained" by her "race." Today the image's outrageousness can provoke surprise, humor and/or culturally relative empathy, reactions that were probably similar in the eighteenth century. Note that Montesquieu names the Armenians as one of several groups subject to persecution in Persia, resulting in "a spirit of dizzying madness" in which reason is no longer operative (*PL* 164–65).

60. John Bowring, *Report on Egypt and Candia, addressed to the Right Honorable Lord Viscount Palmerston . . . Presented to Both Houses of Parliament by Command of Her Majesty* (London: Printed by W. Clowes and Sons, H.M. Stationery Office, 1840), 4.

61. *Encyclopedia of Islam* (Leyden and London: Luza and Co., 1960), 1:32.

62. Julia Pardoe, *The City of the Sultan and Domestic Manners of the Turks in 1836,* 2 vols. (London: Henry Colburn, 1837), 1:104, 114 (hereafter cited as *CS*); Charles White, *Three Years in Constantinople or Domestic Manners of the Turks in 1844,* 3 vols. (London: Henry Colburn, 1845), 2:290.

63. By Lady Mary Wortley Montagu's account, Armenians "are (perhaps) the devoutest Christians in the whole world" (*L* 1:410). Likewise the series title from which this plate is taken affirms its authenticity, as we are assured of the artist's firsthand observation: *Cinquante et une planches, en partie coloriées, pour illustrer le voyage à Athènes et à Constantinople.*

64. "Glimpses of Harem Life," *Bentley's Miscellany* 43 (1858): 513.

65. Lewis's work can be correlated to at least three discourses about the harem, the first of which is eastern and theological, the other two western and political. In one reading the inmate is the personification of the heavenly *houri*; no critics commented this way. Alternatively, the Armenian woman, presumably once a prisoner, accepts her life of luxury as suggested by her placid demeanor here. Thirdly, she rejects it; she finds a way to circumvent some aspect of the institution's oppression in the spiritual protest implied by the nosegay from an outside lover, as suggested in the work's title when it was published in the *Art Journal* of 1858, three years after it was first shown at the Royal Academy. There it is published as *An Armenian Lady, Cairo—The Love Missive* ("British Artists," *AJ* 1858: 43). Lewis's visual language and his title allow ambiguity in the work's meaning, opening it up to multiple interpretations. By 1841 Lewis had done at least two other watercolor sketches having Armenian women in their titles: *Armenian Women at Brussa* and *Armenian Woman, Cairo* (1841), images which may not describe harem women but simply women of that identity whom he encountered on his travels and sketched.

66. John Ruskin, *The Works of John Ruskin,* 39 vols., ed. E. T. Cook and Alexander Wedderburn (New York: Longmans,

Green and Co.; London: George Allen, 1903–12), 14:12 (hereafter cited as *W*).

67. The year 1855 is a watershed in the history of British interventionism on the issue of Muslim slavery. It is the year the British give up their goal of eliminating Muslim slavery as a whole. Henceforth, they would focus on the more practical goal of restricting the slave trade. Also around this time they learn that black and white slavery would be two separate issues for the Muslims, with two different policies. Simultaneously by 1855 the Ottomans were in the process of prohibiting (temporarily) the slave trade in Circassians and Georgians. The British again interpreted this action as a victory for their principles when in fact the action was internally motivated. In subsequent years the British reminded the sultan of his own prohibition of the trade, he promptly ignored such remarks, pointing out the exigencies of war that necessitated such unusual—and temporary—measures (Ehud Toledano, *The Ottoman Slave Trade and its Suppression 1840–90* [Princeton: Princeton University Press, 1982], 117–19).

68. In Mozart's *Abduction from the Seraglio* the proud hero Belmonte announces his true identity as descended from a great Spanish family (*AS* 149). In an earlier version of the story Pasha Selim recognizes him as his long-lost son, and Selim is himself of European descent (Nicholas Till, *Mozart and the Enlightenment* [New York: W.W. Norton and Company, 1992], 106, 115). Thus the two identities, Spanish and Turkish, are blurred.

69. Lewis, *Lewis*, 37.

70. Ibid., fig. 70.

71. *Language and Poetry of Flowers* (London: Milner and Company, c. 1871), n.p.

72. This work too suffers from an identity crisis: *Siesta* is one of its four titles (Wallace Collection, *Summary of Illustrated Catalogue of Pictures* [London: Trustees of the Wallace Collection, 1979], 19). It was acquired by Richard Wallace and presumably accessible to Lewis and five million other viewers in 1872–75 when Wallace's collection was on view at the Bethnal Green Museum as its permanent building was renovated.

73. Meerza Ahmed Tubeeb, "Visits to the Harem," *Blackwood's Magazine* (Edinburgh) 15 (February 1824), 201.

74. See also Bram Dijkstra, *Idols of Perversity: Fantasies of Feminine Evil in Fin-de-Siècle Culture* (New York: Oxford University Press, 1986), 25–63.

75. Tucker, *Women*, 170.

76. Richard F. Burton, *Personal Narrative of a Pilgrimage to El-Medinah and Meccah*, 3 vols. (London: Longman, Brown and Longmans, 1855), 1:87.

77. *British and Foreign Anti-Slavery Reporter* (15 November 1843): 216 (hereafter cited as *ASR*).

78. *Spectator* (4 May 1853): 427 (hereafter cited as *S*).

79. Later in 1855 it appeared at the Paris Exposition Universelle, where it drew mixed reviews from the French critics Edmond About (*V* 32) and Maxime du Camp (*Les beaux-arts à l'exposition universelle de 1855* [Paris, 1855], 317–18), and unqualified praised from Théophile Gautier, who called this woman a savagely coquettish Nubian slave reminiscent of ancient Egyptian idols. To Gautier she was also "a poor barbaric creature with the smile of a sphinx" and a true African Venus (*Les beaux-arts en Europe 1855* [Paris: Michel Levy frères, 1855], 97). For the French as well as the British poetic metaphor masked the issue of slavery. For an American critic's very positive response to this work, see "John Lewis," *(Littell's) Living Age* 31, no. 385 (4 October 1851): 17.

80. He would have himself crowned Emperor Theodore II two years after, though a skirmish with the British led to his suicide in 1868.

81. Nicos Hadjinicolaou, "*La Liberté guidant le peuple* de Delacroix devant son premier public," *Actes de la Recherche en science sociales* 28 (June 1979): 16.

82. Gustave Planche, *Revue des Deux Mondes* 2, ser. 3 (1 April 1834): 58–59.

83. Barthélemy Hauréau, *La Tribune* (15 March 1834): n.p.

84. "C'est la vie tranquille et contemplative de l'Orient . . . c'est un calme, c'est une nonchalance adorable; c'est une béatitude indicible. Sans doute ces femmes ont bu l'opium ou le *hachich*. Sans doute elles se bercent intérieurement de quelque rêve du prophète; mais il n'en transpire rien au dehors, si ce n'est comme un parfum autour de leurs corps voluptueux. Et puis, ce sont des étoffes de soie argentée, transparentes comme la gaze, des tentures éclatantes, des cassolettes et des *narguileck*; et sur tous cela il règne une harmonie et une vapeur qui caresse les longs cils noirs de ces femmes, qui ondoye sur leurs souples vêtements. Devant cette fraîche peinture, on se recueille, on respire doucement, on fait silence, on a peur de dépenser sa vie. C'est un immense contraste avec le caractére française qui n'a jamais songé à economiser le mouvement et l'activité" (Théophile Thoré-Bürger, *Le Siècle* (1837), quoted in Graté, *Deux critiques d'art*, 228).

85. In *Littré*'s *nonchalance* is defined as : "Mollesse, abandon . . ."

86. DelPlato, "Passivity and Politics," 244–51.

87. Elizabeth Gilmore Holt, *The Triumph of Art for the Public* (Garden City, NY: Anchor Press, Doubleday, 1979), 389.

88. *Journal des Débats*, 8 March 1834, n.p.

89. Beatrice Farwell, *Eugène Delacroix, 1798–1863* (New York: Metropolitan Museum of Art, 1955),14.

90. On this motif Delacroix writes: "our French laws are established in the place of brutal despotism" (quoted in Todd Porterfield, *The Allure of Empire: Art in the Service of French Imperialism, 1798–1836* [Princeton: Princeton University Press, 1998], 137).

91. I agree with Porterfield who sees this as a procolonialist image which reworks harem conventions in a more contemporary (and less allegorical) way, though unlike him I think Delacroix is still perceived as a leader of the revolutionary-Romantic School in 1834. Porterfield also makes a case for this painting as part of early ethnographic *rapportage*, while I see it as still occupying the genre of art-for-art's-sake, given the lack of direct critical commentary on Algeria in response to this painting. I have elsewhere argued that Delacroix probably did not enter a harem while on his trip to Morocco in 1832, while Porterfield is more agnostic and claims that this painting has been received as evidence that he had gained access (Porterfield, *Allure of Empire*, 127–38; DelPlato, "Passivity and Politics," 244–51).

92. Griselda Pollock, *Vision and Difference* (London: Routledge, 1988), 54.

93. Yet another postscript to Delacroix's painting is a collection of short stories given the same title first published in French in 1980, Assia Djebar's *Women of Algiers in their Apartment* (Charlottesville: University of Virginia Press, 1992).

94. Jeffrey Coven, *Baudelaire's Voyages: The Poet and His Paints* (Boston: Little Brown and Co., 1993), 33.

95. Charles Baudelaire, *The Painter of Modern Life and Other Essays,* trans. and ed. Jonathan Mayne (New York: DaCapo, 1986), 65.

96. Ibid.

97. Raphael Danziger, *Abd Al-Qadir and the Algerians: Resistance to the French and Internal Consolidation* (New York and London: Holmes and Meier, 1977), 230.

98. These statistics are from 1840–48 (ibid., xi).

99. *Explication des oeuvrages de peinture, sculpture, gravure . . . des artists vivants, exposés au musée royal* (Paris: Vinchon, 1845), 198.

100. *L'Illustration* 5, no. 107 (15 March 1845): 39. Compare Charles Baudelaire's critical comment: "This African painting is colder than a fine winter's day. Everything in it is of a heart-breaking whiteness and brightness. [. . .] It is truly painful to see an intelligent man floundering about in such a mess of horror" (Charles Baudelaire, "The Salon of 1845," in *The Mirror of Art,* trans. and ed. Jonathan Mayne [Garden City, NY: Doubleday, 1956], 7–8).

101. Note Chassériau's *Woman and Little Girl of Constantine with a Gazelle* (See Fig. 4.29); Chassiron's *Jeune Fille Moresque (Tunis)* (See Fig. 5.20) n.d.; Decamps's *An Algerian Woman* (See Fig. 4.32) (1830–32); Renoir's *Women of Algiers* 1870 (See Fig. 4.60); Devéria's, *Tunis* (See Fig. 3.41) from *Les amants de différents pays* 1834–38, reissued 1851. Two more worthy of note and not studied here are Camille Corot's *L'Algérienne* (c. 1870–73) and his *Young Algerian Woman Lying on the Grass* (c. 1871–73).

102. Grosrichard, *Structure du sérail,* 159.

Chapter 3. Depictions of Slavery and the Making of the Harem

1. Albert Smith, *Customs and Habits of the Turks* (Boston: Higgins and Bradley, 1856), 111.

2. Sophie Lane Poole, *The Englishwoman in Egypt: Letters from Cairo, Written During a Residence There in 1842, -3 and -4 with E. W. Lane* (Philadelphia: G. B. Ziegler and Co., 1845), 168. Lane urged his sister to write *Englishwoman in Egypt* (first edition London, 1844) as a source of information about the harem that he felt he could not provide. For biographical information on her see Billie Melman, *Women's Orients: English Women and the Middle East, 1718–1918: Sexuality, Religion and Work* (Ann Arbor: University of Michigan Press, 1992), 74, 332.

3. Tucker, *Women,* 179.

4. Ibid., 181.

5. Ibid., 184.

6. Ibid., 183.

7. John Bunbury, *A Relation of a Journey of the Rt. Honorable my Lord Henry Howard from London . . . to Constantinople* (London: Collins and Ford, 1671), 85, 115; Paul Rycaut, *History of the present state of the Ottoman Empire . . . in three books,* 4th ed. (London: Starkey and Brome, 1675), 69; George Sandys, *Sandys Travailles: Containing a History of the . . . Turkish Empire,* 6th ed. (London: John Sweeting, 1658), 52, 54; Robert Withers, *A Description of the Grand Signor's Seraglio,* in *The English Experience: Its Record in Early Printed Books* (1585; reprint, Amsterdam and New York: Da Capo Press, 1968), 37, 59.

8. E. Phillip LeVeen, *British Slave Trade Suppression Policies 1821–1865,* Dissertations in Economic History (New York: Arno Press, 1977), 83.

9. Tucker, *Women,* 176. Much later Consul General Evelyn Baring Cromer (Lord Cromer) also wished to avoid provoking lower-class Muslims who might inflame Egyptian religious parties against the British (ibid.).

10. Quoted in Toledano, *Ottoman Slave Trade,* 170.

11. Toledano, *Ottoman Slave Trade,* 92–94; *Anti-Slavery Reporter* (21 October 1840): 267 (hereafter cited as *ASR*).

12. Toledano, *Ottoman Slave Trade,* 93.

13. *ASR* 6 September 1843, 166. Mohammed Ali had previously been singled out for condemnation by abolitionist forces for his slave-hunts overseen by white mameluke officers into deep Africa, where he recruited black male slaves to serve in his newly enlarged navy and for domestic building projects. See also: *ASR* 2 December 1840: 311; 9 February 1842: 24; *T* 7 February 1835: 5; John Bowring, *Report on Egypt and Candia, addressed to the Right Honorable Lord Viscount Palmerston . . . Presented to Both Houses of Parliament by Command of Her Majesty* (London: W. Clowes and Sons, H.M. Stationery Office, 1840), 83.

14. Gabriel Baer, "Slavery in Nineteenth-Century Egypt," *Journal of African History* 8, no. 3 (1967): 429–30.

15. Foucault, *History of Sexuality,* 1:26.

16. Ibid., 1:55.

17. Karl Marx and Frederick Engels, *The Communist Manifesto* (New York: International Publishers, 1979), 12–13.

18. Toledano, *Ottoman Slave Trade,* 139–40.

19. Baer, "Slavery," 431–34.

20. Charles White, *Three Years in Constantinople or Domestic Manners of the Turks in 1844,* 2 vols. (London: Henry Colburn, 1845), 2:312. This book containing commentary on the harem saw two editions and was translated into German. Educated at Eton, White (1793–1861) was a decorated soldier attached to the regiment of the Guards in his youth. He wrote six books on a range of topics from the Belgian Revolution to fiction to naval studies.

21. Ibid., 2:304–5.

22. Ibid., 2:309.

23. (1806–1862). Judging from their titles, at least four of her twenty-four books suggest the harem: *City of the Sultan and Domestic Manners of the Turks in 1831* (1837), *Beauties of the Bosphorus* (1838), *Romance of the Harem* (1839), *Rival Beauties* (1857). She also wrote the introduction to one edition of *1001 Days, A Companion to Arabian Nights.* See biographical information on her in S. Austin Allibone, *A Critical Dictionary of English Literature and British and American Authors* (Philadelphia: J.B. Lippincott Co., 1897), and Billie Melman, *Women's Orients,* 331.

24. Julia Pardoe, *Beauties of the Bosphorus* (London: George Virtue, 1838), 128.

25. Ibid.

26. Julia Pardoe, *City of the Sultan and Domestic Manners of the Turks in 1836,* 2 vols. (London: Henry Colburn, 1837), 1:114. (hereafter cited as *CS*).

27. David Urquhart, *Spirit of the East Illustrated in a Journal of Travels through Roumeli during an Eventful Period* (London: Henry Colburn, 1838), 2:370, 410.

28. Edmund Spencer, *Travels in Circassia, Kim-Tartary . . . in 1836* (London: Colburn, 1837), 1:149–51. Neither his birth

nor death date is known, but his first book was published in 1836, his last in 1866, making him roughly contemporary with Charles White and Julia Pardoe. His writing is almost all travel accounts.

29. Kumari Jayawardena, *Feminism and Nationalism in the Third World* (London: Zea Books, 1986), 27.

30. James MacFarlane, *Turkey and Its Destiny: The Results of Journeys . . . in 1847 and 1848,* 2 vols. (London: John Murray, 1850), 1:23.

31. Urquhart, *Spirit of the East,* 2:410.

32. MacFarlane, *Turkey and Its Destiny,* 2:418, 419.

33. Ibid., 2:420.

34. (*W* 29:337). In March 1878 Ruskin recommends to his readers' attention Canon MacColl's article in the *Nineteenth Century,* titled "Current Fallacies about Turks, Bulgarians, and Russians." For his additional comments on the Eastern Question see *W* 29:45–46 and *W* 24:xxxviii.

35. The story was first quoted in Thomas Carlyle's *Past and Present* and then reported in the *Times* on 4 February 1863.

36. Ruskin says of Carlyle's position: "I should dwell, . . . at more length on this subject of slavery, had not all I would say been said already in vain, (not, as I hope, ultimately in vain) by Carlyle, in the first of the *Latter-Day Pamphlets,* which I commend to the reader's gravest reading" (*W* 17:260.) For Carlyle's comments see his Number 1 "The Present Time," *Latter-Day Pamphlets* (Boston: Estes and Lauriat, n.d.), 284–85.

37. In 1873 W. H. Wylde, head of Britain's Slave Trade Department, had drawn the line at the same point, demonstrating a widespread belief in the primacy of the family unit, even when it was Muslim.

38. In chapter four of *Cestus of Aglaia* (1865, 1866) Ruskin takes issue with the universality of liberty, when its advocates claim "that liberty is good for a man, irrespectively of the use he is likely to make of it" (*W* 19:125). Part of this section was reproduced in *AJ* n.s. 5 (July 1865),197–99.

39. By age 40 (1859) Ruskin was reputedly a pedophile (Phyllis Rose, *Parallel Lives: Five Victorian Marriages* [New York: Alfred A. Knopf, 1984], 56). The harem was known to be the home of child brides, many of whom were betrothed before puberty. Ruskin's apparent disapproval of the harem as an inappropriate artistic subject might be considered at least partially a repression of his own penchant for female children.

40. "It is long since I have bought a picture (my son going sufficiently deep into the luxury), but I was tempted by three small ones at the first glance—[Emile] Plassan's Music Lesson, French Exhibition; Lewis's Inmate of the Hareem, Royal Academy; Lewis's Lilies and Roses, Royal Academy. [. . .] As the *Times* calls the Inmate of the Hareem a masterpiece of masterpieces, and the *Spectator* styles it a marvellous gem, it is a pretty safe purchase. I had it at home before the public saw it" (quoted in *W* 14:180). A letter from the elder Ruskin to Lewis suggests their personal connection. On 30 August 1858 John James Ruskin writes to Lewis "I am writing to my Son almost daily–If you can send me a single line to say you are better–it will be a great pleasure to him and to me" (Letter A15, kindly supplied by the late Michael Lewis).

41. William Makepeace Thackeray, *Sketches and Travels in London* and *Notes of a Journey From Cornhill to Cairo,* in *Works of William Makepeace Thackeray,* 26 vols. (Boston: Charles E. Lauriat, 1904), 16:475.

42. Don Herzog, *Happy Slaves: A Critique of Consent Theory* (Chicago: University of Chicago Press, 1989), 1.

43. Smith, *Customs and Habits,* 113.

44. Poole, *Englishwoman in Egypt,* 137.

45. Ibid., 167–68.

46. David Urquhart, *Spirit of the East,* 2:384–85.

47. *ASR* 2 April 1845:68. See also the *Anti-Slavery Reporter* regarding the young Algerian women about to be sold: they did not "appear to be sad or sorry" (17 September 1845:180).

48. M. E. J. Delécluze, *Les Beaux-Arts dans les deux mondes en 1855* (Paris: Charpentier, 1856), 129.

49. Ibid.

50. A. Kevin Reinhart, "The Here and the Hereafter in Islamic Religious Thought," in *Images of Paradise in Islamic Art,* ed. Sheila S. Blair and Jonathan M. Bloom (Hanover, NH: Hood Museum of Art, Dartmouth College [1991]), 17.

51. Elizabeth Gilmore Holt, *The Triumph of Art for the Public* (Garden City, NY: Anchor Press, Doubleday, 1979), 473.

52. Ali Behdad, "The Eroticized Orient: Images of the Harem in Montesquieu and His Precursors," *Stanford French Review* 13, nos. 2–3 (fall-winter 1989), 117–18.

53. Ibid., 117.

54. Robert Walsh, *Constantinople and the Scenery of the Seven Churches of Asia Minor, Illustrated . . . by Thomas Allom,* 2 vols. (London and Paris: Fisher, Son and Co., 1838) 1:38.

55. Jean Baptiste Vanmour, *Moeurs et usages des turcs,* 2 vols. (Paris, 1746), 2:413.

56. Emma Reeve, *Character and Costume in Turkey and Italy: A Description of Eight Turkish and Twelve Italian Plates* (London: Fisher, Son and Co., 1839), 30.

57. Stewart's comment about eighteenth-century books relates here: "an illustration purports to represent the content of the text, but only abstractly and symbolically" (Philip Stewart, "On the 'Iconology' of Literary Illustration," in *Dilemmes du roman: Essays in Honor of Georges May,* ed. Catherine Lafarge [Saratoga CA: Anma Libri and Company, 1989], 256).

58. *Christie, Manson and Woods Artist's Sale Catalog,* London (7 May 1877): 13.

59. Toledano, *Ottoman Slave Trade,* 52.

60. Lewis was in Constantinople only once, according to his biographer Roget, following his stay in Spain and Greece in 1840 (J. Roget, *A History of the Old Water-Colour Society* [London: Longmans, Green and Co., 1891], 140). From Lewis scholars we learn that he was in and around Constantinople from October 1840 until November 1841. In 1842 he traveled from Constantinople to Asia Minor, reaching Cairo the same year. He then settled in Cairo until he returned home to London by 1851. Assuming that Lewis sketched his *Slave Market* or at least a part of it in Constantinople, it can be dated 1840 or 1841.

61. Martin Hardie, *Water-colour Painting in Britain,* 3 vols., ed. Dudley Snelgrove (London: B. T. Batsford, 1968), 3:54.

62. George Keppel (Earl of Albemarle), *Narrative of a Journey Across the Balcan . . . in the Year 1829–30,* 2 vols. (London: Colburn and Bentley, 1831), 2:79; Toledano, *Ottoman Slave Trade,* 52.

63. Spencer, *Travels in Circassia,* 1:149.

64. White, *Three Years in Constantinople,* 2:281.

65. Pardoe, *Beauties of the Bosphorus,* 129; McFarlane, *Turkey and Its Destiny,* 2:406; Smith *Customs and Habits of the Turks,* 111;

1838 Royal Academy Exhibition catalog (quoted in Bendiner, "Wilkie in Turkey," *Art Bulletin* 63, no. 2 [June 1981], 262).

66. The mosque looms ghostlike in the background in William Allan's painting *Slave Market, Constantinople* shown at the Royal Academy in 1838.

67. On Turkey see Toledano, *Ottoman Slave Trade,* 59. On Egypt see Baer, "Slavery in Nineteenth-Century Egypt," 427.

68. Keppel, *Journey Across the Balcan,* 2:79.

69. Smith, *Customs and Habits of the Turks,* 113.

70. Spencer, *Travels in Circassia,* 1:149; White, *Three Years in Constantinople,* 2:282–83.

71. Keppel, *Journey Across the Balcan,* 2:79; White, *Three Years in Constantinople,* 2:283.

72. Keppel, *Journey Across the Balcan,* 2:79 and Spencer, *Travels in Circassia,* 1:149–52.

73. Toledano, *Ottoman Slave Trade,* 54; Tucker, *Women,* 168. Nerval also must go to a private home to find the Abyssinian slave woman he first hopes to purchase (*VO* 45).

74. Toledano, *Ottoman Slave Trade,* 107–8, 116.

75. Tucker, *Women,* 173.

76. This is according to *AJ* 12 (1850):179. I do not deal in this study with the status of male harem slaves, who were often black eunuchs. For information on male servants and slaves, see David Ayalon, "On the Eunuchs in Islam," *Jerusalem Studies in Arabic and Islam* (1979) 1:89–92; "ᶜAbd," *Encyclopedia of Islam* (Leyden and London: Luza and Co., 1960), 1:31; Baer, "Slavery in Nineteenth-Century Egypt," 417–41; Toledano, *Ottoman Slave Trade* [index]; *ME* 1:169 and 225; and Grosrichard, *Structure du sérail,* 183–206.

77. Nadia Tomiche, "The Situation of Egyptian Women in the First Half of the Nineteenth Century," in *Beginnings of Modernization in the Middle East,* ed. William Roe Polk, *et al.* (Chicago: University of Chicago Press, 1968), 172.

78. Compare *ME* 1:61.

79. Depending on local custom, she provided a guarantee which ranged from three days to one year (*Encyclopedia of Islam,* s.v. "ᶜAbd," 26). Lane says that a slave's snoring, grinding her teeth, or talking in her sleep is reason to return the new slave (*ME* 1:236–37). Compare the Armenian saleswomen to whom Montesquieu refers in Letter 79 of *Persian Letters.*

80. One critic calls her "modest" (*ILN* 4 May 1850:300). Yet another calls her "proud and somewhat indignant" (*A* 4 May 1850:480) at being taken a slave, thus countering the impression of her total passivity.

81. Toledano, *Ottoman Slave Trade,* 117–19.

82. Quoted in Margaret Cecilia Annan, "The *Arabian Nights* in Victorian Literature," (Ph.D. diss., Northwestern University, 1945), 13.

83. *Arabian Nights' Entertainment,* trans. Edward Forster (London: Willoughby and Co., c. 1844), 666.

84. On Scheherazade as an intellectual, see Fatema Mernissi, *Scheherazade Goes West* (New York: Washington Square Press, 2001), 43–60.

85. For commentary on the articles of clothing Lady Mary names, see Fanny Davis, *The Ottoman Lady: A Social History from 1718–1918* (Westport, CT: Greenwood Press, 1986), 187–93.

86. Tucker, *Women,* 178.

87. Redi Mowafi, *Slavery, Slave Trade, and Abolition Attempts in Egypt and the Sudan, 1820–1882,* Lund Studies in International History, no. 14 (Esselte Studium [Sweden], 1981), 42.

88. Mowafi, *Slavery, Slave Trade, and Abolition Attempts,* 42.

89. Withers, *Description of the Grand Signor's Seraglio,* 37.

90. Rycaut, *History of the Present State of the Ottoman Empire,* 375.

91. Pointon, *Bonington Circle,* 106.

92. Frank Anderson Trapp, *The Attainment of Delacroix* (Baltimore and London: Johns Hopkins Press, 1971), 42.

93. Historical and Ethnological Society of Greece, *Philhellenika, 1821–31* (Athens, 1975), 1:15.

94. Francis Haskell, "Chios, the Massacres and Delacroix," in *Chios: A Conference at the Homerion in Chios 1984,* ed. John Boardman and C. E. Vaphopoulou-Richardson (Oxford: Clarendon Press, 1986), 343.

95. Nina Athanassoglou-Kallmyer, *French Images from the Greek War of Independence: Art and Politics Under the Restoration* (New Haven: Yale University Press, 1989), 31.

96. Ibid., 29.

97. Eugène Delacroix, *Journal,* trans. Walter Pach (New York: Crown, 1948), 60.

98. Ibid., 67.

99. Ibid., 73.

100. Historical and Philological Society of Greece, *Philhellenika, 1821–31,* 1:5.

101. Quoted in Holt, *Triumph of Art for the Public,* 268.

102. Quoted in Ibid., 251. Compare Victor Hugo's 1828 poem from *Les Orientales* titled "Pirates' Song" in which the youngest nun is captured from a nunnery and sold into a harem. En route the pirates console her with the thought that "You only change your prison dull / For one that's splendid, glowing!" The woman's attitude about harem life indeed changes: "For vain her vow to pine and die / Thus torn from her dear valley: / She reigns" (*SCL* 44–45).

103. Historical and Ethnological Society of Greece, *Philhellenika, 1821–31,* 1:6.

104. Quoted in Holt, *Triumph of Art for the Public,* 252.

105. Quoted in Ibid., 253.

106. Delacroix, *Journal,* 67.

107. Eugène Delacroix, *Correspondance générale,* 5 vols. (Paris: Plon, 1938), 1:132.

108. Britain, France, and Russia joined forces in the Navarino Bay to the southwest of the Peloponnese. On 20 October 1827 they devastated Egyptian troops and turned the war in favor of the Greeks. The allies destroyed sixty enemy ships and lost none of their own. And 8,000 Muslims were killed compared to the allies' loss of 176.

109. Mohja Kahf, *Western Representations of the Muslim Woman: From Termagant to Odalisque* (Austin: University of Texas Press, 1999), 152, 154, 158.

110. Next to Lewis's signature in the lower left corner and written in the same script are the words, "Greek Girl"; the list of illustrations titles this plate *Captive Greek Girl* emphasizing her confinement. It is unknown whether Lewis played more than a merely technical role, perhaps co-designing the plate he drew.

111. Separating flower clusters from the garden or from each other damages them, according to traditions in Persian literature (William L. Hanaway, Jr., "Paradise on Earth: The Terrestrial Garden in Persian Literature," in *The Islamic Garden,* ed. Elisabeth B. MacDougall and Richard Ettinghausen [Washington, DC: Dumbarton Oaks, 1976], 58).

112. Compare Stanislaus Julien's 1824 text, which laments the captured Greek woman's loss of loved one and her alienation from the other harem women:

Ondes pures et sacrées de la mer Egée, vous ne baignez plus le corps éblouissant des vierges de Chios. Lorsque, soir et matin, vous rafraîchissiez leurs chastes attraits, où triomphaient les Grâces, vous dédaigniez les roses de l'Orient. Maintenant vous êtes dans le veuvage; maintenant ces vierges divines sont enchâinées à leurs charmes innocens! (Historical and Ethnological Society of Greece, *Philhellenika 1821–31*, 1:50)

113. Alloula, *Colonial Harem*, 40.

114. The painter-lithographer Adam (1801–66) was prodigious, having drawn more than eight thousand prints; he was better known for his battle scenes (Beatrice Farwell, *Cult of Images: Baudelaire and the Nineteenth-Century Media Explosion* [Santa Barbara: University of California Press, 1977], 128). Born in Paris, he remained there all his life but specialized in drawings of exotic types (Gordon N. Ray, *The Art of the French Illustrated Book, 1700–1914*, 2 vols. [New York: Pierpont Morgan Library and Ithaca: Cornell University Press, 1982], 194).

115. Capture by pirates precedes women being sold into the harem in both Mozart's *Abduction from the Seraglio* and *Lustful Turk* (1828).

116. Bernard Romanin Julien (1802–71), a student of Baron Gros, exhibited from 1833 to 1850 and worked in painting, drawing, and lithographs. Note the following comment from the *Inventaire*, suggesting the commercial success of this type of image: "Julien pour nous est d'abord, jusqu'à vers 1840, un portraitiste fécond et commercial" (Jean Adhémar, *et al. Inventaire du fonds français après 1800* [Paris: Bibliothèque Nationale, 1930–67], 11:532; see also 11:537).

117. The *Inventaire* lists two Fragonards, father and son, as lithographers active in this period. Their *oeuvres* overlap. This image was probably done by the elder, Alexandre-Evariste (1780–1850), who was himself the son of Jean-Honoré (1732–1806), the well-known eighteenth-century rococo painter. Alexandre-Evariste illustrated exotic mores and scenes from antiquity and collaborated on works of the "voyages pittoresques" genre. His son Théophile (1806–1876) often signed his first name to distinguish his work from his father's. He also did eastern works including engravings in an 1837 edition of Gallard's translation of *1001 Nuits* and a "fantaisies orientales," which is, however, about China and not the Middle East (Adhémar *et al.*, *Inventaire* 8:148, 157).

118. There is a second version of this image in the Cabinet des Estampes in which the woman is brunette, perhaps an attempt to lessen the Circassian associations and emphasize the Greek. This other version is by Carriére and published by Benard, rue de l'Abbaye, no. 4.

119. Brown, "The Harem De-historicized," n. 45.

120. Compare Mohja Kahf's astute comment about how actual possession of a harem woman is represented as "somehow 'deadened'—that is, absented or discarded" in contrast to the quest for possession of her. She is the phallus that can never be had; when she is, she is no longer desirable (Kahf, *Western Representations of the Muslim Woman*, 154).

121. Tucker, *Women*, 169.

122. Nerval, *The Women of Cairo: Scenes of Life in the Orient*, 2 vols., ed. Conrad Elphinstone (1926; reprint, Ann Arbor: University of Michigan, 1982), 2:197.

123. Mrs. Pickersgill, *Tales of the Harem (in verse)* (London: Longman, Rees, Orme, Brown and Green, 1827), 15.

124. Likewise Sardanapalus's favorite slave, the Greek Myrrha, is transformed into a sexy warrior who follows him into battle (Byron, *Complete Works*, 211).

125. Leila Ahmed, *Edward W. Lane: A Study of His Life and Works and of British Ideas of the Middle East in the Nineteenth Century* (London: Longman, 1978), 39.

126. Aaron Hill, *A Full and Just Account of the Present State of the Ottoman Empire in all its Branches . . .* (London: G. Parker, 1733), 104.

127. *ME* 1:9; Poole, *Englishwoman in Egypt*, 152. For designs of the lattice work of Egyptian harems, see Lane's *Specimens of Latticework* (*ME* 1:10).

128. In Mozart's *Abduction from the Seraglio* Belmonte puts a ladder up to Constanza's window to rescue her, a motif having great theatrical possibilities in the staging of an opera.

129. A Lady, "A Visit to a Harem," *Chambers's Edinburgh Journal* 5, 109 n.s. (31 January 1846): 66.

130. "Slavery in Turkey," *Englishwoman's Review of Social and Industrial Questions* (15 June 1878): 257.

131. Walter C. James, "Women in Turkey," *Contemporary Review* 34 (1879): 111.

132. Melek-Hanum, *Thirty Years in the Harem or the Autobiography of Melek-Hanum, Wife of H.H. Kibrizli-Mehemet-Pasha* (New York: Harper and Brothers, 1872), 12.

133. Denon, *Travels in Upper and Lower Egypt*, 1:222.

134. Several works cited in this study were done by one or both of the Devéria brothers: Achille (1800–1857), the more famous printmaker who I am assuming did this print, and his younger brother Eugène, better known for his paintings (Farwell, *Cult of Images*, 135).

135. Compare the poem by Arthur William Edgar O'Shaughnessy titled "Zuleika" (1874), in which the forbidden couple escape at night in a bark. His is a reference to Byron's title character in his *Bride of Abydos* (1813) (O'Shaughnessy, "Zuleika," *Poetry of the Victorian Period*, 3rd edition, ed. Jerome H. Buckley and George B. Woods [Chicago: Scott Foresman, 1965], 761–62).

136. Compare Lewis's *A Mameluk Bay, Egypt*, which he exhibited at the R.A. the previous year and which bears some resemblance to the bey in his 1850 *Hhareem. (Mameluk Bay* is illustrated in Mary Anne Stevens, ed. *The Orientalists: Delacroix to Matisse: The Allure of North Africa and the Near East* [London: Thames and Hudson, 1984], 185).

137. 1768–1854.

138. In a similar scene, Sir Lawrence Alma Tadema's *Who Is It?* (1880) showing cloistered women of the ancient past, only one woman is able to see out-of-doors, as the window is unusually high. Her two interested friends must rely on a secondhand verbal account of the scopic privilege she has for their vicarious pleasure. The women are denied sight, while they themselves become the wondrous sight of this picture. They delight the viewer just as visual pleasure is forbidden to them.

Chapter 4. Setting the Stage: Harem Props as Fetishized Accoutrements

1. Sigmund Freud, "Fetishism," *Sexuality and the Psychology of Love*, ed. Philip Rieff (New York: Macmillan, 1974), 216.

2. Lefebvre, *Production of Space*, 17.

3. Schick, *Erotic Margin*, 366.

4. Melman, *Women's Orients*, 129.

5. "Hookah" is Urdu (the principal and Hindustani language spoken in West Pakistan and by Muslims in India) taken from the Arabic *huqqah*, referring to the bottle of cooling water.

6. Ahmed, *Edward W. Lane*, 33.

7. Alloula, *Colonial Harem*, 74.

8. See the watercolor by Preziosi, *A Turkish Cafe* (1854) for a view of that predominately masculine space and the role of chibouks within it (illustrated in Jullian, *Orientalists*, 154).

9. On Preziosi see Victoria and Albert Museum, *People and Places of Constantinople: Watercolours by Amadeo Count Preziosi* (London: 1985); Rodney Searight and Jennifer M. Scarce, *A Middle Eastern Journey* (Edinburgh: University of Edinburgh, 1980–81), 23, 26–27.

10. This is written in 1863, however ("Mysteries of the Seraglio, from *Bently's [sic] Miscellany* [London]," *Eclectic Magazine* [New York] 60 [December 1863]): 467.

11. His words are: "comme un parfum autour de leurs corps voluptueux" and "on respire doucement, on fait silence, on a peur de dépenser sa vie" (quoted in Graté, *Deux critiques*, 228).

12. John Nield's "Turcotoquade" appeared in *L'Image*, 26 July–30 August 1868. This is frame 34 from the August 23 issue.

13. (c. 1825–90). It was probably part of an 1852 series (compare his *Aux bords de la Tamise* and *Aux bords du Tage* illustrated in Farwell, *Cult of Images*, nos. 127–28). He did another album, *Oeuvres de différents pays*, and collaborated on illustrations for *Le journal pour rire* and *La vie parisienne*.

14. Beatrice Farwell, "Manet and the Nude: A Study in Iconography in the Second Empire" (Ph.D. diss., UCLA, 1973), 33.

15. Compare, for example, Hans Makart's 1875 *Death of Cleopatra* (Cassel, Staatliche Kunstsammlungen).

16. "A Visit," 684.

17. Tucker, *Women*, 170.

18. Alloula calls the attention given to the serving of sweetened coffee in early twentieth-century French harem picture postcards a ritual which provides a "long metaphor for sweetness" (Alloula, *Colonial Harem*, 74).

19. John Lewis also seems to subvert the convention of the long-haired servant carrying a tray with her back to us. In his 1859 *Eastern Girl Carrying a Tray* we are granted a front view of the server who smiles broadly and presumably serves willingly, without coercion or the imposition of an unfair hierarchy. This is an ideal kind of social deference: healthy, young, efficient, prettily white-skinned—and happy in the bargain.

20. "A Visit," 686.

21. *Englishwoman's Review* (15 January 1877), 42.

22. Léon Rosenthal, *Du Romantisme au réalisme* (Paris: H. Laurens, 1914), 124–26; Germain Bazin, "Delacroix au Maroc: Au Musée de l'Orangerie," *L'Amour de l'art* 14 (March 1933): 2:1; Raymond Escholier, *Eugène Delacroix* (Paris: Editions Cercle d'Art, 1963), 174, 186.

23. "Women in Morocco," *Hogg's Instructor* 6, n.s. (1851): 382, 384.

24. Thackeray, *From Cornhill to Cairo*, 16:477–79.

25. Unabashedly indebted to Lewis's art, Frederick Goodall paints a 1884 *New Light in the Harem* (illustrated in Alev Lyle Croutier, *Harem: The World Behind the Veil* [New York: Abbeville, 1989], 42) which utilizes a gazelle as well as a bird as part of the narrative. (The last poem in Thomas Moore's *Lalla Rookh*, first published in 1817, is titled "The Light of the Haram.") Here the reclining odalisque leaves the care of the female infant to the black menial, her elbows cocked over her head suggesting her nonchalance. A gazelle is closer to her than the animated baby suggesting her attachment to the animal over the child, a conception dating at least from Mary Wollstonecraft's description of a leisured woman who inappropriately loved her "spoiled brutes that filled the place which her children ought to have occupied" (*VRW* 293). Meanwhile the title of the Goodall painting and the fact that the child is amused by a startled bird, an erotic symbol, suggest that this infant will grow up to take the place of the reclining beauty.

26. Rajaram Narayan Saletore, *Sex in Indian Harem Life* (New Dehli: Orient Paperbacks, 1978), 11. Pardoe writes that a slave holds a "gilded cage," which contains a parrot, itself called "the favourite of the harem" (*CS* 2:214).

27. *Flowers culled from the Gulistan and Bostan of Sadi [13th century] with a Few Specimens of the Mesnavi of Jelal-ud-Din Rumi*, trans. Samuel Robinson (London: Williams and Norgate, 1876).

28. Schick, *Erotic Margin*, 223.

29. Croutier, *Harem*, 20.

30. Two critics confirm this in 1864 in their reviews of John Lewis's *Caged Doves* (*ILN* 7 May 1864: 454; *T* 30 April 1864:14).

31. Pardoe, *Beauties*, 127.

32. Thackeray, *From Cornhill to Cairo*, 16:357.

33. A Lady, "A Visit to a Harem," 67.

34. "Women in the East," *Bentley's Miscellany* 27 (1850): 380.

35. "An Abode of Bliss," *Chambers's Journal of Popular Literature, Science and Art*, 4th ser. 128 (9 June 1866): 366.

36. Two French examples, both by J. B. Greuze, which could be seen in London are: *Girl with Birdcage* (Victoria and Albert Museum) and *Girl with Doves* 1802, purchased in 1848 for the Wallace Collection.

37. Penzer, *Harem*, 16.

38. Presumably W. Bligh Barker (fl. 1835–1850), "a London painter of portraits, genre, flowers and topographical subjects" (Christopher Wood, *Dictionary of Victorian Painters*, 2d. ed. [Suffolk: Antique Collectors' Club, 1978], 35).

39. Lane, too, says pigeon-raising was the work of village peasants (*ME* 1:26).

40. In one of the three letters Ruskin wrote to Lewis, this one in 1859, he urges the artist to look at Brett's painting carefully. "If you will look carefully at Brett's picture you will find it different in execution from every other in the academy. I say this knowingly: his treatment of the wet-colours being peculiar to himself—conditions of [illegible] form and colour in the distance of that picture are of very great interest to me" (Letter A20, received 14 May 1859). Brett had attracted Ruskin's attention with his *Stonebreaker*, shown in the 1858 R.A. Mike Hickox advances a tentative interpretation of the portrait of Madame Loeser as a means for Brett to rehabilitate his reputation as a serious painter in *Review of Pre-Raphaelite Society* 6, no. 1 (Spring 1998): 12–15.

41. The painting was purchased by John Everett Millais and William Holman Hunt. A similar work is Deverell's *Pet Parrot*, in which the same model plays with a grey parrot, a painting that has been interpreted as lubricious (*Pre-Raphaelites* [London: Tate Gallery and Allen Lane, 1984], 114–15).

42. Quoted in Elaine Shefer, "Deverell, Rossetti, Siddal,

and 'The Bird in the Cage,'" *Art Bulletin* 67, no. 3 (September 1985): 447.

43. Ibid., 439, note 11.

44. A rare representation of a dog in the harem is to be found in Jules-Robert Auguste's *Deux odalisques dans un paysage.* Of the dog in Egypt, Lane says it is "considered very unclean: the Shaafees hold themselves to be polluted by the touch of its nose, if it be wet" (*ME* 1:120).

45. Vanmour, *Recueil de cent estampes,* 17.

46. James Augustus St. John and E. Prisse d'Avennes, *Oriental Album: Characters, Costumes and Modes of Life in the Valley of the Nile* (London: James Madden, 1848), 33.

47. Saletore, *Sex in Indian Harems,* 11.

48. "Love and Marriage in Persia," *All the Year Round* 6 (15 February 1862): 488–91.

49. In a related scene, which is not strictly speaking a harem picture as it is set outdoors, Lewis's *Arab Scribe* (1858 R.A.), the interaction of dark-skinned servant with her white mistress is echoed beneath them where two cats doze, one black and one white (reproduced as an engraving in "British Artists: Their Style and Character, J. F. Lewis," *Art Journal* n.s. 4 [1858]:162).

50. The harem belonging to the Veiled Prophet of Khorassan is called "all that busy hive" (Moore, *Lalla Rookh,* 51).

51. "Glimpses of Harem Life," *Bentley's Miscellany* 43 (1858): 515.

52. Annemarie Schimmel, "The Celestial Garden in Islam," in *The Islamic Garden,* ed. Elisabeth B. MacDougall and Richard Ettinghausen (Washington, DC: Dumbarton Oaks, 1976), 17.

53. Carle Vanloo appears to have used a prototype similar to Vanmour's for his mid-century *Une sultane jouant d'un instrument à cordes,* a work commissioned by Madame de Pompadour to decorate her room at the Bellevue chateau. See Pierre Rosenberg and Marie-Catherine Sahut, *Carle Vanloo: Premier peintre du roi* (Nice, Clermont-Ferrand, Nancy: n.p., 1977), 76.

54. Ingres's *Grande Odalisque* (1814) provides one of the models for both women in his work, but the face of Hébert's curvaceous harem woman, unlike Ingres's, is turned completely away only to be given to the viewer in the form of her twin, whose arms and shoulders also recall the woman in the Ingres work.

55. Lesbianism in the harem is discussed in chapter five.

56. Annan, *"Arabian Nights,"* 60.

57. Elisabeth B. MacDougall and Richard Ettinghausen, eds., *The Islamic Garden* (Washington, DC: Dumbarton Oaks, 1976), 8.

58. Schimmel, "Celestial Garden," 31–33. Alternatively, flowers in Paradise can symbolize the call to prayer or be prayers themselves (ibid., 25).

59. Quoted in Holt, *Triumph of Art for the Public,* 473.

60. *Floral Poetry and the Language of Flowers* (London: Marcus Ward and Co., 1877), 12.

61. Peter Hughes, *Eighteenth-Century France and the East,* Wallace Collection Monographs 4 (London: Wallace Gallery, 1981), 13. See also Fig. 5.9 and his *Une sultane jouant d'un instrument à cordes,* which I do not illustrate in this study.

62. On the self-absorbed harem woman see chapter five.

63. Schimmel, "Celestial Garden," 30.

64. David Kunzle, *Fashion and Fetishism: A Social History of the Corset, Tight-Lacing and Other Forms of Body-Sculpture in the West* (Totowa, NJ: Rowman and Littlefield, 1982), 15.

65. Ibid., 14.

66. According to Dumas's report, she was a Jew and not a harem woman, however.

67. "Mysteries of the Seraglio," 467.

68. "An Abode of Bliss," 366–68.

69. "Glimpses of Harem Life," 513.

70. Even Ingres's subtle rendering of the odalisque's eyes and fingertips might be related to Lady Mary's description of eastern women's cosmetics. The right eye of Ingres's odalisque is encircled with shadow but a comparison with his other pictures of harem women shows it is rather incongruously darkened, a details which is unique to this nude. Following her descriptions of their dress, Lady Mary mentions Muslim women's ancient custom of using *kohl* to accentuate the eyes. The "Turks have a custom of putting round their Eyes on the inside a black Tincture that, at a distance or by candle-light, adds very much to the Blackness of them" (*L* 1:327). If he did indeed respond to her description, Ingres misinterpreted her phrase describing where and how *kohl* was used; "on the inside" for Lady Mary meant the material was placed inside the bottom eyelid and washed to all edges of the eyelids. Ingres must have read this phrase to mean around the whole eye structure. As for Turkish ladies' fingernail polish, Lady Mary continues "They dye their Nails rose colour; I own I cannot enough accustom my selfe to this fashion to find any Beauty in it" (*L* 1:327). Ingres allows his viewer to see only one nail, emphasized by his placement of the white curtain edge over it, and it is clearly painted, even allowing for the shadow cast by the curtain.

71. "A Visit to the Harem," 686–87.

72. A Lady, "A Visit to a Harem," 67.

73. The rose and the nightingale are some of the most common metaphors for love in eastern traditions (Schimmel, "Celestial Garden," 37–38).

74. "Love and Marriage in Persia," 489.

75. "Women in the East," 383.

76. Victor Hugo, *Selections Chiefly Lyrical from the Poetical Works,* 50.

77. "An Abode of Bliss," 367.

78. Reinhart, "Here and Hereafter," 17. It seemed impossible for nineteenth-century western thinkers to conceive of multiple partners for women even in utopian communities, as we explore in an unpublished paper (Nancy Yanoshak and Joan DelPlato, "'Community of Women': Alluding to the Elusive in Nineteenth-Century Socialist and Bourgeois Utopias").

79. In the first of his six lectures on sculpture, "Of the Division of Arts," delivered in 1870 Ruskin proclaims "though the idolatry may not have been wholly divine which sculptured gods, the idolatry is wholly diabolic, which, for vulgar display, sculptures diamonds" (*W* 20:212). And again at the first lecture of a series given at the University of Oxford in 1870 "one form of demand for art which is wholly unenlightening, and powerful only for evil;—namely, the demand of the classes occupied solely in the pursuit of pleasure, for objects and modes of art that can amuse indolence or excite passion . . . they are very deadly at present in their operation on sculpture, and on jewellers' work" (*W* 20:26).

80. Quoted in Cairncross, *After Polygamy Was Made a Sin,* 197–98.

81. See also his undated *Eastern Girl Carrying a Tray*, which is not illustrated here.

82. Charles Baudelaire, quoted in Farwell, *French Popular Lithographic Imagery*, 21.

83. Lefebvre, *Production of Space*, 26.

84. Ashcroft, Griffiths, and Tiffin, *Post-Colonial Studies Reader*, 391.

85. Lefebvre, *Production of Space*, 97.

86. The harem and its garden as "containers" become the themes in other harem pictures, chapter six.

87. Çelik, *Displaying the Orient*, 1.

88. Fredric Jameson, "Modernism and Imperialism," in *Nationalism, Colonialism and Literature*, ed. Terry Eagleton, Fredric Jameson, and Edward W. Said (Minneapolis: University of Minnesota Press, 1990), 50–51.

89. Jameson, "Modernism and Imperialism," 51.

Chapter 5. The Harem Fetishized: Harem Women as Immoral

1. Foucault, *History of Sexuality*, 1:121.

2. Mosse, *Nationalism and Sexuality*, 134.

3. Nikki R. Keddie, "Problems in the Study of Middle Eastern Women," *International Journal of Middle Eastern Studies* 10, no. 2 (1979): 240.

4. Spivak, "Can the Subaltern Speak?" 294.

5. Schimmel, "Celestial Garden in Islam," 19–20, 23.

6. Hanaway, "Paradise on Earth," 53.

7. St. John and Prisse d'Avennes, *Oriental Album*, 7.

8. Alexander Pope quoted in Melman, *Women's Orients*, 72.

9. The soulless Muslim woman was a notion some writers attempted to correct because, among other things, it provided a powerful rationale for missionary activity. For example, "It is a vulgar error that Mohammedism declare that women have so souls . . . The mistake should be corrected; for the argument is often used by the friends of Missionary enterprises, and by writers on the evidences of Christianity" ("Does Mohammedism Allow Women Souls?" *The Christian Observer* [London] 44 [February 1844]: 101).

10. Melman, *Women's Orients*, 118.

11. Brief though his description of her is, she might be based loosely on Lady Mary Wortley Montagu, the intellectual feminist whose "Turkish Embassy Letters" had been written and circulated informally by this time, though they were not published until 1763 (posthumously). Montesquieu spoofs her by having Rica comment that she was worthy of the monarch's harem. Lady Mary was referred to in many accounts as "a beauty and a wit."

12. Incidentally, Sir Richard Burton takes issue with "Miss Martineau" and her "heart-broken wail over the degradation of her sex." He rejects her appraisal of the harem resembling "certain haunts of vice in Europe" and claims that human nature is everywhere the same. Eastern women can be either "coy or heroic," a fascinating binary that fails to escape Martineau's conception. He also sees "polyandry" [*sic*] as engendering less jealousy and rivalry than any other society (*PNP* 3:51).

13. Mitchell, *Colonising Egypt*, 68.

14. On the phallic symbolism of the dagger, worn by harem women who are powerful sisters and daughters of the master, see Withers, *Description of the Grand Signor's Seraglio*, 51.

15. A reference to the 1811 massacre of the Mamelukes by Mohammed Ali.

16. A slightly more decorative version of this pair of lithographs survives in the form of Tassaert's 1833 *L'Odalisque coupable* and his *L'Odalisque punie* with captions that seem to blame the woman somewhat more than in the Mendouze-Barathier pair.

17. Caroline Bugler reviews the explanation of the *Illustrated London News*: the standing woman in green with her hand to her face is the guilty one, while her accuser, bent at the waist with intense emotion, clutches the adulteress with one hand and the telltale evidence with the other, addressing her diatribe to the cuckolded pasha. She forms a link between the accused and a more pensive woman on her right whom the *Athenaeum* claims is the guilty woman. But Bugler refutes this possibility by noting this woman is not grimacing but smiling and shields her eyes not out of guilt but in reaction to the strong sunlight. Bugler also has identified the types of flowers in the all-important bouquet and their symbolism: it includes a pansy, asking the recipient to think of the giver; an anemone, symbolizing the giver's feelings of being forsaken; an *hibiscus syriacum*, glorifying the woman's beauty; and roses, symbols of love. In a vase close to the master, Bugler has further identified larkspur, symbol of haughtiness; a scarlet dahlia, indicating instability and again a rose—all to indicate the cuckolded husband's mixed emotions (Stevens, ed., *Orientalists*, 185).

18. *Encyclopedia of Islam*, 1:29.

19. Douthwaite, *Exotic Women*, 100, 129.

20. Withers, *Description of the Grand Signor's Seraglio*, 58–59.

21. Thackeray, *From Cornhill to Cairo*, 16:351.

22. MacFarlane, *Turkey and Its Destiny*, 415. See also "Women in Turkey," *Bentley's Miscellany* 38 (1855): 353.

23. Annie Jane Harvey, *Turkish Harems and Circassian Homes* (London: Hurst and Blackett, 1871), 96 and 38.

24. Melek-Hanum, *Thirty Years in the Harem*, 28.

25. "'Mysteries of the Seraglio,'" 469.

26. As if to indicate an Egyptian locale, Lewis includes a "hieroglyphic": a seated figure with lion head and horns incised in stone to the upper left of the background wall.

27. A woman bearing a similarly covered object is shown to the extreme right in *Intercepted Correspondence* of 1869, suggesting that the revelation took place just at the time, perhaps before a meal, when ablutions would also have been performed.

28. On the harem woman characterized as emanating unbridled sexuality and as adulterous, homosexual, and masturbatory, see Schick, *Erotic Margin*, 14, 213–18 and 222–26.

29. MacFarlane, *Turkey and Its Destiny*, 257.

30. "Glimpses of Harem Life," 515.

31. "An Abode of Bliss," 516–17.

32. "Glimpses of Harem Life," 516–17.

33. On the phallic symbolism of the pipe, see chapter 4.

34. Alloula, *Colonial Harem*, 59.

35. Compare a similar headdress on Lewis's picture of a young pasha, *Prince Hassan and His Servant* and boys in *Interior of a School, Cairo* (illustrated in Lewis, *Lewis*, figs. 42 and 57).

36. See also Withers, *Description of the Grand Signor's Seraglio*, 44.

37. On a debauched and selfish princess who has sex with her slaves see Melek-Hanum, *Thirty Years in the Harem*, 93–94.

38. Grosrichard, *Structure du sérail*, 161.

39. Toledano, *Ottoman Slave Trade*, 18.

40. *Englishwoman's Review* (15 January 1877): 43.

41. Carroll Smith-Rosenberg, "The Female World of Love and Ritual: Relations between Women in Nineteenth-Century America (1975)," in *Signs Reader: Women, Gender and Scholarship*, ed. Elizabeth Abel and Emily K. Abel (Chicago: University of Chicago Press, 1983):27–55.

42. Schick, *Erotic Margin*, 202–7.

43. Alloula, *Colonial Harem*, 96.

44. Withers, *Description of the Grand Signor's Seraglio*, 59.

45. Grosrichard, *Structure du sérail*, 117; Alexander Pope quoted in Melman, *Women's Orients*, 72.

46. See, for example, *Jupiter in the Shape of Diana Surprising Callisto* (1769) or the pendants, *Spring* and *Autumn* (both 1745), all in the Wallace Collection, London.

47. In *The Second Sex* (1949) Simone de Beauvoir writes: "it is institutions that create uniformity. Young and pretty, the slaves of the harem are always the same in the sultan's embrace . . ." She is struggling with the dilemma of equality between the sexes when women are perceived as different from men and as like each other (Simone de Beauvoir, *The Second Sex* [New York: Random House, 1989], 731).

48. Brown, "Harem De-historicized," 62.

49. Rana Kabbani, *Europe's Myths of Orient* (Bloomington: Indiana University Press, 1986), 17.

50. I suspect the same is true of the French word *indolence*. See my commentary on the use of the word regarding Delacroix's 1834 *Women of Algiers*.

51. *Critic* (1850): 253; *Athenaeum* (4 May 1850): 480; Delécluze, *Beaux-Arts*, 129; *Spectator* (1850): 427, respectively.

52. Harvey, *Turkish Harems and Circassian Homes*, 81.

53. Napoleon claims that Arab women are so heavy they can hardly walk and spend much of their lives on divans. See chapter 2.

54. This painting suffers an identity crisis: *Siesta* is just one of four titles it has had (Wallace Collection, *Summary of Illustrated Catalogue of Pictures*, 19).

55. Tubeeb, "Visits to the Harem," 201.

56. See also Dijkstra, *Idols of Perversity*, 25–63.

57. For more on harem mirrors (and fans), see St. John, *Oriental Album*, 8.

58. Syed Hussein Alatas, *The Myth of the Lazy Native* (London: Frank Cass, 1977), 203.

59. Grosrichard, *Structure du sérail*, 177.

60. "Woman in Turkey" (1855): 354.

61. "Love and Marriage in Persia" (15 February 1862): 490.

62. Walther, *Woman in Islam*, 142.

63. Walter B. Denny, "Reflections of Paradise in Islamic Art," in *Images of Paradise in Islamic Art*, ed. Sheila Blair and Jonathan Bloom (Hanover, NH: Hood Museum of Art, 1991), 39.

64. She can also be correlated to utopian notions of androgyny prevalent in France in this period (Albert Boime, "The Case of Rosa Bonheur: Why Should a Woman Want to Be More Like a Man?" *Art History* 4, no. 4 [1981]: 404).

65. Schimmel, "The Celestial Garden in Islam," 14. The souls of the faithful who earn Paradise will also wear "the richest silks, chiefly of green," as Lane claims (*ME* 1:84).

66. Lewis's image implies western standards of modesty, which fetishize female breasts. In fact, nineteenth-century travelers report that in parts of the Muslim world women's faces and arms had to be covered, while their breasts might be partially (or mostly) exposed, especially if they were nursing children.

67. Walther, *Woman in Islam*, 145.

68. See also the figure painted on a ceramic plate, *Young Woman with a Tambourine; A Houri or a Personification of the Sun or Moon* (Metropolitan Museum of Art, New York), illustrated in *Images of Paradise in Islamic Art*, ed. Blair and Bloom, fig. 21.

69. Schimmel, "The Celestial Garden in Islam," 33.

70. In an Iranian miniature painting from about 1630 by Muhammad Yusuf al-Husaini a Persian woman wraps her male admirer's turban around her own head (reproduced in Walther, *Woman in Islam*, fig. 80).

71. (1811–47). He was a correspondent for *L'Illustration* and collaborated with Philipon on *La Caricature* and *Le Charivari*.

72. Farwell, *Cult of Images*, 123.

73. Ibid., 64.

74. In one of the few known harem pictures painted by a woman, Henriette Browne's 1869 *In the Harem* (not illustrated in this study), smoking helps establish the superior status of the woman at left as the more sophisticated senior wife.

75. Farwell, *Cult of Images*, 66. In Parisian brothels Oriental sexual services were available by the 1860s (Griselda Pollock, *Differencing the Canon* [London and New York: Routledge, 1999], 292).

76. "An Abode of Bliss" (9 June 1866): 367.

77. Tucker, *Women*, 150.

78. James C. McCoan, "Slavery in Egypt." *Fraser's Magazine* 95 (May 1877):569.

79. Adalet, "A Voice from a Harem: Some Words About the Turkish Women of Our Day," *The Nineteenth Century* 28 (August 1890): 186–90; Adalet, "Life in the Harem," *The Nineteenth Century* 28 (December 1890): 959–66.

80. Baer, "Slavery in Nineteenth-Century Egypt," 433.

81. Ibid., 438.

82. Ibid., 433–34.

83. *Englishwoman's Review* (15 October 1877): 475.

84. Judith R. Walkowitz, *Prostitution and Victorian Society: Women, Class and the State* (Cambridge and New York: Cambridge University Press), 1980.

85. Georges Guillet de St.-Georges, *An Account of a Late Voyage to Athens containing . . . The Estate . . . of the Present Empire of the Turks* (London: Herringman, 1674), 345.

86. Alexander Pope quoted in Melman, *Women's Orients*, 72.

87. Tucker, *Women*, 182.

88. Ibid., 53.

89. Melek-Hanum, *Thirty Years in the Harem*, 95.

90. The phrase used is "délaissée sans doute" (Delécluze, *Beaux-Arts*, 129).

91. *Spectator* (4 May 1850): 427; *Athenaeum* (4 May 1850): 480; Delécluze, *Beaux-Arts*, 129.

92. Gautier, *Les beaux-arts en Europe, 1855*, 97.

93. The *Art Journal* agrees she looks European but terms this inappropriate: she is "evidently a study from an Englishwoman, an introduction which injures the uniformity of the composition" (*AJ* 12, 1850:179).

94. Walther, *Woman in Islam*, 83.

95. Brown, "Harem De-historicized," 67.

96. Edmond About reports in 1855 that *Hhareem* was sold in London for 25,000 francs. The same amount purchased its printing rights (About, *Voyage à travers l'exposition des beaux-arts*, 31–32). The work was commissioned while Lewis was in Egypt in the 1840s by Joseph Arden (1799–1879), an attorney since 1840 who would become a magistrate in 1875 (Frederic Boase, *Modern English Biography* [London: Frank Cass and Co., 1965] 1:82). In British currency, Arden paid £1,000 for the work, a sum later matched in its reproduction rights. Charles Matthews, a wealthy brewer and art collector, purchased *Intercepted Correspondence* directly from Lewis. Matthews had been one of the original members of the Burlington Fine Arts Club in London in 1867. He amassed a collection of Victorian paintings that included works by Frederic Leighton, John Millais and J. C. Hook as well as Lewis (ibid. 1:795–96). He eventually purchased another of Lewis's harem pictures, *Reception* (1874 R.A.).

97. Apparently Ruskin still valued Lewis's artistic opinions, however. On 26 August 1858 he writes Lewis from Turin, describing the problem he encountered in some of his own drawing and painting (Letter A14, kindly lent to me by the late Michael Lewis).

98. James G. Mandley, *Woman Outside Christendom: An Exposition of the Influence Exerted by Christianity in the Social Position and Happiness of Women* (London: Trübner and Co., 1880), 128.

99. "Glimpses of Harem Life," 514.

100. "Love and Marriage in Persia," 488–89.

101. Walther, *Woman in Islam*, 35.

102. For example: A Lady, "A Visit to the Harem," 66; and "Women in Turkey," 353.

103. On LePrince see Ray, *Art of the French Illustrated Book*, 1:75.

104. In the early 1880s, a period which exceeds the limits of this study, Auguste Renoir painted images of very young girls in the harem. See his 1880 *Girl with Falcon* (Sterling and Francine Clark Art Institute, Williamstown, MA) and 1881 *Algerian Girl* (Museum of Fine Arts, Boston).

105. René Patris d'Uckermann, *Ernest Hébert, 1817–1908*, Notes et documents des musées de France 7 (Paris: Editions de la Réunion des musées nationaux, 1982), 43.

106. Of course, the rococo harem representation could also function as an assertion of social privilege and wealth against the democratic tendencies of the middle class, as it does on the expensive gold box painted by F. N. Génard 1761–1762 (see Fig. 4.8) and in many other Rococo harem scenes.

107. Hill, *Full and Just Account*,102.

108. Lowe, *Critical Terrains*, 52–60.

109. Till, *Mozart and the Enlightenment*, 102.

110. Hill, *Full and Just Account*, 102.

111. The work was retitled at its 1853 exhibition to include reference to a mameluke bey (*Hhareem of a Mameluke Bey, Cairo: The Introduction of an Abyssinian Slave*). This "mameluke" bears a certain physical resemblance to Lewis himself, who wore a beard; Lewis also lived in a mameluke-style house while in Cairo (Stevens, ed., *Orientalists*, 183).

112. In a caricature of their pairing, her servant Blonde, now owned by Osmin, is ludicrously commanded to fall in love with the eunuch at that moment (*AS* 60).

113. In light of this it is noteworthy that Belmonte's submission to Pasha Selim's authority as he asks him to name a ransom for Constanza is a great gesture of humility (*AS* 149), while Constanza's submission was simply untenable.

114. The phrase is Natalie Zemon Davis's in her essay, "Women on Top," *Society and Culture in Early Modern France: Eight Essays* (Stanford: Stanford University Press, 1975), 124–51.

Chapter 6. The Harem Fetishized: Muslim Women as Moral

1. Thomas Carlyle, "The Hero as Prophet: Mahomet: Islam, Lecture 2," *On Heroes, Hero-Worship and the Heroic in History*, ed. Carl Niemeyer (Lincoln: University of Nebraska Press, 1966), 43–76 (hereafter cited as *H*).

2. See Carle Vanloo, *Deux sultanes travaillant à la tapisserie*, 1755 Salon (see Fig. 5.9). See also *ME* 238–39. Also compare Vanmour's *Fille turque qui brode* from *Recueil*, plate 52.

3. Compare Vanmour's *Femme turque filant au tandour* from *Recueil*, plate 47.

4. Pardoe, *Beauties of the Bosphorus*, 126.

5. A friend of the orientalist Richard Burton, the poet Richard Monckton Milnes kept "the largest known collection of pornography in his day," was actively interested in flagellation, and fascinated by sexual deviancy (Kabbani, *Europe's Myths of Orient*, 55). In the Summer of 1849 he proposed marriage to Florence Nightingale, who turned him down (*LE* 12).

6. "Women in the East" (1850): 379.

7. Denny, "Paradise Described," 81.

8. Denny, "Reflections of Paradise in Islamic Art," 39.

9. Arberry, *Koran Interpreted*, 2:253.

10. Ibid.

11. Ibid., 2:198.

12. Ibid., 2:151, 241, 253, 315.

13. Schimmel, "Celestial Garden in Islam," 13.

14. Arberry, *Koran Interpreted*, 2:316, 253.

15. Ibid., 2:229, 253.

16. Ibid., 2:253.

17. In Islam the kiosk of heavenly gardens can be a hexagonal pavilion often of one or two stories (Richard Ettinghausen, "Introduction," in *The Islamic Garden*, ed. Elisabeth B. MacDougall and Richard Ettinghausen, [Washington, DC: Dumbarton Oaks, Trustees for Harvard University, 1976], 9) or sometimes an octagonal structure in the garden of Paradise which is infinite but enclosed (Schimmel, "Celestial Garden in Islam," 16, 21). Walls in Paradise can separate heaven from the desert which is death (Hanaway, "Paradise on Earth," 63).

18. The presence of a third figure was noticed by the *Art Journal* (*AJ* 1857:178). The *Spectator* identifies this as a male figure, either the eunuch guard or the master (*S* 2 May 1857:463).

19. Schimmel, "Celestial Garden in Islam," 22.

20. Or similarly Boucher's *Femme du levant*. Both are from the series of twelve prints entitled *Les figures etrangères*, engraved by F. Ravenet before 1772.

21. Schick, *Erotic Margin*, 7.

22. Reinhold Schiffer, *Turkey Romanticized: Images of the Turks in Early Nineteenth-Century English Travel Literature*,

Materialia Turcica, Beiheft 5, Studienverlag Dr. N. Brockmeyer (Bochum, 1982), 37.

23. Ettinghausen, "Introduction," 6.

24. Ibid., 6–7.

25. Reinhart, "Here and Hereafter," 11.

26. Schimmel, "Celestial Garden in Islam," 30.

27. Denny, "Paradise Described," 87.

28. Schimmel, "Celestial Garden in Islam," 34, 38.

29. Hanaway, "Paradise on Earth," 43.

30. Ibid., 53.

31. The oil on wood painting now titled *Bouquet* signed and dated 1857 is presumed to be *Lilies and Roses, Constantinople,* a work exhibited at the Royal Academy in 1858 (no. 51), judging from close visual correspondences between *Bouquet* and descriptions of *Lilies and Roses.*

32. Like the Pre-Raphaelites with whom he was associated in the early 1850s, Lewis had made copies of the Flemish "primitives."

33. The *Illustrated London News* had urged Lewis to do so as early as 1850 (*ILN* 4 May 1850:300).

34. The Annunciation was also a popular subject with the Pre-Raphaelites. Dante Gabriel Rossetti in 1850 painted one such scene, *Ecce Ancilla Domini!* (Tate Gallery, London).

35. Arberry, *Koran Interpreted,* 2:198.

36. Letter A16 kindly supplied by the late Michael Lewis.

37. Judy Mabro, ed., *Veiled Half-Truths: Western Travellers' Perceptions of Middle Eastern Women* (London and New York: I. B. Tauris and Co., 1991), 9.

38. Lady Augusta Hamilton, *Marriage Rites, Customs and Ceremonies of All Nations of the Universe* (London: Chapple and Son, 1822), 14; Charles White, *Three Years in Constantinople,* 2:300; Harvey, *Turkish Harems and Circassian Homes,* 12.

39. Patrick B. Brantlinger, "Victorians and Africans: The Genealogy of the Myth of the Dark Continent," in *"Race," Writing and Difference,* ed. Henry Louis Gates, Jr. (Chicago: University of Chicago Press, 1986), 186.

40. These studies were sold as a group to the Royal Scottish Academy in 1853.

41. Lewis, *Lewis,* 36.

42. Quoted in Lewis, *Lewis,* 29.

43. St. John, *Oriental Album,* 19–20.

44. *Encyclopedia of Islam,* 1:26.

45. This legitimizing happens in contemporary feminist scholarship on the harem, and rightly so. That the domestic life of the harem had a significant political function in consolidating class and party lines is the point in Rosemary Sayigh, "Roles and Functions of Arab Women: A Reappraisal," *Arab Studies Quarterly* 3, no. 3 (autumn 1981): 270.

46. Lady Mary disagrees with her predecessors, specifically Aaron Hill when she says: "Tis also very pleasant to observe how tenderly he and all his Brethren Voyage-writers lament the miserable confinement of the Turkish ladys, who are (perhaps) freer than any Ladys in the universe, and are the only Women in the world that lead a life of uninterrupted pleasure, exempt from cares, their whole time being spent in visiting, bathing, or the agreable Amusement of spending Money and inventing new fashions" (*L* 1:406). A contemporaneous painting of a harem reception can be considered the visual counterpart to Lady Mary's Turkish Embassy Letters written 1716–18 (though not published until after her death). Jean Baptiste Vanmour, who painted *Reception in a Turkish Harem* also painted Lady Mary in a harem c. 1717 (see Fig. 3.33). See Joan DelPlato, "An English Feminist in the Turkish Harem: A Portrait of Lady Mary Wortley Montagu," in *Eighteenth-Century Women and the Arts,* ed. Frederick M. Keener and Susan E. Lorsch (New York: Greenwood Press, 1988), 163–78. Vanmour's *Reception,* like Lady Mary's writing, is all politeness and propriety and could just as easily represent an aristocratic, all-female social event in Europe except for the eastern decor; women entertain themselves and each other in luxurious surroundings executed on a grand scale. A few children are present proportioned as miniature adults. The veiled guests at right await their imminent recognition by the harem women at large. The architectural structure of Lewis's *Reception* (discussed below) is much like that in Vanmour's work: Lewis has broken the symmetry of the eighteenth-century oil painting but retains the emphasis on windows and fountain pool and focuses more on the social interactions than Vanmour's painting.

47. On the harem bath, which I do not analyze in detail in this study, see Brown, "Harem De-historicized," 58–68.

48. Melek-Hanum, *Thirty Years in the Harem,* 69.

49. Robert Withers comments in 1650 that harem women live like "nunnes" in large nunneries; bedrooms hold nearly a hundred women (*Description of the Grand Signor's Seraglio,* 40).

50. Denon, *Travels in Upper and Lower Egypt,* 1:221.

51. Poole, *Englishwoman in Egypt,* 167.

52. On images of nuns see Susan P. Casteras, *Images of Victorian Womanhood in English Art* (Rutherford, NJ: Associated University Presses, 1987), 129–60.

53. *Pre-Raphaelites* (London: Tate Gallery and Allen Lane, 1984), 87.

54. White, *Three Years in Constantinople,* 2:304–5, 309.

55. "Mysteries of the Seraglio," 469.

56. Respectively: no. 302 (1857):178; 9 May 1857:444; 2 May 1857:463; 1857:209. The *Times* concurs, but uses the phrase "a female servant" (*T* 8 April 1857:7).

57. *Inmate of the Hareem, Cairo* was exhibited at the 1858 Royal Academy (no. 122), along with another harem picture, *Bouquet* (no. 51). *Inmate* survives in a watercolor owned by the Victoria and Albert Museum titled *Life in the Harem, Cairo* signed and dated 1858. I am assuming the oil and the watercolor study for it are nearly identical in composition and narrative. It was Lewis' habit to closely correlate versions.

58. Tucker, *Women,* 170.

59. This fundamental concession to western expectations occurs even though there are other eastern details: the "Cairean" mosque seen out the window, a page from the *Qur'an* and a (pseudo-)Arabic inscription over the doorway.

60. Historical information in this paragraph is from Toledano, *Ottoman Slave Trade,* 140–47, 167–68.

61. David Price purchased this picture (no. 465) and another of Lewis's eastern pictures shown that year, *Bezestein Bazaar of El Khan Khalil, Cairo,* (Stevens, ed., *Orientalists,* 186). Indicating the ongoing popularity of Lady Mary, William Frith showed his painting *An Incident in the Life of Lady Mary Wortley Montagu* at this same R.A. exhibition, a painting which I have analyzed elsewhere.

62. The *Art Journal* fails to specify the attitudes Lewis expresses here, except to say, rather ambiguously, that he has been "curiously faithful in picturing" them (*AJ* 1872:156), testimony to his verisimilitude.

63. In 1882 Edwin Long paints *Babylonian Marriage Market* in which the most desirable women at the marketplace are the whitest, the least attractive darkest, judging from the work's formal arrangement.

64. Schick, *Erotic Margin*, 201.

65. Four years later, however, Lewis's *Intercepted Correspondence* would elicit the judgment that all Lewis's works up to that date were "artificial"!

66. Foucault, *History of Sexuality*, 1:67, 83.

67. Though the *Art Journal* calls this a "wilderness of sweets" (*AJ* 1858:162).

68. *Language and Poetry of Flowers*, 28; *Floral Poetry*, 252.

69. Forbes Watson, *Flowers and Gardens: Notes on Plant Beauty* (London and New York: John Lane, 1901), 83.

70. Ruskin had discussed the two flowers together (*W* 28:163–65).

71. The two flowers compete for a queenly rank in a short poem titled "The Lily and the Rose" by William Cowper (1731–1800), quoted in one of many flower books popular in the Victorian period. The two flowers are united when they are discovered to be on the cheeks of British women; there they are "two lovely foes, / Aspiring to the rank of queen" and "each seeks / The fairest British fair; / The seat of empire is her cheeks; / They reign united there" (*Floral Poetry*, 136-37). Cowper's use of the imperialist metaphor is particularly ironic when applied to Lewis's image, whose connection to imperialism is much more subtle than the poem written nearly twenty years later.

72. John Ruskin was an avid gardener and botanist.

73. Compare the dress worn by Lewis's *Armenian Lady* (1855) (not illustrated).

74. This picture's size (39 by 27 inches), unlike his 1858 *Bouquet* (12 by 8 inches), allows Lewis the opportunity to show his flowers in much greater detail.

75. *Floral Poetry*, 252.

76. Kadiatu Kanneh, "Feminism and the Colonial Body," in *The Post-Colonial Studies Reader*, ed. Bill Ashcroft, Gareth Griffiths, and Helen Tiffin (London and New York: Routledge, 1995), 347.

77. For a good example of this theme in the rococo period, see the libretto to George Frederic Handel's 1707 *The Triumph of Time and Truth.*

78. Reinhart, "Here and Hereafter," 16.

79. Number 2 in a suite of thirty-one images called *Les amants des nations diverses* which was first issued in 1834–38 and again in 1851 (Farwell, *Cult of Images*, fig. 124).

80. Tucker, *Women*, 53; Melman, *Women's Orients*, 108.

81. Paul Taylor, *Dutch Flower Painting, 1600–1720* (New Haven: Yale University Press, 1995), 75–76, 174.

82. For this fact, I am grateful to three Latin scholars: Max Zanders, Marcia Jones, and Edgar Chamorro. Latin titles were assigned by Ruskin to some of his writings. Chapters of *Modern Painters* include "In Montibus Sanctus" and "Coeli Enarrant."

83. The first edition of *Prosperina* did not appear until 1875 (constantly republished until 1886), but it is conceivable that Lewis knew of Ruskin's writings and notes on flowers long before they went to press in 1875, as Ruskin had begun serious flower study in the 1840s.

84. Mitchell, *Colonising Egypt*, 104.

85. Bhabha, "The Other Question," 18–36.

86. Freud, "Fetishism," 219.

87. Bhabha, "The Other Question," 31.

Chapter 7. Conclusions

1. The word is T. J. Clark's (*The Painting of Modern Life: Paris in the Art of Manet and His Followers* [Princeton: Princeton University Press, 1984], 10.)

2. Tucker reports that in 1877 a bilateral agreement was signed under the auspices of the Anti-Slavery Society between Britain and Egypt outlawing the trade in Abyssinian and Sudanese slaves and outlining punishments for offending slave traders; the agreement was a catalyst in the waning of the slave trade. When the British officially occupy Egypt in 1882, they arrested slave traders in Cairo, who were sentenced up to three years of hard labor. And by the year 1887, nearly all the professional slave trading had ended, while clandestine trading continued to some extent. Within Egypt, the slave trade was in effect banned by 1890 (Tucker, *Women*, 172–75).

3. Tucker, *Women*, 192.

4. Ibid.

5. Ira M. Lapidus, *A History of Islamic Societies* (Cambridge: Cambridge University Press, 1988), 610.

6. Yvonne Yazbeck Haddad, Byron Haines, and Ellison Findly, eds. *The Islamic Impact* (Syracuse: Syracuse University Press, 1984), 92.

7. Information in this paragraph is culled from Toledano, *Ottoman Slave Trade*, 168–71.

8. Albert Boime, *Art and the French Commune: Imagining Paris after War and Revolution* (Princeton: Princeton University Press, 1995).

9. Ibid., 7.

10. Boime describes the reactions of Manet, Renoir, and other early Impressionists to the devastation in Paris in 1870–1871 (Boime, *Art and the French Commune*, 46–54.)

11. See Courbet's *Woman with a Parrot*, 1866 (Metropolitan Museum of Art, New York). I have discussed bird iconography in harem pictures in a previous chapter. There are other indicators of an exotic setting, most notably the fine fabrics in curtain and discarded clothing, the spiral column in the upper left corner and the curious object in the lower left (ambiguously rendered in both reproduction and upon firsthand viewing), which may be a Turkish slipper. Roos quotes one critic's reaction to this work, that of Charles du Sault, whose comment suggests the discourse of harem women as an animal and as soulless, both of which I have demonstrated as often referring to the harem woman: "'[Courbet's] conception of life and of art, we have already said it, does not rise above the level of animality. The question of the immortal soul will never be posed in relation to the *Woman with a Parrot*" (quoted in Jane Mayo Roos, *Early Impressionism and the French State 1866–74* [Cambridge: Cambridge University Press, 1996], 52–53).

12. Clark, *Painting of Modern Life*, 78.

13. I do not address the orientalist harem paintings of Camille Corot, who paints an *Odalisque* c. 1870 and a *Young Algerian Woman Lying on the Grass* (1871–c. 1873), which Gary Tinterow calls "*hommage* to Delacroix, made wholesome in Corot's manner," and notes that Robaut watched Corot

painting this work during the siege of Paris in January 1871 (Gary Tinterow, Michael Pantazzi, and Vincent Pomarède, *Corot* [New York: Harry N. Abrams, Inc. and the Metropolitan Museum of Art, 1996], 360–61 and 358).

14. François Daulte, *Frédéric Bazille et les débuts de l'Impressionisme: Catalogue Raisonné de l'oeuvre peint* (Paris: Bibliothèque des Arts, 1992), 128.

15. There has been some debate over their identities. Rewald identifies the following: Edmond Maître is playing the piano, while on the stairs Zola leans over to converse with Renoir, who is seated on a table. Meanwhile Bazille shows his canvas to Manet and Monet (John Rewald, *The History of Impressionism* [New York: Museum of Modern Art, 1961], 234). Champa notes that Manet painted the figure of Bazille (Kermit Swiler Champa, "A Complicated Codependence," in *Monet and Bazille: A Collaboration* [Atlanta and New York: High Museum of Art and Harry N. Abrams, 1999], 73.) Bazille paints on the wall representations of at least two works rejected by the Salon, one he submitted in 1869 and another done by Renoir rejected from the 1866 Salon (Pascal Bonafoux, "Bazille and Friendship, or the Interrupted Lexicon," in *Frederic Bazille: Prophet of Impressionism*, trans. John Goodman [New York: Brooklyn Museum, 1992], 46–47).

16. Bazille writes: "'What pleases me is that there is real animosity directed against us. The fault lies entirely with Mr. Gérôme, who treated us like a band of madmen, saying that he felt it his duty to keep our paintings from being shown'" (Letter 74, 1869, quoted in J. Patrice Marandel and François Daulte, *Frédéric Bazille and Early Impressionism* [Chicago: Art Institute, 1978], 179).

17. Pictorial lesbianism would support Champa's case that Bazille's paintings from this period, including this work, have homoerotic overtones (Champa, "A Complicated Codependence," 72–74).

18. Champa confirms that this work is more traditional than the kinds of experiments Bazille had conducted with Monet, whose influence is absent here (Champa, "A Complicated Codependence," 90).

19. Gary Tinterow, *Origins of Impressionism* (New York: Harry N. Abrams, 1994), 337.

20. Emile Zola, "Art at the Moment," in *Nineteenth-Century Theories of Art*, ed. Joshua C. Taylor (1866; reprint, Berkeley: University of California Press, 1987), 428.

21. The background of Manet's painting was extended into depth to show a stage setting in 1867 (*Manet: 1832–1883* [New York: Metropolitan Museum of Art and Harry N. Abrams, 1983], 146.)

22. Marius Chaumelin, *L'Art contemporain* (Paris: Renouard, 1873), 417.

23. Charles Blanc, *Les Artistes de mon temps* (Paris: Firmin-Didot, 1876), 74. John Gage confirms Blanc's interpretation of Delacroix's treatment of color as relevant to the younger generation of artists. Like Delacroix they were indebted to M. E. Chevreul's scientific studies (John Gage, "Color in Western Art: An Issue?" *Art Bulletin* 72, no. 4 [December 1990]: 529).

24. T. J. Clark addresses the issue of Olympia's absence of pubic hair (*Painting of Modern Life*, 136–37). A series of illustrations he includes in this chapter, "Olympia's Choice," demonstrates the absence of pubic hair in paintings of academic nudes (118–27).

25. See Schick, *Erotic Margin*, 207–9.

26. Clark, *Painting of Modern Life*, 128.

27. On Manet's interest in *ukiyo-e* and other Japanese art, see Champa, *History of Impressionism*, 207–9; Jacques Dufwa, *Winds from the East* (Stockholm: Almqvist, 1981), 51–82; Siegfried Wichmann, *Japonisme: Japanese Influence on Western Art in the 19th and 20th Centuries* (New York: Thames and Hudson, 1999), 22–25.

28. *Flaubert in Egypt: A Sensibility on Tour: A Narrative drawn from Gustave Flaubert's Travel Notes and Letters*, ed. and trans. Francis Steegmuller (New York: Penguin, 1972), 40.

29. Ibid., 76.

30. Clark is writing of the 1860s (Clark, *Painting of Modern Life*, 103). For the 1870s and 1880s see Hollis Clayson, *Painted Love: Prostitution in French Art of the Impressionist Era* (New Haven: Yale University Press, 1991).

31. Bazille's letters from North Africa written a few months before his death reveal some disappointment at the loss of the ideal of a pure Arab culture. He wrote that Philippesville was Frenchified and poor (Letter 88, 30 August 1870, in Marandel and Daulte, *Bazille and Early Impressionism*, 184).

32. Julia Kristeva, "Woman Can Never Be Defined," in *New French Feminisms*, ed. Elaine Marks and Isabelle de Courtivron, (New York: Schocken Books, 1980), 137.

Bibliography

PRIMARY SOURCES

"An Abode of Bliss." *Chambers's Journal of Popular Literature, Science and Art*, 4th ser. 128 (9 June 1866): 365ff.

About, Edmond. *Voyage à travers l'exposition des beaux-arts*. Paris: Hachette, 1855.

Adalet. "A Voice from a Harem: Some Words About the Turkish Women of Our Day." *The Nineteenth Century* 28 (August 1890): 186–90.

———. "Life in the Harem." *The Nineteenth Century* 28 (December 1890): 959–66.

"An African Hareem." *Cornhill* 23, no. 138 (1871): 726–37.

Arabian Nights' Entertainment. Trans. Edward Forster. London: Willoughby and Company, c.1844.

Arabian Nights' Entertainment (The 1001 Nights). Trans. Edward William Lane and ed. Edward Stanley Poole. 1839–41. Reprint, London: John Murray, 1859.

Art Journal. 12 (1850): 179; (1855): 237ff; (1857): 178; "British Artists: Their Style and Character, no. 32, John Frederick Lewis," n.s. 4 (1858): 41–43, 162; 26 (1 June 1864): 163ff; n.s. 5 (July 1865): 197–99; n.s. 8 (1869): 167ff; (1872): 156ff; n.s. 13 (1874): 200; (1877): 138ff; (18 May 1878): 638; 40 (1878): 200.

Athenaeum. (23 February 1850): 210; (4 May 1850): 480; (2 May 1857): 571; (8 May 1858): 596; (7 May 1864): 651; (6 May 1865): 626; (4 May 1872): 564; (30 May 1874): 740.

Balzac, Honoré de. "Seraphita" and "The Alkahest." *La Comédie humaine*. Trans. Katharine Prescott Wormeley. Boston: Little, Brown and Co., 1904.

Baudelaire, Charles. *The Painter of Modern Life and Other Essays*. Trans. and ed. Jonathan Mayne. New York: DaCapo, 1986.

Blanc, Charles. *Les Artistes de mon temps*. Paris: Firmin-Didot, 1876.

Blunt, Mrs. [John Elijah]. *The People of Turkey: Twenty Years' Residence Among Bulgarians, Greeks, Albanians, Turks and Armenians*. 2 Vols. Ed. Stanley Lane Poole. London: John Murray, 1878.

Bonaparte, Napoleon. *Memoirs of the Military and Political Life of Napoleon Bonaparte*. Ed. B. E. O'Meara. Hartford, Connecticut: Chauncey Goodrich, 1822.

———. *Dictionnaire-Napoléon ou recueil alphabétique des opinions et jugements de l'empereur Napoléon Ier* including *Mémoires pour servir à l'histoire de France sous le règne de Napoléon*. 2d ed. 1838. Reprint, Damas Hinard. Paris: Plon Frères, 1854.

Bowring, John. *Report on Egypt and Candia, Addressed to the Right Honorable Lord Viscount Palmerston . . . Presented to Both Houses of Parliament by Command of Her Majesty*. London: W. Clowes and Sons, H.M. Stationery Office, 1840.

British and Foreign Anti-Slavery Reporter. (21 October 21 1840): 267–70; (2 December 1840): 311; (9 February 1842): 24; (6 September 1843): 166; (15 November 1843): 213; (29 November 1843): 221–24; (7 February 1844): 24; (1 May 1844): 74–75; (2 April 1845): 68; (17 September 1845): 180; (1 October 1845): 188.

Bunbury, John. *A Relation of a Journey of the Rt. Honorable my Lord Henry Howard from London . . . to Constantinople*. London: Collins and Ford, 1671.

Burton, Richard F. *Personal Narrative of a Pilgrimage to El-Medinah and Meccah*. 3 Vols. London: Longman, Brown, and Longmans, 1855.

Byron, Lord [George Gordon Noel]. *The Complete Works of Lord Byron*. Philadelphia: David McKay, 1883.

Carlyle, Thomas. *On Heroes, Hero-Worship and the Heroic in History*. Ed. Carl Niemeyer. Lincoln: University of Nebraska Press, 1966.

———. "The Present Time." In *Latter-day Pamphlets*. Boston: Estes and Lauriat, n.d.

Chaumelin, Marius. *L'Art contemporain*. Paris: Renouard, 1873.

Christie, Manson and Woods Artist's Sale Catalog, 7 May 1877.

Clot Bey, A.B. *Aperçu général sur l'Egypte*. Brussels: Meline, Cans et Cie., 1840.

———. *Mémoires of Clot Bey*. Ed. Jacques Tagher. Cairo: L'Institut français d'archéologie orientale, 1949.

Code Napoléon avec les changemens qui y ont été faits par la loi de 3 Septembre 1807. (French-German ed.). Paris, 1807.

Critic. (1850): 253; (1855): 242; (1857): 209.

Delacroix, Eugène. *Correspondance générale*. 5 Vols. Paris: Plon, 1938.

———. *Journal*. Trans. Walter Pach. New York: Crown, 1948.

Delécluze, M. E. J. *Les Beaux-Arts dans les deux mondes en 1855*. Paris: Charpentier, 1856.

Denon, Dominique Vivant. *Travels in Upper and Lower Egypt: In Company with Several Divisions of the French Army, during the Campaign of General Bonaparte in that Country*. 2 Vols. Trans. Arthur Aikin. London: T. N. Longman and O. Rees, 1803.

"Does Mohammedism Allow Women Souls?" *The Christian Observer* 44 (February 1844): 101ff.

Dublin Universal Magazine 13 (February 1839): 137–44.

du Camp, Maxime. *Les Beaux-Arts à l'exposition universelle de 1855*. Paris, 1855.

Dumas, Alexandre. *Adventures in Algeria*. Trans. Alma Elizabeth Murch. 1848–51. Reprint, Philadelphia and New York: Chilton Co., 1959.

Encyclopaedia Londinensis. London, 1810–11.

Encyclopedia Britannica. 8th ed. London, 1853–60.

The Englishwoman's Review of Social and Industrial Questions. Ed. Janet Horowitz Murray and Myra Stark. (15 January 1877): 42–44; (15 October 1877): 475; "Slavery in Turkey" (15 June 1878): 257. Reprint, New York and London: Garland Publishers, Inc., 1980.

Explication des oeuvrages de peinture, sculpture, gravure, . . . des artists vivants, exposés au musée royal. Paris: Vinchon, 1845.

Flaubert in Egypt: A Sensibility on Tour: A Narrative drawn from Gustave Flaubert's Travel Notes and Letters. Ed. and trans. Francis Steegmuller. New York: Penguin, 1972.

Floral Poetry and the Language of Flowers. London: Marcus Ward and Company, 1877.

Flowers culled from the Gulistan and Bostan of Sadi [13th century] with a Few Specimens of the Mesnavi of Jelal-ud-Din Rumi. Trans. Samuel Robinson. London: Williams and Norgate, 1876.

Gautier, Théophile. *Les beaux-arts en Europe 1855*. Paris: Michel Lévy frères, 1855.

"Glimpses of Harem Life." *Bentley's Miscellany* 43 (1858): 508–18.

Guillet de St.-Georges, Georges. *An Account of a Late Voyage to Athens containing . . . The Estate . . . of the Present Empire of the Turks*. London: Herringman, 1674.

Hamilton, Augusta. *Marriage Rites, Customs and Ceremonies of All Nations of the Universe*. London: Chapple and Son, 1822.

A Handbook for Travellers in Turkey in Asia including Constantinople, the Bosphorus, Dardanelles, Brousa . . . and the Plain of Troy. 4th ed. London: John Murray, 1871.

Harvey, Annie Jane. *Turkish Harems and Circassian Homes*. London: Hurst and Blackett, 1871.

Hauréau, Barthélemy. *La Tribune* (March 15, 1834): n.p.

Hill, Aaron. *A Full and Just Account of the Present State of the Ottoman Empire in all its Branches . . .* London: G. Parker, 1733.

Historical and Ethnological Society of Greece. *Philhellenika, 1821–31*. Athens, 1975.

Hugo, Victor. *Selections Chiefly Lyrical from the Poetical Works of Victor Hugo*. Ed. Henry Llewellyn Williams. London: George Bell and Sons, 1885.

Illustrated London News. 16 (4 May 1850): 299–300; 30 (2 May 1857): 571; 30 (9 May 1857): 444; 64 (7 May 1864): 454; 66 (13 May 1865): 451; (24 April 1869): 422; (8 May 1869): 471; (25 May 1872): 502.

L'Illustration 5, no. 107 (15 March 1845): 39.

James, Walter C. "Women in Turkey." *Contemporary Review* 34 (1879): 108–30.

Keppel, George (Earl of Albemarle). *Narrative of a Journey Across the Balcan . . . in the Year 1829–30*. 2 Vols. London: Colburn and Bentley, 1831.

A Lady. "A Visit to a Harem." *Chambers's Edinburgh Journal* 5, 109 n.s. (31 January 1846): 65–68.

de Lamartine, Alphonse. *A Pilgrimage to the Holy Land (Voyage en Orient)*. 1838. Reprint, Delmar, NY: Scholars' Facsimiles and Reprints, 1978.

Lane, Edward William. *An Account of the Manners and Customs of the Modern Egyptians, Written in Egypt During the Years 1833, –34 and –35*. 5th ed. London: John Murray, 1871.

The Language and Poetry of Flowers. London: Milner and Company, c. 1871.

"The Legend of John Belin." *Funny Folks* (26 December 1874): n.p.

Lewis's Illustrations of Constantinople Made . . . in the Years 1835–6, Arranged and Drawn on Stone, from the Original Sketches of Coke Smyth by J. F. Lewis. London: T. McLean, 1838.

"Love and Marriage in Persia." *All the Year Round* 6 (15 February 1862): 488–91.

McCoan, James C. "Slavery and Polygamy in Turkey." *Fraser's Magazine* 18, 106 n.s. (October 1878): 403–13.

———. "Slavery in Egypt." *Fraser's Magazine* 95 (May 1877): 563–70.

MacFarlane, James. *Turkey and Its Destiny: The Results of Journeys . . . in 1847 and 1848*. 2 Vols. London: John Murray, 1850.

Mandley, James G. *Woman Outside Christendom: An Exposition of the Influence Exerted by Christianity in the Social Position and Happiness of Women*. London: Trübner and Co., 1880.

Martineau, Harriet. *Eastern Life, Present and Past*. Philadelphia: Lea and Blanchard, 1848.

Marx, Karl, and Frederick Engels. *The Communist Manifesto*. New York: International Publishers, 1979.

Melek-Hanum. *Thirty Years in the Harem or the Autobiography of Melek-Hanum, Wife of H. H. Kibrizli-Mehemet-Pasha*. New York: Harper and Brothers, 1872.

Montagu, Lady Mary Wortley. *The Complete Letters of Lady Mary Wortley Montagu*. 3 Vols. Ed. Robert Halsband. Oxford: Clarendon Press, 1965.

Moore, Thomas. *Lalla Rookh: An Oriental Romance*. 1817. Reprint, New York: Lincoln Macveagh, The Dial Press, Longmans Green and Co., 1930.

Montesquieu. *Persian Letters*. Ed. and trans. C.J. Betts. London: Penguin, 1973.

Mozart, Wolfgang Amadeus. *Abduction from the Seraglio*. Trans. Ruth Martin and Thomas Martin. 1782. Reprint, n.p.: Boosey and Hawkes, 1962.

Musée du Louvre. *L'Oeuvre gravée de François Boucher dans la collection de E. de Rothschild*. Paris: Editions des Musées Nationaux, 1978.

"Mysteries of the Seraglio, from *Bently's [sic] Miscellany* (London)." *Eclectic Magazine* [New York] 60 (December 1863): 467–71.

Nerval, Gérard de. *Voyage to the Orient*. Ed. and trans. Norman

Glass. 1851. Reprint, New York: New York University Press, 1972.

———. *The Women of Cairo: Scenes of Life in the Orient.* 2 vols. Ed. Conrad Elphinstone. 1926. Reprint, Ann Arbor: University of Michigan, 1982.

Nield, John. "Turcotoquade." *L'Image* nos. 30–34 (26 July-30 August 1868): n.p.

Nightingale, Florence. *Letters from Egypt: A Journey on the Nile 1849–1850.* New York: Weidenfeld and Nicholson, 1987.

O'Shaughnessy, Arthur William Edgar. "Zuleika." In *Poetry of the Victorian Period,* 3rd edition. Ed. Jerome H. Buckley and George B. Woods. Chicago: Scott Foresman, 1965, 761–62.

Pardoe, Julia. *Beauties of the Bosphorus.* London: George Virtue, 1838.

———. *The City of the Sultan and Domestic Manners of the Turks in 1836.* 2 Vols. London: Henry Colburn, 1837.

Phillips, Henry. *Floral Emblems.* London: Saunders and Otley, 1825.

Pickersgill, Mrs. *Tales of the Harem (in verse).* London: Longman, Rees, Orme, Brown and Green, 1827.

Planche, Gustave. *Revue des Deux Mondes* 2, ser. 3 (1 April 1834): 58–59.

Poole, Sophie Lane. *The Englishwoman in Egypt: Letters from Cairo, Written During a Residence There in 1842, -3 and -4 with E. W. Lane.* 1844. Reprint, Philadelphia: G. B. Ziegler and Co., 1845.

Reeve, Emma. *Character and Costume in Turkey and Italy: A Description of Eight Turkish and Twelve Italian Plates. Designed and Drawn from Nature by Thomas Allom, Esq.* London: Fisher, Son and Co., 1839.

Roberts, David. *Views in the Holy Land, Syria . . . Egypt, and Nubia.* London: F. G. Moor, 1842–49.

———. Letter to John Frederick Lewis. 1859.

Ruskin, John. *The Works of John Ruskin.* 39 Vols. Ed. E. T. Cook and Alexander Wedderburn. New York: Longmans, Green and Co.; London: George Allen, 1903–12.

———. Letters to John Frederick Lewis: A14 (26 August 1858); A16 (1856); A20 (received 14 May 1859).

Ruskin, John James. Letter to John Frederick Lewis A15 (30 August 1858).

Rycaut, Paul. *History of the present state of the Ottoman Empire . . . in three books.* 4th ed. London: Starkey and Brome, 1675.

St. John, James Augustus, and E. Prisse d'Avennes. *Oriental Album: Characters, Costumes and Modes of Life in the Valley of the Nile.* London: James Madden, 1848.

Sandys, George. *Sandys Travailles: Containing a History of the . . . Turkish Empire.* 6th ed. London: John Sweeting, 1658.

"Slavery in Egypt." *Frazer's Magazine* 95 (May 1877): 569.

Smith, Albert Richard. *Customs and Habits of the Turks.* 1850. Reprint, Boston: Higgins and Bradley, 1856.

Spectator. (4 May 1850): 427; (2 May 1857): 463; (22 May 1858): 555.

Spencer, Edmund. *Travels in Circassia, Kim-Tartary . . . in 1836.* 2 Vols. London: Colburn, 1837.

Thackeray, William Makepeace. *Sketches and Travels in London* and *Notes of a Journey From Cornhill to Cairo.* Vol. 16. In *Works of William Makepeace Thackeray.* 26 Vols. Boston: Charles E. Lauriat, 1904.

(London) Times. (7 February 1835): 5; (1 May 1850): 8; (28 April 1857): 7; (1 May 1858): 5; (30 April 1864): 14; (29 April 1865): 12; (1 May 1869): 12; (21 May 1872): 7; (26 May 1874): 6.

Tubeeb, Meerza Ahmed. "Visits to the Harem." *Blackwood's Magazine* (Edinburgh) 15 (February 1824): 199ff.

Urquhart, David. *Spirit of the East Illustrated in a Journal of Travels through Roumeli during an Eventful Period.* London: Henry Colburn, 1838.

Vanmour, Jean Baptiste. *Recueil de cent estampes répresentant différentes nations du Levant tirées sur les tableaux peints d'après nature en 1707 et 1708 par les ordres de M. de Ferriol, Ambassadeur du Roi à la Porte et gravées en 1712 et 1713 . . .* Paris: Le Hay, 1714.

———. *Moeurs et usages des turcs.* 2 Vols. Paris, 1746.

"A Visit to the Harem of the Pasha of Widdin." *Fraser Magazine* 18, no. 108 (December 1838): 679–86.

Walsh, Robert. *Constantinople and the Scenery of the Seven Churches of Asia Minor, Illustrated . . . by Thomas Allom.* 2 Vols. London and Paris: Fisher, Son and Co., 1838.

Watson, Forbes. *Flowers and Gardens: Notes on Plant Beauty.* c. 1872. Reprint, London and New York: John Lane, 1901.

White, Charles. *Three Years in Constantinople or Domestic Manners of the Turks in 1844.* 3 Vols. London: Henry Colburn, 1845.

Withers, Robert. *A Description of the Grand Signor's Seraglio.* In *The English Experience: Its Record in Early Printed Books.* 1585, 1650. Reprint, Amsterdam and New York: Da Capo Press, 1968.

Wollstonecraft, Mary. *Vindication of the Rights of Women.* Ed. Miriam Brody. 1792. Reprint, London: Penguin Books, 1988.

"Woman in Turkey." *Bentley's Miscellany* 38 (1855): 349–54.

"Women in the East." *Bentley's Miscellany* 27 (1850): 379–84.

"Women in Morocco." *Hogg's Instructor* 6, n.s. (1851): 382–84.

Woolner, Thomas. Letter to John Frederick Lewis (3 May 1874).

Zola, Emile. "Art at the Moment." In *Nineteenth-Century Theories of Art.* Ed. Joshua C. Taylor. 1866. Reprint, Berkeley: University of California Press, 1987, 420–30.

Secondary Sources

Abu-Lughod, Lila. "Zones of Theory in the Anthropology of the Arab World." *Annual Review of Anthropology* 18 (1989): 267–306.

Ackerman, Gerald. *J. L. Gérôme (1824–1904).* Dayton, Ohio: Dayton Art Institute, 1972.

———. *The Life and Work of Jean Léon Gérôme.* London: ACR, 1986.

Ahmed, Leila. *Edward W. Lane: A Study of His Life and Works and of British Ideas of the Middle East in the Nineteenth Century.* London: Longman, 1978.

———. "Western Ethnocentrism and Perceptions of the Harem." *Feminist Studies* 8, no. 3 (fall 1982): 521–34.

———. *Women and Gender in Islam.* New Haven: Yale University Press, 1992.

———. *A Border Passage: From Cairo to America—A Woman's Journey.* New York: Penguin, 2000.

Alatas, Syed Hussein. *The Myth of the Lazy Native.* London: Frank Cass, 1977.

Alazard, Jean. *L'Orient et la peinture française au 19e siècle.* Paris: Plon, 1930.

Alloula, Malek. *The Colonial Harem.* Trans. Myrna Godzich and Wlad Godzich. Minneapolis: University of Minnesota Press, 1986.

Anderson, Matthew Smith. *The Eastern Question 1774–1925: A Study in International Relations.* London: Macmillian, 1966.

Annan, Margaret Cecilia. "The *Arabian Nights* in Victorian Literature." Ph.D. diss., Northwestern University, 1945.

Ashcroft, Bill, Gareth Griffiths, and Helen Tiffin, eds. *The Post-Colonial Studies Reader.* London and New York: Routledge, 1995.

Athanassoglou-Kallmyer, Nina. *French Images from the Greek War of Independence: Art and Politics Under the Restoration.* New Haven: Yale University Press, 1989.

Baer, Gabriel. "Slavery in Nineteenth-Century Egypt." *Journal of African History* 8, no. 3 (1967): 417–41.

Bailey, Frank Edgar. *British Policy and the Turkish Reform Movement: A Study in Anglo-Turkish Relations, 1826–1853.* Harvard Historical Studies. New York: Howard Fertig, 1970.

Bazin, Germain. "Delacroix au Maroc: Au Musée de l'Orangerie," *L'Amour de l'art* 14 (March 1933) Part 2: 1–4.

Brantlinger, Patrick B. "Victorians and Africans: The Genealogy of the Myth of the Dark Continent." In *"Race," Writing and Difference,* ed. Henry Louis Gates, Jr. Chicago: University of Chicago Press, 1986, 186–222.

Behdad, Ali. "The Eroticized Orient: Images of the Harem in Montesquieu and His Precursors." *Stanford French Review* 13, nos. 2–3 (fall-winter 1989): 109–26.

Bendiner, Kenneth. "The Portrayal of the Middle East in British Painting, 1835–60." Ph.D. dissertation, Columbia University, 1979.

———. "Albert Moore and John Frederick Lewis." *Arts Magazine* 54, no. 6 (February 1980): 76–79.

———. "Wilkie in Turkey." *Art Bulletin* 63, no. 2 (June 1981): 259–68.

———. *An Introduction to Victorian Painting.* New Haven: Yale University Press, 1985.

Benjamin, Roger, ed. *Orientalism: Delacroix to Klee.* Sydney: New South Wales Art Gallery, 1997.

Bhabha, Homi K. "Signs Taken for Wonders: Questions of Ambivalent Authority Under a Tree Outside Delhi, May 1817." In *"Race," Writing and Difference,* ed. Henry Louis Gates, Jr. Chicago: University of Chicago Press, 1986, 163–84.

———. "The Other Question . . ." *Screen* 24, no. 6 (November-December 1983): 18–36.

Blair, Sheila, and Jonathan Bloom, eds. *Images of Paradise in Islamic Art.* Hanover, NH: Hood Museum of Art, 1991.

Blunt, Alison, and Gillian Rose. *Writing Women and Space: Colonial and Postcolonial Geographies.* New York: Guilford Press, 1994.

Boime, Albert. *Thomas Couture and the Eclectic Vision.* New Haven and London: Yale University Press, 1980.

———. "The Case of Rosa Bonheur: Why Should a Woman Want to Be More Like a Man?" *Art History* 4, no. 4 (1981): 384–409.

———. "Gérôme and the Bourgeois Artist's Burden." *Arts Magazine* 57, no. 5 (January 1983):64–73.

———. "Painted Pomp: Setting the World on Fire." *FMR* [Milan] (December 1986): 81–102.

———. *Art and the French Commune: Imagining Paris after War and Revolution.* Princeton: Princeton University Press, 1995.

Bonafoux, Pascal. "Bazille and Friendship, or the Interrupted Lexicon." In *Frederic Bazille: Prophet of Impressionism,* trans. John Goodman. New York: Brooklyn Museum, 1992.

Bourne, Kenneth. *The Foreign Policy of Victorian England, 1830–1902.* Oxford: Clarendon Press, 1970.

Brantlinger, Patrick B. "Victorians and Africans: The Genealogy of the Myth of the Dark Continent." In *"Race," Writing and Difference,* ed. Henry Louis Gates, Jr. Chicago: University of Chicago Press, 1986, 185–222.

Brown, Marilyn. "The Harem De-historicized: Ingres' *Bain turc.*" *Arts Magazine* 61, no. 10 (summer 1987): 58–68.

Bury, Adrian. "Our Great Water Colour Tradition." *The Artist* 52, no. 4 (December 1956).

Cairncross, John. *After Polygamy Was Made a Sin: The Social History of Christian Polygamy.* London: Routledge and Kegan Paul, 1974.

Casteras, Susan P. *Images of Victorian Womanhood in English Art.* Rutherford, NJ: Associated University Presses, 1987.

Çelik, Zeynep. *Displaying the Orient: Architecture of Islam at the Nineteenth-Century World's Fairs.* Berkeley: University of California Press, 1992.

Champa, Kermit Swiler. "A Complicated Codependence." In *Monet and Bazille: A Collaboration.* Atlanta and New York: High Museum of Art and Harry N. Abrams, 1999, 66–95.

Clark, Timothy J. *The Painting of Modern Life: Paris in the Art of Manet and His Followers.* Princeton: Princeton University Press, 1984.

Clifford, James. "Said's *Orientalism.*" *History and Theory* 19 (1980): 204–23.

Codell, Julie F., and Dianne Sachko Macleod, eds. *Orientalism Transposed: The Impact of the Colonies on British Culture.* Aldershot, England and Brookfield, VT: Ashgate, 1998.

Collier, Peter, and Robert Lethbridge. *Artistic Relations: Literature and the Visual Arts in Nineteenth-Century France.* New Haven: Yale University Press, 1994.

Connor, Patrick, ed. *The Inspiration of Egypt: Its Influence on British Artists, Travellers and Designers, 1700–1900.* Brighton: Borough Council, 1983.

Cooper, Robyn. "Millais' *The Rescue*: A Painting of a 'Dreadful Interruption of Domestic Peace.'" *Art History* 9, no. 4 (December 1986): 471–86.

Coven, Jeffrey. *Baudelaire's Voyages: The Poet and His Paints.* Boston: Little Brown and Co., 1993.

Croutier, Alev Lytle. *Harem: The World Behind the Veil.* New York: Abbeville, 1989.

Dakin, Douglas. *British and American Philhellenes during the War of Greek Independence 1821–33.* Thessaloniki, 1955.

Danziger, Raphael. *Abd Al-Qadir and the Algerians: Resistance to the French and Internal Consolidation.* New York and London: Holmes and Meier, 1977.

Daulte, François. *Frédéric Bazille et les débuts de l'Impressionisme: Catalogue Raisonné de l'oeuvre peint.* Paris: Bibliothèque des Arts, 1992.

Davis, Fanny. *The Ottoman Lady: A Social History from 1718–1918.* Westport, CT: Greenwood Press, 1986.

Davis, Natalie Zemon. "Women on Top." In *Society and Culture in Early Modern France: Eight Essays.* Stanford: Stanford University Press (1975): 124–51.

de Groot, Joanna. "'Sex' and 'Race': the Construction of Language and Image in the Nineteenth Century." In *Sexuality and Subordination: Interdisciplinary Studies of Gender in the Nineteenth Century,* ed. Susan Mendus and Jane Rendall. London: Routledge, 1989.

DelPlato, Joan. "An English Feminist in the Turkish Harem: A Portrait of Lady Mary Wortley Montagu." In *Eighteenth-Century Women and the Arts,* ed. Frederick M. Keener and Susan E. Lorsch. New York: Greenwood Press, 1988, 163–78.

———. "Lefebvre's Critique of Space as Interdisciplinary Paradigm: Desire and Colonialism in Three Harem Pictures by Delacroix, Renoir, and Lewis." In *Gendered Landscapes: An Interdisciplinary Exploration of Past Place and Space,* ed. Bonj Szczygiel, Josephine Carubia, and Lorraine Dowler. University Park: The Pennsylvania State University, 2000, 68–81.

———. "Passivity and Politics in Delacroix's 1834 *Women of Algiers.*" In Amy Tucker. *Visual Literacy.* New York: McGraw-Hill, 2002, 244–51.

Denny, Walter B. "Orientalism in European Art." *The Muslim World* 73, nos. 3–4 (July–October 1983): 262–77.

———. "Reflections of Paradise in Islamic Art" and "Paradise Described." In *Images of Paradise in Islamic Art,* ed. Sheila S. Blair and Jonathan M. Bloom. Hanover, NH: Hood Museum of Art, Dartmouth College, 1991, 33–43, 80–92.

———. "Quotations In and Out of Context: Ottoman Turkish Art and European Orientalist Painting." *Muqarnas* 10 (1993):219–30.

———. "Images of Turks and the European Imagination." In *Court and Conquest,* ed. Walter B. Denny *et al.* Kent, OH: Kent State University Museum, 1999, 3–17.

d'Huart, Annabelle and Nadia Tazi. *Harems.* Paris: Chéne, 1980.

Dijkstra, Bram. *Idols of Perversity: Fantasies of Feminine Evil in Fin-de-Siècle Culture.* New York: Oxford University Press, 1986.

Dimopoulos, Aristide G. *L'opinion publique française et la révolution grecque, 1821–27.* Nancy: V. Idoux, 1962.

Dominguez, Virginia R. "Differentiating Women/Bodies of Knowledge." *American Anthropologist* 96, no. 1 (1994): 127–30.

Douthwaite, Julia V. *Exotic Women: Literary Heroines and Cultural Strategies in Ancien Régime France.* Philadelphia: University of Pennsylvania Press, 1992.

Duncan, Carol. "The Persistence and Re-emergence of the Rococo in French Romantic Painting." Ph.D. diss., Columbia University, 1969.

Eagleton, Terry. *Literary Theory: An Introduction.* Minneapolis: University of Minnesota Press, 1983.

Escholier, Raymond. *Eugène Delacroix.* Paris: Editions Cercle d'Art, 1963.

Etienne, Mona, and Eleanor Leacock, eds. *Women and Colonization: Anthropological Perspectives.* New York: Praeger Bergin, 1980.

Farwell, Beatrice. *Eugène Delacroix, 1798–1863.* New York: Metropolitan Museum of Art, 1955.

———. "Manet and the Nude: A Study in Iconography in the Second Empire." Ph.D. diss., UCLA, 1973.

———. *Cult of Images: Baudelaire and the Nineteenth-Century Media Explosion.* Santa Barbara: University of California Press, 1977.

———. *French Popular Lithographic Imagery, 1815–70.* 12 Vols. Chicago: University of Chicago Press, 1981–97.

Foucault, Michel. *The History of Sexuality.* Vol. 1. Trans. Robert Hurley. New York: Pantheon, 1990.

Freud, Sigmund. "Fetishism." In *Sexuality and the Psychology of Love,* ed. Philip Rieff. 1927. Reprint, New York: Macmillan, 1974.

Gage, John. "Color in Western Art: An Issue?" *Art Bulletin* 72, no. 4 (December 1990): 518–41.

Gates, Jr., Henry Louis, ed. *"Race," Writing and Difference.* Chicago: University of Chicago Press, 1986.

Gilman, Sander L. *Difference and Pathology: Stereotypes of Sexuality, Race, and Madness.* Ithaca: Cornell University Press, 1985.

Gordon, David C. *Women of Algeria: An Essay on Change.* Cambridge: Harvard University Press, 1968.

Graham-Browne, Sarah. *Images of Women: The Portrayal of Women in Photography of the Middle East, 1860–1950.* New York: Columbia University Press, 1988.

Graté, Pontus. *Deux critiques d'art de l'époque romantique.* Stockholm: Almqvist and Wiskell, 1959.

Green, Richard. *John Frederick Lewis, R.A. 1805–76.* Newcastle-upon-Tyne: Laing Art Gallery, 1971.

Grewal, Inderpal. *Home and Harem.* Durham: Duke University Press, 1996.

Grosrichard, Alain. *Structure du sérail: La Fiction du despotisme asiatique dans l'occident classique.* Paris: Editions du Seuil, 1979.

Gueroult, Françoise. *Les écoles du nord.* Cherbourg: Musée Thomas Henry, 1973.

Haddad, Yvonne Yazbeck, Byron Haines, and Ellison Findly, eds. *The Islamic Impact.* Syracuse: Syracuse University Press, 1984.

Hadjinicolaou, Nicos. "*La Liberté guidant le peuple* de Delacroix devant son premier public." *Actes de la Recherche en science sociales* 28 (June 1979): 3–26.

Hanaway, William L., Jr. "Paradise on Earth: The Terrestrial Garden in Persian Literature." In *The Islamic Garden,* ed. Elisabeth B. MacDougall and Richard Ettinghausen. Washington, DC: Dumbarton Oaks, Trustees for Harvard University, 1976, 41–67.

Hardie, Martin. *Water-colour Painting in Britain.* 3 Vols. Ed. Dudley Snelgrove. London: B. T. Batsford, 1968.

Harris, Ann Sutherland, and Linda Nochlin. *Women Artists: 1550–1950.* New York: Alfred A. Knopf, 1976.

Haskell, Francis. "Chios, The Massacres and Delacroix." In *Chios: A Conference at the Homerion in Chios 1984,* ed. John Boardman and C. E. Vaphopoulou-Richardson. Oxford: Clarendon Press, 1986.

Herzog, Don. *Happy Slaves: A Critique of Consent Theory.* Chicago: University of Chicago Press, 1989.

Hollenbach, J. W. "The Image of the Arab in Nineteenth-Century English and American Literature." *Muslim World* 62 (1972): 195–208.

Holt, Elizabeth Gilmore. *The Triumph of Art for the Public.* Garden City, NY: Anchor Press, Doubleday, 1979.

Hughes, Peter. *Eighteenth-Century France and the East.* Wallace Collection Monographs 4. London: Wallace Collection, 1981.

Jameson, Fredric. "Modernism and Imperialism." In *Nationalism, Colonialism and Literature,* ed. Terry Eagleton, Fredric Jameson, and Edward W. Said. Minneapolis: University of Minnesota Press, 1990, 43–66.

Jayawardena, Kumari. *Feminism and Nationalism in the Third World.* London: Zea Books, Inc., 1986.

Jobert, Barthélémy. *Delacroix.* Princeton: Princeton University Press, 1998.

Jullian, Philippe. *The Orientalists: European Painters of Eastern Scenes.* Oxford: Phaidon, 1977.

Kabbani, Rana. *Europe's Myths of Orient.* Bloomington: Indiana University Press, 1986.

Kahf, Mohja. *Western Representations of the Muslim Woman: From Termagant to Odalisque.* Austin: University of Texas Press, 1999.

Kandiyoti, Deniz. *Gendering the Middle East: Emerging Perspectives.* Syracuse, NY: Syracuse University Press, 1996.

Kanneh, Kadiatu. "Feminism and the Colonial Body." In *The Post-Colonial Studies Reader,* ed. Bill Ashcroft, Gareth Griffiths, and Helen Tiffin. London and New York: Routledge, 1995, 346–48.

Keddie, Nikki R. "Problems in the Study of Middle Eastern Women." *International Journal of Middle Eastern Studies* 10, no. 2 (1979): 225–40.

Kemp, Wolfgang. *The Desire of My Eyes: The Life and Work of John Ruskin.* New York: Farrar, Straus and Giroux, 1990.

Kristeva, Julia. "Woman Can Never Be Defined." In *New French Feminisms,* ed. Elaine Marks and Isabelle de Courtivron. New York: Schocken Books, 1980, 137–41.

Kunzle, David. *Fashion and Fetishism: A Social History of the Corset, Tight-Lacing, and Other Forms of Body-Sculpture in the West.* Totowa, NJ: Rowman and Littlefield, 1982.

Lapidus, Ira M. *A History of Islamic Societies.* Cambridge: Cambridge University Press, 1988.

Lefebvre, Henri. *The Production of Space.* Trans. Donald Nicholson-Smith. Cambridge: Basil Blackwell, Inc., 1994.

Lehrman, Jonas. *Earthly Paradise: Garden and Courtyard in Islam.* Berkeley and Los Angeles: University of California Press, 1980.

LeVeen, E. Phillip. *British Slave Trade Suppression Policies, 1821–1865.* Dissertations in Economic History. New York: Arno Press, 1977.

John Frederick Lewis, R.A., 1805–1876: Painter of the Desert and Harem. London: Guilford House Gallery, 1977.

Lewis, Michael. *John Frederick Lewis, R.A., 1805–76.* Leigh-on-Sea: F. Lewis, 1978.

———. "The Egypt of John Frederick Lewis." *Art and Artists* 200 (May 1983): 20–22.

Lewis, Reina. *Gendering Orientalism: Race, Femininity, and Representation.* London: Routledge, 1996.

Llewellyn, Briony. "J. F. Lewis on the London Art Market." *Connoisseur* 203 (March 1980):224–27.

Lowe, Lisa. *Critical Terrains: French and British Orientalisms.* Ithaca: Cornell University Press, 1991.

Luebbers, Leslie. "Documenting the Invisible: European Images of Ottoman Women, 1567–1867." In *Print Collector's Newsletter* 24, no. 1 (March–April 1993): 1–7.

Maas, Jeremy. *Victorian Painters.* New York: G. P. Putnam's Sons, 1969.

Mabro, Judy, ed. *Veiled Half-Truths: Western Travellers' Perceptions of Middle Eastern Women.* London and New York: I. B. Tauris and Co., 1991.

MacDougall, Elisabeth B., and Richard Ettinghausen, eds. *The Islamic Garden.* Washington, DC: Dumbarton Oaks, Trustees for Harvard University, 1976.

MacKenzie, John M. *Orientalism: History, Theory, and the Arts.* Manchester and New York: Manchester University Press, 1995.

McLaren, Angus. "Doctor in the House: Medicine and Private Morality in France, 1800–50." *Feminist Studies* 2, no. 23 (1975): 39–54.

Mainardi, Patricia. *Art and Politics of the Second Empire: The Universal Expositions of 1855 and 1867.* New Haven: Yale University Press, 1987.

Manet: 1832–1883. New York: Metropolitan Museum of Art and Harry N. Abrams, 1983.

Marandel, J. Patrice, and François Daulte. *Frédéric Bazille and Early Impressionism.* Chicago: The Art Institute, 1978.

Marcus, Steven. *The Other Victorians: A Study of Sexuality and Pornography in Mid-Nineteenth-Century England.* New York: Basic Books, Inc., 1966.

Massey, Doreen. *Space, Place, and Gender.* Minneapolis: University of Minnesota Press, 1994.

Maubert, Andrée. *L'Exotisme dans la peinture française du 18e siècle.* Paris: E. de Boccard, 1943.

Melman, Billie. *Women's Orients: English Women and the Middle East, 1718–1918: Sexuality, Religion, and Work.* Ann Arbor: University of Michigan Press, 1992.

Mernissi, Fatima. *Beyond the Veil: Male-Female Dynamics in a Modern Muslim Society.* New York: John Wiley and Sons, 1975.

———. *Dreams of Trespass: Tales of a Harem Girlhood.* Reading, MA: Addison-Wesley, 1994.

———. *Scheherazade Goes West: Different Cultures, Different Harems.* New York: Washington Square Press, 2001.

Miers, Suzanne. *Britain and the Ending of the Slave Trade*. New York: Africana, 1975.

Mills, Sara. *Discourses of Differences: An Analysis of Women's Travel Writing and Colonialism*. London and New York: Routledge, 1991.

Mitchell, Timothy. *Colonising Egypt*. Cambridge and New York: Cambridge University Press, 1988.

Mohanty, Chandra Talpade. "Under Western Eyes: Feminist Scholarship and Colonialist Discourses." In *The Post-Colonial Studies Reader*, ed. Bill Ashcroft, Gareth Griffiths, and Helen Tiffin. London and New York: Routledge, 1995, 259–63.

Mosse, George L. *Nationalism and Sexuality: Middle-Class Morality and Sexual Norms in Modern Europe*. Madison: University of Wisconsin Press, 1988.

Mowafi, Redi. *Slavery, Slave Trade, and Abolition Attempts in Egypt and the Sudan 1820–1882*. Lund Studies in International History, no. 14. Esselte Studium [Sweden], 1981.

Nochlin, Linda. "The Imaginary Orient." In *The Politics of Vision: Essays on Nineteenth-Century Art and Society*. New York: Harper and Row, 1989, 33–59.

Ockman, Carol. *Ingres's Eroticized Bodies: Retracing the Serpentine Line*. New Haven: Yale University Press, 1995.

L'Orient des provençaux: Dessins orientalistes. Marseille: Musée Grobet-Labadié, 1982–83.

Les Orientalistes provençaux. Marseille: Musée des Beaux-Arts, 1982.

Ormond, Leonée, and Richard Ormond. *Lord Leighton*. New Haven and London: Yale University Press, 1975.

Les Peintres orientalistes, 1850–1914. Pau: Musée des Beaux-Arts, 1983.

Penzer, N. M. *The Harem*. London: George G. Harrap and Co., 1936.

Pointon, Marcia. *The Bonington Circle: English Watercolour and Anglo-French Landscape*. Sussex: Hendon Press, 1985.

Pollock, Griselda. *Vision and Difference*. London: Routledge, 1988.

———. *Differencing the Canon: Feminist Desire and the Writing of Art's Histories*. London and New York: Routledge, 1999.

Porter, Bernard. *Britain, Europe and the World, 1850–1982: Delusions of Grandeur*. London: George Allen and Unwin, 1983.

Porterfield, Todd. *The Allure of Empire: Art in the Service of French Imperialism, 1798–1836*. Princeton: Princeton University Press, 1998.

Preston, Harley. "The Harem—Painting Behind the Scenes." *Art Bulletin of Victoria* [Melbourne, Australia] no. 28 (1987): 78–90.

The Pre-Raphaelites. London: Tate Gallery and Allen Lane, 1984.

Ray, Gordon N. *The Art of the French Illustrated Book, 1700–1914*. 2 Vols. New York: Pierpont Morgan Library and Ithaca: Cornell University Press, 1982.

Reinhart, A. Kevin. "The Here and the Hereafter in Islamic Religious Thought." In *Images of Paradise in Islamic Art*, ed. Sheila S. Blair and Jonathan M. Bloom. Hanover, NH: Hood Museum of Art, Dartmouth College, 1991, 15–24.

Rewald, John. *The History of Impressionism*. New York: Museum of Modern Art, 1961.

Rodkey, Frederick S. *The Turco-Egyptian Question in the Relations of England, France and Russia, 1832–1841*. University of Illinois Studies in Social Science, 11, nos. 3–4 (September-December 1923).

Roget, J. *A History of the Old Water-Colour Society*. London: Longmans, Green and Co., 1891.

Roos, Jane Mayo. *Early Impressionism and the French State 1866–74*. Cambridge: Cambridge University Press, 1996.

Rose, Phyllis. *Parallel Lives: Five Victorian Marriages*. New York: Alfred A. Knopf, 1984.

Rosenberg, Pierre, and Marie-Catherine Sahut. *Carle Vanloo: Premier peintre du roi*. Nice, Clermont-Ferrand, Nancy, 1977.

Rosenthal, Léon. "Les conditions sociales de la peinture sous la Monarchie de Juillet." *Gazette des Beaux-Arts* 3 (February-April 1910): 93–114, 217–41, 332–51.

———. *Du Romantisme au réalisme*. Paris: H. Laurens, 1914.

Rushdi, Rushad. "English Travellers in Egypt During the Reign of Mohammed Ali." *Bulletin of the Faculty of Arts Fouad I. University* [Cairo] 14, Part 2 (1952).

Said, Edward W. *Orientalism*. New York: Pantheon, 1978.

———. *Culture and Imperialism*. New York: Vintage (Random House), 1993.

Saletore, Rajaram Narayan. *Sex in Indian Harem Life*. New Dehli: Orient Paperbacks, 1978.

Sayigh, Rosemary. "Roles and Functions of Arab Women: A Reappraisal." *Arab Studies Quarterly* 3, no. 3 (autumn 1981): 258–74.

Schick, Irvin Cemil. "Representing Middle Eastern Women: Feminism and Colonial Discourse." *Feminist Studies* 16, no. 2 (summer 1990): 345–80.

———. *The Erotic Margin: Sexuality and Spatiality in Alteritist Discourse*. London and New York: Verso, 1999.

Schiffer, Reinhold. *Turkey Romanticized: Images of the Turks in Early Nineteenth-Century English Travel Literature*. Materialia Turcica, Beiheft 5, Studienverlag Dr. N. Brockmeyer. Bochum, 1982.

Schimmel, Annemarie. "The Celestial Garden in Islam." In *The Islamic Garden*, ed. Elisabeth B. MacDougall and Richard Ettinghausen. Washington, DC: Dumbarton Oaks, 1976, 11–39.

Scott, Joan Wallach. "Gender: A Useful Category of Historical Analysis." In *Gender and the Politics of History*. New York: Columbia University Press, 1988, 28–50.

Searight, Rodney, and Jennifer M. Scarce. *A Mid-Eastern Journey: Artists on their Travels from the Collection of Rodney Searight*. Edinburgh: University of Edinburgh, 1980–81.

Shefer, Elaine. "Deverell, Rossetti, Siddal, and 'The Bird in the Cage.'" *Art Bulletin* 67, no. 3 (September 1985): 437–48.

Smith, Bonnie G. *Ladies of the Leisure Class*. Princeton: Princeton University Press, 1981.

Smith-Rosenberg, Carroll. "The Female World of Love and

Ritual: Relations between Women in Nineteenth-Century America." In *Signs Reader: Women, Gender and Scholarship*, ed. Elizabeth Abel and Emily K. Abel. Chicago: University of Chicago Press, 1983, 27–55.

Spivak, Gayatri Chakravorty. "Can the Subaltern Speak?" In *Marxism and the Interpretation of Culture*, ed. Cary Nelson and Lawrence Grossberg. Urbana-Champaign: University of Illinois, 1988, 271–313.

Stevens, Mary Anne, ed. *The Orientalists: Delacroix to Matisse: The Allure of North Africa and the Near East.* London: Thames and Hudson, 1984.

Stewart, Philip. "On the 'Iconology' of Literary Illustration." In *Dilemmes du roman: Essays in Honor of Georges May*, ed. Catherine Lafarge. Saratoga, CA: Anma Libri and Co., 1989.

Stokes, Hugh. "John F. Lewis, R. A. (1805–76)." *Walker's Quarterly* no. 28 (1929).

Sweetman, John. "John Frederick Lewis, A Centenary Reckoning." 1976.

———. *The Oriental Obsession: Islamic Inspiration in British and American Art and Architecture, 1500–1920.* Cambridge: Cambridge University Press, 1988.

Tapper, Nancy. "Mysteries of the Harem? An Anthropological Perspective on Recent Studies of Women of the Muslim Middle East." *Women's Studies International Quarterly* 2 (1979): 481–87.

Taylor, Paul. *Dutch Flower Painting, 1600–1720.* New Haven: Yale University Press, 1992.

Thornton, Lynne. *Women as Portrayed in Orientalist Painting.* Paris: ACR, 1993.

Till, Nicholas. *Mozart and the Enlightenment.* New York: W.W. Norton and Company, 1992.

Tinterow, Gary. *Origins of Impressionism.* New York: Harry N. Abrams, 1994.

———, Michael Pantazzi, and Vincent Pomarède. *Corot.* New York: Harry N. Abrams and the Metropolitan Museum of Art, 1996.

Toledano, Ehud. *The Ottoman Slave Trade and its Suppression, 1840–90.* Princeton: Princeton University Press, 1982.

Tomiche, Nadia. "The Situation of Egyptian Women in the First Half of the Nineteenth Century." In *Beginnings of Modernization in the Middle East*, ed. William Roe Polk and Richard L. Chambers. Chicago: University of Chicago Press, 1968.

Trapp, Frank Anderson. *The Attainment of Delacroix.* Baltimore and London: The Johns Hopkins Press, 1971.

Treble, Rosemary. *Great Victorian Pictures: Their Paths to Fame.* London: Arts Council of Great Britain, 1978.

Tucker, Judith E. *Women in Nineteenth-Century Egypt.* Cambridge: Cambridge University Press, 1985.

d'Uckermann, René Patris. *Ernest Hébert, 1817–1908.* Notes et documents des musées de France 7. Paris: Editions de la Réunion des musées nationaux, 1982.

Walkowitz, Judith R. *Prostitution and Victorian Society: Women, Class, and the State.* Cambridge and New York: Cambridge University Press, 1980.

Walther, Wiebke. *Woman in Islam.* Trans. C.S.V. Salt. Montclair, NJ: Abner Schram, 1981.

Watt, W. Montgomery. "Carlyle on Muhammad." *The Hibbert Journal* 53 (April 1955): 247–54.

Wilton, Andrew. *British Watercolours, 1750 to 1850.* Phaidon: Oxford, 1977.

Woodhouse, C.M. *The Philhellenes.* London: Hodder and Stoughton, 1969.

Yeazell, Ruth Bernard. *Harems of the Mind: Passages of Western Art and Literature.* New Haven: Yale University Press, 2000.

Zlatnik, Gail Parson. "Myth, Vision, and the Harem in French Painting, From Fontainebleau through the Nineteenth Century." Ph.D. diss., University of Iowa, 1998.

Zonana, Joyce. "The Sultan and the Slave: Feminist Orientalism and the Structure of *Jane Eyre*." *Signs* 18, no. 3 (spring 1993): 592–617.

Reference Works

Adhémar, Jean, *et al. Inventaire du fonds français après 1800.* Paris: Bibliothèque Nationale, 1930–67.

Allibone, S. Austin. *A Critical Dictionary of English Literature and British and American Authors.* Philadelphia: J. B. Lippincott Co., 1897.

Arberry, J. J., trans. *The Koran Interpreted.* New York: Macmillan Company, 1955.

Bénézit, E. *Dictionnaire critique et documentaire des peintres, sculpteurs, dessinateurs et graveurs.* Paris: Gründ, 1976.

Béraldi, Henry. *Les Graveurs du 19e siècle.* Paris: C. Conquet, 1891.

Boase, Frederic. *Modern English Biography.* London: Frank Cass and Co., 1965.

Encyclopedia of Islam. Leyden and London: Luza and Co., 1960.

Graves, Algernon. *Dictionary of Artists who have Exhibited in the Principal London Exhibitions from 1760–1893.* London: H. Graves and Company, 1901.

Samuel Redgrave's Dictionary of Artists of the English School. London: George Bell and Sons, 1878.

Sandby, William. *History of the Royal Academy of Arts.* London: Longman, 1862.

Stephen, Leslie, and Sidney Lee, eds. *Dictionary of National Biography.* London: Oxford University Press, 1973.

Thieme, Ulrich, and Felix Becker. *Allgemeines Lexikon der Bildenden Künstler.* Leipzig: Seeman, 1907–50.

Wallace Collection. *Summary of Illustrated Catalogue of Pictures.* London: Trustees of the Wallace Collection, 1979.

Wood, Christopher. *Dictionary of Victorian Painters.* 2nd ed. Suffolk: Antique Collectors' Club, 1978.

El Hashim, ou le Médecin (Opiz), 129, 134, *141*
Elliot, Sir Henry, 60, 230
embroidery, 106
Encyclopaedia Londinensis, 36, 112
Englishwoman in Egypt, The (Poole), 58, 248 n. 2
Englishwoman's Review, 20–21, 103, 188–89
enlightenment, 195, 201
Entertainment in the Harem (Denon), 35–36, *35*
environment and morality, 165
equality, gender, 200, 201
eroticism: in French art, 25, 46; of garden harem scenes, 206–7; of harem images, 22; of *Hhareem* (Lewis), 85–86; of *In the Bey's Garden, Asia Minor* (Lewis), 217; of *Massacres at Scio* (Delacroix), 91, 93; and music, 136; of roses, 142; and scientism, 25, 110; of shoes, 144; of sleep, 46; of slippers, 143–45; and space, 155–56, 160
escape from the harem, 104–5
Escholier, Raymond, 121
essentialism, 22
ethnicity, 36–39
ethnography. *See* scientism
Eugénie, Empress, 11
eunuchs, 71, 84–85, 129, 134; in *Persian Letters* (Montesquieu), 71, 165, 169, 190, 245 n. 41
Europe, map of, 117
exoticism, 38, 43, 146, 154
Exposition Universelle, Paris, 85, 157, 159, 189
extravagance, 190–91, 224
eyebrows, 43, 236
eyes, 206, 222

fabrics, 64, 72, 150, 172, 180, 205, 208, 232, 233, 234
facial stoicism, 70
Faed, John: *Bedouin Exchanging a Slave for Armour*, 81, *84*, 144–45
families, 19, 191; and the harem, 40, 172, 173, 211; and the slave trade, 67, 249 n. 37
fans, 46, 150, 180, 220
Fantasie de l'Hareme Egyptienne (Dadd), 110–11, *111*
Fantin-Latour, Henri: *Homage to Delacroix*, 232; *Studio of the Batignolles*, 232
Farwell, Beatrice, 11, 12
Fatime (Régnier/Désondré), 125, *135*
Favourite Odalisque, The (Allom), *plate 5*, 120, 180
"Favourite Sultana, The" (Hugo), 189
fear of harem women, 228–29
feathers, 89
Félon, Joseph: *Le harem*, 125, *135*, 145
Female, Eternal, 54
[Female Slave Being Unveiled] (Lane), 86–87, *86*
"female view," 22–24
femininity, 138
feminization of the East, 56
Femme dans son harem, Une ("Stop"), 104, *105*
Femme d'Orient: Childe Harold (Lord Byron) (Pickersgill), 192, *194*, 212
Femme du levant (Boucher), 256 n. 20
Femme esclave, La (Bourdet), 142, *149*, 225
femme fatale, 54, 156, 234
Femme grecque (Devéria), 98, *98*
Femmes au harem. See *Interior of an Egyptian Harem*
Femmes d'Alger dans leur appartement. See *Women of Algiers in Their Apartment* (1834)
Femmes d'Alger dans l'intérieur. See *Women of Algiers in Their Apartment* (1849)
Femme turque filant au tandour (Vanmour), 256 n. 3
fetishism, 12, 26, 110–61; and castration anxiety, 110, 229; and colonialism, 228–29; and difference, 110; and "double attitude," 229; of fabrics, 208; and female breasts, 255 n. 66; of flowers, 208; and genitalia, 110; of skin color, 37
fezzes, 56, 64, 184–85. *See also* hats
figural representation in religious art, 20
Filles turques qui jouent au mangala (Vanmour), 176, *176*
Fille turque jouant du tehegour (Vanmour), 134, *142*
Fille turque prenant le caffé sur la sopha (Vanmour), 120, *129*
Fille turque qui fume sur le sopha (Vanmour), 113, *117*
fingernails, 46, 180, 253 n. 70
Flaubert, Gustave, 237
Fleurs et les femmes, Les, 142
flirtation, 87
flowers, 46, 64, 99, 141–43, 157, 183, 223–24; with broken stalks, 96, 98; and femininity, 138; fetishized, 208; and harem women, 207, 223; and Paradise, 138, 253 n. 58; and prayer, 253 n. 58; and sexuality, 221; symbolism of, 217, 225, 250 n. 111, 254 n. 17. *See also* lilies; roses
Flowers in a Vase (Ruysch), 225, *226*
Foucault, Michel, 14, 19, 25–26, 61, 162, 165
fountains, 64
Fox, Charles: *The Ionian Captive*, 99, *102*
Fragonard, Alexandre-Evariste, 251 n. 117; *La Musulmane imprudente*, 167, *168*, 185; *L'Odalisque Vertueuse*, 96–97, *97*; *La Vengeance*, 167, *169*
Fragonard, Jean Honoré, 251 n. 117; *Happy Lovers*, 199
Fragonard, Théophile, 251 n. 117
France: and Algeria, 50, 53, 54–57, 188, 259 n. 31; and Britain, 31–32, 244 n. 16; colonialism, 32, 36, 54–56; and Egypt, 246 n. 54; and eroticism, 25, 46; and the harem, 33, 167; and harem images, 12, 26, 32, 231–38; and modernism, 53; national character, 32; politics, 52–53, 54; Pre-Impressionism, 231–238; printmaking, 11; prostitution in, 255 n. 75; restoration, 31; romanticism, 110; and Russia, 57; and Spain, 45; and Turkey, 244 n. 16; women of, 69
freedom: of harem women, 63, 108, 215, 257 n. 46, and monogamy, 30; Ruskin on, 67, 249 n. 38; and windows, 103, 104
free love, 21
free will, 69
French animated map of Europe, 115, *127*
Freud, 110, 229
friendship between women, 175
Frith, William: *An Incident in the Life of Lady Mary Wortley Montagu*, 257 n. 61
front-back pairing, 176–77
frugality, 190–91
fruit, 46, 157, 168
fuchsias, 223–24
fur, 72, 89, 232

Gage, John, 259 n. 23
gallantry: male, 200
games, 176

gardens, 204, 206–7, 208, 209, 217, 224
Gardiner, Lady Marguerite, Countess of Blessington (*née* Power), 128
gates, 224
Gates, Henry Louis, 37
Gautier, Théophile, 189, 247 n. 79
gaze, 14
gazelles, 98, 122–23, 252 n. 25
geese, 123
Génard, F. N., 256 n. 106; *Pasha with Odalisque*, 113, *116*
gender, equality, 200, 201; politics, 13, 30; and power, 196
genitalia, 110
Georgia, 39, 43; women of, 20, 39, 42, 85, 221
geraniums, 224
Gérôme, Jean-Léon, 25, 159 n. 16; *Moorish Bath*, 176, *178*, 232; *Slave Market* (ca. 1867), 81, *82*, 232; *Slave Market* (1871), 81, *83*
Giaour, The (Byron), 122, 164
"gild," 227
Giraud, Eugénie, 193; *Interior of an Egyptian Harem*, 113, *118*
Girlfriends, The (Deux odalisques dans un paysage) (Auguste), 155, *157*
Girl Reading a Letter at an Open Window (Vermeer), 213, *214*
girls, harem, 191–92
Girl with Falcon (Renoir), 256 n. 104
God, 207
"Golden Lily." See *Lilium Auratum*
Goodall, Frederick: *Eastern Mother and Child*, 212, *212*; *New Light in the Harem*, 252 n. 25
Gordon, Charles, 40
gossip, 152, 175, 176
Goya, Francisco: *Clothed Maja*, 46, *48*
Graces, Three, 176
Grand Divan, 32
Grande Odalisque (Ingres), 23, 25, 88–89, *90*, 111, 113, 147, 155, 166, 232, 253 n. 70; chibouk in, 113; jewelry in, 147; smoke in, 111; space in, 155
Greece: and Egypt, 90–91; pirates, 94; and Turkey, 21, 98; War of Independence, 59, 75, 90–91, 97; women of, 59, 75, 90–103, 191–92
Greece on the Ruins of Missolonghi (Delacroix), 94
Greek Girl, A (Pickersgill), 99
Greek Girl/Captive Greek Girl (Lewis/Smyth), 95–96, *95*, 105, 191, 221, 250 n. 110
green clothing, 184, 205, 255 n. 65
Grévedon: *Odalisque*, 99, *101*; *Odalisque au bain*, 71–72, *71*; *Sultane à sa toilette*, *71*, 150, 177
Griffiths, Gareth, 11
Grosrichard, 56
Grosvenor Gallery, 212
Guérard: *L'Amour, le vin et le tabac*, 185–86, *186*; *Le lendemain de victoire*, 185, *188*; *Le Pacha, ou la vie dans le sérail, d'après le tableau de Guérard*, 113, *115*, 191, 197, 198; *La Vie au sérail*, no. 1, 115, *126*, 155, 197; *La Vie au sérail*, no. 2, 72, *72*, 115; *La Vie au sérail*, no. 4, 113, *116*, 145
Guet, Charlemagne Oscar: *Narghillet*, 115, *121*

Habesh or *Abyssinian Slave, Cairo* (Mouilleron/Prisse d'Avennes), 49, *52*, 173
hair: braiding, 99; flowing, 43, 71–72; loose, 55, 72, 96, 136; pubic, 235, 259 n. 24
Halil Pasha, 230
Hamilton, Lady Augusta, 211
Handel, George Frederic: *The Triumph of Time and Truth*, 258 n. 77
happiness, 63, 67, 69–74
Happy Lovers (Fragonard), 199
"Hareem, The" (Milnes), 203
Hareem of a Mameluke Bey, Cairo: The Introduction of the Abyssinian Slave (Lewis), 49–50. See also *Hhareem*
harem: decline of, 14, 30–31, 230, 242 n. 36; defended, 21, 40–41, 64–65; defined, 9, 19; female views of, 22–24; male views of, 22; objective representation of, 238–39; popular myths of, 19; as subject for art, 163; and "truth," 9, 11; and the West, 12, 22, 61, 167, 213
"harem": etymology of, 9
Harem, Le (Félon), 125, *135*, 145
Harem (Lewis), 46, *47*, 154
Harem (Rowlandson), 112–13, *114*, 176
Harem/Hhareem (Lewis/Smyth), 105, *107*, 142–43, 177
harem images: British, 12, 25, 32, 230–31; as created for men, 22; French, 12, 25, 32, 231–38; inconsistent with accompanying texts, 64, 74, 75–76, 81, 84, 102; as repetitive, 12; "style" of, 26
Harem Life, Cairo (Lewis), 206
Harem Life—Constantinople (Lewis), *109*, 164; cat in, 129; *Critic* on, 106–7, 163, 213; elevated harem in, 204; fan in, 129, 220; green clothing in, 205; hierarchy in, 220; houris in, 205–6; *Illustrated London News* on, 163; indolence in, 179; lowered eyes in, 206; and *Mérode Altarpiece* (Campin), 208; open window in, 106–7; plumpness of women in, 180; Ruskin on, 66; *Spectator* on, 129; and Van Eyck, 208, 257 n. 32; and Vermeer, 213; and the Virgin Mary, 208
haremlik, 160
Harem Scene (LePrince), 146–47, *150*, 191, 199
Harley, Lady Charlotte, 192
Harvey, Annie, 171, 211
Hashim. See *El Hashim, ou le Médecin*
hashish, 111, 114
hats, 184–85; caps, 185; fezzes, 56, 64, 184–85; headdresses, 43, 173, 254 n. 35; turbans, 46, 188, 255 n. 70
Hauréau, Barthélemy, 51–52, 54
Hay, Robert, 102
health of harem women, 148, 150
heaven, 225. *See also* Paradise
Hébert, Antoine Auguste Ernst: *Deux Odalisques couchées sur la terrasse*, 114–15, *120*, 136, 176–77, 195
hell, 165, 179, 225
"Hero as Prophet, The" (Carlyle): on Islam, 202
"Hetaeria: The Tale of the Greek Slave, The" (Mrs. Pickersgill), 102
Hhareem (Lewis), *plate 1*, 23, *23*, 238; About on, 24; Abyssinian woman in, 49–50, 247 n. 79; ambiguity of, 85–86; animals in, 122–23, 128–29; *Art Journal* on, 70, 255 n. 93; *Athenaeum* on, 70, 106, 128–29, 180, 189–90, 213; colored windows in, 105–6; eroticism of, 85–86; indolence in, 179; jealousy in, 189–90; jewelry in, 154; lowered eyes in, 206; mameluke in, 198, 256 n. 111; master's spatial dominance in, 198; mother in, 173; plumpness of women in, 180; Ruskin on, 66, 163; sale of, 256 n. 96; smiling in, 70
Hickox, Mike, 252 n. 40

hierarchy: chibouk as symbol of, 112, 113–14; and children, 173; and Circassian women, 39; and class, 61; and coffee serving, 117; and ethnicity, 38; and Georgian women, 39; and jewelry, 147; Montagu on, 151; and race, 38–39, 46, 48, 49, 50, 61, 220–22
hieroglyphics, 254 n. 26
Hill, Aaron, 103, 198, 257 n. 46
Historical Male, 54
History of Sexuality (Foucault), 14, 25
Hollier: *L'Odalisque*, 150, *153*
Homage to Delacroix (Fantin-Latour), 232
home: bourgeois, 165, 213; the harem as, 21, 63, 243 n. 12
homosexuality: in Egypt, 34. *See also* lesbianism
"hookah," 252 n. 5
hookahs, 41, 111, 112–17, 136. *See also* pipes
hostesses: harem women as, 215–16
Houri, Eastern Woman with a Hookah (Lewis), 114, *119*, 144, 184, 231, 234, 238, 255 n. 66
Houri in a Paradise Garden (Vali), 185, *185*, 207
houris, 138, 155, 182, 202, 203–6, 223, 246 n. 65; beauty of, 163; doves as symbols of, 123; in gardens, 207; green worn by, 184, 255 n. 65; male, 183; as prostitutes, 182–83, 184; and roses, 138; and the Virgin Mary, 208
Hour of the Ox [Midnight] (Utamaro), *236*, 237
"How Hassan Captured the Bird Maidens," 123
Hugo, Victor: "The Favourite Sultana", 189; "[Juana] The Obdurate Beauty," 44–45, 150; "Moonlight on the Bosphorus," 169; "My Napoleon," 32; *Les Orientales*, 32, 91, 250 n. 102; "Pirates' Song," 250 n. 102; "The Sacking of the City," 91; "The Veil," 73
Hullmandel, C.: *Circassian Slaves, Constantinople*, 41, *41*; *The Odalique [sic] or Favourite of the Harem, Constantinople*, 120, *130*; *Slave-Merchant, Constantinople*, 74–76, *76*, 81, 157
Hunt, William Holman, 213, 252 n. 41
husbands in Paradise, 152

Ibrahim Pasha, 90
iconographical analysis, 13
identification: viewer, 229
identity, 23, 27–29
Illustrated London News, on *Harem Life—Constantinople* (Lewis), 129, 164, 179, 180, 220, 256 n. 18; on *Hhareem* (Lewis), 23, 70, 238, 243 n. 22; on *Intercepted Correspondence* (Lewis), 168, 254 n. 17; on latticed windows, 107; on Lewis, 257 n. 33; on *Lilium Auratum* (Lewis), 221, 231
Illustration, L', 56
illustration: book, 75–76, 249 n. 57
Illustrations of Constantinople (Lewis/Smyth), 95, 105
immorality, 71, 162–94, 179, 201, 228–29
imperialism, 13, 14, 20, 25, 65, 258 n. 71
Imperial Palace, Constantinople, 107
Impressionism, 230
inaccessibility, 209
Incident in the Life of Lady Mary Wortley Montagu, An (Frith), 257 n. 61
India: harems in, 242 n. 20
indolence: and colonialism, 182; of the East, 182; of harem women, 34–35, 46, 47, 66, 128, 179–82; and narcissism, 181; of the Other, 47; Ruskin on, 66; and sexual desire, 179
"indolence," 179, 255 n. 50
In-door Gossip, Cairo or *A Scene in a Hareem* (Lewis), 150–51, 152, 154, *154*, 213–14, 216, 231
infanticide, 174
inferiority of women, 21, 198
infidelity. *See* adultery
Ingres, Jean Auguste Dominique: use of *Turkish Embassy Letters* (Montagu) by, 88–89. Works: *Grande Odalisque*, 23, 25, 88–89, *90*, 111, 113, 147, 155, 166, 232, 253 n. 70; *Odalisque with Slave*, 38–39, *38*, 72, 136, 147; *Turkish Bath (Bain Turc)*, 136, *144*, 177
Inmate of the Hhareem. See *Life in the Harem, Cairo*
innocence: loss of, 225
Institut d'Egypte, 32
intelligence of harem women, 86–87, 199
Intercepted Correspondence (Lewis), *170*, 171, 254 nn. 17, and 27, 258 n. 65; adultery in, 167–68; *Art Journal* on, 24; colored windows in, 105–6; flowers in, 168, 254 n. 17; "mischievous" wife in, 190; mother in, 173; sale of, 256 n. 96; smiling in, 70
Intérieur d'un harem (Devéria), 172, *173*
Interior of an Egyptian Harem (Giraud), 113, *118*
Interior of a School, Cairo (Lewis), 254 n. 35
Interior of the Pavillion du Bosphore, Paris, 1867, 157, 159, *161*
International Congress on Public Morality, 188–89
In the Bey's Garden, Asia Minor (Lewis), 205, 206, 207, 216–17, *218*, 223, 224, 227, 258 n. 74
Ionian Captive, The (Fox/Pickersgill), 99, *102*
Islam: and Christianity, 20, 162, 202; on concubines, 31, 59; and female beauty, 163; and "happy slaves," 71; monolithic, 59; as mysterious, 22; and polygyny, 31; prisoners converted to, 90, 91; on religious art, 20; as sensual, 202; and slavery, 31, 59, 70, 79, 90, 244–45 n. 33; and souls of women, 164–65, 196, 200, 254 n. 9; texts of, 9; on veiling, 73. *See also* Paradise; the *Qur'an*
Ismail, the Khedive, 31, 62

Jal, Auguste, 93, 94
Jameson, Fredric, 159, 160
japonisme, 237
jealousy, 189–90
Jeune Fille Moresque [sic] (Tunis) (Mouilleron/Chassiron), 192, *193*
Jeune grecque, La (Régnier/Leloir), 98, *100*, 122, 191
Jeune grecque sauvée de l'esclavage des Turcs (Loeillot), 94, *95*
jewelry, 42, 43, 46, 55, 145–48, 150–54, 172, 235, 237, 253 n. 79
Jewish women, 56
Josephine, Empress, 34
"Joy For Ever, A" (Ruskin), 153
"[Juana] The Obdurate Beauty" (Hugo), 44–45, 150
Julien, Bernard Romanin, 251 n. 115; *L'Odalisque Vertueuse*, 96–97, *97*
Julien, Stanislaus, 250–51 n. 112
July Monarchy, 50, 51, 53, 54

Ka'ah, A (Lane), 157, *159*
Kadijah, 202
Kahf, Mohja, 94, 251 n. 120
Keepsake annuals, 127–28
Keppel, George, 80
kerchief, 43

Khorassan, Veiled Prophet of, 37, 253 n. 50
"King Baturan Ghur and Husn Banu," 123
kiosks, 205, 256 n. 17
kohl, 253 n. 70
Kristeva, Julia, 239
Kunzle, David, 144

labor, 152–53
Lacambrie: *Costumes turcs*, 125, *134*, 143
"Lady, A,": 103, 148
Lady Adorned with the Ckoor's and Suf'a, etc., A (Lane), 43–44, *45*
Lady in the Dress worn in Private, A (Lane), 223, *224*
Lady Mary Wortley Montagu and Her Son (Vanmour), 103, *104*, 134, 157
Lalla Rookh (Moore), 37, 182, 252 n. 25
Lamartine, Alphonse de: on abduction for the harem, 94; on Armenian women, 43; on British women, 28; on colonialism, 56–57, 72–73; on eastern women, 192–93, 217; on "happy slaves," 72–73; on Islam, 202; on jewelry, 150; on Maltese women, 218; on nonverbal communication, 136; on "primitive" peoples, 164; on race and ethnicity, 37–38; on speechlessness, 193; on Turks, 56, 57
Landelle, Charles: *An Armenian Woman*, 43–44, *45*
Landseer, Edwin Henry: *Miss Ellen ("Nellie") Power*, 127–28, *139*
Lane, Edward William, 248 n. 2; on Abyssinian women, 48, 49; on animals, 123, 252 n. 39, 253 n. 44; on drowning of harem women, 170; on harem mothers, 172; on the hookah, 116; influence on Lewis, 157; on jealousy in the harem, 189; on jewelry, 146; and Nefeeseh, 102, 103; realist techniques of, 24–25; on slave trade, 250 n. 79; on wives in Paradise, 182. Works: *Arabian Nights' Entertainment (The 1001 Nights)*, 87, 123; *A Ka'ah*, 157, *159*; *A Lady Adorned with the Ckoor's and Suf'a, etc.*, 43–44, *45*; *A Lady in the Dress worn in Private*, 223, *224*; *Manners and Customs of the Modern Egyptians*, 43, 102–3, 111; *'Ood*, 134, *142*; *A Performer on the 'Ood*, 134
Lane, R. J.: *Nefeeseh*, 102, *103*
language, 11, 110
Latter-Day Pamphlets (Carlyle), 66
"lazy native" stereotype, 52
Lefebvre, Henri, 10, 21, 30, 110, 154, 242 n. 10
legitimization of the harem, 214–15, 257 n. 45
Lehoux, Pierre François: *Scène de harem*, 172–73, *174*; *Scène familiale en Orient*, 211, *211*
Leighton, Lord Frederick: *At a Reading Desk*, 203, *204*
leisure, 27, 227
Leloir, Héloïse Suzanne (*née* Bouteiller): *La Jeune grecque*, 98, *100*, 122, 191
Lendemain de victoire, Le (Scultz/Guérard), 185, *188*
LePrince, Jean Baptiste: *Harem Scene*, 146–47, *150*, 191, 199
lesbianism, 136, 150, 175–77, 179, 232–33, 259 n. 17. *See also* homosexuality
Lesseps, Ferdinand de, 171
Lewis, John Frederick: in Constantinople, 249 n. 60; and Dutch art, 213; Egyptian home of, 157; eroticism in works of, 25; gazelles of, 122; houris in works of, 204–6; *Illustrated London News* on, 257 n. 33; realist techniques of, 24–25; references to Spain, 46; Ruskin on, 153, 190, 208, 209, 249 n. 40, 256 n. 97; sale of works, 190; and the slave market, 77, 80–81; urged to paint in oils, 208, 209, 257 n. 33; and Van Eyck, 208; women in works of, 163, 164, 243 n. 45. Works: *Arab Scribe*, 253 n. 49; *An Arab Scribe, Cairo*, 225, 227; *An Armenian Lady, Cairo*, 44, 163, 206, 246 n. 65, 258 n. 73; *Armenian Women at Brussa*, 246 n. 65; *Armenian Woman, Cairo*, 246 n. 65; *Bezestein Bazaar of El Khan Khalil, Cairo*, 257 n. 61; *Bouquet/Lilies and Roses, Constantinople*, 207, *208*, 209, 217, 223, 224, 257 n. 31, 258 nn. 71 and 74; *Caged Doves, Cairo*, 125, *136*; *Circassian*, 41–42, *42*, 223, 246 n. 57; *Courtyard of the Painter's House, Cairo*, *159*; *Eastern Girl Carrying a Tray*, 70, 252 n. 19, 254 n. 81; *Greek Girl/Captive Greek Girl*, 95–96, *95*, 191–92, 221, 250 n. 110; Harem, 46, *47*, 154; *Harem/Hhareem*, 105, *107*, 142, 177; *Harem Life, Cairo*, 206; *Harem Life—Constantinople* (*see under title of work*); *Hhareem* (*see under title of work*); *Houri, Eastern Woman with a Hookah*, 114, *119*, 144, 184, 231, 234, 238, 255 n. 66; *Illustrations of Constantinople*, 95, 105; *In-door Gossip, Cairo* or *A Scene in a Hareem*, 150–51, 152, 154, *154*, 213–14, 216, 231; *Intercepted Correspondence* (*see under title of work*); *Interior of a School, Cairo*, 254 n. 35; *In the Bey's Garden, Asia Minor*, 205, 206, 207, 216–17, *218*, 223, 224, 227, 258 n. 74; *Life in the Harem, Cairo*, 67, *68*, 69, 70, 120, 154, 205, 220–21, 223, 257 n. 57; *Lilium Auratum*, 70, 205, *206*, 207, 217, 221, 223, 224, 227, 231, 251 n. 61, 257 n. 62; *A Mameluk Bay, Egypt*, 251 n. 136; *Outdoor Gossip, Cairo*, 231; *"And the Prayer of Faith Shall Save the Sick" (James 5:15)*, 129, *140*, 171, 173, 227, 254 nn. 26 and 27; *Prince Hassan and His Servant*, 254 n. 35; *Reception*, 205, *205*, 215–16, 231, 257 n. 46; *Siesta*, 46, *49*, 180, 205; *Slave Market in the East*, 76–81, *78*, 249 n. 60; *Two Women in a Harem*, 221–22, *222*
Liberal Romanticism, 51, 53
liberation of the harem, 21, 107–8
libertines, 128
liberty. *See* freedom
Liberty Leading the People (Delacroix), 53
Life in the Harem, Cairo (Lewis), 67, *68*, 69, 71, 154, 257 n. 57; clothing in, 205, 223; coffee serving in, 120; smiling in, 70
"Light of the Haram, The" (Moore), 252 n. 25
lilies, 217, 223, 227, 258 nn. 70 and 71
Lilies and Roses, Constantinople (Lewis), 207, *208*, 209, 217
"lilium," 227
Lilium Auratum (Lewis), *206*, 217, 223, 227, 257 nn. 61 and 62; confinement in, 224; hierarchy in, 221; houris in, 207; kiosk in, 205; mimesis in, 231; smiling in, 70
"Lily and the Rose, The" (Cowper), 258 n. 71
literacy, 203
lithography: French, 11
lived reality, 239
Loeillot, Henri Charles: *Combats pour l'indepéndance*, 94; *Jeune grecque sauvée de l'esclavage des Turcs*, 94, *95*
Lola de Valence (Manet, 233, 259 n. 21
London and Westminster Review, 86
Long, Edwin: *Babylonian Marriage Market*, 258 n. 63
Louis XIV, 196
Louis-Philippe, 50
love, 27, 46, 100, 102, 253 n. 73
Lustful Turk, 198, 251 n. 115

lutes, 33, 39, 41, 100, 136, 177. *See also* 'oods
luxuria, 150

Mabro, Judy, 209
MacFarlane, James, 65, 171, 172
Madonna of Humility (Campin), 209, *210*
Maghreb, the, 50
Maghrebian women, 50–56
Mahmud II, Sultan, 90, 184
Maître, Edmond, 259 n. 15
"majesty" of the poor, 191
Makart, Hans: *Death of Cleopatra*, 252 n. 15
Male, Historical, 54
Mameluk Bay, Egypt, A (Lewis), 251 n. 136
mamelukes, 30, 34, 162, 198, 244 n. 27, 254 n. 15, 256 n. 111
Manet, Edouard, 231, 232, 238, 259 n. 15; *Lola de Valence*, 233, 259 n. 21; *Odalisque*, 115, *122*, 234–35; *Olympia*, 184, 185, 232–33, 234, 235, 259 n. 24; *Portrait of Zola*, 237; *La Sultane*, *plate 6*, 10, 235–37
Manners and Customs of the Modern Egyptians (Lane), 102–3, 111
manumission of Egyptian slaves, 31
map of Europe, 117
Marchand d'esclaves (Boucher), 74–75, *76*, 105, 197
Marchande d'oiseaux des tropiques: georgienne, La (Régnier/Barker), 42, *43*, 127
marginalization, 30
"Mariana" (Tennyson), 214
Mariana in the Moated Grange (Millais), 214, *216*, 217
Marie Louise, Empress, 34
marriage, 22, 24, 152, 191
Martineau, Harriet, 12, 165, 254 n. 12; on beauty, 163, 164; on children in the harem, 172, 174; on harem women, 39, 163; on jewelry, 148; on pipes and coffee, 111; on roses, 143; on slavery, 65
Marx, Karl, 61
Massacres at Scio (Delacroix), 91–94, *92*
masters, 195; as benevolent, 64, 69; death of, 74; as enervated, 196; Ruskin on, 217, 220; spatial dominance of, 197–98; as tyrannical, 162, 197–98
Matthew 6:28–30, 227
Matthews, Charles, 256 n. 96
Mauresque (Roubaud), 185, *187*
Maurin, Nicolas Eustache: *Asie: Asia*, 116, *126*, 142; *Constantinople*, 165–66, *166*, 167; *Odalisque au bain*, 71–72, *71*; *L'Odorat, Paradis de Mahomet*, 138, *146*; *Le Songe*, 155, *156*; *Sultane à toilette*, *71*, 150, 177
McCoan, James C., 187
Measure for Measure (Shakespeare), 214
Medora (Bonington), 136, *145*
Mehemet Ali, 146
Melbourne, Lord, 245 n. 50
Melek-Hanum, 103–4, 189
Melman, Billie, 164
melons, 168
memento mori, 225–28
men, 200; animality of, 121; bourgeois, 22; chibouks and, 112, 115; as harem slaves, 250 n. 76; and modernism, 22; Muslim, 20; and polygyny, 19–20; power relationships with women, 197–99, 200, 201; superiority of, 21; as tyrannical, 198; western, 46, 96, 167
Mendouze: *La Musulmane imprudente*, 167, *168*, 185
"Merchant and the Parrot, The" (Rumi), 123
Mernissi, Fatema, 250 n. 84
Mérode Altarpiece (Campin), 208, *209*
Meurent, Victorine, 233
middle class, the, 195, 223; and the harem, 21, 63, 243 n. 12; home life of, 165, 213; men of, 22; and prostitution, 36; women of, 10, 27, 107, 195, 203, 220
Midnight (Utamaro), *236*, 237
Millais, John Everett, 213, 252 n. 41; *Mariana in the Moated Grange*, 214, *216*, 217
Milnes, Richard Monckton, 256 n. 5; "The Hareem," 203
Milton, John, 200
mimesis in art, 230, 231
mind and body, 204
mirrors, 46, 64, 172, 180
Miss Ellen ("Nellie") Power (Landseer), 127–28, *139*
"Mr. Lewis's Oriental paradise," 204
Mitchell, Timothy, 11, 26, 165
mobility: social, 36, 58, 244–45 n. 33
Modern Egyptians (Lane), 43
modernism, 22, 53, 232
modernization of the East, 30–31
Modern Painters (Ruskin), 66, 154, 164
Moeurs d'un sérail, 96–97, 167
Moeurs et usages des turcs, 74, 104
Mohamed Abduh, Sheik, 31
Mohammed Ali, 30, 31, 57, 60, 61, 62, 171, 187, 248 n. 13
Monet, Claude, 259 nn. 15 and 18
monkeys, 125, 175
monogamy, 20, 30, 34, 199, 211, 225
Montagu, Lady Mary Wortley, 45, 175, 253 n. 70; on Armenians, 246 n. 63; on birds, 123; on flower symbolism, 138; on freedom of harem women, 215, 257 n. 46; on gazelle eyes, 122; on harem civility, 215; harem defended by, 21; on harem gardens, 207; on harem hierarchy, 151; on harems as nunneries, 216; on Hill, 257 n. 46; on jewelry, 147; on Lewis' home, 157; on Paradise, 183; on public baths, 179; on punishment of harem women, 169; on the souls of Islamic women, 164; on Turkish baths, 215; *Turkish Embassy Letters*, 88–89, 103, 146, 179, 254 n. 11; on veiling, 246 n. 50
Montaut, Henri de: *Aux bords du Bosphore*, 115, *125*, 145
Montesquieu: on Armenians, 246 n. 59; Douthwaite on, 23–24; on French women, 69; on the liberation of the harem, 31; on Montagu, 254 n. 11; *Persian Letters (see under title of work)*; on Persian women, 69; on Spanish men, 45
Montpellier, 232
"Moonlight on the Bosphorus" (Hugo), 169
Moore, Thomas, 136; on bees, 128; on harem animals, 121; *Lalla Rookh*, 37, 182, 252 n. 25; "The Light of the Haram", 252 n. 25
Moorish Bath (Gérôme), 176, *178*, 232
Moorish Conversation (Delacroix), 142, *149*, 156–57, 199
morality: of art, 67; and beauty, 164; Christian, 162; and environment, 165; of harem women, 203, 208–17, 222–24, 228–29; and jewelry, 147–48, 150; of western women, 182
moral transgression, 20, 36

Morel-Retz, L. P. G. B. ("Stop"): *Une Femme dans son harem,* 104, *105*
Morlon, Paul Emile Antony: *Constantinople,* 115, *119,* 180
Mornay, Charles Edgar de, 156
Morocco, 61–62, 247 n. 91; women of, 50
Mosque of Osmanié, The (From the Slave Market) (Bartlett), 79, *79*
mosques, 78–79, 250 n. 66, 257 n. 59
motherhood, 171–75, 175, 209, 210–12
motifs: contextualizing of, 13
"motility," 229
moucharabic windows, 103–4
Mouilleron, Adolphe: *Cairene Lady Waited Upon by a Galla Slave Girl,* 118, 120, *129*; *Habesh or Abyssinian Slave, Cairo, 52,* 173; *Jeune Fille Moresque [sic] (Tunis),* 192, *193*; *Untitled [Odalisque],* 88, *89,* 199
Mozart: *Abduction from the Seraglio,* 31, 175, 195, 197–99, 247 n. 68, 251 n. 115, 251 n. 128, 256 nn. 112–13
Muhammad, 9, 138, 155, 191, 202, 207
Muhammad Yusuf al-Husaini, 255 n. 70
Murat, Caroline Bonaparte, 23
Murray, John, 165, 245 n. 49
musical instruments, 64, 134, 136–38. *See also* lutes; 'oods
Musique, La (Régnier/Bettannier/Bouvier), 136
Mustafa (son of Sulieman I), 190
Mustafa Effendi, 69
Musulmane imprudente, La (Mendouze/Fragonard), 167, *168,* 185
"My Napoleon" (Hugo), 32
Myrrha, 98, 147, 192, 251 n. 124

nakedness, 81, 91, 94, 197
Narcisse de la Turquie, Le (The Narcissus of Turkey) (Devéria), 142, *148,* 180
narcissism, 180–81. *See also vanitas*
narghiles, 50, 111. *See also* pipes
Narghillet (Guet/Vogt), 115, *121*
narrative and art criticism, 70
Natal, Bishop of, 153
nationality, 36–37, 56
nations: conquered, 37
naturalness: of the harem, 21, 223; of harem women, 55, 238; of the middle class, 223; of polygyny, 196; of slavery, 67
Navarino, Battle of, 94, 250 n. 108
Nefeeseh (R. J. Lane), 102, *103*
Nerval, Gérard de: on Abyssinian women, 48–49; on the Greek profile, 99; on harem women as caged birds, 124; on jealousy, 189; on laughing slaves, 69; on servants, 217; and Zetnaybia, 27–28; *Voyage to the Orient,* 27–28, 37, 104; "Zetnaybia," 37, 245 n. 41
New Light in the Harem (Goodall), 252 n. 25
Nield, John: *Turcotoquade,* 115, *120*
Nightingale, Florence, 39, 103, 165, 179, 256 n. 5
nightingales, 148, 253 n. 73
nonchalance, 52
Noory Osmanya, 79
nuns, 216–17, 257 n. 49

"Obdurate Beauty, The" (Hugo), 150
obsession, 12
Ockman, Carol, 23
Odalique [sic] or Favourite of the Harem, Constantinople, The (Hullmandel/Allom), 120, *130*
"odalisque," 9
Odalisque (Alès), 115, *124*
Odalisque, L' (Colin), 124, *131*
Odalisque (Corot), 258 n. 13
Odalisque (Devéria), 75, *77,* 125, 185
Odalisque (Grévedon), 99, *101*
Odalisque, L' (Hollier), 150, *153*
Odalisque (Manet), 115, *122,* 234–35
[Odalisque] (Mouilleron), 88, *89,* 199
Odalisque (Renoir), 156, *158*
Odalisque au bain (Maurin/Grévedon), 71–72, *71*
Odalisque coupable, L' (Tassaert), 254 n. 16
"odalisque pose", 9, 75, 117, 185. *See also* reclining figure
Odalisque punie, L' (Tassaert), 254 n. 16
Odalisque Vertueuse, L' (Julien/Fragonard), 96–97, *97*
Odalisque with Parrot (Delacroix), 73, 138
Odalisque (with Red Parrot) (Bonington), 125, *132,* 141
Odalisque with Slave (Ingres), 38–39, *38,* 72, 136, 147
Odorat, Paradis de Mahomet, L' (Maurin), 138, *146*
oil painting, 209
Old Water-Colour Society, 23, 49, 85, 189, 225, 238
Olympia (Manet), 184, 185, 232–33, 234, 235, 259 n. 24
1001 Nights, The (Arabian Nights' Entertainment), 42, 86–87, 123, 138
'Ood (Lane), 134, *142*
'oods, 134, 136
opium, 111, 114
Opiz, Georg: *El Hashim, ou le Médecin,* 129, 134, *141*
oppression of harem women, 20–21
Oriental Album, 49, 173
Orientales, Les (Hugo), 32, 91, 250 n. 102
orientalism, 13, 110, 233, 243 n. 24
Orientalism (Said), 13, 243 n. 24
Oriental Love-Letter (Pickersgill), 141, *147*
O'Shaughnessy, Arthur William Edgar: "Zuleika", 251 n. 134
Osmin, 175
Other, the, 27–28, 47; and colonialism, 29, 228–29; desire for, 37; and the Self, 24, 29, 30, 195, 228. *See also* difference
Ottoman Empire, 19, 174–75. *See also* Turkey
Outdoor Gossip, Cairo (Lewis), 231
outdoor harem scenes, 206–8
Oxford English Dictionary, 179

Pacha, Le, ou la vie dans le sérail, d'après le tableau de Guérard (Régnier/Guérard), 113, *115,* 191, 197, 198
pain, 225
pairing, front-back, 176–77
Palais Bourbon, 53
Palanquins d'Isfahan (Philipon), 176, *179*
Palmerston, Lord, 20, 32, 60, 61, 62, 244 n. 16, 245–46 n. 50
Paradise, 71, 152, 256 n. 17; and beauty, 163; butterflies in, 206; fabrics in, 205; and flowers, 138, 253 n. 58; and gardens, 204, 207, 208; green as color of, 205; harems, in, 182; husbands in, 152; Islam on, 204–6, 213, 225; marriage in, 152; music in, 134; as sensual, 202, 203–4; servants' reward in, 213; sexuality in, 182; silence in, 205, 213; spiritual pleasure in, 204; wives in, 152; women in, 183–84. *See also* houris
Paradise de Mahomet, 138, 155

Pardoe, Julia: *Beauties of the Bosphorus*, 79; on drowning of harem women, 170; on "happy slaves," 69; on harem women as caged birds, 123–24; on the hookah, 116–17; on mirrors, 180; on poisoned coffee, 190; political views of, 63; on the slave market, 62, 63; on sleeping harem women, 46–47, 180
Pardoe, Thomas, 63
parents of harem women, 174
Parisian Women in Algerian Costume (Harem) (Renoir), 237–38, *238*
parrots, 123, 252 nn. 26 and 41
Pasha with Odalisque (Génard), 113, *116*
pashas. *See* masters
passion flower, 217
passivity, 52, 86–87
Patmore, Coventry: "Angel in the House," 213
pedophilia, 194, 249 n. 39
Pedrillo, 31, 198
Performer on the 'Ood, A (Lane), 134
peris, 123
Persane boudeuse, Une (Bettannier/Desandré), 27, *28*, 117
Persian Letters (Montesquieu), 23–24, 97, 176, 190, 242 nn. 20 and 33, 244 n. 3, 245 nn. 41 and 42; adultery in, 168–69; on authority of master, 197; on disorder of the harem, 165; eunuchs in, 71, 165, 169, 190, 245 n. 41; on gender and power, 196; jealousy in, 190; lesbianism in, 175; motherhood and sexuality in, 211; on polygyny, 20; powerful women in, 199; Roxana in, 190; on souls of Islamic women, 164–65; on tyranny, 195; unveiling in, 84–85; on women's education, 200
Persian women, 27, 69
Pet, A (Deverell), 127, *138*
Pet Parrot (Deverell), 252 n. 41
phallus: hookah as, 115
philhellenism, 21, 75, 90–91, 93–94, 96, 98, 100
Philipon: *Palanquins d'Isfahan*, 176, *179*
photography, 24
Pickersgill, Henry William: *Femme d'Orient: Childe Harold (Lord Byron)*, 192, *194*, 212; *A Greek Girl*, 99; *The Ionian Captive*, 99, *102*; *Oriental Love-Letter*, 141, *147*
Pickersgill, Mrs., 100, 102; "The Hetaeria: The Tale of the Greek Slave", 102; *Tales of the Harem*, 99–100, 102
pictorial prototypes, 203
pigeons, 123, 252 n. 39
pipes, 27, 46, 64, 111–17, 136, 172–73, 216, 235. *See also* chibouks; hookahs; narghiles; smoking
pirates, 94, 96
"Pirates' Song" (Hugo), 250 n. 102
place, 11, 154
Planche, Gustave, 51
pleasure, 13, 202, 204, 225
plumpness of harem women, 180, 255 n. 53
Pointon, Marcia, 12
politics, 13, 27, 30, 56, 195
polygyny, 34, 36, 40, 67, 162, 196, 221, 245 n. 33; and Christianity, 20; and Islam, 9, 31; and jealousy, 189; and monogamy, 20, 24, 30; and motherhood, 211; and Muhammad, 202; as "natural," 196; and population, 19–20; and prostitution, 36; as weakening men, 19–20
"polysexuality": in the harem, 175
Pompadour, Madame de, 141, 253 n. 53
Ponsonby, Lord, 60, 61
Pontormo, Jacopo da: *Descent from the Cross*, 55
Poole, Sophie Lane, 58, 70, 216; *The Englishwoman in Egypt*, 58, 248 n. 2
Poole, Stanley Lane, 65, 175
"poor" harems, 190–91
Pope, Alexander, 164, 175, 189
poppies, 46, 223, 224
population, 19–20
pornography, 73, 88
Porterfield, Todd, 247 n. 91
Portrait of Zola (Manet), 237
positivism, 9, 24, 110, 160; aesthetic, 24–25, 231, 243 n. 24
possession, 30, 73, 251 n. 120
postcolonialism, 13
power: and beauty, 200; chibouk as symbol of, 112, 113–14; and gender, 196; and jewelry, 146–47; and nakedness, 197; relationships, 13, 197–99, 200, 201; of the spectator, 39; of women, 10, 86–87, 200
prayer, 253 n. 58
"Prayer of Faith Shall Save the Sick, And the" (James 5:15) (Lewis), 129, *140*, 171, 173, 227, 254 nn. 26 and 27
Pre-Impressionism, French, 231–38
Pre-Raphaelites, 214, 217
Preziosi, Count Amadeo: *Trois femmes turcs*, 113, 118, *119*; *A Turkish Cafe*, 252 n. 8; *Turkish Woman Holding a Pipe, with a Black Servant at her Side*, 11, 113, *118*, 242 n. 15
Price, David, 257 n. 61
primitiveness, 19, 43, 122, 164, 191
Prince arménien et sa femme, Un (Duz-Oglou) (Dupré), 43, *44*
Prince Hassan and His Servant (Lewis), 254 n. 35
printmaking: French, 11
prisoners: Arab women as, 28; Armenian women as, 42, 43; converted to Islam, 90, 91; harem women as, 59, 90–103
prisons: "luxurious," 12, 106–7, 108, 141, 224
Prisse d'Avennes, A. C. T. E.: *Cairene Lady Waited Upon by a Galla Slave Girl*, 120, *129*; *Habesh or Abyssinian Slave, Cairo*, 49, *52*, 173
private life, 20
procuresses: slave, 84, 250 n. 79
profile: Greek, 99
progress in art and science, 36
proletariat, the, 66, 220
promiscuity, 162
propaganda, 91
property, 34, 59, 166
Prosperina (Ruskin), 227, 258 n. 83
prostitution, 237–38; in Algeria, 188; bourgeois justification for, 36; in Britain, 188, 188–89; and cigarettes, 185; in Egypt, 187, 187–188, 237; in France, 255 n. 75; and harem women, 182–189, 231, 234, 236–237; and hats, 184–85; and houris, 182–83, 184; and polygyny, 36; and slavery, 187–88
prototypes, pictorial, 203
Proverbs 24:21, 217, 220
pubic hair, 235, 259 n. 24
public life, 20
punishment of harem women, 168, 169–71

"quiet": images as, 213
Qur'an, the, 257 n. 59; on adultery, 168; in harem images, 203;

on houris, 204–205; on Paradise, 204–206, 207, 213; on polygyny, 9; on seclusion of harem women, 9; on veiling, 9, 73

race, 27, 36–39, 46, 48–50, 61, 220–22
racial difference, 48, 56, 118
racism, 61, 65, 69
radical realism, 243 n. 24
rafraf, 206
rape, 198
Ras Kassa, 50, 247 n. 80
Ravenet: *Dame de Constantinople*, 206, *206*
Reading Desk (Leighton), 203, *204*
realism, 24–25, 243 n. 24
reality: lived, 239
reason, 200–201
Reception (Lewis), 205, *205*, 215–16, 231, 257 n. 46
Reception in a Turkish Harem (Vanmour), 257 n. 46
receptivity, female, 52
reclining figure, 43, 46, 72, 75. *See also* "odalisque pose"
Reclining Odalisque (Delacroix), 46, *51*, 180
recognition, rules of, 25
Recueil de cent estampes (Vanmour), 176, 246 n. 59
Redgrave, Richard, 106
Reeve, Emma, 39, 74, 75
Régnier, Claude: *L'Amour, le vin et le tabac*, 185–86, *186*; *Le Chibouk*, 115, *123*; *Constantinople*, 114–15, *119*, 180; *Fatime*, 125, *135*; *La Jeune grecque*, 98, *100*, 122, 191; *La Marchande d'oiseaux des tropiques: georgienne*, 42, *43*, 127; *La Musique*, 136, *143*; *Le Pacha, ou la vie dans le sérail, d'après le tableau de Guérard*, 113, *115*, 191, 197, 198; *Saidah*, 183–84, *184*, 225; *Séraphita*, 183–84, *183*, 225; *La Vie au sérail*, no. 1, 115, 120, *126*, 155, 197; *La Vie au sérail*, no. 2, 72, *72*, 115; *Le Voile*, 88, *88*
relativism, 22, 228
relaxation, 179
religiosity, 203, 209
Renoir, Pierre Auguste, 231, 232, 238, 259 n. 15; *Girl with Falcon*, 256 n. 104; *Parisian Women in Algerian Costume (Harem)*, 237–38, *238*; *Woman of Algiers* or *Odalisque*, 156, *158*, 233–34
representation, 10, 238–39
representation, figural: in religious art, 20
"rescue" of harem women, 94, 96
resistance, cultural, 10; of harem women, 97
Réunion dimanches, 93
Revue de Paris, 93
Rica, 20, 31, 165, 244 n. 3, 245 n. 42
Richardson, James, 61
Roberts, David, 66
Roberts, Emilie, 94
rococo-revivalism, 51, 75, 195, 197
romantic aesthetics, 52
romanticism, 51, 53, 110
Rosenthal, Léon: *Du Romantisme au réalisme*, 121
roses, 138, 142, 143, 148, 166; eroticism of, 142; and houris, 138; and lilies, 223, 258 nn. 70–71; and Muhammad, 207; as symbols of the beloved, 112, 207; as symbols of love, 207, 253 n. 73; as symbols of sexuality, 177, 223
Rossetti, Dante Gabriel: *Ecce Ancilla Domini!*, 257 n. 34
Rossetti, William: "The Bullfinch," 127
Roubaud, Benjamin, 255 n. 71; *Mauresque*, 185, *187*
Rousseau, Jean Jacques, 200
Rowlandson, Thomas: *Harem*, 112–13, *114*, 176
Roxana, 97, 165, 169, 190
Roxana (wife of Sulieman I), 190
Royal Academy, 163, 190, 217, 257 nn. 31 and 57
Royal Scottish Academy, 49
rules of recognition, 25
Rumi, Jelal-ud-Din: "The Merchant and the Parrot," 123
Ruskin, John, 65–66, 258 n. 72; and abolitionism, 66, 67; on animality, 66; on *An Armenian Lady, Cairo* (Lewis), 44; on capitalism, 67, 153; on Carlyle, 249 n. 36; on class conflict, 153; on *Convent Thoughts* (Collins), 217; on David Roberts, 66; on Dutch art, 213; on facial stoicism, 70; on harem as subject for art, 163; on *Harem Life—Constantinople* (Lewis), 66; on *Hhareem* (Lewis), 66, 163; on indolence, 66; on jewelry, 152–54, 253 n. 79; on *Lady with a Dove: Madame Loeser* (Brett), 127, 252 n. 40; on Lewis, 153, 190, 208, 209, 249 n. 40, 256 n. 97; on liberty, 67, 249 n. 38; on *Mariana* (Millais), 214; on masters, 217, 220; on morality of art, 44, 67, 164; on Muslims, 220; pedophilia of, 194, 249 n. 39; on polygyny, 67; on servants, 21, 67; on slavery, 21, 66–67; on *Slave Ship* (Turner), 66, 67. Works: *Cestus of Aglaia*, 220, 249 n. 38; "Of the Division of Arts," 253 n. 79; "Education in Art," 153; "A Joy For Ever," 153; *Modern Painters*, 66, 154, 164, 213; *Prosperina*, 227, 258 n. 83; "The Seven Lamps of Architecture," 152; *Stones of Venice*, 227; *Time and Tide*, 220
Ruskin, John James, 66, 67, 249 n. 40
Russia, and Armenia, 42–43; and Britain, 20, 57, 63, 244 n. 16, 245–46 n. 50; and Circassia, 39, 65; and France, 57, 244 n. 16; and Georgia, 39; and Turkey, 39, 57, 62, 63, 244 n. 16
Ruysch, Rachel: *Flowers in a Vase*, 225, *226*
Rycaut, Paul, 91

Saidah (Régnier/Brochart), 183–84, *184*, 225
Said, Edward, 12, 25; *Culture and Imperialism*, 13; *Orientalism*, 13, 243 n. 24
Salemenes, 31, 138
Salomé (Wilde), 238
Salon (Paris), 10, 91, 232, 237, 259 n. 16
Sardanapalus, 98, 192
Sardanapalus (Byron), 31, 98–99, 136, 138, 147, 192, 251 n. 124
Sardanapalus (Delacroix), 31, 55, 147, *151*
Scène de harem (Lehoux), 172–73, *174*
Scène familiale en Orient (Lehoux), 211, *211*
Scène Orientale (Adam), 96, *96*
Scheherazad, 87, 250 n. 84
Schick, Irvin Cemil, 175, 222, 243 n. 32
scientia sexualis, 25–26
scientific space, 155, 156–57, 160
scientism, 26, 36, 81, 146, 156–57, 206, 243 n. 30; and eroticism, 25, 110; of Gérôme, 25; of Lamartine, 37–38
Scotland, 50
Scott, Joan Wallach, 30
Scultz, *Le lendemain de victoire*, 185, *188*
Seated Sultan with Harem Girl Reposing at His Feet (Decamps), 112, *112*, 191, 197
seclusion of harem women, 9, 10, 20
Second Brussels Conference, 60

Second Sex, The (de Beauvoir), 255 n. 47
seduction, 87–88
Self, the, 23, 24, 29, 30, 195, 228
self-confession, 25–26
self-help, 58
Selim, 31, 198, 199, 247 n. 68
Selim II (son of Roxana), 190
Seneca Falls Convention, 58
"Séraphita" (Balzac), 183, 255 n. 64
Séraphita (Régnier/Brochart), 183–84, *183*, 225
"serraglio," 127
servants, 173; in Britain, 220; eastern women as, 217; and motherhood, 174; musical instruments played by, 136; and Paradise, 213; Ruskin on, 21, 67; and slavery, 21, 220, 221; western, 62, 174, 189, 217
"Seven Lamps of Architecture, The" (Ruskin), 152
sexuality, birds as symbols of, 124; and coffee serving, 120, 252 n. 18; and confinement, 103; and conquest, 30, 244 n. 3; deviant, 26; flowers as symbols of, 177, 221, 223; Foucault on, 14, 25–26, 61; of girls, 191–92; of houris, 203–4; and imperialism, 20; and indolence, 179; and jewelry, 147; lutes as symbols of, 177; and motherhood, 211; 19th century views of, 19, 61; and the Other, 47; in Paradise, 182, 203–4; pipes as symbols of, 27, 112–17; self-confession of, 25–26; and violence, 167; of women, 162, 164–165, 182, 198, 254 n. 28
Shahriyar, King, 87
Shakespeare, William: *Measure for Measure*, 214
shibuks. *See* chibouks
Shields, Rob, 242 n. 10
shoes, 33, 144. *See also* slippers
Siècle, Le, 114
Siesta, La (Bonington), 46, *50*, 117–18, 136, 180, 247 n. 72, 255 n. 54
Siesta (Lewis), 46, *49*, 180, 205
silence, 205, 212–14, 213
silk, 205
skin color: and coffee serving, 117, 118, 120; fetishized, 37; and harem hierarchy, 38–39, 46, 48, 49, 50, 61, 220–22; and racial difference, 48; and stereotyping, 71
Slave Market (ca. 1867) (Gérôme), 81, *82*
Slave Market (1871) (Gérôme), 81, *83*, 232
Slave Market, Constantinople (Allan), 250 n. 66
Slave Market in the East (Lewis), 76–81, *78*, 249 n. 60
slave markets, 73–86; black and white slaves in, 80; in Cairo, 60, 81; children sold in, 80; condemnation of, 63–64; in Constantinople, 80; and Islam, 79; and non-harem women, 79–80, 84, 250 n. 79; Pardoe on, 62, 63; Smith on, 58; Spencer on, 63–64; and unveiling, 73
Slave-Merchant, Constantinople (Hullmandel/Allom), 74–76, *76*, 80, 81, 157, 168
slavery, 21, 27, 35, 58–109; in America, 58, 62; apologia for, 58; black, 62, 66, 80, 85, 221; and Britain, 60, 61, 62, 85, 247 n. 67, 258 n. 2; and Circassian women, 62, 65, 85; and class conflict, 21; and death of masters, 74; decline of, 230; in Egypt, 30–31, 59, 60, 62, 187–88, 258 n. 2; and families, 67, 249 n. 37; and Georgian women, 85; and Greek women, 102; and "happy slaves", 69–74; harem women as masters, 220; and Islam, 31, 59, 70, 90, 244–45 n. 33, 247 n. 67; Lane on, 250 n. 79; male harem slaves, 250 n. 76; in Morocco, 61; Pardoe on, 62–63; and the proletariat, 220; and property, 59; and prostitution, 59, 187–188; Ruskin on, 21, 66–67; and servants, 21, 217, 220, 221; Tucker on, 258 n. 2; in Turkey, 60, 62–63, 230; as voluntary, 58; and western women, 58; white, 62, 66, 80, 85, 221, 230; and women, 200; and the work ethic, 58
Slave Ship (Turner), 66, 67
sleep, 46–47, 180
Sleeper of Naples, 23
slippers, 143–45, 232. *See also* shoes
smiling, 67, 69, 70, 71–72
Smirne (Devéria), 104–5, *106*
Smith, Albert, 58, 69, 80
smoking, 52, 72, 85, 111, 114, 185, 255 n. 74. *See also* pipes
Smyth, Coke: *Greek Girl/Captive Greek Girl*, 95–96, *95*, 191, 221, 250 n. 110; *Harem/Hhareem*, 105, *107*, 142, 177; *Illustrations of Constantinople*, 95, 105
snakes, 123, 128
social character of art, 52
social mobility, 36, 58, 244–45 n. 33
social privilege, 224
Social Science Congress, 153
Solim, 69, 84–85
Songe, Le (Maurin), 155, *156*
Song of Solomon 2:2, 217
souls, and beauty, 163–64; of women, 164–65, 196, 200, 254 n. 9, 258 n. 11
space, 10–11, 26, 110, 154–61, 206, 242 n. 10
Spanish women, 44–48
"spatial disjuncture," 159
spatial dominance, 197–99, 200
spectator: power of, 39
Spectator, 67, 69, 106–7, 129, 163, 179, 180, 213, 220, 256 n. 18
speechlessness, 193
Spencer, Edmund, 63–64, 136, 248–49 n. 28
Spirit of the East (Urquhart), 40, 246 n. 54
Spivak, Gayatri Chakravorty, 12–13, 20, 163
Stendhal, 93
stereotyping, 12, 245 n. 34; of Armenian women, 42, 43; Bhabha on, 29, 65; of eastern women, 56; of harem women, 19, 162–63, 228–29; "lazy native," 52; by nations, 30; of the Other, 27; racial, 37; and skin color, 71; of Spanish women, 47–48
Stewart, Philip, 245 n. 34
St. John, James Augustus, 163
Stonebreaker (Brett), 252 n. 40
Stones of Venice (Ruskin), 227
"Stop" (L. P. G. B. Morel-Retz): *Une Femme dans son harem*, 104, *105*
Stratford de Radcliffe, Lord, 221
Studio of the Batignolles (Fantin-Latour), 232
Studio on the Rue de la Condamine (Bazille), 232, *233*, 259 n. 15
subservience, 35, 212
Sulieman I, Sultan, 190
Sultana Reading in the Harem (Boucher), 104, *105*, 136, 157
Sultane, La (Manet), *plate 6*, 10, 235–37
Sultane (à la toilette), La (Boucher), 180, *181*
Sultane à sa toilette (Maurin/Grévedon), *71*, 150, 177
Sultane et ses domestiques, La (Vanloo), 157, *158*, 172
Sultane jouant d'un instrument à cordes, Une (Vanloo), 253 n. 53
Sultane prenant du café, réprésentée sous les traits de Mme. de Pompadour, Une (Vanloo), 117, *128*, 141

swans, 123
swords, 97, 233

Tales of a Parrot, 123
Tales of the Harem (Mrs. Pickersgill), 99–100, 102
tambourines, 233
Tanzimat, 80
Tapper, Nancy, 29
Tassaert, 254 n. 16
tehegours, 136
Tennyson, Alfred: "Mariana," 214
texts, 11, 13, 25
Thackeray, William Makepeace, 69, 122, 124, 170–71
Thévenot, Jean de, 183
Thiers, Louis Adolphe, 52–53
Thoré-Bürger, Théophile, 52, 53, 73, 114, 138, 247 n. 84, 252 n. 11
three glorious days, the, 50
Three Years in Constantinople (White), 62
Tiffin, Helen, 11
Time and Tide (Ruskin), 220
Times (London), 67, 216, 221, 223, 227–28, 231
tobacco, 111, 114
Toilette, La (Bazille), 232–33, *234*, 259 n. 18
Toledano, Ehud, 80
tourism, 21–22
transgression, 20, 36
transparency of texts, 25, 26
travel literature, 11, 62–65
Travels in Upper and Lower Egypt, (Denon), 32–34, 35–36
Tréhot, Lise, 233
Triumph of Time and Truth, The (Handel), 258 n. 77
Trois femmes turcs (Preziosi), 113, 118, *119*
Trois glorieuses, Les, 50
truth-claims, 11, 22, 26, 33, 35
Tubeeb, Meerza Ahmed, 46, 180
Tucker, Judith E., 9, 30, 230, 258 n. 2
Tunis (Devéria), 166, *167*
Tunisian women, 50
turbans, 46, 185, 255 n. 70. *See also* hats
Turcotoquade (Nield), 115, *120*
Turcs (Devéria), 112, *113*, 197, 225
Turkey, 117; as barbaric, 91; and Britain, 20, 40, 60, 62, 63, 70, 221, 230, 244 n. 16, 247 n. 67; and Circassia, 39; despotism in, 196; and Greece, 21, 98; Lamartine on, 56, 57; modernization of, 31; mothers in, 211; national character, 175; peasants, 191; and Russia, 39, 57, 62, 63; slavery in, 60, 62–63, 230; and the West, 57; white slave trade in, 62; women of, 65, 88–89. *See also* Ottoman Empire
Turkish Bath. See *Bain Turc*
Turkish baths, 215
Turkish Cafe, A (Preziosi), 252 n. 8
Turkish Embassy Letters (Montagu), 88–89, 103, 146, 179, 254 n. 11
Turkish Family Picture, A, 64, *64*, 113–14, 136
Turkish Interior in Cairo, A (Dillon), 157, *160*
Turkish Woman Holding a Pipe, with a Black Servant at her Side (Preziosi), 11, 113, *118*, 242 n. 15
Turkish Woman Smoking (Decamps), *plate 4*, 113
Turk Reposing (Bonington), 112, *112*
Turner, J. M. W.: *Slave Ship*, 66, 67
turquerie, 12
Twelve Lunar Hours in the Pleasure Quarter, 237
Two Women in a Harem (Lewis), 221–22, *222*
tyranny, 31, 162, 195–98, 201

urns, 171, 254 n. 27
Urquhart, David, 245–46 n. 50, 246 n. 52; on colonialism, 41; on concubines, 40; on harem children, 173–74; harem defended by, 40–41, 64–65, 70; on harem as home, 63; on harem women as virtuous, 203; on jealousy, 189; on Napoleon, 40; on polygyny, 40; on slavery, 217; *Spirit of the East*, 40, 246 n. 54; as Turkophile, 40, 246 n. 51
Usbek, 20, 31, 69, 97, 165, 169, 197, 198, 199, 211
Utamaro, Kitagawa: *Hour of the Ox [Midnight]/Courtesan with Lit Taper*, *236*, 237

Vali, Jan: *Houri in a Paradise Garden*, 185, *185*, 207
Van Eyck, Jan, 208
vanitas, 46, 154, 172. *See also* narcissism
Vanloo, Amédée: *La Sultane et ses domestiques*, 157, *158*, 172
Vanloo, Carle: *Deux sultanes travaillant à la tapisserie*, 176, *177*; *Une Sultane jouant d'un instrument à cordes*, 253 n. 53; *Une Sultane prenant du café, réprésentée sous les traits de Mme. de Pompadour*, 117, *128*, 141
Vanmour, Jean Baptiste: *Dame grecque dans son appartement*, 98, *99*, 141; *Femme turque filant au tandour*, 256 n. 3; *Filles turques qui jouent au mangala*, 176, *176*; *Fille turque jouant du tehegour*, 134, *142*; *Fille turque prenant le caffé sur la sopha*, 120, *129*; *Fille turque qui fume sur le sopha*, 113, *117*; *Lady Mary Wortley Montagu and Her Son*, 103, *104*, 134, 157; *Reception in a Turkish Harem*, 257 n. 46; *Recueil de cent estampes*, 176, 246 n. 59
"Veil, The" (Hugo), 73
Veiled Prophet of Khorassan, 37, 253 n. 50
veils, 9, 10, 55, 73, 87, 246 n. 59; unveiling, 73–75, 81, 84–88, 250 n. 80
Vengeance, La (Barathier/Fragonard), 167, *169*
Venus of Melos, 93
verisimilitude, 231
Vermeer, Johannes (Jan): *Girl Reading a Letter at an Open Window*, 213, *214*; *Woman with a Pearl Necklace*, 213–14, *215*
Vernet, Horace: *Capture of the Smala of 'Abd Al-Qadir*, *plate 3*, 54–56
Victoria and Albert Museum, The, 23, 76, 257 n. 57
Vie au sérail, La, no. 1 (Régnier/Guérard), 115, 120, *126*, 155, 197
Vie au sérail, La, no. 2 (Régnier/Guérard), 72, *72*, 115
Vie au sérail, La, no. 4 (Guérard), 113, *116*, 145
viewer identification, 229
Vindication of the Rights of Women (Wollstonecraft), 19–20, 172, 195–96, 199–200, 227
violence, 73, 167, 189
virginity, 91, 93–94, 96, 209, 223
Virgin Mary, the, 208, 209, 212, 217
virtue, 200–201, 203
Vogt, Charles: *Narghillet*, 115, *121*
voicelessness, 12–13
Voile, Le (Régnier/Bettannier/Bouvier), 88, *88*
Voyage to the Orient (Nerval), 27–28, 37, 104

voyeurism, 46, 73, 180
vulnerability, 10, 91, 180

waiting, 212
Wallace, Richard, 247 n. 72
Wallace Collection, 180
Walsh, Rev. Robert: *Constantinople and the Scenery of the Seven Churches of Asia*, 74, 75–76
wantonness, 128
watercolor painting, 86
Watson, Forbes, 223
wealthy harems, 222–24
West, the, 13, 57, 242 n. 29
White, Charles, 62, 211, 217, 248 n. 20; *Three Years in Constantinople*, 62
"white man's burden," 57
white supremacy, 65
Who Is It? (Alma-Tadema), 251 n. 138
wife-selling, 21
Wilberforce, William, 60
Wilde, Oscar: *Salomé*, 238
windows, 103–8, 251 n. 128; barred, 42; colored, 105–6; covered, 141; latticed, 46, 107, 208; open, 99, 103, 104, 106–8; shuttered, 103–4, 105. *See also* doors
wish-fulfillment, 22
Withers, Robert, 91, 169, 175, 183, 257 n. 49
wives in Paradise, 152, 182
Wollstonecraft, Mary: on animality of western men, 121; on the aristocracy, 175, 195–96, 223, 227; on beauty, 163, 225; on childlike women, 191; on civilization, 195–96; on "disregard of order", 165; on education, 199–200; and European society, 201; on French character, 32; on harem as oppressive, 20–21; on indolence, 181; on the middle class, 195, 223; on narcissism, 180–81; on pets, 252 n. 25; on political tyrants, 198; on polygyny, 196; on the souls of Islamic women, 164; *Vindication of the Rights of Women*, 19–20, 58, 172, 195–96, 199–200, 227; on women as caged birds, 123; on women and male status, 197; on women as slaves, 58; on women's power, 200
Woman and Little Girl of Constantine with a Gazelle (Chassériau), 122, *131*
Woman in Moorish Costume (Mauresque) (Bazille), 233, *235*
Woman of Algiers (Renoir), 156, *158*, 233–34
Woman with a Hookah. See *Houri, Eastern Woman with a Hookah*
Woman with a Parrot (Courbet), 258 n. 11
Woman with a Pearl Necklace (Vermeer), 213–14, *215*
women: able to see as men, 24; Abyssinian, 48–50; Algerian, 50–56; and animals, 172, 252 n. 25; Arab, 28, 84; aristocratic, 172, 195–96, 198; Armenian, 42–44, 246 n. 59; and beauty, 164; black, 69–71, 85, 221–22; and "body", 197; British, 27; as childlike, 191, 192; Circassian, 20, 34–35, 39, 41–42, 47, 65, 85, 166, 221; and desire, 164; as despots, 200; Eastern, 28–29, 46, 212; education of, 199; European, 27, 29, 196, 198; as feminine, 23; French, 69; friendship between, 175; Georgian, 20, 39, 42, 85, 221; gossiping, 175, 176; Greek, 59, 75, 90–103, 191–92; as heroic, 99; as hidden, 14, 242 n. 33; idealized, 177, 200, 255 n. 47; inferiority of, 21, 198; Jewish, 56; Maghrebian, 50–56; and male status, 197; as masculine, 23; middle-class, 10, 27, 107, 195, 203, 220; Moroccan, 50; multiple partners of, 152, 253 n. 78; Muslim, 196; passivity of, 52; Persian, 27, 69; possession of, 30; power relationships with men, 197–99, 200, 201; as property, 34; receptivity of, 52; sexuality of, 162, 164–65, 182, 198, 254 n. 28; "silent", 212–214; as slaves, 200; souls of, 164–65, 196, 200, 254 n. 9; Spanish, 44–46, 47–48; spatial dominance of, 199; as territory, 30; Tunisian, 50; Turkish, 65, 88–89; views on the harem, 22–24; vulnerability of, 91; Western, 10, 28–29, 182, 220; white, 70, 85, 221–22; working-class, 66
Women of Algiers in Their Apartment (1834) (Delacroix), 25, *53*, 105–6, 156, 232, 234, 247 nn. 84 and 91; animality in, 121; and French politics, 52–53; hookah in, 114; jewelry in, 147; leftist criticism of, 51–52; "odalisque pose" in, 75; slippers in, 144; unveiling in, 88
Women of Algiers in Their Apartment (1849) (Delacroix), 54, *55*, 105, 232
work ethic, 58
working class, the, 66, 220
worry beads, 33, 74
Wyburd, Francis: *Xarifa: The Zegri Lady Rose Not*, 106, *108*
Wylde, W. H., 249 n. 37

Xarifa: The Zegri Lady Rose Not (Wyburd), 106, *108*

Young Algerian Woman Lying on the Grass (Corot), 258–59 n. 13
Young Turks Movement, 31

Zelica, 136
Zelid, 175
Zelis, 198, 211
Zephis, 175
Zetnaybia, 27–28, 37, 104
"Zetnaybia" (Nerval), 37, 245 n. 41
Zola, Emile, 232, 233, 259 n. 15
"Zuleika" (O'Shaughnessy), 251 n. 134
Zulema, 165, 199